EDUCATIONAL PSYCHOLOGY

Principles and Applications

Third
Edition

John A. Glover
Ball State University

Roger H. Bruning
The University of Nebraska, Lincoln

 HarperCollins*Publishers*

Illustration Acknowledgments

Cover art: "Passage" by Gayle Fitzpatrick.
All cartoons © Sidney Harris. Reprinted by permission.
Unless otherwise acknowledged, all photographs are courtesy of Jenni Bruning.
5 (top): Arthur Grace, Stock Boston.   **5** (bottom): Gale Zucker, Stock Boston.
8: Elizabeth Crews, Stock Boston.   **96**: Mark Antman, The Image Works.
113: Yves Debraine, Black Star.   **166**: Jeffrey W. Myers, Stock Boston.   **202**: Peter Vandermark.   **207**: PICASSO, Pablo. *Baboon and Young*. 1951. Bronze (cast 1955), after found objects, 21" high, base 13¼" x 6⅞". Collection, The Museum of Modern Art, New York. Mrs. Simon Guggenheim Fund.   **216–217**: Scott, Foresman and Company.   **237**: Brent Jones.   **253**: Thomas England.   **266–267**: Bob Daemmrich, Stock Boston.   **277**: Scott, Foresman and Company.   **332**: Peter Vandermark.
357: Scott, Foresman and Company.   **440**: Bob Daemmrich, Stock Boston.
450: Arthur Grace, Stock Boston.   **482–483**: Freda Leinwand, Monkmeyer Press Photo Service.   **493**: Bob Daemmrich, Stock Boston.   **501**: Elizabeth Crews, Stock Boston.   **505**: Elizabeth Crews, Stock Boston.   **507**: Scott, Foresman and Company.

172: Figure 5–5 from Hayes, J. R., & Flower, L. S. Identifying the organization of writing processes. In L. W. Gregg & E. R. Steinberg (Eds.), *Cognitive processes in writing*. Hillsdale, NJ: Lawrence Erlbaum Associates. Copyright 1980 by Lawrence Erlbaum. Adapted by permission.

Library of Congress Cataloging-in-Publication Data

Glover, John A.
   Educational psychology, principles and applications / John A.
Glover, Roger H. Bruning. —3rd ed.
      p.   cm.
   Includes bibliographical references.
   ISBN 0-673-52007-2
   1. Educational psychology.   2. Teaching.   I. Bruning, Roger H.
II. Title.
LB1051.G567   1990   89-39566
370.15—dc20   CIP

23456-VHJ-959493929190

PREFACE

Educational Psychology: Principles and Applications, Third Edition, is designed primarily for future teachers, current teachers who are developing their knowledge and skills, and all others who are involved with the processes of learning and teaching from preschool through adulthood. We believe our book also will be valuable for the general reader—the person who wants to know more about what learning is and how teaching can be more effective.

Three major goals guided our efforts: (1) to help our readers understand the science of educational psychology—particularly in its past and present relationships to psychology and education, (2) to describe as clearly as possible what is known about how students learn, and (3) to help our readers translate this knowledge about learning into strategies for effective teaching.

The major theme of our book is the influence of meaningfulness on learning. We believe that the best, most lasting learning occurs when teaching methods and materials build upon students' present knowledge. Each chapter in our text is based on this premise and is written to demonstrate how all the diverse skills in educational psychology help teachers, in one way or another, do a better job of presenting meaningful instruction to students. We have taken our theme very seriously by trying to create a scholarly yet meaningful text for our own readers.

Many individuals who taught from the first two editions of our book have given us invaluable feedback for the preparation of the third edition. Using their suggestions, we have added considerable material dealing with metacognition, parallel-distributed processing, the ACT* model of memory, the Triarchic theory of intelligence, and domain-specific problem solving. We also have focused more clearly on attribution theory and the role of self-efficacy in student learning. We have not simply added material to the volume, however. Using the feedback we received, we have streamlined our presentation by combining separate chapters on language development and reading into one updated and carefully focused chapter. Similarly, we now have blended the most recent work on creativity into our chapter on problem solving. Finally, rather than devoting an entire chapter to writing instructional objectives, we have included this content in our chapter that introduces measurement to the reader.

The text is organized in a logical, contemporary manner. We devote Part One to cognitive psychology and cognitive development, the most rapidly growing areas in educational psychology. Chapters in this section are "An Introduction to Cognitive Processes," "Memory and Concepts," "Intelligence and Cognitive Development," "Emerging Literacy: Language Development, Reading, and Writing," and "Problem Solving and Creativity." We do not, however, lose sight of the importance of self-understanding and the development of a sense of self. In Part Two we devote Chapter Seven, "Self-Concept and Moral Development," to a discussion of the self-concept, how it develops, and its implications for education, and we discuss moral development and its implications for school behavior. Chapter Eight, "Motivation," reflects the importance of humanistic views of psychology.

The important contributions of behavioral psychology to modern education are detailed in Part Three. We devote Chapter Nine, "An Introduction to Behavioral Psychology," to an outline of behavioral psychology. Chapter Ten, "Social Learning and Modeling," reflects the changing nature of behavioral psychology, and Chapter Eleven, "Classroom Management," contains a wealth of behavioral techniques available to today's teacher. Part Four is devoted to measurement and evaluation. The importance of effective communication in instruction and the basics of educational measurement are described in Chapter Twelve, "An Introduction to Measurement." Chapter Thirteen deals with teacher-made tests, and Chapter Fourteen covers standardized tests. Part Five of the book contains one crucial chapter, "The Exceptional Student."

To make our book more useful and interesting, we have supplemented the basic content with:

1. An outline at the beginning of each chapter.

2. Higher-order objectives, also at the beginning of each chapter, focused on important learning outcomes.

3. Clear and informative illustrations.

4. Detailed lists of applications of the knowledge and skills contained in each chapter.

5. Practice exercises designed to demonstrate the specific knowledge and skills in each chapter.

6. Suggested readings at the end of each chapter identifying sources of more detailed information on specific topics of interest.

7. A detailed glossary at the end of the text.

A unique feature of our text is the practice exercises. Each has been field-tested on thousands of students over the years, is keyed specifically to a critical issue or skill, and allows you to experience a concept directly or practice an important skill. We believe you will find the exercises worthwhile and illuminating.

We believe our text fairly and professionally represents educational psychology. Clearly, our emphasis on contemporary cognitive psychology is a departure from most traditional texts, as is our interpretation of cognitive, humanistic, and behavioral psychology. Our inclusion of an entire chapter on language development, reading, and writing also is a departure from traditional textbooks. We believe all teachers, not just those of the early elementary years and those who teach "language arts," must be able to deal with problems associated with the development of communication skills.

Acknowledgments

In the development of this text we owe thanks to many, many people — too many to list in this brief space. Special thanks are due, however, to Mylan Jaixen, who saw us through the first two editions at Little, Brown. We also want to extend our heartfelt thanks to Chris Jennison, Manager, Education Book Group, Scott, Foresman, who greatly eased the process of bringing out this third edition. In addition, many thanks are owed Anita Portugal, Developmental Editor, and Phil Herbst, Project Editor. We cannot forget the debt of gratitude owed David Moshman (a developmentalist's developmentalist), Royce Ronning (a true cognitive psychologist), and John Zimmer (the last practicing metaphysician).

We want to express our great appreciation to a very special group of scholars whose attentions to our manuscript were invaluable. First, we wish to acknowledge once again our first edition reviewers: Walter Brown, formerly of the University of Washington; Steven L. Christopherson, The University of Texas at San Antonio; Richard I. Fisher, Colorado State University; Janice Hayes, Middle Tennessee State University; Wayne Kirk, Winona State University; John Long, University of Rhode Island; Wayne Mollenberg, University of New Mexico; Robert Trimble, University of Missouri, Columbia; and Joan R. Yanuzzi, Indiana University of Pennsylvania.

Second, we express our gratitude to our colleagues who provided suggestions for improving the second edition and for reading the revised manuscript: Karen Block, University of Pittsburgh; Theodore

Coladarci, University of Maine; Charles H. Gregg, The University of Utah; Donald A. Moroose, Fairmont State College; Alan N. Rudnitsky, Smith College; Angela R. Taylor, University of Maryland; Suzanne P. Waller, The University of Wisconsin—Milwaukee; and Barry J. Wilson, University of Northern Iowa. We believe the hours that they spent reviewing various drafts of our manuscript contributed considerably to our ability to reach our goals of comprehensive content and clarity of expression.

Third, we want to thank the reviewers of our third edition: Donald Moroose, Fairmont State College; Richard J. Mueller, Northern Illinois University; Dale Dinnel, Western Washington State University; Carla Mathison, San Diego State University; Ann Pace, University of Missouri, Kansas City; Henry T. Clark, Pennsylvania State University; Joan S. Timm, University of Wisconsin—Oshkosh; Ray Buss, University of Northern Iowa; Barry Wilson, University of Northern Iowa; Karen Block, University of Pittsburgh; William J. Gnagey, Illinois State University; William Burgess, University of San Francisco; Edward Kobesky, Luzerne County Community College; and Charles Gregg, University of Utah. Their careful attention to detail helped us pull together what we believe is the best edition yet of *Educational Psychology: Principles and Applications*.

Fourth, it is important to single out Henry T. Clark, Pennsylvania State University. Henry gave us inordinate amounts of time in developing both our second and our third editions. Henry's insights into the field of educational psychology gave us very great help.

We have a special feeling also for the many individuals who appear in the text's photographs. They include staff and students of Zeman Elementary School, Lakeview Elementary School, Everett Junior High School, Southeast High School, Pound Junior High School, and Southeast Community College of Lincoln, Nebraska.

Finally, we want to thank our wives, Theresa and Mary, and our families for their support as we worked on the book. Their encouragement and love gave us more than words can describe.

John A. Glover
Roger H. Bruning

OVERVIEW

CONTENTS

CHAPTER
1

An Introduction to Educational Psychology

ABOUT TEACHING
- [ ] Excellence in Teaching
- [ ] Teaching as Art and Science

EFFECTIVE TEACHERS
- [ ] Fostering Thinking Skills
- [ ] Building Self-Concept and Motivation
- [ ] Managing Classroom Environments
- [ ] Delivering Instruction
- [ ] Evaluating Learning
- [ ] Meeting the Needs of Special Students
- [ ] Remaining Lifelong Learners

EDUCATIONAL PSYCHOLOGY AND EFFECTIVE TEACHING
- [ ] A Definition of Educational Psychology
- [ ] Looking Ahead

SUMMARY

SUGGESTED READINGS

OVERVIEW

Remember the teachers everybody sought out—teachers whose classes were always full and who made their students work hard but helped them to enjoy it? You can be remembered this way by your students, although you may feel you still are a long way from being such an admired teacher. Research on the skills effective teachers possess shows that they are not mysterious, magical traits that only a chosen few can hope to have. Most of these skills are straightforward and can be learned through study and practice.

Educational psychology can help you to acquire many of the skills of an excellent teacher through its focus on the major concerns of teachers—how people learn, how best to help them learn, and how to evaluate that learning (Hilgard, 1987). As Gagné has stated, "current theory and research in psychology provide rich sources of ideas that cry out for application to the educational scene" (Gagné, 1987, p. 381).

The major purpose of this book is to help you to see how to apply the principles and research methods of psychology to your own teaching. To help you understand more specifically what you'll be learning to apply, we first will provide you with some information about the way in which educational psychologists view the teaching and learning process.

About Teaching

Excellence in Teaching

Everyone knows something about teaching. Parents teach their children. Children teach each other. Adults teach themselves all kinds of things. If everyone knows something about teaching, then why does anyone need a course in educational psychology? Aren't teaching and learning inevitable, natural processes? If someone knows a great deal about a subject such as history, isn't it a simple matter to teach it?

The answer is yes and no. No doubt, there are a few people who are "naturals" at teaching; even without formal training, they have many of the skills of outstanding teachers. By fortunate circumstance—having a parent who is a skilled teacher, for instance—these people have acquired the qualities of organization, personality, and the ability to motivate students. Most teachers, however, work hard to obtain these skills. They build on their strengths. They also realistically assess their weaknesses and overcome them. Their teaching is built on a firm base in psychology, and it is as consistent as possible with current knowledge about human learning and development.

Excellent teachers are made, not born. It isn't enough just to suppose that one can teach; an array of demonstrable skills and knowledge is needed to ensure student learning. We don't trust ourselves to the care of a doctor, lawyer, or dentist unless we have the utmost confidence in his or her skills. Neither should we assume that children will be entrusted to us if we cannot show our excellence as teachers. None of us wants to be under the tutelage of a teacher who is not highly competent. Consider Socrates' comments about a teacher, Protagoras.

> You are going to commit your soul to the care of a man whom you call a Sophist. And yet I hardly think that you know what a Sophist is; and if not, then you do not even know to whom you are committing your soul and whether the thing to which you commit yourself be good or evil. (*Plato*, Dialogues, "*Protagoras*")

We don't often think about how distinguished teachers acquire and perfect their skills. The best teachers, of course, have many fine attributes in addition to teaching skills—they know a great deal about students, they enjoy students, and they are knowledgeable and enthusiastic about their subject matter. Educational psychology is not designed to develop your proficiency in a subject matter area, although the principles of educational psychology certainly can be applied to your own studies, as we demonstrate and encourage in our Practice Exercises. This text does not presume to be able to help you enjoy your prospective students, although as your teaching skills improve so will your enjoyment of teaching and of students. What educational psychology offers you is the psychological knowledge about learners necessary to develop instructional skills for effective teaching

Teaching as Art and Science

Whenever teaching is discussed, an inevitable question is whether teaching is an *art* or a *science*. Many people prefer to consider teaching to be an art because teachers must draw upon individual experiences, emotions, and values that seem to occur outside the province of science (see Benton, in press). Others have focused on teaching as a science in which the critical aspects of instruction are reduced to elements that can be studied by the scientific method (e.g., Skinner, 1984). Who is right? Is teaching an art or a science? We believe teaching is both an art and a science.

The complex, demanding profession of teaching requires artistry *and* scientific knowledge. As an art, teaching surely engages the emotions, the values, and, some would say, the souls of all who teach well. Many teachers are as deeply involved in their work—the development of students—as painters, sculptors, and musicians are in producing their masterpieces. Good teachers are creative; they solve problems by inventing teaching methods and materials. Education as a science draws upon psychology, sociology, anthropology, ethology, biology, medicine, and many other scientific disciplines to develop effective instruction. Teachers use many of the methods of science, such as hypothesizing, experimenting, and observing outcomes.

Science and artistry are inextricably intertwined in good teaching. The goal of this text is to help you acquire the skills and knowledge generated by science to complement your artistry, just as a painter uses scientifically derived principles of light, shading, and perspective to produce art forms.

Psychology tries to translate human experience into a set of scientific principles.

"I love hearing that lonesome wail of the train whistle as the magnitude of the frequency of the wave changes due to the Doppler effect."

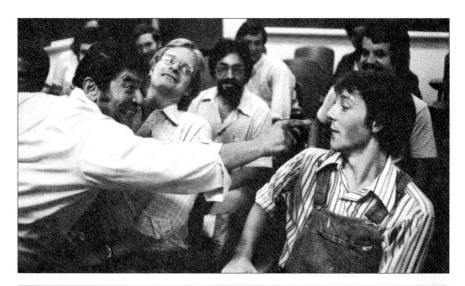

Teaching is both an art and a science. A complex, demanding profession, it combines artistry and scientific knowledge.

Effective Teachers

Everyone has experienced good teachers and bad teachers. What are the differences between them? Are effective teachers more intelligent? Are their personalities better suited to teaching? Are some people just born to teach? These are important questions that have been addressed by careful research. The research generally has shown that factors such as intelligence and personality are less important than the skills teachers use in class (see, e.g., Evertson & Smylie, 1987). Research has identified many skills that make a difference in the quality of instruction. Good teachers are able to develop student thinking, facilitate student development, manage classrooms effectively, deliver high-quality instruction, evaluate learning, and adapt to changing requirements.

Fostering Thinking Skills

Perhaps the major goal of education is to develop students' abilities to think. To meet this goal, teachers must understand how thinking (cognition) operates in human beings. The concept of meaningful learning is especially important to the development of student thinking (J. R. Anderson, 1985); effective teachers are able to make learning activities meaningful.

Meaningful learning occurs when students are able to relate new information to what they already know (DiVesta, 1987). Thus, a knowledge of how new information may be made meaningful to students is critical. This knowledge is gained from first understanding the processes of perception and attention, which determine to a great extent what students will be able to remember.

Another key to providing meaningful learning for students is knowledge of human memory (Solso, 1988). Not only must new learning build upon prior knowledge, but students should be able to organize their new learning logically in their memories so that it is available for continued learning. Curricula are designed so that the information contained in one course builds on prior courses as it lays the foundation for future learning. Teachers should thoroughly understand human memory so that their instruction takes advantage of curriculum structure and increases students' mastery of educational goals.

Effective teachers are sensitive to individual differences in how students think. One set of differences is in overall cognitive ability, that is, intelligence (Hunt, 1988). Of equal importance to effective teaching is an understanding of cognitive development (Glover, Ronning, & Bruning, in press). The logic and reasoning of the typical six-year-old are not the same as those of a nine-year-old. Important changes in thinking continue to take place throughout life at different points for different people. A third, more general set of individual differences in cognition is known as cognitive style, which generally refers to the characteristic ways in which individuals perceive and deal with information (Wittrock, 1986). Ineffective instruction seldom takes cognitive differences into account and results in "learning activities" that are unsuited to many students. Effective teachers, in contrast, are aware of cognitive differences and consider them carefully when planning instruction (Wittrock, 1986).

One of the most crucial aspects of facilitating students' cognitive abilities is understanding the development of language. There is an increasing recognition that all teachers must be able to understand how children's language abilities develop; they must be able to provide instruction in reading and writing, the most important of all academic skills. The alarmingly high illiteracy rates in the United States are such that all teachers must be committed to developing the reading and writing abilities of students.

The development of problem-solving skills in students also is achieved by effective teachers who understand the importance of problem solving in modern life and emphasize it in many ways in their instruction (Lesgold, 1988). Effective teachers also foster creative thinking; they understand the conditions that lead to creative thought and arrange learning activities to help develop creativity.

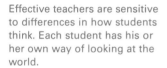

Effective teachers are sensitive to differences in how students think. Each student has his or her own way of looking at the world.

Effective teachers are able to establish rapport quickly.

Building Self-Concept and Motivation

Excellent teaching involves more than enhancing students' cognitive abilities (Evertson & Smylie, 1987). Effective teachers are able to establish a rapport with their students from the beginning. They interact freely and easily with class members, and students perceive them as warm and authentic (Rogers, 1983). They emphasize cooperation rather than competition in their classrooms, which results in more positive learning experiences for their students (Johnson, 1988). The learning process, rather than its products, is emphasized (Johnson, 1988). Their important overall goals are to improve relationships among students and to continually nurture the growth of students' self-esteem (Johnson, 1988). Effective teachers understand the development of self-concepts in their students and structure classroom activities in ways that foster the formation of positive self-concepts.

The ability to enhance student motivation is one of the hallmarks of good teaching (Brophy & Good, 1986). Students' positive self-concepts increase their motivation to achieve in the classroom, but excellent teachers also understand other factors involved in motivation. Whether this means finding ways to help students meet their personal needs, developing students' interests, or aiding students in gaining insight into their own behaviors, effective teachers have skills to foster motivation in students.

Managing Classroom Environments

Effective teachers have pleasant, organized, and productive classrooms (Evertson & Smylie, 1987). In contrast, ineffective teachers have difficulty in providing conditions that lead to harmonious and productive behavior. Perhaps the most striking difference between them, however, is the ability of effective teachers to prevent problem behaviors. Effective teachers are highly sensitive to what is happening in their classrooms and are able to head off trouble. They can manage many student activities simultaneously and thereby prevent discipline problems. The adage that an ounce of prevention is worth a pound of cure certainly applies to classroom management.

The best teachers also provide excellent role models and help students learn how to work happily, cooperatively, and usefully with others. Unfortunately, ineffective teachers sometimes model undesirable qualities ("blowing up" when frustrated or angered, for instance) and often do not understand their role in helping students to learn by imitation and observation. Most people see the school as an arena in which students learn many of the social skills they need to function throughout life. Effective teachers understand the factors that affect social behavior and recognize their role in the social development of their students (Bandura, 1986).

Delivering Instruction

Effective teachers are able to communicate to students what they are expected to learn. Evertson and Smylie (1987) reviewed the research that has contrasted effective with less effective teachers. They found that effective teachers were far better organized than their less effective counterparts and that they clearly informed students of what was to be done and how it was to be done. This ability to communicate goals and objectives to students has far-reaching effects. It influences how students prepare for class, what they do in class, and what portions of reading materials they attend to. Clear goals also affect how teachers prepare for and conduct their classes (Gagné & Driscoll, 1988).

The most competent teachers are able to determine where to begin instruction with each student. Gagné and Driscoll (1988) point out that effective teachers prepare for instruction at the students' level, provide individualized instruction where necessary, and pace instruction properly. Poor instruction frequently bores good students and frustrates less able students. The best teachers provide something for everyone—all students are challenged because materials are suited to their varying capabilities.

Evaluating Learning

Good instruction is evaluated carefully and constantly adjusted. Students receive prompt and relevant feedback about their learning. Poor instruction, on the other hand, is characterized by inappropriate, irrelevant evaluations of student learning and sometimes by no evaluations at all. Effective teachers possess a whole host of evaluation skills that allow them to determine how well students are learning. This information, obtained from both well-constructed, teacher-made evaluation instruments and standardized tests, helps good teachers to adjust their instructional procedures. Student learning is greatly facilitated by feedback received from careful evaluation.

Meeting the Needs of Special Students

Excellent teachers are able to orchestrate challenging learning experiences for all students (Brophy, 1982; Brophy & Evertson, 1976; Brophy & Good, 1986). In particular, they adapt their instruction to the needs of both exceptionally talented and handicapped students. Poor instruction ignores the needs of individual students, a guarantee that many will never reach their potential. Effective teachers take into account the specific needs of individual learners, including the disabled and the nondisabled.

Good teachers are constantly giving thoughtful reactions to what students are doing. Careful feedback like this greatly facilitates learning.

Remaining Lifelong Learners

The best teachers are dedicated lifelong learners. Not all teachers are good learners, however. Oscar Wilde reflected the feeling of some people when he wrote: "Everybody who is incapable of learning has taken to teaching" (Wilde, 1904). This skeptical attitude about teachers is, unfortunately, partly correct even today in that some teachers seem to stop learning when they begin teaching. The changing world passes them by and soon leaves them unprepared to teach effectively. In contrast, excellent teachers keep abreast of new developments in their subject matter areas and continually improve their already outstanding teaching skills. The best teachers are always learning—they are themselves dedicated students.

Educational Psychology and Effective Teaching

A Definition of Educational Psychology

It would be as absurd for one to undertake to educate the young with no knowledge of . . . psychology, as for one to attempt to produce a sonata while ignorant of the phenomena of sound. (Louisa Parsons Hopkins, *Educational Psychology*, 1886, p. 3)

A common belief among those of us who call ourselves educational psychologists was expressed clearly by Hopkins in the first book to be entitled *Educational Psychology*. We believe the best teaching can happen only when teachers thoughtfully apply the principles of psychology.

In simple terms, educational psychology is that branch of psychology devoted to the application of the principles of psychology to educational settings. Most educational psychologists, however, would argue that educational psychology is much more than the simple application of already discovered psychological principles to educational systems. Indeed, educational psychology is its own discipline with its own goals, research agenda, and infrastructure. It has a unique history in academia and has been blessed with contributors of uncommon ability and foresight.

Educational psychologists function in many different roles. Some educational psychologists design curricular materials for the schools, some evaluate educational programs, and others develop sophisticated computer-assisted instructional materials for business, industry, and the armed forces. Many educational psychologists teach and are integral parts of teacher-preparation programs. A significant number of educational psychologists perform research in attempts to better understand the teaching-learning process.

Educational psychologists investigate human learning, human development, and teaching methods in their research by applying the scientific method to questions educators have about the learning-teaching process. One of the major tasks of educational psychology is conducting research on the most effective ways to teach. In the previous section we listed the skills and the kinds of knowledge effective teachers possess. This list was the product of research by educational psychologists on the differences between effective and ineffective teachers.

Research in educational psychology lies along a continuum from basic to applied, with most falling somewhere in between (Berliner, 1985; Glover & Ronning, 1987; Melton, 1959; Wittrock, 1967). Basic research is conducted to answer fundamental questions about the nature of learning or teaching without concern for any direct applications of the results. An example of basic research is an investigation of how finely people can discriminate between different musical tones. The answer is of great interest to many persons and is relevant to the teaching of music, but it may not have any direct impact on teachers. At the other end of the spectrum, applied research is conducted to find solutions to actual educational problems. Suppose members of a curriculum committee are developing reading materials for sixth-graders and they want to know the best kind of study questions to give the students. A research study designed to answer this question would be directly applicable for these educators and probably for many other teachers as well.

Research at all levels from basic to applied helps us to improve education. Principles from basic research are the foundation for much of our current understanding of children's thinking and motivation. Applied studies have often helped the educational community to test these principles in complex settings such as in reading programs or mathematics curricula. Research at all levels contributes to the theory and practice of education.

There is more to educational psychology, however, than research. Teachers must be able to use research results. Finding out, for example, that mnemonics (memory aids) are helpful for many students doesn't benefit anyone unless teachers learn to use them. So if you ask, "How can educational psychology help me become a more effective teacher?" the answer lies in your ability to learn and employ the skills, knowledge, and principles generated from psychological research. A careful examination of the next few paragraphs outlining the rest of the book will help you to see what skills and knowledge you will acquire in your study of educational psychology.

Looking Ahead

The first major part of the book, "Cognitive Psychology Applied to Teaching," is designed to help you attain a broad understanding of human cognition and to apply this understanding to your teaching. Chapter Two, "An Introduction to Cognitive Processes," introduces you to the study of thinking and provides specific information about the processes of perception and attention. A discussion of short- and long-term memory and a brief history of cognitive psychology are followed by applications of cognitive psychology to teaching.

Chapter Three, "Memory and Concepts," continues the discussion of human cognition. Specifically, Chapter Three describes both historical and current views of memory, with emphasis on the application of memory research to teaching. Concepts, a central feature of memory, are discussed, and effective methods for teaching concepts are described. Chapter Four, "Intelligence and Cognitive Development, "focuses on individual differences in cognitive functioning and the nature of cognitive development. The chapter emphasizes the application of developmental theories in teaching. Chapter Five, "Language and the Development of Literacy," begins by reviewing a crucial aspect of cognition, how language develops. The chapter then focuses on two highly important cognitive skills, reading and writing. Chapter Six, "Problem Solving and Creativity," presents methods by which teachers can help students become better problem solvers and can help facilitate the development of their creativity.

The second major part of the text, "Self-Concept and Motivation," examines the importance of students' self-concepts and outlines methods whereby teachers can motivate their students' classroom performance. Chapter Seven, "Self-Concept and Moral Development," traces the development of self-concept and closely examines the implications of self-concept for academic achievement. Later in the chapter, the focus is on moral development and the relation of moral development to students' behaviors in educational settings. Chapter Eight, "Motivation," surveys several important views of motivation and draws on them to present a set of guidelines for motivating student behavior.

The next major part of the text, "Guiding Classroom Behavior," emphasizes the prevention of problem behavior. Chapter Nine, "An Introduction to Behavioral Psychology," provides a thorough description of behavioral psychology, a discipline that views learning from a perspective quite different from that of cognitive psychology. The principles of behavioral psychology are reviewed and applications for teachers are described. Chapter Ten, "Social Learning and Modeling," presents a theoretical perspective, social learning theory, that integrates cognitive and behavioral psychology. We discuss the learning of social behaviors, especially through observation, with particular emphasis on classroom interactions. Chapter Eleven, "Classroom Management," draws on the theories presented through the first ten chapters of the text to describe specific methods of modifying student behavior.

Chapters Twelve through Fourteen constitute the next part of the book, "Educational Measurement and Evaluation." Chapter Twelve, "Planning for Meaningful Learning," will help you to translate broad educational goals and the principles of cognitive and behavioral psychology into specific statements about your students' abilities. In addition, the chapter outlines the concepts, principles, and basic issues underlying educational measurement. Chapter Thirteen, "Teacher-Made Tests," applies the principles from Chapter Twelve to the planning of tests and other measures. It will help you learn to design measurement instruments that will lead to sound decisions about student learning and provide excellent feedback on student progress. In Chapter Fourteen, "Standardized Tests," you will learn about using standardized tests in making educational decisions.

The final part of the text, "Special Needs Students," includes extremely important information for teachers. Chapter Fifteen, "The Exceptional Student," highlights characteristics of the children educators often refer to as "special." Information about a wide range of exceptionalities, from visual impairment to giftedness, is presented along with a description of the mainstreaming process.

Summary

To teach effectively requires both artistry and a knowledge of the principles of effective instruction. Educational psychology is a source of many principles upon which teachers can draw. These principles come from research—both basic and applied—conducted to study how people learn and develop and to find the best ways to help them learn. Educational psychology provides both general principles that underlie all teaching methods and specific skills that help a person become a more effective teacher. Its ultimate value lies both in its contribution to theory and in its applications, as teachers provide students with successful and enjoyable learning experiences.

Suggested Readings

Bagley, W. C., Bell, J. C., Seashore, C. E., & Whipple, G. M. (1910). Editorial. *Journal of Educational Psychology, 1,* 1–3.
> *This editorial, which appeared in the first issue of the* Journal of Educational Psychology,*provided an early definition of the field that still is important in our thinking about educational psychology.*

Glover, J. A., & Ronning, R. R. (1987). About educational psychology. In J. A. Glover & R. R. Ronning (Eds.), *Historical foundations of educational psychology* (pp. 3–15). New York: Plenum.
> *This chapter traces the evolution of educational psychology from its beginnings to contemporary times. It also provides an overview of the relationship between psychology and the field of education.*

Hopkins, L. P. (1886). *Educational psychology.* Boston: Lee and Shepard.
> *This little volume, written by Louisa Parsons Hopkins, was the first book to have educational psychology in its title. The book is worth reviewing in order to obtain a sense of how much we've changed over the years.*

James, W. (1899). *Talks to teachers on psychology and to students on some of life's ideas.* New York: Holt.
> *William James' book is the classic volume describing the application of psychology to teaching. Not only are the ideas in this volume still fresh, but it contains a great deal about the background of our field.*

Klausmeier, H. J. (1988). The future of educational psychology and the content of the graduate program in educational psychology. *Educational Psychologist, 23,* 203–220.
> *Herbert Klausmeier's review paper is a good source of ideas about the future directions of educational psychology.*

PART ONE

The central issues of cognitive psychology concern the ways in which human beings understand, remember, and use information. Most teachers, of course, have a strong interest in these same topics. The six chapters in this first part are devoted to cognitive psychology and its application to education.

Chapter Two, "An Introduction to Cognitive Processes," provides an overview of the study of human thought, with particular emphasis on a model of human thought and the basic processes of perception and attention. Chapter Three, "Memory and Concepts," is directed to the functioning of human memory and to how teachers can facilitate students' memory for new information. Central to the discussion in Chapter Three is the role of concepts in teaching. Chapter Four, "Intelligence and Cognitive Development," describes perspectives on intelligence and their use in effective teaching practices. In addition, Chapter Four recounts the unfolding of cognitive development and provides guidelines for how teachers can employ their knowledge of cognitive development to improve instruction.

Related to an understanding of cognition and cognitive development is a knowledge of how language develops, the topic opening Chapter Five. Basic information about the processes involved in reading and writing complete Chapter Five. Chapter Six, "Problem Solving and Creativity," addresses two additional important aspects of cognition: how people solve problems and creative thought. The teacher's role in developing students' problem-solving skills and enhancing their creative abilities is described.

Cognitive Psychology Applied to Teaching

CHAPTER
2

An Introduction to Cognitive Processes

OVERVIEW

Just for a moment, take a little trip with us in your imagination. You're standing in front of a floor-length mirror admiring yourself. Suddenly you become aware of a young child standing a little to the side and behind you, looking rather seriously at herself. First she moves one hand and then the other. She stares intently at her mirror image. She then tugs at your sleeve.

"I don't understand it," she says. "Why is it that I'm turned around in the mirror, so that my right hand is my left hand and my left hand is my right hand?" "Hmm . . ." Giving yourself a moment to think, you begin to search your mind for an answer she can understand. You mentally bounce light rays off the mirror. But she goes right on, ". . . but my head isn't at the bottom, and my feet aren't at the top! How is it that I'm reversed sideways but not up and down? Why aren't I standing on my head in the mirror?" "Mmmm . . ." you say.

Sometimes a child can ask a seemingly simple question that can momentarily perplex you and force you to think hard to come up with an explanation. Her questions and actions also give us a number of hints about the workings of the child's mind as she observes herself, does things such as moving her hands to test the effect, recognizes an apparent paradox, and then poses a puzzling question.

The processes of the child's mind—her mental activities—generally are referred to as **cognitive processes.** Cognitive processes include all the many fascinating functions of the mind—recognition, remembering, self-awareness, thinking, reading, writing, problem solving, and creativity. Your reactions to the child's questions in our story likewise fall into the realm of cognitive processes. As you read the story, you understood the meaning of the sentences and may have imagined the scene. Perhaps you tried to recall certain optical principles from a distant science class. Finally, you may have thought about the problem and about the explanation you would give the child.*

How we think, what and how we remember, and how we solve problems all are cognitive processes of great interest to psychologists. These same cognitive processes are crucial to teachers, who are responsible for guiding all forms of learning. In fact, many educators would suggest that the primary role of teachers is the development of students' cognitive processes.

In this chapter we introduce you to cognitive psychology, the systematic study of cognitive processes; and we outline a model of human thought that should help you to better understand how students acquire, retain, process, and create information. We then develop this model of cognitive processes in detail in Chapters Three through Six. These chapters stress both the research on which an understanding of cognitive processes is based and applications of the principles of cognitive psychology to teaching.

---

*Actually, the image is not "reversed." The reflection is of what is opposite to it at every point on the mirror.

| OBJECTIVES | After reading this chapter, you should be able to meet the following objectives. |

1.   Relate a model of cognitive processes to classroom learning.

2.   Translate the major principles of cognitive psychology into a set of instructional procedures in your subject area.

The Nature of Cognitive Processes

All cognitive processes are invisible. This fact, though obvious, implies a basic difficulty in the study of cognitive processes. Consider what can be observed when one form of cognitive processing—reading—occurs.

Suppose we have given a student a ten-page essay on the nature of the Rumanian government. The student looks at the title, and we watch as her eyes flick back and forth down the first page. In a few moments she turns the page, and we continue observing her as she reads through the essay. Finally, after ten minutes or so, she announces that she has finished the essay. What happened? What have we seen? We've seen eye movements, hand movements, head movements, and perhaps some movements of the lips. But have we seen any cognitive processes? No. From our observation of this student we will have very little information about any of her mental activities. Did she learn anything? Did she comprehend the information? Will she remember any of it this afternoon or a month from now? We simply don't know. Because cognitive processes are not visible, we are forced instead to use indirect methods to assess them.

Think for a moment about other examples of cognitive processes. Perhaps you have had a roommate who suddenly discovered a way of solving a set of math problems. Maybe you have seen a small child figure out how to open a box. Or possibly you've watched as a person puzzled out the meaning of an unfamiliar term in a textbook. What happened? What did you see? No matter how many examples you consider, have you ever seen anything other than the *results* of cognitive processes? Cognitive processes, whether in reading, solving problems, or listening to a lecture, never can be observed directly. We can only observe the results of these processes—that is, changes in behavior—and make inferences about the processes.

In our example of the student who read the essay, we could infer some things about her cognitive processes if her experience (reading)

Cognitive processes can never
be studied directly.

altered her behavior. One way to do this would be to first assess the
student's prior knowledge of the Rumanian government by asking her
a series of questions. Her answers would constitute behaviors (talking
or writing) that we could observe and analyze. After she read the essay,
we could ask her the same questions about Rumania. If she could
answer the questions she could not answer before, we would infer she

had learned the answers from her reading. We could, of course, further test her knowledge and determine which parts of the essay she remembered best, which parts she confused with her knowledge of other things, how the writing styles in different sections of the essay influenced her memory, and so on. This procedure—looking at changes in behavior as a result of experience—is the major research methodology employed by psychologists and educators who study cognitive processes.

The invisible nature of cognitive processes places researchers in much the same position as astronomers who study black holes. Black holes are celestial bodies possessing such strong gravitational forces that not even light can escape from them. Astronomers can never directly observe black holes and, thus, must try to understand them by studying the effects these invisible objects have on other parts of the cosmos. Similarly, psychologists and educators can never study cognitive processes directly and so have based their studies on the observable outcomes of mental activity.

A Model of Cognitive Processes

When scientists wish to understand complex processes, they often attempt to construct a *model* of what they are studying. Constructing a workable and accurate model of the DNA molecule, for example, was a major step for researchers in biology and genetics toward understanding the mechanisms by which genetic information is transmitted. Similarly, cognitive psychologists have constructed models of cognitive processes. Many of these models picture the human being as an information-processing system (see Dellarosa, 1988; Lesgold, 1988; Newell & Simon, 1956). Information-processing models have guided the rapid development of cognitive theory and research in recent years.

In the following chapters, we discuss in detail important cognitive processes such as memory, concept learning, reading, writing, problem solving, and creativity as well as the collection of high-level cognitive processes that fall under the label "intelligence." In addition, we describe the course of cognitive development and how language develops and becomes an integral part of cognition. To help you understand how these aspects of cognition fit together, we have chosen an **information-processing model** of cognition as the organizing feature for the next several chapters. This model is presented in Figure 2–1.

FIGURE 2–1   INFORMATION-PROCESSING MODEL OF COGNITION

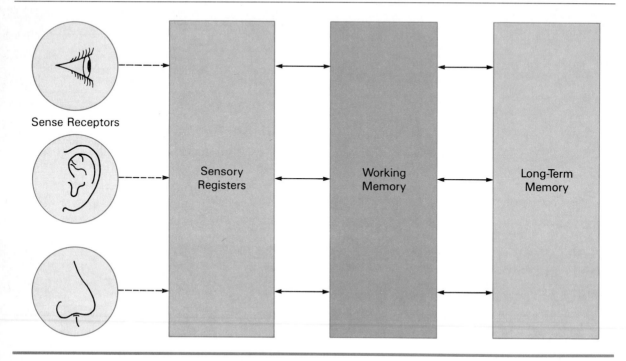

Sense Receptors

Sensory Registers

Working Memory

Long-Term Memory

As you can see, it contains several components: sense receptors, sensory registers, a working memory, and a long-term memory. Each plays a vital role in our abilities to process information.

Sense Receptors

Our primary contact with the world and the information in it is through our **sense receptors**. These organs—such as our eyes, ears, and nose—allow us to make contact with the environment. Each type of sense receptor is sensitive to a particular class of **stimuli** (singular, *stimulus*), events that can cue or prompt actions on the part of the learner.* A word such as *stop* in this sentence is a visual stimulus. It may be a cue for you to take such actions as looking at the word, or momentarily stopping in your reading. Other types of stimuli are auditory (for example, a spoken word or the sound of a train whistle), olfactory (the scent of a peach cobbler), tactile (the feel of a baseball), and kinesthetic (the feel of your muscles as you write a sentence).

---

*Note that this definition of the term *stimulus* is somewhat different from that given in Chapter Nine, in which we take up behavioral psychology.

Regardless of their type, sense receptors convey information about stimuli into our information-processing system.

An impairment in a sense receptor obviously has an important effect on how a learner processes information. Children who are deaf from birth, for example, live in an environment in which auditory stimuli play no part. Visual and tactile stimuli are thus especially critical. In fact, recent research indicates that deaf children's cognitive processes may develop quite differently from those of hearing children (see Rodda & Grove, 1987). Such differences have important implications for how teachers work with children. Our chapter "Special Needs Students" explores the implications of sense receptor impairment for learning. Our primary reason for introducing sense receptors here is to show that they are the critical first component in the human information-processing system.

Sensory Registers

One of the most important cognitive processes is **perception**. Perception is more than sensing something in the environment; it is the process of determining the meaning of what is sensed (Watt, 1988). That is, an element of the environment (a stimulus) is perceived when a person can give meaning to that stimulus. The difference between sensing and perceiving a stimulus is analogous to the difference between seeing something (a blur in the corner of your eye, for instance) and knowing what you've seen (a bird flying toward you).

Our primary contact with the world and the information in it is through our sense receptors.

Before a person can determine the meaning of stimuli, a number of cognitive processes must be carried out. Each process takes time, and thus perception is not instantaneous. This fact poses an interesting problem for psychologists who have tried to model cognitive processes. Since the environment often changes very quickly (as when students view a film or listen to directions), many stimuli disappear long before there has been enough time for the processes involved in perception to be completed. This would seem to indicate that the analysis of stimuli would abruptly cease when the stimuli disappear. This doesn't happen, however (at least with most persons), because human beings possess "holding systems" that briefly maintain representations of stimuli so that perceptual analyses can occur (Solso, 1988; Watt, 1988). These holding systems are the **sensory registers**.

The importance of sensory registers can be seen in almost every classroom situation. Consider the role of sensory registers as teachers give spoken directions to students. Once an instruction has been given, there is no physical trace of it. Unless listeners can briefly maintain words in some form, perception and understanding cannot occur. Imagine the difficulty, indeed the impossibility, of trying to follow directions if each word disappeared before its meaning could be determined.

There probably are different registers for each of our senses (see Watt, 1988). Each is vital to perception, but other components of cognition are equally involved in giving meaning to stimuli. One of these components is long-term memory, the permanent repository of knowledge about the world (Solso, 1988).

Long-term Memory

The permanent repository of information we have accumulated from the world around us is represented as the **long-term memory** component of our cognitive model. We can recall at will many events from our past, such as a birthday party at a friend's house, a particularly beautiful sunset, or a first date. Even in those cases when we are not consciously recalling our experiences from long-term memory, however, they affect our perception. Consider, for example, the following:

Did you see the duplicate word in each triangle? Many readers do not. Because of our prior learning, we usually don't read each word as an individual, separate unit; most readers instead perceive the phrase as a whole. As Smith (1988) has pointed out, good readers often are likely to make mistakes in their perception of individual words because as they read they predict what the words or phrases will be. Thus, students' perceptions depend to a large extent on what they already know. From the perspective of cognitive psychology, as Ausubel (1960) noted many years ago, perception occurs when stimuli become meaningful to students, that is, when students have prior knowledge that enables them to give meaning to new information.

Working Memory

In addition to sense receptors, sensory registers, and long-term memory, the final component of the model of cognitive processes is **working memory**, in which perception is guided, decisions are made, problems are solved, and new knowledge is created. In short, working memory is the part of the model in which thinking occurs.

Working memory corresponds to what most people call consciousness (Hitch, Halliday, Schaafstal, & Schraagen, 1988). Our working memory guides the process of transforming and analyzing stimuli in order to compare them to what is in our permanent memory* (Solso, 1988). Working memory also can be conceived of as the component in our model in which decisions about incoming stimuli are made (Andre, 1987).

Learning cannot occur without perception. Unless information has meaning, no understanding can develop. Stimuli must be recognized, classified, and distinguished from other stimuli in order for meaningful learning to take place. Until children recognize what words are and what their boundaries are and distinguish words from other stimuli (letters, numbers), they are likely to have great difficulty learning to read (Ehri & Wilce, 1985; Tierney, Anders, & Mitchell, 1987). Many young children simply do not perceive words as units, even though they can combine and recombine them in sentences (Goeslan, Oberg, & Smith, 1984). As we will see in Chapter Twelve, "Planning for Meaningful Learning," the process of assessing students' present perceptions and planning new instruction so that it builds on their current knowledge is a key component of effective teaching.

---

*The transformation and analysis process is usually referred to as **pattern recognition** (Watt, 1988). There is a large body of research in cognitive psychology devoted solely to investigating how this process occurs.

PRACTICE EXERCISE 2–1   PERCEPTION AND COGNITIVE PERFORMANCE

This practice exercise is a simple one. First we would like you to read the sentence in the box below.

> FINISHED FILES ARE THE RESULT
> OF YEARS OF SCIENTIFIC STUDY
> COMBINED WITH THE
> EXPERIENCE OF
> MANY YEARS.

Now we want to count the *F*s in the sentence. Count them just once. Then turn to page 47 to check your count.

An important cognitive process closely linked to working memory is **attention**. Attention can be defined as the overall distribution of mental activity to the tasks an individual performs (Hunt, 1988). Students are limited in the number of things they can focus on at a given time. A student, for instance, may be faced simultaneously with a teacher's explanation of a geometry problem, snow falling outside, thoughts of what to buy a parent for her birthday, a whispered discussion of who's dating whom, and the smell of food from the cafeteria. Obviously, all these events cannot receive equal attention, and so an important consideration is what events the student attends. The procedures described in Chapter Eleven "Classroom Management," can help a teacher control distractions in the classroom. Regardless of how carefully a classroom is organized and managed, however, attention is still a cognitive process (Halpain, Glover, & Harvey, 1985). Consider what happens when a student is carefully taking notes during a lecture. The student selects some of what the instructor says and copies it down, while ignoring or transforming other information. Some questions raised by class members will be carefully scrutinized, and other questions will be largely ignored as the student looks over his or her notes. Even when students are engaged in careful study, they are attending selectively to various aspects of their environment.

The most recent research on attention processes suggests that the selection of stimuli occurs *after* a preliminary meaning has been assigned to stimuli in the working memory* (Watt, 1988). Those materials and activities most likely to get students' attention are those to which they can assign meaning. New learning builds on prior learning.

Another component of working memory, **short-term memory**, was regarded by many early information-processing researchers (e.g., Waugh & Norman, 1965) as a repository for briefly storing incoming information. Although more recent conceptions of memory do not emphasize a separate short-term memory, the initial processing, rehearsal, and transfer of incoming information are together regarded as one of the most critical functions of the working memory. If incoming stimuli are not sufficiently processed, forgetting can occur in only a few seconds. Constant rehearsal of new materials often is necessary, particularly if there are many separate bits of information. If you are distracted between the time you look up a phone number and the time you dial the phone, for example, you may completely forget the number. Similarly, students trying to take notes may lose their place if too much information is given to them in too short a time and their short-term memories become overloaded. Once information is transferred to long-term memory, however, it is much less likely to be lost since long-term memory is much less fragile.

In addition to the working memory's function of briefly holding new information, it also contains information called up from long-term memory. It is the arena in which memories interplay with new information. That is, working memory is where thinking goes on (Hitch et al., 1988): remembering good times, thinking about the answer to a trivia quiz ("What line precedes the line 'A woman's work is never done'?"), solving problems ("Let's see, if I brace this board with a brick . . ."), considering alternatives ("Do I want to go to the movies or read another chapter of educational psychology?"), filing away things to be remembered ("I've got to remember to tell Jane to call Susie"), analyzing thoughts ("I can't believe I could be so forgetful"), and creating new knowledge ("Eureka! $E = mc^2$").

As you can see, the overall model of information processing stresses the interplay of cognitive functions. Perception depends on incoming stimuli, information in long-term memory, and decisions in

---

*Broadbent (1958) articulated the first modern cognitive theory of attention and suggested that selection occurs in the sensory registers *prior* to perception. While his theory is now viewed as too simplistic (see, e.g., Watt, 1988), his view of attention selection in the sensory registers focused a great deal of research activity on this important process (Yost & Watson, 1987).

the working memory. Attention depends on perception (with all its constituent processes) and decisions in the working memory. Recall depends on the working memory and long-term memory but is influenced, of course, by perception. In the same way, problem solving, creativity, and other cognitive processes all result from an interaction of cognitive functions.

The Role of Knowledge

All cognitive processes are directly influenced by knowledge. A recent study by Recht and Leslie (1988) demonstrates just how powerful knowledge can be. To set the stage for their study, it is important to point out that one of the most common findings in educational research (dating back at least to Huey, 1908) is that good readers remember more about what they read than poor readers. In fact, this very common-sense finding is almost a definition of good and poor reading.

Recht and Leslie wondered about the role of knowledge in what people remember about reading materials. Unfortunately, this question is difficult to address because good readers tend to know more about almost everything than poor readers—presumably because good readers gain so much knowledge from their reading. Recht and Leslie, however, found a topic for which knowledge was independent of reading ability: baseball.

In their study, Recht and Leslie tested more than 600 seventh- and eighth-grade students for their knowledge of baseball. They also checked the students' scores on a standardized test of reading ability. These procedures allowed Recht and Leslie to place 64 of the students into 4 groups of 16 each: (1) good readers who knew a great deal about baseball, (2) good readers who knew very little about baseball, (3) poor readers who knew a great deal about baseball, and (4) poor readers who knew very little about baseball.

On an individual basis, the 64 students then were given a brief passage describing one half of an inning of a baseball game. The students were asked to read the passage carefully and were allowed to work at their own pace. After they finished reading, they were tested over their ability to remember the passage's contents. The results of the study showed that poor readers who knew a great deal about baseball remembered as much as good readers who knew a great deal about baseball. Further, poor readers who knew a great deal about baseball remembered more than twice as much of the passage contents than good readers who knew very little about baseball. Poor readers who knew very little about baseball, as one might expect, remembered the least.

The results of Recht and Leslie's (1988) study fit into a consistent pattern observed in recent years (see Taft & Leslie, 1985). Prior knowledge about a topic is directly related to the amount of new information students are able to remember about that topic. Knowledge, though, affects more than what students remember. Knowledge influences their ability to think, to solve problems, to explain—all their cognitive processes.

Consider, for example, two kindergartners of equal ability listening to their teacher read the story "Pickles, the Fire Cat." One child, Brad, clearly imagines Pickles because he has a cat at home. Brad knows a lot about cats and easily understands those parts of the story that focus on Pickles. Katie, sitting next to Brad, isn't learning much about Pickles. Katie doesn't have a cat and has only seen them on television or in other people's yards. However, Katie's mother is a firefighter. Katie knows what a fire station looks like, what a hook-and-ladder truck is, and knows a lot about fires. What Katie understands best about the story are those segments focused on the fire station and the work of the firefighters. It should come as no surprise that Brad and Katie differ in what parts of the story they pay careful attention to, what kinds of scenes they imagine, and what parts of the story they remember best. Their cognitive processes were guided by their knowledge.

Finally, knowledge is the key to an important concept described years ago by Ausubel (1960)—meaningfulness. New information is meaningful when it can be related to what is already known. The meaning that we give to information organizes our perception, attention, short-term memory, long-term memory, and ability to integrate all these components into problem solving and creativity.

Metacognition: Thinking About Thinking

One important way that information is made meaningful is through metacognition. **Metacognition** means, literally, thinking about thinking (Armbruster & Brown, 1984) and is a process that occurs in the working memory. Over the past few years, research on how students think about their own cognitive processes has given us considerable

As this girl does her own measurements as she works math problems, her growing knowledge about her own thinking—her metacognition—helps her judge whether the problem solving approaches she selects are likely to be successful.

insight into the human information-processing system and has suggested many important applications for teaching.

In general, there seem to be two closely related types of metacognition: (1) knowing about cognition and (2) monitoring and regulating cognition (Baker & Brown, 1985; Cross & Paris, 1988). Knowing about cognition can be seen when students are aware of their own cognitive abilities. For example, a student who knows he has a poor memory for assignments may make it a point to systematically record each of his daily assignments in a notebook. Similarly, a teacher who wants to remember students' names may make it a point to use a seating chart the first few days of school to help her match names with faces. As another example, a second student who knows she can learn to solve math problems much more effectively by reading the instructions in her text than by listening in class may pay little attention to a teacher's explanation and instead focus on the material in her book. Each of these examples shows individuals' awareness of their own thought processes and is thus metacognitive.

The second type of metacognition, thinking that monitors and regulates thinking, refers to activities students engage in to help them better perform cognitive tasks (Cross & Paris, 1988). Often, students are not even aware of such self-regulating activities. For example, good readers are seldom aware of monitoring and regulating their reading until something—seeing an unknown word or not being able to integrate a new sentence with a previous one—alerts them to a problem in their reading. At that point, good readers may reread the passage, try to use context to determine a word's meaning, or even consult a dictionary. Their self-monitoring and self-regulation allows them to take appropriate steps if there is some difficulty.

As one might imagine, students' abilities to perform cognitive tasks are related to their metacognitive abilities. To return to the reading example we used above, good readers typically have good metacognitive skills. They monitor their own reading and make adjustments—slowing down for difficult material, planning to reread very abstract articles, and taking notes while reading complex histories. Good readers also monitor and regulate their reading with little conscious effort. Only when a problem occurs, such as when a sentence makes no sense, do they become consciously aware of their comprehension monitoring and take steps to remedy the situation.

Poor readers, in contrast, often are unaware of their own approaches to reading. They may attempt to process many different kinds of reading materials in the same way. Further, they typically do not monitor or regulate their reading in effective ways—poor readers often do not seem to know when they are not comprehending a passage, and, if they do become aware of a problem, they may not know what to do about it (see Cross & Paris, 1988).

The Development of Metacognition

When students of different ages are asked to rate the importance of ideas in brief passages, a very clear developmental trend is observed (Jacobs & Paris, 1987). Eighteen-year-olds who are good readers consistently are able to rate ideas at four levels (i.e., "most" to "least"). In contrast, twelve-year-old good readers usually can identify only the most and least important ideas in passages. Ten-year-olds typically can pick out only the most important ideas, and eight-year-olds have great trouble making any distinctions at all among the ideas in passages (see Brown & Smiley, 1977). Students' abilities to identify main ideas can be improved (see Stevens, 1988), but the difference across ages remains.

As yet, research on metacognitive development is still in its beginning stages. However, as we will see in Chapter Three, "Memory and Concepts," there has been considerable work on one important facet of metacognitive development—metamemory. Here we will limit ourselves to pointing out that metacognitive skills seem to be relatively late in developing (Jacobs & Paris, 1987) and that the instruction children receive should be closely linked to their metacognitive skills (Stevens, 1988). As Jacobs and Paris (1987, p. 275) have noted in their review of metacognitive instruction, "It is clear that children's awareness about reading and their use of effective strategies can be promoted by instruction."

Facilitating Students' Metacognition

Ann Brown, of the University of California–Berkeley, has done pioneering research on metacognition and has written extensively about the applications of this research to teaching (e.g., Armbruster & Brown, 1984; Brown, 1987). Below, we summarize a series of guidelines drawn from Brown's work designed to help teachers improve their students' metacognitive abilities.

1. *Students should be helped to understand that different learning activities make different demands on them.* For example, elementary students learning new vocabulary words need to learn that reading over a word list and even memorizing it is not the best way to learn to use new vocabulary. More effective is learning the definitions of words and practicing their use in as many settings as possible (e.g., in conversations, in discussions, in written assignments, in talking with parents). Similarly, high school students who will be tested by an essay examination need to learn to study differently than if they were to be tested by, say, a true-false test. An essay examination will require the ability to relate concepts, to give examples not described in the text, and to evaluate arguments. All these activities, of course, are far different from what most true-false or multiple-choice tests require. In general, research on metacognition suggests that teachers need to teach more than content; they also must teach students how to evaluate and how to prepare for learning tasks.

2. *Students should be taught that there are many clues to how materials are organized.* Headings, introductions, summaries, signals (e.g., "number one . . .," "the most important is . . .") all provide important information about which aspects of a reading assignment are especially important.

3. *Teach students that awareness of their own cognition can make a big difference in learning.* For example, students should learn that when they link new information to what they already know, the likelihood of remembering it increases. Similarly, students should know that their own motivation to learn makes a big difference in how well they learn.

Also, students should be helped to discover their strong and weak points (e.g., whether they benefit most from lectures, reading, questions, or discussions) and take them into account when learning new material.

4.   *Instruct students in basic metacognitive strategies.* Two especially good metacognitive strategies, for instance, are summarizing and self-questioning. Research shows that when students develop their own summaries or "maps" of reading materials and lectures, their memory for the content increases (Glover, 1989). In the same way, learning to use self-questioning during reading and listening to lectures helps students remember important information (Andre, 1987).

The Development of Cognitive Psychology

Contemporary cognitive psychology, which heavily emphasizes the interplay of cognitive functions and the role of meaningfulness in learning, is a rather recent development in psychology. Its origins can be traced to Ausubel (1960), to Bruner (Bruner, Goodnow, & Austin, 1956), and to the publication in 1967 of Ulrich Neisser's influential book, *Cognitive Psychology*. Yet today's cognitive psychology has deep roots; it is built on a long history that dates back to the very beginnings of the science of psychology. Cognitive psychology, in fact, can be said to have three distinct histories: an early period of steady growth (1880 to 1925), an intermediate period in which most American psychologists' efforts were in areas outside of cognitive psychology (1926 to about 1960), and a recent period in which advances have been rapid and dramatic (Anderson, 1985; DiVesta, 1987).

Structuralism

Most historians of psychology pinpoint the origin of psychology as a science at about 1878 in Würzburg, Germany, when Wilhelm Wundt set up the first experimental psychological laboratory (Baars, 1986; Boring, 1950; Dellarosa, 1988; DiVesta, 1987; Wertheimer, 1978). Wundt established his laboratory for the express purpose of studying the structure of consciousness (DiVesta, 1987), a goal within the general domain of cognitive psychology. Wundt's psychology, called **structuralism**, had three major aims: (1) to identify the most basic cognitive processes; (2) to ascertain how the elements of thought and thought processes are combined and to determine what laws govern their combination; and (3) to determine the relationship of cognitive to physiological processes (Titchener, 1909). Structuralism was the forerunner not only of cognitive psychology but of all other experimentally oriented schools of psychological thought* (Lundin, 1985).

Structuralism was the first coherent school of thought in psychology. It was replaced, however, by other theoretical perspectives that proved more attractive to most American psychologists. The failure of structuralism, in their eyes, was that its subject matter was extremely specific (the structure of consciousness and nothing else), that it was inflexible in changing to fit new evidence and concerns in psychology, and especially that its method of gathering data (introspection, which involves having experimental subjects report their mental events) was inadequate.

Functionalism

The first school of thought to set itself in opposition to structuralism was **functionalism**,[†] which was concerned with developing techniques in psychology and education that would be applicable to everyday problems. It was the first truly American psychology, and it was based on the ideas of William James.[‡] James was a genius who cannot be placed into any specific school of thought (Keller, 1937, 1965). He was much less an experimentalist than were the structuralists. James is credited, however, with articulating the first scientific theory of memory, in which he outlined short- and long-term memory processes, well in advance of contemporary theories of memory. His *Principles of Psychology*, published in 1890, was the foundation for functionalist theory.

The objectives of functionalism were to determine "(1) how mental activity goes on, (2) what it [mental activity] accomplishes, and (3) why it takes place" (Keller, 1937, p. 77). In contrast to structuralism, func-

---

*Psychology has tended to develop in such a way that clusters of individuals who share theories and investigative methods have often worked somewhat separately from those with different views. For example, cognitive psychologists and behaviorists (see Chapter Nine) have very different views of what is important to investigate; they are concerned with the nature of thought or of observable behavior, respectively. In educational psychology it is important to remain open to both points of view.

---

†The name *functionalism*, surprisingly, was coined by the structuralist E. B. Titchener in his 1898 paper "The Postulates of a Structural Psychology," in which he outlined the differences between the budding functionalist position and his own.

---

‡William James obtained the funds for a psychological laboratory at Harvard in 1875 but allowed the lab to be closed down after only a few months of operation. Hence, he actually established the first laboratory for psychology but is not given the same kind of credit awarded to Wundt (DiVesta, 1987; Murray & Rowe, 1979).

tionalism was a pragmatic, application-oriented psychology. Functionalists were extremely interested in pursuing the educational implications of psychology (Carr, 1925). Strongly influenced by Darwinian evolutionary theory, functionalism was a psychology that focused on the adjustment of organisms to their environment (Baars, 1986). While functionalism did employ introspection as an investigative method for a period of time, new observational methods quickly supplanted introspection as the major source of data.

Functionalism, centered in the work of John Dewey and James Angell at the University of Chicago, replaced structuralism as the major school of psychological thought in the United States. Its influence has been long-lived—contemporary psychology remains functional in its orientation (Hilgard, 1987). Functionalist approaches are extremely important in shaping contemporary theories of cognition (e.g., see Sternberg & Smith, 1988) and in guiding our concepts of what educational psychology should be.

Gestalt Psychology

Between about 1925 and 1960, American psychology was dominated by what came to be known as a behavioral view of psychology, or, simply, *behaviorism*. Behaviorism, at least in its early forms, was a strong reaction to the structuralist and functionalist positions and their emphasis on the study of cognitive processes. Led by John B. Watson, the behaviorists argued that all subjective and introspective data on cognitive processes should be ruled out and that the goal of psychology should be to predict and to control behavior, not to study mental processes (Watson, 1913).

So rapid was the growth of behaviorism and so powerful was its influence that its rise ushered in the second phase of the history of cognitive psychology, a dormant phase. The preoccupation of American experimental psychology with behaviorism was not absolute, although, compared to behaviorism, cognitive psychology was proceeding at a snail's pace in the United States. A few psychologists such as Arthur Melton (see Chapter Three, "Memory and Concepts") continued to study cognitive processes, particularly memory; but the major new influence in cognitive psychology came, not surprisingly, from outside the United States—from the German school of **Gestalt psychology** (DiVesta, 1987). Major interests of Gestalt theorists were in the areas of perception and problem solving.

Gestalt psychology, which we examine in greater detail in our chapter "Problem Solving and Creativity," was founded by Max Wertheimer, Wolfgang Köhler, and Kurt Koffka. *Gestalt* in the closest possible English translation means form, shape, or configuration

(Lundin, 1985). Gestalt theorists held that psychological experience could not be broken down into elements or pieces that could be studied separately, as the structuralists, functionalists, and behaviorists believed. Instead, experiences are perceived as an organized field of events that interact and mutually affect one other (Dellarosa, 1988). Gestalt psychologists argued that people do not perceive or react to individual elements in their environments; rather, they react to their total experiences. The total experience is different and perhaps greater than the sum of the parts.

By 1925, two major Gestalt psychology books had been published in the United States, and, ultimately, Wertheimer, Köhler, and Koffka all emigrated to the United States to escape the oppression of the growing Nazi movement in Germany. The impact of Gestalt psychology is such that Hilgard (1987) has said that the Gestalt psychologists were the intellectual forefathers of a large part of what now is called cognitive psychology. Gestalt psychology no longer exists as a separate school of thought; it has become an integral part of cognitive psychology.

Contemporary Cognitive Psychology

Cognitive psychology has experienced a resurgence in the past two decades, as psychologists have renewed their long-term interests in the mental processes critical to teaching and learning. Led by such psychologists as Jerome Bruner and David Ausubel, cognitive psychology clearly entered its modern era with the publication in 1967 of Ulrich Neisser's *Cognitive Psychology*. What does modern cognitive psychology stress? According to DiVesta, "the emphasis is on the total instructional event of which the learner is a part. The situational demands, the characteristics of the learner, the task demands, the purpose of the learner, and so on *interact* to determine the quality and texture of an event such as a teaching or learning episode." Cognitive psychology emphasizes the active and constructive role of the student in the context of a learning situation. Students construct meaning and create their own realities, rather than responding in an automatic way to their environments (Glover, Ronning, & Bruning, in press). The underlying theoretical perspective of the cognitive approach is that information processing is the most critical human activity. The primary function of the human mind is to seek, gain, store, remember, and use information about the world (Sternberg & Smith, 1988).

The continuing influence of functionalism and Gestalt psychology is undeniable (Dellarosa, 1988), but events outside of psychology also have provided resources for psychology's renewed interest in cognition. The most important of such events was the development of the high speed computer in the 1940s. DiVesta (1987) suggests that com-

Students actively process information. Here a student seeks clarification from a teacher about how to proceed in a problem she is working on.

puters have had three major effects on the new cognitive movement: (1) computers have served as an information-processing *model* for human thought; (2) computers are used to *test cognitive theories* through simulations of human thought; and (3) the study of artificial intelligence (such as that of chess-playing computers) has become a *source of ideas* for cognitive psychologists. Additionally, advances in other fields, especially linguistics (the study of language) and information theory in mathematics provided new ways of thinking about cognition (Hayes, in press).

As important as these advances in other sciences were, cognitive psychology would not have reemerged as a strong alternative to behaviorism had it not been for the dissatisfaction among many psychologists with the ability of a purely behavioral psychology to address important issues in such areas as language and problem solving (DiVesta, 1987). Behaviorism certainly has not lost its influence in American psychology. Nonetheless, many psychologists and educators consider cognitive psychology to be more useful in the study of mental processes central to teaching and learning. Each psychology, cognitive and behavioral, has focused on somewhat different aspects of human activity—cognitive psychology has focused on human mental processes and behavioral psychology on the effects that external events have on the actions of individuals. These interests are not exclusive, of course, and you will find members of both schools of thought holding views compatible with the other position. In educational psychology, in particular, both cognitive and behavioral psychology provide vital information for effective teaching.

Applications for Teaching: A Cognitive Perspective On Student Learning

No psychology, no matter how interesting, is useful unless it can be related to actual situations and problems. Thus we need to ask, "How does cognitive psychology view the teaching and learning process?" By applying some of the tenets of modern cognitive psychology to the learning process, we can derive a set of statements about students and how they learn best. We will present more detailed applications in Chapters Three through Six where we discuss the major processes of cognition.

1. Students are active processors of information. Students actively process information. They are not sponges or receptacles into which knowledge is poured. They relate each new thing they hear or see to what they already know. They classify, make guesses and formulate hypotheses, interpret, and read between the lines.

Suppose that a ninth-grade English class reads the following segment of a poem in a unit on irony.

> "Now tell us what 'twas all about,"
> Young Peterkin, he cries;
> And little Wilhelmine looks up
> .with wonder-waiting eyes;
> "Now tell us all about the war,
> and what they fought each other for?"
> "It was the English," Kaspar cried,
> "Who put the French to rout;
> But what they fought each other for
> I could not well make out.
> But every body said," quoth he,
> "That 't was a famous victory."*

Each reader will process the information contained in these lines in his or her own way. Some will have vivid images of young Wilhelmine or of a battle

_____
*From "The Battle of Blenheim," by Robert Southey.

scene. Others may think about the odd names or spend time trying to figure out the meaning of the words *'t was*. Some will begin memorizing the stanzas or will wonder about the author—whether he was English or French, for instance. Still other students will completely reject the idea of learning anything at all from a poem such as this; it simply is not meaningful to them.

As you think about the variety of potential information-processing activities, you should realize that what is learned will depend not only on the actual content but also on what students already know and on how they process the information received. As a teacher you can influence not only the selection of content but these two factors as well. The effective teacher will choose content that is or can be made meaningful to the student. Learning activities can also be skillfully guided by methods such as questioning and role playing so that students learn processes of inquiry as well as the basic information.

2. Students' knowledge influences all their cognitive processes. What students pay attention to, what they perceive, what they remember, how they solve problems, how they read, and what they create all are influenced by what they already know. Learning is most likely when new information is related to knowledge students already possess. Teachers must develop methods of finding out what students know about various topics (e.g., pretesting, questioning, making brief writing assignments) and relate to-be-learned material to that which students already know. Effective teachers discover what their students know and adjust their instruction accordingly.

3. Learning occurs when information is meaningful to students. Psychologists long have made a distinction between types of stimuli. At a most basic level, stimuli are events that cue or prompt learners' actions, such as a teacher's instructions to take out a sheet of paper, the distribution of handouts for students to read, or questions posed at the end of a lesson. On the other hand, there is the *interpretation* of the meaning of any stimulus. An instruction to take out a sheet of paper may be interpreted by some students as punishment for poor class recitation; a question may stimulate a great deal of thought from some students and not arouse the slightest interest in others. Cognitive psychologists emphasize the aspect of interpretation — the meaning learners give to stimuli, not the stimuli themselves.

In a cognitive approach to teaching, the greatest emphasis is on the *process*, not the products, of learning. What is important for these girls is that they are talking about their assignment and giving each other feedback on their thinking. What they learn from this particular assignment is less important.

From a cognitive perspective, learning and memory must be *constructed* by learners. Effective learning is interactive and interpretive, not passive and receptive. Meaning is not something that "sits out there" in the teacher's lecture or in the text; meaning results from learners' processing of the information that has been heard or read. Several factors determine whether information will be meaningful. Some relate to the students themselves. Do the students have prior knowledge or interest in this topic? Can they relate the information to things they already know? Does the topic match their intellectual abilities or is it too difficult or too easy? Other factors are linked to what the teacher does to interest and involve the students in learning. Can the teacher relate this topic to student concerns? Can the information be acquired in activities the students enjoy, such as projects or games, or written in ways that capture the students' interest? Meaningfulness emerges out of the mixture of topic, activities, and prior knowledge. Learners and teachers together make meaning.

PRACTICE EXERCISE 2–2   MEANINGFULNESS AND LEARNING

As you can see from this chapter, one of the major principles of cognitive psychology is that information is better learned and retained if it is meaningful. If materials, such as a list of words, are not particularly meaningful in and of themselves, most people automatically will do something to make them more meaningful.

To demonstrate this point, we would like you to try a little experiment in memory. You need three or four friends and these words:

Muskrat, blacksmith, panther, baker, wildcat, Howard, Jason, printer, chemist, radish, mushroom, Otto, plumber, pumpkin, chipmunk, Amos, Wallace, parsnip, milkman, druggist, leopard, woodchuck, Adam, grocer, Simon, Owen, lettuce, giraffe, turnip, garlic, rhubarb, typist, eggplant, Noah, zebra, donkey, Gerald, dentist, otter, parsley, spinach, Oswald, weasel, broker.*

To begin the experiment, tell your participants, either individually or as a group, that you will read them a list of words and that they will be asked to recall as many of them as possible. Read the list at a rate of about one word every three seconds. After you finish reading the whole list, tell them to start writing the words they recall as rapidly as possible. You should allow five minutes for recall from the time you tell them to start recalling. Turn now to page 47 for our comments on the results you should see.

———

*This list is based on a classic study by Bousfield (1953), and the methods of your experiment roughly parallel his.

4. How students learn is as important as what they learn. If you ask some people what education is, they will say that education is the "transmission of information"; that is, each new generation learns information discovered by earlier generations. Cognitive psychologists emphatically disagree with this position.

In a cognitive approach, there is greater emphasis on the processes of learning. If we can learn how to learn, then we can use these skills over and over. Getting the right answer to a single word problem is not particularly important from this standpoint; but knowing how to solve word problems is. Knowledge is not especially useful for its own sake; as we know, today's knowledge is quickly outdated. Bruner has said that to be used effectively knowledge must be "translated into the learner's way of attempting to solve a problem" (Bruner et al., 1956, p. 53).

Fourth-grade students, for example, may be studying a unit on the prairie pioneers and the great migration westward in nineteenth-century America. As part of this unit, students may learn that gold was discovered in California in 1848, that the Oto were a Plains Indian tribe, that Father Marquette was a missionary, and that a famous landmark of the Oregon trail was Chimney Rock. While this knowledge may be useful, a cognitive approach would put more emphasis on helping students to think and to make guesses and hypotheses about why things happened as they did. In short, the goal of the cognitively oriented teacher is to build curiosity, inquiry skills, and motivation to learn more.

Methods of teaching might include questions about which students can venture guesses ("Why did the pioneers travel in large groups in wagon trains while crossing the prairie?"), questions of value ("Were the Indian scouts who worked for the army at Ft. Kearny heroes or traitors to their people?"), and problems requiring the students to design solutions ("Imagine that you and your pioneer family are camped on the prairie on a stormy night in September. You have about three months more to travel before you reach your destination. Lightning strikes several times on the grass-covered hills surrounding you, and within moments a huge fire is roaring down on you, driven by terrific winds. The oxen are unhitched from the wagon, and you have less than a minute to save yourselves and whatever you can carry into and across a nearby stream. In your group, decide which of the contents of your wagon *must* be saved. Remember, you have less than a minute to save whatever you can, so you will have to decide."). In each case—asking students to guess, to evaluate, or to solve problems—the goal is not just to teach facts and figures but to develop students' abilities to think.

5. Cognitive processes become automatic with repeated use. The old adage "practice makes perfect" applies to mental processes. Initially, we must analyze stimuli such as words and patterns part by part and piece by piece in order to make sense out of them. In children who are just learning to read almost every word must be produced by laborious attention to such features as letters and phrases and, often, through a process of "sounding out." Skilled readers, in contrast, seldom devote their attention to decoding and to conscious attempts at recognition. Instead their processes of recognition are almost, if not completely, automatic (LaBerge & Samuels, 1974; Palmer & Jonides, 1988). Skilled readers read to get the meaning of what they read. Only when they are confused about meaning (for example, you read in a dialogue, "Yes, I occasionally suffer from pursy") do skilled readers pay conscious attention to deciphering the meaning of words.

Automatic processing and recognition are processes that take a long time to develop. Months or years may pass before students' reading processes become automatic. Some students' reading never does become automatic, and they must always pay attention to decoding. Chess masters who can instantly recognize and reproduce extremely complex patterns of chess pieces are estimated by Simon and Chase (1973) to have spent between 10,000 and 50,000 hours of their lives at a chessboard. This obviously is a long time, but it is not out of line with the time many adults have spent practicing their reactions in a variety of physical skills or in reading.

Thus, an important long-term goal of education is facilitating students' information-processing skills so that they occur rapidly and automatically. More than accuracy is often needed. The foreign-language student who cannot respond automatically in a conversation and must, for example, search for words and try to think of what to say, is not in a very comfortable position when trying to converse with a native speaker. The goal of much instruction, then, is to produce cognitive processes that are rapid, fluent, and automatic.

6. Metacognitive skills can be developed through instruction. Students' abilities to perform many cognitive tasks (e.g., reading, writing, solving problems) depend in large part on the effectiveness of their metacognitive skills (Weinert & Kluwe, 1987). Students need systematic instruction and guided practice in learning to understand and adapt to the demands of different learning tasks, in using the structure of reading materials to enhance their comprehension, in discovering their own cognitive abilities, and in acquiring effective metacognitive skills such as summarizing and self-questioning.

Metacognitive skills generally have been thought to be late to develop and to result from years of practice (Baker & Brown, 1985). Ghatala, Levin, Pressley, and Lodico (1985), however, found that second-graders could learn to use metacognitive skills with relative ease. More recently, Stevens (1988) found success in teaching metacognitive skills to remedial students from grades six through eleven. Similarly, Cross and Paris (1988) found that curricula focused on metacognitive skills were effective in helping third- and fifth-graders become more effective readers. Apparently, students of almost any age can benefit from instruction in metacognition. Teachers should focus not only on students' thinking skills but also on how their students think about their own thinking.

7. The most enduring motivation for learning is internal motivation. Long ago, Bruner and his coauthors (1956) captured the motivating qualities of engaging a student's curiosity, interest, and sense of discovery: "Our attention is attracted to something that is unclear, unfinished, or uncertain. We sustain our attention until the matter in hand becomes clear, finished, or certain. The achievement of clarity or merely the search for it is what satisfies" (p. 114).

In the view of cognitive psychology, children are responsible for their own cognitive development. They learn by interacting with the world around them. When experiences confirm their present knowledge, their mental structures become more stable. If new experiences do not fit with their present understanding, however, the understanding must eventually be reorganized to fit the new experiences. Conflict between an old way of thinking and new experiences is the basis for cognitive growth and change (Piaget, 1970a). (This aspect of cognitive development will be explored in detail in Chapter Four, "Intelligence and Cognitive Development.") Not only is this conflict the basis for intellectual growth, it is also highly motivating as children test their present ways of thinking against new experiences and the thinking of others.

8. There are vast differences in students' information-processing capabilities. In any classroom, you will see a wide range of differences in students' abilities to process and retain information. Some students will be excellent memorizers and able to learn long lists of facts such as state capitals, spelling words, chemical names, or authors and their works. Others may not retain such information easily but may be better at understanding and remembering the sense of what has been said. Metacognitive abilities also will differ greatly, some students showing much greater awareness of their own thinking skills. We will examine one important category of cognitive differences, intelligence, in Chapter Four. In both Chapter Four and Chapter Twelve, "Planning for Meaningful Learning," we will examine ways of adapting instructional methods to take students' cognitive differences into account. In addition, a variety of the methods described in our chapter "Classroom Management" will help you structure your classroom in ways that will better enable you to take individual differences into account.

PRACTICE EXERCISE 2–3   APPLYING PRINCIPLES OF COGNITIVE PSYCHOLOGY

One test for the value of ideas is whether they can be applied. The principles of cognitive psychology will be most valuable if you can apply them to your own teaching.

Listed below are the six major principles of cognitive psychology that relate to instruction. Briefly describe four teaching activities in your subject area and at the grade levels you hope to teach that are based on one or more of these principles. For each activity, indicate the number of the principle (or principles) that most closely relates to the activity.

Principles

1. Students are active processors of information.

2. Students' knowledge influences all their cognitive processes.

3. Learning occurs when information is meaningful to students.

4. How students learn is as important as what they learn.

5. Cognitive processes become automatic with repeated use.

6. Metacognitive skills can be developed through instruction.

7. The most enduring motivation for learning is internal motivation.

8. There are vast differences in students' information-processing capabilities.

Teaching Activities   Related
                                                                 Principles

1. _____

   _____   _____

   _____

2. _____

   _____   _____

   _____

3. _____

   _____   _____

   _____

4. _____

   _____   _____

   _____

Summary

Thinking, remembering, and problem solving are the major interests of cognitive psychologists. Teachers also are vitally concerned with cognitive processes because of their need to develop these abilities in students.

Contemporary cognitive psychology uses many of the terms of information-processing theory to model and explain cognition. Major elements of an information-processing model of cognition are sense receptors, sensory registers, long-term memory, and working memory, as well as the processes of perception and attention.

Human information processing is active and dynamic. Incoming information is related in working memory to already-stored information from long-term memory. Many parts of this modern view of cognition can be traced to earlier concepts of cognitive processes held by the structuralists, the functionalists, and Gestalt psychologists.

In general, a cognitive view of teaching portrays students as active processors of information. Cognitively oriented teachers recognize the importance of determining what their students know and basing instruction on students' level of knowledge. They also recognize the need to develop students' metacognitive skills and to take individual differences in cognitive abilities into account. Thus, teachers need to consider each learner individually in planning instruction. A cognitive approach to teaching also is based on the ideas that students learn best if materials are meaningful and that processes are just as important as content in learning. A detailed study of cognitive processes leads to many specific suggestions for teachers, which are outlined in detail in later chapters.

Suggested Readings

Baars, B. J. (1986). *The cognitive revolution in psychology.* New York: Guilford Press.

> *This is an excellent history of contemporary cognitive psychology. Contributions by such notables as B. F. Skinner, Howard Rachlin, George A. Miller, Noam Chomsky, Ulric Neisser, and Ernest Hilgard make this book a cornerstone for any student wishing to build a foundation of knowledge in contemporary psychology.*

DiVesta, F. J. (1987). The cognitive movement in education. In J. A. Glover & R. R. Ronning (Eds.), *Historical foundations of educational psychology.* (pp. 203–236). New York: Plenum.

> *This outstanding chapter, based on a synthesis of years of cognitive work in educational psychology, provides an overview of the impact of cognitive psychology on instructional practices.*

Glover, J. A., Ronning, R. R., & Bruning, R. H. (1989). *Cognitive psychology for teachers.* New York: Macmillan.

    This volume is an introduction to all aspects of cognitive psychology. It is designed for upper-level undergraduate education majors who have had material similar to that covered in this book.

Neisser, U. (1967). *Cognitive psychology.* New York: Appleton-Century-Crofts.

    Neisser's book, along with that of Bruner, Goodnow, and Austin (1956), is credited with marking the onset of contemporary cognitive psychology. Neisser's book was state-of-the-art in the late 1960s.

Solso, R. L. (1988). *Cognitive psychology* (2nd ed.). Boston: Allyn and Bacon.

    This book is a good intermediate-level introduction to cognitive psychology.

Sternberg, R. J., & Smith, E. E. (Eds.). (1988). *The psychology of human thought.* New York: Cambridge University Press.

    This collection of chapters on various topics in cognitive psychology is an excellent source for in-depth information.

Comments on Practice Exercise 2–1

There are 6 *F*'s in the sentence. Most adults count only three *F*'s on their first try! Why? Perception is the key. As adult readers, we have long since learned to look for the *meaning* of words, phrases, and sentences. The cognitive processes that we use to extract meaning from written materials are so well practiced that they occur almost automatically. We have learned to pay attention to the words that usually carry the most meaning in sentences, particularly nouns and verbs. Prepositions such as the word *OF* are barely attended to, if at all. Cognitive processes relating to meaning are so automatic, however, that they are hard to shut down. Even while concentrating on this easy task, many readers completely fail to see the *F*'s that appear in the *OF*'s. In this task, meaningfulness *interferes* with successful performance.

Comments on Practice Exercise 2–2

As you probably noticed as you read over the list, the words come from four categories: animals, names, professions, and vegetables. The interesting thing about many people's recall of the list is that they tend to recall many of the words in related clusters—not in the exact order they learned the words. This shows that they have been active rather than passive processors of the information you have given them.

    More specifically, they already have the concepts of animals, names, professions, and vegetables well learned. Once they recognize that the new learning—the list of words—can be made more meaningful in terms of categories, associations and clustering can take place.

Learning is made easier (although this memory task is not an easy one) because the learners have made it more meaningful.

You will also notice differences in recall among your learners. Some will recall more than others, and each person's order of recall will be his or her own. You may also notice that the words at the beginning and the end of your list are somewhat more likely to be recalled. Generally, memory researchers have theorized that words at the beginning are better remembered because they are interfered with less by other words; words at the end are remembered better because they are still being rehearsed in working memory close to the time of recall.

CHAPTER

3

Memory and Concepts

OVERVIEW

We all know about memory. Some experiences are easy to remember, even years after their occurrence. Other things, such as all the names and dates students sometimes cram into their heads the night before a test, often are forgotten in a matter of hours. Students "try to remember" many things, including the names of new acquaintances, the phone number of a favorite pizza parlor, twenty French words for tomorrow's quiz, or the formula for nitroglycerin.

As teachers, we believe that knowledge should be beneficial to students long after they have left our classes. Educational experiences, no matter how interesting, have little or no use unless they can be remembered and somehow later applied. Effective teachers provide instruction that makes it likely that students will recall important information long after their formal education has been completed. These teachers expect more than just a temporary change in what their students know.

One aspect of becoming an effective teacher is developing an understanding of human memory. This chapter will provide you with an overview of theories of memory and with a set of teaching applications based on those theories. We also will examine the central feature of human memory, the concept, and discuss the most effective ways to teach concepts.

OBJECTIVES

After reading this chapter, you should be able to meet the following objectives.

1. Apply eleven guidelines drawn from memory research to your teaching.

2. Determine the defining attributes of a concept.

3. Teach a concept to another person using the steps outlined in the chapter.

4. Teach yourself a concept following the model presented in the chapter, and compare the results to your usual approach for learning new concepts.

5. Use the SQ3R method to improve your studying, and help someone else use the method to improve his or her studying.

Memory

As we saw in Chapter Two, thinking requires the storage of prior experiences in an organized fashion—a memory. Thinking doesn't include only perception of present happenings in our environment. Prior experiences drawn from memory also influence the way we interpret events. In Chapter Two we discussed some important aspects of cognition, including perception, attention, and the working memory. In this chapter we focus primarily on long-term memory—the retention of information over a period of days, weeks, months, and even years.

Memory researchers have used a wide range of learning tasks in their studies. Some researchers, in order to study memory in its purest state, have emphasized extremely simple learning tasks. These scientists have investigated so-called rote memory—the memory for single words, simple pictures, and syllables. Others have focused primarily on higher levels of learning and memory, choosing to study how concepts, principles, and written passages are remembered. They have concentrated on a form of memory in which the information to be learned and recalled is akin to that of most people's everyday experiences. These two traditions have led to different theories of memory and, as we will see, to different applications for teachers.

An understanding of memory will help you to make better decisions about your teaching methods that will result in improved memory for your students. To help you understand current theories of memory, we will first examine some theories that originated in the early work of the great pioneer of experimental memory research, Hermann Ebbinghaus (1850–1909). These theories, decay theory and interference theory, were developed and tested mainly through the use of rote-learning methods invented and used by Ebbinghaus.

Decay Theory

One of the first concerns of psychology was memory (Ebbinghaus, 1913), and the earliest psychological theory of memory was **decay theory**. Decay theory was simple, straightforward, and based on common sense: memories fade (decay) with the passage of time. Memory was thought to be like a photograph left in the sun. At first the image is sharp and clear, but the passage of time (plus the sun and rain) gradually fades the picture, until it is not discernible at all. This theory could be tested by two of its predictions. First, the more time that passes after learning some materials, the less well those materials will be remembered. Second, faster presentation rates of material to be learned should result in better memory because there is less time for forgetting. (That is, if it takes an hour to present some information, you have fifty-nine minutes to forget the first part of it; if the same material is presented in ten minutes, you have only nine minutes to forget the first part of it.)

For all its appeal to common sense and simplicity, decay theory was found to be inaccurate by research done in the 1920s and early 1930s. Jenkins and Dallenbach (1924), for example, tested decay theory in a study requiring two subjects to learn lists of ten nonsense syllables on two different occasions. After learning the initial list, the subjects were tested after one, two, four, and eight hours. One of the subjects participated during the daytime, while the other participated at night. The daytime subject was awake between the time he learned the list and the time he was tested, going about his normal daily activities. The subject who participated at night slept during the interval. After this phase of the experiment was completed, the subjects reversed their daytime and nighttime roles for the learning of the second list of nonsense syllables.

If decay theory were correct, there should have been no differences in forgetting between the person who slept and the one who stayed awake. Forgetting would be governed solely by the passage of time. Another hypothesis, however, was that newly encountered information might *interfere* with what had already been learned. If this interference theory were correct, the subject who was awake would forget more than the sleeping subject because there are more possibilities of interference in the awake state. The results of both phases of the study clearly supported the interference theory. The subject who slept in each phase of the experiment remembered about six out of ten of the nonsense syllables, while the subject who was awake recalled only one out of ten.

Thus, decay theory could not account for common phenomena observed in memory research. Theories that do not explain what happens in experiments are discarded, and scientists must formulate new theories to explain what has been observed. In this case, decay theory was replaced by the theory that better explained the experimental results—interference theory.

Interference Theory

The phenomenon of one learning task interfering with the performance of another is known as *interference*. Interference theories have been with us since Jenkins and Dallenbach's (1924) early formulation. Researchers still consider interference theory valid for explaining rapid loss of memory of such items as word lists and names, and, thus, it has direct implications for classroom teachers. It seems to be less applicable, however, to meaningful learning.

Specifically, interference theory holds that forgetting occurs as time passes because new, conflicting information enters memory and interferes with the original learning. Passage of time is not the important factor. Instead, the amount of interfering information a person processes in memory during a given interval accounts for most of the lapse in memory.

We can see how interference theory explains memory loss in an example drawn from everyday experience. Suppose you are enrolled in an American literature course and an American history course during the same semester. Not surprisingly, your professors manage to schedule their first examinations on the same day. As a typical student, you do a lot of your studying the night before the exams. First you study the literature for several hours, and then you study the history. Exhausted, you climb into bed and sleep until ten minutes before your literature test. You dash to the classroom and take the test, working as hard as you can. During the literature test you have several lapses of memory and confuse some of the names and dates from the history course with facts from the literature course.

This case illustrates **retroactive interference**; that is, later learning interferes with the recall of prior learning:

Retroactive Interference
Learn Task #1 → Learn Task #2 → Recall Task #1.
Having to learn Task #2 makes recall of Task #1 poorer.

Retroactive interference studies show that groups given new materials to learn (Task 2) between the time they learn materials (Task 1) and try to recall them (Recall Task 1) remember *less* than groups who are not given the new, interfering materials* (see Chechile, 1987). Almost all interference studies, unlike our example, have been laboratory studies that used lists of nonsense syllables (such as *paz, nic, xom*) paired with nouns as the materials to be remembered. This procedure, which dates back to the work of Ebbinghaus (1913), has been used to reduce possible contamination of the results stemming from the participants' prior knowledge.

Another form of interference, **proactive interference**, also commonly occurs in our daily lives; here, prior learning interferes with current learning.

---

*Note that Jenkin and Dallenbach's study (1924) was a study of retroactive interference.

Proactive Interference
Learn Task #1 → Learn Task #2 → Recall Task # 2.
Having to learn Task #1 makes recall of Task #2 poorer.

In both retroactive and proactive interference, the similarity of the learning tasks influences the degree to which interference occurs (Chechile, 1987; Dempster, 1985). Generally, the greater the similarity of the two learning tasks, the greater the likelihood of interference. If you were first to memorize a list of numbers and then a second list of numbers, for example, interference would be more likely than if you first memorized a list of names and then a list of numbers.

There have been several attempts to explain proactive interference (see Chechile, 1987; Dornic, 1983; Wickens, Moody, & Vidulid, 1985), but none has been able to account fully for the experimental results, that is, to answer the question of why previous learning interferes with the recall of new learning. Nevertheless, interference theory is still very much alive today even though some of its predictions are not conclusively supported by research (see Chechile, 1987, for a recent attempt to explain interference based on contemporary views).

Unless instruction is meaningful, little is likely to be retained. Here the instructor helps make learning photography principles meaningful by relating them to projects the students now have in progress.

Interference theory, while valuable for understanding rote memory, has not been shown to be applicable to higher levels of learning. For this reason alone, other theoretical perspectives were necessary to account for how we remember and forget concepts, principles, rules, and other higher forms of learning. We will examine these theories after we look at some ways to make materials that are usually learned by rote more meaningful.

Mnemonics: Making Nonmeaningful Material More Meaningful

As we saw in Chapter Two, the key to all aspects of information processing is meaningfulness. To be most efficient and useful, new learning must somehow be linked to information already in long-term memory. Unfortunately, though, not all material is meaningful to students at the time it must be learned. For example, foreign-language students often are asked to learn large numbers of vocabulary words, second- and third-graders are required to learn "math facts" (e.g., $9+9=18$, $7\times9=63$), beginning chemistry students must learn the periodic table of the elements, and so on. Such material must be mastered, but often is difficult to make meaningful to students.

One method for relating "low-meaningful" to "high-meaningful" materials is the use of **mnemonics**. Mnemonics are rhymes, words, or images—anything familiar—that are paired with new information to make it more memorable (Carney, Levin, & Morrison, 1988; Higbee & Kunihira, 1985). The rhyme "i before e except after c" is a mnemonic that helps students to remember a spelling rule. In much the same way, beginning musicians use the mnemonics *Every Good Boy Does Fine* and FACE to help them recall the lines E, G, B, D, and F and the spaces F, A, C, and E of the treble clef. Teachers often use mnemonics in their instruction (Carney et al., 1988; Higbee & Kunihira, 1985), and students report that they frequently use mnemonics in learning new information (Kilpatrick, 1985).

Most effective mnemonics use imagery (Levin, 1985), and simply advising students to use mental images can give them a powerful mnemonic tool. As Begg and Azzarello (1988) have observed, imagery can significantly enhance recall for many kinds of materials. Several relatively simple but effective systems of mnemonics involving imagery can be learned by students and used for remembering many types of information (Glover, Timme, Deyloff, & Rogers, 1987; Pressley, 1985). Four of these are the link method, the method of loci, the peg or hook method, and the keyword method.

Typically, learning how to forget is not a problem for students.

The Link Method. The link method is especially suited for learning lists of items. In this method, a person forms an image for each item on a list of items to be learned. Each image then is pictured as "interacting" with the image of the next item on the list. That is, the images are linked in the imagination. In a simple example, if you were trying to remember to buy chicken, cheese, apples, and soup at the grocery store, you might visualize a sequence in which a chicken picked up a piece of cheese, melted the cheese onto an apple, and dropped the cheese covered apple into a bowl of soup. The interactive image makes it likely that the recall of each item will cue the recall of the next item. A great advantage of this method is its simplicity. No external scheme or set of materials needs to be learned.

The Method of Loci. The method of loci dates back to the ancient Greeks. According to Bower (1970), Cicero attributed the origin of this method to the Greek poet Simonides. Simonides had recited a poem to assembled guests at a large banquet and, following his oration, had been called outside. At that very moment, the roof of the great hall collapsed, killing everyone who remained inside. The corpses were so mangled that not even relatives could identify them. Simonides came forward, however, and was able to name each of the many corpses by their locations in the wreckage of the huge hall. This feat of memory convinced Simonides of a very useful method for remembering: use a set of locations in which you can place images of things to be remembered.

In the modern use of the method of loci, learners think first of a series of ten to twenty well-learned locations (such as points on a path taken daily, rooms in one's house, or locations on a campus) and then "place" each item from the list to be learned at one of the locations. Usually learners are advised to imagine themselves walking and visiting each location in order. On this "walk" each item in the list is visualized as located in one particular location. To recall the items, then, learners are encouraged to "walk" along the path once more and to "look" at each location in order to recall the item placed there. Generally, this method helps learners both in recalling the items and in placing them in the proper order, since "traveling the path" helps the person recall items in the right sequence.

The Peg Method.   In the peg, or hook, method, learners memorize a series of "pegs" on which information can be "hung" as it is learned. Pegs can be any well-learned set of items; the most popular scheme and one often investigated in research is a rhyming peg system (for example, one is a bun, two is a shoe, three is a tree . . .). Each peg is easy to visualize—a bun, a shoe, a tree, and so on.

Once the pegs are memorized, they can be used to help remember a series of items in order. The first step is to form an image of each item interacting with its assigned peg. If the first item on a list were *book*, for instance, the book might be imagined as sandwiched between the halves of a bun. The second item would be imagined as interacting with a shoe, and so on through the list. The peg method is especially helpful for learning to perform the steps in complex tasks such as operating machinery (Glover, Timme, Deyloff,& Rogers, 1987).

The Keyword Method.   The keyword method also uses imagery but differs from the link method, the method of loci, and the peg method in its use. While the three mnemonics we have described above are most useful for remembering lists of information, the keyword method is best suited for learning new vocabulary. There are two stages in the keyword mnemonic, an acoustic link and an imagery link.

When new vocabulary is being learned, a student must first find a "keyword" that sounds like a part of the to-be-learned word—the acoustic link (Levin, 1985). For example, a good keyword for the word *conflagration* is *flag*—*flag* is similar to the second syllable of con*flag*ration, and flags are easily imagined, making the second stage of imaging easy.

Once a keyword has been chosen, the student links it to an image. In this process, the student must imagine a visual image of the keyword interacting with the meaning of the to-be-learned word (Levin, 1985). In this instance, a student might envision a flag on fire. Then, when the student is tested and sees the word conflagration on the exam, it should evoke the keyword *flag*, which should then cause the student to remember the vision of a flag on fire.

In the past few years, a great deal of research has been done on the keyword method. In general, the results have been very positive for students of all ages (see Pressley, Levin, & Delaney, 1982), across different languages (e.g., Presley, 1987), for the learning of facts other than vocabulary (Levin, 1985; Pressley et al., 1982), and even when learning from reading materials (McCormick & Levin, 1984). Of all the mnemonic techniques currently available, the keyword mnemonic is perhaps the most applicable to classroom use (Pressley, 1987).

The success of the mnemonics we've described hinges on their ability to help learners relate the familiar (in the form of a well-learned mnemonic or a well-known keyword) to the unfamiliar (the items to be learned). A critical factor in using mnemonics successfully is that the learner must be completely comfortable with them. Their use must be automatic, or nearly so. There typically are very few problems in obtaining automaticity with the method of loci, for instance, if the mental walk encompasses familiar locations. For the peg system, however, some effort must be expended to develop a completely familiar and useful mnemonic. If the peg system is not very well learned, it is unlikely that students will find it effective or continue to use it. The keyword method also requires practice for it to be effective. Students must be comfortable in choosing a keyword and developing an image that has the meaning of the to-be-learned word interacting with the keyword. In mnemonics, as in any skill, "practice makes perfect."

Information-Processing Theory

The limitations of interference theory caused memory researchers to look for other explanations of how meaningful materials are remembered. A general theoretical framework that has been very useful in accounting for memory for concepts, principles, and rules is information-processing theory.

PRACTICE EXERCISE 3–1   USING A MNEMONIC

There isn't a better way to make a fair decision about the worth of mnemonics than to try them. For many people, the method of loci is a good starting point because it is easy to use for many different types of information.

We suggest that you try the method for a week. You may want to use it to remember your shopping lists, important compounds in a chemistry class, body parts for physiology (by forming an interactive image of each part and its label and placing the image in the location), or important events in history. Try to do each of the following, in order, to give the method a fair test.

1. Make sure you know your mnemonic well before you try to use it.

2. Take mental "walks" through the locations until you have the order well learned.

3. Place the items to be remembered in the locations, with one and only one in each location.

4. If you study the list of items again, place them in the same locations each time.

5. Use the method with several different types of information.

After using the method for at least a week, make a judgment about how well the method of loci has worked for you. For what kinds of materials was the method most useful? Did you become more comfortable with the mnemonic with repeated use? Are the loci you chose the best for you? After you make changes to suit your needs you should have a versatile and powerful mnemonic to help you in many situations.

As we suggested in Chapter Two, information-processing theory came into being both as an alternative to competing theories and as a result of technological advances in other sciences. As you recall, information-processing theory portrays humans as active processors of information and states that memory cannot be studied without understanding what the learner does with new information and how meaningful the information is to the learner. In this theory, human beings are seen as information-processing systems (Dellarosa, 1988). This view suggests that memory is a process of (1) encoding (or placing

What the learner does is critical to memory. The activities of this student in chemistry lab help make the concepts and principles he learned in class more meaningful and hence memorable.

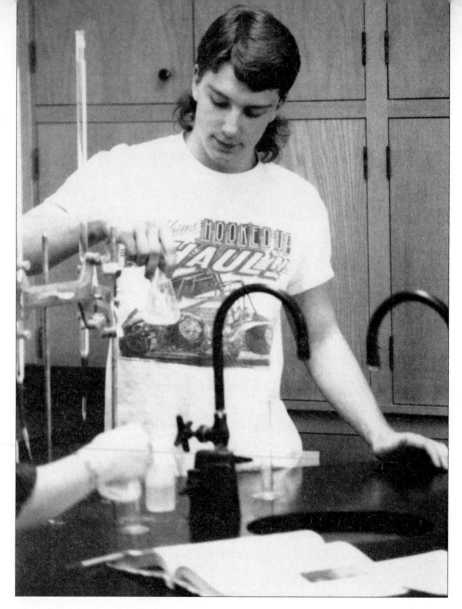

into memory) information registered by the sense organs, (2) storing the information, and (3) retrieving or remembering it when necessary.

Early variations of information-processing theory were mechanistic and somewhat overreliant on computer models. Contemporary researchers still find the computer metaphor to be a useful tool for thinking about memory (see McClelland, 1988), but they increasingly have looked for more flexible ways of depicting human memory. Three flexible ways of thinking about memory are levels-of-processing, schema theory, and parallel distributed processing.

Retrieval is recall of stored information. Understanding this story about kangaroos requires students to retrieve previously stored information.

Levels-of-Processing and Elaboration-of-Processing

In 1972, Fergus Craik and Robert Lockhart published an extremely influential paper. In it they argued that the structure of memory (i.e., short-term, long-term, etc.) was not nearly so important as the things people did while learning. They further hypothesized that memory is a direct function of *depth of processing*: the more deeply or carefully new information is analyzed by the learner, the more likely it will be recalled in the future.

As an example, consider two students of equal ability given the same amount of time to work on a paragraph. The first student has been asked to count the number of three-letter words in the paragraph by circling each. The second student, meanwhile, has been asked to replace as many words in the paragraph as possible with their synonyms. Now, if we surprise both students with a test over the contents of the paragraph, who would you suppose would remember more of the content? From Craik and Lockhart's (1972) perspective, the answer would be the person who more carefully analyzed the material. In this case, the person who counted the three-letter words had to perform only minimal analyses. This person did not even have to deal with the meaning of any aspects of the paragraph in order to complete the task—a clear instance of *shallow* processing. On the other hand, the person who had to identify synonyms had to perform some rather complex analyses. This person had to understand the meaning of each of the words—an example of relatively *deep* processing.

In study after study (see Walker, 1986), Craik and Lockhart's predictions have been verified. No matter what kind of materials, students who engage in deep processing remember more than students who engage in shallow processing. Recent research in this tradition has refined psychologists' ideas about how best to describe differences in how students encode new information. These refinements have led to the idea of *elaboration-of-processing*, which grew directly out of levels-of-processing (Craik & Tulving, 1975).

In an elaboration-of-processing view, students' memory depends on how elaborately they encode information (McDaniel, Einstein, & Lollis, 1988; O'Brien, Shank, Myers, & Rayner, 1988; Walker, 1986). That is, as students use more and different ways to encode materials, their memory for the information should improve. For example, when a student reads a paragraph, answers questions she has asked herself about the paragraph, and summarizes the paragraph to herself, her memory for that material should be far better than if she merely rereads the paragraph three times. Whether the concept is depth of processing or elaboration, the key determiner of memory is what students *do* as they attempt to learn. As educators, we must be aware that learners need to be active processors of information, not merely passive recipients of new material.

Schema Theory

A second current perspective on memory that stresses the importance of what learners do while learning is **schema theory**. The idea of schemata (the plural of schema) has been used in memory research since at least the time of Bartlett (1932) and is one of the major conceptions of Jean Piaget's (1896–1980) theory of cognitive development (which we will examine in detail in Chapter Four). Over the years, theorists have used the concept of schemata in different ways. As we will see in Chapter Four, "Intelligence and Cognitive Development," the term *schemata* has a somewhat different flavor in theories of cognitive development than it does in memory research. Here, we will follow the lead of R. C. Anderson (1984) and McKoon and Ratcliff (1988) in describing a schema theory of memory.

Schemata are knowledge structures in memory that contain elements of related information and provide plans for gathering future information. For instance, a young child may have a schema for "birthday party." In that schema may be knowledge that birthday parties typically take place on somebody's birthday, that presents are given to the person whose birthday it is, that games are played, and that refreshments are served. The child has a framework for understanding about birthday parties; he "knows all about" birthday parties. Similarly, a student may have a schema for division problems (e.g., "Four girls have twenty four cookies they want to share equally. How many cookies should each girl receive?"). In the student's schema may be basic information about the nature of such problems, procedures for solving some types of division problems, and some idea of what a reasonable answer might be. Well-developed schemata guide the student as he or she attempts to identify relevant information and select different strategies for solving the problem (Anderson, 1984; McKoon & Ratcliff, 1988).

The content and organization of schemata vary both among individuals and within the same individual over time (Gerrig, 1988). A young astronomy buff, for example will have far more complex information about, say, telescopes than a student who is not interested in the topic. In one sense, the astronomy buff's telescope schema may be viewed as being much more extensive than a telescope schema possessed by another student. Most likely, however, the astronomy buff's knowledge consists of several related schemata, all containing different but related information about different types of telescopes (e.g., refracting telescopes, reflecting telescopes, and radio telescopes), their use, and their relationship to the study of various astronomical phenomena.

From a schema-theory perspective, the more a student knows about a topic, the easier it is to learn more about the topic. For example, a student who already learned the Fortran computer language will more rapidly and effectively learn BASIC, another computer language, than a student who has not previously learned Fortran. This is because the knowledgeable student already possesses a great deal of understanding about the structure and uses of computer languages. In other words, the student has schemata to which new information can be directly related, resulting in interconnections of old and new information.

Schemata can be activated through recall of old information or by new information. New information may be related to one or more schemata, and as it is correctly identified and matched to schemata (a process referred to as **instantiation**), the schema with the greatest number of instantiations is activated. An example of **schema activation** (or its failure) can be seen in the following sentence drawn from Bransford and McCarrell (1974):

> The house was small because the sun came out.

The sentence is gramatically sound, and each of the words should be familiar to you. However, the sentence probably doesn't make sense because you cannot activate an appropriate schema. You have no framework within which to understand it. Notice what happens to your understanding of the sentence, however, when the word *igloo* is given as a clue. Now, with an appropriate schema—that for igloos—activated, the sentence should make sense.

From the perspective of schema theory, students' understanding of the world and, therefore, what they will remember depend on the information they encounter, the information they already have, and the way in which they interact with the information. Meaning is constructed on the basis of students' knowledge about the world (Gerrig, 1988). One last example, drawn from a study conducted by Anderson, Reynolds, Schallert, and Goetz (1977), should help make this point. Read the following paragraph, and decide who or what Tony is:

> Tony slowly got up from the mat, planning his escape. He hesitated a moment and thought. Things were not going well. What bothered him most was being held, especially since the charge against him had been weak. He considered his present situation. The lock that held him was strong, but he thought he could break it. He knew, however, that his timing would have to be perfect. Tony was aware that it was because of his early roughness that he had been penalized so severely—much too severely from his point of view. The situation was becoming frustrating; the pressure had been grinding on him for too long. He was being ridden unmercifully. Tony was getting angry now. He felt he was ready to make his move. He knew that his success or failure would depend on what he did in the next few seconds.

What did you decide about Tony? Many readers decide Tony is a prisoner in a jail—there are enough elements in the paragraph that match their schema for prisoner that this decision makes very good sense. However, other readers, especially those who have participated in wrestling or who are wrestling fans, conclude instead that Tony is a wrestler in a difficult match. For these readers, the elements in the paragraph are more likely to activate their schema for wrestling than their schema for prisoner. Not surprisingly, readers who believe that Tony is a prisoner remember very different things about the paragraph than do readers who think that Tony is a wrestler. What students remember about the information they encounter depends not only on the information itself but on what is already known (the relevant schema) and on whether they activate that information.

Making Meaningful Materials More Meaningful. As we've seen, materials that initially have little intrinsic meaning are better learned if they can be related to something meaningful. The same principle holds true for the learning of meaningful materials; they, too, are better learned if linked to what students already know. There are two procedures related to schema theory—advance organizers and schema activation—that can be used to further enhance the meaningfulness of higher-order learning materials. We will discuss each below.

Advance Organizers. One well-known approach for relating new reading material to what students already know is the use of **advance organizers** (Ausubel, 1960, 1980). Advance organizers are abstract, general overviews of new information read in advance of the new information. Like schema theorists, Ausubel asserted that new information is most easily learned when it can be linked to stable cognitive structures the learner already has. According to Ausubel, the advance organizer provides a kind of "scaffolding" to which the more detailed material that follows can be related. Thus, advance organizers are constructed to help learners tie new information into their existing knowledge.

Recently, schema theorists (e.g., Derry, 1984; Mayer, 1984) have used schema theory to explain how advance organizers work. Derry (1984), for example, has suggested that advance organizers operate by (1) activating relevant schemata for to-be-read material and (2) correcting the activated schemata so that the new material can be linked to them. The reader's knowledge base and the new information form a more extensive schema that contains both the original and the new information.

The concept of advance organizers has received some rather strong criticism over the years (see, e.g., Anderson, Spiro, & Anderson, 1978). However, the results of recent research on advance organizers (e.g., Corkill, Glover, & Bruning, 1988) suggest that they have a consistent, if moderate, facilitative effect on readers' memory for prose. In addi-

Before beginning instruction on a new topic, many teachers ask children to talk about what they already know about the topic, or associate with it. The resulting "schema map" helps children relate their own concepts to the content of instruction and helps make it meaningful.

tion, it seems that advance organizers are especially helpful if students *carefully* study them prior to moving on to the reading passages (Dinnel & Glover, 1985). The idea of employing prefatory material to help make reading materials more meaningful to readers remains a popular one and is an area of continuing research interest to educators and psychologists (Corkill et al., in press).

Schema Activation.   A more general procedure for enhancing the meaningfulness of new material can be referred to as **schema activation** (Rowe & Rayford, 1987). Schema activation refers to techniques designed to activate relevant schema prior to and during a learning activity. For example, prior to a lesson on mammals, fourth-grade students can be asked to describe the characteristics of their own pet cats and dogs in order to activate relevant schemata. Similarly, high school students preparing for a lesson on fascism can be asked to talk about their knowledge of dictatorships as a means of activating some relevant schemata. Senior literature students, as another example, can be led in a discussion of, say, male and female roles before beginning to read one of Ernest Hemingway's novels.

The reasoning underlying the idea of schema activation is that students at any level will have *some* relevant knowledge to which new information can be tied. A group of fourth-graders we know, for instance, learned about a part of Einstein's theory of relativity by first thinking of examples of acceleration (riding in a car, a roller coaster), and then doing a simple experiment in which a half-full bucket of water was spun around in a circle over their heads without spilling any. They then discussed why the water stayed in the bucket and related this (the acceleration pushing the water to the bottom of the bucket regardless of what position it was in) to their own experiences with acceleration. (One girl had experienced a ride at an amusement park in which the riders stood against the walls of a large cylinder and were spun around faster and faster. Then, the floor dropped out of the cylinder, and the riders were held on the wall of the cylinder by the force of acceleration. Her knowledge of acceleration was very personal!)

With their schemata for acceleration presumably activated, the students were told an edited version of one of Einstein's stories in which they were encouraged to respond to the teacher's questions:

Teacher:	Let's suppose that three of us are in an elevator without any windows. How would gravity feel to us?
Student A:	Just like now. We'd feel the same. (A brief discussion followed.)
Teacher:	Suppose we had a special elevator, and instead of being on Earth, we were in space?
Student B:	We'd be weightless like on the space shuttle. (Another brief discussion followed.)
Teacher:	OK. Now, suppose that a spaceship got behind us and pushed us (accelerated us like in a car) so that the push of the acceleration was just the same as the pull of gravity on Earth. How could we tell we were in space?
Student C:	We could look outside.
Teacher:	Remember, we don't have any windows.
Student D:	You couldn't tell. It would feel just the same. (A long and hearty discussion followed.)
Teacher:	What do you think about gravity and acceleration?
Several students:	They're the same thing!

The relationship of gravity and acceleration is, of course, a very sophisticated concept that most adults really don't understand. By carefully activating her students' relevant schemata, however, this teacher was able to help her students learn and remember fundamental aspects of a very difficult concept.

Schema activation *is* a general technique. It can involve having students generate examples from their experience, review previous learning, and use the context in which new material is presented (Bridge, 1987). Essentially, any teaching activity that helps students build conceptual bridges between what they already know and what they are to learn can be thought of as schema activation.

Parallel Distributed Processing

A third way of thinking about human memory is **parallel distributed processing** (McClelland, 1988). Parallel-distributed-processing (or, more simply, PDP) theorists argue that humans are far more flexible than computers because humans can simultaneously consider many pieces of information. Processing occurs in *parallel*, along many dimensions at the same time. In reading, for example, processing isn't seen as moving from decoding the individual letters to decoding the words to comprehending meaning. Instead, PDP theorists believe that processing moves ahead on many different levels at once. Decoding and comprehension are thought to occur in parallel.

Beyond the idea of parallel processing, McClelland (1988) holds that another major difference between PDP and other cognitive models is that in most models, knowledge is stored as a static copy of a pattern. When access is needed, the pattern (e.g., the schema) is found in long-term memory and copied into working memory. In PDP, however, the patterns themselves are not stored. Instead, what is stored are the *connection strengths* among processing units. These connection strengths allow the patterns to be recreated when the system is activated. In this view, memory is distributed over the connections among a very large number of processing units. Thus, our comprehension of the word "butter" in the sentence, "The butter melted in the sun" occurs through the activation of connections among a large number of processing units. These processing units include those for letter perception, word meanings, syntax, and those related to the sentence's context.

PDP has received a great deal of research attention in the past few years (see McClelland, 1988), but its future is still unclear to us. However, the notion of processing many items in parallel is highly appealing because it seems to describe many of the functions of human cognition (e.g., reading, problem solving). Further, PDP may help us see how best to design practice situations in which students may develop skills requiring the simultaneous processing of many bits of information.

Metamemory: Thinking
About Memory

Metamemory is one aspect of the broader topic of metacognition we introduced in Chapter Two. Metamemory specifically refers to knowledge people have about their own memory. Examples of metamemory include understanding that a long list is harder to remember than a short list and knowing that a reading assignment for next week's test requires more intensive study than a phone number to be remembered for a few minutes. While such knowledge seems to be second nature to adults, children develop it only gradually.

Three related skills are involved in metamemory (Kail, 1984): awareness, diagnosis, and monitoring. We will examine the development of each of these skills in more detail next.

Awareness.   An effective memory requires being aware of the need to remember. For example, if your instructor tells you that you will be tested on this chapter, you know that you are being asked to remember the information it contains. Your awareness influences how you read; you may spend more time on some sections than others, reread some parts, highlight some ideas, or jot down important points.

When does this awareness develop? The answer to our question isn't absolutely clear-cut (Borkowski, Milstead, & Hale, 1988), but research suggests that even preschoolers know something about the importance of remembering. One method that has been used to determine how aware children are of their memories involves contrasting their memory for things when (1) they merely observe them and (2) they are told to try to remember them. If there are differences between (1) and (2) and these differences increase with age, then we have evidence that children understand something about memory and that their understanding increases as they grow older (Borkowski et al., 1988). The technique we've described, called a *differentiation technique,* was used by Acredolo, Pick, and Olson (1975) in an early study of children's metamemory.

Acredolo et al. (1975) took preschoolers and other children on short walks through several hallways. On the walks, the experimenter dropped her keys and then picked them up. Later, the children were asked to find the place where the keys had fallen and were fairly accurate. When children were led to a particular site and *asked* to remember it, however, their accuracy in finding the site again was considerably greater. The better performances showed that even young children have some awareness of their own memories and how to improve them. Without this awareness, of course, the instructions would have had no effect.

Awareness of one's need to remember does not develop all at once. The study we described above and many other studies (e.g., DeLoache, 1986; Pillow, 1988; Scholnick & Wing, 1988) have shown that children's understanding of their own memories and even their understanding of mental activities such as remembering, knowing, forgetting, and guessing change only gradually throughout childhood.

Diagnosis.   Beyond simple awareness of the need to remember is the need to diagnose the requirements of tasks, especially as they relate to one's own abilities. Some memory tasks are more difficult for us than others. For example, as adults we know it is much easier to learn the names of two new students than the names of a roomful of students, and we know that a list of five new vocabulary words is more easily learned than a list of twenty-five new words. We are making an *assessment of task difficulty* based on our knowledge that the number of items makes a great difference in how hard something is to remember.

Likewise, we easily can recall which of our three roommates were at a meeting, in contrast to reporting on the presence of three people whom we know only slightly. We know *familiarity* reduces the difficulty of remembering information. As another example, we cringe at the lecturer who presents material in rapid-fire fashion but begin to feel more comfortable when we discover that she hands out and follows an outline. In this case, we know that our memory can be overloaded by too much information coming too fast but that a meaningful structure such as an outline can help ease the memory load.

Even little children know that these same variables—number of items, familiarity, speed of presentation, and organization of information—affect the difficulty of memory tasks. Young children's diagnostic skills, however, are very rudimentary (Brainerd & Pressley, 1985; Borkowski et al., 1988; Pillow, 1988) and develop slowly. Even so, effective teachers can enhance children's diagnostic skills by providing appropriate instruction and practice.

Diagnosing *retrieval demands* also is an important part of the diagnostic aspect of metamemory. Retrieval demands refer to the kind of memory performance required at the point of recall. For instance, most of us would prepare differently for a true-false or multiple-choice examination than we would for an essay test—we judge that the retrieval demands will be different. In the same way, knowledge that we will have to explain a poem to our class will spur us to do a great deal of preparation.

Retrieval demands also vary for children. For instance, does a child simply need to recognize information, recall it verbatim (word for word), or perhaps just "tell it in her own words"? By ages five or six, children begin to understand these distinctions and grasp their implications for memory (see Pillow, 1988; Sodian & Wimmer, 1987). To more closely examine children's knowledge of retrieval demands, Kreutzer, Leonard, and Flavell (1975, p. 43) told their subjects the following story: "The other day I played a record of a story for a girl. I asked her to listen carefully to the record as many times as she wanted to so she could tell me the story later. Before she began to listen to the record, she asked me one question: 'Am I supposed to remember the story word for word, just like on the record, or can I tell you in my own words?'" We realize, of course, the reason for the girl's question—requiring verbatim recall of an entire story makes a much more severe demand on memory than simply highlighting it. But do children understand the reason for the question?

Kreutzer et al. (1975) found that kindergarten to second-grade children did not understand the reason for the question. Children from the upper grades, however, knew its significance. Most of these older children said the girl needed to know because it would affect the difficulty of remembering and the way she would listen to the story.

In another study reported by Kreutzer et al. (1975), children were asked whether it would make any difference to their recall if, in phoning a friend, they got a drink between the time they were told the number and when they actually called. Again, kindergarten and first-grade children showed less awareness of the need to phone first (although it was still their most frequent choice) than did children in grades three and five. Thus, like children's knowledge in other areas of metamemory, awareness of the effects of delay on memory develops only gradually.

Monitoring.   A final category of metamemory is *monitoring*. Skilled learners constantly decide how well remembering is progressing as they study. They determine what is well learned, what is close to mastery, and what requires additional effort (Kail, 1984; Pillow, 1988). This knowledge is vital for successful memory performance in many settings.

One example of the development of monitoring was reported by Goodman and Gardiner (1981), who gave children lists to memorize and tested their memory after several lists were learned. After the test, each of the words was presented individually to the children, and they were asked to judge whether they had recalled or forgotten each item. The youngest children in the study, six-year-olds, could make the judgments with some accuracy, but the ability to identify what had and had not been learned increased steadily with age. This ability to accurately monitor memory performance continues to increase into adulthood (see Borkowski et al., 1988).

Memory monitoring is important because it allows us to concentrate our efforts on what still needs to be learned. An interesting early study by Masur, McIntyre, and Flavell (1973) illustrates this point. Masur et al. asked students to study a set of pictures for forty-five seconds and then tested their ability to recall the pictures. After the test was completed, the students (first-graders, third-graders, and college students) were allowed to pick half of the pictures for an additional forty-five seconds of study. This pattern continued for several trials, with the students always allowed to pick half of the pictures for further study. Third-graders and college students almost always picked the pictures they had failed to recall for additional study. First-graders, however, picked about equal numbers of recalled and unrecalled pictures to study. They apparently did not see the usefulness of studying items they did not already know in order to learn the total list.

Summary of Metamemory. As we have seen from research on metamemory, children undergo important developmental changes in their awareness of the need for memory, their ability to determine memory requirements and to choose strategies for remembering, and their monitoring of the effectiveness of the strategies. Even preschoolers know that they need to remember things and that the amount of information influences their ability to remember it. Not until middle childhood, however, do children become aware that different retrieval requirements (e.g., verbatim or paraphrase recall) create vastly different memory demands and that certain strategies for remembering are better than others.

To understand memory it is necessary to understand what a person does with new information, what that person already knows, and what that person knows about memory. Memory cannot be isolated and studied without examining all aspects of the human mind and, in particular, the *actions* taken by the learner. It is this continually evolving view of memory, which takes both the material and the learner into account, that allows us to develop guidelines for teaching to enhance our students' memory.

Applications for Teaching: Enhancing Students' Memory

By following the eleven guidelines we have drawn from research in memory, you can help your students remember new information more effectively.

1. Make new information meaningful by helping students mobilize existing schemata. Encoding is most likely to occur when the learner activates a framework of understanding in which to represent new information. If students simply read a passage or listen to a lecture without activating appropriate schemata, many will fail to encode the ideas. Students possess many schemata that can provide organization for their experiences. To help them better retain new information, give them analogies (e.g., a cheetah is a lot like a leopard) or otherwise help them to associate structures they already have with what they are now trying to remember (e.g., "Washington's army was very cold and hungry that winter. Have you ever been really cold, where you didn't have enough clothes on? Can you tell me about it?"). What seem like obvious links from what students already know to what is to be learned may not be nearly so obvious to them. Teachers need to help students to activate schemata appropriate for new learning.

2. Learners should be active rather than passive. For new information to be remembered it must be rehearsed. You can be assured that rehearsal is going on if your learners are actively involved in a task rather than passively listening or observing. Active learning also means practice. For learning both in and out of school to be effective, learners must practice using new information. Where possible, practice should be free of distractions and uninterrupted.

3. Have students generate rather than reread to-be-learned materials. Self-generated material is better remembered than material that is merely read (Slamecka & Katsaiti, 1987). Students' memory will be improved by practicing their remembering (generating from memory) rather than merely reading and rereading material. Generating may be especially helpful for increasing the ease with which vocabulary words, math facts, word spellings, and basic concepts are acquired (Greene, 1988).

4. Test frequently. Testing gives students an opportunity to rehearse to-be-remembered information (Foos & Fisher, 1988; Glover, in press). The "testing" effect (see Glover, in press) refers to the finding that students who are tested over material ultimately remember more than students who are not tested. This pattern of results holds for both simple and complex learning outcomes and fits well within a theoretical framework based on elaboration-of-processing.

5. Mnemonics should be used when appropriate. A great deal of learning in school requires students to commit fairly large amounts of verbal material to memory. Foreign language vocabulary words, names of countries, dates and names in history, and plant phyla, for example, all are essentially rote information when first encountered. Nonetheless, such learning is often critical to successful performance in many classes. By helping students tie new information into existing memory structures through the use of mnemonics, teachers can enhance students' learning and the subsequent memorability of this kind of information.

6. Avoid interference in your class. Give quizzes and examinations at the beginning of the day or the period if you can arrange it. Those teachers who insist on covering new materials during the first part of the period and then give quizzes on old information during the last part of the period are setting up events that almost certainly will result in both proactive and retroactive interference (and frustrated students). Also try to avoid interference with other classes: when possible, do not give an examination on a day when your students must take another examination.

7. Teach your students to "overlearn" information. Many students practice new learning only until they can perform one error-free repetition of the material. If they are learning definitions of several accounting techniques, for example, they may practice until they can recall the list of definitions once without error. This minimum level of learning is extremely susceptible to interference. Almost any unexpected occurrence, anxiety, or loss of attention can be catastrophic for recall.

Overlearning is the continued practice of an errorless recitation and can be a great help in reducing interference effects. If learners keep track of how many times it took them to reach the first errorless recall and then practice the materials that many more times, overlearning is fairly well assured and interference is much less likely.

8. Point out the implications of remembering new information. If students are to remember a series of complex steps for, say, installing brakes in a car, stress the possible outcome if the steps are not correctly remembered. Motivation to remember is a powerful incentive for students to rehearse newly learned material.

9. Have students picture where and how they will have to remember information. Pairing learning with the cues students will use to remember helps students organize their memory (Tulving, 1985). When the situation arises in which recall must occur, the association of the situation and the information to be recalled is likely to be automatic. Many times information is in memory but simply is not associated properly with the situation at hand. Effective teachers point out those situations in which recall of information is likely to be required.

10. Encourage students to think about their memory abilities and strategies. Having students think about their own memory will help the development of their metamemory skills, and this will in turn improve their memory performance over the long run. Effective teachers especially stress the importance of awareness, diagnosis, and monitoring.

Point out the implications of remembering. If students understand *why* remembering something is important, they will be more likely to remember it. This art teacher's example of how perspective is used in drawing makes his instruction more meaningful and therefore more memorable for his students.

11. Have students spread apart their study sessions. The "spacing" effect refers to the finding that to-be-learned information is better recalled when study sessions are spaced apart rather than massed together (Dellarosa & Bourne, 1985; Glover & Corkill, 1987). The reason that spaced-apart sessions have an advantage over massed sessions is clear. During massed study sessions, students engage in complete encoding processes only on their first encounter with the to-be-learned material. On subsequent encounters with the material, they do not have to encode it fully because some of the information still is readily accessible in memory. When study sessions are spaced apart, however, each session requires full encoding processes. In simple terms, materials studied in spaced-apart sessions receive more processing and more complete processing than materials studied in massed sessions (see Dellarosa & Bourne, 1985; Glover & Corkill, 1987).

Categorizing Information: Concepts

Earlier in the chapter we stated that human memory can be organized into specific categories. One way in which we can think about categories in memory is through the use of concepts. **Concepts** are classes of stimuli (information) that people group together on the basis of some perceived commonalities. Concepts help us to reduce the complexity of the world by allowing us to place new information in already existing "compartments" of knowledge. The first time we see an old crop-dusting biplane, for example, we don't have to learn very much about it because we can place it into our memory under the category "airplane"; that is, we can identify it as an object that is an example or instance of the concept of airplane. Some new information, of course, must be placed into its own separate category; when this happens a new concept must be learned.

Memory is systematic. One way of thinking about the systematic nature of human memory is to consider the relationships among different concepts. Concepts can be organized into hierarchies; some concepts are more general (e.g., animals) and some are more specific (e.g., dogs, cats). Two or more concepts can also be related to each other in the form of rules or principles (Gagné, 1987). Consider the following statements:

1. All mammals have four-chambered hearts.

2. Sentences must contain a subject and a verb.

3. All satellites are in orbit.

4. Green plants produce chlorophyll.

Each of these statements is a principle. In the first, the concept of mammal is related to the concept of a four-chambered heart. The second principle relates the concept of sentence to the concepts of subject and verb. The concept of satellites is related to the concept of orbit in the third principle, and the concept of green plant is related to the concept of chlorophyll in the fourth.

The following sections are designed to help you understand concepts and principles and to help you learn how to teach concepts to your students.

Concept Attributes

As we have noted, concepts are classes of stimuli people group together on the basis of some perceived similarities.* These classes of stimuli may be objects (caps, balls, tetrahedrons), persons (lawyers, midgets, clowns), events (parades, picnics, fairs), or ideas (envy, beauty, ambition). People place particular stimuli (examples of concepts) into specific categories as a result of the similarities they perceive. If stimuli do not fit into a given category ("No, that was not an egret we just saw"), they are nonexamples of a concept. As we'll see, part of our task in guiding our students' learning is to reduce concepts to the most important similarities so that students can distinguish examples from nonexamples.

These similarities across examples of a concept are called **attributes**. Attributes can refer to size (an ocean is bigger than a pond), shape (a triangle has one shape, a square another), color (oranges are orange, grapes are not), or use (desks are primarily for writing, tables are primarily for eating). Some attributes are necessary to define a concept while others are not. The necessary attributes are known as *defining attributes*. As you begin to identify the defining attributes of concepts on your own, you will find a good dictionary very valuable. Perhaps the best way to explain this idea is to look at a series of concepts.

Concept 1: Cup.   What makes a cup a cup? What is "cupness"? Most of us can conjure up a vision of an object that is fairly small, circular on top, designed to hold liquid, with a small handle on it. All of us can imagine a cup and recognize one when we see one. But what are the defining attributes of a cup? Let's look at some attributes of cup to determine what its defining attributes are.

What are cups made of? They can be glass, plastic, ceramic, metal, paper, or styrofoam. It seems that the material from which an object is

---

*The concepts formed by each individual usually have some unique features. Each person forms concepts and adds to them on the basis of experience. However, in education we try to help students understand concepts in the same way. We might think of dictionaries as standards for defining concepts.

made does not matter in determining whether it is a cup. The material from which a cup is made is an attribute but not a defining attribute.

What kinds of shapes do cups have? Some cups are half spheres, some are squares, some are cylinders, and some have other, very strange shapes. Shape is an attribute of cups, but it is not a defining attribute.

What about size? Some cups are the size of thimbles. Some can hold as much as a pint. It appears, however, that when an object is much larger than pint-sized it is no longer a cup but is a mug. So size is a defining attribute of cups. Cups must be relatively small.

Does color matter? Cups may be of any color without affecting their cupness. Color is an attribute of cups but not an important one.

Cups differ from some small glasses only because they are designed to protect the drinker from the heat of the liquid they contain while glasses do not. So the ability to insulate must be a defining attribute of cups.

Do all cups have handles? No. Some do and some don't. Evidently having a handle is not a defining attribute of cups. Use, however, is a defining attribute. Cups, unlike many other objects, are used to hold hot liquids.

We instantly recognize cups, but to teach the concept we must analyze it. So far we have identified several attributes of the concept "cup" without exactly determining which attributes make a cup a cup. In fact, there is a combination of attributes that, taken together, define the concept "cup." A cup is a small (the attribute of size) drinking container designed for hot liquid substances (the attribute of use). Glasses are like cups but need not be small and need not hold hot drinks. Mugs typically are considered to be larger than cups. So the defining attributes of the concept "cup" are size and use. All the other attributes, including several we did not list, are not important to defining "cup."

Concept 2: Ring.   What makes something a ring? Without listing all the possible attributes of rings, we can see that the defining attributes of rings are that they can be affixed to a finger somehow and that they are worn for ornamentation. All the other attributes are unnecessary to defining rings. Color, size, shape, form, materials, and so on are not necessary to define the concept "ring."*

---

*The concept "ring" could be defined more generally to include washers, targets, and so forth. We have chosen one aspect of the concept because it allowed us easily to describe the attributes that define the concept.

PRACTICE EXERCISE 3–2   LISTING CONCEPT ATTRIBUTES

We have listed a series of concepts below. Read them and then list the defining attributes of each concept. You may check your responses against ours at the end of the chapter, on page 91.

1. envelope

2. clock

3. distillation

4. opera

5. referendum

6. over

7. estrange

8. harmony

Concept 3:   What properties (attributes) must an object have in order to be considered a pencil? We'll define a pencil as a long, narrow object that contains a dry substance used to mark a surface. Only four attributes are necessary to define "pencil": they are used to mark something, they are longer than they are wide, they contain a marking substance, and they have a protective covering over the marking substance. The four attributes will allow persons to place common lead pencils, carpenters' pencils, grease pencils, mechanical pencils, and graphic arts pencils all into the category "pencil."

Types of Concepts   Although there are many kinds of concepts, three are most common: conjunctive, disjunctive, and relational. The concepts we have talked about thus far, those that are defined by common attributes, are **conjunctive concepts. Disjunctive concepts** are concepts defined by statements of "either *A* or *B*." A strike in baseball, for instance, is either a ball pitched through a certain zone (one attribute), or a foul ball when there are less than two strikes (another attribute), or a foul tip that is caught with two strikes (another attribute), or a ball that the batter swings at and misses (another attribute). A strike is either *A* or *B* or *C* or *D*. Another example of a disjunctive concept is a point in tennis. A player scores a point when the other player hits the ball out of the boundary lines, strokes the ball into the net, misses a ball hit to him or her, double-faults in serving, touches the net with his or her racquet, and so on. A point is A or B or C or D (Hampton, 1988).

Relational concepts are defined by a relationship between two or more of a concept's attributes. Direction and distance are the most common relational concepts. Direction is described by giving a relationship between two or more points (west, thataway), as is distance (about two miles from here). "Over," "under," "beside," and "before" (in fact, many prepositions) are relational concepts.

Concept Prototypes

Not all theorists believe that concepts have well-defined boundaries and that all instances of a concept fit equally well into the category under consideration. For example, some of the colors we call "green" seem greener than others. Similarly, some cars seem more "car-like" than others, some balls more "ball-like," and some shirts more "shirt-like." Rosch (1977) and other contemporary researchers (e.g., Busemeyer & Myung, 1988; Nosofsky, 1988) have shown that many concepts have a **prototype**—a clear case that is a good example of the concept. For example, if we asked a group of people to rate a large number of instances of the concept of bird (e.g., cardinal, ostrich, kiwi, or hawk), we would probably find that most people would agree that a bird such as a robin would be the most "bird-like." Busemeyer and Myung (1988) have argued that most concepts are represented in memory as prototypes. These prototypes contain the most typical attributes of concepts, and the various instances of a concept share these attributes to some degree (e.g., cardinals and robins clearly share many attributes). In their view, the boundaries between concepts are ill-defined and judgments about borderline cases (e.g., bats as an instance of bird or whales as an instance of fish) are very difficult (see also Rosch, 1977).

Whether we think of concepts in terms of prototypes or as well-defined categories of information, they are central to our understanding of memory. In the next section, we will examine how concepts fit into current theories of memory.

Relationships Among Concepts: Network Models of Memory

Many psychologists who study memory cast it into two forms, episodic and semantic, although some theorists (such as Anderson, 1985) have argued against this distinction. Endel Tulving (1985) has used the term **episodic memory** to refer to memories of our personal experiences. Any memories we have about the events in our lives, such as "Yesterday I purchased a new book," or any recall of a conversation with a friend are examples of episodic memory (Tulving, 1985).

Much of what is stored in our memory, however, is not associated with any specific time or place from our past. If you remember the fact that birds fly or that 1816 was the "year with no summer," these memories are not episodic. Memory that is not episodic is referred to as **semantic memory**. Concepts and principles—knowledge not tied to memories of specific events—can be considered part of semantic memory. Much of the learning that occurs in school involves semantic memory. And, while there are several different models of semantic memory, the form of model most relevant to educational theory is the network model (Anderson, 1985; Yantis & Meyer, 1988).

Collins and Quillian's Model.   Some theorists have suggested that items stored in semantic memory are connected in a giant network. The most influential of these network models of semantic memory has been that developed by Collins and Quillian (see Yantis & Meyer, 1988). Figure 3–1 presents a hypothetical memory structure based on the original network model of Collins and Quillian (1969).

You can see that the concepts in Figure 3–1 are organized in a hierarchy based on subordinate-superordinate relations. The superor-

FIGURE 3–1   A NETWORK MODEL OF SEMANTIC MEMORY

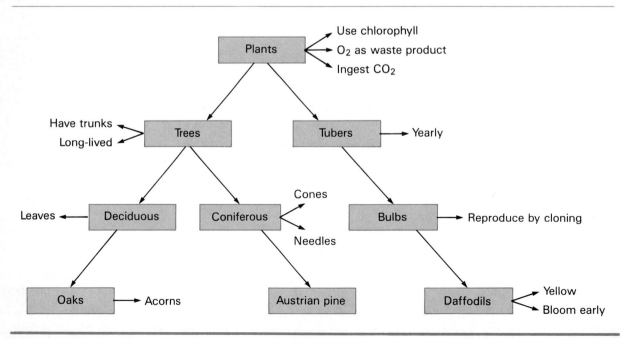

dinate of *oaks* is *deciduous*, the superordinate of *deciduous* is *trees*, and the superordinate of *trees* is *plants*. You can also see that attributes defining each concept are stored only at the point in the hierarchy corresponding to that concept. This way of thinking about storage is known as *cognitive economy*. An example of cognitive economy is the placement of *have trunks*, an attribute of all trees. It is stored only in the general category *trees* and not in any subordinate items, because all trees have trunks.

To test their model Collins and Quillian performed an experiment in which subjects were required to answer yes or no to simple questions such as the following:

1. Do oaks have trunks?

2. Do oaks lose their leaves in the winter?

3. Do oaks have acorns?

These three questions represent different semantic levels of information contained in Figure 3–1. The question "Do oaks have trunks?" can only be answered with information stored with *trees*, which is two levels away from *oaks*. The answer to the second question can be obtained from information stored at *deciduous*, one semantic level away from *oaks*. The last question can be answered from the information at *oaks* itself. Collins and Quillian believed that subjects' reaction times to such questions would test their views of how information is stored in memory. They predicted longer reaction times for information further removed in the structure from the semantic level of the concept.

Their findings were as predicted. Reaction time was shortest for questions like number 3, longest for questions like number 1, and intermediate for questions like number 2. Collins and Quillian concluded that subjects who were asked about *oaks*, for example, first entered the category *oaks*. If the information necessary to answer the question was located there, the response time was short. If the necessary information was at a different semantic level, however, subjects still would enter at *oaks* but then go up the hierarchy stopping at each level, one step at a time, until they found the answer to the question. This extra processing would account for the longer times necessary to answer questions at semantic levels above or below the entry point.

Anderson's ACT* Model.   The most comprehensive current network model is the Adaptive Control of Thought (ACT*) model developed by J. R. Anderson (e.g., 1983, 1985; Jones & Anderson, 1987). The ACT* model, based on the earlier Human Associative Memory (HAM) model developed by Anderson and Bower (1973), differs from the

Much knowledge is procedural, a "how-to" kind of knowledge. This girl's ability to use her scissors skillfully is based on procedural knowledge.

Collins and Quillian model in some important ways. First, Anderson does not agree with the semantic-episodic memory distinction we have described. Instead, his model posits two distinct kinds of knowledge—declarative knowledge and procedural knowledge. Second, the ACT* model is much broader than the Collins and Quillian model; it attempts to provide a single uniform theoretical framework for all aspects of thinking.

In Anderson's view, **declarative knowledge** refers to facts and beliefs that we have about the world. For example, declarative knowledge includes the fact that Thomas Jefferson was the third president of the United States, that we like blueberry-cheesecake ice cream, and that yesterday, one of the authors of this book had a salad for lunch. In Anderson's model, declarative knowledge combines episodic and semantic memory.

The second form of knowledge Anderson describes is **procedural knowledge**. Procedural knowledge is what we know how to do. For example, riding a bicycle, tying a shoe, doing long division, and bunting a baseball all are elements of procedural knowledge. Anderson suggests that there are two separate knowledge systems in memory: a network system much like that proposed by Collins and Quillian for declarative knowledge and a separate system for procedural knowledge. Because of the complexity of his model, we will focus here on Anderson's declarative system.

In Anderson's terms, declarative knowledge is made up of a network of nodes connected by links of varying strengths. Stored in the nodes are propositions. Propositions can be thought of as "complete" ideas, "the smallest unit about which it makes sense to make a judgment of true or false" (Anderson, 1985, pp. 114–115). Thus, "artichokes," "debate trophy," and "bread" would not be propositions (they are concepts); but the knowledge represented by the sentences "Most people hate artichokes," "Al won a debate trophy," and "That bread is stale" would be propositions. Thus propositions, like principles, involve combinations of concepts.

At any given time, some of the nodes are active (i.e., the propositions stored in the nodes are being thought about), while others are inactive. As learners shift from one area of thought to another (e.g., from thinking about, say, Hannibal crossing the Alps to Dickens's *Great Expectations*), relevant nodes are activated, and the activation spreads among the relevant nodes. Simultaneously, irrelevant nodes are deactivated. It is the idea of spreading activation that Anderson uses to account for data such as those gathered by Collins and Quillian on subjects' reaction times to different sorts of questions.

Even though we have barely skimmed the surface of Anderson's theorizing, we can see that the ACT* model is detailed and complex. It has also, however, been a very effective model that has helped us understand how information is related and remembered. Because Anderson has proposed separate memory systems for declarative and procedural knowledge, his model is able to deal with a wide range of cognitive functions.

An Evaluation of Network Models.   Network models such as Anderson's continue to be developed and refined and spur a great deal of research (McNamara & Healy, 1988; Shoben & Ross, 1988; Yantis & Meyer, 1988). We cannot say at this point what final form these models will take and which will prove to be most nearly correct.

From the point of view of teachers, however, the central idea of **network models**—that concepts and propositions are stored within large networks of related ideas—is an extraordinarily powerful one. Network models draw our attention to the idea that new knowledge must be linked with prior knowledge. The greater the number of links of new information with old information, the more stable the new information becomes. As the number of links to new knowledge increases, the new knowledge also is more readily accessible because multiple pathways have been established for reaching it.

From the standpoint of network models, both initial learning and recall can be thought of in terms of spreading activation within a network of related ideas. In initial learning, the deeper and more active the processing, the more knowledge in the network will be activated and the greater the number of links established. Elaborated encoding increases the chances of rich, stable learning. At the time of recall, the greater the number of nodes the student previously has activated in learning and the greater the number of pathways the student can activate in trying to remember, the more likely recall will be.

Of course, the point of building models of memory is to attempt to understand how individuals organize and structure their knowledge. Insights gained by memory theorists into this process will help you do a better job in one of your major roles as a teacher—helping students master and remember new concepts and principles.

Applications for Teaching: Improving the Teaching of Concepts

Learning concepts is a lifelong endeavor, and guidance is important for learners who must master new concepts. A great deal of research has focused on procedures used in teaching concepts. Here we have identified a six-step process for teaching concepts that stresses a combination of several of the most effective procedures examined in research.

1. Present the student with a well-prepared instructional objective. As we discuss in detail in Chapter Twelve, the first step in all instruction is the clear communication of what is to be learned.

2. Dispense with all the unnecessary attributes of a concept. As in our examples of the cup, ring, and pencil, only the defining attributes of concepts should be stressed at the beginning of instruction. Take the concept you are going to teach, and list all the attributes you think describe it. Then determine which attributes actually define the concept.

3. Link the new concept to what students already know. Many times students do not (or are not able to) associate new concepts with their present knowledge. Schema activation through analogies, examples, and metaphors can help students relate new information to what they already know. Having students describe what they know

about related concepts is also a good way of helping them build conceptual bridges between new and already learned information. In addition, if the learners do not have the necessary vocabulary to learn a new concept, you must first teach them the language. New concepts are built on old concepts, and concepts are organized in hierarchical networks with links between the elements. The understanding of new concepts (such as "amerce") is unlikely unless the concepts are defined and explained in terms of existing concepts ("amerce" means "to punish").

4. Present the learners with both positive and negative examples of the concept. If you were teaching the concept "reptile," you might present some reptiles (positive examples) and some nonreptiles (negative examples).* You would then point out or ask leading questions to elicit student identification of defining attributes of rep-

_____

*Positive examples are usually more important than negative examples (Hampton, 1988). In the case of reptiles, pictures or descriptions are preferable to a roomful of animals, although you might be able to obtain lizards or small snakes in the spring and fall. Nonreptilian animals such as goldfish, frogs, mice, and birds can probably also be obtained fairly readily; some of your students may have them as pets.

tiles. You would also give students practice with feedback in discriminating defining and nondefining attributes.

The use of many positive and negative examples enables students to differentiate between those things that are classed into a concept and those that are not. Students also should provide examples from their own experiences. This increases students' depth of processing and helps them fit the new information into already existing memory structures.

5. Encourage students to be active and provide feedback for their responses. Students cannot obtain the best possible practice (trying out their learning to see if it is correct or incorrect) without participating and receiving feedback, which in this case is information about how well they have learned. Students who aren't completely sure whether a small furry animal is a mammal need to try out their thinking and have you react to it. Also, don't limit your feedback only to the *outcomes* of concept learning; focus on the mental processes your students are using (Andre, 1988). By probing student thinking, you not only learn about the quality of their learning but help them to gain metacognitive knowledge about their own thought processes.

6. Evaluate the learning of the concept. We are not finished with instruction until we determine how well our students have mastered the concepts. Most instructors hope that students acquire more than just a verbal definition of a concept. Simply defining a word is a low level of concept use. Instead, we expect students to be able to recognize examples and nonexamples of concepts and to use concepts in their thinking. Evaluation should be planned accordingly.

Examples of Teaching Concepts
Mr. Jones teaches many concepts to his sixth-grade students during the year. Let's examine how he taught some of his students the concept of "levee" by following our six-step process.

Mr. Jones started his lesson by providing his students with a set of objectives. Among them was

the following: "You will be able to correctly identify eight out of ten objects as levees or nonlevees on your next quiz." Mr. Jones's second step was to reduce the number of attributes of "levee" to the least possible number. He did this by defining "levee" as "an embankment raised to prevent a river from overflowing." The attributes were use (preventing a river from overflowing) and form (an embankment). So "levee" was a simple conjunctive concept with two defining attributes.

In order to link the concept to what students already knew, he wrote the words "levee" and "embankment" on the chalkboard and asked the students to pronounce them. All his students could say "embankment" and "levee" very easily. Some, in fact, began to break into songs about levees before he could proceed with his lesson. Stopping the singers, he then spent some time having the students describe examples of levees they had seen and recounting visits to places where embankments were used for many purposes. He then shifted the conversation somewhat and had students recount their knowledge of the damage caused by floods, and, in particular, he focused on a news report that had been presented the previous day by one of the students.

To follow the fourth step of the process, Mr. Jones showed the class some large photographs representing both positive and negative examples of the concept "levee." As he presented each card he reminded the students that they were looking for objects that were embankments built to prevent a river from overflowing. The first picture was a photograph taken of a mound of earth being bulldozed up against a small river. Mr. Jones asked his class if this picture was a levee. The class responded that it was, although several students pointed out that the bulldozer might be building something else and had incidentally piled up the earth along the river. He then held the picture closer to those students so they could see the embankment receding into the distance along the river. They then decided it was a levee. Mr. Jones complimented the class on its responses and went on to describe the process of building a levee. Here he was getting at another instructional objective—the effects of new construction on wildlife habitats.

Mr. Jones then showed pictures of several examples and nonexamples of levees: a dam, a bridge abutment, a bridge under construction, sandbag levees, a pier, rock levees, boat ramps, ski ramps, and other assorted constructions along rivers and other bodies of water. He continually had the students respond to the pictures while he provided feedback.* He also asked students to give examples from their own experiences.

Toward the end of the period, Mr. Jones had presented several positive and negative examples of levees in addition to his instruction on ecological concerns. To quickly evaluate student learning, he passed out a brief quiz that consisted of hand-drawn pictures of several positive and negative examples of levees. The students were instructed to label the items as levees or nonlevees. He then had the students score their own papers as he called out the correct responses. He answered a few questions requiring a "judgment call" and then, on the basis of looking over the papers quickly, determined that his class had mastered the concept of levee.

This example is a relatively simple one. It is easy to think of positive and negative examples of levees. Many other concepts are much more difficult to teach and require considerably more effort on the part of the teacher and the learner. A good example can be taken from an adult's self-initiated learning.

Let's suppose that Mr. Jones is a person of many interests, among them astronomy. A budding stargazer and reader of astronomy books, he has decided to build a telescope to further pursue his hobby. He has chosen to build a telescope rather than purchase a completed one for several reasons—cost, the chance to learn about how tele-

*You should notice that Mr. Jones was doing what all teachers do—blending the teaching of several concepts into one lesson. While the concept "levee" was being taught he was also describing other waterway constructions and making points about ecological concerns.

scopes work, and the general need for involvement in a meaningful project. Mr. Jones, however, has never had formal instruction in the areas of physics, optics, or astronomy.

As Mr. Jones pores over several telescope catalogs, it becomes apparent that, although he already knows quite a bit about astronomy, he must better understand several concepts before he can make an intelligent decision about purchasing a telescope kit. Among the concepts he must refine are those of refracting and reflecting telescopes.

Mr. Jones sets an informal objective for himself: "to be able to completely understand refracting and reflecting telescopes." Then he determines the defining attributes of refracting and reflecting telescopes by going to his local library and checking out several books and pamphlets. He then reads through the simplest materials he could find and determines that a refracting telescope uses lenses to bend and focus light while reflecting telescopes use mirrors for the same purpose. Mr. Jones can see that the defining attributes are the use of lenses or mirrors for forming images of distant objects. He rehearses this information so that he will have it available any time he needs it.

As Mr. Jones reads more, he learns many different concepts ("focal length," "resolution," and so on) and builds a broader vocabulary. He sees varied examples of both reflecting and refracting telescopes, from small ones he might consider building to Mt. Palomar, the largest in the United States. He flips from picture to picture, back and forth, until he can readily identify each type of telescope.

As Mr. Jones studies, he asks questions of himself. He is not just the learner—he is actively involved in many other ways as the initiator, teacher, and evaluator of his lesson. He finally evaluates himself by checking his definitions against the books and also by sketching reflecting and refracting telescope diagrams and comparing his diagrams with those in some of his books. After a few more weeks of study, he is ready to try his hand at building a telescope. He elects, incidentally, to construct a reflector.

PRACTICE EXERCISE 3–3   PLANNING FOR CONCEPT TEACHING

This exercise consists of two steps: (1) observing concept teaching in one of your classes and (2) planning for your own teaching of a concept. As a first step, we would like you to use the following form and to observe concept teaching in a classroom. Any class is acceptable, but it would be best to observe a class in the subject area and grade level you will teach.

1. Type of class and grade level of students:

2. Concept being taught was:

3. Was the concept defined? _____ If so, how?

4. What relevant (defining attributes) of the concept were presented?

5. What examples of the concept were given?

6. Were nonexamples given? _____ If so, were they helpful?

7. How did the teacher try to link the new concept to what the students already knew?

8. From the presentation you observed, estimate the percentage of students who could:

    _____ Write a definition of the concept

    _____ Recognize almost every example of the concept

    _____ Explain the concept clearly to another student

9. Give an overall rating of the effectiveness of the concept teaching you saw:

1	2	3	4	5	6	7
A waste of time; no one understood.			Most persons had some understanding, but more learning needed.		Everyone understood and can now use the concept.	

Now, as a second step, select a concept from your subject area and select someone who has not yet learned the concept (a classmate, friend, student in a school, or group of students). Plan how you would teach the concept by using the following steps:

1. The concept is

2. Definition of the concept

3. Relevant attributes

4. Good positive examples of the concept

5. Negative examples of the concept (select those that the student might possibly confuse with positive examples)

6. Domain to which the concept applies

7. The ways I will help students link this concept to their present knowledge

If possible, go ahead and teach the concept. Use the kind of questions you used in your observation of concept teaching to have your pupil give you feedback on how well you presented the concept and how well he or she understood it.

Organizing Personal Study to Improve Memory

Understanding the process of memory and the process of forgetting allows teachers to adapt techniques to help their students more effectively learn and remember new information. A method of study described by the late Frank Robinson in his book *Effective Study* (1972) still fits well within our current knowledge about memory. Robinson's general method has been demonstrated to be successful in helping students above the elementary level learn more effectively, and his work has been incorporated in several recent approaches to improving study skills (e.g., Meyer, Young & Bartlett, 1988; Singer & Donlan, 1988). We have found Robinson's method to be especially effective for independent study assignments such as reading this book. It can be taught to students to improve their study habits and to increase the quality of their learning of concepts and principles. As you look over the steps listed below, you will see that they are designed to help make new information meaningful, to keep students actively involved in learning, and to provide occasions for practicing newly learned information.

Step 1: Survey. When any new material is to be learned, the first step is to survey it—to look it over—in order to familiarize yourself with the information and to determine exactly what your task is and is not. You are seeking to make the task meaningful in the sense in which we have described meaningful learning. You probably can best complete the survey step by looking over the chapter summary. This will tie the chapter's information to your past experience and help you activate relevant knowledge.

Step 2: Question. The questioning step helps you to become actively involved with the material. As you look over the chapter, convert the headings and subheadings into open questions. Also ask yourself questions about the content: What is the author trying to accomplish with this chapter? How does the information in this chapter tie into things I already know? What experiences have I had related to the information in this chapter? The idea is to specify your own objectives as questions and to relate the new materials to what you have already learned. This step greatly increases the meaningfulness of new information and gets you actively involved. It also helps you anticipate test questions.

Step 3: Read. Read the material. As you read, try to answer the questions you formulated in Step 2 and link what you are reading to what you already know.

Step 4: Recite. As soon as you finish reading a section, stop and try to answer the questions you asked about it. This active practice helps you give meaning to the passage by relating the material to previously learned information.

Step 5: Review. The review process saves some time because it does not require you to reread all the material you have studied. Rather, you focus on questions you found difficult and study the difficult portions of the material until you can answer the questions. This step is your evaluation of learning and gives additional practice in those places where you need it.

The mnemonic to remember this process is SQ3R: *Survey, Question, Read, Recite,* and *Review*. Not only can you use this process to enhance your study skills, you can also teach it to others. Your future students can benefit as much from instruction and practice in study skills as you can.

PRACTICE EXERCISE 3–4   TEACHING YOURSELF A CONCEPT

> We spend much of our adult lives teaching ourselves new concepts. Choose a concept you would like to learn, and teach it to yourself following the steps listed below. Place your responses in the spaces indicated. Keep in mind that we seldom learn new concepts out of context; that is, when you are learning new things you probably will learn many new concepts, just as Mr. Jones did when he was learning about telescopes.
>
> 1. Set an informal objective to master a new concept.
> 2. Determine the defining attributes of the concept.
> 3. Think of what you already know about this area, and jot down related concepts.
> 4. If you need to learn new vocabulary, indicate what vocabulary you need to learn.
> 5. Identify several positive and negative examples of the concept. List them here, and note how they affect your learning of the concept.
> 6. Describe specifically how you learned about the concept (other than reading).
> 7. What did you do to evaluate the results of your learning? Do you now have the level of understanding of the concept you need?

Summary

In this chapter we outlined theories of human memory, including decay theory, interference theory, and three dimensions of an information-processing perspective—levels-of-processing, schema theory, and parallel distributed processing. We then reviewed metamemory and its development. The study of memory led us to a series of guidelines to apply to teaching and studying.

Memory is systematically organized, and the central feature of memory for declarative knowledge is the concept. Concepts were defined as were attributes and defining attributes. The way in which concepts are organized in memory was examined by reviewing two network models, the original Collins and Quillian model and the more ambitious ACT* model of J. R. Anderson. A six-step process for teaching concepts was described together with a general study method—survey, question, read, recite, and review (SQ3R).

As we have emphasized in our introduction to cognition in Chapter Two, meaningfulness is a key feature in human memory and concept learning. In Chapter Two we examined the role of meaning in perception, attention, and working memory. Here we devoted our discussion to critical aspects of the repository of knowledge about the world—long term memory—that allow people to give meaning to what they learn. We also focused on how children's metamemory—thinking about their memory—develops and influences memory capabilities.

In the next chapter, "Intelligence and Cognitive Development," we examine the issue of cognitive development much more fully as we explore the concept of intelligence. An understanding of basic cognitive processes is important for effective teaching but so is knowledge of the nature of cognitive development and knowledge of individual differences in overall human cognitive abilities.

Suggested Readings

Craik, F. I. M., & Lockhart, R. S. (1972). Levels of processing: A framework for memory research. *Journal of Verbal Learning and Verbal Behavior, 11,* 671–684.

> *This classic article first set out the "levels" position. The ideas in this paper have stimulated a significant amount of research on memory. The metaphor of "levels of processing" remains an extremely useful one for educators.*

Farr, M. J. (1988). *The long-term retention of knowledge and skills.* New York: Springer-Verlag.

> *Farr's volume is a valuable resource for thinking about how knowledge and skills are remembered, especially in terms of strategies for improving students' long-term retention.*

Gorfein, D. S., & Hoffman, R. R. (1988). *Memory and learning: The Ebbinghaus Centennial Conference.* Hillsdale, NJ: Erlbaum.

> *This set of readings presents an outstanding overview of a century's worth of progress in the study of human memory.*

McClelland, J. L. (1988). Connectionist models and psychological evidence. *Journal of Memory and Language, 27,* 107–123.

> *McClelland's article introduces a special issue of the* Journal of Memory and Language *devoted entirely to new developments in memory theory. Centered on the new research on parallel distributed processing (PDP), this issue of the journal provides a technical exposition of new directions in memory research.*

Weinert, F. E., & Perlmutter, M. (1988). *Memory development: Universal changes and individual differences.* Hillsdale, NJ: Erlbaum.

> *Weinert and Perlmutter have edited an outstanding volume. Especially valuable are chapters on metamemory and schema theory. We strongly recommend this book.*

Answers to Practice Exercise 3–2

1. encloses other objects, nonrigid
2. tells time
3. uses heat, separates chemical substances
4. staged play, major part of story conveyed by song
5. popular vote, decides public issue
6. immediately above another object, not touching other object
7. alienated, removed from
8. agreement, pleasant arrangement

As you can see, the defining attributes of these concepts vary from very simple to moderately complex. If you want to consider one that is really complex, try to obtain your class's consensus on the defining attributes of "love."

OVERVIEW

Intelligence, the ability to profit from experience, can be considered the summation of all the cognitive functions we have discussed thus far. A common theme of Chapters Two and Three was an information-processing approach to cognition. Our perspective in this chapter will change somewhat, although we remain in the general area of cognition. The reason for our shift in emphasis was first clearly expressed by Cronbach (1957) several years ago. He pointed out at the time that there appeared to be two disciplines in psychology that should have been interacting but were not. On the one hand was *psychometry*, a specialty in psychology devoted to measuring differences between people (including intellectual differences). On the other hand was *experimental psychology*, which, when humans were the subjects, was devoted to the investigation of psychological processes. One aspect of experimental psychology was the study of cognitive processes. While the group of psychologists interested in psychometry was engaged in measuring *differences* in the intellectual abilities of people, experimentalists were studying the *processes* that underlay these differences. Neither group (with the exception of Cronbach) paid much attention to what the other was doing. This state of affairs, however, has begun to change in the last few years (Carroll, 1987; Hunt, 1988; Sternberg, 1988; Waters, Brock, & Malus-Abramowitz, 1988).

In our discussion of cognitive processes we have necessarily emphasized the tradition of experimental psychology. As important as this tradition has been to our understanding of human cognition, we must leave experimental psychology for a time and turn to psychometry in order to begin to understand the ways in which intelligence has been measured. We will trace the history of psychometric views about intelligence as psychometry and experimental psychology began to find common ground in information-processing theory (Hunt, 1988). We will also review Jean Piaget's developmental theory, which he developed in reaction to psychometric approaches (Inhelder, de Caprona, & Corno-Wells, 1988) and which became a major influence on contemporary cognitive psychology and education. Then, we will return to an information-processing perspective, focusing on how Piaget's theory and information-processing views have become synthesized in a contemporary view of cognitive development.

OBJECTIVES
After reading this chapter, you should be able to meet the following objectives.

1. Describe the implications of individual differences in intelligence for your teaching practices.

2. Indicate the effect your knowledge of the nature-nurture controversy will have on your practices as a teacher.

3. Recognize how developmental theories of intelligence affect the decisions you will make as a teacher.

Psychometric Approaches to Intelligence

Intelligence Tests

The idea that humans possess intellectual abilities that can be accurately measured dates back at least to Sir Francis Galton's 1869 book *Hereditary Genius*. Galton's conception that there were different limits to each person's intellectual abilities set the tone for much of modern psychometry's views on intellectual ability (Jensen, 1987; Plomin, 1987). As important as Galton's pathfinding was, however, it was not until after the turn of the century that the assessment of intelligence got its real start.

The Binet and Simon Scales.   In 1904, the French Minister of Public Instruction called together a commission of learned people concerned with education—physicians, educators, public officials, and scientists—and asked them to investigate the problems of teaching so-called feeble-minded children. As it turned out, the most important work accomplished by this commission was performed by a psychologist, Alfred Binet, and a physician, Theodore Simon. Their efforts were to have a permanent impact on both education and psychology.

Binet and Simon believed that before any instructional programs could be developed, some method was needed for measuring the general cognitive functions of the children the programs were trying to help. Working from this assumption, Binet and Simon constructed a test designed to measure intelligence. Their test was based on the following definition:

> It seems to us that in intelligence there is a fundamental faculty, the alteration or the lack of which is of the utmost importance for practical life. This faculty is judgment, otherwise called good sense,

practical sense, initiative, the faculty of adapting one's self to circumstances. To judge well, to comprehend well, to reason well, these are the essential activities of intelligence. (*Binet & Simon, 1905, p. 246*)

Their test consisted of a series of problems Binet and Simon believed could be solved with little influence from children's backgrounds and required reason and judgment rather than rote memory. An indication of what the original test demanded can be seen in some of the expectations Binet had for "normal" children's performance at different ages:

Age 3   Points to nose, eyes, and mouth when asked.
Age 5   Can count four coins.
Age 7   Identifies and shows left ear and right hand.
Age 9   Can relate familiar words to other concepts.
Age 12 When given three words, can employ them in a sentence. (*Binet & Simon, 1911, p. 91*)

As we'll see later in this chapter, a hotly debated topic is whether such items (which also appear on current intelligence tests) are truly environment- and background-free.

Between 1905, when the first version of the Binet-Simon test appeared, and 1911, when the last version was published, Binet revised and refined his test. During this time and in the years following the appearance of the 1911 version, Binet and other psychologists observed that retarded children who were tested and then retested at a later date fell further and further behind their "normal" peers.

Binet found that the ratio of mental age (the average age of children who got a given number of items correct) to chronological age typically remained almost constant as children developed. For example, a child who at age five had a mental age of three would be likely to obtain a mental-age score of six at the age of ten, both mental ages being three-fifths of "normal."

This observation of a relatively constant ratio of mental and chronological age led to the expression of intelligence test results as the **intelligence quotient**, or **IQ**. IQ was defined as the ratio of mental age to chronological age multiplied by 100 (to create a whole number):

$$\frac{\text{mental age}}{\text{chronological age}} \times 100 = \text{IQ}$$

A five-year-old with a mental age of three would have an IQ of 60 ($3/5 \times 100 = 60$). Likewise, an eight-year-old obtaining a mental-age

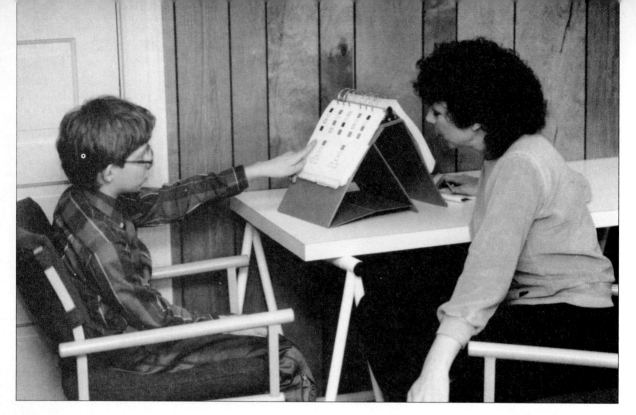

Individual intelligence tests provide one estimate of intellectual ability.

score of 10 would have an IQ of 125 ($10/8 \times 100 = 125$). IQs calculated in this manner have come to be known as **ratio IQs**.

The Binet-Simon test and its later revisions formed the keystone of efforts to measure intellectual abilities. It should be pointed out, however, that the Binet-Simon test in no way was a measure of underlying cognitive processes, such as those that are components of modern information-processing models. There only was the conjecture that responses to the test items involved "judgment," "practical sense," "initiative," and other rather loosely defined qualities thought to be important for academic success.

The Stanford-Binet.   The next important event in the development of measures of intelligence took place in the United States and was guided by L. M. Terman. Terman tried out Binet's materials as well as other tests, including some of his own devising, on nearly three thousand children. He then arranged these tests into mental-age levels and published them in 1916 as the Stanford Revision of the Binet-Simon test.

For twenty years the 1916 Stanford Revision was *the* test of intelligence in the United States, the standard against which all new measures of intelligence were judged. During that time, however, it became apparent that it was unsatisfactory in some ways. Its major shortcomings were that it was not appropriate for adults nor for very young children. Also, there was only one version of the 1916 test. Because of these problems, Terman and Maud Merrill published a revision of the Stanford-Binet in 1937. The 1937 version had two forms and was extended upward so that it was appropriate for adults and downward so that it could be used for children as young as two. The typical procedure for calculating mental age was not employed when the test was used to assess the intelligence of adults. That is, no one expects a fifty-year-old person to have twice the mental capacity of a twenty-five-year-old. Instead, the chronological age of adults was "corrected" to fit into the old formula (Terman & Merrill, 1937).

The Stanford-Binet was revised again in 1960 and in 1986. In general, the best items from previous versions of the test have been retained, while poorer and outdated items have been replaced. Over the years, the Stanford-Binet has continued to be the standard of reference for all intelligence tests (Gronlund, 1985; Naglieri, 1988; Sternberg, 1987).

There have been two major changes in the later revision of the Stanford-Binet. First, while the early versions relied heavily on the language ability of the person being tested, the newer versions have included performance tests thought to be freer of language bias. That is, tests emphasizing language were noted to unfairly penalize people who did not speak English as their native language. To supplement language-oriented tasks, tests requiring nonverbal performances were developed. An example is the form-boards task, which provides a board with holes into which test takers must fit blocks of the correct size and shape as rapidly as possible. Additionally, in the newer versions of the Stanford-Binet, IQ no longer is calculated with the mental-age/chronological-age equation. Instead, IQ is expressed as a standard score (see Chapter Fourteen).

The Wechsler Scales. Another major event in the assessment of intellectual ability was the development of the Wechsler Scales. There are three major differences between the Wechsler Scales and the Stanford-Binet tests: (1) the Wechsler Scales were originally designed for adults, while the Stanford-Binet was first developed for children; (2) the Wechsler Scales are organized by subtests rather than age levels; and (3) the Wechsler Scales yield both a verbal and a nonverbal IQ (Naglieri, 1988). There is very little difference between the utility of the Wechsler Scales and that of the Stanford-Binet—people will score nearly the same on both tests (Lukens, 1988). The Wechsler Scales include the Wechsler Adult Intelligence Scale, Revised (WAIS–R; Wechsler, 1981), the Wechsler Intelligence Scale for Children, Revised (WISC–R; Wechsler, 1974), and the Wechsler Preschool and Primary Scale (WPPSI; Wechsler, 1967).

Group Intelligence Tests.   Another important development in the assessment of intelligence was the creation of group tests of intelligence. Group tests, as the term implies, are designed to be given to a group of people at one time and so have a large advantage over individually administered tests, such as the Stanford-Binet and the Wechsler Scales, in terms of the time required to administer them. Because of the large role of reading and other language-related skills required to perform well on such tests, however, they have been severely criticized by many people and have been banned as discriminatory in some states. We will explore group tests in more detail in our chapter on Standardized Tests, but we note here that they all were developed with either the Stanford-Binet or the Wechsler as the standard of comparison (Gronlund, 1985; Sternberg, 1988).

Psychometric Theories of Intelligence

To understand how psychometrists view intelligence, it is helpful to recount some of the ideas of D. O. Hebb (1949). Hebb suggested that a distinction should be made between what he called Intelligence A and Intelligence B. He referred to Intelligence A as the innate, inborn intellectual capacity possessed by a person and Intelligence B as the average or typical level of intellectual functioning demonstrated by a person. Hebb did not claim that there were two different kinds of intelligence; but he did argue that, while neither Intelligence A nor Intelligence B was truly observable, Intelligence B was far more open to measurement. Hebb suggested that testing could allow a fairly accurate estimate of Intelligence B but that an accurate measurement of Intelligence A would be far more difficult to obtain. Most psychometrists have focused on Intelligence B in their attempts to define and measure intelligence.

There are several ways of defining intelligence (Brown, in press). Three common views are as follows (Michael, in press):

Intelligence is learning ability.

Intelligence is a person's ability to adapt to his or her environment.

Intelligence is the ability to think abstractly.

These three definitions, of course, do not necessarily exclude one another, but they do represent distinct positions about Intelligence B. The first definition emphasizes people's receptiveness to education; the second, the way in which people deal with new situations; and the third, people's capabilities for verbal and mathematical reasoning. When we think about the definitions, it becomes clear that learning ability must depend to some extent on adaptive skills and abstract thought. Similarly, adaptability seems to depend in part on learning ability. And while abstract thought may not necessarily overlap with adaptability, the concepts that allow abstract thought must be learned in the first place. This high degree of agreement among the three definitions indicates that psychometrists are in fairly close accord in their views. It also shows the difficulty in describing and defining intelligence apart from scores on intelligence tests (Jensen, 1987; Sternberg, 1988).

As it turns out, the questions on intelligence tests that best relate to overall performance on the tests are those that require numerical or verbal reasoning (Jensen, 1985). From the perspective of intelligence tests, therefore, a reasonable definition of intelligence would be ability in numerical and verbal reasoning. That certain types of test items relate well to overall test performance, however, has not put to rest the debates on the true nature of intelligence (Eysenck, 1987; Jensen, 1985).

Two general theories of intelligence could be applied to any of the three preceding definitions: the general-factor theory and the multifactor theory. Both theories are based on the statistical analysis of large numbers of intelligence test scores, which allows psychologists to identify the factors that best relate to overall test performance. General-factor theories of intelligence (see Eysenck, 1987; Spearman, 1927) suggest that all human intellectual abilities have in common a general factor, which Spearman called the g factor. Spearman described the g factor as the mental energy that supports all mental activities and suggested that some mental operations require more g than do others. He also described some specific factors(s) in intelligence. Despite Spearman's ideas about specific factors, he believed that intelligence tests should measure g and that, in fact, a good, single test could do so.

Multifactor theories of intelligence (see Guilford, 1959; Thurstone, 1938) are based on the position that intelligence is best defined by *separate* factors or underlying abilities. Thurstone (1938) suggested that six factors make up intelligence and that each is involved in several intellectual operations (six factors follow on p. 100).

Number factor (NA): Ability to perform mathematical operations with speed and accuracy

Verbal factor (V): Ability to perform on tests of verbal (language) comprehension

Space factor (S): Ability to manipulate an object in space in one's imagination

Word fluency factor (W): Ability to think rapidly of individual words

Reasoning factor (R): Ability to determine rules through deductive or inductive thought

Rote memory factor (M): Rapid memorization ability

For Thurstone these six factors are the primary mental abilities. Because he thought them to be relatively independent, he expected that people could score well on one or more of these factors while scoring poorly on others. As it turned out (Sternberg, 1987), Thurstone never obtained data that fully supported the existence of six independent factors, and he concluded that there must be an underlying general factor that influenced each of the six primary mental-ability factors.

High verbal individuals rapidly convert symbols into thought. The printed symbols in this book are readily understood by the high verbal student.

The most famous of the multifactor intelligence theories was put forth by J. P. Guilford (1959), who developed a model containing one hundred twenty separate factors. As intriguing as a model containing one hundred twenty factors might be, Guilford's model has not received extensive support (Jensen, 1987) except for the distinction he made between convergent and divergent (creative) thought. In Chapter Six we will see the importance of Guilford's contributions to current conceptions of creativity.

The issue of whether intelligence is related to a single or multiple factor still is debated today (see Dinsmore, 1987; Eysenck, 1987), but analyzing factors in a test does not appear to take us any closer to understanding the cognitive processes underlying intelligence-test scores (Carroll, 1987; Hunt, 1988). Such research has dealt primarily with the types of test items that best predict overall test scores; generally, it has not addressed cognitive processes.

Information-Processing Approaches to Intelligence

As we have seen, a psychometric approach is a widely used way of trying to understand intelligence. Psychometricians have been most concerned with how to measure intelligence and with predicting other performance, such as classroom learning, from these scores. In contrast, psychologists with an information-processing perspective seldom have been concerned with measurement of overall intellectual abilities but have instead emphasized the study of thought processes (Hunt, 1988).

You will recall that the first suggestion for research integrating psychometric and cognitive psychology came from Cronbach (1957), an esteemed psychometrist and educational psychologist. It wasn't until the 1970s, however, that such research began in earnest (e.g., Hunt, 1978; Hunt, Frost, & Lunneborg, 1973; Lansman & Hunt, 1982; MacLeod, Hunt, & Mathews, 1978).

Research on individual differences in information processing is based on the observation that there are several "bottlenecks" in the processing system (Hunt, 1988; Sternberg, 1985). For example, far more information in the environment is available to children than can be held in the sensory registers. Further, only a fraction of what is held in the sensory registers can be accessed by the working memory. As we have noted, working memory has a limited capacity (Sternberg, 1988), and only a portion of the information held in it is passed on to long-term memory (Sternberg, 1988). These bottlenecks in the processing system, along with the obvious differences in scores people obtain on measures of intelligence, led several theorists (e.g., Hunt, 1988; Jensen, 1987; Sternberg, 1985) to propose that differences in cognitive abilities were the result of differences in individuals' information-processing systems.

Hunt's Approach

For instance, Hunt and his colleagues (e.g., Hunt, 1988; Hunt & Pellegrino, 1985; Palmer, MacLeod, Hunt, & Davidson, 1985) have suggested that there are three potential sources of individual differences in information processing: (1) knowledge, (2) mechanics of information processing, and (3) elementary information-processing programs. Differences in knowledge (contained in long-term memory) clearly influence what students attend to, what they perceive, and the likelihood that they will pass new information into long-term memory. For example, a student who is faced with a word problem in mathematics and who has knowledge of how to solve such problems probably will notice relevant aspects of the problem, assign appropriate meanings to its various aspects, and is very likely to append any new information to the already existing store of knowledge in long-term memory. In contrast, a student who has little knowledge about word problems is unlikely to know what to focus on, may not understand parts of the problem, and is unlikely to tie this experience into relevant knowledge structures.

Hunt's second source of individual variations in cognition, the mechanics of information processing, refers to the "hardware" component of the information-processing system (Hunt, 1988). Hunt has proposed that there are capacity and duration differences in the sensory registers. In addition, he has suggested differences in capacity, duration, and speed of information manipulation in working memory. Finally, he has also posited differences in speed of access to long-term memory.

Hunt (1988) also has suggested, however, that "hardware" (i.e., structural) differences have to be considered in light of differences among individuals' *elementary information-processing programs*. In Hunt's view, humans must possess

> simple strategies that are used as steps in virtually every larger problem. Examples are the strategy of repeating names that are to be remembered or the strategy of checking an answer after it has been developed but before it is publicly enunciated . . . much of what we refer to as general intelligence is based on the facility with which one uses such general information processes. (p. 93)

The three sources of individual differences in information processing have received considerable research attention (see, e.g., Kail, 1988). Differences in knowledge have been the most frequently investigated, usually in psychometrically oriented research. We know, of course, that there are large individual differences in knowledge. Here, however, we will focus specifically on research that has examined differences in the mechanics of information processing and elementary information-processing programs.

In their research, Hunt and his colleagues typically have selected a measure of verbal ability (the Washington Pre-College Test, WPCT) as the instrument to identify groups of students with test-measured high-verbal ability and low-verbal ability. Working with a sample of undergraduates at the University of Washington, they determined that the WPCT reflected verbal intelligence in much the same way as did the verbal component of most intelligence tests.

In a series of experiments, Hunt and his colleagues identified students who scored in the upper quartile (the top 25 percent) and the lower quartile (bottom 25 percent) of the WPCT, who then were required to perform a series of memory tasks. Overall, the research found that students in the upper quartile (high-verbals) differed from those in the lower quartile (low-verbals) in several interesting ways.

High-verbals manipulate information in working memory more quickly than do low-verbals.

High-verbals remember information in correct order better than low-verbals.

High-verbals can retrieve greatly overlearned information (such as the letters of the alphabet) more rapidly from long-term memory than can low-verbals.

High-verbals convert symbols in written form into thought more rapidly than do low-verbals.

Further research has supported the findings of Hunt and his colleagues. For instance, a study by Ellis, Deacon, and Woolridge (1985) compared the performance of normal and mildly retarded young adults on a memory task in which an intervening task (counting backwards) was used to keep the subjects from rehearsing the information. Their results indicated that the normal group recalled significantly more information at each interval. The results, of course, fit the general trend observed by Hunt et al. between high-verbal and low-verbal subjects and extend it to contrasts between normal and mildly retarded individuals. Likewise, Raz, Willerman, and Yama (1988) found that the ability to process auditory information was closely related to intelligence test scores.

A similar pattern of results also has been obtained by Cohn, Carlson, and Jensen (1988), who examined information-processing differences between gifted and normal adolescents. In the Cohn et al. study, the gifted students consistently outperformed the normal sample on working memory, perception, and access to long-term memory tasks. Likewise, Schofield and Ashman (1987) found that gifted students outperformed high-average students on measures of information processing while the high-average students similarly outperformed low-average students.

Thus, a clear trend emerges when we examine individual differences in information-processing research. People who obtain high scores on psychometric measures of intelligence outperform people who obtain low intelligence-test scores on a wide range of basic information-processing tasks. This pattern of results is in general agreement with what psychometric theories of intelligence have long asserted (Binet & Simon, 1905; Spearman, 1927; Thurstone, 1938). Apparently, psychometric tests of intellectual ability do measure differences in how people process information (Ellis, Palmer, & Reeves, 1988; Small, Raney, & Knapp, 1987).

In the past few years, several distinguished psychologists have begun to explore ways in which the measurement of information-processing differences might replace or at least supplement some of the traditional psychometric tests of intelligence (Carroll, 1987; Hunt, 1988; Jensen, 1987; Sternberg, 1988). Hunt (1988), for example, argues that there now is a highly sophisticated technology available, both in equipment and in statistics, to permit a thorough exploration of this possibility. Although he does not see the use of information-processing measures (such as the speed of manipulating information in working memory) as totally replacing traditional intelligence tests, his general feeling is that studying information-processing performance can improve the assessment of intelligence.

Sternberg's Triarchic Theory

Among contemporary psychologists, Robert Sternberg of Yale University has developed the most ambitious theory of intelligence based on an information-processing perspective (e.g., 1988). In his view, there are three major aspects of intelligence: (1) performance components, (2) knowledge-acquisition components, and (3) metacomponents. A brief discussion of each of these aspects follows.

Performance components are cognitive processes involved in completing tasks. Consider the following analogy: Sternberg is to theories of intelligence as Fergus Craik is to (a) cheeseburgers, (b) foreign diplomacy, or (c) theories of memory. What kinds of cognitive processes did you employ in choosing the best answer? Sternberg (1987, 1988) suggests several processes (components, in his terms) are involved. We will describe four as examples so you can get the flavor of Sternberg's approach.

Among the performance components involved in solving the problem are *encoding*, in which information from the problem is placed into memory, and *inferring the relations* in the problem statement (i.e., you infer that the relationship of Sternberg to theories of intelligence is that Sternberg has developed one). Another performance component is *mapping higher-order relations*. That is, to solve the problem, you must determine that the relationship of Sternberg to theories of intelligence is the same as the relationship of Fergus Craik to theories of memory. A fourth performance component necessary to solve the problem is the *response*—in other words, choosing the answer.

The second major aspect of intelligence described by Sternberg focuses on *knowledge-acquisition components*. People use these components to determine whether information is worth learning. If so, people then use knowledge-acquisition components to make the information meaningful by relating it to prior knowledge.

Performance and knowledge-acquisition components alone are insufficient to account for intelligence. A third set of components, *metacomponents*, is needed to describe how people direct their performance and knowledge-acquisition components. Metacomponents are "executive processes." Metacomponents are responsible for understanding the nature of problems, deciding which performance components should be used in dealing with a particular problem, selecting strategies for combining performance components in order to handle problems, and keeping track of what has been accomplished and what remains to be completed in order to solve the problem.

Sternberg depicts differences in intellectual functioning as due to differences in the three aspects of intelligence. In particular, he argues that intellectually advanced individuals spend more of their time on metacomponential processing. Further, he sees the major developmental changes in intellectual functioning as due to the increasing sophistication of metacomponential processing. For Sternberg, major differences in intellectual ability are due to executive functions.

Intelligence and the Nature-Nurture Question

Why do some people have a higher measured intelligence than others? One way to try to answer this question is to compare the intelligence test scores of people with differing degrees of genetic (nature) and environmental (nurture) similarity. To understand the research methods used to investigate this issue, it is important first to review some basic facts about genetic relationships. Table 4–1 presents a series of genetic relationships among individuals (e.g., parent-child or identical twin to identical twin). As you can see, identical twins share all of their genetic materials in common. The proportion of genetic materials shared between other sibling pairs (nonidentical twins and other brother-sister combinations) is .50—siblings have one-half of their genetic makeup in common with each other. Likewise, the proportion of genetic materials shared between parents and their children is .50—each child receives only one-half of a parent's genetic material. Finally, total strangers share no genetic materials in common beyond their basic humanity.

These facts led scholars interested in the **nature-nurture** issue to formulate an interesting hypothesis: if heredity were the only influence on the development of intelligence, the correlation of intelligence test scores among individuals should be highly similar to the proportion of genetic materials they share in common. That is, since the proportion of genetic materials shared between identical twins is 1.00, the correlation of intelligence test scores between identical twins also should be

TABLE 4–1	GENETIC RELATIONSHIPS AND EXPECTED INTELLECTUAL RELATIONSHIPS		
Relationship	*Proportion of Genetic Material Shared*	*Expected Correlation of Intelligence*	*Observed Correlation of Intelligence*
Identical twins reared together	1.00	1.00	.90
Nontwin siblings reared together	.50	.50	.50
Parent-child living together	.50	.50	.50
Unrelated strangers	.00	.00	.02

The numbers given in this table are correlations. Correlations describe the extent to which scores are related. A correlation close to 1.00 indicates a high degree of relationship, while a correlation of .00 indicates no relationship at all.

Identical twins usually are similar in intelligence regardless of where they are raised.

about 1.00. Likewise, since the proportion of genes shared between nontwin siblings is .50, the correlation of intelligence measures between nontwin siblings should also be about .50. In addition, the correlation of intelligence test scores between parents and their children should be about .50, while the correlation of intelligence test scores among unrelated individuals should be close to 0.00 (see Table 4–1).

Things are not as simple, however, as the hypothesis we outlined above might make them seem. First, even the very best measures of intellectual ability are not perfect (Sternberg, 1988). For many reasons, the same person taking the same intelligence test on two or more occasions seldom will obtain identical scores. Typically, when the same person takes the same test several times (or takes different versions of it), the correlation among the test scores is about .90—a very high correlation but certainly not a perfect one.

Second, genetically related individuals usually live in similar environments. For example, the vast majority of identical twins grow up in the same home, as do most nontwin siblings. Hence, comparing the intelligence test scores of, for example, identical twins reared in the same environment doesn't really help us to determine the relative effects of heredity and environment because we don't know whether their scores are (1) due to genetic similarities or (2) because they were raised in the same home.

One way to examine the nature-nurture issue is to compare the correlation of intelligence test scores between identical twins reared in the same environment with those between nontwin siblings reared in the same environment. It turns out that the correlation of intelligence test scores between identical twins reared together is about .90 (just about the same as if one person were tested twice), while the correlation of intelligence test scores between nontwin siblings is about .50 (P. E. Vernon, in press). Hence, heredity seems to play a relatively important role in determining intelligence.

A better approach to the nature-nurture question in intelligence, however, is to determine the correlation of intelligence test scores among family members reared in separate environments. Such a method should eliminate the environment as a factor in the development of intelligence. Any relation that remains should be due to heredity.

The results of such "family members reared apart" studies (e.g., Bergeman, Plomin, DeFries, & Fulker, 1988) generally have provided consistent results pointing to the importance of heredity. For example, Joseph Horn (1983, 1985) has reported on a wide-ranging study of the nature-nurture question in which he employed data from the Texas Adoption Project, one of several national projects in which the development of adopted children is being carefully monitored. As a part of this project, Horn obtained intelligence test scores from parents and children in three hundred adoptive families and also from the biological mothers of the children. Horn then compared the relationship of the adoptive parent-child intelligence with the biological mother-child intelligence. The results indicated a very powerful role of heredity in determining children's intelligence. Similar results have been reported throughout the United States and Europe (see Bergeman et al., 1988; Scarr, 1988; Tambs, Sundet, & Mangus, 1988).

It is critical, however, that we not make the mistake of presuming that heredity is all-important in determining children's intellectual abilities. Even though recent studies of the nature-nurture issue have eliminated many methodological problems that plagued early research (see Scarr, 1988, for comments on those problems), environmental influences also are powerful. For example, in a recent study, Duyme (1988) examined the relationship of academic failure and children's adoptive parents' social class. Each of the eighty seven children in Duyme's study (conducted in France) was given up for adoption at birth and entered the adoptive parents' home before age three. Then, late in adolescence, Duyme examined the children's success in school.

The most important finding in Duyme's study was the significantly *negative* relationship between failure in school and adoptive parents' social class (− .37). That is, as adoptive parents' social standing increased (from poor up through middle class to upper-middle class), the likelihood of school failure decreased.

Although there still are disagreements about the relative contribution of heredity and environment (see Sternberg, 1988), the conclusion we can reach from research focusing on this issue is that neither heredity nor environment completely "controls" intellectual abilities (see Table 4–2). Although the exact contribution of the two factors is unclear, it is well established that a complex interaction of nature and nurture is responsible for intellectual differences.

Does the nature-nurture issue make any difference to teaching? On the one hand, even the strictest proponent of the genetic viewpoint concedes that 20 to 25 percent of intelligence is environmentally determined (Jensen, Lawson, & Paul, 1988). On the other hand, environmentalists allow that heredity determines at least one-fourth of the variation in intelligence (Bardis, 1985). It would seem that the utility of the argument really boils down to how well teachers can nurture students' intellectual development. As teachers, we are responsible for helping all of our students grow to the fullest extent possible, regardless of their intelligence test scores.

TABLE 4–2   THE CORRELATION OF INTELLIGENCE FOR PERSONS OF VARYING GENETIC AND ENVIRONMENTAL SIMILARITIES

Relationship	*Correlation*
Identical twins reared together	.90
Identical twins reared separately	.74
Heterozygotic twins of same sex reared together	.60
Heterozygotic twins of different sex reared together	.55
Nontwin siblings reared together	.50
Nontwin siblings reared separately	.25
Foster parents and foster children	.20
Unrelated children reared in the same home	.20
Unrelated strangers	.02

Note that both genetic and environmental factors vary. These factors range from identical genetic makeup and highly similar environments (in the case of identical twins reared together) to no genetic similarity and no environmental similarity (in the case of unrelated strangers).

**PRACTICE EXERCISE 4–1   INTELLIGENCE AND COGNITIVE PROCESSES —
WHAT DO PRACTICING TEACHERS THINK?**

Most teachers have developed their ideas about teaching well beyond those they had in teacher training. One area where views often change is that of intelligence and its measurement. In this exercise, we want you to take advantage of teachers' experiences by interviewing one or more experienced teachers on the topic of intelligence and cognitive development. The following questions should lead you to some interesting responses about intelligence. You should also add questions of your own. If you can, get permission to tape record your interview so that you will have it available to analyze in more detail.

Questions for the interview

1. What is your definition of intelligence?

2. Do differences in intelligence affect what you do in your classroom?

3. As a teacher, what do you think of IQ test scores as a measure of intelligence?

4. Have you ever made use of IQ test scores in your work with students?

5. Cognitive style refers to the way in which students usually approach problems — for example, impulsively or with reflection. Do you notice differences in cognitive style in your students and, if so, how does this affect your teaching?

6. What cognitive processes (examples might be memory, visualizing, or problem solving) do you most hope to change in the students you teach?

7. Is there a special researcher or theorist whose views on memory, thinking, or cognitive development have had a great effect on you?

PRACTICE EXERCISE 4–1   CONTINUED

Your own questions:

8. _____

_____

_____

9. _____

_____

_____

10. _____

_____

_____

After you have finished your interview, judge your results (and, if possible, compare them to your classmates') on the following criteria:

1. Would you say that the teacher you interviewed is negative, neutral, or positive about the use of intelligence test scores as indicators of general mental ability?

2. Do his or her views seem valid, in your opinion? If so, why? If not, why not?

3. Do his or her views seem consistent with those of most other teachers?

4. If this person's views were your own, would they make you a better (a more humane, effective) teacher or would they make you worse (less humane, ineffective)?

A Developmental View of Intelligence: Jean Piaget

So far in this chapter we have presented an overview of the psychometric approach and have seen how the research from an information-processing perspective gives us insight into individual differences. Both the psychometric and the information-processing viewpoints, however, have some limits in scope, especially in describing how intelligence *develops* in human beings and what factors influence that development. This section of this chapter is devoted to the most comprehensive contemporary theory of intelligence, that of Jean Piaget.

Piaget (1896–1980) was a true giant in psychology, greatly affecting its development (see Flavell, 1980). In fact, much of current cognitive psychology has been influenced by the pioneering work of Piaget (DiVesta, 1987). A discussion of Piaget's theory will allow us to present a fuller, more descriptive picture of human cognition.

Piaget began his work in biology, publishing his first paper in his midteens. He earned his doctorate in biology at the age of twenty-two but soon became interested in psychology. His first efforts in psychology were in the study of psychoanalysis, where he developed his observational method of research (Inhelder et al., 1988), but his major interest in intelligence sprang from the two years he spent standardizing tests of intelligence in Theodore Simon's laboratory.

> This initiation had two effects. First, he was able to go beyond the categorization of children's answers as "right" or "wrong." Further questioning enabled him to establish how and why a reply took the form that it did. This is the line of investigation that was to be Piaget's principal preoccupation throughout his career. Second, and as a corollary to this, Piaget became disenchanted with psychometrics—and has remained so [to his death] . . . believing that other methods . . . permit the investigator to go beyond statistical recording of surface data to the analysis of process itself. *(Lunzer, 1976, p. xii)*

Piaget's ideas about intelligence were to have a profound impact on the field of education.

Why is Piaget's theory of importance to the educator and so widely applied to thinking about education? First, it is a theory that describes how thinking develops in human beings from birth to adulthood. As teachers, you will be working with students at different stages and levels, and changes occur rapidly. Second, Piaget's theory has touched on almost all aspects of human intellectual functioning, including imitation, perception, language, logic, memory, judgment, reasoning,

Jean Piaget: Much of what cognitive psychology is today has been influenced by his theories about the development of intellectual processes.

and play. Piaget's theory, articulated in more than two hundred articles and dozens of books, is truly a comprehensive theory of the mental activity we call thinking and encompasses all aspects of human thought. Third, Piaget (and to an even greater extent his coauthor, Barbel Inhelder; see Inhelder et al., 1988) was concerned with education during his career. Several of his books and articles and hundreds of publications by other authors have related Piaget's theory to the practice of teaching.

Obviously, the lifework of Jean Piaget cannot be distilled into a few pages. What we will do is set out the basic principles of his theory, relate them to other views of human cognition, and stress some educational applications.

Intelligence as Biological Adaptation

Piaget viewed the development of intelligence as one way in which people adapt to the world. Humans are biological organisms who must develop means of fitting into their environment in order to survive. Intelligence is "a particular instance of biological adaptation" (Piaget, 1952, pp. 3–4), an achievement that allows people to interact effectively with the environment (Inhelder et al., 1988).* Intelligence has its own tendencies toward development, organized by biological mechanisms within the individual.

This perspective is important. Piaget conceived of cognitive growth as proceeding by stages from the innate reflexes of a baby to an adult's capability for abstract, logical reasoning. According to Piaget's view, the mechanisms and states of cognitive development are universal, but each individual's cognitive development is unique. Each person's environment puts specific demands on that person. Thus, cognitive growth is governed both by universal processes of intellectual development and by the specific kinds of experiences people have. As we proceed with our discussion of Piaget's theory, this basic principle must be kept in mind.

Cognitive Organization and Adaptation

According to Piaget, cognitive growth occurs as the intelligence of the individual adapts to the demands of the environment. But how does cognitive adaptation operate? Piaget does not provide a simple answer to this question. In his view, adaptation is linked to the way in which people organize the environment they encounter.

> From the biological point of view organization is inseparable from adaptation. They are two complementary processes of a single mechanism, the first being the internal aspect of the cycle of which adaptation constitutes the external aspect. *(Piaget, 1952, p. 7)*

To comprehend cognitive organization and adaptation, it is important to understand five concepts basic to Piaget's theory: schemes, schemata, assimilation, accommodation, and equilibrium. These are the concepts Piaget used to explain how and why cognitive development occurs (Inhelder et al., 1988; Piaget, 1977; Piaget & Inhelder, 1973).

---

*Piaget did not use the term *intelligence* to refer only to the abilities usually measured by standardized tests of intelligence. Rather, he talked about intelligence as the totality of the mechanisms of thinking and adaptation available to humans. Intelligence is present in all human actions and perceptions.

Schemes and Schemata.   Piaget suggested that humans have two forms of knowledge about the world—operative and figurative. Operative knowledge is knowledge of how to perform actions such as tying shoes, writing a letter, or grading a paper. Figurative knowledge is knowledge of facts—that birds have wings, that mammals have a four-chambered heart, the name of the president of the United States, and so on. These two types of knowledge are represented in two kinds of structures—*schemes* and *schemata*.

For Piaget, **schemes** are the inferred cognitive structures by which people represent their knowledge for operations. That is, a scheme is a cognitive structure for performing an activity. A baby, for example, has a scheme for responding to a favorite toy that may relate to grasping it and putting it into his or her mouth. **Schemata** (singular, *schema*) are the cognitive structures (similar to the way schemata were defined in Chapter Three) by which children and adults intellectually organize figurative knowledge. For instance, a child may have a schema for "bird" that is very broad (undifferentiated). As the child acquires new information, the schema will change, so that he or she can differentiate bats from birds. Further, some anomalous kinds of birds, like penguins, might not be properly classed until the information in a child's schema for bird has increased to the point that the child can recognize the similarities between penguins and other birds.

In infancy, many of the child's cognitive structures are reflexive—schemes inferred from regularities in behavior, such as sucking and grasping objects. Such cognitive structures are very closely linked to the infant's actions. Adults, in contrast, have evolved a vast array of quite complex and abstracted cognitive structures, including both schemes and schemata, that permit them to distinguish a multitude of different events, concepts, and objects.

Schemes and schemata become progressively more complex with development but are derived from the early, simple cognitive structures of infancy and childhood. The processes by which schemes and schemata are modified are assimilation and accommodation (Inhelder et al., 1988).

Assimilation and Accommodation.   Assimilation and accommodation are the two complementary processes by which experiences are integrated into cognitive structures. A person experiences an event in terms of existing schemes and schemata. **Assimilation** is the process of relating new information to existing cognitive structures. **Accom-**

modation is the process of *modifying* existing cognitive structures to the particular aspect of the environment one is assimilating.

Piaget (1963) used the following example to help explain the concepts of assimilation and accommodation:

> Laurent (age 10 months) is lying on his back but nevertheless resumes his experiments of the day before. He grasps in succession a celluloid swan, a box, etc., stretches out his arms and lets them fall. Sometimes he stretches out his arm vertically, sometimes he holds it obliquely, in front of or behind his eyes, etc. When the object falls in a new position (for example, on his pillow), he lets it fall two or three times more on the same place, as though to study the spatial relation; then he modifies the situation. *(Piaget, 1963, p. 269)*

In Piaget's view, baby Laurent was understanding his environment (the celluloid swan, the box, and the other toys) by acting on it (grasping and dropping the items). Piaget argued that the actions Laurent could carry out were schemes and that the process of using these schemes to make sense of the world was assimilation. Laurent, for instance, assimilated the toy swan to his grasping scheme. However, grasping (or any scheme, for that matter) won't work in exactly the same way for different objects. Grasping is different for a toy swan, a box, or a plush bunny. Consequently, Laurent had to accommodate his grasping scheme to the unique characteristics of each item he picked up. Changes in cognitive structures (schemes and schemata) are necessary for children to adjust to the impact of experiences that cannot be assimilated into existing cognitive structures. As the situation demands, the child must construct new cognitive structures into which information can be assimilated.

While it is possible to think about the two processes as separate functions, they always occur together. Consider the case of a child who sees a cow for the first time but already has a schema for horses (figurative knowledge). "What's that?" asks a parent. "A horsie," answers the child. The child has taken new information (seeing the cow) and assimilated it into the schema for horse. To allow this assimilation to occur, however, the horse schema was slightly modified (accommodated) so that the new information would fit. With further experience, however, the child's cognitive structures will be adapted (accommodated) so that a new schema is formed into which the child's perceptions can be assimilated. When the child sees a cow and recognizes it as such, he or she has formed a new cognitive structure for cow that is different from the one for horse.

Equilibrium.   Piaget refers to *equilibrium* as a balance between assimilation and accommodation. Obviously children cannot always assimilate or they would end up with a few very, very large cognitive structures and be unable to detect differences in the things they perceive. Likewise, children cannot solely accommodate because this would result in a huge number of schemes and schemata, each representing only a little of their experience, and they would not be able to detect similarities. There must be a balance between assimilation and accommodation.

Piaget contends that the child strives for equilibrium. The overriding principle is that mental growth progresses toward more complex and stable mental structures. When structures cannot easily assimilate new experiences, there is an imbalance between assimilation and accommodation. A sense of *disequilibrium* motivates the person to seek equilibrium. (See Chapter Nine for different views of motivation.) Equilibrium is achieved as stimuli are assimilated into modified or new cognitive structures.

Children constantly strive for equilibrium as they seek an organization that will be internally consistent for them. This organization, however, need not be and often is not the same as an adult's organization. There is no such thing as an incorrect organization from Piaget's perspective, only less complex and consistent organizations.

Factors Influencing the Development of Cognition

Piaget (1976, 1977, 1978) suggested that four general factors influence the development of human thought: (1) biological maturation, (2) experience with the physical environment, (3) experience with the social environment, and (4) equilibration. Biological maturation refers to the growth and change of biological structures in individuals. As children mature, their physical structures become more complete, and they are able to experience their environment in more sophisticated ways. Hence the quality of their thought changes. Piaget (1978), however, is very explicit in pointing out that intelligence is not genetically programmed and that biological maturation works in combination with other factors.

> We cannot assume there exists a hereditary program indulging the development of human intelligence, there are no innate ideas. . . . The effects of maturation consist essentially of organizing new possibilities for development; that is, giving access to structures which could not be evolved before these possibilities are offered. But between possibility and actualization, there must intervene a set of other factors such as . . . experience and social interaction. *(Piaget, 1970, pp. 719–720)*

In other words, while Piaget acknowledges the importance of biological maturation, the actual fulfillment of intellectual capabilities is created by children's interactions with their environment.

One form of children's interaction with the environment is their experience with the physical world. Piaget categorized such experience into two major forms: physical and logical-mathematical. *Physical experience* "consists of acting upon objects and drawing some knowledge about the objects by abstraction from the objects" (Piaget, 1978, p. 231). A child may discover, for example, that wooden objects float by placing objects made from various materials in a bathtub. The child's interaction with the environment results in the acquisition of knowledge about some of the physical properties of objects—"wooden things float." While a considerable amount of cognitive development is guided by physical experience, logical-mathematical experience also is important.

Logical-mathematical experience occurs when "knowledge is not drawn from the objects, but it is drawn by the action's effects upon the objects" (Piaget, 1978, p. 231). Piaget provided a classic example of logical-mathematical experience in a story he often related about the childhood experiences of one of his friends. The child (about four or five years of age at the time) was playing with some pebbles in his garden. He placed them in a row and counted them up to ten. He then re-counted them from the opposite direction and still found ten. The boy found this fact fascinating. He then put the stones in a circle and counted them—still ten. Ultimately, the boy put the pebbles into several configurations, always counting them and always finding ten. The boy discovered that ten items are ten items no matter how they are arranged. He did not discover anything about the properties of pebbles themselves as would be the case in physical experience but rather discovered knowledge about an action he took (counting). The boy could have made the same discovery (configuration does not affect number) with marbles, twigs, beans, or frogs (providing they did not hop away!). The properties of the objects were not relevant to the boy's discovery.

Physical experience is an important factor influencing cognitive development. Obviously the kinds of experiences children have with their physical environment will affect the development of their thought processes to a considerable extent. Piaget, however, suggested that children's experiences with the social environment are just as important. The social environment (other people) provides opportunities for children to learn a great many things. Piaget's major focus in this area was on children's learning of language. Language, of course, plays a crucial role in permitting children to represent actions in their thoughts. However, language does not produce the development of intelligence but rather serves to facilitate its growth.

The fourth fundamental factor in cognitive development is the process of equilibration (Piaget, 1978). Piaget believes that children actively participate in their cognitive development through **equilibration** (Piaget & Inhelder, 1969), which is the child's system for regulating and integrating the changes brought about by maturation, physical experience, and social experience. Through assimilation and accommodation, equilibration moves the person from a state of disequilibrium to a state of equilibrium.

Operations and Stages of Cognitive Development

Cognitive changes are the results of developmental processes. Piaget felt that cognitive development is a coherent sequence of successive, qualitative changes in cognitive structures. The cognitive development process is logical and orderly, with each change based on prior structures and processes. Piaget (1973) categorized cognitive development into four general stages as follows:

> The **sensorimotor stage** (birth to approximately two years). During this stage children's actions become more and more intentional and integrated into patterns. Cognitive development can be observed as children display awareness of themselves and their surroundings and respond consistently to similar stimuli.

> The **preoperational thought** stage (approximately two to seven years). During this stage children rapidly develop language and conceptual thought.

> The **concrete operations** stage (approximately seven to eleven years). Children develop the ability to apply logical thought to concrete problems during this stage. Their thinking, however, is still quite closely linked to their immediate experience.

> The **formal operations** stage (from approximately age eleven on). Cognitive development may reach its highest level during this stage. By the age of fifteen or sixteen (approximately), many children are able to apply logic to a variety of problems, although some people never fully develop formal operational thinking.

Each of Piaget's stages is frequently given with the ages of children who possess cognitive structures characteristic of that stage. Piaget did not mean these chronological dates to be rigid. Rather, they are general approximations of where *most children* of certain ages are likely to be in their intellectual development. The stages are sequential, but children need not complete all of one stage before entering the next. A child in the preoperational stage may perform some functions characteristic of both the sensorimotor and concrete operations stages, for instance. Piaget does assert, however, that all children must pass through the same stages in the same order, although not necessarily at the same rate.

An extremely important concept for understanding Piaget's stages of development is the idea of operations (Piaget & Inhelder, 1969; Inhelder et al., 1988). An **operation** is a scheme whose major characteristic is that it can be reversed. If we took the square root of 49 to obtain 7, we know as adults that we can reverse this operation and square 7 to get back to 49. Understanding that two rows of five beads contain the same number of beads even if we lengthen or compress one of them also is an operation, as is understanding that the volume of water in a container doesn't change when we pour it into a container of another shape. Adults understand clearly that each transformation is reversible to its former state; most young children, however, do not.

While many rules and specific facts are not operations (knowing that school buses are yellow, that dogs bark, or that snow is white), operations rather than the specific facts of learning are central to intelligence as Piaget saw it. Thus you can best understand Piaget's stages of development by examining the operations that children can

During formal operations, the individual can construct hypotheses and test them logically. Here, in her ninth-grade shop class, a student must predict what will happen to types of wood when they are used for different functions and explain why.

master during each one. Few if any operations are present during the initial two stages, sensorimotor and preoperational, but operations gradually develop during what is called the concrete operational stage.

The Sensorimotor Stage.   The sensorimotor stage, like the following stages of development, is divided into substages. The first substage, immediately following birth, is dominated by reflexes such as sucking and by random body movements. During the second substage (from two weeks to four months of age), infants assimilate their cognitive structures to familiar experiences and accommodate and develop new cognitive structures for strange new objects (a bottle instead of the breast, grasping a toy). The third substage (four to eight months of age) is characterized by infants' developing sense of cause and effect, a sense that will continue to be refined. Infants learn cause and effect from their interactions with their environment—the last time the baby slapped the bottle, he got milk and so now he begins to develop a scheme for slapping the bottle. Or the last time the baby was on her back she kicked with her right knee and elbow and rolled over. The next time she is placed on the floor on her back she uses the same set of movements to roll over.

In addition to a rudimentary understanding of causation, children in the third substage of the sensorimotor period rapidly develop the ability to coordinate their vision with their touch. They can now grasp what they see and actively manipulate objects. This coordination of actions leads to experiences that in turn allow for greater cognitive development and their cognitive structures become more complex. A further general characteristic of the first three substages is that infants appear to have no conception of time—only the here and now matter.

By the fourth substage (eight to twelve months), however, infants usually develop some concept of the future. The baby crying to be picked up hushes when she hears her father walking down the hall toward her room. She understands that comfort is only a few seconds away.

By the age of twelve months, object permanence usually is understood. Objects removed from the direct vision of infants seem to no longer exist for them. Around twelve months, however, children show an understanding that just because an object is out of their immediate sight it need not be gone. Their actions demonstrate that they can think about objects without having to see them. One-year-old children can be observed playing "peekaboo" with objects, covering and uncovering them. They will also remember that your piece of candy still exists even if you hide it.

By the beginning of the fifth substage (twelve to eighteen months), children begin to experiment with their world. They throw, bite, spit out, rearrange, and break objects just to see what will happen. At dinner a child may drop a spoon on the floor over and over as he or she experiments with the effects of dropping the spoon. Experimentation soon leads to problem solving. Where a baby might once have stood by the crib and cried until a parent came to get his blanket for him, he now grabs a corner of it and pulls it through the bars. Later he pulls a stool to the edge of the crib and reaches over the side for objects. Children in the fifth substage also increase their imitation of other people. Stick your tongue out at a baby of this age, and she may stick hers back out at you!

During the sixth substage (eighteen to twenty-four months), children can better represent objects cognitively. They are beginning to abstract and to "think," and this allows them to develop new ways of solving problems. A child who remembers that the jar lids are in the box at the back of the bottom drawer in the kitchen can carry out a sequence of actions based on that knowledge. If she can think about playing with the lids, she may walk to the kitchen, open the drawer, get out the box, and play.

The ability to visualize objects and people and to predict simple outcomes of actions readies children for the next stage of development. No longer will cognition focus primarily on physical activities: in the preoperational stage the emphasis shifts to *symbolic* learning.

The Preoperational Stage.   The preoperational stage was so named by Piaget because children do not possess operations at its outset. The story of the preoperational stage is one of acquiring cognitive operations. There are, however, many other activities of preoperational children. Language acquisition is one of the most important. Two-year-olds have a vocabulary of about two hundred words, but by the time children start school at age five their vocabularies will likely consist of thousands of words. Words are important in ways beyond the obvious need to communicate. Words are symbols and as such children use them to structure their worlds. Initially, children assign definitions to words that suit themselves. Their meanings may be very different from those an adult would give the words.

One interesting characteristic of preoperational children is egocentrism. **Egocentrism** means, quite literally, believing that you are at the center of the universe. One of the authors asked his three-year-old daughter why the sun was shining. She answered, "Because it wants to." "Oh," said the author, "why does it want to?" "Because I like to play outside," she answered.

Because they organize their worlds around their own points of view, preoperational children are quite likely to be unable to see things "objectively" (Inhelder et al., 1988). Adult reasoning will often not be effective, and an adult may despair at how self-centered a preoperational child can be. Asking a preoperational child to go downstairs and play because you must wash the dishes can be very frustrating when the child cannot see why you should bother with the dishes.

Preoperational children also cannot perform the operation of conservation. **Conservation** means understanding that such features as number, mass, and area are not changed by superficial transformation of an object or set of objects. There are different forms of conservation, including conservation of number, area, length, and volume. Preoperational children, for example, do not conserve number. If a five-year-old is shown two rows of ten pennies, one longer than the other, and is told that she may have the row she wants, she likely will choose the longer one. If you ask why, you're likely to receive an answer like "Because it's the biggest." Although this answer is illogical to us as adults, it is perfectly logical within the child's own cognitive structures.

During a Saturday lunch at the home of one of the authors, both his two-year-old and four-year-old were given little pieces of cake for dessert. Both pieces were the same size, but the author inadvertently broke the two-year-old's into pieces as it was removed from the cake pan. As both girls started to eat, the four-year-old remarked, "I'm almost full. I'm glad I didn't get as much as my sister." She had not yet acquired the operation of conservation of volume.

The major feature of operations is reversibility, and preoperational children cannot conserve because they cannot reverse processes in their minds. A broken piece of cake cannot be reconstructed mentally into a whole piece. Likewise, the conservation of number, area, and length all require reversibility, the recognition that things can be transformed back to the way they were before.

One characteristic of preoperational children is the endless number of questions they ask. "Why did the puppy run across our yard?" "Why is that a tree?" "Why are airplanes loud?" Such questions require answers that are reasonable for the children within their own frame of reference. If you answer the question "Why are clouds white?" with a monologue about the reflection and absorption of different wavelengths of light, your answer likely will be lost on a preoperational child. A response stressing things that the child knows may help:

"What white things do you know about?" (The child names some.) "What is the same about them?" (The child makes some guesses.) "See, clouds are kind of like a clean, fluffy ball of cotton. They look white because of how the light shines on them and because they don't have much dust or rain in them."

Preoperational children begin to develop a more accurate sense of time. They can store information for future use. Their sense of time may still be somewhat different from that of an adult, however. In telling a story, a child of one of the authors began, "Once upon a time, far, far away—in Kansas City—and long, long ago—last Tuesday . . ." She understood the past but her ideas of "long ago" were rather different from her father's.

The Concrete Operations Stage.   Piaget so named the stage of concrete operations because children during this stage can deal with concrete problems in logical ways. "Concrete" refers to the actual presence of objects and events. Concrete-operational children can master conservation problems and understand reversibility if materials

And, of course, some of us never leave concrete operations.

" . . . and *this* is for those drug-resistant microbes."

are physically present. A child at this stage can cognitively restructure a broken-up piece of cake into the size and shape it once was.

In this stage children can group objects on the basis of color, size, shape, or other similarities, and they can consider more than one attribute of objects simultaneously. Given cubes and balls of two colors, concrete-operational children can group by all round and blue things, all square and brown things, and so on. They also can answer questions like "Are there more balls or brown objects?" Piaget referred to such reasoning abilities as **decentration**; children no longer center on only a single attribute of objects as they did in the preoperational stage.

Visual problems are solved more readily than verbal problems during the stage of concrete operations. Word problems—"There are four boys in the room. Ed is taller than Bill. Joe is shorter than Sam. Bill is taller than Sam. Who is the shortest?"—will likely only confuse concrete-operational children. However, if you were to draw pictures of Ed, Bill, Sam, and Joe on the blackboard and ask, "Who is the shortest?" children at this stage would answer your question easily.

Abstract thought is not highly developed in concrete-operational children. This means that such children can accept reality more readily than hypothetical conditions. If you were chatting with a group of concrete-operational children and said something like "Suppose the sky were green," you would likely hear a chorus of "No, it isn't! The sky

In the concrete operations stage, learning is closely linked to children's concrete experiences with the world.

PRACTICE EXERCISE 4–2   CONSERVATION

One of the most fascinating things about Piaget's theory is that conservation or the lack of it is so easily observed in preoperational children. To help you get a better feel for conservation, we urge you to locate a three- to five-year-old child and try some things. The child can be your own, a sibling, a nephew or niece, or the child of a friend—it makes no difference. After you've chatted for a while and the child is comfortable in your presence, ask if he or she would like to play a brief game. If so, try some of the following conservation problems.

Conservation of Number

Make two equal rows of similar objects (marbles, chips, blocks) on a table. Be careful to make the spaces between the objects the same. Each object should have a corresponding object across from it. Ask the child, "Which row has more or do they have the same?" Most preoperational children will answer that both rows have the same amount. Now, with the child watching, increase the spaces between the objects in one of the rows. Again ask the child, "Which row has more or do they both have the same?" Children who cannot conserve number will answer that the longer row has the most. Their judgment is affected by the change in distance between the objects. You may then want to have the child count the objects and try rearranging them in several ways. The child who cannot conserve will continue to err in his or her judgment.

First Trial			Second Trial	
				0
0	0		0	0
0	0		0	
0	0		0	0
0	0		0	
0	0		0	0
				0

Conservation of Area

Make up two green cardboard sheets to use as "fields of grass." You will also need two small models or cutouts of cows and a number of barns (such as the hotels in a Monopoly game). Ask the child to

PRACTICE EXERCISE 4–2   ***CONTINUED***

pretend that the two identical cardboard sheets are fields of grass. Then place a cow in the middle of each field. Substantiate with the child the equality of the fields of grass ("Do both cows have the same amount of grass to eat or does one cow have more?"). Now place a barn in the *middle* of one field and ask, "Does this cow have the same, more, or less grass to eat than that other cow?" After the child responds (most will say the cow now has less), place a second barn in one of the corners of the other field. Ask the same question again. From this point, place two barns at a time; in one field place the barns in a scattered, random way, and in the other place the barns along the edge starting in the child's left-hand corner. Each time you place a pair of barns, reask the question about the amount of grass available. Most young children will make errors in their judgments. To them the scattered barns mean less grass to eat, while the barns all in a row leave more for the cow.

First Trial   **Second Trial**

        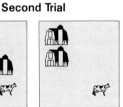

Conservation of Volume

Conservation of volume can be tested with water and three containers, two identical and one different. Fill the two identical containers with the same amount of water. Ask the child to substantiate the equality of the water. (You may need to add a bit of water to one or the other container to satisfy the child that the amounts are "exactly the same.") Then pour the water from one of the containers into another container of a different shape. Now ask, "Do these containers have the same amount of water to drink, or does one have more water to drink?" Point to the appropriate glasses as you ask the question. Children who cannot conserve volume will inform you that the amounts of water in the two containers are not

---

equal when water from one of the containers has been poured into another of a different shape. Their explanation of why this is so may surprise you.

First Trial   **Second Trial**

---

is blue." Or if you asked them, "What would happen if we found out that cars could run on water?" you'd likely get back, "But water won't work." Both these hypothetical situations require manipulation of abstract ideas. Concrete-operational children are unlikely to be able to think that way. A given set of assumptions cannot be used by concrete-operational children unless they correspond exactly to how they have learned to perceive the world.

This close adherence to concrete experience leads to an interesting change from the preoperational stage. Rather than imagining all kinds of fantastic events, concrete-operational children are addicted to literal facts. "No, Papa, you can't load the dishwasher like that. That isn't how Momma does it." "No, Momma, that's not how to play dolly. You *have* to do it this way." Concrete-operational students see teachers as unfair if they test more than literal meaning or rote recall. The middle elementary school years are a time of learning the facts, the dates, and the classifications of things. This sticking to the facts will soon be left behind as children enter formal operations.

The Formal Operations Stage.   Piaget named this stage formal operations because children now can perform operations that require formal logic (Piaget, 1969, 1970). Many of the characteristics of adult thought develop in this period. Abstract thought is present, allowing children to begin to handle questions they stumbled over when they were concrete operational. If you toss out the thought "Suppose the sky were green" to formal-operational youngsters, they may think you are silly but they could deal with the notion. "I'd guess that everything would have a different color. I wonder if the sunsets would be blue or red or what?"

In the formal operations stage, the individual can construct hypotheses and test them logically. Formal-operational students are beginning to think like adults in evaluating their own reasoning. The thinking of other persons likewise is critically evaluated by formal-operational children. There is some egocentricity, but it is different from that of earlier years. Rather than believing that they are at the center of all things, they believe that they are in the spotlight and that others are watching and evaluating their actions. This feeling of being in the spotlight accounts for some of the acting-out behavior of adolescents.

Evaluating one's own thinking leads to introspection and to the assumption of adult roles. Formal-operational students often become concerned about society, their roles in it, and what might make it better. Much of the disaffection adolescents have for society and its ground rules is a result of a newly developed ability to think critically about and evaluate the world.

As we noted earlier, not all persons ultimately develop the ability for abstract thought and formal operations. Environmental deficiencies may reduce the effects of physical experience and social interactions. Many children never have enough stimulation to take full advantage of their maturation. Even some college students and adults remain at the level of concrete operations in many areas of their thinking.

In summary, Piaget's concept of development can be captured by the following. Development proceeds through a continuous process of generalizations and differentiations, and the continuity of development is achieved by a continuing unfolding (Case, Hayward, Lewis, & Hurst, 1988). Each level of development finds its roots in a previous phase and continues into the following phase. Each phase entails a repetition of the previous level of cognitive development, but with different cognitive organization. Previous behavior patterns are sensed as inferior and become part of the new superior level. Piaget's view is that the natural tendency of human intelligence is to be "active and constructive" (Inhelder et al., 1988), and cognitive processes make an active contribution to any interaction that humans have with their environments. Each person creates a unique understanding of the world through his or her own construction and organization of experience.

Implications for Teaching

In general, psychometric approaches have not led to many direct applications for the classroom teacher. Instead, intelligence testing has been used most extensively as a part of decisions about placement in and selection of students for educational programs (see Chapter 14). There are, however, some elements of psychometric approach important for classroom teachers.

The measurement of intelligence has, without a doubt, led to a general understanding that there are individual differences in cognitive abilities among the students in any given classroom (Waters et al., 1988). This recognition has led a great many educators to emphasize individualized instruction in order to meet the needs of each student. We also stress the need to individualize instruction; but like many others (Dick & Carey, 1988; Gagné, 1987), our emphasis is on the analysis of what students currently know or can do and what is to be learned, rather than on measured intelligence (IQ).

A word of caution. The measurement of intelligence is a complex and controversial topic and contains many pitfalls for the unwary. We feel that, in general, intelligence-test scores should be interpreted with extreme care. IQ scores are simply scores on a test and should not be taken as measures of "potential," "capacity," or "innate ability." To do so is to risk stereotyping a student—as "gifted," "retarded," or a "slow learner." These IQ-related stereotypes are so strong that teachers (and professors) actually have been known to disregard evidence before their eyes (the achievement of a particular student, for instance) in favor of a single indicator of the student's abilities (the IQ score). It is better to pay less attention to what a score "predicts" and instead to observe what students do or do not do in your class.

As we indicated, the information-processing theory of intelligence is still in its infancy, especially as it relates to the cognitive processes of attention, perception, long-term memory, and problem solving in the working memory. Some theorists, however, have stressed a number of applications of an information-processing approach. Bruner (1982), for example, has pointed out that effective instruction should use all the available ways that children can represent their experiences. Younger students especially should be allowed to engage in grasping, touching, feeling, and other hands-on experiences. Later, students should still have these kinds of experiences, but instruction should begin to include pictorial and other imagery-based representations. As cognitive development continues, students should receive instruction emphasizing symbols (concepts, principles) as well as a continuation of the other, more basic forms of representation.

Like Piaget, Bruner views intellectual growth as developing from the child's interaction with the teacher, other students, and instructional materials. Student involvement is one key to meaningful learning. Another is that knowledge should be structured so that it can be grasped by students. This structuring requires that the teacher analyze the knowledge and organize it for presentation to students.

Bruner sees the processes of intellectual development as self-motivating. He deemphasizes the use of external or "extrinsic" forms of incentives for learning. To Bruner, "the will to learn is an intrinsic motive, one that finds both its source and its reward in its own exercise." External rewards, in his view, can get learning under way and maintain it, but the bases for long-term learning are natural and spontaneous—human curiosity, playfulness, a natural motivation toward competence, and the desire to imitate others.

There are many parts of Piaget's theory of intellectual development that should affect teaching decisions. Teachers must remember that cognitive development is not automatic. The processes of assimilation and accommodation depend on both physical experience and social interactions. The kinds of schemes and schemata that students develop depend on the kinds of experiences they have. As a teacher, you influence these experiences to a great extent. The richer, more diversified experiences you provide for students, the more elaborate their cognitive structures will be.

Applications for Teaching: Piaget's Theory

The preceding implications lead to some practical applications we have adapted from Piaget's writings.

1. Remember that students construct their knowledge. Piaget emphasized that students are not simply empty containers to be filled with information. Instead, he stressed that students make sense of their environment and actively construct their own knowledge. From this perspective, it would be an error to teach students division as if the students only needed to imitate the mechanical processes for getting the answer. Students learning division already have considerable knowledge of numbers and arithmetic. They assimilate the teacher's instruction to what they already know and

actively construct a conception of division. Teachers who know this can present material more effectively. They understand the kinds of mistakes students commonly make in assimilating the new ideas to their prior knowledge (e.g., concepts of multiplication or subtraction) and in trying to construct their own new understandings.

2. Focus on internal motivation. Piagetian-oriented educators usually do not put much stress on external rewards for good performance. From Piaget's perspective on equilibration, genuine intellectual development is its own reward. As students overcome earlier contradictions, they move from disequilibrium to equilibrium. Knowing more about mathematics, for instance, will help students to obtain sensible answers to math problems, which leads them to feel the real satisfaction of genuine understanding. Piagetian-oriented teachers, of course, do not believe that there is no place for external rewards; they simply do not believe that external rewards are the most important basis for students' learning. Effective teachers allow children to experience challenge and success.

3. Recognize the developmental basis for learning. Since children learn by assimilating new experiences to prior knowledge, that prior knowledge provides the basis for learning. Faulty or poorly-organized prior knowledge may make genuine understanding of new material impossible. Students with no conception of chemical structure, for example, may learn by rote to get correct answers to chemistry problems. Unfortunately, they are very unlikely to understand the point of what they are doing or to remember it for very long. When teachers present new information, they should ask themselves what prior knowledge the students need to understand it and take steps to find out if the students have that knowledge.

4. Aim for moderate levels of novelty. Students learn best if presented with new material slightly beyond their present understanding. If a teacher presents material that is already understood, there obviously is nothing to be learned. On the other hand, if a teacher presents information that is too novel, the student will be unable to assimilate it to their present schemata. Moderately novel material is different enough to present a satisfying challenge but familiar enough to be meaningfully assimilated. The student who understands simple division, for example, may be ready for long division but not for algebra.

5. Value the students' points of view. The student who does not understand may not simply lack knowledge but may have an entirely different way of looking at things. From Piaget's perspective, it is important to determine how the student *does* understand things, even if that understanding is not "correct." In fact, the more unusual a student's point of view, the more important it is for the teacher to be aware of it in order to help the student move toward better understanding.

6. Use individual conferences. Although individual sessions with students are time-consuming, they provide teachers with insights that other sources of information (e.g., standardized tests) cannot. For example, a student may be having difficulty with division because an incorrect procedure is being applied. By having the student solve a series of division problems, observing the steps the student takes and questioning the student about each step, a sensitive teacher may gain considerable insight into the student's understanding of the division process and may be able to correct the problem with relative ease.

An Information-Processing Approach to Cognitive Development

In recent years, several individuals have begun to formulate theories of cognitive development based on an information-processing perspective (e.g., Case, 1984; Siegler, 1987; Sternberg, 1988). Robert Siegler (1987), for instance, credits Piaget with important work on children's acquisition of knowledge and has proposed that information-processing analyses of Piagetian tasks are valuable for better understanding the component processes involved in thinking through problems. More specifically, Siegler has performed a detailed analysis of Piagetian tasks by determining the kinds of rules children follow in solving problems. He then has helped students acquire those rules that will allow for better task understanding.

Current Theories

Robert Sternberg (1988), whom we mentioned earlier in our discussion of information-processing approaches to intelligence, also has written extensively about cognitive development. Like Siegler, Sternberg has focused on an information-processing analysis of tasks, but his emphasis has been more on the kinds of items found in psychometric tests of intelligence. His theory of intelligence is extremely broad ranging and includes information-processing analyses of tasks similar to those employed by Piaget.

Among contemporary information-processing theorists, Robbie Case perhaps has come closest to a synthesis of Piagetian and information-processing theories. Case makes extensive use of information-processing concepts, but at the same time sees Piaget's theory as the basis for understanding cognitive development. Case, in fact, refers to himself as a "neo-Piagetian."

Case's theory of cognitive development (1984a, b; Case et al., 1988) focuses primarily on the working memory (see Chapter Two). In Case's view, working memory capacity has two aspects—operating space and short-term storage space. **Operating space** is used for actually processing information, while **storage space** is used for holding information in order to allow for processing.

For Case, changes in cognitive development do not result from an overall change in working memory capacity but from an increased efficiency in operating space. When we see that a twelve-year-old finds the task of writing a sentence easier than an eight-year-old, for instance, Case would suggest that it is because the twelve-year-old has a more efficient operating space. This leaves more storage space available for the task.

Case argues that very specific practice at a task (e.g., counting) is not the major reason for changes in the efficiency of operating space. Instead, Case employs Piagetian reasoning—changes in operating space are due to the interaction of biological maturation and experience. From Case's viewpoint, biological maturation refers to the growth and refinement of the neurological structures involved in cognitive processes. Generally, as children mature, their neurological structures become more and more efficient. In terms of experience, it is the integration of existing schemes into new schemes that help account for changes in operating-space efficiency. For example, an efficient scheme for, say, finding the main idea in a story will take up relatively less operating space than an inefficient scheme, thus leaving more storage space in working memory for holding critical information.

Case suggests that there are four general processes involved in the integration of schemes: (1) problem solving, (2) exploration, (3) observation and imitation, and (4) mutual regulation. In *problem solving*, old schemes are combined in new ways as integrated, higher-order schemes in order to achieve goals. For example, a student trying to look up vocabulary words in a dictionary might learn to find them more efficiently by "bracketing" the letters of the vocabulary words within the letters of the "guide" words at the top of each page. The newly discovered process is an integrated "alphabetize and search" scheme that combines many separate subprocesses into a more streamlined approach (consider, in contrast, the inefficient effort of a student who starts with identifying the first letter and then the second letter, the third letter, and so on). Such an integrated scheme, of course, would require far less operating capacity than a less efficient scheme, leaving more storage space available for the task.

Exploration, in Case's view, is similar to problem solving, but the integration of schemes is based on pure curiosity rather than on achievement of any specific goal. For example, the student who is curious about a hand-held calculator may play with it and discover the ability to perform several operations in a sequential order and, hence, form a rudimentary, integrated scheme for solving equations.

The third process described by Case is *observation and imitation*, in which students watch and mimic the behavior of others. A physics student may, for instance, watch her teacher solve a vector problem on the board and then imitate the teacher's actions with another problem. If the imitation is successful, it may help integrate already existing schemes into a new scheme for vector problems.

The final scheme integration process described by Case is *mutual regulation*, a continuing interchange between two people that involves more than simple imitation. Mutual regulation can be seen, for example, when a student is having difficulty reading a topographic map and asks the teacher for help. If this results in the student being able to read contour lines where before he or she could not, then a new, higher-order scheme has been integrated out of already existing schemes (e.g., map legends or altitude markers).

Status of Information-Processing Views

Although they seem promising, in some ways it is still too soon to attempt to evaluate the utility of information-processing theories of cognitive development. They have been consistent with the general information-processing model we presented in Chapter Two and compatible with the major theory of cognitive development, that of Jean Piaget. Even though Piagetian-oriented theorists are somewhat uncomfortable with the specific nature of some information-processing theories (see Siegler, 1987), it would seem that integrative approaches such as Case's can continue to lead to fruitful research and classroom applications.

Applications for Teaching: Information-Processing Views

The applications in this section have been adapted in part from Case's work (e.g., 1984a; Case et al., 1988).

1. Relate your methods and materials to desired cognitive processes. Carefully observe your students so that you can predict the kinds of strategies they are likely to use when they attempt to learn new concepts and solve problems. You also need to determine what kinds of conceptual and problem-solving strategies are most appropriate for new tasks so that you may help students acquire them.

2. Make sure activities give feedback to students on the quality of their thinking. Set up your instruction so that the limitations of students' current strategies and hypotheses will be readily apparent to them and so that they will see the need for applying other approaches to a situation.

3. Reduce the memory requirements to a minimum. Implicit here is the development of new or modified cognitive structures through the processes of accommodation and assimilation. As teachers, we want development to proceed, but always without introducing too much disequilibrium. Successful cognitive growth is most likely when the memory demands of new tasks are kept at a reasonable level.

4. Use student "errors" to gain insight into their thought processes. Any "mistakes" that students make in their reasoning are actually excellent indicators of the nature of their thought processes and the level of cognitive development they have reached. Carefully note them and use them to adjust your instruction. You may infer which operations students can perform and which ones have yet to develop. In Piaget's view, all external experiences are translated through internal mechanisms. As Furth (1989) said, "the educator provides, the child decides." The child's present intellectual mechanisms are the key to his or her further intellectual development.

5. Use a variety of visual aids to present new information. Different kinds of visual aids (graphics, charts, photographs, drawings, and many more) should be used to convey new information. Since almost all students think somewhat concretely about some topics, you can aid their understanding of new materials by reducing the amount of abstract information they must deal with.

6. Allow students the opportunity to manipulate objects directly. Just as visual aids provide a great help in learning new material, the chance to actually handle objects can greatly assist in the acquisition of many new concepts.

7. Expect large differences in students' cognitive development. Keep in mind that there will be great variation in the levels of cognitive development in any group of students. In a fifth-grade class, for instance, there will be some children who are primarily concrete operational, some who are well into formal operations, and some with the characteristics of both levels.

Make sure activities provide feedback to students on the quality of their thinking.

Summary

Intelligence involves all the human cognitive processes. As Binet said, "To judge well, to comprehend well, to reason well, these are the essential activities of intelligence." Although there is some agreement about the general nature of intelligence, psychologists have studied and used the concept in quite different ways over the years.

One method of studying intelligence has been through the use of tests. Psychometric (testing) approaches have concentrated on the measurement of intelligence. Individual intelligence tests such as the Wechsler and Stanford-Binet have been the major method of measuring intelligence, although group intelligence tests also have been commonly used.

More recently information-processing theory has been applied to the study of intelligence. Information-processing variables such as memory and reaction times have been shown to be related to scores on traditional intelligence tests and may account for much of the individual differences in measured intelligence.

Yet another way of thinking about intelligence is from a developmental perspective, which emphasizes changes in intellectual qualities with experience. The foremost cognitive-developmental theorist is Jean Piaget, whose views have greatly influenced psychologists and educators. His theory holds that intelligence is part of the biological adaptation of the human being to the world. Through the processes of assimilation and accommodation, learners acquire and modify their cognitive structures. These cognitive structures organize learners' experiences and make them meaningful.

Development of cognition, according to Piaget, occurs by stages. The sensorimotor stage reveals a shift from simple reflexive reactions in infants to the beginning of ideas of causation and future time. In the preoperational stage, language acquisition is prominent. Children are egocentric, believing themselves to be the center of the universe. They also typically do not conserve; they do not understand that superficial changes in form and shape do not alter qualities of volume, number, and mass of objects and materials.

In concrete operations, conservation is attained, but thinking is closely linked to the here and now. Abstract thinking develops more fully in the last stage, formal operations.

Recently, information-processing based theories of cognitive development have been formulated. Among several theories, that of Robbie Case has come closest to a synthesis of Piagetian and information-processing based views. Case has hypothesized that changes in cognitive abilities are due to increasing efficiency in the working memory's operating space, which leaves increased storage space in working memory. Changes in operating space efficiency are thought to result from the integration of schemes into higher-order schemes.

A major application from the study of intelligence has been a recognition of the need for teachers' planning to take individual differences into account. Cognitive-developmental theory provides us with an understanding of cognitive changes with age. The teacher needs to be aware of the cognitive level of the students and to make instruction consistent with their cognitive structures. Good teachers help their students organize and reorganize their experience in increasingly more complex and adequate ways. They recognize that students' own intellectual constructions are the keys to further cognitive development.

Suggested Readings   Broughton, J. M. (1987). *Critical theories of psychological development.* New York: Plenum.

>   *Broughton's selection of readings provides a rich and comprehensive view of theories of human development. This volume is especially recommended for students seeking to expand their breadth in the area.*

Forman, G., & Pufall, P. B. (Eds.). (1989). *Constructivism in the computer age.* Hillsdale, NJ: Erlbaum.

>   *The continuing influence of Piaget's work is seen in this excellent volume in which a Piagetian perspective is used to analyze recent developments in instructional technology.*

Inhelder, B., de Caprona, B., & Cornu-Wells, A. (Eds.). (1988). *Piaget today.* Hillsdale, NJ: Erlbaum.

>   *Barbel Inhelder, Piaget's best-known collaborator, and her associates have assembled an outstanding volume reflecting the richness of Piaget's continuing influence on developmental psychology.*

Sternberg, R. J. (Ed.). (1987). *Advances in the psychology of human intelligence.* Hillsdale, NJ: Erlbaum.

>   *Sternberg's edited volume presents an excellent set of readings emphasizing research-oriented views of human intelligence.*

Vernon, P. E. (in press). The nature-nurture problem. In J. A. Glover, R. R. Ronning, & C. R. Reynolds (Eds.). *Handbook of creativity research.* New York: Plenum.

>   *The late Philip E. Vernon, a renowned researcher in the area of human abilities, presented a highly cogent and insightful discussion of the nature-nurture issue in his last published work.*

CHAPTER 5

Language and the Development of Literacy

In Chapter Two, "An Introduction to Cognitive Processes," we focused on the nature of thinking and described a model of human cognition. In Chapter Three, "Memory and Concepts," we explored an important part of cognition, memory and its organization, while Chapter Four, "Intelligence and Cognitive Development," described general trends in intellectual development. Although it is implicit in our discussions in these chapters, one of the most critical aspects of human cognition has not yet been addressed—language and the development of literacy.

An obvious characteristic of human thought is its relationship to language. If we ask you, for example, to remember the house you grew up in, you may generate an image, but you will use language to describe it. Similarly, if an exam question requires that you discuss schema theory, you will recall information in your memory and express it in language. Almost all instruction relies on language. As a teacher you will employ language both in providing instruction and giving feedback. Further, you often will teach language in both its oral and written forms; a major goal of our educational system is helping students acquire excellent language expression skills. Of course, the most central academic skills of all, reading and writing, are complex activities directly based on language understanding.

Effective teaching requires a knowledge of how children's linguistic abilities develop. In the first part of this chapter, we trace the early course of language development. We then shift our focus to the critical cognitive skill of reading. We examine its components and then the stages in learning to read. Finally, in the last part of the chapter, we discuss writing and the development of students' writing skills.

1. Identify characteristics of language development that will affect your choice of teaching methods.

2. Trace developmental changes in children's language abilities.

3. Describe techniques you can use to facilitate children's language development.

4. Describe a basal reading series by examining the types of reading activities appearing at each level in the series.

5. Develop increased flexibility in your own reading.

6. Identify procedures for helping students become better readers.

7. Describe a program that will help students become better writers.

Development of Language

Most people think of children's language beginning with their first words. In fact, however, learning to speak is only one of many major achievements in learning language and is built on many earlier experiences. One such set of experiences involves the perception of language.

Early Language Perception

Research by Coltheart (e.g., 1987) and others has shown that the human infant comes equipped with the capability to recognize speech sounds. A series of experiments by Eimas (1985), for example, has shown that even very young infants—as young as three or four weeks old—can recognize differences in sound that are important in language. This capability is so well developed that Eimas and others have argued that human infants must have special, innate mechanisms for acquiring and using language. Because of these inborn mechanisms, even very young babies very quickly learn to perceive language.

Obviously, young infants cannot record their perceptions directly. Therefore, researchers in this area have used a research approach called a high-amplitude sucking procedure (Petitto, 1988) in which infants suck on a pacifier as they listen to sounds much like those in human speech. This is no ordinary pacifier, however; it is hooked to a pressure detector, which in turn is attached to recording instruments. The key to this procedure is a process called *habituation*, in which infants are known to slow their sucking rate when exposed to a familiar stimulus but to increase it when they detect something new or novel.

Imagine a baby in an infant seat, sucking on the pacifier and listening to a syllable, /ba/, generated by a computer and presented over and over. Since the infant becomes familiar with the sound as it is pronounced repeatedly, the sucking rate gradually slows. Now, however, the syllable is changed to /pa/. When this change occurs, the rate of sucking increases, often dramatically, and we know the baby has recognized the difference in sound. As Eimas points out, even very young infants can distinguish among different speech sounds. Because such recognition occurs so early in life, it is unlikely that it has been learned. A simpler explanation of this ability is that babies are born with perceptual mechanisms specifically designed for speech sounds (Cromer, 1988). In other words, human infants seem biologically prepared to recognize and use language.

Indeed, newborns and young infants do seem to show tremendous sensitivity to language. From the very beginning of life, babies can be

As this baby's name is called, he turns his head and gazes at the caller. Even very young infants show extraordinary sensitivity to language.

In early language development, parents often imitate their children to draw them into using language.

soothed by gentle speech (Anisfeld, 1984). They show preferences for their mothers' voices over others' voices (Ellis & Beattie, 1986). Also, adults begin talking to their children almost from the moment of birth (Slobin, 1988), which provides language for them to react to. Further, caregivers use a special form of communication—**motherese**—that may make infants' speech perception and communication easier.

When adults talk to infants, they usually do so during shared activities such as feeding, bathing, and dressing (Coleman, 1988). From the earliest point of life on, these shared activities help give meaning to language and vice versa. Language and activities stimulate and complement one another. Because parents see their infants as social beings from the beginning, they engage them in "conversations," ask them questions, and give them information. Even though the infant initially has little or no awareness of what is being said, the stage is being set for the meaningful use of language.

We often think of children imitating adults, but in the first year of language development, parents often imitate their children. They comment on their infant's actions and often repeat or exaggerate the child's vocalizations. For instance, a baby may stretch its arms upward and yawn, and its mother will comment, "Oh, you're so tired, aren't you!" Likewise, an infant may babble, /pa/ /pa/ /pa/ /pa/, and we can note the father faithfully imitating, /pa/ /pa/ /pa/ /pa/! Such exchanges between adults and infants help draw infants into the language and into the social community. These social interactions build intimacy between adults and children, enhance babies' interest in their surroundings, and provide them with stimulation for their language development (Anisfeld, 1984; Ninio & Snow, 1988).

Early Speech Production   There are two major periods in creating and perceiving speech. The first, the prelinguistic period, lasts from birth to around the child's first birthday. The second, called the *linguistic period*, continues from that point on (Anisfeld, 1984; Levy, 1988). In the prelinguistic period, infants' speech does not contain meaning. Although infants vocalize a great deal and do affect adults with their vocalizations, their major purpose seems simply to practice making sounds. Only in the linguistic period does sound-making become linked to meaning.

The earliest and most obvious form of infant vocalization is crying. Crying starts from the moment of birth, and babies cry when they are hungry, cold, uncomfortable, or want to be held. Crying is produced by breathing out, and it consists of sounds much like vowels produced in a series. A crying sequence can last up to five minutes or longer (Petitto, 1988). Crying is not learned but has a biological basis.

While crying signals discomfort, another biologically determined type of vocalization, cooing, signals more pleasurable states. Cooing is the sound babies often produce when their parents smile at or talk to them. Cooing is somewhat closer to speech than crying because cooing contains both consonant and vowel sounds (Anisfeld, 1984; Petitto, 1988).

The next stage of vocalization occurs at about six months of age when infants begin to babble. Babbling is playful speech that has no meaning. When children babble, they produce a tremendous variety of speech sounds. They seem to be practicing sound-making in general; the great range of sounds children make in babbling is produced by chance as all the possibilities of their vocal apparatus are tried out. Interestingly, the sounds produced in babbling at first show almost no trace of the particular language used in the child's home. Infants in English-speaking homes, for instance, babble almost identically to those in, say, Japanese-speaking homes. Even deaf babies babble in this "universal language" (Rodda & Grove, 1987), although in their case, vocalization quickly begins to drop off because there is no auditory feedback.

First Words

Two streams of language development, communication and vocalization, develop side by side during the first year of life. On the one hand, infants and adults have been communicating through shared activities and adult language use from the very beginning. By about a year of age, infants have a clear sense of the role of language in communication and can understand a great deal of it. For example, eight- or nine-month-old children, when asked, may be able to point to their noses, mouths, or eyes. On the other hand, they also have been exercising their sound-making capabilities by crying, cooing, and babbling. While these two streams, communication and vocalization, mostly are separate in the first year of life, in the second they merge. Making sounds becomes a mode of communication.

The combining of communication and vocalization signals the beginning of the *linguistic period*, the beginning of true language (Petitto, 1988). What we observe is a transition from nonmeaningful vocalization (babbling) to meaningful speech (the baby's first words). Although the shift is not sudden, it is possible from about nine months of age onward to identify elements of speech that correspond to words. Infants' speech sounds begin to contain more and more features of the mother tongue. Whereas babbling infants speak a "universal language," infants speaking their first words do not.

When children move from the babbling state to their "first words," their verbal output may drop dramatically (Maratsos, 1988). To some parents, at least, it almost may seem as if their children have stopped talking. The reason for this lies in the shift from nonmeaningful to meaningful sound-making. When children babble, they are not restricted by meaning; any sound they make is fine. When they begin to talk, however, their sound-making must be confined to the sounds of a particular language—it must be meaningful.

Infants' first words are quite different from adult words. They often are mispronounced by adult standards. Frequently, too, they are given generalized meanings that do not correspond to those of adults (e.g., the word *bite* is used by one of our nephews to stand for something to eat, something to drink, and even to communicate that he wants a kiss!). Also, depending on the context and on how the word is said, a single word (e.g., "mah") can be used by a child to identify something or somebody (saying "mah" when her mother enters the room), to express a need (the baby says "mah" and extends her arms to be picked up), or to label an object linked to someone (saying "mah" when she sees her mother's shoe). Because a given word clearly is used in different ways, some believe that first words are best viewed as one-word sentences (holophrases) used to express a variety of meanings (Braine, 1988).

First words typically accompany infants' direct experiences—they "go with" certain things or actions. For instance, children may say "bye-bye" while waving good-bye as a parent leaves for work. Speech is a part of the total activity pattern of the parent leaving and the child waving. Because this language use is not clearly separable from action patterns, it has been labeled *presymbolic*. In the presymbolic stage, words accompany actions. Gradually, however, words are separated from actions and come to be more and more free of context—more *symbolic*, or representational.

As we indicated earlier, first words often are highly personalized. Since children's experiences are quite limited, word use tends to conform to their subjective understanding of the world rather than to "objective" adult standards. If children hope to communicate with others, however, an important change needs to occur. Language is a social activity, in which word meanings are shared by all speakers of the language. Words that only the child or perhaps his or her parents can understand have extremely limited utility.

When children discover that language is the same for everyone—that words are symbols with shared meanings—there is often a period of extremely rapid vocabulary growth. Whereas children may acquire only ten or twenty new words between twelve and eighteen months, new words are learned much more rapidly between eighteen and twenty-four months. The rate is extremely high; sometimes as many as sixty or more words are learned a month (see McKeown & Curtis, 1987).

First Sentences

After a period of single-word utterances, children begin to produce simple sentences. Children usually first create two-word sentences (duos) and then longer ones. The following duos are typical of early two-word sentences (Braine, 1988).

big ball	more juice	two bread
big plane	more catch	two fly
big stickie	more dice	two daddy
big blue	more bee	two spoon
big duck	more duck	two squirrel
big lamb		

As you can see, a major characteristic of duos is that a few words are used in mostly fixed positions (e.g., big, more, two) and are combined with other, less regularly used words. Braine (1988) called these fixed words *pivots* because sentences seemed to hinge on them. Braine called the other words *open words*—new vocabulary that readily could be substituted for one another.

Even though such sentences seem very simple to adults, single units of meaning are being combined into more complex, unitary ideas (Braine, 1988). They have a *syntax*, or structure—each sentence conveys relationships between ideas. Most authorities believe that syntax appears when children reach the stage of combining words in sentences, although some feel that single words, used in various contexts, function much like sentences (Braine, 1988).

Context is very important to the interpretation of childrens' early sentences just as it is to the interpretation of first words. "Mommy shoe" may be said when the child sees his mother putting on her shoe, when he sees her shoe lying on the floor, or when the child himself wants his mother to help him put on his shoe. Of course, when children begin to use inflections (e.g., -'s, -ed) to convey such ideas as possession or past tense, depending on context for interpretation diminishes.

Children start using sentences shortly after beginning their vocabulary growth spurt. Once they begin to make sentences, sentence use accelerates rapidly while single-word use declines. Sentences become more and more elaborate as children seem to build from simple utterances to more complex ones. Often, children will "assemble" sentences from simple parts. It is as if they cannot put together a complex sentence all at once but must take its parts and assemble it gradually. Braine (1987) has called these sequences of increasingly elaborate utterances *replacement sequences*. Table 5–1 shows examples of replacement sequences recorded between the ages of twenty and twenty-two months, from one of our daughters.

TABLE 5–1	EXAMPLES OF REPLACEMENT SEQUENCES

Dink. Dink pop. [Dink is drink.]
Pick. Pick-e-up.
Pick. Pick up-a-me.
Dink. Me dink. Dink water me.
Mik. Dink mik.
Blankie. I want blankie.
Fred. Ride Fred. Pull Fred. [Fred is a toy horse.]
Peepeye. Play peepeye. ["Peepeye" means peekaboo.]
Kiki. Where Kiki? ["Kiki" means Kitty.]
Noonals. Me hab noonals. ["Noonals" is noodles.]

Replacement sequences may account for as much as 30 or 40 percent of what a child says during the period after the second birthday and, as mentioned, seem to occur because more complex sentences are too difficult to make all at once. Gradual assembly allows children to create more complex sentences from simpler parts. Soon, however, children seem to be able to produce full sentences first and then break them down into their component parts (e.g., "Billy jump out too. Jump out too") (see MacWhinney, 1987).

Emergent Literacy

By the age of three and one-half or four, many of the essential elements of language have been mastered. Most children have a relatively large working vocabulary and use words effectively to refer to things and actions. They also know a great deal about syntax and can combine words into many types of sentences. In addition, they are skilled at the basics of conversation and can talk about a variety of topics with their peers, older children, and adults. A significant challenge, however, lies ahead—learning to read and write. To become literate, children must apply their knowledge of spoken language—their vocabulary, their knowledge of syntax, and their understanding of the uses of language—to decoding and comprehending written language.

For most children, learning to read and write is a natural next step in their language development. Far in advance of actually "learning to read," for instance, many children already know much about reading. Before they enter school, for example, most children know that the purpose of reading is to get meaning, that the context for print (e.g., illustrations) often provides clues for meaning, and that knowing how to read is important (McGee, Lomax, & Head, 1988). For most children, becoming literate is not "either-or" but a gradual process of "emergent literacy" (Teale & Sulzby, 1986).

Emergent literacy is not automatic, however. It depends heavily on children's early experiences with language (Teale & Sulzby, 1986). Giving young children the opportunity to talk about their experiences and helping them learn new words, for instance, are very important. Perhaps most critical, however, are children's early experiences with books. Parents' reading to children not only develops children's vocabulary and knowledge of language structure but also instills in them a sense of reading as an important and enjoyable activity. When parents read to them, children find that reading is pleasurable and soon come to see reading as something they want to do for themselves.

As we noted earlier, children usually learn to read easily when they have good language experiences and when they have been exposed to reading throughout early childhood. Interactions with literate adults, adult modeling, children's own self-explorations, and, of course, for-

When an older child reads to younger children, both are likely to benefit. Reading becomes a shared language activity in which both learn about the topic, each other, and language itself.

mal instruction in reading set the stage for this significant achievement. For some children, however, the process can be considerably more challenging. For instance, many children of kindergarten age have an incomplete knowledge about language sounds and how they can be divided—knowledge vital to "sounding out" (decoding) words. Others do not know the alphabet, do not have a concept of "word," or are unable to group sequences of sounds into syllables or words (Ehri & Wilce, 1985). As you can imagine, without these skills, learning to read and to write is very difficult. When children lack these skills, teachers need to be especially adept at drawing out the knowledge that will help children succeed in beginning reading instruction (Norris, 1988).

Summary of Language Development. Children's language development is a continuous process starting at birth. At first, their language is largely *receptive*; they respond to language but do not create it. By one year, however, children begin to produce language—first single words, then simple two-word sentences, and soon more elaborate constructions. During the very rapid growth in language knowledge in the preschool years, the groundwork is being laid for the significant achievements of literacy—knowing how to read and to write—and the first hints of literacy begin to emerge for many children. For children who are exposed to books and who have been read to, a sense of what reading and writing are "all about" is acquired. This awareness and children's general language skills are critical factors in determining how easy or difficult it will be for them to learn to read and to use written language in communication.

▌ *Applications for Teaching: Language Development Research*

The following applications are drawn from the research on language development.

1. Talk to infants. Although talking to infants comes naturally to most people, remember that children's experiences from birth prepare them to use language. Young babies may not understand what you say, but it is important that you are talking to them. By hearing you speak, they learn to link language with other activities. At first infants rely heavily on context for comprehension but quickly learn to understand spoken language both with and without context.

2. Be responsive to infants' vocalizations. Like any other human action, vocalization is affected by feedback. Just as talking to infants comes easily for most adults, so too does their reacting to babies' vocalizations. However, some adults are more responsive than others. Through your reactions, children are encouraged to vocalize, and gradually they learn how and when to use language.

3. Ask children to describe their experiences. As children tell about things they have seen or heard, they develop the ability to express themselves and learn conversational skills. With very young children, you may need to prompt some of what they say. Patience is often important as children search for words and ways of stating their ideas. Soon, however, they will speak much more easily. Like other skills, speaking requires practice.

4. Read to young children regularly. Literacy emerges from early language experience. Adults who read to children not only expose them to language and create a pleasurable event but they convey knowledge about reading as a meaningful activity. Generally, those children who have been read to learn to read earlier and more easily than those children who have not had similar experiences.

5. Encourage children to read. Reading is a key to a variety of desirable language development outcomes. Other things being equal, for instance, the more children read, the larger their vocabularies are likely to be. Reading exposes children to different styles of written language. Also, as children make the transition from "learning to read" to "reading to learn," reading becomes one of the most important and efficient avenues for acquiring new information.

6. Set aside time every day for conversations with children. Children best learn to use communication skills when they use them regularly. Frequent conversations with an adult can facilitate critical thinking skills, vocabulary growth, social skills, and, simply, keeping in touch with children's feelings and needs. There is no substitute for regular, extended conversation with adults (Gottlieb & Williams, 1987).

About Reading

Just exactly what is this process called reading? Perhaps a good starting point is the definition offered by Harris and Sipey (1983): "Reading is a meaningful interpretation of written or printed verbal symbols" (p. 3). Beck (1984) has described it as a "meaningful encounter with text" (p. 4). While the term *reading* sometimes is used loosely to refer to a wide range of activities that revolve around gaining information, such as "reading" defenses in football or "reading" public opinion on a particular issue, we don't think of such processes as falling within the usual definition of reading. Reading almost always is a meaningful activity. It involves more than matching up sounds with symbols on a printed page. It is a cognitive process in which readers' perspectives and reading processes have much to do with what they learn. Reading is a skill we all take for granted, but it is a complex, sophisticated process that includes many different components.

Components of the Reading Process

A Writing System.   The use of written symbols to represent spoken language is one of the great achievements of human history. Writing has made it possible to expand communication not only across space but across time as well. Many of the greatest accomplishments of the human race—our science, our literature, and the recording of our history—are dependent on the written word. Because reading can supplement or replace listening, written language also transforms how education takes place.

Most spoken languages are represented in some system of writing. These writing systems vary tremendously, but they share a number of common characteristics. Writing is patterned, has gaps between units, is composed of parallel lines of print, and has various forms (such as cursive and printed letters) that usually are not mixed (Ellis & Beattie, 1986). Most languages are written from left to right, although some are written from right to left (Hebrew) and others from top to bottom (Japanese). There doesn't seem to be any particular advantage to reading in one direction or another; we just adapt to whatever system our native language uses.

Although the use of pictures and drawings to communicate appeared some 20,000 years ago (Tzeng & Hung, 1981), the earliest form of writing appeared about 6,000 years ago in Egypt. This form of writing, in which each word is represented by a symbol, is called **logographic**. Not only did Egyptian written language (e.g., hieroglyphics) evolve this way but also modern Chinese, another logographic language (Ellis & Beattie, 1986). Logographic languages ordinarily have many thousands of distinct characters, which must be memorized as part of the process of becoming literate. Some of the symbols, called *pictograms*, are carryovers from the earlier, picture-drawing stage. Thus, a picture of a tree might represent the word *tree*. A written language composed only of pictograms, even a series of them, has serious difficulty in representing abstract concepts, however.

Other languages evolved in a different way. These languages, called **phonographic languages**, do not use symbols directly to represent the meaning of words but rather their sounds. One interesting but primitive form of phonographic language is the *rebus*, such as the one pictured in Figure 5–1, in which pictures or symbols represent sounds. As you can see if you try to construct a rebus, its utility is extremely limited, mostly because of the difficulty in finding enough unambiguous pictures.

FIGURE 5–1   A SIMPLE REBUS

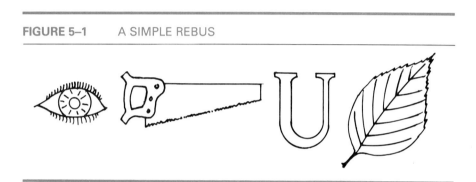

A much more complex and useful phonographic language system is the **syllabary**, which has a written symbol for each syllable in the spoken language. Syllabaries permit a relatively small number of symbols to be used to write down all the words and sentences of a language. Each unit of writing corresponds to a unit of speech. For instance, Japanese has two distinct syllabary forms—Hiragana and Katakana—in which there are symbols for consonants and consonant-vowel combinations. A third form of Japanese writing, Kanji, is logographic.

Perhaps the most significant development in the evolution of phonographic languages, however, came with the invention of the alphabet, in which characters symbolize vowels and consonants. The advantage of an alphabet is that its symbols represent both the individual sounds and the meanings of words. **Alphabetic writing** first developed in Greece in a span of about two hundred years during the first millennium B.C. (Ellis & Beattie, 1986). English and most other European languages are alphabetic. Another advantage of an alphabet for representing language is that it represents a vast spoken language with only a few symbols. English, for example, uses only twenty-six letters to represent all its sounds. In contrast, mastery of the Chinese language logography may require knowledge of as many as fifty thousand distinct symbols.

Some alphabetic languages, such as Finnish, possess a strict (regular) relationship between the writing system, the orthography, and the spoken language sounds. In other words, the relationship between spelling and pronunciation is regular—words are pronounced the way they are spelled. Other languages, in contrast, are much less regular. For instance, English pronunciations may differ for similar spellings (consider *plough, rough, though*). Such variations make beginning reading more difficult and have led to such inventions as the Initial Teaching Alphabet, in which each English sound is given its own symbol.

Eye Movements and Fixations.   One of the few observable aspects of reading is the movement of the eyes across the printed page. Eye movements in reading are not smooth like those we make when looking at slowly moving objects but are a series of start-stop jumps across a line of print. The jumps are called **saccades**, while the periods of time in which the eyes come to rest are called **fixations**. The eye movements in reading are much like those involved in looking at various objects in a room: the eyes jump from point to point (Ellis & Beattie, 1986).

Each saccade is very rapid, taking only a few thousandths of a second, and usually covers about seven to nine characters on a line (Just & Carpenter, 1987). The eye is essentially blind during the saccade. Most information is processed during fixations, which take up more than 90 percent of total reading time (Just & Carpenter, 1987).

Almost every content word (noun, verb, adjective, and so on) is fixated at least once during ordinary reading. When readers are given text materials matched to their reading level, they average about 1.2 words per fixation. Words not fixated are usually short words, such as *the, of,* and *a* (Just and Carpenter, 1987).

When good readers encounter simple materials such as a child's story, however, they usually skip more words. In difficult materials, however, there are many more regressions in which the eyes return to an earlier position. Unfamiliar words, for instance, are fixated repeatedly as readers attempt to comprehend their meaning (Just & Carpenter, 1987).

The eye fixations (given in seconds) of a college student reading a passage about weightarms are shown in Figure 5–2. As you can see, this reader spent the most time on words important to understanding the passage, such as the key word *weightarms*. The student also spent somewhat longer times on the last words in sentences, presuma-

---

FIGURE 5–2   EYE FIXATIONS OF A COLLEGE STUDENT READING A
PASSAGE (IN SECONDS)

	.267	.283		.200	.350	.283	.283	.733		.333
The	Egyptian	engineer	of	5,000	years	ago	may	have	used	a

	.266	.183	.467	.200			1.201		.333	
simple	wooden	device	called	a			weightarm	for	handling	the

.367		1.151		.583	.568		.417	.267	.183		.217
2½	to	7	ton	pyramid	blocks.	The	weightarm	is	like	a	lever

		.600	.167	.200	.617			.267	.367
or	beam	pivoting	on	a	fulcrum	...	Weightarms	may	

	.256	.283			.234	.384		.216	.356	
have	been	used	to	lift	the	blocks	off	the	barges	which

.267		.250	.433	.899
came	from	the	upriver	quarries.

Source: Adapted by permission from Carpenter, P., and Just, M. A., What your eyes do while
your mind is reading. In K. Rayner (Ed.), *Eye movements in reading: Perceptual and language
processes.* New York: Academic Press, 1982. Used by permission.

---

bly attempting to integrate the information in the just completed
sentence.

   Some of the information we have just presented traces back to early
studies of eye movements in reading from the first part of this century.
That early work, in particular, is a tribute to scientific resourcefulness
and, perhaps, to the perseverance of the subjects. One successful early
method was that of Huey (1908), in which he attached a suction cup to
the surface of the eye and, by mechanical and electrical means,
recorded eye movements by markings on a smoked drum. Modern
methods involve the reflection of regular or infrared light off the
cornea of the eye and then recording the light on a film or videotape of
what the person is looking at.

   The most advanced research techniques for the study of eye
movements in reading now link computers to eye-movement recording
devices. This enables investigators to perform sophisticated research
on the perceptual and cognitive processes involved in reading. For
example, these studies demonstrate that readers generally cannot
process information from their peripheral vision. Only seven or eight
letters can be processed meaningfully in a single fixation (Just &

Carpenter, 1987). Thus, some of the more extravagant claims for taking in information during speed-reading have been shown to be physically impossible. Such research also has shown that eye-movement patterns tend to change as people acquire increased skills in reading, with fixations becoming somewhat shorter and regressions fewer. Figure 5–3 shows the contrast between the fixations of a skilled and an unskilled reader.

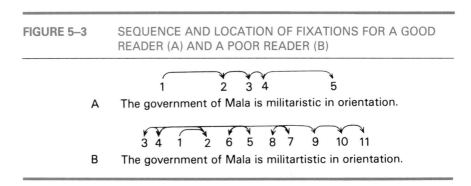

FIGURE 5–3   SEQUENCE AND LOCATION OF FIXATIONS FOR A GOOD
READER (A) AND A POOR READER (B)

Such data, however, sometimes have been misinterpreted. Some people have thought that since good readers' fixations are short and their regressions few, training poor readers to make "better" eye movements should help them become better readers. This thinking unfortunately confuses cause with effect. Do eye movements determine the success of reading, or are they caused by the student's reading skills? Most serious scholars in the area of reading research conclude that the brain, rather than the eye, is the key to reading (see Just & Carpenter, 1987). For most students, information processing controls the physical activities of reading rather than the other way around. Good readers do move their eyes efficiently, but practicing eye movements will not improve reading. Efficient eye movements are caused by reading well.

An Information-Processing Model of Reading. Marcel Just and Patricia Carpenter (1987) have developed a useful model of the major cognitive processes involved in reading, which we present in modified form in Figure 5–4. As you can see, it has a great deal in common with the information-processing model of cognition we presented in Chapter Two. This is natural because reading is a cognitive activity. In Just and Carpenter's model of reading, the activities and processes by which information is taken from the text are depicted on the left. The reader encounters new information through reading and assigns it preliminary meaning. Long-term memory, pictured on the right, likewise contributes to the reading process. Memory for alphabet characteristics, concepts, word order, the structure of passages and prior information all influence reading.

FIGURE 5–4   A MODEL OF COGNITIVE PROCESSES IN READING

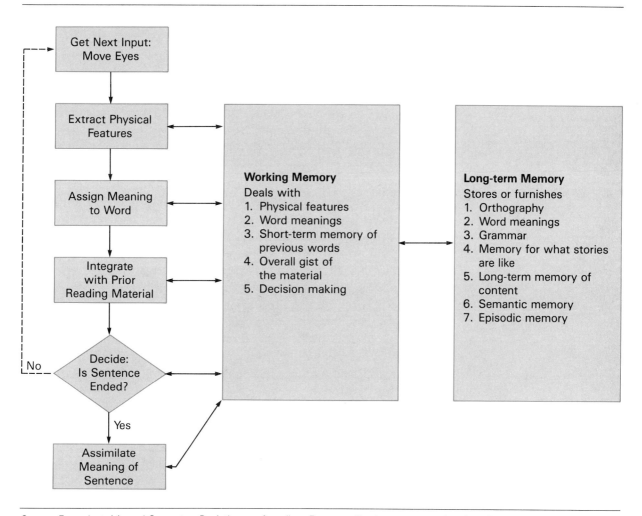

Source: From Just, M., and Carpenter, P., A theory of reading: From eye fixations to comprehension. *Psychological Review*, 1980, *87,* 329–354. Copyright 1980 by the American Psychological Association. Adapted by permission of the authors.

The main activities of reading, like all other cognitive processes, occur in working memory. In Just and Carpenter's view, incoming information and prior knowledge interact in working memory, each influencing the other. On one hand, our schemata affect the information we can take in and the way in which we take it in (that is, the way we read). On the other hand, our existing knowledge is modified and transformed by new content. As with all cognitive activities, reading is a dynamic, interactive process. The meaning that students obtain while reading is influenced by the content of what they read, their prior knowledge, and their goals for reading. An expert in reading who is writing a review of this chapter, for example, might pay attention to different things (style, level of sophistication, breadth of coverage) than would a student taking his or her first course in educational psychology.

Attention.   To read effectively, readers must devote their attention to the task (Garner, 1987). We all are aware of the effects distractions can have upon our reading. When our attention wavers as someone speaks to us or when we become sleepy, we find it difficult to understand what we are reading.

Another aspect of attention is more subtle, but equally important. As we read, our attention can be directed to an infinite variety of things—the words themselves, concepts associated with the content we are reading, or to our own emotions. To a great extent, these cognitive processes determine what we learn. Out of numerous stimuli that we could pay attention to, we select only a few. For instance, the page you are looking at now has a great many features to which you could pay attention—for example, the page number, the type of print used, and the texture of the paper. As adult readers, however, we usually concentrate mainly on the meaning or gist of a passage. In fact, we typically are not particularly aware of the surrounding features or even the individual letters or the words we read. Our attention usually is focused on those features that help us comprehend the meaning of what we are reading.

One reason our attention is so selective, as we noted in Chapter Two, is that our capacity for processing incoming information in working memory is very limited (Halpain, Glover, & Harvey, 1985; Smith, 1988). Attention can be shifted quickly from one feature of a text to another, but large amounts of information cannot be processed simultaneously. The limited capacity of working memory often creates a bottleneck for incoming information.

Many reading problems involve faulty attention, as when students simply do not spend enough time reading or when they try to study

Studying is more effective when there are few distractions and when students learn to use such techniques as previewing, outlining, and summarizing. At its best, studying is a meaningful activity involving an active learner.

under distracting conditions. Such problems often can be very effectively dealt with by using some of the behavioral self-management procedures we discuss in Chapter Eleven. Other attention problems occur when students are reading but their reading processes are misdirected or inefficient. Their reading strategies may not be appropriate for their purposes. Reading to prepare for a speech or for a discussion with a professor requires quite different patterns of attention than does reading one's favorite novel on the bus going home. We discuss a number of approaches for improving reading strategies later in this chapter.

Decoding and Comprehension. The cognitive processes involved in reading may be divided into two stages (Smith, 1988). Obtaining the meaning of individual words (identifying the physical features and assigning meaning in Just and Carpenter's model) is referred to as **decoding**. The second stage of reading, **comprehending**, refers to the processes whereby the reader gains an overall understanding of the content.

Decoding occurs when readers consciously direct their attention to individual words, or it may occur automatically after much practice (Smith, 1978). For example, you probably did not stop to decode the word *practice* in the previous sentence—your decoding was automatic. According to Samuels (1988), skilled reading of reasonably familiar materials involves automatic decoding of word meanings while the reader's attention is directed to the comprehension of what is being read. In his view, this process is somewhat analogous to a skilled musician's being able to concentrate on the expressive aspects of music rather than on the individual notes. If a reader encounters an unfamiliar word or if the materials become difficult, however, decoding is no longer automatic. In such instances, decoding itself occupies the reader's attention (Just & Carpenter, 1987). We may say a difficult word to ourselves (for example, "ex-ig-u-ous") and use a sounding-out process in an attempt to decode it.

An important part of learning to read with comprehension is the development of fluent decoding skills. Beginning readers need to learn to recognize the distinguishing features of letters, syllables, and words automatically (Palincsar, Brown, & Martin, 1987). When the processing of letters or words is automatic, readers can concentrate their attention on comprehension. When poor or immature readers need to devote most of their attention to decoding letters and words, comprehension is more difficult and less likely to occur (Hedley & Hicks, 1988; Samuels, 1988).

Stages in Learning to Read

Learning to read often is considered to occur in stages, beginning with the transition to reading and culminating in the refinement of reading skills in high school and adulthood (see Glazer & Searfoss, 1988). Each stage has its unique challenges that readers must meet in order to progress. The first challenge comes in the transition to reading.

The Transition to Reading

While the skills on which literacy depends emerge gradually during the preschool years, there nonetheless is a clear progression from a point at which children cannot read to the point when it can be said that they are "readers." Ehri and Wilce (1988) have proposed four stages. Initially children are nonreaders. As they move into reading, they typically first use visual cues and then gradually start to use phonetic cues. Finally they master the full system of relationships between letters and letter-combinations to the sounds of oral language.

Nonreaders.   Nonreaders are not able to read words in isolation. For instance, if they are given a list of simple words (e.g., *bat, hit, do*), they cannot read any of them. As we discussed earlier, however, many nonreaders will be aware that words do mean something and that books, newspapers, and advertisements contain information. Some even can "read" signs and logos—for instance, the word *Pepsi* or *MacDonalds* in context—but their reading is more of the context than the print. When the words are taken out of context, they no longer are recognized.

Visual-Cue Reading.   The first "real" reading takes place when children can recognize isolated words in print. For many, their initial recognition is based on *visual cues,* such as the shape of the word or distinctive features of letters. Reading using only visual cues, however, is a kind of paired-associate task (see Chapter Three) of linking how a word looks with its pronunciation and meaning. Since visual cue reading relies on distinctive features of words (which are quickly exhausted) and because associations between words and meanings are arbitrary, visual-cue reading seldom is effective and soon is abandoned by most readers.

Phonetic-Cue Reading.   To read competently requires attention to phonetic (sound) cues in letters and words. Phonetic-cue readers begin to do so by using their knowledge of the alphabet to associate words with their pronunciations. For instance, a child may be able to read the word *giraffe* by recognizing the letters "g," "r," and "f" in the word and linking the letter names to the word (i.e., gee-are-eff = "giraffe"). Almost all letter names (except "y" and "w") contain sounds that can be used to make phonetic associations (Ehri & Wilce, 1988). Since these associations are not arbitrary, they are easier to remember than the visual cues of letters and word shape.

Phonetic-cue readers are more effective than visual-cue readers. However, since they do not use all the information in words (e.g., ignoring the vowels in "giraffe") and because letter names often are not the same as their sounds, they have trouble with many new words. To be a full-fledged reader, a more systematic approach is needed.

Systematic Phonemic Decoding.   Children become "real readers" when they begin to read with comprehension and accurately identify similarly spelled words. **Systematic phonemic decoders** can do this. They not only have learned the alphabet, but they are able to distin-

Children should be read to frequently. Research has shown that experiences with reading in early childhood relate to later skill in reading.

guish each of the meaningful sounds or **phonemes** that words contain (cuh—ah—tuh, CAT vs. buh—ah—tuh, BAT). They understand how spellings correspond to pronunciations. For children learning to read English, this means that they have mastered a very complex mapping system tying more than forty sounds (the phonemes of English) to a huge number of letters and letter combinations.

When to Begin?   When should children begin to read? A number of children, especially those who have been read to and who have had excellent language experiences, may already be readers when they enter school. Others may begin to read during kindergarten. Many educators feel, however, that for most children formal reading instruction should not begin until first grade.

Part of this feeling stems from an influential early study by Morphett and Washburne (1931), who concluded that the best time to begin instruction was when children had reached a mental age (see Chapter Four) of six years and six months. Although this study was quite defective from a scientific standpoint, it became an important part of a general belief among reading teachers that reading instruction shouldn't begin until age six or later. Thus, most reading instruction in the United States now begins in the first grade, when the majority of children reach the mental age of six years and six months.*

Some authorities (see Alexander, 1988; Karlin & Karlin, 1987) have shown that precocious (early) readers benefit from their early start; but, of course, it is recognized that most such readers learned to read on their own without benefit of formal instruction. While some studies show positive effects of early reading instruction, the question of when formal reading instruction should begin is still open (Kontos, 1988). Obviously, there is a very wide range of individual differences in reading, and no one age standard fits everyone. More important is the question of how well the abilities of a given child match those required by beginning reading instruction. A well-rounded approach to prepare a child for reading requires attention to individual abilities and building foundations for literacy through rich experiences with language.

———

*This belief is not universally held. Reading instruction begins at age five in such countries as Great Britain and Israel and not until age seven in Denmark, Sweden, and the Soviet Union.

Applications for Teaching: Guidelines for Facilitating the Transition to Reading

For parents and teachers who would like to work with children on developing prereading skills, we suggest the following principles. They emphasize development of reading and reading-related skills in a positive atmosphere that is likely to stimulate a child's interest in reading.

1. Reading and reading enjoyment should be modeled (see Chapter Ten). Children can learn about the importance and fun of reading from what they see adults do.

2. Children should be read to frequently. Reading to children not only provides a model of reading and aids in the development of literacy but helps them discover that reading is enjoyable and that printed symbols have meanings. Of course, reading to children also helps develop their vocabularies as they encounter new words (Alexander, 1988).

3. Do not pressure a prereader to master reading-related tasks. If a child sees reading as enjoyable, he or she will usually develop the appropriate prereading skills. When reading activities become pressured, children may stop seeing reading as fun and seek to avoid the activities (Beardsley & Marecek-Zeman, 1987).

4. Children should be taught how to pay attention prior to any formal reading instruction. Paying attention, following directions, and staying on task are requirements for any kind of learning, especially learning to read. Behavioral approaches (see Chapters Eight and Eleven) often can be used effectively to teach general attentional skills.

5. Games and exercises can be used to develop the general motor and perceptual skills necessary for reading. Simple discrimination tasks, eye-hand coordination activities, scribbling, and drawing should all be encouraged.

6. All children should be examined for any possible perceptual problems that might interfere with reading. Problems in visual and auditory perception should be identified early and treated if possible. Reading is difficult enough for many children without their having to cope with additional problems.

Beginning Reading

A variety of methods for teaching beginning reading have come and gone over the years. Methods of teaching reading, perhaps more than methods in any other instructional area, have been promoted with great zeal and attacked with equal vigor. Today, hundreds of commercial programs are available that draw from a variety of theoretical approaches.

One common approach to beginning reading is phonics. **Phonics** emphasizes decoding of sounds from letters and words, particularly the learning of letter-sound relationships and using these relationships

---

PRACTICE EXERCISE 5–1   REVIEWING A READING SERIES

There are a large number of commercially available programs for teaching beginning reading. Committees of teachers and others usually choose a reading program series for a school after careful examination of several series.

Analyze the program series used in your local school system (sample sets are available at your school or from your college elementary teacher education program) on one or more of the following dimensions.

1. *What is to be learned at each level of the series?* What are some of the key elements being taught at each level of the basal reading series? How are new concepts introduced?

2. *Are the skills of reading taught effectively?* Are all important reading skills covered? Is enough time devoted to critical topics, and is the method of teaching concepts usually clear?

3. *What roles are portrayed in the reading materials?* Are male and female roles stereotyped? Are families always depicted as "typical" families? Are there any ethnic or racial biases?

4. *How are illustrations used?* How are pictures used in relation to the content? Do they provide context or do they distract? Are they clear and attractive?

5. *What are the usual outcomes of stories?* Are they unrealistically positive and Pollyannaish, or do they depict real-life outcomes for children?

6. *What are the settings for the stories?* Are settings rural or urban, are they imaginary or real? Would they be interesting to a child?

---

to decode word meanings. Some phonics approaches teach the letter-sound patterns in relative isolation (how to pronounce *sp, st,* and *br*), while others employ phonics within words and stories.

Another approach is *language experience,* which emphasizes the relationship of reading to children's general language experiences. Reading is viewed as the process of relating written to oral language. Children's own oral stories about themselves, their families, or their neighborhoods may be written down to become the basis for reading.

Most current instructional methods, however, are *eclectic,* combining these and other approaches. Basal readers are the most prominent examples of eclectic reading instruction. Basal readers are coordinated sets of texts, workbooks, and activities used in most American schools. Diverse aspects of reading such as learning letter sounds and sound blends and using context to extract meanings may be included in the same basal series. While basal readers have been criticized for many reasons (unrealistic content, cultural and ethnic biases, sexism, among others), the majority have been adjusted, and they continue to form the core of most children's beginning reading experiences.

A major report summarizing research on beginning reading also has concluded that there is no single key to children's successful reading. This report, *Becoming a Nation of Readers* (1985), was prepared by the Commission on Reading of the National Academy of Education and funded by the National Institute of Education. According to the report, in beginning reading instruction it is critical to build on children's prior knowledge. New learning must be linked to existing schemata. Another key is emphasizing children's oral and written language by having children talk and write about their experiences. In addition, parents and teachers should model skilled reading by reading aloud to children. Further, both oral and silent reading by the children should be encouraged. Phonics, the report stresses, has a place in beginning reading but should be kept simple. The central theme of all effective early reading instruction, however, is making sure children *understand* what they read. Unless children understand that reading is a *meaningful* activity, they quickly come to view it as tedious and boring and see themselves as poor readers or nonreaders.

Applications for Teaching: Guidelines for Teaching Beginning Reading

Some reading experts view beginning reading as a set of skills that can be separated into parts — such as the ability to discriminate between letters, the ability to blend sounds, and so on. In contrast, Frank Smith (1988) takes the position that reading is more a process of bringing meaning to print than of decoding. For Smith, reading is a process of testing hypotheses and making guesses about what is on the page. The major objectives in learning to read are understanding that print is meaningful, understanding that words are language, and getting the chance to learn to read through frequent practice.

We generally agree with Smith's position. Such practices as insisting on perfection in reading, teaching letters and words in isolation, and discouraging use of one's own knowledge can interfere with children's experience of reading as meaningful and enjoyable (Commission on Reading, 1985; Smith, 1988). A certain way to ensure that some beginning readers will fail is to demand conformity and to force children to work toward the impossible criterion of perfection in reading. The following guidelines stress meaningfulness in learning to read and the individual nature of this process. Following them should benefit all beginning readers.

1. Make reading and activities associated with reading enjoyable. To become good readers, children must devote time and effort to reading activities. These activities should be enjoyable so that children will want to read rather than avoid reading. For many children, beginning reading is hard work, and hard work is more palatable when it's fun.

2. Stress experiences that will lead to success. It is important to carefully plan beginning reading activities for students so that they experience feelings of success in reading. Not only must the activities allow for success, but each child should feel a sense of genuine accomplishment.

3. Emphasize meaningful reading experiences. As we have stressed throughout this book, learning is best when experiences can be related to what students already know, when new experiences are meaningful. From this perspective, the teacher should carefully choose or construct reading materials that employ the vocabulary and concepts that are a part of students' prior knowledge (Combs, 1987).

4. Use a variety of instructional methods in reading instruction. No single method is the magical key to success. Instruction in reading at this crucial time should be geared as much as possible to individual needs.

5. Have students reread materials with which they are already familiar. Students need to gain confidence in reading and experience the sense of "I can really do it!" Having students reread materials they already have mastered is one way to foster feelings of confidence in reading (Atwell, 1985; Reitsma, 1988).

6. Stress accomplishment rather than errors. Beginning readers will make mistakes. The emphasis should be on recognizing improvement rather than on pointing out mistakes.

In teaching beginning reading, time should be set aside for children to use the library.

7. Allow guessing. Beginning readers, by using pictures or the verbal context of stories, are often able to guess words as they read. This is not a bad approach. As adults we often guess the meanings of unfamiliar words on the basis of context. Fluency in reading is more important in beginning reading than perfection (McKeown, 1985).

8. Practice, practice, practice. The evidence is clear and direct. The more students read, the better they will read (Anderson, Wilson, & Fielding, 1988). As in developing any other skill, practice is necessary to improve upon students' ability to read.

9. Identify possible perceptual problems, and have them treated as rapidly as possible. Despite the fact that most schools require a check on children's visual and auditory abilities prior to kindergarten, some problems are not identified. If you suspect a perceptual problem, notify the parents and appropriate school authorities as soon as possible. Beginning reading is difficult enough without the presence of uncorrected perceptual problems.

10. Include self-directed reading activities. Set aside some time at least once a week when the students may use the school library to choose books to read on their own.

11. Encourage reading at home. Anderson, Wilson, and Fielding (1988) recently have reported on the strong link between reading at home and children's reading abilities. Reading at home has very positive effects on children's development of reading skills. In addition, children's pride in their new skills can be enhanced by reading to appreciative parents and siblings. Also, don't forget to encourage parents to continue to read to their children. It is not only an enjoyable activity but one with demonstrated beneficial effects on children's reading skills (e.g., Morrow, 1988).

The Middle Years: Developing Comprehension and Vocabulary

Once students have acquired basic decoding skills, full emphasis can be placed on comprehension. Reading comprehension goals include recognizing the main thought in a passage, predicting outcomes, and following written directions (Palincsar et al., 1987). By the middle elementary grades, the emphasis thus has shifted from learning *to* read to learning *through* reading. Reading now is more and more functional. Students read in order to obtain instructions, to enjoy themselves, and to learn.

An especially important aspect of reading comprehension is vocabulary development. Much, if not most, of the vocabulary development that takes place during the elementary and secondary school years comes from reading (Nagy & Herman, 1987)—by students encountering unknown words as they read.

Learning words in this way is a slow, incremental process, however. A single contact with a word usually produces only a small amount of learning. Only after students encounter a word several times are they likely to fully comprehend it; the chance of learning a significant amount from reading a word in text is not more than about 10 percent (Nagy, Anderson, & Herman, 1987; Nagy & Herman, 1987). The sheer volume of reading that students typically do in and out of school,

As these children explore the globe to find examples of islands and peninsulas for their geography class, they are putting not only their map skills but also their reading and writing skills to work. They are reading to learn.

however, makes reading a vital mechanism for acquiring new vocabulary. A typical fifth-grade student, for instance, reads about 300,000 words just from books *outside* of school (Anderson et al., 1988). When the reading *in* school is added to this total, the estimate moves to about a million words a year read for an average fifth-grader. As children read and as the same new words are encountered again and again, their meanings gradually become clear.

For instance, in a story a girl is reading in English, she might see the word *gibber* for the first time in a sentence that says, "Nathan began to gibber like a monkey." Even though she initially has no idea what *gibber* means, the sentence reveals that gibber is a kind of action and something both Nathan and a monkey can do. At this point, however, the girl might not even pause to "figure out" the word. Later, in another story, reading the sentences, "No one could understand him. He was speaking gibberish," the girl may recall that she earlier had read the word *gibber* and may infer than *gibber* and *gibberish* (which she does have some idea about) might be related; both could have something to do with talking nonsense. As students make these kinds of connections and learn to use the context of words to figure them out, word meanings are gradually built up.

If much of a person's vocabulary is acquired from context during reading, it is likely that children who read more will have larger vocabularies. In fact, the amount children read on their own does differ dramatically (some children read twenty or thirty times as much as others), and the amount read seems to be closely related to vocabulary size (Wilson, 1985). It seems logical, then, for both teachers and parents to encourage reading so that all children can tap this important source of vocabulary growth. Reading contests, brief oral reports about books read, and providing the opportunity for students to share feelings and perspectives gained from reading are only a few of the many ways teachers can encourage their students to read.

Applications for Teaching: Guidelines for Developing Comprehension and Vocabulary

Several possible applications for developing reading comprehension can be drawn from the research on reading.

1. Use prereading discussions and advance organizers to help students better comprehend new reading materials. Prereading discussions both actuate students' knowledge and build their interest. Advance organizers, brief prefaces to reading materials, help students relate the new information in the text to their existing knowledge structures. (Advance organizers are discussed in more detail later in this chapter.) Both can help students activate their prior knowledge to make reading more meaningful.

2. Help students understand the purpose for their reading. Knowing the purpose for reading usually helps students' comprehension. Also, the point of view that students take in reading affects which content they will learn and which they will not (Anderson, 1984; Vosniadou, Pearson, & Rogers, 1988).

3. Give students feedback on their reading performance. Practice with feedback on different comprehension tasks (such as requiring students to summarize orally a short passage, asking them to judge the validity of inferences from a passage) is necessary to continue to sharpen reading skills. Students should be given frequent practice in reading for comprehension and receive feedback for their efforts (Stevens, 1988).

4. Encourage students to use context to build their vocabularies. Reading is the key to vocabulary development. Help students recognize that the context for unknown words contains many clues to their meanings. Also, the words themselves often contain clues. Students who recognize these clues will be better "word learners."

PRACTICE EXERCISE 5–2   DEVELOPING READING FLEXIBILITY

One way to become a better reader is to develop flexible reading rates. Obtain some reading materials that require varying rates: careful, normal, rapid, and skimming. A textbook, for example, would be read carefully. A novel or short story would be read normally. Any review materials—perhaps the rereading of a textbook chapter—can be read rapidly, while a newsmagazine can serve as an excellent source for material to skim.

When you have obtained the appropriate reading materials, estimate the number of words (a per-line count multiplied by lines on a page or in a column will do) so that you can have approximately 2,500 words from each source. When you have done this, read each item as you customarily would read it, and time yourself. Then divide 2,500 words by the number of minutes and seconds you spent reading to get words per minute. Your words per minute rate should be different for the different styles of reading. If this is the case, fine. If not, decide whether you need to slow down or speed up some of your reading.

Practice reading at different rates for different purposes. To do this, use your careful reading rate and the normal rate you just measured as your starting point. Was your normal rate comfortable? Could you easily recall the material you read? If your careful rate was not slower than your normal rate, ask yourself if you learned more while reading carefully than while reading normally. If so, speed up your normal rate. If not, slow down your careful rate. A general rule of thumb is that rapid reading ought to be between 25 and 50 percent faster than normal reading, and skimming should be between 50 and 100 percent faster than normal. If you didn't obtain differences close to this, practice rapid reading and skimming by reading standard lengths of materials with a timer set to go off at a time that indicates a certain rate of reading. Your goal, of course, is to try to read the passage before the time goes off while retaining as much comprehension as possible.

The Adult Reader

As students proceed through junior and senior high school into adulthood, the demands on their reading abilities become more complex. One particularly important demand is the need to develop flexible reading rates (Harris & Sipey, 1985). That is, readers should learn to vary their rates in accord with the demands of different reading tasks. Harris and Sipey suggest four rates appropriate to different purposes: skimming, rapid, normal, and careful.

Skimming rate:	Appropriate to finding references, getting the general point or gist of an article
Rapid rate:	Used to reread familiar material, to get information for temporary use
Normal rate:	Used in finding answers to questions, noting details, and relating details to main ideas
Careful rate:	Employed to master content, to read poetry, to learn details in sequence

Harris maintains that flexibility can be taught but that most persons are not flexible readers (Harris & Sipey, 1985).

The majority of readers with about a twelfth-grade education have a silent reading rate of about 200 words per minute (Harris & Sipey, 1985), but there is a wide range of individual differences. Interestingly, silent reading rates tend to be about the same rate at which persons can listen and comprehend speech. As we have previously noted, the controlling factor in reading comprehension seems to be how the information is processed rather than the physical activities of reading.

Adjunct Aids for Comprehension.   Techniques designed to facilitate students' comprehension of reading materials are called **adjunct aids**. How they affect reading comprehension has been the topic of a great deal of research, and there are several applications that are especially helpful for teachers. Most of the research on adjunct aids has grown out of the early work of Ausubel (1960, 1980) and Rothkopf (1970). In general, adjunct aids can be classed into one of four categories: objectives, questions, advance organizers, and active response modes (Anderson, 1981). We will examine each of the adjunct aids more closely below.

Objectives are statements of the learning that should occur from reading a set of materials (see Chapter Twelve). Objectives can be written at several levels of sophistication from very simplistic (names, facts, figures) to very complex (analysis of content, evaluation of ideas). Researchers commonly investigate the effects of objectives by examining *intentional learning* (the learning of information specified in the objectives) and *incidental learning* (the learning of information *not* specified in the objectives). In general, when the amount of time spent reading is not a concern, research supports the following statements: (1) unsophisticated, lower-order objectives increase intentional learning at the expense of incidental learning; (2) sophisticated, complex objectives increase intentional learning but have little or no effect on incidental learning; and (3) objectives are most beneficial if they require complex cognitive activities (e.g., analysis), if only a few are used, and when they are distributed throughout a passage (Andre, 1987).

Not all the results of research on the use of objectives as adjunct aids to reading have been positive, however (See Andre, 1987, for a good review of the area). When the time allotted for reading is the same for groups of students given objectives as it is for those not given objectives, there is often no positive effect of objectives on overall comprehension. Nonetheless, objectives have been observed to increase intentional learning in almost all studies.

Students can be asked to answer questions as they read. In general, when the amount of time spent reading does not matter, the following conclusions are true: (1) questions requiring complex processing result in greater overall recall of content than questions requiring only simple processing, (2) questions presented prior to the reading material facilitate intentional learning but have no particular effect on incidental learning, and (3) questions that follow the reading increase intentional learning significantly and also produce smaller but reliable increases in incidental learning (see Halpain et al., 1985; Wong, 1985). When the amount of time is the same for readers with and without questions, however, questions have a smaller effect on comprehension (Wong, 1985).

Advance organizers are overviews of major ideas in reading materials (see Chapter Three, "Memory and Concepts"). They are written at a high level of abstraction as a "framework" for what will follow. They are not intended to provide specific information (Ausubel, 1960, 1980). Early research on advance organizers had many methodological flaws (see Faw & Waller, 1976; Mayer, 1979, for discussions), and these reports are of dubious value. However, more recent work indicates that if the organizers themselves are well learned, comprehension of subsequent reading materials is facilitated (Corkill, Glover, Bruning, & Krug, 1988). In addition, organizers seem to have a positive effect on transfer and appear to be most useful for facilitating recall among students of low ability or poor educational backgrounds (Corkill, 1988).

Active response modes are activities such as underlining, highlighting, and note taking. Although some research results suggest that causing students to use such active response modes has no effect on comprehension (see Kiewra, in press), more recent work has generally indicated that note taking and summarizing may be a valuable means of helping students to remember new information from reading passages and integrate it with their existing schemata (Kiewra, in press).

Applications for Teaching: Guidelines for Using Adjunct Aids

An overall view of the research supports the following uses of adjunct aids by classroom teachers.

1. Write objectives at higher levels of learning. Objectives and questions are most effective in increasing intentional learning when they require sophisticated thinking (see Chapter Fourteen) (Andre, 1987; Halpain et al., 1985).

2. Allow time for using adjunct aids. Readers utilizing adjunct aids need more time for reading than when adjunct aids are not used. To quote Reynolds, Standiford, and Anderson (1979), "time is cheap and achievement is dear."

3. Use advance organizers when introducing unfamiliar topics. Advance organizers seem especially helpful for novel material. They are particularly effective for students with poor backgrounds and students who learn somewhat slowly (Corkill et al., 1988).

4. Encourage note taking. Note-taking skills, especially those in which students organize new information into meaningful frameworks, should be taught as a means of helping students integrate new knowledge into their existing memory structures (Kiewra, in press).

5. Avoid trivial objectives. Objectives and questions should deal with meaningful aspects of the reading materials. A few meaningful objectives can effectively guide student learning.

6. Use objectives and questions when you wish to target learning. Do not use objectives or questions unless you are willing to give up some incidental learning. Students will invest most of their learning time on topics you single out in your questions or objectives (Halpain et al., 1985).

7. Distribute the adjunct aids throughout the materials. Objectives and questions should be distributed such that one or two are presented every so often within a relatively short segment of the reading materials.

About Writing

Complementary to the cognitive skill of reading is writing, the production and organization of connected written discourse. Like reading, writing almost always is meaningful (Whiteman, 1983); it involves more than scratching or typing a series of symbols on a page of paper. Writing is a cognitive skill that is influenced by the writer's perspective, understanding of the intended audience, ability to use the language, and many other factors. While the cognitive processes involved in writing are complex and interrelated, they can be understood readily through the use of an information-processing model of writing.

An Information-Processing Model of Writing

John Hayes and Linda Flower (e.g., Carey & Flower, in press; Geisler, Kaufer, & Hayes, 1985) have formulated a very helpful model of the cognitive processes involved in writing. A simplified version of their **information-processing model** is pictured in Figure 5–5. As you can see, the model's emphasis is on working memory, with three major processes occurring here: planning, translating, and reviewing. We will examine each more closely in the following sections.

FIGURE 5–5   THE FLOWER AND HAYES MODEL OF WRITING

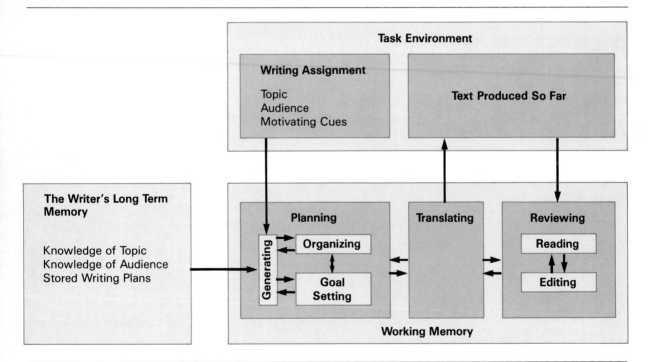

Adapted from Flower & Hayes, 1983.

Planning.   Planning involves setting writing goals based on information from the task environment and long-term memory. The *task environment* may include a teacher's assignment ("Write a two-page essay on the role of the 'yellow press' in the Spanish-American War"), feedback from a teacher ("This paragraph needs a good topic sentence"), and information about who the audience will be ("The best essay will be published in the school newspaper," or "We will be reading our paragraphs out loud in class"). Each of these kinds of information, of course, influences a student's planning.

Information from **long-term memory** may incorporate factual information ("I need to work in the fact that William Randolph Hearst's newspapers were particularly likely to engage in 'yellow press' "), knowledge of different forms of writing ("Let's see, a good essay should have a snappy topic sentence"), and an understanding of the audience ("Ms. Smith likes alliteration; I'll work some into this paragraph"). Clearly, the knowledge a student has about the audience, about the form of writing to be produced, and about writing in general makes a big difference in the quality of planning (Englert, Stewart, & Hiebert, 1988). In part, the individual differences we see in students' abilities to write are due to knowledge differences.

Three subprocesses are thought to be involved in planning: generating, organizing, and goal setting. *Generating* refers to obtaining relevant information from long-term memory ("What was the name of that ship sunk in Havana harbor?") and the task environment ("Hmmm. It has to be two pages long"). *Organizing* involves selecting and organizing information into a plan for writing ("Let's see, I'll start by defining 'yellow journalism,' then I'll give some reasons for it. After that, I'll work in some of Hearst's activities and describe how the American public was influenced by the papers. I think I'll finish with the sinking of the battleship *Maine* and how the papers urged a declaration of war"). Finally, *goal setting* is the subprocess in which the writer evaluates the relevance of information he or she has available ("As neat as old Teddy Roosevelt is, he doesn't really fit here. Maybe the press's relationship with Congress does, though").

As you can see, the subprocesses of planning are highly interactive and dependent on one another. Goals can hardly be set without generating information. The generation of information will influence goal setting. Decisions in goal setting will then further influence what new information is generated and how it is organized.

Generating information, organizing it, and setting writing goals compromise the planning stage of writing.

Translating. The second major process in the Flower and Hayes model is translating, in which the student's thoughts are translated into phrases and sentences. According to Hayes and Flower (1986), the writing completed during translating is usually in the form of complete sentences, often followed by self-questioning ("Let's see, how do I want to say that there were some questionable issues surrounding the sinking of the *Maine?*").

Translating begins with the first part of the writer's plan ("I'll define 'yellow journalism' "), which is then transformed into phrases or a sentence ("What's a good way to say that?"). When one sentence is completed, the writer typically asks himself or herself a question about the next part of the writing plan and how he or she wants to express it. The next sentence is then written and the writer once again returns to the plan. This process is cycled over and over until the writing assignment is complete.

The quality of the translating process depends on the quality of planning, the writer's knowledge of the content area, and the writer's knowledge of syntax—how to put words together in a correct fashion. Translating and planning are highly interactive because the writer must return to the plan over and over again during writing and because the writing plan may change if there are problems in translating ("Drat! I can't remember the name of the correspondent in Havana. I'll have to be more general").

Reviewing.   Reviewing is the third major process in the Hayes and Flower model. In reviewing, the writer improves the quality of what he or she has written by reading and editing. In *reading* the finished product (or a part of it), the writer is sensitive to ideas from the plan that have been left out, superfluous information that detracts from the quality of writing, and mechanical errors. *Editing* involves rewriting, moving materials from one place to another, and changing wording. Clearly, the writer's knowledge of writing, especially its mechanics, are important for revising.

Reviewing interacts with both planning and translating. In order to properly review a written work, the writer must refer back to his or her goals. In addition, new information may need to be generated to enhance the written product, or a check for extraneous material may need to be performed. Reading and editing, of course, require translating as parts of a passage are rewritten and other parts are checked for clarity and grammatical correctness.

Applications for Teaching: Improving Students' Writing

Beyond helping to clarify the cognitive processes involved in writing, the Hayes and Flower model has some important implications for teaching writing. Following is a set of guidelines for improving students' writing based on the Hayes and Flower model and on our review of the literature on teaching writing.

1. Stress goal setting. To write well, students must know what their goal is (Applebee, 1988). Younger students can be helped to set writing goals by prompting them to jot down story ideas, what feelings they want to share, or what idea they want to describe. After writing, they can be asked to compare the goal they set for themselves with what their writing actually tells. Older students can be helped to set goals by first writing a very brief précis or summary of what they are working on. A comparison of the finished product to the précis is a helpful way of checking to see if their goals have been met.

2. Encourage the use of outlines for planning. Research on the composing process has consistently shown that outlining improves the quality of writing (Hull, 1987). Outlining is a skill in and of itself and should be taught. Especially with beginning or poor writers, outlining what is to be written should precede any writing. Outlining also can be helpful in reviewing what has been written.

3. Encourage idea generation. A characteristic typical of skilled writers is their ability to think of many different ideas related to the topic they are writing about (Quinn & Matsuhashi, 1985; Raphael & Kirschner, 1985). As we will see in Chapter Eight, there are some effective ways to enhance students' generation of ideas that teachers can employ with a minimum of effort.

4. Emphasize the evaluation of resources. Writing goals can be met only when students have the necessary resources (Hayes & Flower, 1986; Raphael & Kirschner, 1985). For example, if a third-grader wants to write on "how volcanoes work," she must first find and then learn the content she will incorporate in her paper. Students' evaluation of resources can be facilitated by having them study the goal and outline they've developed and having them ask themselves if they have the information to complete the writing task. If they do not have the necessary resources, library skills may have to be taught in order to help students learn how to gather needed resources.

5. Focus student planning on the communication of meaning. Good writers plan the meaning they are going to communicate to readers, while poor writers focus their planning on mechanics (Diamond, 1985). The mechanics of writing *are* important, but the major emphasis in composition should be on the expression of meaning (Geisler, Kaufer, & Hayes, 1985).

6. Provide extensive practice in writing. To learn to write well, one must write often and learn to improve. The consensus of scholars is that the poor quality of so many students' writing skills is due to the fact that they are not required to write enough (see Applebee, 1988).

7. Have students practice revising their papers. Skilled writers typically make the revision of their papers an important part of the writing process (Hull, 1985). Students should be encouraged to set papers aside for a day or so and then critically reread them. Often, it is helpful for students to read their papers aloud to someone else, as they may hear errors they do not "see." Revising is especially helpful if students have stated a goal for their paper and developed an outline (Odoroff, 1985). The paper can then be checked to see if it meets the criteria they set.

8. Have students correct and rewrite papers. Feedback is beneficial only if the learner uses it to improve his or her performance. One way to improve students' use of feedback is to require that they correct and rewrite graded papers. Students should not see rewriting as a form of punishment, however, but as a way of better expressing themselves. The benefits of rewriting should be stressed to students. Rewriting not only focuses students' attention on the feedback they have received but also gives them practice in writing correctly.

9. Employ peer editing. One way to help students learn to do a better job of revising their own papers is to have them edit the papers of their classmates (Benton & Blohm, 1985). Students can be assigned to teams of two each who first plan and write a paper and then trade papers for editing. Each student then edits the other's paper for meeting its goal and following its outline. In addition, the editor also should check for coherence and mechanics. Editing is a skill in its own right and can be developed only through consistent practice.

10. Encourage writing in all classes. The teaching of writing is not just the responsibility of language arts and English teachers. Writing is an extremely useful tool for teachers in all content areas. Not only does writing allow students to organize their own thinking about concepts and issues, but it gives teachers considerable insight into their students' understanding (or lack of understanding). Well used, writing can give students a unique way of better understanding a topic, expressing themselves, and getting feedback. Science, math, business, and social studies teachers need to go beyond merely having students write, however, by giving their students detailed feedback on how effective their writing is.

Summary

Humans have a special aptitude for language. From earliest infancy, babies can distinguish between important categories of speech sounds and can produce sounds. The earliest sound-making—crying and cooing—is biologically determined. Similarly, babbling seems to be "built in" to the development of human infants and begins at the age of about four months. In babbling, a huge number of sounds are produced, but they have no meaning. At about the age of one, children utter their first words. Vocalization and communication have been developing side by side in the first year; now they become linked in meaningful speech.

By about eighteen months of age, children begin to combine words into sentences. Inflections soon appear but often are overgeneralized (e.g., "Papa goed," "two peoples"). Vocabulary growth undergoes a spurt at about the same time, and as many as several words a day can be learned. By three and one-half or four, many of the basic elements of language are established, and some of the basic foundations of literacy are beginning to emerge.

A major accomplishment of the early elementary years is becoming literate—learning to read and write. Reading involves several components. The major observable aspect of reading is the movements made by the eyes. Eye movements across the printed page are referred to as saccades, while the stops are called fixations. Information is gathered during the fixations. Patterns of saccades and fixations vary considerably between good and poor readers. Training eye movements in order to improve reading is not effective, however, because these movements are controlled by the student's cognitive processes.

Reading is a dynamic, interactional process with both the content and the reader contributing to what is learned. Attention, as in all cognitive processes, is essential to reading. The cognitive processes in reading can be viewed in two stages: decoding (obtaining the meaning of individual words) and comprehending (understanding the gist of what is read). Good readers decode automatically and concentrate on comprehension, while poor readers struggle with decoding and often comprehend far less.

Learning to read occurs in stages: the transition to reading, beginning reading, and the continuing development of comprehension skills and vocabulary in the middle grades. At each level, learners' goals are different. Early on, children need to "crack the code" in order to learn to relate printed information to the oral language they already know. By middle-elementary grades, children are "reading to learn" as reading becomes a way to gather information. Teachers, of course, need to recognize that each stage of reading has its own demands for instruction.

Writing is the complementary process to reading. Like reading, writing is complex, involving a wide range of cognitive activities. In the cognitive model developed by Hayes and Flower, three major processes in writing occur in the working memory: planning, translating, and reviewing.

When they plan, writers generate ideas, organize their thoughts, and set goals. Generating ideas involves selecting information from the task environment and long-term memory. Organizing results in a plan for writing. Goal-setting refers to determining the purpose for the writing task.

In translating, the second major process, writers turn ideas into phrases and sentences, while reviewing refers to a writer's evaluation of a written work after it has been completed. Reviewing includes two subprocesses, reading and editing, which improve the final product.

The model of writing proposed by Hayes and Flower and a review of research led to a set of guidelines for teaching writing. These guidelines stress the importance of practice and feedback. They also emphasize the communication of meaning rather than the mechanical aspects of writing.

Suggested Readings

Alexander, J. E. (1988). *Teaching reading*, 3rd ed. Glenview, IL: Scott, Foresman.
> *Alexander's book is typical of texts designed for preservice educators wishing to learn about how to teach reading. The contents of this book are well within reach of any reader of the current chapter.*

Ellis, A., & Beattie, G. (1986). *The psychology of language and communication*. New York: Guilford.
> *This volume is written at an introductory level and is an excellent source for students who wish to expand their knowledge of language.*

Just, M., & Carpenter, P. (1987). *The psychology of reading and language comprehension*. Boston: Allyn and Bacon.
> *Just and Carpenter's volume provides an excellent description of reading processes. Although written for advanced students, the volume is highly readable and within the grasp of students who have completed this chapter.*

Kessel, F. (1988). *The development of language and language researchers.* Hillsdale, NJ: Erlbaum.

   Kessel's edited volume is an excellent compilation of readings in language and language development. Most striking is its commentary on the field of language study.

McKeown, M. G., & Curtis, M. E. (Eds.). (1987). *The nature of vocabulary acquisition.* Hillsdale, NJ: Erlbaum.

   McKeown and Curtis have edited an extremely interesting book focused on a very specific area of language development, vocabulary acquisition. Students interested in vocabulary development will find the book a rich source of ideas.

Tierney, R. J., Anders, P. L., & Mitchell, J. N. (1987). *Understanding readers' understanding.* Hillsdale, NJ: Erlbaum.

   This edited book is an excellent source of readings focused on reading comprehension.

CHAPTER
6

Problem Solving and Creativity

Problems may be defined simply. Any time a person wants to be doing something else or wants to be somewhere else but is unable to make it happen, a problem exists. Problem solving is a highly sophisticated form of learning (see Ausubel et al., 1978; Gagne, 1987). Problems and the search for solutions to them are a part of every person's life. Historically, teachers have aspired to teach their students to reason, to think, to create, and to be responsible citizens. Even critics of schools who want a return to the basics do not dispute these goals. They may differ in how such goals should be achieved but not on the centrality of these goals for education.

A common theme runs through all these goals: education should prepare students for dealing with their future life conditions. The eminent educational philosopher John Dewey long ago identified this process of "dealing with life conditions" as problem solving (1910). He reasoned that living and learning consisted of confronting and solving series of problems and that every human action (including the decision not to respond) represented a choice among alternatives. Dewey and his followers held that if there were no alternatives or choices—that is to say, no problems—then individuals would probably not learn.

Dewey and other adherents to this view pointed out that while each human act occurs in response to a problem, there is great variation in the solutions people devise. Simply, some solutions are better than others. The goal of education in their eyes becomes that of improving the problem-solving abilities of all students.

We have included this chapter to help you provide your future students with learning experiences that will improve their abilities to deal with life's problems—experiences that will develop their problem-solving abilities and help them become more creative problem solvers. We begin by briefly surveying some historical approaches to problem solving and examining the information-processing approach to problem solving. Then we focus on research that examines the role of knowledge in problem solving. Next, we examine applications from problem-solving research that will help you enhance the problem-solving ability of your students. Finally, we examine creativity and ways in which you may help your students become more creative.

OBJECTIVES

After reading this chapter, you should be able to meet the following objectives.

1. Improve the efficiency of your own problem solving.

2. Solve problems by using each of the heuristic methods described in this chapter.

3. Develop a strategy for teaching problem solving to your students.

4. Write a description of the process you follow in solving a problem with an unknown number of solutions. Identify the solution paths, problem spaces, and problem searches you utilize.

5. Engage in self-management activities that will enhance your own creative abilities.

Problem Solving

We begin our discussion of problem solving by examining a set of historically important views of the problem-solving process. Although each of these perspectives was developed not long after the turn of the century, they remain important to our understanding of problem solving. The three historical perspectives we examine are those developed by E. L. Thorndike, by John Dewey, and by Wolfgang Köhler of the Gestalt school. The three views form the foundation for modern views of problem solving.

E. L. Thorndike's Trial and Error Approach to Problem Solving

E. L. Thorndike (1879–1949) was one of the earliest and perhaps the greatest learning theorist of all time. His interests were far ranging, spanning almost all areas of contemporary educational psychology. In his lifetime, Thorndike published 507 books, journal articles, and monographs. His influence on early American psychology was so great that Edward Tolman, an eminent learning theorist in his own right, suggested that the "psychology of learning . . . has been and still is a matter of agreeing or disagreeing with Thorndike" (1939, p. 11).

FIGURE 6–1   THORNDIKE'S PUZZLE BOX

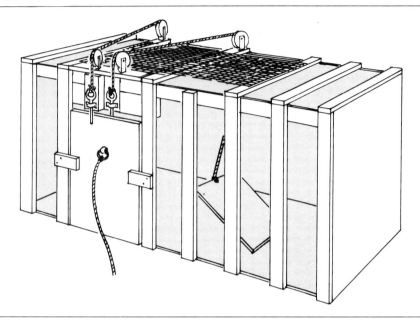

Source: E. L. Thorndike, Animal intelligence. *Psychological Review Monographs*, Supplement 2, #8, 1898. Copyright 1898 by the American Psychological Association. Adapted by permission of the American Psychological Association.

In his most famous series of experiments, Thorndike (1898, 1911) placed cats (and, less well remembered, dogs) in wooden cages. The cages were constructed in various ways, typically with a handle sticking up from the center of the cage so that any firm touch on the handle would open a door and allow escape (see Figure 6–1). Thorndike arranged events so that each cat was hungry when placed in a cage and food was available to it if it could figure out how to get out of the cage. The situation the cats found themselves in, of course, fits our definition of a problem—being in one situation, wanting (presumably) to be in another, but not knowing how to get there.

Thorndike observed the cats carefully and kept detailed records of their movements as they tried to escape. He noted that the cats would try several behaviors until they hit the handle by accident. He further noted on repeated trials that the cats made their escapes more and more quickly. Ultimately, when the cats were placed in the cage, they would almost immediately perform the handle-pushing behavior that got them out of the cage during previous trials. The cats' actions led Thorndike to explain such problem solving—and all learning, for that matter—as *trial-and-error* learning.

From his experiments with cats, Thorndike concluded that their learning was incremental (that improvement was gradual, coming in small bits and pieces). He further suggested that their problem solving was not directed by thinking or reasoning:

> The cat does not look over the situation, much less think it over, and then decide what to do. It bursts out at once into the activities which instinct and experience have settled on as suitable reactions to the situation, "confinement when hungry with food outside." It does not ever in the course of its success realize that such an act brings food and therefore decide to do it and henceforth do it immediately from decision instead of impulse. *(1898, p. 45)*

Thorndike was later to argue that all mammals, including humans, learned and solved problems in much the same way (1911). For Thorndike, human problem solving was similar to that of lower organisms in that it was built on trial and error, it was incremental, and it proceeded without thinking or reasoning.

John Dewey's Pragmatic Approach to Problem Solving

While John Dewey is best known as a philosopher of education, he spent several years at the turn of the century immersed in the development of the functionalist school of psychology (Charles, 1987). As we discussed in Chapter Two, functionalists were concerned with developing techniques in psychology and education that would be applicable to real-world problems (Carr, 1925; Charles, 1987). This emphasis on the application of psychology to education was apparent in all of Dewey's work and definitely influenced his thoughts about problem solving.

From his many observations, Dewey described a sequence of steps that effective problem solvers followed (1910, 1933). These steps still are used in the development of programs to teach people various aspects of problem solving (see Cormier & Cormier, 1985; Dixon, 1987).

Presentation of the Problem.   Clearly, problem solutions cannot occur unless individuals encounter problems. In this step, two kinds of directions are taken by psychologists who work with the development of problem-solving skills (Dixon, 1987). First, in training oriented toward solving personal problems, emphasis is placed on helping people become aware of problems they may not have previously noticed. Second, in more formal problem-solving training, emphasis is placed on the teacher's role in clearly presenting problems. The teacher must ensure that all the information necessary to solve a problem is either presented to students or has been previously mastered by them.

Problem Definition.   Defining the problem is crucial to solving it. Almost any problem can be defined in several ways, and each definition is likely to lead to different attempts to solve it. Training in problem solving stresses students' abilities to define problems in as many ways as possible to provide the widest array of subsequent activities that will lead to problem solutions (Dixon, 1987). An example of such problem solving can be seen in a person who wants but cannot afford a new stereo. Is this problem one of making more money, saving more money, altering attitudes toward a new stereo, or obtaining credit? The problem can be defined in each of these ways and each definition leads to different actions on the part of the problem solver. Certainly, helping students visualize many ways of solving problems has a greater chance of leading them to satisfactory solutions (Dixon, 1987).

Development of Hypotheses.   Once a problem is defined, the next step is to make as many hypotheses as possible for solving the problem. The more hypotheses or alternatives a person generates, the greater the chances that a satisfactory solution will be found. Procedures for facilitating the generation of alternatives are described later in the chapter.

Testing Hypotheses.   Generating a large number of hypotheses for solving a problem places problem solvers in the position of having to choose among the hypotheses. That is, if a student develops several hypotheses for obtaining a stereo, he or she will have to settle on one of the alternatives. For this reason, psychologists who train students in problem-solving skills emphasize the testing and evaluation of hypotheses (Cormier & Cormier, 1985) in terms of the potential benefits they provide and their possible drawbacks. Because most of the problems students encounter (choosing a major, finding a date, purchasing a stereo, and the like) can be solved in a variety of ways, possible solutions should be carefully explored before a decision is made.

Selection of the Best Hypothesis.   Once a person has evaluated the possible ways in which a problem can be solved, he or she should choose the most attractive hypothesis. Psychologists stress the use of decision-making skills in this step of the problem-solving process (see Dixon, 1987). Typically, students are asked to weigh the advantages and disadvantages of each possible hypothesis and to select the hypothesis that promises the greatest advantages.

Solutions to problems are often seen in flashes of insight.

Insight: A Gestalt View of Problem Solving

As we saw in Chapter Two, Gestalt psychology arose in the early part of the twentieth century in reaction to structuralism and functionalism. Not surprisingly, the Gestalt view of problem solving was quite different from that of either Thorndike or Dewey. Wolfgang Köhler, the founder of that branch of Gestalt psychology most concerned with problem solving, suggested that problems bring about a cognitive imbalance in people, an imbalance that they seek to resolve. That is, problems spur people into action until the problems are solved and cognitive balance is achieved. Köhler also suggested that people ponder problems, examining all the parts of problem situations, until they suddenly see solutions in flashes of insight. Köhler strongly disagreed with Thorndike's view that problem solving was a trial-and-error process. He argued that there are no intermediate, incremental steps and that problems are either solved or unsolved with no points in between.

Köhler based his writings on a famous series of experiments he conducted using apes (1925).* The animals were placed in problem situations where available objects, if properly used, could be employed to achieve a solution to the problem. In one of these experiments, fruit was suspended from the wire roof of the cage in such a manner that it could be reached only by stacking up several boxes scattered on the cage floor. The purpose was to see if the apes would use the materials available to them to obtain the fruit.

In general, Köhler's apes behaved in ways that could be called insightful. When the apes found solutions, these solutions appeared to be sudden and complete. Köhler extended his hypotheses to human

---

*Not as well remembered is the fact that Köhler also did problem-solving research with chickens. Apparently apes were better for demonstrating insight than were chickens!

beings (as supported originally by Alpert, 1928, in a study with human children) and found basically the same results. We can summarize the Gestalt description of problem solving and contrast it with Thorndike's and Dewey's description as follows.

Identification of the Problem.   Like Dewey, Köhler suggested that a problem had to be recognized before any action could take place. Thorndike's position, of course, also included the presentation or recognition of a problem as the beginning point in the search for problem solutions.

Incubation Period.   Köhler's observations led him to conclude that problem solvers engaged in considerable thought during early phases of problem solving. This incubation or presolution period, Köhler felt, was characterized by the problem solver mentally trying out a number of possible solutions. Such cognitive activity, of course, was denied in Thorndike's view of problem solving. It fit well, however, with Dewey's description of the hypotheses-generation and testing steps, although Dewey was less concerned with specific cognitive functions.

Insight.   When a correct hypothesis was hit upon during the incubation period, the solution occurred suddenly and completely. Köhler called this understanding of problem solutions *insight*. Here Köhler was in direct conflict with Thorndike's trial-and-error approach, but he was again not far afield from Dewey. Dewey, however, did not directly concern himself with the concept of insight in problem solving (1910, 1933).

Memorability of Insightful Solutions.   Köhler believed that problem solutions achieved through insight were extremely memorable. The memorability of problem solutions was not described by Thorndike; Dewey felt that the problem solver had to work to retain the solution for possible future use.

Generalization of Insightful Solutions.   For Köhler, as for Dewey, the generalization of knowledge was important. Köhler considered generalization a natural outcome of insight, while Dewey thought more effort was required by the problem solver. Thorndike also discussed generalization but from a perspective that did not include cognition.

The Gestalt view of problem solving is compatible with that of Dewey, although it clearly places much more emphasis on cognitive factors such as incubation and insight. There is much less agreement between the Gestalt view and Thorndike's. For Gestalt psychologists, problem solving and all human learning were seen as insightful, all-or-none, and controlled almost totally by thinking.

Current Approaches to Problem Solving

In recent years psychologists following an information-processing approach have developed computer models of human problem solving. These models and the research they have generated have given rise to many ideas about how the human mind operates during problem solving. Information-processing psychologists believe the most important facet of problem solving is the construction of a problem representation (see Hayes, in press–a; Stein, in press).

To construct a **problem representation** a person must understand four aspects of a problem: (1) the initial state, (2) the goal state, (3) the operators, and (4) precisely how the operators are restricted or unrestricted. The initial state is the situation in which a person finds himself or herself when a problem is recognized. Suppose you are playing chess and your opponent makes a move and places your king in check. A complete understanding of your current position in the game is essential to solving your problem. Many college students have

Incomplete problem representations cause difficulties in solving problems.

"I think you should be more explicit here in step two."

trouble deciding on their major. A successful resolution of this problem depends in large part on their ability to understand their initial state, in this case, their academic strengths and weaknesses, financial position, likes and dislikes, knowledge about professions, and so on. Clearly, the more adequately students understand their initial state, the more effective they will be at solving problems.

The goal state is simply the outcome a problem solver seeks. Clearly understanding the goal you want to reach is extremely important. The chess example presents a relatively straightforward goal state—taking the king out of check. The problem of choosing a major is a different matter. Students' goals often are not clearly defined; it thus is very difficult for them to determine what actions to take in choosing a major. When goals are understood clearly, the paths a person can take become much more explicit.

In addition to an understanding of the initial and goal states, a good problem representation includes an understanding of the operators, which, in information-processing terminology, are the actions a person can take in solving a problem. Consider the chess problem again. If you find yourself in check, you have very few actions open to you—you are limited to moving chess pieces or withdrawing from the game. In more ambiguous problems such as choosing a major, the number of operators available to problem solvers is far greater. Among the operators a student may choose are sampling courses in different areas and seeking vocational counseling. Information-processing psychologists suggest that the more we understand about the actions we can perform in solving problems—that is, the more we know about our operators—the more effective we will be in solving problems.

Understanding the restrictions on operators is the last feature of problem representation. Operators often have restrictions or limits and problem solvers must understand them if they are to fully comprehend a problem. The operator of moving chess pieces is restricted in several ways. Some of the spaces on the playing board will contain other pieces, and so you cannot move your pieces onto those locations, kings can only move one space at a time, knights must move in an L-shaped pattern—each piece has a set of restrictions placed on its use. A chess problem is not solvable unless the restrictions on the operators are understood. In the more personal problem of choosing a major, restrictions are defined both by the situation (a course, for example, necessarily lasts a certain number of weeks) and by the person involved ("I can't afford to just take courses until I find something that I like").

The way in which people represent problems determines the actions they consider to solve the problems. If we find ourselves at one end of a field and we want to be at the other, our operator may be walking. However, there are many paths we could take in using our operator. Those paths that connect the initial state to the goal are known as **solution paths**. The total number of actions a problem solver considers possible (whether correct or incorrect) is called the **problem space** (Figure 6-2). As Hayes (in press–a) points out, problem spaces are determined by problem solvers themselves, not by the problems. That is, possible actions are identified by the problem solver. There may be more possible actions than those allowed by the restrictions on the operators (for example, responding to the chess problem by making two moves in a row) or fewer possible actions (for example, not recognizing that one of the pieces can be moved to protect the king).

Let's take a look at some problems that illustrate the information-processing view of problem representation.

> Ed is running for his life from a tribe of hostile cannibals. He has reached a river and must cross it to save his life. Ed has rapidly constructed a small raft from readily available materials in the forest and is now ready to paddle across the river. He has a problem, however; he has only one source of food, a bunch of bananas. He must take these with him or he will surely starve. Ed also has his pet chimpanzee along. Ed wants to save his chimp from certain death by taking him across the river. To further complicate matters, Ed has a leopard that he has raised since it was a cub, and Ed knows he needs the leopard for protection on the other side of the river. All this is trouble enough, but the situation is further compounded by the following: (1) Ed can take only one of the three things across the river with him at one time; (2) if Ed leaves the chimp with the bananas, the chimp will eat them all; (3) if Ed leaves the leopard with the chimp, the leopard will kill the chimp. How can we advise Ed in solving his problem? Remember, since there are piranha in the river, Ed and all of his belongings must cross the river on the raft; they can't swim across.

Many people have trouble with river-crossing problems. Once people are reminded that Ed can take objects across the river in *both* directions, however, they typically solve the problem easily. That is, once people understand the restrictions clearly, they can solve the problem.

Your reaction to the river-crossing problem can be used to make some points about problem representation. Ed's problem was to get himself and his belongings across the river. Luckily, many problems

FIGURE 6–2   A REPRESENTATION OF PROBLEM SPACE

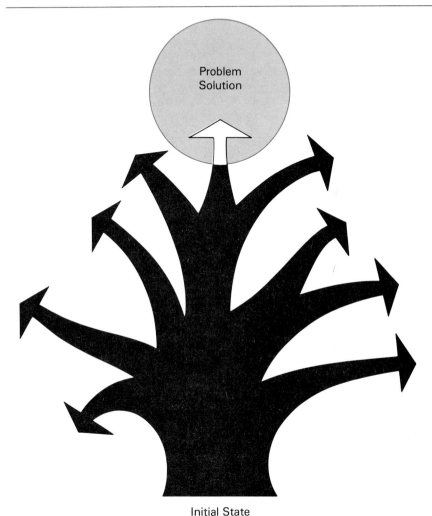

Problem
Solution

Initial State

clearly specify actions (operators) we can take to get from where we are (the initial state) to where we want to be (the goal state). Ed's operator was paddling across the river on a raft. Unfortunately, there were restrictions on Ed's operator (as there are in most problems), things that could happen if his belongings were left in the wrong combination. Obviously, if you want to successfully solve a problem such as Ed's, you must represent all you know about the problem in your thinking. Leaving any information out of your representation of a problem is likely to lead to an incorrect solution.*

Although many problems present all four necessary components very clearly, some do not, and so problem solvers must infer them from available information. No doubt you have seen the following type of problem.

> Joe, Schmoe, and Moe all live on the same block. They live in red, green, and blue houses. Joe doesn't live in the green or the blue house. Schmoe doesn't live in the green house. What house does each person live in?

While the initial state and the goal in this problem are clearly presented, the operators (identifying the person about which most is known) and their restrictions (we must infer that only one person lives in each house) aren't mentioned directly. You, or any other problem solver, often must infer information to develop a complete problem representation. Such problems may not necessarily be any more difficult than others; they simply require more inferences.

Problems such as the two we have presented can be defined clearly. The initial state, the operators, the restrictions on the operators, and the goals are fairly obvious. Unfortunately (or fortunately, depending on your point of view), real-life problems (such as choosing a major) are seldom as easily defined as those we have described (Dixon, 1987). **Ill-defined problems** (Hayes, in press–a) require the problem solver to contribute actively to the representation of the problem. Consider a problem involving the construction of a bridge somewhere in rural Arizona. The initial statement of the problem was presented as follows:

1. A two-lane blacktop road is to be constructed between towns *A* and *B*.

2. A river crosses the proposed path of the road at point *C*.

3. The river is dry six months of the year but reaches to within three feet of its banks at the crossing point after spring flooding two out of every five years. The other three of the five years, the river reaches within ten feet of the bank top.

4. The river has flooded over its banks once in the last seventy-five years.

---

*One solution: (1) take chimp across and leave it; (2) return; (3) take bananas over and leave them; (4) take chimp back to original side and leave it; (5) take over leopard and leave it with bananas; (6) return; (7) bring chimp across.

5. The bridge's load will be light except for occasional farm machinery.

6. Money is definitely a factor. The cheaper you can build the bridge, the better.

A sample of engineers shown this problem statement reacted differently, but we have chosen one set of responses to demonstrate how a problem solver actively constructs the representation of the problem.

The engineer (along with all those in our sample) first started with a series of questions. He requested pictures of the location, geologists' reports, governmental specifications for bridges, and an environmental impact study. After examining the requested materials, the engineer began to redefine the problem.

"OK, it looks like we have a couple of choices at least. . . . . The flooding—I don't think it's going to be a problem. We won't need to worry about that. I don't think we'll need any suspension—could do it but—no, it would be a big cost factor."

As he continued, he introduced additional concerns (such as load requirements the bridge must satisfy) and made decisions about their relative importance. Ultimately, he reconstructed the problem based on his experience and on his evaluation of the current situation. The problem he ended up solving was largely of his own making.*

Ill-defined problems require that we make decisions to fill in gaps in the problem definition and try out some tentative solutions before we settle on a satisfactory answer. Obviously, the more we know about various aspects of a problem (underlying concepts, principles, and information), the better we are able to address it.

Domain-Specific Knowledge

As we've noted, the quality of solutions depends in part on how much problem solvers know about different aspects of the problem. For example, if we give a group of senior music majors a problem requiring them to determine the most economical way to ship supplies to a lunar colony, we are apt to obtain less effective solutions than if we pose the

---

*Our example illustrates the role of social issues in public problem solving. Obviously, our engineer in defining the problem might adversely affect people with heavy equipment or those who wish an unimpeded stream flow. Their rights in the matter could only be preserved by their involvement in the problem-definition stage.

same problem to senior physics majors. Conversely, if we asked the physics majors to solve a problem requiring the composition of a sonata, we would obtain less sophisticated answers than if we gave the problem to the music majors.

Knowledge about a specific area is referred to as **domain-specific knowledge**. Typically, physicists know more about the domain of physics than do most musicians, while musicians know more about the domain of music than do physicists. Not surprisingly, experts in a specific area can usually do a better job of solving problems in their domain than can novices. However, experts don't simply have more domain-specific knowledge; their knowledge also is better organized (e.g., Chase & Simon, 1973; Dee-Lucas & Larkin, 1988; Larkin, 1985; Novick, 1988).

An example of differences in both the extent and organization of knowledge can be seen when we consider how a senior engineering student reacted to the bridge construction problem we presented earlier: "A simple three-piling iron bridge should do the trick. It should withstand any flood, and it will hold the heavy machinery." Unlike the expert in our previous example, the novice engineer did not request additional information, nor did he redefine the problem. He failed to do these things because he lacked knowledge—he didn't know the importance, for example, of an environmental impact statement. Knowing less than the expert was only a part of the difference, however. The organization of the expert engineer's knowledge allowed him to understand that we had not given a complete problem statement and that he needed to elaborate and redefine the problem. Where the novice had one solution, a three-piling bridge, the expert had several.

The differences in domain-specific knowledge between novices and experts also are seen clearly in a study conducted by Feltovich (1981). Feltovich employed two specialists in congenital heart problems (each of whom had at least twenty years of experience) and two fourth-year medical students (who had covered congenital heart problems in a course and had observed several patients with such problems). All four of the participants were given the same information about a hypothetical patient and were asked to make a diagnosis (solve the problem).

The differences between the experts and novices were clear. First, the experts tended to entertain several hypotheses at one time, while the novices considered each hypothesis one at a time. Second, the experts discarded hypotheses only when they encountered evidence that ruled them out completely. In contrast, the novices tended to go from hypothesis to hypothesis depending on the most recent bit of information they had obtained.

The fact that the experts could consider several hypotheses at once, ruling one out only when clear evidence was presented against it, indicates that the *quality* of their knowledge differed from that of the novices (Feltovich, 1981). Considering multiple hypotheses requires a better organization of knowledge and a more effective means of employing knowledge.

More recently, Myles-Worsley, Johnston, and Simons (1988) examined the role of expertise for radiologists. As with Feltovich, Myles-Worsley et al. found that expert radiologists (physicians who have specialized in reading x-rays) were able to deal with more information simultaneously than novices and that they better organized that information in memory. These differences appeared across four different levels of expertise (from novices without experience to "advanced" experts who averaged twenty two years of experience in radiology), indicating that as knowledge of an area increases, the ability to deal with new knowledge related to that area becomes more and more efficient.

One of the more unusual studies in recent years to focus on the role of knowledge in problem solving was conducted by Ceci and Liker (1986, 1988), who examined the role of knowledge in handicapping harness races (i.e., predicting and betting on races). They found, as has been the case in all studies of expertise, that experts were better at problem solving than were novices. Expert handicappers were able to juggle mentally several possibilities simultaneously and drew on a much larger store of information than less knowledgeable handicappers. Most startling, though, was the finding that handicapping performance was unrelated to measures of intelligence. Knowledge and the organization of knowledge rather than intellectual abilities was the determining factor in the handicappers' performance.

In general, then, it would seem that to be an excellent problem solver in any domain requires that a great deal of knowledge be acquired and organized. Simply, one cannot be an expert solver of, say, classroom management problems without knowing a great deal about classroom management and without having that knowledge well organized. As crucial as the development of problem solving skills is, there is no substitute for acquiring and organizing knowledge. Indeed, knowledge ultimately may be as important or more important than the abilities measured by tests of intelligence (see Ceci & Liker, 1988; Detterman & Spry, 1988).

Methods of Solving Problems

In the information-processing approach, problem solving is visualized as a search for a path to a solution. If there are many possible paths with wrong turns or dead ends, a problem is more difficult than if there are only a few incorrect paths. As we shall see, the number of paths to choose from is not as important as how problem solvers go about their searches.

Suppose a plane is reported down somewhere in a twelve-county area of western New York state. The plane must be found before nightfall because a storm is sweeping off Lake Erie. The odds of finding the plane in any one county are then one in twelve. Easy, right? Now suppose that there are twelve twenty-five-square-mile townships in each county. The plane could be in any one of them. So instead of twelve possibilities, we must now check 12 x 12, or 144, possibilities. Assume a ground party can effectively search only five square miles a day—one-fifth of a township. In a ground search, we must then check 12 x 12 x 5, or 720, places. Of course, we could make the problem much larger—five states with two hundred counties and so on until the number of possibilities to check becomes enormous.

Even such a problem is very small compared to the search involved in deciding the next move in a chess game, despite the fact that chess moves are well-defined problems. Newell and Simon (1972) estimate that there are about 10^{120} possible paths on a chess board, more paths than there are stars in the sky or grains of sand on the earth. So whether you are looking for a lost plane or planning a chess move, the way in which you go about solving the problem is important. You must develop systematic methods of searching problem spaces and increasing the chances of a correct choice, or you will never reach the solution to many problems.

Problem-Search Techniques

There are two basic approaches to problem searches: random and heuristic. In a **random search**, chance alone determines whether the goal is reached, as in the case of Thorndike's cats. Random searches are the simplest but least efficient of all problem-solving approaches. They are conducted without any knowledge of which paths would be more favorable for reaching the goal. Simply looking for the downed plane in one of the 144 townships without any planning or strategy would be a random search. Unless the problem space is very small, random searches are ineffective for almost all problems, although many students (and teachers) employ them from time to time.

A better way to search for a problem solution is the **heuristic* search**. Hayes defines heuristic searches as those in which problem solvers use knowledge to find promising paths to the problem solution or goal. Knowledge of the plane's probable route, last radio transmission, and citizen reports would help change a random search into a heuristic one. There are three general kinds of heuristic approaches: proximity searches, pattern matching, and planning (Hayes, in press–a).

Proximity Searches.   **Proximity searches** involve actions that allow the problem solver to get closer and closer, by approximation, to the problem solution. One form of proximity search is "hot-and-cold." For those of you who don't remember, hot-and-cold is a game that requires a hidden object, a seeker of the object, and an audience who knows where the object is. As the seeker moves closer to the object, the audience calls out "hotter," and as the seeker moves away from the object, the audience calls out "colder." Watch children play hot-and-cold sometime and you'll see a search pattern guided by information about the problem. Typically, children use cues to find hidden objects fairly effectively.

Those of us who have not actually played the game have probably still used the hot-and-cold method. Recently, one of the authors stopped his car and heard a low hissing sound. He walked around the car, moving toward the location where the hiss sounded and away from the areas where the sound was weak until he located a leaking hose under the hood. Similarly, a faint radio transmission that either strengthened or weakened as a search party changed directions could guide rescuers to a downed plane. Such information, whether it is the response "hot" or "cold," a hissing noise, or a radio transmission, helps us reduce the number of pathways and thereby makes our problem searches more effective.

A version of a hot-and-cold search can be seen in a teacher's attempt to develop practices that best promote student learning and satisfaction. Ms. Rose understands that some people believe a class conducted in small discussion groups is best, that others argue for the use of lectures, and that still others feel simulations and games are best to promote learning. Ms. Rose knows that experts disagree, but she can't very well support her own research program to find out what will work best with her students. She can, however, use a proximity approach to solve her problem. She can take one step (perhaps using a

---

*From the Greek word *heuriskein*, which means to discover or find.

simulation) and see what effect this has before going further. Over several weeks she can try many things, continuing to do those that increase student learning and satisfaction while dropping those that do not seem to help her reach her goal. After a lot of trial and error, Ms. Rose is likely to reach the goal of teaching her class in an effective way. As in all proximity searches, she may not find the best possible solution, but she should find one that works reasonably well.

Another form of proximity search is known as **means-ends analysis**, which is similar to hot-and-cold with an important difference. In hot-and-cold, only one way is used to get closer to the goal—walking around a car or varying instructional methods, for instance. In means-ends analysis, there are choices to be made among differing methods (means) of approaching the goal. A means-ends analysis involves breaking a problem down into component parts or subproblems and then using whatever means are available to solve each subproblem (called a **reduction goal**). As each subproblem is solved, the problem solver moves closer to the ends (called **apply goals**) he or she desires.

A chemistry student attempting to identify an unknown substance would apply a means-ends analysis. The student can use a series of reagents, a spectrographic analysis, a light absorption test, or a flame test. Often these procedures are used in sequence with successive tests made on the basis of the findings of previous tests.

In another example of means-ends analysis, suppose you get a flat tire in a sparsely populated rural area. You have an excellent spare tire but unfortunately you have no jack with which to raise the car. Here the initial state and the final goal are both clear. You want to "move" from a flat tire that has made your car undrivable to an air-filled tire.

Typically, you would follow these steps when you have a flat tire:

1. identify the problem
2. loosen the lug nuts
3. jack up the car
4. remove the lug nuts
5. remove the flat tire   reduction goals
6. put spare tire on
7. screw on lug nuts
8. lower car
9. tighten the lug nuts
10. operate the car in a normal fashion (apply goal)

When you remove the possibility of using a jack, however, you have a problem within a problem. The new, major problem is gaining access to the tire, an apply goal located between steps 2 and 3. Everything you do to gain access to the tire is a reduction goal. Building a ramp, using a fence post and rocks to raise the car, and putting the car up on the rocks are all possible reduction goals that help you on your way to actually changing the tire.

Means-ends analysis can best be thought of as a problem search that emphasizes the various means you have to reach the ends, your goals. Anytime you make a series of secondary moves to reduce the difficulty of a problem, you have engaged in a form of means-ends analysis.

Hayes (in press–a) uses the analogy of a stack of plates to picture the progression of goals in a means-ends analysis. He describes goals as placed on top of one another, much like dishes in a cafeteria, so that as one is removed another pops up until you come to the final goal. Figure 6–4 allows us to picture the working of means-ends analysis as

FIGURE 6–3   A PLATE-STACK REPRESENTATION OF REDUCTION AND APPLY GOALS

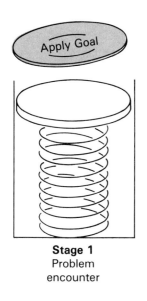

Stage 1
Problem
encounter

Stage 2
Ready to solve
problem, one
goal at a time

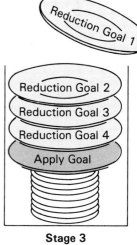

Stage 3
Reduction goal 1
is reached,
ready for
reduction goal 2

Source: J. R. Hayes, *Cognitive Psychology: Thinking and Creating.* Homewood, Illinois: Dorsey. Copyright © 1978 by Dorsey Press. Used by permission.

PRACTICE EXERCISE 6–1   PROBLEM SOLVING IN REAL LIFE

We believe problem solving is like any other form of learning—you get better with practice. Each of the steps we outlined earlier can be put to use in solving problems in your own life. The key to improvement, though, is to practice solving problems systematically.

Of course you need a problem to solve. Pick one that is important to you—choosing a major if you don't have one, for instance, or finding a good apartment at a reasonable price. Perhaps your problem is an interpersonal one. In any event, once you settle on the problem, follow the steps below in working out a solution. If you're like many people, using this guide will help you solve problems more effectively (Dixon, 1987).

1. *Define the problem.* State the problem as clearly as you can.

    _____

    _____

2. *Identify your reasons for wanting to solve the problem.* First,

    what will happen if the problem stays unsolved? _____

    _____

    _____

    What will happen if the problem is solved? _____

    _____

    _____

3. *Test several hypotheses for solving the problem.* Try out a number of strategies. For each, list its assets and its liabilities. As sources for ideas, think of what has worked for you in the past. Also, what do others suggest as ways to solve the problem?

Strategy	*Assets*	*Liabilities*
a. _____	_____	_____
	_____	_____
	_____	_____

PRACTICE EXERCISE 6–1   *CONTINUED*

b. _____ _____ _____

_____ _____

_____ _____

c. _____ _____ _____

_____ _____

_____ _____

Write the alternative you judge to be the best.

_____

4. *Try out your hypothesis.* Test out your approach and see how it works.

What went right? _____

What went wrong? _____

5. *Is the problem solved?* _____ Yes _____ No. If no, what do you need to do now in order to move toward solving the problem?

follows. An apply goal is at the bottom of the stack, with the reduction goals pressing it down. As each reduction goal is met, the problem solver moves to the next until the apply goal is reached.

Pattern Matching.   **Pattern-matching** searches involve an examination of a problem, identification of it, and then an attempt to locate a problem in memory that is of the same pattern. In other words, problem solvers ask themselves, "Have I been in similar situations before, and can I apply the solution I learned then to the current problem?"

Clear examples of pattern-matching approaches can be seen in the game of chess (Lesgold, 1988; Simon & Chase, 1973; Simon & Gilmartin, 1973). Simon and his associates contrasted pattern-recognition abilities of novice and master chess players. They determined that a major difference between them was that masters had stored thousands

Planning allows us to be better problem solvers. These students anticipate problems by thinking through the next step of their experiment.

of chessboard patterns in their memories while the novices had stored relatively few. The far greater availability of recognizable patterns in the memories of chess masters presumably results in their greater ability to play chess.

Pattern-matching problem searches also are used by classroom teachers. The experiences gained in teaching as well as in reading and advanced classwork help teachers recognize various patterns of educational problems and their solutions. When a new problem emerges—a student who does not learn or who is disruptive, for example—pattern matching can be one approach to finding possible solutions. Similarly, by recognizing a learning difficulty as a failure in, say, memory or attention, the teacher can apply solutions that have worked for these problems in the past.

Planning.   A critical aspect of problem solving often occurs prior to the actual search. Planning allows us to engage in proximity and pattern-searching approaches in advance of trying to solve the problem. Planning for problems can be seen in architects' scale models, a graphic layout of an assembly line, a sketch of a plan for a flower garden, a computer simulation of economic trends, or a term-paper outline. Planning allows us to test problem solutions with minimal expenditure of money, effort, and risk.

Applications for Teaching: Helping Students Become Problem Solvers

Training for problem-solving skills (see Cormier & Cormier, 1985; Dixon, 1987; Haley, 1987) typically has followed the sequence of steps shown in our outline. In addition to the training literature, we can apply a number of the insights gained through the information-processing approach to our goal of teaching students to be effective problem solvers.

1. Give students a chance to become problem solvers. Too often, teachers feel that they must present factual information to students in the form of names, dates, and figures. Most students are far more interested in and stimulated by a well-chosen problem. Of course, effective teachers exercise care in their selection of problems. We need to be sure that students have the necessary background to enable them to solve the particular types of problems we present. Problems must fit into previous knowledge to be meaningful.

2. Help students define problems. Students will define problems (create their own problem spaces) according to their perception of the information they are given (Flowers & Garbin, in press; Hayes, in press–a). Teachers should help students define their problem space by exploring what their initial state is, what their goal is, what operators are permitted, and exactly what restrictions are placed on the operators. Effective problem solvers also question the reliability of information and continue to search for reliable data even after the initial problem space has been constructed. They also understand clearly which parts of the problem are really data and which parts are inferences (Metcalf & Wiebe, 1987).

3. Encourage students to make hypotheses. The more hypotheses generated, the more likely a good solution. Bransford and Stein (1984) have suggested that problem solvers need to give attention to more than one part of the problem. In other words, the search for solution paths should not be unnecessarily restricted. On the other hand, problem solvers should try to avoid making the same assumptions for similar looking problems. Pattern matching may not always be a useful heuristic. Students should be taught not only to look for similarities to past problems but to search carefully for dissimilarities.

4. Have students test their hypotheses. Hypotheses can be tested in two ways: by thinking them through in the planning stage or by actually testing them. Either way, students should always be encouraged to be systematic and to avoid random searches.

Effective hypothesis testing is based on the previous stage of planning. Since your task as a teacher is to help students acquire useful processes for solving problems, you should be prepared to spend much of your time evaluating the models, diagrams, and outlines of hypotheses students make in the planning stage. Equally vital is giving your students feedback on their hypotheses as they test them on the actual problem.

Systematic heuristic methods can be taught. Specific instructions can be given, along with many broadly based examples, for students to use hot-and-cold and means-ends analysis on assigned problems. Students can be required to describe their problem searches orally or in writing.

Similarly, pattern matching can be practiced. In mathematics or the sciences, for instance, students can be taught to relate new problems to methods they previously used with similar problems. Pattern matching can be useful in every class, from social studies to science to literature.

Problem solvers always should avoid jumping to conclusions in the hypothesis-testing stage (Dixon, 1987). The first solution is not necessarily the best solution. Problem solvers should always be taught to go further than the most obvious answer, even if that answer eventually works. Proximity methods often yield solutions that are not the best ones. Solutions should therefore be checked against outside criteria whenever possible.

Finally, if a hypothesis is unsuccessful, students should be taught to try another (Larkin, 1985). Persistence in problem solving is admirable, but students should recognize blind alleys. Students need to learn that it may be necessary to test several possible pathways before they find the solution path.

✸ 5. Help students judge the value of their solutions. Some problems have many solutions, but only one can be chosen. Factors such as cost, time, accuracy, and completeness often must be taken into account in judging the worth of a solution. In social problems, issues of ethics and morality may also enter in. Students therefore should be encouraged to practice rank-ordering of a problem solution based on several criteria. Criteria such as those above are especially important when we consider that most of the problems students will face in life will be ill-defined. For most such problems, a large number of problem definitions is possible, with an even larger number of potential solutions. Since the solutions to many problems (building highways to meet transportation needs, for example) may lead to other problems in related areas (inner-city deterioration, air pollution), testing solutions against multiple criteria becomes especially critical.

✸ 6. Help students avoid rigidity. Students' abilities to solve problems are strongly influenced by their predispositions to perceive, approach, and

attempt solutions in certain ways. Some of these predispositions are useful to problem solving. Difficulty arises, however, when old problem solutions don't quite fit new problems but seem to. As Dixon (1987) has pointed out, variety and novelty in problem-solving tasks are key elements in the continued development of effective cognitive strategies. Additionally, the problem of rigidity is greatly reduced when teachers emphasize the processes involved in solving problems rather than just the correct answers.

Having students orally define problems is an excellent way of determining whether they have created a good problem representation.

Creativity

If we watch enough students solve problems, sooner or later we will see different, unusual, and perhaps even strange solutions. If such solutions, despite their oddness, result in acceptable problem resolutions, then we would refer to them as *creative*. Creative problem solving, in other words, has two characteristics: novelty (i.e., unusualness) and value (i.e., it must be appropriate to the demands of the task in question).

Creativity has proven an extremely difficult topic to study. As Brown (in press) has noted, there are basic disagreements among psychologists about whether creativity is a cognitive, personality, or environmental characteristic, or some combination of all three. There also are severe problems in the various instruments that have been designed to measure creativity (see Michael, 1988), leading Hocevar (in press) to argue that the only acceptable way of predicting a person's future creativity is not by tests but by judging previous creative accomplishments. In spite of such problems, however, the importance of creative problem solving to our society is undeniable, and there have been a number of research findings with direct implications for classroom instruction.

Frame of Reference

One way to make the study of creativity less difficult is to recognize that there are different perspectives from which creativity can be viewed. For our purposes, the most important are personal and societal (see Glover et al., in press). At the personal level—that is, with respect only to ourselves—each of us can be creative. People have the potential of being creative—acting in novel but valuable ways—when they decorate their houses or apartments, dress differently, or engage in a hobby. From a personal frame of reference, any facet of life holds the potential for creative behavior.

A far more rigorous test of creativity occurs within the societal frame of reference. At this level, a person's problem solutions must be novel and valuable to society at large in order to be called creative. Books, plays, movies, and scientific inventions, for example, are subject to evaluation from a societal frame of reference. Professional peers, such as fellow teachers, would be within this frame of reference. Scientific innovations are reviewed by other scientists, for example; and novels and plays are reviewed by literary and theater critics as well as the population at large. Ultimately, a few works identified as creative stand the most rigorous test of all—time. For instance, Shakespeare's writings speak to some basic truths about humanity that transcend time; his insights from hundreds of years ago seem just as powerful now as when he conceived them. Other accomplishments, such as Madam Curie's discovery of radium or Mendel's explanation of the laws of genetics, have stood the test of time because they have been shown to be turning points in the development of fields of knowledge.

Much research on creativity has focused on both the personal and societal frames of reference. In the next section, we examine factors associated with creativity at the societal frame of reference and then proceed to factors that appear to lead to enhanced creativity in each students' personal frame of reference.

Creativity at the Societal Level

It isn't hard to draw up a list of works that have been creative at the societal level: Chaucer's writings, Dickinson's poems, Newton's invention of the calculus, and so on. In fact, entire books have been filled with lists of creative accomplishments. And, while we may quibble about exactly what things to include (e.g., Rosemary Rogers' novels and Francis Ford Coppola's movies may or may not belong), there is no question that each year brings outstanding scientific discoveries, exciting new music, marvelous new writings, and eye-pleasing art—things that society judges to be highly creative. To nurture creative abilities in our students requires that we understand what it is that makes highly creative individuals special. A great deal of research in the past thirty-five years has focused on exactly this issue.

John R. Hayes (1988a, in press–b) has devoted much of his career to the study of outstandingly creative individuals. He has identified individuals whom society has honored as highly creative in some way and then contrasted them with "normal" people. Three findings from Hayes' research seem especially relevant. They concern the role of knowledge, intelligence, and motivation in creativity.

Knowledge.   What is the role of knowledge in creativity? Most people would agree that scientists must spend a great deal of time and effort learning their fields in order to do highly creative work. There is sometimes the sense, however, that the same level of knowledge and skill is not necessary for literature and the arts. Some people seem to believe that highly creative musicians, artists, and writers have such "genius" that their works pour forth without preparation. Two recent studies conducted at Carnegie-Mellon University cast very strong doubt on this point of view.

Picasso put a toy automobile and a cooking pot (the handle is the tail) to an unusual use in his fanciful *Baboon and Young* (1951).

In the first study, Hayes (1988b) analyzed the lives of the seventy-six composers mentioned in Schönberg's *The Lives of the Great Composers* (1970). Hayes found that more than 99 percent of these composers' best-known works were written after the composers had been "on the job" for at least ten years. Even the child prodigy Mozart, who essentially became a musician at age four, did not produce any work recognized as creative until about the age of twelve—after Mozart already had spent eight years composing and studying music. In the same paper, Hayes also reported that the notable works of 131 great painters almost uniformly were produced after they had practiced their craft for at least six years. In the second study, Wishbow (1988) performed an analysis of sixty-six eminent poets and found that none wrote a notable poem sooner than five years into their careers. Fifty-five of the sixty-six produced no memorable work earlier than *ten* years into their careers.

Like every other aspect of cognition we have examined, creativity is directly linked to knowledge. In simple terms, it is not possible to be a creative architect, physicist, writer, or musician without a great deal of knowledge. This knowledge may be self-taught (as is sometimes the case for musicians, writers, and artists) or obtained through formal schooling (as is almost always the case with scientists). To do work that will be recognized as outstanding requires that years be devoted to gaining knowledge of a field. Knowledge alone, however, is not enough to explain why some people are creative and others are not. Many highly knowledgeable people do not solve problems in creative ways. Other variables must be involved.

Intelligence.   What is the relationship between creativity and intelligence? Several investigators, most notably Roe (1953) and MacKinnon (1968), have examined this question by testing the intelligence of highly creative individuals. In general, highly creative individuals are more intelligent than the average person on the street. For example, the IQs of the individuals included in Roe's and MacKinnon's studies (noteworthy physicists, biologists, social scientists, mathematicians, and architects) ranged from 120 to 177. However, even while these highly creative individuals had higher-than-average intelligence test scores, they were no brighter than their noncreative colleagues (Hayes, in press–b). That is, there is no difference in the IQ scores of, say, highly creative biologists and noncreative biologists.

How can it be that highly creative people are more intelligent than average but no more intelligent than their uncreative colleagues? The answer would appear to be that like knowledge, intelligence does not tell the entire story of creativity. Some other variable must underlie what we refer to as creativity.

Motivation.   Ultimately, it seems that almost all creative acts recognized at the societal level require enormous effort. Hayes (in press–b) points out that highly creative individuals often are totally absorbed by their work. Hayes' colleague, Herb Simon, for example, reports spending about one hundred hours a week working on the problem whose solution resulted in his Nobel Prize (Hayes, in press–b). Further, creative individuals often are not satisfied with work for work's sake. They seem satisfied only with originality—solutions that show clear evidence of creativity.

Biographies of highly creative people support the notion that they are highly motivated to produce original work (Hayes, 1988a). Creative members of all professions (writing, science, art, music) tend to produce works at an earlier age, to produce far more, and to keep producing longer than their peers. Hayes (in press–b) put it in the most direct terms: "Creative people work very hard."

Summary of Creativity at the Societal Level. What makes people highly creative? The answer to that question likely will require years of additional research. At this point, though, it probably is safe to say that high levels of creativity require great amounts of knowledge, higher-than-average levels of intelligence, and extraordinary motivation. Only a tiny fraction of our society will ever make the efforts involved in seeking high levels of creative performance. Just as most of us cannot imagine spending six hours a day practicing swimming or gymnastics (the level of effort required to compete at championship levels), few of us are willing to devote one hundred or more hours per week to writing the great American novel, composing the next legendary hit song, or trying to unravel the secrets of "brown" stars. From our personal frames of reference, however, all of us can become more creative.

Applications for Teaching: Facilitating Students' Personal Creativity

Even though most of our students will not go on to become famous writers, scientists, musicians, or artists, each can have his or her personal creative abilities improved through careful classroom practices. E. Paul Torrance (see Torrance, 1988) has devoted much of his career to procedures designed to facilitate creativity in the classroom. The following principles are taken in large part from Torrance's work but also are based on the general literature on facilitating students' creative abilities.

1. Strange, unusual, and odd questions from students should not be discounted. Learners who have creative questions may leave you wondering about the relevance of what they have asked. You cannot afford to react negatively to such questions. If learners see they cannot ask their "good" questions, they just won't ask them. Far too often, we find that students who ask unusu-

al questions are told, "Be quiet," "Don't get smart," or "Go look it up." By accepting strange and unusual questions, of course, you run the risk of spending some time with questions that really are irrelevant. Students can enjoy asking questions designed to get the teacher off the track. This is a minor problem, however, if students learn to ask creative questions. If you can't answer the question (such as "Why do pandas have six fingers?"), let learners see that you welcome such questions and try to help them find the needed answers (Isaksen & Parnes, 1985; Moses, 1985).

Encouraging unusual and challenging questions can result in an increase in students' overall creative behaviors. Once students see they can really ask you what they want to know and not worry about your reaction, creative behavior tends to generalize to other areas (Isaksen & Parnes, 1985).

2. Try to find something positive in all ideas. Tagging some ideas and questions as "stupid," "bad," or "irrelevant" will reduce the chances of students asking better questions. The best approach is to follow up "bad" questions with some of your own that require the learner to think through the problem (Moses, 1985). When learners evaluate their own thinking, they are far less likely to inhibit future questioning.

3. Make it a point to systematically reward creativity in your students. Many studies have shown that rewarding creative activities increases their number (see Sternberg, 1988b).

4. Expect and demand creativity from your students. In those situations where you tell learners you expect them to be creative and where creativity is a part of the overall performance you will judge, you will find more creative behaviors (Sternberg, 1988b; Taylor, 1984).

5. In terms of grading, creativity ought to be an extra. Requiring creativity for a grade is somewhat unfair—after all, you will be making a subjective judgment about how creative a student's efforts are. Creativity should be rewarded, but in the form of extra credit (Moses, 1985).

6. Model creative behaviors. Several studies (see Sternberg, 1988b) report that those students who are exposed to a creative model act more creatively than do students who are exposed to models that aren't particularly creative. So if you are serious about enhancing the creativity of your students, model originality in your own classroom behaviors. You also can invite your creative colleagues for occasional guest appearances.

Strange questions should not be discounted. Try to find something positive in all ideas and follow up "bad" questions with some of your own that require the learner to think through the problem.

PRACTICE EXERCISE 6–2   DEVELOPING CREATIVITY

The best way to practice helping someone develop his or her creativity is to start with yourself. This activity is based on a series of research studies we have conducted over the years. To start, sit down in a quiet place with paper and pencil. Now think about buttons. You are probably wearing some buttons. Make a list of all the unusual uses you can think of for buttons. Don't worry about your ideas being odd or strange; no one will see them but you. In your unusual uses you may employ as many buttons as you wish of any size you wish. Stop reading and complete the activity now! If you read on to this line, you are fudging. Complete the activity first.

Finished? Good. Now score your list. How many ideas did you list? The number of uses you listed is your *fluency* score. How many *different* kinds of ideas did you list? Count only the number of really different ideas you listed; that number is your *flexibility* score. *Originality* will have to wait because it can't be scored on this list.

What you have done so far may be thought of as identifying your reference point for increasing creative responding. Below is a list containing ten objects commonly found in settings where you might be taking a course in educational psychology.

1. pencil

2. chalkboard eraser

3. book

4. paper clip

5. trash can

6. ashtray

7. bookend

8. rubber eraser

9. cellophane wrapper

10. roll of masking tape

These ten items will be the stimuli for your development of unusual uses over the next ten days.

continued

PRACTICE EXERCISE 6–2   CONTINUED

To make the activity a little more rigorous, let's set some daily goals. Whatever your fluency score was on the first list, try to increase it by 3 every day. Try to increase your flexibility score by 2. You will want to increase your originality score by 1 each day, but you won't have a reference for it until you complete the second list.

To help you work at this task, choose your favorite daily activity — watching television, reading, talking on the phone, whatever — and engage in this activity *only* if you meet the goals.* If you increase your fluency score by 3 tonight, for example, give yourself the pleasure of watching television. By the way, be sure to choose an activity that you really enjoy. An activity you don't care much about doesn't help motivate you to work hard on the task.

When you complete the second list based on the stimulus "pencil," score fluency and flexibility as we've already described. Then compare your list to the list you generated for "buttons." Count every idea on your "pencil" list that is in no way mentioned on your "button" list, and add the total to determine your first originality score.† Suppose you write that a pencil could be used "to make a prop to hold open a window" on the second list. If on the first list, you suggested that a button could be used "to prop open a window," then you cannot consider the same response to "pencil" original. An original response must be different from all previous responses. Your goal is to increase your originality score by at least 1 every day. Stay with this activity for ten days and compare your final performance with your original score.

In order to increase the utility of your creativity training, add a second component to your tasks on about the fifth day. For ten days (the last five of the Unusual Uses activity and five more) write out a problem that occurred during the day. Such problems might include finding a parking place on the campus, replacing a button on a shirt

---

*After having hundreds of college students perform this activity, we found that the daily increases we gave above were reached by almost all students. The required increases may not seem very challenging, but after ten days your fluency score will have increased by 30, and the other scores will increase greatly as well. These overall increases *are* impressive.

---

†Originality must be scored differently here from the way we described it earlier because you are the only reference point. At first, being more original will seem simple. It will become more difficult by the time you get to lists 5 and 6.

PRACTICE EXERCISE 6–2   *CONTINUED*

you are wearing, figuring out how to get a date with someone, and so on. Each day, list as many possible solutions to the problem as you can think of. Once again, try to raise your fluency score by 3, your flexibility score by 2,and your originality score by 1 daily.

If you want to go one step further after your two tasks are finished, work on generalizing what you have learned. Try to generate as many possible ideas as you can for each problem that comes up during the day. It will probably be difficult for you to keep track of them, but it is the general approach to problems we are concerned with, not keeping day-to-day running lists.

It is creativity in everyday life that is important. Thinking of odd uses for buttons is pretty far removed from real-life problems, but developing your skills with such activities is a good starting place. Ultimately, you want to approach important problems with high levels of fluency, flexibility, and originality. By developing your creativity, you will do a better job of solving *all* the problems you encounter, from gardening to social interactions. Becoming more creative requires work, but you can do it.

Summary

We began the chapter by examining historical views of problem solving. Thorndike's research led him to describe problem solving as an incremental, trial-and-error form of learning that did not involve thinking or reasoning as we usually define such terms. Köhler, a Gestalt psychologist, envisioned problem solving as an all-or-none insightful process closely governed by reasoning; while Dewey, ever the pragmatist, concentrated on the sequence of steps people follow in problem solving. Dewey's notions have led directly to the development of programs designed to facilitate problem-solving skills. Information-processing approaches to problem solving borrow from the works of Thorndike, Köhler, and Dewey as well as from the rich tradition of memory research. The information-processing view of problem solving emphasizes what a person does with the information: constructing problem representations, building problem spaces, and testing hypotheses.

A critical factor influencing the quality of solutions problem solvers formulate is their domain-specific knowledge. In general, the more a person knows about a particular domain, the more efficiently he or she is likely to solve problems in that area. Differences between experts and novices in an area go beyond the sheer amount of knowledge they possess, however, and include the ways in which their knowledge is organized.

There are two basic approaches to solving problems: random and heuristic. In the long run, random methods clearly are inferior to heuristic methods. Heuristic approaches include hot-and-cold, means-ends analysis, pattern matching, and planning strategies. Ill-defined problems require problem solvers to analyze and specify the problems before experimenting with different solutions. Such problems are best solved through the heuristic strategy of systematic planning, which involves visualizing and testing alternative solutions by various analytic procedures such as diagrams, flow charts, or computer simulations.

Creative problem solutions—unique and novel responses to problems—can be viewed from two frames of reference: personal and societal. At the societal level, creative problem solutions require great amounts of knowledge. Further, creative individuals tend to score higher than average on measures of intelligence. However, the factor that seems to best separate highly creative individuals from their colleagues in the same fields is motivation. Highly creative individuals work very hard and work hard at being original.

At the personal level, you should expect to find creativity in all your students. Every student is creative at one time or another; some students, of course, are creative more often. You also can expect to be able to increase your own levels of creativity and apply the principles described in this chapter to enhance the creativity of your students.

Suggested Readings

Glover, J. A., Ronning, R. R., & Reynolds, C. R. (Eds.). (in press). *Handbook of creativity research*. New York: Plenum.
This edited volume cuts across all areas of research on human creativity.

Haley, J. (1987). *Problem-solving therapy* (2nd ed.). San Francisco: Jossey-Bass.
Haley's volume remains the single best exposition of how contemporary views of problem solving may be used in dealing with interpersonal problems.

Hayes, J. R. (1988). *The complete problem solver* (2nd ed.). Hillsdale, NJ: Erlbaum.

> *Hayes' volume is one of the finest books ever written about human problem solving. We strongly recommend it.*

Kuhn, D., Amsel, E., O'Loughlin, M., Schauble, L., Leadbeater, B., & Yotive, W. (1988). *The development of scientific thinking skills*. Orlando, FL: Academic Press.

> *Although this text is not restricted to problem solving, it is a marvelous vehicle for charting the development of scientific thinking skills in students.*

Sternberg, R. J. (Ed.). (1988). *The nature of creativity*. New York: Cambridge.

> *Robert Sternberg's excellent volume contains outstanding chapters from some of the best researchers in the area of creativity. We strongly recommend this book as a supplemental reading.*

PART TWO

A critical educational goal is ensuring that students learn to like and appreciate themselves. Another is motivating them to achieve in the classroom. In Part One, we focused on cognition and cognitive development and the teacher's role in enhancing students' cognitive growth. In this part, we examine the development of self-concept, morality, and aspects of motivation. Chapter Seven, "Self-Concept and Moral Development," outlines the development of self-concept and emphasizes the implications of self-concept for academic achievement. Later in the chapter, the focus is on moral development and the relation of moral development to students' behavior in educational settings. Chapter Eight, "Motivation," surveys several important views of motivation and builds on them to present a set of guidelines for motivating students.

Self-Concept and Motivation

CHAPTER 7

Self-Concept and Moral Development

OVERVIEW

The first six chapters of our text introduced you to one very important way of understanding students—through the use of cognitive psychology. Students, however, are more than collections of cognitive abilities. Each one has a unique identity and a special sense of self. This sense of self, which has far-reaching implications for how students perform in school, will be discussed in the first part of this chapter.

The sense of self includes students' moral values. Moral values, of course, vary from student to student and, within the same student, vary across time. Students' moral development also influences many of their school-related behaviors, and so we describe the course of moral development in the second part of the chapter. Later, in Chapter Eight, we will see how teachers can integrate their knowledge of self-concept and moral development with basic principles of motivation.

OBJECTIVES

After reading this chapter, you should be able to meet the following objectives.

1. Describe the implications of the development of students' self-concepts for your teaching.

2. Describe the effect your knowledge of moral development will have on your teaching.

3. Describe the effect your knowledge of causal attributions will have on your classroom practices.

Establishing a Sense of Self—the Self-Concept

A **self-concept** is a person's total view of him- or herself (Hamachek, 1987). If we could place a student in a situation in which she felt absolutely free to describe herself as openly and accurately as possible, the resulting description—"intelligent," "hard working," "caring," "mature," "responsible," "insightful," etc.—would capture the essence of her self-concept.

Self-concepts are not static and unchanging (Hamachek, 1987). They are shaped by experience and how people interpret their experience—receiving an A on an arithmetic test ("I'm pretty good at arithmetic"), driving in the winning run in a softball game ("I'm a solid hitter"), misspelling eight out of ten words on a test ("I'm a rotten speller"), and playing well at a piano recital ("I'm a good pianist"). The beliefs that grow out of experience form the basis of how people see themselves.

Each person has a unique identity and a special sense of self.

Self-concept, however, is more than just self-description. While experiences help shape people's self-concepts, their self-concepts also influence the kinds of experiences they have (Dweck & Leggett, 1988). For example, consider two girls of equal ability on the same softball team. One girl believes she is a good hitter, the other believes herself to be a poor hitter. The "good hitter" is likely to talk one of her parents or siblings into pitching to her in the backyard as often as she can. Further, she probably will participate in "pick-up" games in the neighborhood and take every other opportunity she can find to hit softballs. All of this practice, of course, is very likely to make her a better hitter, and so she probably will experience more success as a hitter, confirming her self-belief. In contrast, the girl who believes she is a poor hitter is much less likely to enjoy hitting and probably does many other things besides practicing batting between games. A skill such as hitting a softball hardly can improve without practice,and so she is unlikely to do well in her next game, thereby confirming her self-belief.

A similar example can be drawn about two boys of equal ability in a high school chemistry class. One believes himself to be "good at science"; therefore he reads articles and books about science in his spare time, joins the school science club, and eagerly does his assignments for chemistry class. Not surprisingly, he does well and confirms his self-belief. The other boy, who believes he is a "poor science student," avoids reading about science, has no extracurricular activities involving science, and puts off doing his chemistry assignments (if he does them at all) until the last moment. This second boy is likely to have his self-belief confirmed as well.

The Formation of Self-Concept

Where do self-concepts come from in the first place? The development of the self-concept begins with an awareness of the self as an entity separate from the rest of the environment (Hart, 1988b). Some research designed to pinpoint the age at which self-awareness emerges has examined how babies react to mirrors. In some studies, researchers have put marks on babies' faces (e.g., with rouge) and then let them look in mirrors. Most twenty-month-olds react to seeing a mark on their faces in the mirror by touching the mark. Fifteen-month-olds, however, do not (Brooks-Gunn & Lewis, 1984). The fact that twenty-month-olds touch the marks on their faces indicates that they have self-awareness, a conception of themselves.

Preschoolers' self-understanding is dominated by the physical self.

Other studies (see Brooks-Gunn & Lewis, 1984) indicate that babies begin to react to mirrors in a self-conscious way at about eighteen months. Making faces, acting silly, being coy, or appearing embarrassed all are signs of self-awareness. Apparently, self-awareness is established at about eighteen months of age. From this point on, the formation of the self-concept becomes more complex and sophisticated (Cote & Levine, 1988).

"I" and"Me."   Damon and Hart (1982) proposed that an important distinction (first made by William James) is useful in understanding self-concept. The distinction is between **"I"** and **"Me"** (see also Hart, 1988a, 1988b).

Whenever you think about yourself, you play two different roles in the process. There is the *you* doing the thinking and the *you* being thought about. From your point of view, you can say that "I think about me" involves an "I" doing the thinking (the subject) and a "Me" that is thought about (the object). Below we will first review the development of the "Me" and then trace the development of the "I."

Development of the "Me."   Hart (1988b) suggests that the "Me" includes four aspects of the self: the physical self, the active self, the social self, and the psychological self. As one would expect, the *physical self* includes one's bodily characteristics, name, and material possessions. The *active self* includes a person's behaviors and abilities, while the *social self* involves group memberships, social characteristics, and social relations. Last, the *psychological self* includes beliefs, feelings, psychological traits (e.g., honesty or modesty), and thoughts.

Although all aspects of the self are important, the emphasis on each changes during development. Preschool children's self-understanding is dominated by the physical self. They think of themselves in terms of their physical characteristics and possessions (e.g., "I have brown eyes," "I have a choo-choo," "I am little"). When preschoolers do talk about behaviors (the active self), social interactions (the social self), or feelings (the psychological self), these usually are described as though they too were physical attributes (e.g., "I jumped to the couch" rather than "I am a good jumper"; "My friends are named Joe and Alice" rather than "I am a friendly person"; and "I have a funny feeling inside" rather than "I am a sad person").

During the elementary-school years the emphasis shifts from the physical to the active self. More specifically, self-understanding focuses on general capabilities in relation to other children. For example, an eight-year-old might define herself as the best skater in her neighborhood, while a ten-year-old might stress that he is the best sledder

The active self includes a person's behaviors and abilities.

"I want to experience a warm climate, fly through the air, see some color, eat a peach—I want to love!"

on his block. As is the case with preschoolers, characteristics of the physical, social, and psychological selves can be seen, but elementary-school children emphasize these aspects of their selves in activity-related ways (e.g., "I'm the best sledder because I'm the strongest" or "I make friends faster than anybody in my room").

By junior high school, the social self becomes most important. This is evident in self-descriptions such as "I'm friendly" or "I'm shy," which directly involve relations with other people. Characteristics related to the physical, active, or psychological self generally are seen in terms of social relations. So, for instance, being a good athlete or student, if it is seen as the reason for being popular, might be important to an eighth-grader's self-concept.

High-school-age students typically emphasize the psychological self. Their self-concepts center on their personal philosophy, beliefs, and thoughts (e.g., "I am a conservationist," "I'm a nonconformist," or "I'm a political activist"). By this age, physical, active, and social characteristics are crucial to the self-concept only if they have psycho-logical dimensions. Group membership, style of dress, hairstyle, or political activities may be important to the self-concept, but only if they reflect deeply held personal beliefs.

To summarize, the "Me," includes physical, active, social, and psychological aspects. These four aspects of the self, however, are not equally important at all ages. The physical self predominates among

224

The self-understanding of an elementary school child focuses on activity-related aspects of self. This child might regard herself as the best in her class at standing on her head.

preschoolers. As development unfolds, the emphasis of the self-concept shifts to the active self, the social self, and finally to the psychological self.

Development of the "I."   The "I" refers to the subjective self who organizes and interprets experience. Understanding one's "I" is based on several dimensions: continuity, distinctiveness, volition, and self-reflectivity. We examine each of these dimensions below.

Continuity refers to individuals' sense that they remain the same person over time ("Sure, I've changed since going to college, but I'm still the same person"). Preschoolers' sense of continuity is based on continuity of name and physical features ("I'm the same person I was before 'cause my name is still Sandy and my hair is long"). As students grow older, their understanding of continuity becomes more and more focused on psychological characteristics (e.g., "I'm still the same person because I believe in the same things.")

Distinctiveness refers to people's sense of individuality ("I can tell you about seeing this morning's sunrise, but no one else can experience things from my perspective in the same direct way I do"). Young children understand they are distinct from other people because their names are different and because they have different physical features (e.g., red hair, freckles). As children develop, physical characteristics become less important while psychological attributes become more important to a sense of distinctiveness. For example, a young boy might see himself as different from Joe because they have different names. An older boy might differentiate himself from Joe because he understands that he has a unique, personal point of view that Joe can learn about but never directly experience.

Volition refers to individuals' sense that they are active agents with free will ("If I decide to go to a movie instead of a play, *I* make that decision; it doesn't just happen to me"). Preschool children think of volition in physical terms ("I am my own boss . . . my brain thought it and my arm did what my brain thought up"). As development continues, children increasingly understand their actions in terms of active decisions made by a conscious mind (Bullock & Lutkenhaus, 1988). Ultimately, they even may begin to see the role of unconscious factors and self-deception. A high school senior, for example, might notice that he isn't preparing as well for his music lessons as usual and think about unconscious factors that could be responsible (e.g., "Am I afraid of success?" "Do I really want to avoid going to the conservatory next year?"). Such questions, of course, would never occur to an eight-year-old.

Finally, *self-reflectivity* is the ability of the self to consider its continuity, distinctiveness, and volition (e.g., "I know that I am I, a unique, continuing person with free will"). Early in life, self-reflectivity is restricted to an awareness of physical characteristics and typical activities. Over time, it includes behavioral capabilities and, by late adolescence, the recognition of conscious and unconscious processes.

Self-Concept as Personal Theory.   In recent years, Carol Dweck and Ellen Leggett (e.g., Dweck & Leggett, 1988) have taken a more cognitive approach to the idea of self-concept. From their perspective, self-concepts depend on how people view their personal characteristics (e.g., intelligence, empathy, integrity)—they have "theories" about themselves. Further, Dweck and Leggett (1988) argue that there are two kinds of views people take about their personal characteristics—entity-oriented or incremental. Children with *entity-oriented* theories believe that their personal characteristics (such as intelligence) are fixed or uncontrollable. Children with *incremental* theories believe their characteristics are "malleable, increasable, controllable qualities" (p. 262).

In Dweck and Leggett's view, the two types of theories lead to different kinds of self-concepts. Entity-oriented children (or "theorists," as Dweck and Leggett like to refer to them) see themselves as a "collection of fixed traits that can be measured and evaluated" (p. 266).

Adolescents see themselves as distinct because they understand they have a unique, personal point of view.

In contrast, "incremental theorists" see themselves as a dynamic, changeable set of qualities that is "evolving over time through the individual's efforts" (p. 266).

Whether children see themselves as fixed or changing makes a profound difference in how they see their world and what they do. Students who see their personal traits as fixed and unchangeable are unlikely to believe that efforts devoted to studying, practicing a musical instrument, or mastering a physical skill will be of benefit. In contrast, students who believe they are changeable also are confident that they can change themselves through their own efforts—study and practice are seen as important to self-development.

Dweck and Leggett (1988) have not yet fully examined how the two different types of self-concepts develop. However, it is clear that children's goals and the ways they evaluate them are important (e.g., Elliott & Dweck, 1988; Leggett & Dweck, 1986). Self-improvement goals, in which children attempt to increase knowledge, enhance skills, or otherwise change things about themselves, seem to be associated with the development of incremental theories of the self. Performance goals ("I'm going to make an A," "I'll win the race"), in contrast, are associated with entity-oriented theories. As one might guess, teachers are an important influence on the kinds of goals students select, and as we see in Chapter Eight, proper goal selection is an important part of motivating academic performance.

A Summary of Self-Concept Formation.   We have described self-concept formation in terms of the development of the "Me" and the "I." Each dimension plays a role in self-concept, although the importance of each changes as development proceeds. In general, young children's self-concepts are tied to their physical nature. As time passes, the self-concept focuses more on psychological concerns.

Students' self-concepts have a profound influence on their performance in school. In particular, it seems that whether children see themselves as entity-oriented or incrementally changing has direct implications for academic motivation. Of course, as we saw at the outset of the chapter, children's self-concepts do not occur in a vacuum. Through their interactions with other people, children come to see themselves as good students, friendly people, and trustworthy friends or as lazy, inept, and incompetent. As we'll see below, there is a great deal that teachers can do to facilitate the development of children's self-concepts.

Educational Implications of Self-Concepts Research

In the large amount of research that has been done on the development of children's self-concepts, five aspects of the self appear time and again (see Cote & Levine, 1988; Hart, 1988a; 1988b; Lapsley & Power, 1988; Rogers, 1983). These aspects are that (1) each person strives for a consistent self-concept, (2) behavior is consistent with the self-concept, (3) experiences inconsistent with the self-concept are seen as threatening, (4) the self-concept changes as a result of learning and maturation, and (5) there is a relationship between the kinds of goals students strive for and the formation of their self-concepts. From this perspective, students who see themselves as academically inept (as part of an overall view of self) will act in ways consistent with this view (such as avoiding academic tasks) and actually may feel threatened by the possibility of academic success. Conversely, students who view themselves as good students usually act like good students (by studying, doing in-class assignments, and so on) and are bothered by experiences (such as receiving a bad grade) that counter this view. From this frame of reference, self-concept is a critical factor in determining students' academic performance. Since an accurate self-concept is necessary for full functioning, a major goal for educators should be to foster the development of realistic and accurate self-concepts in their students.

Applications for Teaching: The Development of Positive Self-Concepts

The following are several guidelines drawn from research on self-concept that will help you facilitate the development of your students' self-concepts.

1. Give students ample opportunities to participate in class. Teachers must be aware that not all the students will have equal opportunities or inclinations to become involved in class discussions. They need to structure nonthreatening and supportive classroom environments so that differences of opinion are welcome and each student's opinions are valued. Small groups in particular can offer the opportunity for each student to engage in discussion. Encouraging students to participate and sincerely valuing their comments will help them develop more positive self-concepts.

2. Allow students to express their feelings. Students need to learn more than subject matter content in school; they should learn about themselves and how to accept their feelings. Teachers can provide a warm, accepting environment that allows for the expression of emotion. Accepting students also means accepting their feelings (Rogers, 1983), even if those feelings may be negative or even hostile.

3. Provide a classroom atmosphere of acceptance. Acceptance means taking students for what they are, but it doesn't mean that teachers have to accept specific student behaviors. We can reject a particular behavior (such as hitting another student) while still accepting the person. Try to separate the rejection of acts from the rejection of people. It is better to say "Susan, I cannot tolerate

your being late" than it is to say "Susan, I can't tolerate you anymore."

4. Establish clear classroom rules. Communicating rules for conduct and expectations for academic tasks and enforcing them in a fair and firm manner help students see that we expect them to live up to certain standards. By enforcing rules and guidelines, we tell students we care about them and that they can depend on us to be fair.

5. Stress activities likely to lead to success. As we pointed out at the beginning of the chapter, success and failure have powerful effects on students' self-concepts. It is difficult to think of oneself as a "good student" or a "hard worker" if success is never experienced in academic settings. Instead, continued failure is likely to lead to self-concepts that include descriptions such as "I'm no good in school" or "I'm lazy." Students with such self-concepts, of course, will act in ways consistent with them—avoiding academic activities and neglecting their work.

6. Stress self-improvement goals. Self-improvement goals are associated with the development of incremental theories of the self. When children believe they can change themselves through their own efforts, academic achievement becomes far more likely. Self-improvement goals also are more congruent with becoming lifelong learners than are performance goals. Indeed, any of us can work toward self-improvement and feel real satisfaction as we see ourselves change. Performance goals, in contrast, seldom lead to the same kinds of satisfaction.

Moral Development

An important part of how we view ourselves is our sense of right and wrong—our morality. Because of the obvious implications children's morality has for school (and other) behavior, a great deal of attention has been devoted to the study of morality and its development. Before we discuss moral development, however, it is important for us to examine some difficult issues.

First, ideas about right and wrong vary from place to place. For example, while most Americans consider having more than one wife or husband to be wrong (in fact, there are laws against it), some cultures practice polygamy as a matter of course, attaching great prestige to those who have many spouses. Similarly, incest is morally repugnant in most cultures, but it was an approved practice among royalty in ancient Egypt, and certain forms have occurred in other areas of the world. Finally, even murder was practiced as an important religious ceremony by the Thugees of India as recently as the early part of this century.

A second issue involves who decides what is morally correct. Most of us quickly could agree on the importance of such qualities as trustworthiness, honesty, truthfulness, and the need to respect the rights of others. Once we get beyond such global concepts, however, agreement is much harder to find. Consider, for example, the very different positions taken by thoughtful, mature people on issues such as abortion, nuclear power, nuclear disarmament, capital punishment, and U.S. support for nondemocratic governments. Who decides which view is morally correct?

A third issue is whether the schools should teach moral values. Even if a majority of people within a school district agreed on moral values, should schools teach them? The issue is a long way from being resolved, especially when we consider controversies surrounding topics such as sex education, biological evolution (a moral issue in some parts of the country), and the contents of books (books have been banned from some school libraries because they contained passages about sex, alcoholism, depression, or atheism).

Despite difficult issues in the study of moral development, it is clear that students' moral values are affected by their teachers and other students. While there is disagreement about the role teachers should play, an understanding of moral development remains important.

Students do bring up moral issues, and decisions must be made about dilemmas involving morality. In short, there is no way to escape the fact that teachers are involved in students' moral development. In this part of the chapter we will examine two different theoretical perspectives on moral development. A knowledge of each will help you make better decisions about the moral development issues you encounter as a teacher.

Kohlberg and Stages of Moral Development

One of the major theories of moral development was formulated by the late Lawrence Kohlberg (e.g., 1958, 1984, 1987) in the 1950s. Kohlberg's theory is cognitive-developmental in origin and is based on ideas about moral development originally proposed by Jean Piaget (see Chapter Four). Kohlberg argued that there are five discrete stages of moral development (Kohlberg, 1984, 1987). Unlike Piaget's developmental stages, however, Kohlberg's stages of moral development are not tied to specific ages (Kohlberg, 1987). Kohlberg (1958) originally proposed six stages of moral development. However, he reformulated his theory by deleting the sixth stage just prior to his death. We will examine each of the five stages included in Kohlberg's revised theory.

Stage 1: Heteronomous Morality. For children at Kohlberg's first stage, moral behavior is heteronomous (under external control). A behavior is moral if it doesn't get punished. Immoral behaviors are punished because they are immoral, and they are immoral because they are punished. Good and bad are inherent in behaviors. For example, stealing is wrong to stage 1 children in the same way that grass is green. When a stage 1 child is asked why it is wrong to steal, the child will probably respond "because it's stealing," and believe that this statement settles the issue.

Stage 2: Individualism and Exchange. For children at this stage, moral actions amount to doing things that further one's own interest, while allowing others to do the same. Stage 2 children know that other people have their own interests that differ from or even conflict with their own. In order to get what they want from other people, stage 2 children understand that they must recognize and respond to others' needs. Morality involves making fair deals and equal trades with other people.

Stage 3: Mutual Expectations and Interpersonal Conformity. From Kohlberg's (1987) perspective, stage 3 marks the onset of what he called "conventional morality." At this stage, children value relationships based on mutual trust and loyalty. Other people no longer are seen as objects to be manipulated in order to reach some goal. Stage 3 children try to live up to the expectations of people close to them and work at fulfilling various roles (e.g., being a good brother). Youngsters at this stage see themselves as moral because they genuinely care about others and want to be seen as good people. Individual interests take a back seat to mutual agreements and shared moral values. Further, moral development at this level involves being able to see things from the perspective of other people (e.g., "I'll bring in Mary's skates. If I were her, that's what I'd expect.").

Stage 4: Social System. People who move into stage 4 still possess "conventional morality" but at a more sophisticated level than at stage 3. Rather than basing moral values on immediate interaction with others, stage 4 morality relies on an abstract understanding of society as a whole. Appropriate roles and rules are established by society. Individual relations still are important, but they are understood from the perspective of society's legal, social, or religious systems. Morality is defined as meeting social and/or religious responsibilities, upholding the law, and contributing to society and its institutions. People at stage 4 meet obligations and preserve social structure. Antisocial behavior is seen as wrong because if everyone behaved antisocially, the system would break down.

Stage 5: Social Contract. Kohlberg argued that stage 5 involves "postconventional morality." Stage 5 individuals raise basic questions about the need to follow laws and about how laws are determined by society. They take a *prior-to-society perspective*. That is, they understand that if a group of rational people existed without any social structure, a mutually beneficial society soon would emerge. Such a society would include fair procedures for determining laws and agreements about abiding by those laws. People at stage 5 further understand that laws usually should be followed because they have resulted from a social contract, an implied agreement among the members of a society. In addition, stage 5 thinkers are aware of the basis for social commitments and freely meet them. However, laws and social commitments are not accepted blindly. Instead, they are evaluated on the basis of "the greatest good for the greatest number" (the principle of *utility*) and whether or not they respect absolute rights such as life and liberty. On this basis, then, stage 5 individuals see that laws typically should be obeyed but that a given law or even an entire social structure or religious system may be rejected if it violates the intrinsic worth and dignity of individuals. For example, a stage 5 person in Nazi Germany would have understood the need to follow a society's rules but would have made a rational decision to break its laws because of the persecution of the Jews. Similarly, a stage 5 thinker in our society might see the value in most of our laws but protest specific issues (e.g., the death penalty) because they seem to violate the concept of a rational social contract. For stage 5 thinkers, the social system is important, but it does not have the last word in moral correctness. Societies themselves can be evaluated on a moral basis.

The Process of Moral Development.   How do children move from one stage of moral development to the next, and why do some people progress further than others? In attempting to answer these questions, Kohlberg (1987) took a cognitive-developmental approach. He believed that moral dilemmas and responses of other people to those dilemmas bring about cognitive conflict or disequilibrium (see Chapter Four), which can be resolved by constructing more adequate moral structures. Kohlberg also argued that general cognitive abilities are important in moral reasoning. For example, stage 4 reasoning requires a highly abstract understanding of social structure, while stage 5 involves the even more abstract concept of moral values existing prior to society. Kohlberg acknowledged, however, that while cognitive development (attaining formal operations, for example) does not ensure advanced moral development, it may be a necessary condition for it to occur (Kohlberg, 1987).

Beyond general cognitive development, however, Kohlberg's major emphasis in accounting for moral development was the increasing ability to take others' perspective (e.g., Kohlberg, 1984). In Kohlberg's theory, each stage requires more sophisticated perspective-taking than the preceding stage. For instance, stage 2 thinking involves a recognition that other people have perspectives different from one's own, while perspective-taking in stage 3 demands a sophisticated coordination of many points of view. Stage 4, of course, is even more demanding because it requires taking the perspective of society as a whole. Stage 5 requires yet more abstract perspectives—perspectives outside of and logically prior to society.

Assessing Moral Reasoning.   How is a person's level of moral reasoning to be determined? Kohlberg employed interviews with subjects in which moral dilemmas are presented and followed up by a series of questions. The questions are designed to determine how the subjects reasoned their way through the dilemma. Kohlberg's most famous interview story is the so-called "Heinz" dilemma.

> In Europe, a woman was near death from a special kind of cancer. There was one drug that the doctors thought might save her. It was a form of radium that a druggist in the same town had recently discovered. The drug was expensive to make, but the druggist was charging ten times what the drug cost him to make. He paid $400 for the radium and charged $4,000 for a small dose of the drug. The sick woman's husband, Heinz, went to everyone he knew to borrow the

money and tried every legal means, but he could only get together about $2,000, which is half of what it cost. He told the druggist that his wife was dying, and asked him to sell it cheaper or let him pay later. But the druggist said, "No, I discovered the drug and I'm going to make money from it." So, having tried every legal means, Heinz gets desperate and considers breaking into the man's store to steal the drug for his wife.

1. Should Heinz steal the drug?

2. Why or why not?

3. Does Heinz have a duty or obligation to steal the drug?

4. Why or why not?

5. If Heinz doesn't love his wife, should he steal the drug for her? (If subject favors not stealing, ask: Does it make a difference in what Heinz should do whether or not he loves his wife?)

6. Why or why not?

7. Suppose the person dying is not his wife but a stranger. Should Heinz steal the drug for a stranger?

8. Why or why not?

9. Is it important for people to do everything they can to save another's life?

10. Why or why not?

11. In general, should people try to do everything they can to obey the law?

12. Why or why not?

13. How does this apply to what Heinz should do? *(from Kohlberg, 1984)*

Kohlberg didn't determine people's stage of moral development merely by looking at the answers they give to such dilemmas (e.g., "Yes, Heinz should steal the drug"). Instead, he examined the reasoning employed to justify the solution. Of course, analyzing a person's moral reasoning through such a procedure is extremely difficult. In fact, the most recent version of Kohlberg's scoring manual is hundreds of pages long! Not surprisingly, there has been considerable interest in simplified methods of assessing moral reasoning.

Among the alternatives to Kohlberg's interview strategy for assessing moral development is the *Defining Issues Test* developed by James Rest (1983). Rest's test is based on the idea that people at different stages of moral development differ in what they see as the major issues in resolving a moral dilemma. His test contains six dilemmas (three drawn directly from Kohlberg) with a set of twelve issue-statements for each. In the set of statements following the Heinz dilemma, for example, are issue-statements similar to the following: "Shouldn't the community's laws be upheld?" and "Isn't it only natural for a loving husband to care so much for his wife that he'd steal?" From Rest's perspective, a stage 3 subject would identify the second issue-statement as most important, while a stage 4 subject would select the first one. By having subjects rank order the importance of the issue-statements in each set following a dilemma, each person's level of moral development can be determined.

Criticisms of Kohlberg's Theory.   In the past several years there has been considerable criticism of Kohlberg's work. One criticism has been that Kohlberg's original work was based almost solely on male subjects and that his theory is biased toward males (Gilligan, 1982; Gilligan & Attanucci, 1988). Recent work, however, shows no differences in the stages of moral development attained by males and females (see Miller & Bersoff, 1988; Snarey, Reimer, & Kohlberg, 1985; Vasudev, 1988).

A second criticism is that different studies have used different methods to assess moral development. Of course, the result of employing many different measures of moral development is that we cannot be sure that the same things are being measured in different studies. This issue is a problem, and research comparing the various methods of assessing stages of moral development must be conducted before it can be resolved.

A third criticism of Kohlberg's work is the lack of cross-cultural validation of his ideas. That is, the early work of Kohlberg and others in the area focused almost exclusively on testing subjects in the United States. Studies in Turkey (Nisan & Kohlberg, 1982) and Israel (Snarey et al., 1985), however, have produced results similar to those obtained in the United States (see also Boyes & Walker, 1988).

Another early criticism of Kohlberg's work centered on the fact that very few people were found to be thinking at stages 5 and 6. In response to this criticism, Kohlberg reevaluated his theory (1987) and described the general trend of moral development as a progression from stages 1 to 5, with stage 6 being set aside. According to Kohlberg's last works (1984, 1987), most ten-year-olds are at stage 2, with some also at stages 1 and 3. During adolescence, stage 3 reasoning is dominant, but students at stage 2 still appear as do a few students who

PRACTICE EXERCISE 7–1   IDENTIFYING STAGES OF MORAL
                                DEVELOPMENT

Below are a set of statements. For each, decide which of Kohlberg's
five stages is best illustrated. Keep in mind that in real life, isolated
instances of moral reasoning usually are ambiguous. This is why
Kohlberg's assessments depend on detailed interviews and complex
scoring methods. Our answers appear on page 244.

1. You should be nice to other people so that when you want
   something, they will be nice to you.

2. Breaking a law is justified if that law violates basic principles
   of equality for all.

3. People should never break the law. Even if they dislike a law,
   people must remember that if everyone broke laws they
   disliked, the result would be the destruction of our society.

4. As a social worker you should report that a "divorced"
   couple really is living together in order to gain extra welfare
   payments. Even if you have great sympathy in a particular
   case, you must do your duty. The rules may be harsh, but
   society is counting on you to do your job.

5. Your sister has special obligations to you, as a sister, and you
   in turn have obligations to her, as her sister.

6. Congress shall make no law respecting an establishment
   of religion or prohibiting the free exercise thereof; or
   abridging the freedom of speech or of the press, or the right
   of the people peaceably to assemble and petition the
   government for a redress of grievances.

7. Robbery is a crime because it is wrong.

8. You can't run wild doing whatever you want because this
   might get in the way of someone doing what she wants.
   You have to see things from other people's perspective, too.

9. You shouldn't take a friend's candy bar because it would
   destroy the relationship of trust between the two of you.

10. You shouldn't take things from people because they might
    take things away from you, too.

11. You should always obey your father. Why? Because he's your
    father!

12. You should be honest at all times because it is important to
    be a moral person whom others can depend on.

have progressed to stage 4. Stage 4 reasoning, while appearing in some people early in adolescence, does not become dominant until people are in their twenties. Finally, stage 5 reasoning does not appear until the twenties and remains a rare attainment.

The last and perhaps most telling criticism of Kohlberg's approach is that his methods measure how people think about moral decisions, not how they would actually behave. Kohlberg (1987) acknowledged this criticism and indicated that research must begin to focus on how well his evaluations of moral development predict actual moral behavior. To date, limited research evidence does support the predictability of moral behavior from Kohlberg's stages (Hart, 1988a), but a great deal of work remains to be completed.

A Social Learning View of Moral Development

In contrast to Kohlberg, some theorists hold that children acquire their moral values primarily through the observation and imitation of other people. In their view, a social learning perspective, children imitate what they see other people doing as long as the actions they observe do not lead to punishment.

Bandura (1986) has argued that children imitate more than behaviors. He suggests that they also take on the standards of behavior and personal characteristics of people they admire. At first, this imitation centers on the parents, but as children mature they are more and more likely to identify with others (e.g., peers, teachers, professional athletes, rock stars, media figures). Inevitably, as children's identification shifts from parents to others, conflicts in moral standards arise. Ultimately, a person's morals are formed from a combination of the values adopted from parents, those modeled after other significant people, and the consequences of holding these values to the developing person.

Kohlberg agreed that imitation is an important process in moral development. However, as we have seen, he placed far greater emphasis on the role of cognitive development (especially perspective-taking) in accounting for the changes we see in people's moral values. Recent advances in social learning theory also have come to place more and more emphasis on cognition in moral development.

Social Cognition

In recent years, several psychologists working in the general area of social learning have turned to analyses of social cognition in order to explain complex processes such as moral development. Children's increasing knowledge of *why* they and other people act as they

A person's moral values are formed from a combination of values adopted from parents and other significant people.

do is a critical component of moral development. Consider the following situation:

> Sandy's fifth-grade teacher was asking the children in her room questions about a vocabulary exercise they were to have completed the night before. Sandy got a new kitten last night and forgot all about her assignment. When it was Sandy's turn to answer the teacher's question, she guessed at the answer and got it right. Sandy knew that the reason for her success was good luck. How do you think she felt?
> A. thankful
> B. surprised
> C. happy

If you'll examine the options presented above for a moment, you'll see that they fall into two categories—those reactions dependent solely on the outcome (C, happy, in this instance) and those that require a more subtle understanding of the situation (A and B). This second category of alternatives can be referred to as **causally linked** because they take into account the reasons behind the outcome.

Outcome-dependent reactions to events are determined entirely by their results—feeling happy when a test is passed, when a new doll is obtained, when a hug is received, or feeling sad when a toy is broken, a test is failed, or a mitten is lost. Although all of us have such reactions to events, they are relatively unsophisticated because they focus only on outcomes. More sophisticated reactions focus not only on outcomes but on *why* outcomes happen (Graham, in press).

Imagine, for instance, how you might have reacted in Sandy's place. True, you'd probably feel happy (mildly pleased might be a more apt description for most of us), but wouldn't surprise or thankfulness be a more appropriate description? After all, the question was answered correctly on a lucky guess. Similarly, let's suppose that you forget to study for the next examination in this course (obviously, an unlikely possibility) and fail it. How would you react? You probably would feel sad, but wouldn't anger (at yourself) or shame be better descriptions? Instead of focusing on the outcome and feeling sad, it is far more probable that you'd emphasize the *cause* of the outcome in your reaction.

The analyses we make of situations for which we seek "why" answers are called causal attributions. Our feelings and reactions emphasize the *cause* of an outcome.

The idea of outcome-dependent and causally linked reactions to events can be applied to moral reasoning (Yuille & Perner, 1988). For example, we may feel anger and repugnance if we hear on the radio that a person has killed his aged father. If we discover later that the parent was suffering from extremely painful terminal cancer and that the son turned himself in to the authorities immediately after the event, we might have a very different reaction—pity, sadness, and confusion about what is right in such situations. Similarly, if we hear that someone has robbed a convenience store by threatening the cashier with a knife, we might react with a harsh moral judgment about the perpetrator of the crime. Later, however, when we find out that the robber was destitute and stealing money to feed her baby, we probably would revise our judgment. Returning to the example of Heinz, which we described earlier in the chapter, the odds are very good that we would make a different moral judgment if we found out that Heinz had plenty of money in his bank account.

The analyses we make of situations for which we seek "why" answers are referred to as **causal attributions** (Graham, in press). In an interesting early study, Weiner (1980) examined how causal attributions influenced college students' judgments. The participants in this experiment were randomly assigned to one of three conditions and asked to read a description of a hypothetical event. The descriptions Weiner used (1980, p. 677) were as follows:

1.   At about 1:00 in the afternoon you are walking through campus and a student comes up to you. He says that you do not know him, but that you are both enrolled in the same class and he has happened to notice you. He asks if you would lend him the class notes from the meetings last week. He indicates that he needs the notes because he skipped class to go to the beach.

2.   At about 1:00 in the afternoon you are walking through campus and a student comes up to you. He says that you don't know him, but that you are both enrolled in the same class and he has happened to notice you. He asks if you would lend him the class notes from the meetings last week. He indicates that he needs the notes because he was having difficulty with his eyes, a change in type of glasses was required, and during the week he had difficulty seeing because of eyedrops and other treatments.

3.   At about 1:00 in the afternoon you are walking through the campus and a student comes up to you. He says that you do not know

him, but that you are both enrolled in the same class and he has happened to notice you. He asks if you would lend him the class notes from the meetings last week. He indicates that he needs the notes because he was having difficulty with his eyes, a change in type of glasses was required, and during the week he had difficulty seeing because of eye-drops and other treatments. You notice that he is wearing especially dark glasses and has a patch covering one eye.

When the participants finished reading the passage they were assigned, they were asked to imagine that the event actually had occurred and to describe their feelings toward the student trying to borrow class notes. Not surprisingly, the most positive feelings were generated by the last situation, in which the "note-borrower" was wearing very dark glasses and an eye patch. The least positive feelings were generated by the "note-borrower" who had been to the beach. Although Weiner's study did not examine actual behavior, if behavior is, in fact, governed by our causal attributions, the student with the eye patch would be far more likely to obtain notes from his classmates than the student who went to the beach.

The kinds of causal attributions made by the participants in Weiner's (1980) study were fairly sophisticated, with many expressing skepticism about the students with eye trouble and others looking for hidden motives in the "note-borrowers." Such sophisticated reasoning, of course, is common in adults but not in young children (see Fabes, Eisenberg, McCormick, & Wilson, 1988). As children develop, their abilities to make causal attributions improve apace with their cognitive development. In consequence, moral judgments depend more and more on the interpretation of events rather than on the events themselves. In early childhood, moral judgments are outcome dependent. An act is wrong if it is wrong, regardless of the causes (e.g., stealing is wrong, even if a starving family can find no other way to eat). By middle childhood, the emphasis is more on the causes of events (why things happen), and by adulthood our moral judgments are based primarily on causal attributions.

As you can see, the idea of causal attributions in moral development is similar in many ways to Kohlberg's views on perspective-taking. In both cases the focus is on understanding the causes for people's behavior. However, while Kohlberg emphasized discrete stages, researchers in social cognition do not. From a social cognition perspective, moral judgments depend on our cognitive abilities. As cognitive development proceeds, we are better and better able to analyze situations in answer to our "why" questions, and so our moral judgments become more and more sophisticated.

Applications for Teaching: Fostering Moral Development

Although controversy surrounds the role of moral education in the schools, we have seen that moral development is an inescapable part of the schooling process. As teachers understand more about moral development, they are better able to make excellent teaching decisions about moral issues. Our guidelines here are based on the work of Kohlberg (e.g., 1984, 1987), and Weiner (1986).

1. Don't avoid moral issues. Students should be encouraged to discuss moral issues that come up in school or elsewhere in their lives. Teachers should participate in these discussions by asking questions that will help students identify the moral conflicts involved. If you wish to structure such discussions, you can use hypothetical issues (such as the Heinz dilemma). When the discussion flags, it is wise to model your own use of moral reasoning and perspective-taking.

2. Emphasize moral reasoning. When dilemmas are discussed, students may change the focus of the session to nonmoral issues. When students get off track, redirect them to moral aspects of the problem. Also, follow up student opinions by asking them "why questions" that cause them to think about and describe their reasoning.

3. Stress perspective-taking. Encourage students to see issues from the perspective of the different people involved. Also, as different points of view emerge in class discussions, try to get students to think about issues from the perspective of other students. With younger children in particular, it often helps to have them act out the roles of some of the characters in a dilemma. In the Heinz story, for instance, one student could play the role of Heinz, another could take the part of his wife, and a third student could take the druggist's role.

4. Stimulate student-to-student interactions. Encourage students to interact with each other, not with you. Using small groups and arranging seats in a circle can facilitate this process.

5. Don't be "the authority." Another characteristic of many classroom discussions is that students view the teacher as an authority, the final arbiter of right and wrong. After getting discussions started, you should try to stay out of them, other than keeping the students focused on the moral issue at hand and making them give their reasons for opinions. It *is* difficult to avoid giving answers to dilemmas, but students will gain far more if they are allowed to work through moral issues among themselves.

6. Consider the students' level of moral development. Although determining the precise level of student reasoning is not necessary, teachers need to keep in mind the kinds of moral reasoning that students are likely to use. By understanding the level of moral reasoning students use, teachers are better able to question them in ways that nudge them toward more sophisticated levels of reasoning.

7. Emphasize generalization. It is one thing to employ, for example, stage 4 reasoning in a class discussion and another to use such reasoning with personal issues. Moral development isn't simply a matter of moving from one stage of reasoning to the next. Students need practice in employing their newly emerging reasoning skills on a wide variety of topics.

8. Provide a supportive atmosphere. Discussion of moral issues is risky business for students. Any time moral issues are examined in a group setting, conflict occurs. Students may come to question and possibly even abandon old ways of thinking. Such challenges are important for moral development, but they should happen in a classroom atmosphere of cooperation and trust. Help your students see that disequilibrium leads to further development and that questioning another person's reasoning is not the same thing as questioning his or her value as a person.

Summary

The self-concept is a person's total view of him- or herself. It is shaped by and shapes experience. Development of the self-concept begins with an awareness of self at about eighteen months of age. The "I" of the self-concept is the subject doing the thinking, while the "Me" of the self-concept is the object. There are four aspects of the "Me" that change in emphasis during development: the physical self, the active self, the social self, and the psychological self. Early in life, self-understanding is dominated by the physical self. During the elementary school years, the emphasis shifts to the active self. By junior high school, the social self becomes most critical to self-understanding, while most high-school-aged students focus on the psychological self in their self-understanding.

The "I" of self-concepts refers to the subjective self who organizes and interprets experiences. Four dimensions of the "I" are continuity (people's sense that they remain the same person over time), distinctiveness (people's awareness that they are unique), volition (individuals' beliefs that they are active agents with free will), and self-reflectivity (the ability of the self to consider its continuity, distinctiveness, and volition).

Students' self-concepts have a profound influence on their school performance, especially in terms of the types of goals they select. Students with entity-oriented theories about themselves tend to select performance goals, while students with incremental theories strive for self-improvement goals. Teachers can do a great deal to facilitate the development of children's self-concepts, especially by providing classroom experiences that allow children to achieve success and develop positive views of themselves.

An important part of how we see ourselves is based on our moral values. Lawrence Kohlberg fashioned the major theory of moral development. In his view, there are five stages of moral development. These stages are not tied to ages, and not all people pass through all the stages.

In the first of Kohlberg's stages, heteronomous morality, moral behavior is what doesn't get punished. Moral behavior in the second stage, individualism and exchange, is characterized by doing things that further one's own interests, while allowing others to do the same. Stages 3 and 4 are stages of "conventional morality." People at stage 3 see themselves as moral because they genuinely care about others and want to be seen as good people. Stage 4 involves an abstract under-standing of society as a whole and an adherence to the laws of society. "Postconventional morality" appears in stage 5. People at stage 5 can see that societies can be immoral and govern their own behavior on the basis of the greatest good for the greatest number.

Other views of moral development are provided by social learning theorists. According to Albert Bandura, moral values are learned by imitation of parents, peers, and teachers. In the newly emerging social cognitive perspective, the emphasis is on children's developing abili-ties to make causal attributions—to understand the "why" behind events.

In this chapter, we reviewed the development of self-concept and morality. We build on both of these issues in the next chapter, "Motiva-tion," in which we examine the role of motivation in teaching and learning.

Suggested Readings

Gilligan, C., & Attanucci, J. (1988). Two moral orientations: Gender differences and similarities. *Merrill-Palmer Quarterly, 34,* 223–238.

> *This monograph-length article and the subsequent commentary by Vasudev provide an excellent summary and critique of contemporary moral development theory.*

Kohlberg, L. (1987). *Childhood psychology and childhood education: A cognitive developmental view.* New York: Longman.

> *This volume is the last of Kohlberg's major contributions. It is an especially fruitful source of ideas for moral education.*

Kohlberg, L. (1984). *Essays on cognitive development: Vol. II. The psycholo-gy of moral development.* New York: Harper & Row.

> *This book presents a collection of Kohlberg's writings on the psychology of moral development. It is the most complete presentation of his theoretical views.*

Lapsley, D. K., & Power, F. C. (1988). *Self, ego, and identity.* New York: Springer-Verlag.

> *Lapsley and Power's book is an excellent compilation of contemporary perspectives on self-concept.*

Rogers, C. R. (1983). *Freedom to learn for the '80s.* Columbus, Ohio: Merrill.

> *The late Carl Rogers' book is an excellent source for teachers. We strongly recommend it to anyone working with children.*

Answers to Practice
Exercise 7–1

1. Stage 2. The person making this statement could see that doing good may be to one's own advantage. The morality is strictly "you scratch my back, I'll scratch yours."

2. Stage 5. This statement clearly shows a prior-to-society perspective. In this person's view, laws that violate basic principles should be resisted. Breaking laws for this reason is quite different from breaking laws (e.g., cheating on one's income tax) because it is in a person's *own* self-interest.

3. Stage 4. The person uttering this remark is fixed on the standards of society and the need to maintain them.

4. Stage 4. The acceptance of the social system takes the form of insisting on the need to fulfill abstract social roles, regardless of personal feelings.

5. Stage 3. The emphasis here is on fulfilling one's role, but it is in terms of immediate relationships.

6. Stage 5. Surprise. This is the First Amendment to the United States Constitution. It demonstrates a stage 5 perspective in specifying that Congress may not make laws that violate individuals' fundamental rights, even if a majority of the people support those laws.

7. Stage 1. What's wrong is what's wrong and that's that.

8. Stage 2. The "tit-for-tat" nature of stage 2 thinking is clear.

9. Stage 3. This person's statement is based on the idea that a betrayal of a relationship is immoral.

10. Stage 2. "You take care of me; I'll take care of you."

11. Stage 1. This statement clearly indicates a heteronomous respect for authority.

12. Stage 3. Here the motivation to be honest is not based just on the expectation of getting some return from other people (as in stage 2). Instead, there is a real desire to be a good person who is honest. However, the statement doesn't really indicate a grasp of social structure (stage 4) or of social contract (stage 5).

CHAPTER
8

Motivation

Most motivational theorists are concerned with the development of human potential. In applications to education, particular emphasis has been placed on the students' feelings of worth and on their personality development. A major concept is that of the self. Knowledge of one's self and a good self-concept (see Chapter Seven) are keys to motivation and to achievement.

From this theoretical viewpoint, often labeled *humanistic*, students should be free to choose and to seek out new learning. The teacher should not act as an authoritarian director but should be responsive to student needs. The learner is all-important, the teacher much less so. Teachers should be accepting of students and their behavior. They should allow them to seek and discover. Humanistic theorists such as Carl Rogers, whom we discussed in Chapter Seven, and Abraham Maslow believe a supportive and nonthreatening environment reduces external threat and contributes to the possibility of genuine learning.

After reading this chapter, you should be able to meet the following objectives.

1. Describe the implications of Maslow's theory for your practices as a teacher.

2. Discuss the classroom implications of attribution theory.

3. Describe the effect your knowledge of achievement motivation will have on your teaching practices.

4. Outline the applications of motivation theory for your teaching.

Maslow's Theory of Motivation

The late Abraham Maslow, considered by many as the founder of humanistic psychology (e.g., Corey, 1977; Hamachek, 1987), developed a theory of motivation that has had significant effects on American education. His theory is based on the idea that gratification of needs is "the most important single principle underlying all development" (Maslow, 1968, p. 55). For Maslow the most important feature of motivation, "the single, holistic principle that binds together the multiplicity of human motives," is the tendency for new, higher needs to emerge as lower needs are gratified (Maslow, 1968, p. 55). As very basic (lower) needs are met—such as a need for safety—other needs replace

The desire for security and affection is basic to all human beings. Basic needs must be met before higher level needs can develop.

them as motivating forces. People's motivation derives directly from their needs and human behavior is therefore oriented toward need gratification (see Maslow, 1987*).

Maslow postulated seven basic levels of needs: physiological, safety, belongingness and love, esteem, self-actualization, knowing and understanding, and aesthetics. Maslow referred to the first four as **deficiency needs** because humans are motivated to fulfill them as a

---

*Maslow's classic volume, *Motivation and Personality*, recently was revised by Robert Frager, James Fadiman, Cynthia McReynolds, and Ruth Cox.

"Is this it? Is this self-actualization?"

result of deficits—lack of food, lack of safety, the absence of love, and lack of esteem. Maslow suggested that people were motivated to gratify the last three needs, which he called **being needs**, when their deficiency needs were met. Being needs are motivating not because of deficits but because of basic human desires for self-actualization, knowledge,and aesthetics (Maslow, 1987).

A Hierarchy of Needs   Maslow proposed that the needs in his system were steps to be completed in a progression toward self-growth. They are *hierarchical*, that is, one level of need must be met before the next becomes motivating. Maslow's hierarchy is presented in Figure 8–1. Until physiological needs are gratified, humans do not strive for safety needs. Similarly, until safety needs are gratified, humans do not seek to gratify love needs, and so on. While we can think of obvious examples

FIGURE 8–1   MASLOW'S HIERARCHY OF NEEDS

Aesthetic needs

needs to experience
and understand beauty
for its own sake

Needs to know

curiosity, a need to learn
about the world to satisfy
the basic growth urge of
human beings

Needs for self-actualization

the striving for "the full use and
exploitation of talents, capacities,
potentialities" (Maslow, 1970, p. 150)

Needs for esteem

needs for self-respect, a feeling of
adequacy, competence, mastery

Needs for love and belongingness

needs for affection, feeling wanted, roots in
a family or peer group

Needs for safety

avoidance of danger and anxiety, desire for security

Physiological needs

needs for food, drink, sleep, and so on

Source: Adapted from Maslow, 1970.

of people who do not fit this hierarchical scheme (such as the painter who goes without food and comfort for extended periods of time and devotes herself fully to aesthetic pursuits), the general pattern was of greatest theoretical interest to Maslow. The motivating needs in a person's life are those that are deficient and, later, when these deficiency needs are met, those that reflect the innate human desire for self-actualization, knowledge, and aesthetics.

Implications for Teaching

Maslow's theory often has been applied as a framework for thinking about student motivation. Teachers should do everything possible to help students satisfy their deficiency needs because an inner motivation for knowledge simply will not develop until these basic needs have been met. Teachers are not always able to intervene in children's lives to the extent necessary to fulfill deficiency needs, however. They cannot replace the love a child is not receiving at home, nor can they ensure the satisfaction of safety needs away from the school. Teachers, instead, are in the position of providing a classroom environment that fulfills deficiency needs to the greatest possible extent. They also act as children's advocates in helping others, primarily parents, provide an environment in which deficit needs are met outside the school. A common example of the advocacy role is the teacher who discerns that a child is the victim of abuse at home and who then initiates actions to remedy the problem.

When being needs are considered, teachers should do everything possible to make the acquisition of new knowledge attractive to students (Maslow, 1968). Intertwined in the development of attractive, meaningful learning experiences is the facilitation of decision making among students (Vander Meij, 1988). Similarly, Maslow has stressed that decisions leading to self-growth can be facilitated by "making the growth choice positively attractive and less dangerous and by making the regressive choice less attractive and more costly" (1968, p. 59). Simply stated, students need to be encouraged toward self-growth.

Of the theoretical perspectives we have examined thus far in the text, Maslow's theory is most compatible with Jean Piaget's view of motivation. The best learning, according to Maslow, is self-motivated. Like Piaget, Maslow's proponents would suggest that children, when given the opportunity, will make wise choices for their learning. Maslow's position leads naturally to the basis for "free education," an approach in which teachers arrange attractive and meaningful learning situations from which students may select those they find personally valuable. In this approach, the principles of teacher-directed classroom management are secondary to the motivating power of

PRACTICE EXERCISE 8–1   YOUR PERSONAL HIERARCHY OF NEEDS

An analysis of our motivation patterns often gives us a revealing look at ourselves. Think back over your activities in the past forty-eight hours. Associate as many of your activities as you can with the levels in Maslow's hierarchy. Then make an estimate of the proportion of your total waking time devoted to activities at each level of need. Be honest in analyzing your motivations. If you went to class because a quiz was given, you may not want to place this activity in the category "Needs for knowledge."

Percent of Time	*Needs*	*Your Actions*
_____	*Aesthetic needs:* needs to experience and understand beauty for its own sake	
_____	*Needs for knowledge:* curiosity, a need to learn about the world to satisfy the basic growth urge	
_____	*Needs for self-actualization:* the striving for "the full use and exploitation of talents, capacities, potentialities" (Maslow, 1970, p. 150)	
_____	*Needs for esteem:* needs for self-respect, a feeling of adequacy, competence, mastery	
_____	*Needs for love and belongingness:* needs for affection, feeling wanted, roots in a group	
_____	*Needs for safety:* avoidance of danger, anxiety; desire for security	
_____	*Physiological needs:* needs for food, drink, sleep, and so on	

Note: Are your activities generally related to the being needs or the deficiency needs? Are there any problems in seeking to fill needs primarily at one level or another? Is the pattern you indicated one that you will always be satisfied with?

students' self-chosen learning activities—the learning experience itself becomes its own reward.

A humanistic approach to teaching requires that teachers return to the theme we have taken up in each chapter of this book: the necessity for (1) determining students' current abilities and needs and (2) deriving meaningful instruction. As we will see, this theme also is present in other views of motivation.

Aspirations and the Need for Achievement

Another theoretical perspective that considers differences in students' motivation to achieve in school is referred to as *achievement motivation* (Ames & Archer, 1988). Achievement motivation theory is based on the early works of Hoppe (1930), Sears (1940), McClelland (1961), and Atkinson (e.g., 1967); it emphasizes the role of goals and students' success and failure experiences. We will begin our examination of this area by reviewing early work.

Hoppe's early work (Hoppe, 1930) described people's experiences with success and failure. He noted that people raised their levels of aspiration after successes and lowered them after failures. Hoppe felt that these changes in levels of aspirations protected people from

Knowledge of one's self and a good self-concept are keys to motivation and achievement.

Success helps students set reasonable and accurate goals. The feedback from successful performance not only encourages students but helps them judge their capabilities.

experiencing continued failure or from the kind of overly easy achievement that does not give a feeling of accomplishment. People choose a level of aspiration to balance two conflicting tendencies: the wish to succeed at the greatest level possible (which tends to increase aspirations) and the desire to avoid the disappointment that accompanies failure (which tends to lower aspirations). Hoppe also felt that the balancing mechanism could be thrown out of kilter. People who set unrealistically high goals inevitably fail and, conversely, people who set goals at a low level do not obtain any satisfaction from their accomplishments. For Hoppe, the idea was for students to set their levels of aspiration at realistic levels—achievable but satisfying.

A decade later, Sears (1940) affected the development of achievement motivation theory through an interesting experiment she conducted on the aspirations of elementary school children (Maehr, 1984). She identified three groups of upper elementary children: a "success" group (children with a consistent history of academic success in all areas), a "failure" group (children with a consistent record of academic failure in all areas), and a "differential" group (children with consistent records of success in reading but with records of failure in mathematics). The children in these groups were given a series of twenty speed tests in reading and math. After each test, the children were asked to estimate how long it would take them to complete the next test. Half of the children, those in the "success condition," were given lavish praise for their performance after most, but not all, of the tests. Likewise, the other half of the children, the "failure condition," were given severe criticism after most but not all of the tests.

The results indicated that the children in the success condition made accurate estimates of their performances on the speed tests—their goals were set at or slightly above their actual performance. This result was observed regardless of whether the children were from groups with prior success, failure, or differential records. On the other hand, children in the failure condition had much greater discrepancies between their goals and their actual performance. There also was a striking effect on how they set goals—some children set impossibly high goals while others set ridiculously low ones. Not surprisingly, the most powerful effects of the failure condition were on students with failure and differential backgrounds. Children with consistent histories of academic success (the success group) were somewhat better able to cope with repeated criticism of their performance, evidencing a more accurate and less variable pattern of goal setting.

This study provided confirmation of Hoppe's earlier ideas and reemphasized the effect of success and failure on aspirations. Success brought about fairly high but accurate aspirations, irrespective of the students' history of success or failure. Repeated failure, in contrast, seemed to cause students—especially those with histories of failure—to aspire either to unrealistically high or very low goals.

McClelland (e.g., 1961) continued work on **achievement motivation theory**, studying conditions under which people acquire their needs to achieve. One of McClelland's early coworkers, Atkinson, went on to formulate the basis for contemporary achievement motivation theory (see Maehr, 1984). In a series of experiments reminiscent of those conducted by Sears, Atkinson (1965, 1966, 1967) demonstrated that success-oriented people tend to set personal goals of intermediate difficulty while people with high levels of anxiety about failure often set goals that are either too high or too low. Atkinson has suggested that the unrealistic goal setting of anxiety-filled people allows for rationalization—"Nobody can blame me for failure because my goal was so high" or "With my goal set so low, how can I fail?" He observed that the tendency to be successful is affected by the likelihood of success and the attractiveness of its achievement. Conversely, the need to avoid failure develops when people experience repeated failure.

Modern views of achievement motivation still emphasize the effects of success and failure but now include different kinds of student goals (Dweck, 1988). Ames and Archer (1988), for example, make the same type of distinction between the kinds of goals that we discussed in Chapter Seven—between self-improvement and performance. Students with these different kinds of goals achieve at different levels. Because students who strive for self-improvement goals believe their efforts will make a real difference, they achieve at higher levels than students who set goals based on personal ability. In addition to these basic differences in achievement and beliefs about the value of effort, students with self-improvement goals also use more effective study strategies, prefer challenging tasks, and have more positive attitudes toward their coursework. Students with performance goals, on the other hand, tend to blame their ability levels for poor achievement and do not believe that their achievement is related to effort (see Ames & Archer, 1988, p. 264).

Can the kinds of goals students strive for be changed? Ames and Archer (1988, p. 264) report that "when students perceived their class as emphasizing a . . . [self-improvement] goal, they were more likely to report using effective learning strategies, prefer tasks that offer challenge, (and) like their class more . . ." Apparently, when teachers model the effects of effort, stress goals associated with each individual student's improvement over previous performance, and help students focus on how effort makes a difference, students can become oriented toward self-improvement. Helping students seek self-improvement, of course, is a major goal of any teacher. When students strive for self-improvement, they make real efforts to achieve. This, of course, is all we can ask of any student.

Attribution Theory

One way of thinking about achievement motivation uses the general framework of **attribution theory**. Attributions, as we saw in Chapter Seven, refer to people's interpretations of experience. Attribution theory helps us understand how students explain their successes and failures and how those explanations affect future achievement-oriented behavior. The foundation for attribution theory was set by the work of Fritz Heider (1944, 1958) and was later expanded and refined by Julian Rotter (1966), Bernard Weiner (e.g., 1985), and H. M. Lefcourt (1976).

Explanations of Success and Failure

Attribution theory suggests that people use one of seven different forms of explanations for their successes or failures: ability, effort, mood, difficulty of task, teacher bias, luck or chance, and unusual help from others (for a full discussion, see Dweck, 1988). If students fail a test, for example, they often ascribe their failure to (1) "not studying" (lack of effort), (2) the hard test (difficulty of task), (3) feeling emotionally drained when they took the test (mood), (4) studying the wrong thing (luck or chance), (5) capricious teacher behavior (teacher bias, e.g., "The teacher wanted to give me an F"), or (6) personal shortcomings (ability, e.g., "I've always been bad at math"). While ability, effort, mood, difficulty of task, teacher bias, and luck or chance often are used to explain both failures and successes (e.g., "I've always been good at English," "I studied hard for the test"), unusual help from others (7) is an attribution usually made only when an unexpectedly good performance occurs (e.g., "I'd never have passed without Ann's help"). Although one could suggest there are other possible explanations for successes or failures (e.g., "The directions were unclear," or "The room was so hot") (see Weiner, 1985; Wigfield, 1988), attribution theorists generally subsume any explanation not mentioning the seven attributions described above under the label of luck or chance.

Students' explanations of their successes and failures provide information about their locus of control (Wigfield, 1988). **Locus of control** refers to where a person feels the control of his or her successes and failures lies, that is, whether it is internal or external to him or her. Students with an internal locus of control are likely to attribute their successes to ability and effort and their failures to lack of effort. Students with an external locus of control are likely to believe that their successes and failures are governed by task difficulty, chance, lack of ability, mood, bias, or unusual help from others.

Students with an external locus of control are likely to think that their own efforts make little difference in achievement. After all, from their perspective, external factors are in control. Motivating such "external" children may be very difficult. Consequently, an important question is whether or not a student's locus of control can change. A recent study by Wigfield (1988) indicates that both age and experience of past success or failure have powerful effects on students' attribu-

Student explanations of success and failures provide information about their locus of control. This student has been asked to summarize his successes and failures on each project in this class. Such summaries provide valuable insight into student thinking.

tions. In general, as children become more mature and as they experience more success, their attributions become more and more internal. Perceptions of success, of course, depend on how well teachers are able to help students pursue realistic self-improvement goals.

Success Seekers and
Failure Avoiders

Success seekers are students who have a history of successful achievement in schools. They generally are self-confident and have strong achievement motivation and an internal locus of control. Success fosters success because it confirms their ideas about their abilities. Failure, for success seekers, is a signal that in the particular task in question they made a misjudgment about how much effort was required for success (Covington & Omelich, 1985). Failure seldom is taken as an indication of lack of ability; instead, it is a sign that more effort is necessary (Covington, 1985).

Failure avoiders, on the other hand, have very little confidence. Many have performed poorly in school and are likely to have an external locus of control. Achievement motivation seldom is internal, and failure avoiders depend heavily on external factors (approval, praise) for their motivation. Because they have a poor opinion of their own abilities, they try to avoid failure and thereby the loss of external support, that is, the approval of others. Failure also can be avoided by

Success seekers are students who have a history of successful achievement.

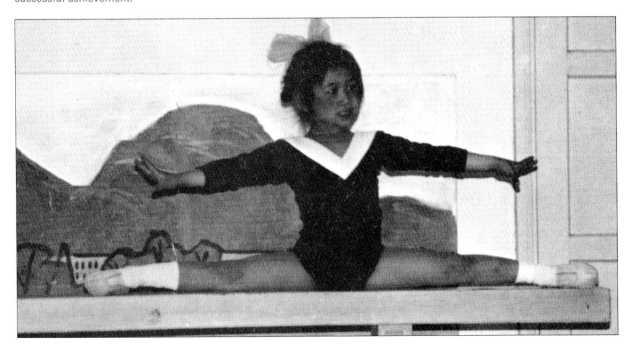

PRACTICE EXERCISE 8–2   ANALYZING ATTRIBUTIONS

Postmortems on athletic contests, writing or speaking competitions, music contests, and games all prompt people's explanations of why things went right or wrong. During the next week, observe at least one person who is talking about a success and another person who is describing a failure. Television interviews are a good source of such individuals, as are the newspapers. The "succeeder" or "failer" may be describing his or her own action or be serving as the spokesperson for a group (a football coach explaining a victory or a loss, for instance). Successes may include winning a race, being chosen as a representative or leader, or receiving an honor. Failure likewise may be observed in a variety of endeavors. Record below as specifically as you can what the person says about success and failure and compare your notes with those of others in your class. Does any pattern appear? Specifically answer the question of whether the attributions you observe are the kinds you hope your students will make about their own successes and failures.

Success Experience

The success was _____

The person was _____

To which of the following did the person attribute his or her success? (Give a quote from the person about the attribute he or she cited.)

Ability _____

Effort _____

Ease of task _____

Good luck or other factors _____

---

setting unrealistic goals, by lack of effort, or by false effort—you cannot really fail, for example, if you haven't really tried. Each of these strategies, however, actually makes further failure almost inevitable. Repeated failures continue to affirm the failure avoiders' belief in their poor ability.

Failure avoiders take failure as an indication of poor ability (Covington & Omelich, 1985), but they tend to attribute success to luck, chance, or ease of task. It seems that both success and failure may

---

PRACTICE EXERCISE 8–2   *CONTINUED*

How realistic/accurate were the attributions, in your estimate?

_____

_____

_____

_____

Failure Experience

The failure was _____

The person was _____

To which of the following factors did the person attribute his or her failure? (Give a quote from person about any factor he or she cited.)

Ability _____

Effort _____

Difficulty of task _____

Bad luck or other factors _____

How realistic/accurate were the attributions, in your estimate?

_____

_____

_____

_____

---

damage future achievement among failure avoiders—success because it results in less future effort (Barker & Graham, 1987) and failure because it confirms poor self-esteem and results in greater efforts to avoid failure without increased efforts to achieve. As Barker and Graham (1987) pointed out, however, the long-term effects of success in ability tasks (as opposed to tasks governed by chance) generally are positive. With continuing success, students can develop a more internal, more realistic locus of control and increase their motivation.

Applications for Teaching: Motivation Theory in the Classroom

1. Help students satisfy their deficiency needs. *Physiological needs*. Teachers can help students meet their physiological needs by some fairly straightforward actions. Especially for younger children, arrange for routine snack or drink breaks. Be aware that some of your students may not have had breakfast (and possibly no supper the night before). Where there is a need, encourage student participation in breakfast and lunch programs—many are free to students from low-income families.

Allow occasional breaks in classroom instruction. It is especially critical to be flexible in setting break times for small children, for whom naps or quiet times are important parts of the school day. A time to stretch is equally important for older children and adults.

Try to keep your room comfortable. A classroom that is too warm or too cool is not a good place to work. Remind students of the need for sweaters or the benefits of removing jackets. Be sure to ask your students about the classroom's comfort level.

Keep an eye out for students who seem to be feeling ill, and make sure that you are aware of any special health problems among your students. A student who does not feel well will almost never benefit from instruction.

Safety needs. Do everything possible to make students feel comfortable and secure in your classroom. Always avoid the use of ridicule or embarrassment in dealing with children. Instead, try to provide a warm, accepting classroom environment with firm and consistent guidelines. Our discussion of classroom management in Chapter Eleven should help you create such an atmosphere.

Do not allow students to bully or intimidate other students. Students need to be free from fears, including fears of physical abuse at the hands of older students. Incidents of intimidation and violent acts can and do occur in many schools.

School authorities need, therefore, to work doubly hard to make the school and its grounds a safe haven for all children.

Needs for love and belongingness. While teachers cannot replace parental love, they can help students develop a sense of belonging to the classroom. Little things can be important. Learn the names of each student as soon as possible. Make your comments to students personal and specific. Let students know that you care about each one of them.

Arrange one-to-one sessions with each child as frequently as possible. If practical, meet with the parents of each child. Encourage group activities that allow students to share personal experiences with each other. Not only do you want to show that you care about each student, but also you want to develop mutual concern among the students, based on successful cooperation.

Needs for esteem. The needs each child has for esteem from others and for self-esteem can be gratified to a great extent by judicious classroom management. Avoid comparisons between students. Students are unique individuals with specific strengths and weaknesses. Build on strengths, and avoid emphasizing weaknesses.

Promote cooperation and sharing to the greatest extent possible. Not only will this facilitate belongingness, but also it will be an aid in replacing competitive patterns of behavior (see Johnson, 1988).

In Chapter Twelve, "Planning for Meaningful Learning," we recommend setting individual goals for students and providing praise for their mastery of the goals. These procedures are especially appropriate for building students' concepts of themselves as successful learners. Give slower-learning students individual help in attaining their goals, and make sure you sincerely praise them when they achieve their goals.

Little things can be important
in satisfying needs for love and
belonging. For this first-grader,
a special place with the teacher
gives her a feeling of being
cared about.

2. Help students develop the desire to meet their being needs. According to Maslow's hierarchy of needs, self-actualization, knowing and understanding, and aesthetic needs can only come into play when deficiency needs are met. Helping students develop their being needs depends on the teacher's ability to structure meaningful and attractive learning activities. As much as possible, learning should be self-guided. Students can be helped to see the potential outcomes of certain decisions. As a teacher, you can help present choices that encourage growth as more attractive and less threatening than choices that limit growth.

Growth takes place when the next step forward is subjectively more delightful, more joyous, more intrinsically satisfying than the previous gratification. . . . The new experience validates itself rather than . . . any outside criterion. It is self-justifying, self-validating. (Maslow, 1968, p. 45).

Every action the teacher can take to make learning activities and growth choices more attractive is a step in the direction of facilitating internally motivated learning among students.

3. Promote feelings of success. Feelings of success will help your students develop realistic self-expectations, increase achievement motivation, and heighten positive self-regard. Several procedures teachers may use to promote feelings of success are readily available.

First, your activities and assignments should make student success likely. As we will see in Chapter Twelve, the goals you set for instruction should represent reachable and meaningful accomplishments. Each student should work for objectives based on his or her needs.

Second, provide students with accurate, specific, and personal feedback on their performance. As we will point out in Chapter Thirteen, effective instruction requires high-quality evaluation. Good evaluation allows students to gain maximum insight into their performance. Attributions of their successes and failures are thus much less likely to be distorted.

Third, do not be afraid to use reinforcement procedures as a part of your motivation plan. Consider the use of the approaches we discuss in Chapter Eleven, "Classroom Management," as a way of promoting feelings of success. Rewards for appropriate classroom behavior can certainly bring about feelings of satisfaction.

4. Help students develop achievement motivation. Some students, regardless of how well you satisfy their deficiency needs, promote the desirability of meeting their being needs, and enhance their feelings of success, still are likely to hold back from aspiring to goals at a challenging yet reachable level. There are, fortunately, some general approaches teachers may employ to help students acquire achievement motivation.

First, model appropriate achievement motivation, and arrange for other models with whom your students can identify. In modeling achievement motivation, point out how you select attainable yet challenging goals. Describe how goals that are too easy and those that are unattainable can be both impractical and frustrating. Emphasize self-knowledge in setting goals. When you employ other persons to model achievement motivation, choose realistic models. Millionaires and professional athletes, for example, may not be particularly good models for most children's achievement, in spite of the excitement they may generate. Instead, choose people who have accurately assessed their own abilities and have consistently set and met reasonable goals. It also seems especially important to choose a wide variety of models in order to avoid stereotypes of success and opportunity as limited by sex, ethnic group, or other characteristics.

Second, teachers can systematically encourage students to set improvement goals and gently discourage their use of performance goals. In individual sessions, have students describe their goals in several areas of classroom life. Show interest in and praise self-improvement goals. Try to help students restate performance goals in self-improvement terms. As Ames and Archer (1988) have noted, students are far more likely to work hard and enjoy their classes when they are striving for self-improvement goals.

Third, most students need practice in setting realistic goals. It is a good idea for teachers to help students set concrete goals and keep a log of their progress toward meeting them.

Finally, let students know you believe they will achieve at a high level. Stipek and Daniels (1988) recently reported significant declines in students' perceptions of self-competence as they moved through elementary school—kindergarteners had much greater faith in their abilities than did fourth-graders. These changes in views of the self are related to achievement motivation (March, Byrne, & Shavelson, 1988). Since the classroom environment is so critical to how children see their own abilities (Stipek & Daniels, 1988), teachers must find ways to help children believe that they will experience success. One way of moving toward this goal may be very simple. Haynes and Johnson (1983) informed one group of college freshmen that they were likely to perform very well during the upcoming semester, while another group was not given such motivation. The results of their study indicated that letting students know that their instructors believed that they would do well led to heightened levels of student self-expectancy and higher grades. In short, when the teachers in Haynes and Johnson's study conveyed the expectation that students probably would do well, the students believed it and in fact, they achieved at a higher level than other students.

5. Avoid frequent competition. In any competition someone must lose. Continued losing, as we have seen, leads students to set unrealistic goals. Teachers need to emphasize cooperation, students' competition with their own past achievement, and a wide range of activities that allow all students a chance to succeed. As we will see in Chapter Ten, "Social Learning and Modeling," the use of small groups can greatly facilitate the development of cooperative behaviors (see Johnson, 1988).

We are not suggesting that schools portray an unrealistic view of the world. Competition, of course, is an inescapable part of life. Nonetheless, students need to be nurtured in their achievement-related activities. Preparation for competition comes from success, not from failure. Stifling someone's potential for achievement in school through ill-conceived competition cannot possibly benefit the student or society.

6. Take advantage of students' interests. Students' interests are a significant source of motivation (Feather, 1988), and teachers often use interests to heighten motivation to achieve. New learning is always built on previous knowledge (see Chapter Two, "An Introduction to Cognitive Psychology"), and the relationship of new topics to students' interests should be pointed out. Students who are interested in the weather, for example, are involved in a topic closely aligned with many other physical sciences. Effective teachers employ novelty, contrast, and humor to perk up students' curiosity about new topics. Novelty by itself often is enough to kindle students' curiosity, leading to extended interests (Evertson & Smylie, 1987).

Not all topics are immediately interesting to students, however. Memorizing "math facts" (e.g., 6 x 3 = 18), for example, may seem irrelevant to many elementary school children, regardless of how important these facts may be to the later development of skills in long division and multiplication. In such cases, methods that employ incentives and rewards may be required.

7. Help students develop a balanced locus of control. Students should not attribute all the causes for success or failure to their own efforts. Students inclined to blame all their failures on a lack of effort, for example, have an unrealistic view of the world. Similarly, students who attribute all their success to external factors and none to their own efforts are unlikely to become self-directed, achievement-motivated adults. A balance between the two extremes is desirable, and recent research (see Borkowski, Weyhing, & Carr, 1988) suggests that teachers may influence the attainment of this balance by systematically encouraging appropriate attribution statements.

To help students attain a balanced locus of control, reward accurate causal attributions. Have students rethink and rephrase statements in which they do not appropriately accept responsibility for their own actions. Conversely, students need to become aware of self-statements indicating too much acceptance of responsibility.

Your feedback can help students internalize reasonable standards of self-responsibility.

Summary

Building on the foundation of Chapter Seven, "Self-Concept and Moral Development," we explored the concept of motivation in this chapter. Abraham Maslow's theory of a hierarchy of needs stresses satisfaction of students' deficiency needs so that higher levels of needs (being needs) can be gratified. Maslow's work has provided a theoretical basis for much of the work on self-concept (see Chapter Seven) and is related to Jean Piaget's theory of motivation (see Chapter Four, "Intelligence and Cognitive Development"); it has provided the foundation for the humanistic approach to education.

Achievement motivation theory has emphasized the importance of success in students' aspirations and need to achieve. Students' perceptions of success and failure depend on the types of goals they pursue; self-improvement goals result in greater achievement motivation than performance goals. Attribution theory is closely related to achievement motivation theory; it suggests that failure and success have differential effects depending on the kinds of attributions students make about their experiences.

Motivation theories have many implications for classroom teachers. Students' motivation can be developed by providing a classroom environment that both provides for successful experiences and takes advantage of intrinsically motivating factors.

As we'll see in the next part, "Guiding Classroom Behavior," there are other views of motivation that stress the importance of the external environment and how it influences behavior.

Suggested Readings

Covington, M. V. (1985). Strategic thinking and fear of failure. In J. Segal, S. Chipman, & R. Glaser (Eds.), *Thinking and learning skills: Relating instruction to research.* (pp. 389–416). Hillsdale, NJ: Erlbaum.
> *Martin Covington's chapter is an excellent overview of his work on success seekers and failure avoiders.*

Dweck, C. S. (1988). Motivation. In R. Glaser & A. Lesgold (Eds.), *The handbook of psychology and education.* (Vol. 1, pp. 187–239). Hillsdale, NJ: Erlbaum.
> *Carol Dweck's chapter provides an outstanding survey of contemporary approaches to motivation.*

Maslow, A. H. (1968). *Toward a psychology of being* (2nd ed.). New York: Harper & Row.

Maslow, A. H. (1987). *Motivation and personality* (3rd ed.). New York: Harper & Row. Revised by Robert Frager, James Fadiman, Cynthia McReynolds, and Ruth Cox.

Maslow, A. H. (1971). *The further reaches of human nature.* New York: Viking.
> *These three books are Maslow's best works, and they provide a comprehensive description of his theory. The richness and subtlety of Maslow's ideas are not fully apparent without reading the original works.*

Weiner, B. (1985). An attributional theory of achievement motivation and emotion. *Psychological Review, 92,* 548–573.
> *Bernard Weiner's review paper is a comprehensive description of attribution theory.*

PART THREE

One of the most important functions of the teacher is the guidance of classroom behavior. In Part One we emphasized the teacher's role in facilitating the cognitive growth of students. In Part Two we examined the part teachers play in motivating students. In this part, we examine how teachers can structure classrooms so that maximum and enjoyable learning results. Chapter Nine, "An Introduction to Behavioral Psychology," presents an in-depth examination of a theory of human behavior that, in contrast to cognitive psychology and motivation theories, describes the effect of external events on student behavior. Chapter Ten, "Social Learning and Modeling," presents a theoretical perspective that combines important aspects of cognitive and behavioral theories. Chapter Eleven, "Classroom Management," is devoted to the application of the principles discussed throughout the first ten chapters of this volume to the management of student behavior.

Guiding Classroom Behavior

CHAPTER
9

An Introduction to Behavioral Psychology

The first eight chapters of our text focused primarily on how events internal to the person influence student behavior. In this chapter we turn to a different way of thinking about human behavior—behavioral psychology. While cognitive psychology emphasizes the ways in which perceptions and thoughts affect behavior, and theories of motivation stress self-understanding, behavioral psychology emphasizes how events *external* to the person affect behavior. Less attention is devoted to internal events. Clearly, to fully understand people's actions, we must be aware of the effects of cognition, motivation, *and* the external world. The study of behavioral psychology expands our knowledge of human learning. Moreover, principles of behavioral psychology have been applied successfully to a host of educational problems, most notably those we refer to as discipline problems. In this chapter we examine the basic principles of behavioral psychology, and in Chapter Ten we will see how these principles can be applied to achieve social learning goals in education.

OBJECTIVES

After reading this chapter, you should be able to meet the following objectives.

1. Analyze your behaviors by identifying the discriminative stimuli, the responses, and the consequences of the responses.

2. Devise a procedure whereby you can strengthen a response in a student.

3. Devise a procedure for extinguishing a student's inappropriate response.

4. Apply the principles of self-management to alter one of your behaviors.

About Behavioral Psychology

From its beginnings early in this century, behavioral psychology has emphasized three premises. First, behavioral psychology attempts to be "objective, ruling out all subjective data or interpretations in terms of conscious experience" (Fancher, 1979, p. 319). Objective observations of behavior are the major source of data for behavioral psychologists. Second, the goal of behavioral psychology is to "predict and control behavior" (J. B. Watson, 1913, p. 158), where **behavior** is a general term denoting any observable action of a person. Descriptions of thought processes are generally seen as outside the bounds of behavioral psychology, although recent developments in "cognitive behaviorism" have begun to recognize the utility of analyzing internal events (Meichenbaum & Turk, 1987). Third, behavioral psychologists see fundamental continuities of behavioral principles across all animal species. The principles derived from studies of animal behavior may be used to explain aspects of human behavior (Hersen & Last, 1988).

Behavioral psychology focuses on observable events—what people do and say. It is the study of behavior as it interacts with the environment. In order to grasp fully how the behaviorist conceives of learning, it is necessary to examine some basic concepts of the behavioral approach.

Stimuli

A person's environment—all that a person perceives external and internal to the body—is seen as being made up of stimuli. **Stimuli** are perceivable units of the environment that *may* affect behavior.* Stimuli can be of any size (a group of students, a teacher, one button on a student's shirt) and may be perceived through any one sense (a beam of light through a window can be seen but not perceived in other ways) or a number of them (a desk can be seen, tasted, smelled, felt, and even heard). In the behavioral approach, stimuli are not defined by their

---

*Behavioral psychologists typically do not consider perception to be a cognitive process as it was described in Chapter Two.

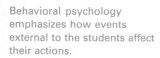
Behavioral psychology emphasizes how events external to the students affect their actions.

form or size but rather by their effect on behavior. Hence we may perceive either a very faint musical tone or an entire song as a single stimulus.

Behaviorists are interested in how stimuli (sometimes referred to as *stimulus situations*) affect behavior. That is, what kinds of responses do people make to various kinds of stimuli?

Responses

Responses are reactions by organisms to stimuli; they may be complex or simple. A bright light in the eye causes the iris to contract. A tap on the knee causes leg muscles to respond with a jerk. A teacher's question results in a student saying yes in response. A dial glows on an instrument panel, and the pilot responds by carefully looking at several other dials and then at the engines for smoke or other signs of trouble.

Even the simplest responses are complex in that they are made up of several component responses. The apparently simple response of saying yes really is a series of responses involving the eardrum, the aural-neural system, the brain, effector neural pathways, the jaw, tongue, throat muscles, and the muscles that control breathing.* A more complex response such as using a pay phone contains several identifiable components: inserting the coin, listening for the dial tone, dialing the number, listening for a ring or a busy signal, and so on. Any response can be divided into subcomponents. Responses merely are convenient units to use in talking about behavior. We usually speak of any reaction as a response whether it is composed of few or many component responses. So we may refer to both a slight muscle movement and a professor's long-winded answer to a question as one response.

Early Views of the Interaction of Stimulus and Response

Historians of psychology typically break the development of behavioral psychology into early and contemporary phases (Boring, 1950; Fancher, 1979; Kratochwill & Bijou, 1987). Early behaviorism was characterized by an emphasis on a type of learning called classical conditioning. To understand classical conditioning, it is necessary to examine two broad classes of stimuli, neutral and unconditioned stimuli.

---

*From a strictly behavioral perspective, of course, thoughts are not considered to be responses because they are not observable.

Neutral Stimuli

Neutral stimuli are stimuli that have little or no effect on behavior. To understand neutral stimuli, consider how you have been reacting to your environment as you read this book. Did you occasionally hear faint sounds of traffic or people in nearby rooms? Could you hear the sound of air-conditioning or heating units? Perhaps you heard the wind outside and the sound of birds. If you were aware of these stimuli as you read, but were unaffected by them, they were neutral stimuli for you. Likewise, the smell of library stacks, the color of the walls in your study room, or the pressure of your feet as you sit probably have had no particular effect on your behavior. All of these things, until we directed your attention to them, were neutral stimuli. Unless stimuli somehow change behavior they are neutral.

The majority of stimuli we perceive are neutral. Neutral stimuli, however, can acquire properties that affect your behavior. We will examine these properties in greater detail as we consider other types of stimuli.

"Perhaps, Dr. Pavlov, he could be taught to seal envelopes."

Unconditioned Eliciting
Stimuli

Unconditioned eliciting stimuli* are stimuli that cause involuntary responses (**reflexes**) to occur. A bug flying in your eye (an unconditioned stimulus) will elicit (cause) a blink (an involuntary response). You cannot avoid blinking in the presence of such a stimulus. Likewise, an ice cube slid down your back will cause your back muscles to contract. By gritting your teeth, you may be able to inhibit screaming or waving your arms, but the cold from the ice cube will cause your muscles to contract. We're all aware of reflexive responses and might not give them much thought in terms of educational applications, but it was the discovery by Ivan Pavlov that neutral stimuli can acquire the properties of eliciting stimuli that launched behavioral psychology in the first place.

Pavlov, a physiologist, had just completed the research on digestive processes that was to win him the Nobel Prize when he became interested in some related phenomena observed during his classic research. Pavlov had fitted dogs with tubes connected to their mouths so that he could measure how much they salivated under different conditions. As part of his research into the digestive process, he had his laboratory assistants place meat powder in the dogs' mouths. Meat powder, of course, is an unconditioned stimulus for the reflex of salivation. There's nothing surprising about this, but Pavlov also noted that certain other stimuli present at the time of inserting the meat powder came to elicit salivation by themselves. The most striking example of this was Pavlov's observation that the dogs began to salivate when they saw laboratory assistants enter the laboratory—whether or not they carried food with them (Pavlov, 1928). The dogs had learned to salivate at the sight of laboratory assistants alone.

The kind of learning Pavlov witnessed in his dogs is now called **classical conditioning**, or **respondent conditioning**. We can diagram the process of classical conditioning as follows:

Stage 1   An unconditioned (eliciting) stimulus elicits a response

Unconditioned Eliciting Stimulus	$\longrightarrow$	Unconditioned (reflexive) Response

---

*Conditioning is a technical term for learning. Unconditioned eliciting stimuli, therefore, are stimuli that do not need to be learned in order to elicit (cause) a reflexive response.

Stage 2   A neutral stimulus is paired with the unconditioned stimulus

| Neutral Stimulus | + | Unconditioned Eliciting Stimulus | $\longrightarrow$ | Unconditioned Response |

Stage 3   After several pairings, the neutral stimulus becomes a conditioned stimulus, eliciting the response on its own

| Conditioned Eliciting Stimulus (formerly the neutral stimulus) | $\longrightarrow$ | Conditioned Response |

Thus, a neutral stimulus can function as an unconditioned eliciting stimulus by being paired with it on several occasions. When the formerly neutral stimulus can itself bring about the reflex, it is called a **conditioned eliciting stimulus**, while the reflexive response it causes now is referred to as a **conditioned response**. In Pavlov's laboratory, the sight of the laboratory assistant became a conditioned eliciting stimulus for the conditioned response of salivation. Subsequent research has shown that many emotional and physiological reactions in humans (for example, fears, increased heart rate) are learned through the process of classical conditioning.

The fact that neutral stimuli can come to elicit responses was seized upon by John Watson (e.g., Watson, 1913), who believed that classical conditioning could be used to explain much, if not all, human behavior (see Gormezano, Prokasy, & Thompson, 1986). Watson's research and especially his books and articles designed for the general public had a tremendous impact on psychology. Not long after Watson stopped writing in psychology, about 1930, however, it became apparent that classical conditioning could explain some, but certainly not all learning. Other theorists, most notably B. F. Skinner, began to examine stimuli and responses from a different point of view.

Contemporary Views of Stimulus and Response

Rather than using the reflex as the basic unit of analysis for learning, Skinner argued that most animal and human behavior is controlled by events that precede *and* follow the behavior. Skinner referred to this form of learning as **operant conditioning**. The whole tone of modern behaviorism was set by Skinner's detailed analysis of how antecedent (preceding) events and consequent (following) events affect behavior. In general, antecedent events tell us what to do, and consequent events either strengthen or weaken our behaviors (Williams, 1987). Table 9–1

TABLE 9–1   SOME BEHAVIORS WITH THEIR ANTECEDENTS AND CONSEQUENCES

Antecedent	Behavior	Consequence
Teacher asks a question	Student gives the correct answer	Teacher praises student
Girl sees toy on steps	Girl picks up toy	Mother kisses girl
Phone rings	Professor picks up phone	Someone screams obscenities
Child sees shoe untied	Child ties shoe	Child feels more comfortable
Teacher says, "Any questions?"	Student asks, "Why is the sky dark at night?"	Class laughs
Radio alarm comes on very loud	Sleepy person turns it down	Person goes back to sleep
Girl says, "Hello"	Boy says, "How are you doing?"	Girl smiles
Boy feels nervous	Boy ducks behind locker out of sight of new girl	Boy feels calmer
Man enters dark room	Man flicks light switch	Light bulb pops; man is shocked

---

presents a series of behaviors with their antecedents and consequences.

The behaviors depicted in Table 9–1 were initiated by their antecedents; the antecedent events served as cues for the behaviors. The behaviors were then either strengthened or weakened by their consequences. We can make guesses about which of the behaviors were strengthened and which were weakened, but we cannot actually determine how the behaviors were affected by their consequences without first examining some concepts basic to contemporary behaviorism. We begin with a discussion of reinforcing stimuli, consequences that strengthen behavior.

Reinforcing Stimuli   Reinforcing stimuli are stimuli that, when applied to behaviors, strengthen them. Technically, they increase the probability of a behavior's occurrence in specific future situations (Skinner, 1938). The term **reinforcing stimulus**, or simply **reinforcer**, was coined by B. F. Skinner. His observations of laboratory animals' behavior indicated that some stimuli strengthened behaviors. This principle was not novel—it had been put forward by E. L. Thorndike forty years before (he called such stimuli *satisfiers*) and had been hinted at in the writings of Alexander Bain in the mid-1800s—but Skinner's rigorous research and his ability to popularize ideas firmly established the principles of reinforcement.

Reinforcers are defined by the effect they have on behavior. If a stimulus strengthens a behavior, it is by definition a reinforcer. It does

Positive reinforcers strengthen behaviors they follow. Here, a stamp and a positive comment are reinforcers for a good performance.

not matter what the stimulus looks like, feels like, tastes like, or what someone might intend for it to do. If a stimulus strengthens behavior, it is a reinforcer.

Some reinforcers follow behaviors. These are termed **positive reinforcers**. If giving a small boy a hug after he says "thank you" increases the likelihood of his saying "thank you" in similar situations in the future, the hug was a positive reinforcer. Reinforcers may also occur prior to the behaviors they strengthen. These are referred to as **negative reinforcers**. Suppose a teacher shuts a window to stop some loud construction noises from interfering with classroom activity. If she is more likely to shut the window in similar circumstances in the future, the construction noise was a negative reinforcer. We'll examine the differences between positive and negative reinforcers more carefully later in the chapter.*

The term *reinforcement* is not synonymous with the term *reward*. Rewards are given with the intent of strengthening a behavior. We know, of course, that rewards don't always work as intended. We can, for example, compliment a child in front of her friends for sharing her toys. If we then see that the child is embarrassed by our actions and *stops* her sharing behavior, we would be painfully aware that our "reward" was unsuccessful in strengthening her behavior. We may have intended the compliment as a reward, but it certainly did not act as a reinforcer.

Any time you hear someone say, "I tried reinforcement but it didn't work," you are listening to a person who does not clearly understand reinforcement. We can determine whether stimuli are reinforcers only by observing the effect they have on behavior. If a stimulus does not strengthen a behavior, it is not a reinforcer. Only through behavior analysis can we label a stimulus as reinforcing or not reinforcing.

Reinforcement is a complex idea. There are different ways in which reinforcers can be categorized, and it is necessary for us to consider several aspects of reinforcement in order to fully understand it. One way to think about reinforcers is by categorizing them as primary and secondary reinforcers.

---

*The terms *positive* and *negative* have nothing whatever to do with "positive" or "negative" behaviors, "positive" outlooks on life, or other familiar uses of the terms. They merely were used by Skinner to refer to two kinds of stimuli that strengthen behaviors in different ways.

Primary reinforcers strengthen behavior because of our biological nature. Food and drink are primary reinforcers.

Primary Reinforcers. **Primary reinforcers** are stimuli that strengthen behaviors because of our biological nature. They are innately reinforcing: We need them for individual survival or survival of the human race. We need not learn about primary reinforcers in order for them to be effective.

Primary reinforcers include food, water, air, tactile contact, climatic comfort, rest, affection, and sexual stimulation. These reinforcers generally are thought of as physiological. Newborn infants, for example, do not encounter breast milk until birth, but breast milk will serve as a reinforcer for hungry infants from the first time they consume it. Likewise, newborns do not get cold prior to birth, but the escape from cold is reinforcing the first time it occurs. Children may learn to cry because crying results in relief from discomfort—Mama or Papa comes running at the sound of baby's cries, removes the discomfort, and thereby reinforces crying.

Secondary Reinforcers. Many of the stimuli that function as reinforcers are not primary reinforcers. **Secondary reinforcers** are formerly neutral stimuli that have acquired some of the reinforcing value of primary reinforcers by being paired with them or with other secondary reinforcers. The phenomenon is very similar to the pairing process in classical conditioning by which neutral stimuli come to elicit a conditioned response. In this case, however, the neutral stimulus is paired with a consequence of behavior. The sound of the words "I love you," for example, has no biological value to anyone. But if "I love you," is spoken each time an infant is fed, cleaned, hugged, and provided with primary reinforcers, the sound of *these words alone* will acquire the ability to strengthen behavior in the absence of primary reinforcement. Similarly, money has no biological value in and of itself. You cannot obtain much nourishment by eating dollar bills, and they won't directly provide you with affection, comfort, or sexual stimulation. And yet, we all are aware that money often is very powerfully reinforcing. Why? Because money is paired with so many other reinforcers: food, drink, and a host of other reinforcers all can be obtained in exchange for money.

Most reinforcers (praise, smiles, new clothing, record albums) are secondary reinforcers. Certainly, any observation of classroom behavior would demonstrate that students do a great many things, appropriate and inappropriate, in order to obtain praise from the teacher, good grades, free time, peer approval, laughter, and other secondary reinforcers. One important task of the teacher, as we will see in Chapter Eleven, is the establishment and use of *effective* secondary reinforcers.

Potency of Reinforcement.   You may wonder what we mean by "effective" reinforcers. We define the effectiveness, or **potency**, of reinforcers by examining their ability to strengthen behaviors. The greater the probability that a stimulus will strengthen a behavior, the more potent it is said to be. Money is likely to be a more potent reinforcer for maintaining ditch-digging behavior than is free dirt, for example.

The potency of a given reinforcer varies greatly among people. Books may be a highly potent secondary reinforcer for some people but have a very small behavior-strengthening effect on others. Thus, some students purchase books frequently, while others spend money on other things. Most stimuli will be reinforcing at different levels for the individual students in any class you teach. Praise may be a reinforcer for some students, but not for others; grades, attention, or free time may be strong reinforcers for some of your students but much weaker reinforcers for others.

The effectiveness of reinforcers also varies within the same person. While food is reinforcing when we're hungry, even the thought of food can be nauseating after we have overeaten. Similarly, a drink of water usually isn't a potent reinforcer for a person who has just finished a large iced drink. The fact that reinforcers often lose their potency as they are acquired in large amounts or in great numbers is referred to as **satiation**. Satiation can occur with both primary and secondary reinforcers. After a while, for instance, praise can lose its potency as a reinforcer if it is experienced too frequently.

The Premack Principle.   Some helpful ideas about reinforcement potency come from the work of David Premack. In his first studies Premack altered the probabilities of rats' running and drinking by depriving them of access to water or to a running wheel. When they were deprived of water, drinking would serve to reinforce running. When denied access to the running wheel, the rats would drink water in order to run. Premack maintained (1965, pp. 143–144) that this principle makes it unnecessary to know much about a learner's history of reinforcement. The reinforcement value of an event can be predicted from present-day levels of activity. Premack's findings were formalized into a principle: *Of every pair of responses or activities in which an individual engages, the more probable one will reinforce the less probable one.* In everyday terms, preferred activities will reinforce activities that are less preferred.

Homme, DeBaca, Devine, Steinhorst, and Rickert (1963) applied the **Premack Principle** in a nursery school where three of the children were extremely disruptive. The children spent a great deal of time running around, screaming, pushing furniture, and playing games. These behaviors had a higher probability of occurrence than did sitting quietly and attending to classroom events. Homme instructed the children to "sit quietly" so that they could then run, scream, and play for five minutes after accomplishing the "quiet behavior." The use of high-frequency behaviors as a reinforcement for competing responses was effective. The disruptive children learned to sit quietly and attend to teachers and other learning experiences within a week or two. In general, the Premack Principle has proved to be a highly effective approach to identifying reinforcers at all age levels (Witt, Elliott, & Gresham, 1988).

Delay and Frequency of Reinforcement.   Any delay in administration of positive reinforcement increases the probability that other responses will occur between the response you are attempting to strengthen and the reinforcer. When such delays occur, it is likely that these intervening responses rather than the desired response will be strengthened by the reinforcer. The principle is especially critical when working with young children and students who have trouble paying attention to tasks. An example can be seen in a teacher who decides not to interrupt a boy who finally is doing his in-class work in order to praise him. However, the boy soon starts to look around and bother his classmates. The teacher *then* speaks to him and says, "You were doing so well." The teacher has, of course, delayed the praise until the boy no longer was doing his work. Instead of reinforcing working, the teacher most likely has reinforced the boy's looking around and bothering other students.

The effects of reinforcement also are correlated with the frequency of reinforcement. Generally, the more often reinforcers are experienced, the more potent their effect. Increases in size or amount beyond some minimum level, however, seem to have little effect on the potency of reinforcers. A child probably won't practice the piano for three hours to obtain a single star, but if she will practice one hour for six stars, increasing the reinforcer to sixty stars per hour is unlikely to have any effect.

Effectiveness of Positive Reinforcement in the Classroom.   Just how well does deliberate positive reinforcement of desired behavior work for teachers? Does it work for all teachers or only for some? Thompson and his colleagues (1974) attempted to answer these questions by training teachers in fourteen classrooms in techniques of positively reinforcing appropriate conduct while ignoring inappropriate, disruptive behavior. A control group of teachers in an adjoining school was given no training. The results were clear-cut. In the experimental classrooms the frequency of appropriate behaviors greatly increased, while in the control classes appropriate behaviors actually decreased.

More recently, Williams (1987) has surveyed approaches to classroom management and concluded that the most successful approaches employ positive reinforcement for appropriate behavior rather than emphasizing a decrease of inappropriate behaviors. Williams recommended that courses with practical experiences in classroom management should be included in basic teacher-education programs.

Schedules of Reinforcement.   Reinforcement often occurs intermittently. Sometimes our actions are reinforced and sometimes they are not. The relationship of the number of reinforcers to the number of behaviors is called a **schedule of reinforcement.** *Schedule* does not necessarily mean that someone arranged or "scheduled" the reinforcers—schedules of reinforcement can occur naturally or be set by the teacher. They are determined either by the ratio of reinforcers to responses or by the time interval between reinforcers. The ratio or

TABLE 9–2   SCHEDULES OF REINFORCEMENT

Type and Definition	*Examples*
Continuous Reinforcement (CRF)	
Provision of a reinforcer for each act or response.	1. Teacher praises the student every time she contributes to a discussion. 2. Child puts a gold star on a chart each time he brushes his teeth.
Intermittent Schedules	
Fixed ratio (FR): Reinforcers given on a 1:2, 1:3, 1:4, etc., ratio to responses. An FR 50 or FR 75 means that every fiftieth or seventy-fifth response is reinforced.	1. Coach gives a "credit" for every fifth push-up or pull-up (FR 5 schedule). 2. A boy gives his dog a bite of meat for every third time the dog jumps through a hoop (FR 3). 3. A teacher gives a sticker for each ten words spelled correctly (FR 10).
Variable ratio (VR): Similar to FR, except reinforcers are given on a random basis. They average one reinforcement per n number of responses. VR 10 means one reinforcer is given for every ten responses, but the reinforcement may occur after the first, second, third, eleventh, or eighteenth response.	1. Mother gives one "special reward" per week after daughter has cleaned her room (VR 7). The reinforcer may be given on any day, but its use averages once per week. 2. Teacher nods and smiles at student on the average of once for each ten words the student pronounces correctly in reading an assignment (VR 10).
Fixed interval (FI): Reinforcement given for first response following an arbitrary time period. The time period is usually in minutes. FI 7 minutes means that the first response following the passage of a seven-minute interval is reinforced.	1. Shop teacher comes by student's work station every ten minutes and gives approval for the first on-task behavior noted (FI 10 minutes). 2. A girl receives a mark from her father for every ten minutes of practicing the piano (FI 10 minutes).
Variable interval (VI): Similar to FI, except time intervals are randomly chosen around an average interval length.	1. After time periods of approximately nine, fifteen, eleven, fourteen, and eleven minutes (VI 12 minutes) the teacher notifies groups in a simulation game that they have earned another point by brainstorming new ideas.

interval can be fixed or variable. Table 9–2 provides examples of the various types of schedules of reinforcement as they relate to instruction and classroom management.

Continuous reinforcement (CRF) is typically most useful at the beginning of learning and for strengthening weak responses. A student memorizing a new set of number facts or learning how to assemble her clarinet should receive reinforcement at first for each correct response. Continuous reinforcement typically yields the fastest rates of learning and the highest rates of continued responding.

Shifting from a continuous-reinforcement schedule to a variable schedule constitutes one step of the process known as *leaning* of reinforcement. By continuously and gradually moving to a leaner reinforcement schedule, it is possible to reduce reinforcement to practically zero but still maintain the behavior.

Fixed-ratio (FR) schedules also produce high rates of responding, but rates may be rather erratic. Performance typically slows down or stops after a reinforcement and then resumes and picks up speed near an anticipated reinforcement. Many natural work and study situations operate on a fixed-ratio schedule. We study by reading a fixed number of pages, completing so many questions in a workbook, or solving a certain number of problems. As we near our goal, we tend to work more and more quickly.

Variable-ratio (VR) schedules tend to reduce the pause that occurs right after reinforcement in the FR schedule, thus producing steady, consistent effort. Most slot machines and dice games provide reinforcement (winning) on a VR schedule. If you can imagine the so-called compulsive gambler inserting coins and pulling the lever of a slot machine hour after hour in a casino, with an overall loss of money, sleep, and meals, you understand what we mean.

Fixed-interval (FI) and *variable-interval* (VI) schedules produce steady responding but at a somewhat lower rate than ratio schedules. Variable-interval schedules are particularly useful for developing good work habits. Classroom teachers use variable-interval schedules to increase students' abilities to work steadily and productively. Periodic checks on student seatwork, done with a smile and friendly attention to the work, can effectively reinforce good study habits.

Superstitious Learning.   We all are familiar with the common superstitions of our culture: black cats crossing your path bring bad luck, breaking a mirror brings seven years' bad luck, "step on a crack, break your mother's back," and so on. Most superstitions are believed only by the very young or the remarkably gullible and are probably learned by seeing older or more authoritative persons model them.

A pervasive type of superstitious learning, however, comes from accidental reinforcement and affects us all from time to time. We occasionally receive reinforcement on an accidental basis and may make erroneous connections between some act and the receipt of a reinforcer. Consider, for example, a second-grader studying her spelling list in preparation for a test the next day. Where she usually would print her words three or four times each, today she employs cursive style for the first time. Further, let's suppose that instead of missing two or three words, as is usually the case, she spells them all correctly on the test. It should come as no great surprise that this chain of events leads to our hypothetical student's use of cursive every time she studies spelling in the future.

Teachers should recognize the frequency with which children make such spurious connections between "cause" and "effect." The resultant behavior is not stupid or silly, nor does it represent deception. It sometimes can be very difficult for a child to detect that a "consequence" has nothing to do with a behavior since it may be mixed with actual consequences for functional activities.

Negative Reinforcement.   There are times when people act to decrease stimuli. If you are in a small room into which a loud rasping sound (so-called white noise) is piped, you will be exceedingly uncomfortable. If there is a brightly lit switch on one wall and the noise is either stopped or reduced when you touch the switch, you quickly will learn to touch the switch when you hear the noise. Reducing a noxious stimulus is reinforcing since the responses that reduce it are strengthened. As we mentioned before, this form of strengthening response is usually called negative reinforcement, and the stimulus is termed a negative reinforcer. Most events we consider embarrassing, frightening, painful, disgusting, tasteless, or offensive can function as negative reinforcers. When we act in ways that reduce pain, embarrassment, or disgust and our actions are strengthened, the actions have been negatively reinforced.

Three classes of behavior are strengthened through negative reinforcement: escape, avoidance, and aggression. All are means of reducing noxious stimuli.

Escape behavior is learned by removing oneself from unpleasant situations. A young girl, for example, may run into her house when a playmate starts hitting and taunting her. Likewise, a schoolboy may feign an injured knee and leave a rough soccer game. Escape reduces the noxious stimuli.

Escape behavior can *generalize*. That is, it can appear in situations other than the situation in which it originally occurred. The girl in our earlier example may start running into the house when she sees her aggressive playmate approach or when she hears other children arguing. The boy may start limping as he walks by the soccer field. If these events occur, the children will be acting in anticipation of an event, avoiding the aversive situation. The response patterns we refer to as "anxiety," "worry," "timidity," or "fearfulness" usually involve avoidance behavior, as do lying, making alibis, and cheating. These avoidance behavior patterns are learned (through negative reinforcement) because they are successful at reducing contact with negative reinforcers.

Aggression consists of responses that act directly on negative reinforcers. Turning off a squawking radio is an "aggressive" act, as would be destroying it with a hammer. One is a socially acceptable response, the other is not, especially if the radio belongs to someone else.

Punishing Stimuli

Any consequent event (a stimulus that follows a behavior) that reduces responding is a **punishing stimulus**, or punisher. Punishers are the opposite of positive reinforcers, which strengthen the responses they follow. In defining a punisher, the characteristics of a stimulus make no difference. If candy, money, or praise lead to decreases in behavior, they are punishers. If nagging, spankings, and loss of privileges do not decrease responding, they are not punishers and so should not be termed as such, regardless of how painful or unpleasant they seem to be.

Just as there are no universal reinforcers available to teachers and parents, there are no universal punishers. For humans, context often determines whether an event is punishing or reinforcing. Prepubescent boys may react to praise from female teachers as punishing, but only when other boys are around. Similarly, a young girl may react positively to attention from a boy when they are alone but find his attention "disgusting" (punishing) when they are with her friends.

Our society frequently employs punishment and the threat of punishment in its efforts to control human behavior. Lawful behavior is at least partly motivated by threats, fines, and loss of jobs or families, which are the consequences for unlawful behavior. Likewise, schools frequently employ threats of suspension, failure in courses, and corporal punishment as motivators for cooperating and studying. Presumably, appropriate social acts thus are negatively reinforced because they enable us to avoid the threatened punishment. They also permit us to enjoy the positive reinforcers that are contingent upon acceptable behavior. Despite the prevalence of social usage, teachers are well advised to make very limited use of punishment because it usually works against them, making it impossible to achieve their educational goals (McDaniel, 1980; Williams, 1987). Positive reinforcement of desired behavior usually works far better.

Yet teachers and parents continue to use punishment as a primary strategy (Hersen & Last, 1988; McDaniel, 1980). Why do adults continue to make use of punishment if its results are deleterious? An analysis suggests that four separate processes are in effect: (1) ignorance of alternatives to punishment (Yule & Carr, 1988); (2) negative reinforcement of the person administering the punishment by the immediate decrease in problem behaviors (Pfiffner, Rosen, & O'Leary, 1985); (3) social expectations that adults will punish children (Pfiffner et al., 1985; Ashman & Conway, 1988); and (4) the "visibility" of many problem behaviors.

Most teachers can verbalize the limitations of punishment, but many still continue to use it. To some degree this seems a matter of negative reinforcement of the *teacher's* behavior. Punishment does, by definition, reduce responding. A teacher *can* control some problems, for example, by sarcasm or threats to call the principal. To the extent that the troublesome behavior ceases immediately, there is an increased probability that the teacher will use sarcasm or threats again. This is negative reinforcement of the teacher's behavior.

Discriminative Stimuli: Stimulus Control of Behavior

We have discussed behavior as mainly under the influence of consequent stimuli—reinforcers and punishers. Behavior obviously also is influenced by antecedent stimuli. When we travel from home to work, for example, cues along the way control our turns, speed, stopping, and starting so that we arrive precisely at the right place, on time, and without traffic tickets.

The cues in the environment that "tell us what to do" are termed **discriminative stimuli**. If we wish to leave an unfamiliar building, an exit sign would be a cue. Likewise, if we are chatting with someone as we enter a library and see a large "no talking" sign, it is a cue to stop talking. Those stimuli that indicate that a behavior will be reinforced in their presence are usually referred to as S^Ds ("Ess Dees," a form of technical shorthand). Those stimuli that indicate a response is inap-

Discriminative stimuli are cues for our behavior. As this student types information into the computer, the computer screen provides him with discriminative stimuli for the actions that he will take next.

propriate (will not be reinforced) also are discriminative stimuli but are labeled **S$^\Delta$s** ("Ess Deltas"). A lecture, for example, is an S^D for listening and note taking and an S$^\Delta$ for speaking out. The teacher's questions, on the other hand, are S^{D}s for speaking out and S$^\Delta$s for note taking.

The effect that discriminative stimuli have on behavior is referred to as **stimulus control**. Discriminative stimuli do not control behavior in the sense that eliciting stimuli control reflexes in classical conditioning. When an eliciting stimulus, such as a bug flying in one's eye, occurs, the reflex *must* follow it—the reflex is involuntary. The behaviors that follow discriminative stimuli are voluntary—they need not occur. We answer the question "What time is it?" not because we have to but because we typically have been reinforced in the past for answering similar questions. Likewise, we follow an instructor's directions to read the next chapter not because the instructor controls our behavior but because we have learned that we are likely to gain reinforcement or at least avoid punishment by reading the assignment.

Stimulus control can be very powerful and quite automatic. A teacher's instruction to "take out a sheet of paper" or "open your books to page 34" typically will be followed by most class members quickly and without question because of past reinforcement for these actions. How do such stimuli come to be able to "control" our behavior? That is, how are discriminative stimuli formed from neutral stimuli? We best can answer this question by looking at an example of discrimination learning.

Discrimination Learning.   The process of learning to respond to just one stimulus in a whole field of stimuli is referred to as discrimination learning. Let's assume you have an antique automobile. It has a number of unfamiliar knobs and dials whose function you don't understand. You turn the key and step on the starter. The motor turns over but does not catch. You try again and again, meanwhile pulling and turning knobs and switches. After you pull a particular knob, the motor catches and roars reassuringly. The next time you try to start it, you mess with the knobs and switches again, but somewhat sooner you pull the "magic" knob and the motor catches again. Thereafter, you pull the knob labeled "choke" almost automatically as you turn the key and step on the starter.

Notice that we have refrained from saying that the choke "causes" behavior. You can look at the choke knob all day, but if you do not attempt to start the engine, you will not touch the choke. It is the *consequence* of pulling the choke that determines whether it is pulled.

Generalization.   Always working as a counter to discrimination learning is the process of **generalization**. Generalization is the making of the same response to two or more differing stimuli. Very young children, for example, after learning to say "daddy," may call all men "daddy." Mothers usually step up discrimination training at this point, reinforcing the child for applying the label correctly and gently punishing its misapplication.

The process of generalization is a marvelous labor saver. Since we can generalize, we do not have to undergo a new learning process each time we encounter a slight variation of a stimulus. Think of the effort required to relearn how to open a door each time we came to one if we could not generalize across all knobs, latches, pulls, and electronic aids from two or three basic types. Similarly, consider the savings in effort and time that result from learning the concepts of "animal," "plant," and "automobile" (see Chapter Three, "Memory and Concepts"). People are able to respond to these concepts rather than relearning responses for each new animal, plant, or automobile they encounter. Think especially of the convenience of a number system that applies to all objects and events regardless of size, shape, color, or context. The quantity "five" is constant regardless of its use with groups of humans, pencils, roses, or books.

To some degree, generalization is automatic. A young child will call any color "red" that is more red than orange or purple. Only with reinforced practice is each of the large variety of reds, pinks, burgundies, and maroons identified. The degree of generalization depends on the amount of similarity between stimuli. Colors that differ only by a few wavelengths of light are usually given the same label (burgundy and maroon, for example). The less similarity between stimuli, the less likely that they will evoke the same response. If, for example, we reinforce a little girl for saying "yellow" to light of a certain range of wavelengths, we may find that she says "yellow" to light that extends from near-orange to chartreuse. But she will make the response "yellow" more slowly and with more qualifiers the farther the light is from the original reinforced stimulus.

Many "inappropriate" behaviors are actually instances of incorrect generalization. Some children who learn their social behaviors in a setting that reinforces competitiveness and aggression, for example, may not fit well into the school setting. They have overgeneralized the competitiveness and aggressiveness. In such situations the teacher may need to help children through a discrimination-learning process.

Shaping

As we will see in Chapter Ten, "Social Learning and Modeling," many human behaviors are learned through observation (including reading and listening), but there is an important learning process that is governed primarily by antecedent and consequent events. **Shaping** is

Shaping is learning through successive approximations.

the learning of a response through reinforcement of successive approximations of that response. Consider how a child learns to print her name. Because her parents have systematically reinforced drawing, Jane likes to draw. Further, Jane's attempts to draw letters have been profusely reinforced by her parents. One day Jane works diligently to draw a reasonable facsimile of her name. When she finishes, she shows it to her parents, who are reinforced by Jane's obvious genius and hug, kiss, and greatly praise Jane for printing her name. Like most children, Jane likes to be hugged, kissed, and praised, and so she makes another attempt at printing her name. This time, though, the parents are hesitant to lavishly reinforce Jane for repeating the same level of behavior. The parents make comments about how to improve the printing as well as providing some modeling (how to make a *J* frontward instead of backward). As we follow Jane's progress over the next several weeks we see that she must make better and better approximations of printing her name correctly in order to receive reinforcement. Finally, she is able to print her name very well.

Shaping can be seen when children learn to use a pencil, to ride a bike, to somersault, and so on. Any time a behavior is learned primarily by reinforcement of successive approximations, shaping has occurred.

Extinction

It does sometimes happen in real life that we try, try, and try again but see no desirable effects from our efforts. Typically, unreinforced trying tapers off and eventually ceases. **Extinction** is a process in which a response occurs less and less frequently as a function of nonreinforcement. It occurs whenever reinforcers are discontinued. It is not the same as forgetting, although, as we explained in Chapter Three, some of what we call forgetting actually may be extinction. If you learn to read but are no longer reinforced by reading, the *amount* of reading will decrease, but you will not have forgotten how to read. Extinction reduces performance, not knowledge.

The gradual nature of extinction is important. If a behavior stops abruptly, it probably has not been extinguished. It more likely has been suppressed by punishment or threat of punishment.

Recovery After Extinction.   Extinction may be followed by a spontaneous recovery. Suppose a small child's whining is ignored by his mother and it ceases. The next night, the child may start whining again. The whining response has recovered some portion of its original strength. It likely will not persist as long on successive recoveries if the mother continues to ignore it, but it is likely to start up again and again.

Consider also what can happen if a kindergarten teacher tries to extinguish a child's demanding behavior by ignoring it. After two or three days of successfully ignoring the child's demands, she decides the child has been doing well. Upon the next demand by the child, she stops and gives him a hug and tells him he has been doing "real good" for several days. Chances are that the demanding behavior will resume at full strength. The teacher has, through this process, inadvertently reinforced "demanding behavior" on a variable-ratio schedule. Many parents create a similar problem when they attempt to ignore their children's inappropriate behaviors and fail. The result actually may be to strengthen the undesirable behavior.

Extinction and Response Strength.   When reinforcers are removed for a given behavior, the behavior sometimes increases in strength before gradually becoming extinct. Resistance to extinction often is taken as a measure of response strength. Responses that take five hundred unreinforced trials to extinguish are considered to be stronger than responses that extinguish after fifty trials without reinforcement. This fact has been used to test the effectiveness of differing schedules of reinforcement. By and large, responses that have been maintained on a variable ratio or variable-interval schedule are the most resistant to extinction. For this reason, it is advisable to use continuous reinforcement to develop a desirable response and then to shift to one of the variable schedules for maintenance of the response.

Extinction of Classically Conditioned Responses.   Classically conditioned responses extinguish when the conditioned eliciting stimulus is repeatedly applied in the absence of the unconditioned eliciting stimulus. Suppose a dog has been conditioned by the use of meat powder to salivate at the sound of a buzzer. If we sound the buzzer time after time without ever again pairing it with meat powder (or some other unconditioned eliciting stimulus), the dog eventually will stop salivating at the sound of the buzzer.

Spontaneous recovery also occurs with partially extinguished classically conditioned responses. Suppose we extinguish the dog's salivation to a buzzer on Monday. If we return to the laboratory on Tuesday and again sound the buzzer, the dog will likely salivate to some extent. As in operant conditioning, however, the conditioned reflex will be far weaker than it was originally. Similar patterns have been observed in human classical conditioning, particularly of emotional behavior.

Self-Management

Is it necessary for *all* cues and consequences to come from the external environment? There are several indications that they do not need to—that individuals can prompt and reinforce themselves to bring about behavior change. This process has come to be called *self-management* or *self-control*, and it has been widely promoted as a useful procedure in counseling and education.

In self-management, the environment should prompt desired responses.

The term *self* as it is used here does not imply that the environment is not involved in behavior change. What it means is that one response is controlling another. A boy may clap his hand over his mouth to keep from screaming. A girl may jam her fist in her pocket when she is angry to keep from striking another girl. Such actions occur naturally and frequently in all our lives. Psychologists who use self-management procedures have extended the process and developed means of training individuals in making self-management responses to achieve a growing list of behavior-change objectives. Several aspects of self-management have been shown to extend students' control over what they do. These include stimulus control, self-monitoring, self-reinforcement, and cognitive self-instruction.

Stimulus Control.   Stimulus control (see our previous section on discriminative stimuli) refers to a situation in which a person's frequency of responding is increased in one setting and decreased in others (Watson & Tharp, 1985). If you set up an environment (a desk or an area in a room) in which study and only study takes place and is reinforced, then this setting soon will be a place in which studying will occur easily and reliably. We often are not careful about establishing stimulus control, however. Certain places and times for studying (trying to read late at night while lying on your bed or while listening to records) are not S^Ds just for studying but are also S^Ds for behaviors other than studying (such as falling asleep or listening to the music).

The general approach taken in establishing stimulus control as part of self-management is to arrange the environment so that desired responses will be prompted and reinforced. Thus a study carrel is used exclusively for studying, we use note cards to prompt our observations for a creative-writing class, and a bedside clipboard is available to record our impressions of the day. Distractors should be reduced to a minimum; the other activities are not to take place in the controlled environment. The more an environment becomes linked with one activity, the better the stimulus control will be.

Self-Monitoring.   Self-monitoring is a technique in which students record their own responses. The responses recorded may be "good" or "bad" from the students' and others' viewpoints. Examples of self-monitored responses in schools and classrooms include participating in class discussions, meeting new people, completing homework and in-class problems, practicing an instrument, and swimming laps. Students' records of these kinds of responses frequently have a significant effect on how often the behaviors occur. The records can also be the basis for fruitful discussion with parents, teachers, and counselors.

The effect of self-monitoring is often strong. In the area of study skills, for example, Mace and Kratochwill (1988) report that students who monitor their own studying in combination with being given advice on study skills significantly improve their grades. Further, these students improve far more than students who use the knowledge of study skills alone. Indeed, monitoring alone often is sufficient to change behavior in a desired direction.

Self-Reinforcement. Another approach to self-management involves students reinforcing themselves for desired responses. Watson and Tharp (1985), Kazdin (1988), and Hayes et al. (1985) have concluded that self-reinforcement is an effective way for students to learn to control their actions. Kazdin (1988) has argued that in many cases, self-reinforcement is just as effective as reinforcement administered by external sources. Teachers often first establish a reinforcement system, especially with younger students, and then move to arrangements in which self-monitoring is combined with self-reinforcement. Although there is an occasional tendency for standards to become more lenient (Kazdin, 1988), this tendency can be countered by periodic prompting and by reinforcement for maintaining high standards.

Cognitive Self-Instruction. Recently many behavioral psychologists have become more and more interested in "covert" behaviors—what people say to themselves and how these statements affect their actions. Because these psychologists' interest is in the effect of cognitive processes on behavior but because their methods of analysis are derived from behaviorism, this new approach has been referred to as a cognitive-behavioral approach.

A simple illustration of how a self-statement might affect behavior can be seen in a common approach to dealing with provoking circumstances. People often tell themselves, "Now count to ten!" to lower their chances of doing something rash. Less obvious, but equally important, are the effects of students' statements to themselves when they are criticized, when they meet with failure or success, or when a situation might call for an extra degree of patience or restraint. In early work in this area, Meichenbaum (Meichenbaum & Turk, 1987) has shown that teaching impulsive children to instruct themselves as a form of self-guidance significantly improved their performance on a variety of tasks. Related work (see Watson & Tharp, 1985) has shown that many

---

PRACTICE EXERCISE 9–1   MODIFYING YOUR OWN BEHAVIOR

Using the principles outlined in this chapter, devise a procedure to modify one of your own behaviors. You may wish to quit smoking, alter your eating so that you lose weight, change your study habits, or develop an entirely new behavior such as reading the biographies of famous psychologists (well, *someone* might want to do that). Follow the guidelines below.

1. Clearly define the behavior. Describe the behavior you wish to alter in observable and measurable terms.

2. What are the S^Ds or S^{Δ}s for the behavior? If you wish to establish an entirely new behavior (such as keeping a diary, reading research in educational psychology, and so on) you will need to select one or more S^Ds.

3. What are the consequences of the behavior? Be sure to specify the immediate consequences. Increased reading may make you better equipped for solving world problems, but this long-term consequence is not as important as the immediate consequence to your behavior change.

4. How will you alter the consequences of your behavior in order to strengthen or weaken it? If you want to strengthen a behavior, carefully select a reinforcing consequence you can hold contingent on the behavior's occurrence. If you want to extinguish the behavior, how will you remove reinforcing consequences?

5. Keep a daily record of your performance.

---

people who have consistent high anxiety overreact to painful stimuli, show a lack of self-control, and talk to themselves in inappropriate ways. They often label events incorrectly or have unreasonable expectations about what they do. Teaching these people to say different things to themselves often changes their reactions.

Cognitive self-instruction has been shown to be effective in a variety of studies with school-age children (Hersen & Last, 1988; Kamfer & Schefft, 1988), and its use has become more common in classroom settings (Billings & Wasik, 1985; Will et al., 1988). Working with students to help them identify their "self talk" about what happens to them is likely to become an effective way of altering overt behaviors in the classroom and school. As Scott et al. (1988) have pointed out, however, more research is needed to evaluate fully the worth of cognitive interventions in producing self-control.

Summary

In this chapter we outlined the principles of behavioral psychology. In general, five kinds of stimuli have different effects on our behavior. Neutral stimuli are perceived but have little or no effect. Unconditioned stimuli, both primary (those needed for biological reasons) and secondary (those that are learned), strengthen our behaviors and may take the form of positive reinforcement (following behaviors) or negative reinforcement (preceding behaviors). Punishing stimuli weaken behaviors, while discriminative stimuli are cues for behavior.

Behavioral psychologists usually decribe two major types of learning—classical conditioning and operant conditioning. In classical conditioning, a neutral stimulus is paired with an eliciting stimulus until the neutral stimulus can bring forth a response by itself. In operant conditioning, behaviors are strengthened or weakened by their consequences. Learning new behavior through reinforcement of successive approximations of the behavior is termed *shaping*, while the cessation of a behavior when reinforcement is withdrawn is known as *extinction*. The principles of behavioral psychology can be applied by individuals to their own behaviors. This process, known as *self-management*, is becoming a more common part of what teachers may impart to their students.

Suggested Readings

Hersen, M. & Last, C. G. (Eds.). (1988). *Child behavior casebook*. New York: Plenum.
> *Hersen and Last's edited volume presents a broad array of students' problems and how they are solved. Focused primarily on behavioral interventions, the book is very well done.*

Pavlov, L. P. (1928). *Lectures on conditioned reflexes*. (W. H. Gantt, Trans.). New York: International Press.
> *This collection of Pavlov's original experiments gives the reader the full flavor of his experimental work.*

Skinner, B. F. (1968). *The technology of teaching.* New York: Appleton-Century-Crofts.

> *Written more than twenty years ago, Skinner's book remains one of the best expositions of how operant psychology can be applied in educational settings.*

Watson, D. L., & Tharp, R. G. (1985). *Self-directed behavior.* (4th ed.). Monterey, California: Brooks/Cole.

> *Now in its fourth edition, Watson and Tharp's book is one of the best volumes available about the application of behavioral psychology to everyday life.*

Witt, J. C., Elliott, S. N., & Gresham, F. M. (Eds.). (1988). *Handbook of behavior therapy in education.* New York: Plenum.

> *Advanced chapters on nearly all aspects of behavior change in the schools are presented in well-organized fashion in this comprehensive handbook.*

CHAPTER

10

Social Learning and Modeling

OVERVIEW

It may seem difficult to reconcile differences among the various theoretical perspectives we've discussed. There is, however, an important theoretical position that helps us bridge the apparent gaps among the theories. *Social learning theory* tempers behaviorism by emphasizing the role of cognitive processes in the acquisition and regulation of behaviors (Hilgard, 1987; Zentall & Galef, 1988). Social learning theory falls in between the extremes of behavioral and cognitive theories and probably is a position of moderation accepted by the majority of contemporary psychologists (Hilgard, 1987; Peters & McMahon, 1987).

This chapter is based primarily on Albert Bandura's (e.g., 1986) social learning theory. Our primary emphasis is on social behaviors, which we first define before we move on to an examination of the applications of social learning theory to the classroom.

OBJECTIVES

After reading this chapter, you should be able to meet the following objectives.

1. Identify patterns of behavior that represent social learning in yourself, your acquaintances, and your future students.

2. State how a cooperative program with parents or other adults could be used to improve social behavior in your classes.

3. Describe the kinds of assistance you would give parents concerned about some aspect of their child's social development, such as timidity, aggressiveness, lying, or selfishness.

Social Behavior

Social behaviors are the sum total of people's interactions within a particular environment or geographic location.* Social behaviors are prompted by the actions of other people and usually are reinforced or punished by others as well. They are clear examples of the interaction of behavior and environment. To better visualize this relationship, look at the social interchanges depicted in Table 10–1. In each instance there are many alternative responses the individuals could have made. The child in Case 1, for example, could have said "None of your business" or

---

*Although we will limit ourselves to social behavior among humans, other species—chimps, gorillas, and wolves, to name only three—display very complex social behaviors.

TABLE 10–1   SAMPLES OF COMPLEX SOCIAL INTERACTIONS

Case	Initial Cue	Response, Consequence, Cue	Response, Consequence, Cue	Response
1	Mother asks, "Where are you going?"	Child stops running, smiles, says, "Outside."	Mother pats child and gives a hug, says, "Put on your coat, it's cold."	Child says, "OK." Gets coat, leaves.
2	Teacher asks discussion question.	Student makes humorous reply.	Teacher frowns, says it's a serious topic.	Student says topic is stupid.
3	Child sees older friend entering car.	Child smiles, waves, shouts, asks to accompany friend.	Friend hears a shout, looks, sees child, returns wave, but shakes head.	Child continues waving and shouts angrily as car drives away.
4	Girl sees boy stumble and fall.	Girl runs, helps him to his feet, asks if he's OK.	Boy shakes head, mumbles "Yes," then hurries away.	Girl turns and walks in other direction.
5	First student bumps into classmate near drinking fountain.	Second student shoves first student, who is slightly hurt. Second student remains at fountain.	First student says, "You son of a . . . ," kicks second student, and raises fists.	Second student calls a friend, and they both hit first student several times.
6	Girls standing near basketball court.	Boy begins a fancy dribble. One girl points at him.	Boy dribbles faster, passes to teammate, girls yell at him.	Boy demands ball, shoots a ridiculously long shot, misses. Girls laugh.

falsified his intentions by saying "To the bathroom." The helpful girl in Case 4 could instead have laughed at the boy, pushed him down again, or looked the other way. The people in our examples made one set of responses but not others. Why? Because in their past learning, such events as a question from mother or the sight of a playmate in pain have become generalized discriminative stimuli for certain responses. The reinforcers for learning these responses are the reactions of other people, who act in reinforcing ways or stop acting in aversive ways.

The behaviors illustrated in Table 10–1 represent only a small segment of the literally thousands of differing responses referred to as social behaviors. There are so many that we cannot possibly list or even think of them all. In fact, we usually speak of social behaviors in terms of *response categories* rather than as discrete acts. Many children, for example, exhibit a pattern of related responses we label "oppositional behaviors." These responses are made to requests, directions, orders, or demands from other people. They may vary from a child simply saying "No" to standing behind a tree and brandishing a stick when asked by a teacher to enter a game with other children. Oppositional behavior also can consist of a child sitting rigidly in a chair and clamping her mouth tightly shut when offered a spoonful of medicine or holding on tightly when asked to relinquish a toy to another child. In all cases, the category of "oppositional behavior" includes social behaviors that serve to negate requests.

Table 10–2 presents a list of categories of social behaviors that have frequently appeared in the literature on social learning.

TABLE 10–2   EXAMPLES OF SOCIAL BEHAVIOR CATEGORIES

Category of Social Behavior	Examples
Affiliative	Smiles, attends to others, speaks and greets, frequently expresses pleasure at others' company, seeks company
Assertive	Speaks often of own or others' equal rights, expresses feelings easily, refuses to be unnecessarily manipulated or "sold," speaks out against infringements of rights. Rejects unwanted attention with tact.
Aggressive	Hits frequently, physically abusive, makes verbal demands, argues often, uses trickery or misleading language to control, coerces others
Dependent	Asks for help, frequently complains of inability to meet requirements, expresses fear of making mistakes, waits for others to initiate action
Sharing	Frequently offers to assist, encourages, divides materials or time
Moral-ethical	Expresses social rules for correct conduct and acts accordingly, expresses guilt or remorse at violations, predicts effects of own and others' actions on future welfare
Nonassertive	Avoids social conflict, acts to avoid evaluative situations, does not protest when rights are violated, excuses those who make errors, avoids strangers or situations where there are many strangers
Deviant	Makes violent, unprovoked attacks on others, accuses others, hallucinates, is nonresponsive to actions of others, self-stimulates, is nonresponsive to social reinforcement or punishment
Deceitful	Lies or acts to mislead others either to gain a reinforcer or to avoid a punishment
Sex role	Acts similar to own gender in own culture, states desire to be member of own or opposite gender, selects same or opposite sex as love or sex partner(s)
Cooperative	Accepts assignments to carry out joint tasks, seeks out opportunities to work with others, joins in common tasks for common benefit, expresses his preferences for doing things with others, denies own immediate gain for activities that benefit whole group
Competitive	Frequently acts to best others, expresses preferences for competition in occupation or in recreation pursuits, denies losing or debates about "who lost," shows evident signs of distress over losing

Social learning theory emphasizes the role of cognition in regulating behaviors.

Reciprocal Determinism

Each of the categories in Table 10–2 is an interaction between two or more people. Bandura (1986) views such interactions as examples of **reciprocal determinism**. In reciprocal determinism interpersonal and nonsocial environmental factors come together as interlocking determinants of each other. Reciprocal determinism holds that the behavior of individuals occurs because of prior interactions with other people *and* with the immediate environment. Diagrammatically, the relationship looks like this:

The behavior (B) of an individual is seen as being determined by prior learning (P) and the present environment (E). The arrows indicate that the influence can be in any direction.

Reciprocal determinism, according to Bandura, predicts that the relative strength of interpersonal behavior will vary with changes in environmental factors. Sharing and competitive behaviors, for example, usually are thought to be types of interactions determined by past learning. In times of extended drought or other hardships, however, sharing and competition may change considerably. Prior learning interacts with the present environment to determine behavior (Kruglanski & Mayseles, 1988).

Generality of Social Learning

Social behaviors tend to be quite generalized (see Bandura, 1986; Zentall & Galef, 1988). That is, they are likely to appear in a variety of settings involving many different people. Social behaviors also tend to be fairly stable, persisting over long periods of time. An individual who acts aggressively in one situation, for example, usually will be aggressive in many similar situations. Likewise, the shy student in the classroom probably will be shy in many similar settings in the future.

Social learning theory explains this generalization by hypothesizing the existence of mediating responses. **Mediating responses** are considered to be symbolic events (thoughts). They usually consist of images or verbal responses that people think of when they encounter stimuli. These mediating responses help determine one's overt actions, which then are reinforced or punished by the reactions of other people.* We can picture the chain of events in social behaviors as follows:

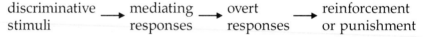

discriminative → mediating → overt → reinforcement
stimuli   responses   responses   or punishment

Suppose that Jane is walking home from school when she encounters another little girl whom she has never seen before. Further imagine that this unknown child slips on some ice and falls down. This situation—seeing another child in distress—is a discriminative stimulus for several possible mediating responses on Jane's part. Mediating responses generally provide people with a label for an event they witness (Jane thinks, "That little girl is hurt"), a course of action to follow ("I should help her get up and see if she needs a doctor"), and an anticipation of the outcome of the course of action ("Maybe she'll be my friend if I help her"). On some occasions, mediating responses may include cautions. Consider the thoughts one may have about stopping to help a motorist in distress: "Maybe he needs help but then again maybe he's trying to lure people into a trap so that he can rob them."

Most mediating responses are easily remembered. The images and verbal responses occur so readily that they are available in almost every social situation. This may account for the consistency in most people's social behaviors. Changes in social behavior *can* occur if new mediat-

---

*Note that this view of "thoughts" is rather different from how cognitive psychologists see things (see Chapter Two).

ing responses are learned. Therapists, for example, have reported successful treatments based on training their patients to label events in new ways and to describe themselves more favorably (see Dryden & Golden, 1987; Fishman, Rogers, & Franks, 1988).

Social Learning Processes

The Role of Reinforcement

Reinforcement and the shaping of responses are important factors in social learning (see Peters & McMahon, 1987). Bandura (1986) has argued, however, that while reinforcement procedures may be used alone, they often are inefficient. There are usually much faster ways to teach complex behaviors.

Consider, for example, how long it would take a teacher of the Russian language to use shaping alone to teach his or her pupils to pronounce a five-word sentence in Russian. Reinforcement by itself could get the job done, but at terrific expense in time and effort. It is

Most social behavior is learned through observation and imitation.

much simpler to provide a model of Russian pronunciation for the students to imitate. Observation and imitation, not shaping, constitute the process by which almost all social learning occurs.

Reinforcement has a role in social learning, however. It determines two things: whether a response will be attempted again and the rate of improvement in speed and accuracy of an imitation. If a child pronounces a word he has heard his parents say, he will attempt to say it again if he is reinforced. Improvement occurs when reinforcers are provided.

An example of modeling and reinforcement in social learning can be seen in an early study by Barton and Osborne (1978), who reported on a procedure they employed to increase sharing behavior in a kindergarten class of five hearing-impaired children.

All these children were reasonably bright but had severe hearing impairments and poor speech development. Unfortunately, they did not share things well and frequently fought. Each child wanted what others had and tried to take it. Their social interactions apparently resembled those of typical two-year-olds.

The teacher used the experimental procedure during a free-time period in which toys were distributed in the regular classroom. The nonsharing students were required by the teacher to share toys with the other students. When they failed to share, the teacher demonstrated the required sharing and had the students practice sharing. Praise and other rewards were given for sharing. Children who refused were removed from the group for brief periods.

The combination of modeling and reinforced practice led to large increases in sharing for all the children. Verbal interchanges among the children also increased. All changed behaviors continued for the entire fifteen-week follow-up period. The increased sharing (up to three times the level noted prior to the study) generalized to another classroom and also was observed when the children were with another teacher.

A similar study conducted by Bryant and Budd (1984) confirmed the results reported by Barton and Osborne. In this instance, teacher praise and **modeling** substantially increased sharing among six behaviorally handicapped preschoolers. Interestingly, the rate of these children's negative interactions also was reduced, apparently as a by-product of the increased sharing. More recently, Greenwood, Carta, and Hall (1988) reviewed the literature in this area and reported that combinations of *modeling* and reinforcement are highly effective means of classroom management.

Social behavior is affected by anticipated as well as actual consequences. A child will work for extended periods of time not only for immediate reinforcement but also for an anticipated reward, say a weekend movie. Probably if the child were informed that the movie was no longer available, the chore-related behavior would cease.

Social learning research has shown that direct reinforcement and punishment are not always necessary for social learning to occur. When we see others receive rewards or punishers for engaging in an act, the likelihood of our acting in the same way will be affected. Usually, seeing others succeed increases the chances we will try the same behavior. The effect of observing others receive reinforcement has been labeled *vicarious reinforcement* (Bandura, 1986; Cautela, 1984). Observing others receive punishment for a particular act, of course, reduces the probability of our attempting it (vicarious punishment).

Bandura and others have suggested that observing reinforcement or punishment has another important effect: establishing the relative value of consequences. Suppose one student sees another receive a sticker for the completion of several workbook pages. The first child then wants one, too; and so she carries out the same task to earn the sticker just because she saw another child reinforced with one. Suppose the next day she observed a third child rewarded with two stickers for doing the same task. When the first child is again given her reward of a single sticker for her activity, she is likely to become angry or hurt (typical responses to a punisher, not to a positive reinforcer). The child's vicarious experiences have altered the reinforcement value of the sticker—reversed its value, in fact. Observation establishes rewards and punishers as relative values, not as absolute events (Peters & McMahon, 1987).

The importance of observed consequences will be discussed further in the section on modeling. Most behaviors related to our values, self-esteem, career interests, and even our ambition are developed as a result of observing other people achieve satisfaction from carrying out certain tasks. Observation also is a more rapid process for developing secondary reinforcers than the pairing of reinforcers described in Chapter Nine. Observing a single instance of another child experiencing satisfaction with a successful performance in spelling or math often will establish success as a reinforcer. Fears and anxieties also are quickly learned. No one is certain just why vicarious reinforcement and vicarious punishment are so effective, although Bandura (1986) suggests that vicarious consequences act through four related functions: information, motivation, valuation, and influence.

Information function.   Observing others receive reinforcement usually permits a clear view of the connection between an act and its consequence. It also informs the observer about situations in which consequences differ, so that discriminative stimuli are quickly established (Zentall & Galef, 1988).

Motivation function.   Motivation to continue despite failure is improved by seeing others obtain reinforcement for the same behavior (Bandura, 1986; Kann, 1984). Further, observing other people being reinforced for a behavior on a variable schedule is more likely to bring about persistence than observing others reinforced on a continuous schedule.

Valuation function.   New reinforcers can be established through observing others' reactions. Students can develop new preferences (secondary reinforcers) and even come to have positive reactions to previously disliked objects (Higgins & Morris, 1985; Schunk, 1987). Similarly, observed punishment can either lower or raise the status of engaging in various acts. An individual imprisoned for upholding his beliefs and principles, for example, may be praised, whereas an individual imprisoned for abusing a child is reviled. In one case, observation of punishment increases the likelihood of imitation. In the other case, the observed consequence reduces the probability of imitation.

Influence function.   Children who see others react favorably to rewards for completing a task tend to increase their own efforts to complete tasks (Cautela, 1984; Schunk, 1987). When models reject rewards, students' levels of behavior drop significantly. Similarly, Bandura (1986) has noted that children will adopt work standards when they see other children achieve satisfaction by setting their own standards. Interestingly, when children adopt the high-performance standards they observe in others, they tend to generalize the standards to other times and places. Handwriting is a good example. A person who has a "perfect" model of script as a criterion works to achieve that model and is displeased with scrawled messages wherever and whenever he or she produces them.

The generalization of standards and self-reinforcement of effort are forms of self-management (see Chapter Nine) or, to use another label, a value system. In any case, we are talking about a widespread and powerful influence on the behavior of students. Teachers who hope to prepare students to be self-managers will need to be skilled in the application of the principles of observational learning.

Models who are similar in age and sex to learners tend to have the greatest impact.

Modeling and Imitation   Observational learning requires models. The model can be live, of course, but a movie, videotape, or illustrated story also may function well. A model can be provided by an oral discussion in which an older person asks a series of questions such as the following:

> "Will the dog run toward us?"
> "Will he be glad to see us or mad at us?"
> "How could we show him we want to be friends?"
> "How would he act when we show him we are his friends?"
> "Would it be fun for him to act that way?"

A teacher demonstrating an act to a child also is providing a model. Bandura (1986) has noted that modeling processes are sources of many attitudes and personal styles.*

---

*For a review of the treatment of children's fears, see Ollendick and Francis (1988). Specific uses of modeling can be seen in the treatment of fears of visiting the dentist (e.g., Klesges, Malott, & Ugland, 1984), fears of seeing a therapist (Weinstein, 1988), and fears of animals (see Dryden & Golden, 1987).

The precise form of modeling makes little difference to the basic process. The effect generally is the same whether information is conveyed through examples, pictures, or words. Behavioral demonstrations may be more effective for learners who have language limitations, but that is a matter of adapting the process to students' needs, not a change in the basic process.

Among normal children, **imitation** is a naturally developing ability. Reissland (1988) observed imitation in babies who were less than *one hour* old. Meltzoff (1988) reported that infants imitate with ease and that even babies only a few weeks old are able to remember previously imitated actions for as long as one week. Imitation does not necessarily develop on its own among intellectually handicapped children, however. They must learn to imitate others (Abravenel & Gingold, 1985). Some disabled children will observe modeled behavior but will make no effort to imitate it. Imitation, however, can be taught. In an important early study, Baer, Peterson, and Sherman (1967) worked with three severely retarded children, repeatedly reinforcing them for imitating appropriate eating and self-care behaviors, and found that the children's imitative responses increased and generalized.*

Once imitation has been established, learners usually apply their ability to imitate to the rapid acquisition of large numbers of social and academic behaviors, including speech and conversation, moral-ethical judgments, creativity, and sensitivity to others (see Table 10–2). Reinforcement in real life then usually leads to relatively widespread generalization. Also, once behaviors are established in one or a few individuals, modeling and imitation contribute to their diffusion to other people. The diffusion process is often helped by mass media, which explains how fads and fashions can sweep entire regions or countries almost overnight.

A good example of research on imitation in the classroom can be seen in a study by Alvord and O'Leary (1985). They employed slide-tape models and stories of sharing behavior with a group of nursery school and kindergarten children who initially had a very low rate of sharing. After only three days of seeing such models, the children had

---

*If you have slow-learning children in your classroom, you may be interested in additional readings on the process and advantages of using reinforcement methods to train them in generalized imitation: Henry (1987), Matson & Ollendick (1988), Reichle, Siegel, & Rettie (1985), Sang (1987), and Schwartz & Leonard (1985).

significantly higher rates of sharing. Children in a control group, who had heard only animal stories and saw slide-tapes without sharing, did not change their behaviors.

Another study demonstrating the educational utility of modeling was performed by Pluck, Ghafari, Glynn, and McNaughton (1984). In this experiment, parents were asked to model reading and reading enjoyment for children. The results indicated a significant increase in children's own reading. In addition, children's reading during leisure time seemed to generalize to settings outside the home.

A final study was conducted by Henry (1987), who employed modeling and reinforcement procedures to change the behaviors of hyperactive children. His results indicated that compliant behaviors increased as a result of both reinforcement and modeling procedures. A combination of modeling and reinforcement, however, was the most effective. The effectiveness of modeling depends on a number of factors. Modeling that employs "actors" who are very similar to learn-

"YOU MUST REALIZE THAT DESIRE IS THE CAUSE OF ALMOST ALL UNHAPPINESS — BUT, JUST OUT OF CURIOSITY, WHERE COULD I GET A SUIT LIKE THAT?"

ers in age, sex, and occupation tends to have the greatest impact. Modeling that employs higher-status or more expert "actors" also is effective, as is modeling portraying receipt of higher-value reinforcers. The correlates of modeling effectiveness must be interpreted cautiously, however; the status and characteristics of the models are most important if reinforcement is vague, far in the future, or rather probabilistic. If the reinforcers are abundant and potent, the status and character correlates of the model are of less significance (Blake, Austin, & Lowenstein, 1987; Galifret-Granjon, 1985; Sang, 1987).

Observational learning, of course, does not always produce desirable behaviors. Bizarre actions, strange beliefs, poor speech patterns, and high levels of competitive, aggressive, or even criminal behavior can be learned through modeling just as readily as can prosocial

---

PRACTICE EXERCISE 10–1   THE IMPACT OF MODELING AND IMITATION

Modeling and imitation are important learning processes. In growing up, everyone is influenced by models. For most of us, a few people have been models for behaviors that we now consider particularly important. We have imitated them consciously or unconsciously, and, from our standpoint, the behaviors we have acquired may be good or bad.

We would like you to think of a person from whom you acquired one or more important behaviors through modeling and imitation. By answering the following questions, you will have a chance to reflect on why you adopted the behavior.

1. The model was _____

2. Your behavior pattern that resembles that of the model is

    (was): _____

    _____

3. What reinforcers (or punishers) did you observe the model

    receive for his or her behavior? _____

    _____

    _____

behaviors (see Greenwood, Carta, & Hall, 1988; and Schunk, 1987, for comprehensive reviews). One area of great concern is the effect television has on children's behavior. Although the effects of television on social development are difficult to separate from other developmental influences (Bridges, Harnish, & Korber, 1987), television clearly has been shown to have an impact on the social learning of both children and adults (see Brocks, Armstrong, & Goldberg, 1988; Gilley, 1988; Kniveton, 1987). For example, Friedrich and Stein (1975) found that when children viewed only small amounts of "Mister Rogers' Neighborhood," increases occurred in such behaviors as cooperation, helping, sharing, and empathy. More recently, Elliott and Byrd (1984) found that even watching only a fifteen-minute show about disabilities could markedly improve viewers' attitudes toward handicapped people. In

---

PRACTICE EXERCISE 10–1   CONTINUED

4. Did you consciously decide to adopt the behavior?

   _____ Yes _____ No

   If yes, what factors influenced your decision? _____

   _____

   _____

5. Which of the following describe the model's relationship to you?

   a. *Age:* _____ Older _____ Same age _____ Younger

   b. *Sex:* _____ Same _____ Opposite

   c. *Relationship:* _____ Parent _____ Other older relative

   _____ Brother or sister _____ Friend _____ Other

6. Briefly analyze the reinforcement (or punishment) *you* subsequently received for adopting the modeled behavior: _____

   _____

   _____

addition, Landers (1988) has reported on children's increased sharing, greater tolerance for social differences, and cognitive gains as a result of watching "Sesame Street" on a regular basis. Other authors (e.g., Reiser, Tessmer, & Phelps, 1984) have obtained similar results in the development of prosocial behaviors. These positive aspects of television as a social learning medium have resulted in some authors' prescriptions for selectively employing television to augment social learning both in the home and in the classroom (Dunn & Cardwell, 1984; Liebert & Sprafkin, 1988; Singer & Singer, 1984).

Television also can be a potent source of negative social behaviors, however. In general, research has consistently demonstrated that violent television programs increase the likelihood of violence among viewers (Liebert & Sprafkin, 1988; Singer & Singer, 1984). In terms of direct reactions to televised violence, children tend to become frightened when presented with even small segments of violent programming (Landers, 1988; Singer & Singer, 1984), with the effects most notable among younger children and those who discriminate least well between fantasy and reality (Sprafkin, Gadow, & Kant, 1988). In fact, the overall results of research on television viewers indicate that habitual viewers have a distorted, fearful perception of the world (Bridges et al., 1987; Singer & Singer, 1984). Another negative finding concerns sex roles. Sex-role stereotypes are prevalent in general programming, especially commercials, resulting in direct effects on viewers (Holtzman & Akiyama, 1985). Gilley (1988), for example, found less self-confidence and less independent judgment among female viewers of traditional commercials than among viewers of commercials altered to avoid sex-role stereotypes. Finally, high levels of television viewing are linked to poor reading and poor academic performance (Ritchie, Price, & Roberts, 1987).

A few authors view television as a relatively benign social influence with a very small likelihood of harmful effects (Gunter & Furnham, 1985); some suggest it is a moderately effective (but repressive) way of propagating cultural values; while others believe television has the potential for doing great harm (Gilley, 1988). Regardless of which view is correct, it seems that the evidence supports moderation in television viewing and careful monitoring of the television programs children watch (Liebert & Sprafkin, 1988; Singer & Singer, 1984). Ultimately, the effects of television will be determined by the responsibility adults assume for the well-being of children.

Applications for Teaching: Instructional Goals and Observational Learning

Observational methods of instruction for both social and academic goals have a long history. In academic areas, teachers traditionally have included films, photographs, and demonstrations as means to improve students' mastery of the goals of instruction. Although not all the implications of the research on observational learning for classroom instruction are completely understood, a number of procedures can be recommended. We have listed general teaching procedures for the use of observational learning in instruction based on the research on modeling and imitation.

1. Use modeling and imitation in your instruction. Use models or demonstrations to convey complex instruction, especially when your ob-

Demonstrate physical activities without verbalization. Without talking, the instructor carefully shows students how to use a gauge.

jectives (a) involve combinations of cognitive and motor acts (as in teaching the pronunciation of foreign words); (b) involve the use of several muscle movements (as in handling or using tools); (c) involve applying safety rules; (d) require students to make fine discriminations of dial or gauge readings; or (e) specify a rigid adherence to a standard procedure such as using laboratory equipment for making various tests and analyses. In other words, don't depend on verbal instruction alone to develop learning as complex as these examples.

2. Make use of negative models in combination with positive models. A student who uses poor grammar will benefit not only from hearing correct grammar, but also by seeing it contrasted

with his or her present repertoire. Videotaped pairs of good and bad examples of grammar may be very helpful in changing the student's behavior.

3. *At first, direct your demonstration to one student.* When personally modeling a procedure, such as making a motion in a meeting controlled by parliamentary procedure, select one student to stand or sit at the front of the group and demonstrate the correct actions to him or her. After the demonstration, ask the student to model the procedure to the class, with members prompting the student as required to give a correct demonstration.

4. *Demonstrate physical activities without verbalization.* Show a procedure completely without words. Then repeat the action, labeling each part verbally. It will also often be useful to add two more steps: have the students "talk you through" the process, then, "talk themselves through" with peers providing prompts and feedback.

5. *Plan and rehearse all modeling procedures.* Only by going through the process can you be sure that all needed materials are available and that they will work as expected.

6. *Do not be afraid to repeat demonstrations.* Learners can be easily distracted at critical points during observational learning experiences. If possible, remove distractions. If this is not possible, repeat the demonstrations.

7. *Always talk about the knowledge that is called upon to solve problems.* Carefully model rational approaches to problems, then provide reinforcement for imitation. Give plenty of opportunity for students to practice with reinforcement.

8. *Model behavior in a setting similar to that in which learners will use the new skills.* In other words, use field trips, simulations, and hands-on experiences where possible.

Applications for Teaching: Social Goals and Observational Learning

Classroom-based approaches for helping students meet social learning goals have received considerable attention in the last several years (e.g., Kohler & Fowler, 1985). Effective procedures have been reported in schools for increasing sharing and altruistic behaviors (Alvord & O'Leary, 1985); decreasing aggressive acts (Carr & Durand, 1985; Carden-Smith & Fowler, 1984; Matson & Ollendick, 1988); improving verbal interactions with others (Dougherty, Fowler, & Paine, 1985; Odom, Hoyson, Jamieson, & Strain, 1985); and reducing racial prejudice (Aronson, Blaney, Sikes, & Snapp, 1978). The features these studies and a host of other social learning studies have in common provide several guidelines for you to help your students meet social learning goals. Here are six.

1. *Clearly define the social behaviors to be developed.* You and a student with a "temper problem," for example, may agree that angry feelings should be talked about with the person the student is angry at. The student should explain why he or she is angry. (The goal here is for the student to learn to talk out differences instead of settling them by physical means.)

2. Privately praise each time you observe a student exhibiting the desired social behavior. You might say, "Jim, I thought that was great the way you told Ann that she was not to tease you any more. She stopped, and you didn't get mad."

3. Try to show both the expected behavior and its consequences. Coach students to role-play various behaviors, and have them portray the consequences they would likely receive from each behavior.

4. Follow role-playing episodes with a discussion of the situation. Include appropriate alternative behaviors and their consequences. Negative consequences for inappropriate social behaviors should be discussed. You might say, "Let's see, when the guide is showing us around the museum, what could happen if we didn't follow her directions?" Several answers are appropriate and could be prompted and praised: "Other classes might not get to take a field trip to the museum" or "Other people who are touring the museum may be distracted."

5. Use small-group projects that require a division of labor. Require each person to undertake one or more assignments (Hall et al., 1988). Structure small groups so that there is a rotation of several social roles among all the students. Not all instruction should be conducted in small groups, of course, but use them enough to give students several opportunities to have a unique, identifiable contribution and to receive credit.

6. Practice social skills in as many settings as possible. The emphasis on social learning should extend over the entire school day and be included in as many classes as possible in order to result in generalization.

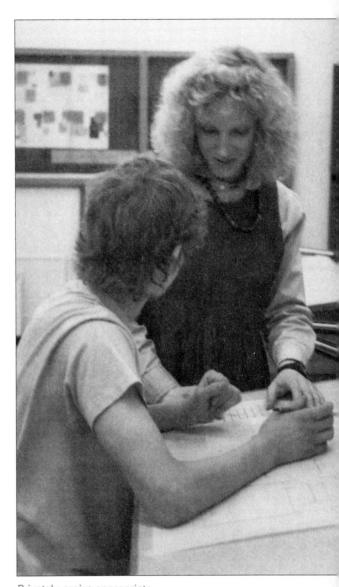

Privately praise appropriate social behavior. As the teacher interacts with the student, she compliments him on his helping another student earlier in the class.

PRACTICE EXERCISE 10–2   BEHAVIOR MODELING

Many if not most physical activities are learned through modeling and imitation. The goal of this practice exercise is for you to teach someone a behavior sequence through the use of modeling. The following are examples of the kinds of behaviors you could model:

The toss and serve in tennis

Operating a ditto, mimeograph, or other office machine

Making a transparency in a media center

Creating a file for a word processing program on a microcomputer

Assembling a clarinet

The behavior sequence you choose should be complex enough so that some learning is necessary, but easy enough to be completed in a few minutes. First identify your behavior sequence and a "student" who will benefit from learning it. Then identify the steps of the sequence so that each part can be demonstrated separately if necessary. Next determine what you need to focus the learner's attention on at each step and what (if anything) you need to say at each step. An abbreviated example for the toss and serve in tennis is given below. Following it is a form for planning and evaluating your behavior modeling sequence.

Sample Plan for Modeling the Toss and Serve to a Junior High School Student

Step in Demonstration	Draw Learner's Attention To	Verbal Comments
1. Holding ball properly	How hand grips ball	"Hold the ball like this, between the thumb and first two fingers."
2. Racquet back, preparing for the serve	How elbow is lifted; position of racquet head	"Lift your elbow like this"; "Scratch your back with your racquet."
3. Toss	Lifting of the ball	"Imagine you're pushing the ball up a pipe. . . ."

Planning Form: Teaching Through Modeling

Behavior to be taught _____

Student _____
(brief description)

PRACTICE EXERCISE 10–2   CONTINUED

Step in Demonstration	Draw Learner's Attention To	Verbal Comments
1. _____	_____ _____ _____	_____ _____ _____
2. _____	_____ _____ _____	_____ _____ _____
3. _____	_____ _____ _____	_____ _____ _____
4. _____	_____ _____ _____	_____ _____ _____
5. _____	_____ _____ _____	_____ _____ _____
6. _____	_____ _____ _____	_____ _____ _____

Problems that arose during your teaching session _____

_____

Your overall evaluation of your teaching _____

_____

_____

The Ethical-Moral Dilemma

Methods for altering student behaviors in the classroom usually raise some ethical questions; but since most such procedures result in changes useful for fostering academic learning, they are not often a source of continuing controversy. Many social behaviors, however, are linked to political philosophies, patriotism, sexual morality, religious beliefs, and even concerns about national security. What the schools do in the area of social development is everybody's business.

Consider competitiveness. This is a category including several related behaviors that some people consider to be highly useful. Much of our political-social system is organized to encourage and benefit from competition. Many people therefore believe schools should systematically do what they can to develop increased levels of competitiveness. Others point out, however, that competitiveness is also associated with insensitivity to human needs, anti-intellectualism, and even criminal behavior and that the schools should counter competitiveness by emphasizing sharing, cooperation, and helpfulness.

Teachers disagree about whether competition is desirable. Many believe competition helps prepare students for later life. Others point out that competitiveness can have many negative side effects.

There are no easy answers about which social learning goals should be established in the schools. There are not even fully satisfactory mechanisms to resolve the issues. There is no escape from making a decision, however. If schools or families choose to ignore such matters on the assumption that children's "natural" tendencies will determine development, they in reality are deciding to let other social influences take over. If schools and families do not employ learning processes, it is safe to assume that peer groups, television, movies, and other factors will control children's social development.

Is it preferable for the peer group or the media to influence social development? Should we intervene and counter some of the peer and media influence? Who should decide what sort of people our students should become? We have no final answers to these issues. We are quite sure that neither psychology nor any other single profession shall ever have the final answers, nor do we believe they should. While many psychologists have spoken out on the consequences of extreme aggressiveness in children, for example, it is not up to psychologists alone to determine how to reduce aggressive behaviors. Such decisions, one would hope, will be forthcoming from a decision-making process involving everyone.

Summary

Social behavior underlies the processes of education. While reinforcement-based classroom management techniques can be effective, most social behaviors related to attitudes, values, and preferences are much more effectively taught through the application of social learning theory.

Central to social learning theory is observational learning. In general, many skills and behaviors are learned more effectively through observation than through reinforcement alone. Observational learning helps determine individual reinforcers and punishers as well as group standards of conduct.

Teachers need to be aware of the power of modeling and imitation for classroom instruction and for student social development. Ethical issues in the use of social learning techniques must be considered, however. Classroom teachers must decide about the extent to which they will emphasize values and ethics as a part of their teaching responsibilities and make decisions about the social learning goals they will pursue.

Suggested Readings

Bandura, A. (1986). *Social foundations of thought and action: A social cognitive theory.* Englewood Cliffs, NJ: Prentice-Hall.
   This recent volume provides the best description of Bandura's theory.

Liebert, R. M., & Sprafkin, J. (1988). *The early window: Effects of television on children and youth* (3rd ed.). New York: Pergamon.
   Liebert and Sprafkin's book is an excellent publication on the influence of television. We highly recommend this book, now in its third edition.

Miller, N. E., & Dollard, M. J. (1941). *Social learning and imitation.* New Haven: Yale University Press.
   The basis of modern-day social learning theory is presented in this now-classic text. The content helps readers understand the influences of early psychology on the development of modern views of social learning.

Singer, J. L., & Singer, D. G. (1984). Psychologists look at television: Cognitive, developmental, personality, and social policy implications. *Annual Progress in Child Psychiatry and Child Development, 11,* 466–506.
   This review of research is useful to anyone wishing to learn about research on the effects of television.

Zentall, T., & Galef, B. G. (Eds.). (1988). *Social learning: A comparative approach.* Hillsdale, NJ: Erlbaum.
   Zentall and Galef have compiled an excellent edited volume focused on social learning theory. We recommend this volume to readers wishing a better theoretical foundation in the area.

CHAPTER
11

Classroom Management

OVERVIEW

Student behavior has been of concern to teachers for as long as there has been education. Even Socrates complained that his students "love luxury. They have bad manners and contempt for authority. They show disrespect for their elders and love chatter in the place of exercise" (Plato, *Republic*). While there have been growing concerns that today's students misbehave more frequently and more severely than their predecessors, there is little evidence to support this idea (Blechman, 1985). Nonetheless, the ability to deal with student behavior is a vital component of effective teaching. Effective instruction requires the ability to guide students' classroom behavior in ways that will result in the best possible atmosphere for learning (Brophy & Good, 1985).

A variety of experts have made many recommendations about classroom management. The best evidence, however, may come from the direct observation of how effective teachers structure classroom environments to contribute to learning. Evertson and Smylie (1987) report that the most important factors in directing student behavior are teacher actions that increase the time students spend in profitable learning activities. Better organization and transitions between activities make discipline problems much less likely to occur.

These observations have been amply confirmed (see Witt et al., 1988). One important way that effective teachers differ from less effective teachers is that they *prevent* behavior problems in their classrooms by keeping students involved in meaningful learning activities. This chapter is designed to help you acquire the skills that lead to effective classroom management.

OBJECTIVES

After reading this chapter, you should be able to meet the following objectives.

1. Develop a classroom management plan that will prevent problem behaviors.

2. Devise procedures for dealing with students who present special behavioral or academic problems.

3. Implement procedures for preventing or correcting behavior problems.

Applications for Teaching: General Principles of Classroom Management

In the last few years, the term *classroom management* has referred primarily to a behavioral approach for guiding classroom behaviors (Kazdin, 1988; Williams, 1987). While behavioral psychology provides some extremely important insights into the complex processes involved in guiding student activity, we cannot lose sight of the cognitive nature of human beings and the self-directed nature of learning. Successful classroom management requires a blending of cognitive, behavioral, and humanistic views of human behavior. The following eight principles of effective classroom management were drawn from all three views.

Meaningful activities prevent many classroom management problems. Students who are engaged in interesting projects seldom misbehave.

1. Provide meaningful learning activities. A classroom in which students have meaningful and challenging work is a key to preventing problems (Evertson & Smylie, 1987). Classroom disruptions are much less likely when students are interested in their work. As we stated in Chapter Two when we discussed cognitive processes, learning will be enhanced if the information is made meaningful to students.

How can you provide meaningful learning activities for your students? In a general educational psychology text we cannot give you specific suggestions about what materials and activities to select for your subject area and teaching level. One factor, however, is your knowledge of students—their interests, ways of thinking, and readiness for new learning tasks (Good & Brophy, 1985).

2. Provide a supportive classroom environment. As we saw in Chapter Eight, learning and self-growth are not likely to occur unless students' deficiency needs are met. The classroom must be a place in which children's physiological, safety, belongingness, and esteem needs are satisfied to the greatest extent possible. Clearly, a teacher cannot replace parents and provide the love and care that children must have. But teachers can certainly assure students' safety in the classroom and develop students' feelings of belonging to the class group. Esteem, in large part, is dependent on how teachers interact with students (Dweck, 1988). The acceptance of each student as a unique person and sincere praise for good effort go a long way to facilitating students' attainment of esteem needs (Dweck, 1988).

3. Provide opportunities for successful learning. The old saying "success breeds success" is no less true in the classroom than elsewhere. All students should have the opportunity to experience success in your classroom, from contributing something useful to a group discussion to seeing their progress in spelling. Success need not mean competing favorably with others; an improvement in one's own performance is an important source of success experience (Dweck, 1988).

Effective teachers plan activities that are challenging but allow a great likelihood for success. Generally, tasks that are too easy become boring and uninviting, and tasks that are too hard result in failure. The correct choice of learning activities for students is a crucial component of effective classroom management (Evertson & Smylie, 1987). When failure is frequent or when success is too easy, students become disenchanted with learning activities and look for other, more rewarding things to do (Good & Brophy, 1985). Too often, these other things disrupt the classroom.

4. Help develop students' self-improvement goals. As we saw in Chapter Eight, the kinds of goals students work toward have an effect on their achievement-related behaviors (Dweck & Leggett, 1988). In short, students who work toward self-improvement goals are far more likely to

be engaged in productive classroom behaviors than students pursuing performance goals.

5. Provide knowledge of results. The feedback teachers give students for their efforts is closely related to success. Feedback—knowledge of results—is an important part of motivating students to persist in learning tasks and in determining how much they learn (Kulhavy, in press). Students need to know how they are performing. Feedback not only permits students to judge their success, but it also contributes to the development of their own standards of excellence. In Chapter Thirteen, "Teacher-Made Tests," we present guidelines for providing appropriate feedback. In general, appropriate feedback facilitates students' motivation to engage in learning tasks, making it less likely that misbehavior will occur.

6. Share decisions with students. Students need to feel a sense of control in what they do (Dweck, 1988). Unfortunately, students in poorly managed classrooms often feel they have little or no control over their learning. When they feel they are giving the teacher only what he or she wants, motivation to continue working is greatly reduced (Good & Brophy, 1985).

Effective teachers allow students to play an important role in determining their own learning experiences. They often let students make decisions about what, when, and how learning will occur. Such shared decision making helps students feel they are in control. When students believe they have a significant say in classroom activities and decisions, motivation is enhanced, and the possibilities of misbehavior are reduced (Glasser, 1986).

7. Plan for "bad" days. No matter how well even the most effective teacher plans classroom activities, lessons sometimes do not work. Events (e.g., car trouble, illness in one's family) sometimes get in the way of adequate planning. On those days when even the best lessons aren't working or when preparation wasn't as complete as possible, teachers should be ready with preplanned "emergency" activities. Effective teachers anticipate having bad days in the school year and develop activities designed specifically to cover them. Such activities, of course, must be general enough to be useful on almost any day of the year but meaningful enough to keep students fully engaged.

8. Strengthen appropriate behaviors. Virtually all successful classroom management programs are based on *strengthening* appropriate behaviors (e.g., Matson & Ollendick, 1988), not on punishing misbehavior. Appropriate behaviors — those that lead to the most rapid and enjoyable learning in the classroom — compete with inappropriate behaviors — those that interfere with learning. Students cannot solve math problems and talk out of turn at the same time. These behaviors compete; that is, only one can happen at any one time. When appropriate behaviors are the norm, misbehavior is rare. This is the basis of a problem-prevention approach (Evertson & Smylie, 1987).

In sum, these eight guidelines emphasize that the hallmark of effective classroom management programs is *preventing* problems, not merely coping with misbehavior (Witt et al., 1988). They are compatible with more specific approaches to classroom management, including Canter's "Assertive Discipline" (e.g., Canter, 1986) and Gordon's "Teacher Effectiveness Training" (e.g., Gordon, 1977). In the next few pages, we present two particularly well-known views of how a problem-prevention approach to classroom management should proceed.

Glasser's Approach to Problem Prevention

William Glasser (1969, 1986) has developed a widely known model for preventing behavior problems. Glasser has reasoned that misbehavior and failure to learn from school experiences go hand in hand, a position in close accord with our discussion of motivation in Chapter Eight. Failure, he argues, leads to emotional reactions that reduce the likelihood that students will behave rationally and learn from the consequences of their behavior. Success, on the other hand, encourages rationality and learning from the behavioral consequences. To prevent behavior problems by increasing students' success and reducing failure, Glasser proposed the following guidelines:

Be personal. Use personal pronouns and express care for students.

Refer only to present behavior. Ask (in effect) "What are you doing now?" Avoid quizzing students about past behavior.

Stress value judgments by students. Ask if what students are now doing is helpful to them.

Plan with students for alternative behaviors. Involve students in decision making.

Be committed to the plan. Show your commitment by checking progress and providing positive reinforcement for meeting the goals of your plan.

Plan with students for alternative behaviors. Planning helps both teacher and student identify desirable outcomes.

Do not accept excuses. Don't discuss excuses and alibis with the students.

Do not punish. Punishment removes responsibility from the students.

Glasser's seven general guidelines are sensible and fit within the cognitive, humanistic, and behavioral framework for problem prevention we described earlier. If teachers are impersonal and distance themselves from students, it is extraordinarily difficult to convince students that teachers care. Referring to past mistakes gives students the feeling that they never can win—that what they did last week, last month, or last year forever shapes how teachers see them. Requiring students to make value judgments asks them to evaluate the worth of their behaviors. Planning for alternative behaviors clearly is required. Many students have not thought about acting differently; unless they are helped to plan alternatives, change is very difficult. Teachers must be committed to any plan designed to help students change their behaviors—if the teacher isn't committed to the plan, why should the student be committed? Excuses, Glasser contends, are of no value. We all have excuses for mistakes, but the real point is avoiding the same mistakes in the future. Finally, Glasser is adamant about not punishing students. Punishment, in his view, places the responsibility for student behaviors on the teacher, not on the student where it belongs.

PRACTICE EXERCISE 11–1   USING GLASSER'S PRINCIPLES IN ANALYZING
A CLASSROOM SITUATION

As we have indicated, Glasser has stated seven principles in his success-based program of classroom management:

1. Be personal.

2. Refer only to present behavior.

3. Stress value judgments by students.

4. Plan alternative behaviors with students.

5. Show commitment by checking and reinforcing progress.

6. Do not accept excuses.

7. Do not punish.

Analyze the situation below in terms of these seven principles by listing the parts of the conversation in which the teacher applies Glasser's principles and the parts where her performance could have been improved by applying his principles. When you have finished, go to the end of the chapter and check your analysis with ours.

Imagine the setting: Bill, a senior, has received a low grade on an examination in English that covered six weeks' study of the writings of Poe and Hawthorne. The next exam is in three weeks. Bill has come in after class to talk about his grade, and the following conversation ensues.

1. *Teacher:* Hello, Bill . . . come on in and sit down.
   Bill: (Slowly taking a seat) Well, I suppose you know why I'm here. . . . I'm pretty upset about the grade you gave me on the exam. I'm gonna end up ineligible for track for sure! Do you know what my parents are going to do when they find out that I'm not eligible for the track team? They're going to kill me. They'd planned on going up to Kirkville to see me run. Now all that's shot.

continued

2. *Teacher:* I'm sorry, but the examination was graded fairly. You just didn't do very well, Bill. Also, I think that you can improve enough on the next test to avoid a failing grade for this quarter.
   Bill: (Upset) I thought I did pretty good. . . . I think I know this stuff. It wasn't like I didn't study or anything.

3. *Teacher:* Bill, it's always the same story with you. I get tired of hearing how you studied and all. Last semester you said the same thing whenever you got a bad grade.
   Bill: Well, it's true. . . . I study but I still get bad grades from you. I don't think you're ever fair to me when you grade my tests.

4. *Teacher:* I think I have a reputation for being fair to students. . . . *(A period of silence)* Bill, I'm not sure we're getting anywhere by arguing about this exam. I'm sure you don't like the consequences—I know I don't—but I think we need to talk about ways to make sure the problem doesn't occur again. My goal is to have you coming out of this course as a good writer knowing about American literature. And I hope we like each other, too.
   Bill: You're not going to change my grade. . . .

5. *Teacher: (Firmly)* No, Bill.
   Bill: No?

6. *Teacher:* No. . . . It wouldn't be fair to the others in the class, and it wouldn't really indicate what you know about Hawthorne and Poe, would it? We have another test coming up in three weeks. I think we might talk about some ways of preparing for it that will help you do better on that one.
   Bill: But I *did* prepare. . . . I studied real hard and—

7. *Teacher: (Gently interrupting)* The next test will cover several of the early twentieth-century writers. *(Checking her lesson plans)* It looks like we have six more class sessions before that exam. Let's talk about some specific things you

might want to do before the next exam to make sure your performance is as good as I know it can be.
Bill: Well, I could come to class . . . *(Smiles a little)*

8. *Teacher: (Laughing)* Well, I guess that's a start. But how about the studying? How do you generally go about getting ready for tests, Bill?
Bill: Well, on this one I pretty much sat down and read over all the stuff you assigned the night before the test.

9. *Teacher: (A little mischievously)* And the result?
Bill: Not too terrific, I guess.

10. *Teacher:* Could we think a bit about approaching this test a little differently? We agree that neither of us is too happy with the outcome.
Bill: For sure!

11. *Teacher:* One thing I've found helpful is for students to work out a schedule for preparing for an exam that starts about a week before the exam takes place. That way, a person doesn't get caught at the last minute. If you'd be willing to draw up a plan for how you might prepare this time, I'd certainly be happy to meet with you after class tomorrow and have a look at it. We also could meet a couple of days before the exam and see how your preparation is coming.
Bill: Sounds reasonable. I'll have something tomorrow.

Positive uses of Glasser's principles

Glasser's principle (by no.)   Teacher comment or question (by no.)

Failure to use Glasser's principles

Glasser's principle (by no.)   Teacher comment or question (by no.)

A Behavioral Approach to Problem Prevention

Contemporary behavioral approaches to classroom management are based primarily on behavioral psychology and social learning as discussed in Chapters Nine and Ten. Behavioral approaches draw specific attention to the antecedents and consequences of behavior that teachers manage in order to increase or decrease behaviors. From this perspective, then, the first step in a preventive approach is to select the behaviors you want to increase.

Desirable Student Behaviors

As a teacher, you first need to decide what goals are most important for your students. Most teachers hope that students will become better self-directed learners, that they will improve their ability to analyze and solve problems, and that they will become more creative. A prerequisite for reaching goals such as these is a smoothly operating and goal-oriented classroom. Following is a list of general student behaviors, with specific examples, that can contribute to productive activity in most classes, regardless of classroom goals. Their occurrence will tend to produce an atmosphere in which learning can take place. An important additional effect is that if students do these things, discipline problems become less likely.

Paying attention to class activities:

☐ Looking at the teacher or other students who are giving a demonstration

☐ Turning to pages of texts when requested

☐ Asking relevant questions

Working as a cooperating member of a class or group:

☐ Participating in discussions, planning sessions, and the like

☐ Volunteering for tasks

☐ Speaking quietly and calmly when disagreeing

☐ Maintaining an even temper and being friendly

☐ Congratulating others on their efforts

☐ Sharing praise with the group

☐ Obtaining permission before speaking out or acting in ways that might distract other students

Initiating learning activities:

- ☐ Exploring ideas
- ☐ Obtaining extra resources for learning
- ☐ Seeking additional instruction
- ☐ Practicing on one's own
- ☐ Helping other students with assignments

Observing safety rules:

- ☐ Walking in crowded places or in halls and stairs
- ☐ Checking clearances when carrying objects
- ☐ Following specific safety rules in class

Our list, of course, is not all-inclusive and will not fit every situation. You may well see some changes or additions you would make. Playground supervisors, shop teachers, music teachers, and parents at home all are in settings that differ from traditional classrooms. They must formulate their own set of problem-solving behaviors. Nonetheless, a difference in appropriate behaviors across situations does not change the basic principle: Simply, discipline problems will be minimal if students are active and productive.

Three Keys to an Effective Behavioral Approach

In an early study of classroom management, Becker, Madsen, Arnold, and Thomas (1967) began a program of research that identified three simple but critical principles of effective behavioral classroom management: (1) have rules for what is expected of students, (2) give praise for appropriate behaviors and indicate what the praise is for, and (3) ignore minor problem behaviors. These three principles can be used to guide all your teaching activities. They have been confirmed in numerous studies with children of various ages and social and ethnic backgrounds (see Hersen, 1988; Kazdin, 1988). Consistent use of these principles results in improvement in student conduct and academic performance (see Canter, 1986, for a thorough discussion).

Rules. Rules are a part of every well-run classroom. They convey to students an idea of what is expected of them. Rules may be written or oral and may be stated positively ("Put all materials away after you finish") or negatively ("Do not interrupt when another person is speaking"). To make your rules most effective, the following suggestions may be helpful.

There are some misbehaviors that cannot be ignored. You may want to decide in advance what behaviors cannot be allowed in your classroom.

Keep rules to a minimum. Ideally, you should have only as many rules as you can monitor yourself—five or six at a maximum.

Describe appropriate activities as clearly and positively as possible.

Always include a description of the positive effects of following a rule. Involve students in the formulation of classroom rules. The more students are involved in determining rules, the more likely they are to follow them.

Introduce rules with an explanation of why they are necessary and discuss them thoroughly (Evertson & Smylie, 1987). Discuss what these expectations mean for each student.

As we noted in Chapter Ten, if the behavior you are asking your students to perform is complex and can be stated only rather abstractly, demonstrations or modeling may be superior to rules. A demonstration of how to use laboratory equipment or the materials in a learning resource center usually is better than instructions or rules about those procedures. Many safety-related behaviors are best demonstrated ("Now look how I keep my hands on the wood and still guide it through the saw. You could get your hand caught if you don't hold it like this"). As with rules, always indicate the positive effects of imitating a model.

PRACTICE EXERCISE 11–2   ANALYZING STUDENT BEHAVIOR

One very useful skill you can perfect is that of identifying productive and nonproductive student behaviors and analyzing why they occur through a behavior analysis. Set a goal for yourself of identifying at least five behaviors of each type (productive and nonproductive) in any setting in which there are individuals learning — in residence halls, in the library, in classes (lectures, discussions, lab sessions), at meals, in meetings, during tests, at social events, and on the job.

List on the following form the productive and nonproductive behaviors you observe. Also list the antecedents and consequences in order to analyze what might be maintaining each behavior. For each, briefly comment on the likely consequences of continuation of this behavior on the student's ultimate academic and social achievement. If possible, share your observations with your instructor and classmates.

Productive Behaviors

Antecedents	Behavior	Consequences	Possible Long-Term Outcomes

Nonproductive Behaviors

Antecedents	Behavior	Consequences	Possible Long-Term Outcomes

Praise and Other Positive Consequences.   Rules alone seldom will keep their influence; they prompt but do not maintain appropriate behavior. In the long run, the consequences of behavior become a critical factor. A student may start out following a classroom rule by being cooperative, for example. However, if there are no discernible benefits or if the student finds that competitiveness rather than cooperation actually is reinforced, the new behavior will soon die out. Teachers must provide consequences consistent with rules to maintain appropriate behaviors.

Effective teachers use their reactions as consequences for student behavior (Matson & Ollendick, 1988). A smile, a word or two of sincere praise, and a careful examination of students' work are examples of teachers' actions likely to reinforce appropriate behavior. Another way to say this, as we stressed in Chapter Eight, is that effective teachers allow students to experience success.

In effective classroom management, positive reinforcement from teachers is contingent on appropriate student behavior. Contingent reinforcers are closely linked to desired student actions; that is, praise and attention (indications of success) are offered on those occasions when desired behaviors occur. The teacher intentionally links his or her attention to appropriate behavior. On the other hand, if praise and attention are unconditional (noncontingent), students are likely to use unproductive ways to gain the teacher's attention.

In early research on classroom behavior and praise, overt praise was generally thought to be universally good—the more praise, the more positive the environment and the better the learning experience (Winett & Winkler, 1972). Two cautions are in order, however. First, praise must be sincerely offered (Hughes, 1988). Extremely frequent use of verbal praise is likely to be justifiably perceived as insincere and probably will have no effect and may even have negative effects (Witt et al., 1988). Second, the effectiveness of praise may depend on several variables. Most successful teachers in schools in the lower socioeconomic strata use praise and gentle encouragement as their basic approach. Successful teachers in the higher socioeconomic levels at times tend to use more critical and demanding approaches. Also, praise coaxed out of teachers by students tends to have negative effects on learning. Public praise of individuals in front of the entire class as a basic teaching approach also tends to reduce achievement levels, but praise offered privately for achievement has very positive effects (see Evertson & Smiley, 1987).

Ignoring Inappropriate Behavior.   The natural inclination of many teachers is to correct or criticize a misbehavior. In some cases, this may be acceptable, as when the teacher perceives that more severe problems are likely to develop soon. Many minor misbehaviors, however, should be ignored (Becker et al., 1967; Matson & Ollendick, 1988) since one of the most common and most powerful reinforcers in the classroom is teacher attention and praise. When students obtain attention for inappropriate behavior it is probable that they will continue to misbehave in order to obtain additional reinforcement.

Withholding attention for inappropriate behavior often will lead to the behavior's extinction. Teachers should be careful to consider three points in ignoring behavior, however. First, during extinction things often get worse before they get better. That is, misbehavior frequently increases when it is first ignored, presumably because the students are not obtaining expected reinforcement ("She didn't pay any attention to me. Didn't she hear me? Maybe I'd better talk louder"). Second, ignoring usually does not result in rapid decreases in behavior. As a rule, misbehavior is maintained on some form of variable schedule of reinforcement, and when reinforcement is withdrawn, many unreinforced instances of the misbehavior will occur before it ceases. Third, and most important, positive reinforcement (attention and praise) for alternative behavior must be plentiful. Merely withholding reinforcement for misbehavior is not nearly so effective as coupling it with positive reinforcement for appropriate behavior. In fact, ignoring *alone* can sometimes lead to greater levels of misbehavior.

Small misbehaviors often can be ignored safely. Students' attention is not always constant, and occasional lapses can be expected.

Some misbehaviors, of course, cannot be ignored. Actions that threaten you or your students, self-injurious behaviors, severe disruptions, violations of safety rules, and similar incidents must be corrected immediately. For such problems we suggest some of the specialized techniques described in the next section.

Some Specific Interventions for Managing Inappropriate Behavior

When behavior problems arise in the classroom despite the teacher's best efforts to prevent them, intervention techniques may be effectively employed. It is interesting to note that most research in classroom management has investigated various techniques for correcting already existing behavior problems rather than methods of preventing problems in the first place (Kazdin, 1988). We suppose that researchers' emphases on correction rather than prevention is a direct result of the severity of some problems and the importance attached to correcting them (Williams, 1987). In this section we briefly describe some of the more widely used (and more widely investigated) techniques for correcting behavior problems once they have started.

The Token Economy

The **token economy**, pioneered by Ayllon and Azrin (1968), is a systematic method of providing students with immediate reinforcement for appropriate behavior. Rather than relying on praise or other sources of social reinforcement, the token economy utilizes a concrete form of secondary reinforcer—tokens. The tokens (points, check marks, "smiley faces," poker chips) are presented to students contingent on their performance of appropriate behaviors specified by the classroom rules. Different behaviors in an economy will earn differing numbers of tokens: Coming to class on time might earn two tokens, while turning in completed homework might earn five.

Typically, tokens can be exchanged at the end of a period of time (usually one class period; sometimes as long as one week) for backup reinforcers (Williams, 1987). The backup reinforcers are, in a sense, purchased by students with their tokens. A student may earn enough tokens to purchase the last fifteen minutes of a period for free time, or he or she may be able to purchase the opportunity to do an especially

There are, however, better ways of guiding student behavior.

"Sure there's a way to discipline them. Yell at them."

interesting activity. Attractive backup reinforcers are an important component of token economies (Witt et al., 1988).

Most token economies also include a response-cost feature (Kazdin, 1988). That is, tokens are taken away from students if they misbehave. Some token economies also place a ceiling on how many points students may lose before they are suspended from the classroom. The point of the response cost, of course, is to weaken inappropriate behavior. The ceiling is used to place a limit on misbehavior.

Token economies have been effective at many age levels and across almost all subject areas (see Witt et al., 1988). In general, the major advantages of the token economy are immediate, concrete reinforcement; high flexibility in student choice of backup reinforcement; student expectations for reinforcement that cue teacher behaviors; and ease of program revision. In situations where a high degree of control is needed, the token economy may be a good intervention.

Token economies should include the following components:

A set of instructions that specify the expectations held for students

Tokens that can be accumulated over time

Guidelines for awarding or taking away tokens

A procedure for identifying effective backup reinforcers

A guide for exchanging tokens for backup reinforcers

The Good Behavior Game

The **Good Behavior Game**, developed by Barrish, Saunders, and Wolf (1969), is another effective method for managing behavior. The game requires that a class be divided into two or more teams that compete to see which team can gain the most points through appropriate behavior. The winning team typically gains an attractive reinforcer for the entire group, such as early recess, free time, or, with younger students, consumables such as an extra carton of milk.

Each team's score depends on the behavior of each team member, and so it is possible for one highly disruptive student to cause a team to lose. This possibility, however, has not been encountered often (see Kazdin, 1988). Further, the game is usually set up so that any team can win if it obtains 80 percent of the score of the winning team.

The Good Behavior Game actually is a variant of the token economy (Witt et al., 1988). Points (or tokens) are given to teams for appropriate behavior of team members, and points are subtracted for the misbehavior of any team member. The game differs from the token economy in the use of group goals and group-contingent reinforcement. That is, the backup reinforcers are given to a group for group behavior. The advantages of the Good Behavior Game include those of the token economy plus a high rate of student participation, peer reinforcement for earning points, and the gamelike nature of the process. The Good Behavior Game has been especially effective with elementary students (see Hersen & Last, 1988).

The Good Behavior Game should include the following components:

Instructions that describe the teacher's expectations

A set of guidelines that specify the behaviors that will gain or lose points

A description of how the game will be administered

A procedure for selecting group backup reinforcers

Group Contracts

Group contracts are agreements negotiated between groups of students and a teacher. They specify both student and teacher behavior (Homme, Csanyi, Gonzales, & Rechs, 1969). There are three important characteristics of group contracts. First, the teacher and students negotiate each item to be included in the contract. The teacher may wish to include certain behaviors to be reinforced, while the students may wish to include others. A negotiation time of several class periods often is necessary to come to a consensus about the contents of the contract.

The second feature is that students voluntarily enter into contracts. Any student in the class may choose *not* to sign the contract and thereby continue with whatever classroom management approach was in effect earlier. Such nonsigning students, of course, receive none of the benefits of the contract. Nonsignees may choose to enter into an agreement at any time during the contract period, however (Witt et al., 1988). The choice is entirely voluntary.

The third component of a group contract is that the teacher also agrees to be held accountable for certain responsibilities. If the teacher agrees to grade and return homework in twenty-four hours, for example, this is just as much a part of the contract as any behaviors the students agree to perform.

Group contracting has been found to be effective with students of all ages and across many different subject areas (Kazdin, 1988). The advantages of group contracting include those of the token economy plus the attitudinal benefits of negotiation and voluntary participation.

The components of a group contract are:

A description of the overall rules for the classroom

A description of the behaviors of the students and the teacher

An explanation of the way in which the system will be administered

A renegotiation date

The signatures of the agreeing parties

Individual Contracts

The techniques we've discussed so far all are designed for implementation with an entire class. There are times, however, when teachers do not want to employ a comprehensive management procedure but instead want to work with only one or two students. An **individual contract**, sometimes called a **contingency contract**, is an agreement that a student will change a behavior in return for reinforcement (Kazdin, 1988). The use of an individual contract can be seen in the following example.

A teacher reported on a sophomore student who very defiantly placed her head down on her desk every day and kept it there during the entire class period. Other teachers reported that the girl's behavior was the same in their classes. The teacher and the student arrived at a contract whereby the student would be ready to discuss the answers to two questions that would be asked at the beginning of every class. After giving the two answers, the girl would receive a "pass" for the day and could then rest her head on her arms and go to sleep. The teacher agreed that the girl would not be called on again during the class period and that she would receive a satisfactory grade on her report card. Getting the girl to answer only two questions a day obviously was not all that was desired. This represents only the starting place in a management plan. Ultimately full participation in class was expected. Contracts frequently start with just one small step and progress gradually until the final goal is reached.

The girl responded very well to the contract. At first she answered the two questions and then put her head down as agreed. Subsequently, she began to stay alert and to participate in discussions for longer periods of time. At the end of three weeks, she was alert during the whole period and frequently was volunteering answers. She continued, however, to visit the teacher after class to get her two special questions for the next day's class. During these private contacts, the teacher gave her sincere praise for participation.

Individual contracts have been used with students of all ages (Witt et al., 1988) and in many different settings. Major advantages are their flexibility—they can be employed for a wide range of behaviors—and the fact that they can be negotiated with individual students to meet individual needs.

To be most effective, individual contracts always should specify positive changes in behavior and contain the following components:

The names of the agreeing parties

A definition of the agreed-upon student behavior and an acceptable performance level

Specification of the agreed-upon teacher behavior or other reinforcers

The signatures of both parties

The techniques we have described so far have emphasized the strengthening of appropriate behaviors. There are times, however, when teachers need to suppress a misbehavior. One method, time-out, has proved to be an effective procedure for decreasing inappropriate behavior.

Time-Out

Time-out is the brief removal (for three to five minutes) of a child from a reinforcing setting to one that is not reinforcing. It generally is thought of as a mild punishment technique. Its basic purpose, however, is not to punish the child but rather to interrupt reinforced misbehavior. Generally, time-out is used when peer attention maintains the inappropriate behavior or when the teacher judges that the behavior must be dealt with quickly. Time-out is not a solution; it always should lead to the use of a more positive behavior-management program (Witt et al., 1988).

Time-out is not recommended for older students, but it has been found effective with elementary school children (Hersen & Last, 1988). Generally, time-out has its greatest effect when the environment from which a child is removed is highly reinforcing. Time-out also seems to be more advantageous when children are removed for brief periods of time and when children are not totally isolated, although total isolation has been used for severe behavior problems (Dangel & Polster, 1988).

Time-out has been found to be effective in school, home, and institutional settings. Its advantages include the rapidity with which it can be employed and the fact that teachers can employ it for a day or two while planning positively oriented behavior-management programs. Time-out, however, has received some strong criticism (see Witt et al., 1988), mostly owing to misuses. Because of the potential for misuse, these detailed rules should be carefully adhered to in using this procedure:

1. Obtain the consent of parents and/or legal guardians of all students involved. Explain the procedures in detail, including (1) the behaviors for which time-out will be invoked, (2) how it will be explained to the students, (3) the duration of the time-out and how often it will be utilized, (4) follow-up provision of reinforcers, and (5) the theory and research basis for using the system.

2. Prepare the student. Explain the process by pointing out that the ultimate purpose is to teach the student better control when angry, excited, or upset. Carefully describe the student behaviors that will lead to time-out.

3.   Where possible, use nonisolation techniques (Kazdin, 1988). Place the child at the periphery of the group with instructions not to interact with the class for a few moments. If the child stops behaving inappropriately, allow a few minutes to pass, and then have the child return to his or her original place in the group. Use isolation as a backup consequence if the behavior does not stop when the child is placed at the edge of the group.

4.   If isolation is used, make sure that the time-out room is comfortable, well lit, and not frightening to your students. You do not want to provide a place to go for fun, but you don't want to alarm anyone, either. The point is to provide a setting that gives few opportunities for reinforcement.

5.   When a student misbehaves, accompany him or her to the time-out area. Ask the student to sit quietly and review what led up to the misbehavior. Then ask the student to describe what he or she might have done differently to avoid the problem.

6.   Notify the student when time is up (three to five minutes), and escort him or her back to the classroom.

7.   Remind students that they can decide for themselves when it would be best to use time-out. Offer sincere praise to students who act to prevent problems. Recognize that it is difficult to walk away from trouble in order to cool off.

Home-Based Contingencies

The techniques we have described are designed for in-school administration. Many times, however, it is useful to involve parents in behavior management. Parents usually appreciate involvement in the school's efforts. One way to foster their participation is through the use of home-based contingencies.

Home-based contingencies are behavior-management programs in which the backup reinforcers are administered at home by the parents (Williams, 1987). Home-based contingencies may be adapted for use with token economies or individual contracts, or they may evolve from an agreement that a student's achievement of specific goals during the day (as determined by the teacher or by agreement of the teacher and parents) will result in backup reinforcement from the parents.

The usefulness of home-based contingencies has been demonstrated with students of all ages and across many different settings (see Kazdin, 1988). There are several advantages of home-based contingencies. First, the parents are fully involved in the program, supporting the teacher's actions. Second, with parental involvement, the behavior-change program is far more likely to be consistent and effective. Third, parents have a wider range of reinforcers (money, special snacks, weekend activities, ball gloves) available for their children's behavior than do teachers. Fourth, a load is removed from the teacher (administering backup reinforcers), freeing him or her for other duties.

For home-based contingencies to be implemented, several conditions should be met:

1. An agreement must be reached about which behaviors will be reinforced, what constitutes an acceptable level for the peformance of the behavior, and which method of recording the behavior will be used.

2. The parents must be willing to become fully involved in the program and consistently administer the backup reinforcers.

3. There must be an effective method of communicating with the parents. Frequently, daily "report cards" are used in which the teacher records the student's level of goal attainment and indicates whether the student is to be reinforced.

Other Techniques

In the past two decades, researchers in education and psychology have developed a large number of specialized techniques for behavior management that go beyond those discussed here (see Table 11–1). Many are not suited for classroom use—particularly some developed especially for implementation in psychiatric hospitals—and others are effective only for a limited group of behaviors ("overcorrection," for example, is an effective technique for reducing some but not all behaviors). Overall, the techniques surveyed in this chapter should be sufficient for most teachers' purposes. Certainly, given teachers' knowledge of the underlying theory, they may develop their own effective approaches to classroom management or adapt those described by others. Readers wishing to expand their knowledge of specific techniques in behavior management should consider further reading (see Dangel & Polster, 1988).

TABLE 11–1   REPRESENTATIVE STUDIES IN BEHAVIOR MANAGEMENT*

Authors	Subjects' Grade Level	Techniques	Processes and Results
Barton & Osborne (1978)	Preschool; kindergarten (learning-impaired)	Required practice with reinforcement	Students who did not share toys practiced sharing. Teacher praised sharing. Sharing increased threefold over fifteen-week follow-up.
O'Connor (1973)	Preschool	Modeling and reinforcement	Modeling alone, then reinforcement alone, then combination of the two improved and increased social interactions. Modeling was needed for new behaviors to persist.
Taylor & Kratochwill	Preschool	Selective teacher praise	Messy kindergartners selectively were praised by teacher for placing paper towels in waste receptacles, flushing toilets, and turning off faucets. Target behaviors improved markedly within twelve days.
Odom et al. (1985)	Handicapped preschoolers	Token economy	A token economy was used with the peers of three handicapped preschoolers to increase the handicapped children's social interactions. Although the number of social interactions greatly increased, no generalization to other settings was observed.
Kohler & Fowler (1985)	Kindergarten and first grade	Social skills training package	Three children with poor social skills were trained to invite their peers to play and to use social amenities in their interactions. These children received significantly more invitations to play with others and no longer were regarded as having poor social skills.
Roberts et al. (1987)	First- and second-graders	Self-instruction and self-reinforcement	Training children in self-instruction coupled with reinforcement for self-instruction yielded significant academic gains.
Pfiffner & O'Leary (1987)	First- through third-graders	General management system	Positive and negative consequences were needed to change behaviors. Positive consequences alone were less effective than the combination.
Pfiffner et al. (1985)	Second- and third-graders	Praise and individualized reinforcers for performance	Praise alone had minimal effects on the behaviors of eight second- and third-graders with behavior problems. Reinforcers tailored to each child's individual needs were effective.
Humphrey (1978)	Sixth-grader	Contract with peer teacher-helper reinforcement	Older student was trained to reinforce a sixth-grader, who had a poor attendance record. Attendance improved to almost 100 percent.

TABLE 11–1   *CONTINUED*

Authors	Subjects' Grade Level	Techniques	Processes and Results
Bologna & Brigham (1978)	Upper elementary	Instruction plus tokens and self-monitoring	Students were instructed, then reinforced for use of new vocabulary in essays. Token reinforcement produced more use of new words and better-quality essays.
Bornstein et al. (1977)	Upper elementary	Assertion training; modeling-rehearsal	A group of over-cooperative, excessively shy, and over-conforming eight- to eleven-year-olds were given assertiveness training. Significant increases in assertive behavior were obtained.
Reese et al. (1977)	Junior high	Token economy plus praise and contracts	Program across entire urban school in low-income area was effective in bringing about increases in attendance, completion of assignments, and grades. Standardized test results did not change, however.
Hayes et al. (1985)	College students	Self-reinforcement	Self-reinforcement was more effective when contingencies were made public. When students who used self-reinforcement told other people what they were doing, the procedure was more effective than if they kept it to themselves.
Rudd & Geller (1985)	College students, staff, and faculty	Incentives	After public announcements, the campus police at Virginia Tech recorded the license plate numbers of drivers using shoulder belts. Then, once every three weeks all the license plate numbers were put in a raffle drawing. Ten winners each three-week period received gift certificates. Faculty and staff significantly increased usage of seat belts.
Crowell et al. (1988)	Adults	Instructions, feedback, and praise	Instructions, feedback, and praise increased the customer service behaviors of bank tellers by 12 percent.
Diament & Colletti (1978)	All levels	Training of parents to use reinforcement	After eight weeks of training, parents were successful in reducing behavior problems in the home and improving relationships with their learning disabled children.

*The techniques and management problems described in this chapter, and others like them, have been researched extensively. Several recent books describe the research and extrapolate the findings. New research appears constantly in respected educational and psychological journals. Professional meetings are devoted exclusively to behavior-management research, for instance, the annual convention of the American Association of Behavior Analysis. It is impossible to cite even a portion of these numerous studies in this chapter. We have, however, summarized several representative studies in this table.

Summary

In this chapter we saw that the principles of cognitive, behavioral, and humanistic psychology can be applied to the management of classroom behavior. Eight general principles of classroom management are meaningful learning activities, supportive classroom environments, opportunity for successful learning, development of self-improvement goals, feedback for learning, sharing decisions with students, planning for "bad" days, and strengthening appropriate behavior. Glasser's success-based approach to classroom management emphasizes the principles of humanistic psychology but is compatible with behavioral psychology. Behavioral procedures involve the teacher's analysis of the antecedents and consequences of behavior in preventing problem behaviors. The principles of rules, praise, and ignoring provide an effective means of increasing appropriate behavior and thereby decreasing misbehavior.

When prevention techniques fail, as they sometimes will, several specific techniques are available for teachers: token economies, the Good Behavior Game, group contracts, individual contracts, time-out, and home-based contingencies. Each of these techniques is based on the principles of behavior analysis, and each can aid teachers in managing their classrooms more effectively.

Suggested Readings

Canter, L. (1986). *Assertive discipline*. Santa Monica, CA: Canter and Associates.

> *Lee Canter's "assertive discipline" is a mainstream approach to classroom management that draws directly on the principles described in this chapter.*

Froyen, L. (1988). *Classroom management*. Columbus, Ohio: Merrill.

> *Len Froyen's book takes a straightforward and traditional behavioral approach. A strength is the volume's readability.*

Glasser, W. (1986). *Control theory in the classroom*. New York: Harper & Row.

> *An updating and expansion of his earlier views, William Glasser's newest volume is highly recommended.*

Greenwood, C. R., Hops, H., & Walker, H. M. (1988). *Pass: Program for academic survival skills—A classroom behavior management system*. Delray Beach, Florida: Educational Achievement Systems.

> *The system developed by Greenwood et al. is a good one and is recommended for teachers with severe classroom behavior problems.*

Jones, F. H. (1988). *Positive classroom discipline*. New York: McGraw-Hill.

> *Jones' volume presents a good introduction to classroom behavior management.*

Witt, J. C., Elliott, S. N., & Gresham, F. M. (1988). *Handbook of behavior therapy in education*. New York: Plenum.

> *This edited volume is a comprehensive source book for teachers and psychologists.*

*Comments on Practice
Exercise 11–1*

Here is our interpretation of the conversation between the teacher and Bill. The numbers are keyed to the teacher's comments.

1.   The teacher makes a friendly, personal greeting (Principle 1, Be personal).

2.   The teacher avoids being manipulated and suggests alternative actions, indirectly, for improving on the next test (Principle 4, Plan alternative behaviors with students).

3.   Oh, oh! The teacher slips a little here and becomes irritated and critical (Principle 7, Do not punish). Also, she refers to past behaviors on Bill's part ("Last semester you said the same thing . . .") and violates Principle 2 (Refer only to present behavior).

4.   Still a little defensive, the teacher comes back at Bill and violates Principle 7 (Do not punish). However, she then turns things around, pointing toward more productive behaviors (Principle 4, Plan alternative behaviors with students, and possibly Principle 3, Stress value judgments by students). She also shows concern for Bill (Principle 1, Be personal).

5.   The teacher remains firm.

6.   The teacher calls for a value judgment by the student about the fairness of changing a grade (Principle 3, Stress value judgments) and guides the conversation toward planning for the future (Principle 4, Plan alternative behaviors with students).

7.   The student is making a form of excuse by shifting the blame from himself. The teacher doesn't accept it (Principle 6, Don't accept excuses) and moves again to planning for the future (Principle 4, Plan alternative behaviors with students).

8.   The teacher shows a personal interest in Bill (Principle 1, Be personal) and continues planning activity (Principle 4, Plan alternative behaviors).

9. The teacher draws the student's attention to the conse-
    quences of his previous behavior by questioning the out-
    comes of his method of study for the last exam (Principle 3,
    Stress value judgments by students).

10. The teacher continues to help the student think about the
    outcomes of one course of action (Principle 3, Stress value
    judgments by students) and about planning for the next
    test (Principle 4, Plan alternative behaviors with students).

11. The teacher shows her interest and commitment to Bill's
    welfare by offering to review his progress in advance of the
    test and early enough so that changes can be made in the
    plan if necessary (Principle 5, Show commitment by check-
    ing and reinforcing progress). Student success is the goal.

PART FOUR

In the previous sections of this book we examined various aspects of development, learning, and motivation. Although an understanding of these issues is important, more is required to ensure effective instruction. Teachers must be able to translate their knowledge into meaningful learning activities and evaluate the learning that takes place. Part Four of our text is designed to help you to do just that—apply the principles of development, learning, and motivation to the design and evaluation of your classroom instruction.

Chapter Twelve, "An Introduction to Measurement," focuses on two closely related topics: planning instructional activities and measuring learning outcomes. The chapter begins by describing the process of formulating meaningful instructional objectives. Beyond their role in guiding instruction, however, well-written objectives also affect the decisions teachers make about measurement. The second part of Chapter Twelve reviews basic concepts in educational measurement. The topic of measurement is at the heart of all educational decisions. How to ensure the meaningfulness of learning, how to grade students, how to motivate them, how to give them feedback, how to pace instruction, how to evaluate your own performance as teachers—each decision relies on the measurement of student learning. The more confident you are that your measurement reflects your educational goals, the more confident you can be that the decisions you made are sound. Chapter Thirteen, "Teacher-Made Tests," will help you move toward competence in using a wide variety of measurement techniques. Finally, Chapter Fourteen, "Standardized Tests," provides you with information on the use and interpretation of standardized tests employed in our schools.

Educational Measurement and Evaluation

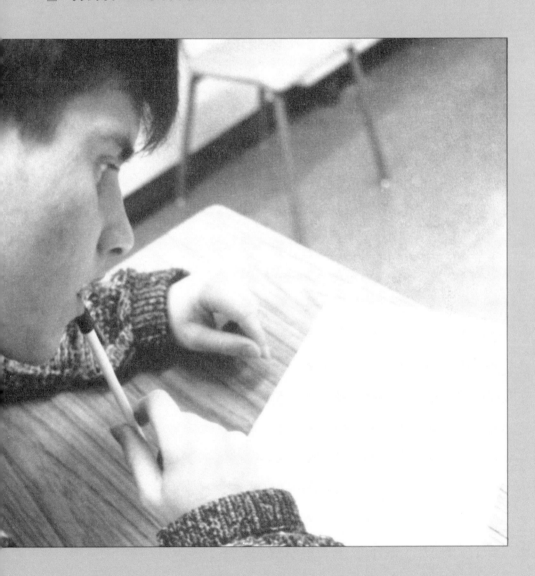

CHAPTER
12

An Introduction to Measurement

OVERVIEW

As you begin planning for teaching, you will have to come to grips with a crucial issue: What will be the goals of your instruction, and how will you communicate those goals clearly to your students? The research on effective teaching has shown that one significant difference between effective and ineffective teachers is how well they convey goals and expectations to students (Evertson & Smiley, 1987). The first part of this chapter will help you master important skills in developing instructional objectives.

Decisions about how to measure student learning are as important as decisions about what to teach. In fact, the most fundamental decisions you make as a teacher may be those about measurement. Measurement is at the heart of all education. The second part of this chapter will help you develop and select the best possible measures of student performance. It describes the purposes of measurement and introduces you to the general categories of measurement used in education. The principles that underlie good educational measurement also are outlined, and they are further elaborated in Chapters Thirteen and Fourteen. We hope they will become a basic part of your teaching.

OBJECTIVES

After reading this chapter, you should be able to meet the following objectives.

1. Identify correctly and incorrectly written instructional objectives.
2. Correctly write cognitive, psychomotor, and affective objectives.
3. Identify steps for improving the reliability of measures.
4. Suggest procedures for improving the validity of measures.
5. Select the appropriate form of measurement for a variety of decisions in which measurement and evaluation are required.

Goals and Objectives

The basic reason we provide instruction for people is to meet *educational goals*—those statements that describe outcomes of education that contribute to society's functioning (Gagné & Driscoll, 1988). There obviously are many things people must be able to do to help a society work smoothly. General abilities such as reading, writing, and arithmetic are recognized as important for everyone. More specific skills such as building houses, preparing food, and repairing cars also are important functions people must perform.

As you decide on the educational goals you will emphasize in your teaching, you will draw on your knowledge of cognition and learning, ideas about what students will need for success in subsequent courses, your concepts of what students will be doing when they leave school, your own interests and values, a sense of society's needs, and tradition. Many of these goals will be stated explicitly in textbooks, curriculum guides, school regulations, and the like. Let's take a look at some representative goals taken from curriculum guides and see how they might fit into teaching.

The students will understand our democratic government.

The students will develop the abilities to solve mathematical problems encountered in day-to-day life.

The students will enjoy reading.

The students will protect our environment.

As you can see, these goals are very general statements describing what students should achieve after fairly extended periods of time (anytime from one semester to twelve years). They state what students will work toward, and they may guide both instruction and the student's learning.

As laudable as the instructional goals listed above are, they leave teachers with a *measurement* problem. That is, teachers must decide what they will *measure* to determine how well the students have met the goals. Let's examine the goals one at a time and see what they tell us to measure.

The students will understand our democratic government. As important as this goal is, what do we make of the term *understand*? Is this a purely cognitive goal? Are students merely expected to think about democratic government? Does "understand" mean "write a paper about," does it mean "identify the correct answers on a multiple choice test," or could it mean "compare and contrast with a dictatorial form of government"? If understanding our democratic government were one of your goals for students, you would need to determine just what it is specifically that you mean by this. You can thereby be effective in your instruction, so that students know how and what to study and so that you will have standards by which to measure what they have learned.

The students will develop the abilities to solve mathematical problems encountered in day-to-day life. The problem of what to measure doesn't seem to be as severe with this goal as it was with the first one. However, we really haven't specified which mathematical abilities are necessary to deal with everyday life. It seems that students ought to be able to count, add and subtract, divide and multiply, figure percentages, use decimals, use fractions, and solve for an unknown. Do students really have to be able to do all these things? If so, *how well* must they be able to do them? Again, it would seem that an interesting measurement problem needs to be solved before helping students work toward meeting this goal.

The students will enjoy reading. Obviously, having students enjoy reading is desirable. Again, however, the goal needs to be translated into a more specific form so that teachers will know what to measure in order to determine if the goal has been met. In other words, a measurement decision is required before this goal can be translated into teaching and learning activities.

The students will protect our environment. Having the students protect the environment also seems to be a worthwhile goal, but it also needs clarification. What will you measure to decide that your students are protecting the environment? You must decide what this goal will mean in the daily classroom experience of your students.

The general point is that goals, while they are useful guides for teachers and students, often are not specific enough for the purposes of measurement. More specific statements—**instructional objectives**—are needed to determine how learning will be measured.

Instructional Objectives

Instructional objectives are explicit statements of what students will be able to do as a result of instruction. They differ from goals because they very clearly describe what aspects of learning are to be measured. Educational goals are stated broadly because we recognize that teachers will adapt their instruction to fit their specific teaching situations. In contrast, teachers generally write instructional objectives themselves based on curriculum guides, text materials, and so on, and prepare them to fit the needs of their own students.

Suppose we were working on the educational goal "The students will understand our democratic government." Obviously, many different learning outcomes would be measured to determine if students have met this goal. An example of one instructional objective that could be taken from this goal is "The students will describe the three branches of the federal government." This objective gives us a very specific learning task to measure. Either students can describe the three branches of government or they cannot.

Suppose we then were to assess the mastery of this objective with some questions on an in-class examination, and no students could answer them correctly. Further suppose that the students all did fairly well on every other question. Evidently, something went wrong, and somehow we didn't teach what we thought we were teaching. On the other hand, if every student had done well on those questions and we had known that they hadn't mastered the material prior to our instruction, then we would have reason to believe that we had done an effective job of teaching.

The objectives we derive from educational goals dictate the measurable skills and knowledge we want students to master as part of the attainment of each goal. When students master our objectives, we can be as certain as is possible in education that they are progressing toward the educational goals and that we and our students are succeeding.

Components of Instructional Objectives	Instructional objectives typically have three components (Mager, 1962; 1976): An action verb, criteria for performance, and a description of the conditions under which the learning will be assessed. We will look at each of these three components in turn and see why each is an important part of a good instructional objective.

Action Verbs. The verb chosen for an instructional objective is crucial. The verb we choose must describe a *measurable* learning outcome. Only action verbs fall into this category (Ebel & Frisbie, 1986).

In order to demonstrate just how important the choice of verbs is in writing objectives, we will consider some verbs taken from objectives that do not clearly specify the behaviors expected of students. Remember the teacher who wanted you to "understand" the causes of the American Revolution? Wasn't it frustrating when you then took an exam on this unit and were expected to "list five causes"? Or how about hearing that the only objective was that you "appreciate Shakespeare" at the end of a literature class? Remember when it took 190 out of 200 correct matches of quotations to characters for you to have "appreciated Shakespeare" enough to earn an A? Or how about the all-time favorite, "be aware of"? Sadly, "be aware of" almost always turned into "define" on a test.

Instructional objectives help guide student efforts. Because he has a clear idea of what he is to do, this boy is able to work steadily on his own.

Just what does all this mean? Your instructional objectives must be clear to *all* students. The verb you use in an instructional objective is a key component of clear communication. If you are planning to use a multiple-choice or true-and-false test to evaluate your students' abilities to recognize new concepts, why tell them you want them to "appreciate," "understand," "be aware," or "know"? If you want them to recognize, say so. A clearly stated objective might say, "In a set of ten sentences, students will be able to recognize each instance that verb number is not in agreement with the subject of the sentence." The objective tells the students exactly what you expect. They will be able to better prepare for tests, and you will be able to plan more effective instruction. Objectives that specify student behaviors using action verbs such as "construct," "compare and contrast," "define," and "describe" allow you to say exactly what you mean. If you ask students to list ten metallic elements you can see how to teach for this outcome, how to evaluate student learning (either they can list them or some part of them or they cannot), and students can see exactly how to prepare.

We do not say that words like "appreciate," "understand," and "be aware of" do not indicate important outcomes for your students. In fact, we expect you to "appreciate" the benefits of using good instructional objectives. Both the communication of expectations and the evaluation of learning, however, are enhanced through the use of more specific action verbs in your objectives.

Criteria for Performance.   The second major component of instructional objectives, criteria, describes the level of performance you expect from students (Gagné & Driscoll, 1988). If students are to discuss a topic, how many points must they include? How long should their answer be? Is there some particular order in which they should present ideas? Does neatness count? What or how much will you tell students you expect to see in their behavior? In short, *how good is good enough?*

Anytime you develop an instructional objective you also should determine the quality of student responses that will be acceptable. Giving students the criteria on which their performance will be judged will help them prepare, it will help you plan your instruction, and it certainly will guide your evaluation.

Description of Conditions for Assessment.   The third component of good instructional objectives is an indication of the conditions under which students' performances will be evaluated (Gagné & Driscoll, 1988). Imagine that an objective asks you to list and describe five major causes of World War II. Would you prepare differently for this assignment if your assessment were to be based on an essay exam in class, on

Instructional objectives must be clear to all students. Students who know the objectives for learning will progress much more rapidly than those who don't.

**PRACTICE EXERCISE 12–1   IDENTIFYING GOOD AND POOR
INSTRUCTIONAL OBJECTIVES**

We have listed ten instructional objectives below. Read each one carefully, and determine whether it is properly written. If it is improperly written, write on a separate sheet of paper a brief statement telling why, and rewrite it properly.

1. The students will develop an awareness of the influence of the Spanish culture on the American Southwest. An essay examination in class will be used to assess their learning.

2. On a short-answer examination, students will define the concept of alliteration correctly and write three examples they have seen in current magazines.

3. When dissecting a frog, the students will identify organs of the digestive system.

4. The students really must know the multiplication tables for an in-class oral quiz tomorrow.

5. The students will conceptualize two higher-order forms of problem solving to be brought to bear on tomorrow's laboratory experiment.

6. The students must have a firm grasp of elementary algebra. They will have to demonstrate their knowledge on an in-class examination and score at least 70 for their performance to be acceptable.

7. When presented flash cards of words containing the letter combination *ph*, the students will correctly pronounce the words in eighteen of twenty instances.

8. The students must remember the major reasons for the downfall of the Roman Empire. They will have to know them for tomorrow's quiz.

9. Given a fifty-word speed test in class, the students will type at a rate not less than ten words per minute with fewer than two errors.

10. Given a worksheet containing twenty addition problems requiring regrouping, the students will solve seventeen correctly during class.

Now that you have responded to each of these objectives, compare your answers to ours at the end of the chapter.

an oral exam in the instructor's office, on a speech you presented to an American foreign policy seminar in which the secretary of state was a participant, or on an at-home, open-book exam? Every person we have ever asked has said "Yes, I would prepare quite differently." Describing the conditions of assessment also helps you plan your instructional activities and your means of assessing the students, and it certainly helps students prepare.

Types of Objectives

On any given day a high school student may learn things as diverse as a new principle in mathematics, how to operate a machine, and a new attitude toward a different culture. These kinds of learning differ greatly from each other, and these differences have formed the basis for systems of classifying objectives. Such systems provide distinctions helpful in writing objectives as well as in devising methods of instruction and evaluation.

While many classifications of objectives have been put forward over the years, the most widely accepted has been a taxonomy of educational objectives (*taxonomy* is another way of saying "classification system") developed by Benjamin Bloom and his associates (Bloom, 1964; Bloom, Englehart, Furst, Hill, & Krathwohl, 1956). Bloom's taxonomy, as it is known, classified objectives into three major domains (categories) of learning: cognitive, psychomotor, and affective. **Cognitive objectives**, as you might guess from the first section of this text, specify processes primarily related to intellectual activities, such as defining, evaluating, recognizing, and reasoning. A teacher helping students learn a new concept or principle is trying to assist them in meeting a cognitive objective. **Psychomotor objectives** describe skilled physical movements such as those required in typing, operating machinery, and playing a musical instrument. Students learning to operate a lathe, for example, are attempting to master several psychomotor objectives. **Affective objectives** deal with feelings, attitudes, values, and preferences. An example of an affective objective is to develop a respect for another culture's way of life.

Very few of the things we expect students to learn are contained exclusively in one of the three domains of objectives (Gagné & Driscoll,

Learning suffers when objectives are missing or poorly stated.

"I'm usually three days ahead of a regular class, one day ahead of the fast learners and two days behind a classful of them."

1988). When students learn to operate a machine, for example, they not only learn skilled physical movements but also a set of facts and rules governing the use of the machine. Likewise, when students learn to value another culture, they learn some basic facts about that culture. Even "purely" cognitive processes have some affective components, as, for example, when students enjoy solving difficult math problems. Despite the fact that cognitive, psychomotor, and affective learning often occur together, it is helpful to examine each domain separately in order to formulate specific objectives.

Cognitive Objectives   Cognitive objectives specify behaviors that can be used to infer changes in students' cognition. Bloom's taxonomy (1956) describes six major levels into which cognitive objectives may be classified: knowledge, comprehension, application, analysis, synthesis, and evaluation (see Table 12–1). We will examine each in turn.

Knowledge.   The first of the six levels of learning Bloom discusses is knowledge. Knowledge-level learning is the ability to recall or identify information (Bloom et al., 1956). We referred to this as rote learning in Chapter Three. A question such as "What is the capital of Connecticut?" requires learning at the knowledge level. Students need not understand anything about capitals in order to demonstrate knowledge-level learning about capitals. They only need to be able to recall a term ("Hartford") or other information.

An example of a knowledge-level objective is "On an in-class quiz, the students will be able to write the names of the capitals of at least ten states." As you can see, knowledge-level objectives may require only the most rudimentary learning. Some, however, can be very complex

---

TABLE 12–1   ACCEPTABLE VERBS FOR USE IN INSTRUCTIONAL OBJECTIVES AT THE SIX LEVELS OF BLOOM'S TAXONOMY

Levels of Learning	*Acceptable Verbs*
Knowledge	Define, distinguish, identify, recall, recognize
Comprehension	Conclude, demonstrate, differentiate, draw, explain, give in your own words, illustrate, interpret, predict, rearrange, reorder, rephrase, represent, restate, transfer, translate
Application	Apply, classify, develop, employ, generalize, organize, relate, restructure, transfer, use
Analysis	Analyze, categorize, compare, contrast, deduce, detect
Synthesis	Combine, constitute, derive, document, formulate, modify, organize, originate, produce, relate, specify, synthesize, tell, transmit, write
Evaluation	Appraise, argue, assess, decide, evaluate, judge, standardize, validate

Source: Based on a more detailed table by Metfessel, Michael & Kirsner in "Instrumentation of Bloom's and Krathwohl's taxonomies for the writing of behavioral objectives." *Psychology in the Schools*, 1969, *6*, 227–231.

(such as memorization of the periodic table of elements). Whether they are simple or complex, it is relatively easy to assess students' mastery of such objectives. Either the students can or cannot perform the behaviors called for in the objectives.

Comprehension.   Comprehension-level learning is more complex. Comprehension of information requires that a student put information into his or her own words (Bloom et al., 1956). Answering a question such as "Describe the geographical areas of the state of Tennessee in your own words" requires comprehension-level learning, as does an objective such as "On a take-home essay, the students will accurately portray the plot of *The Velveteen Rabbit* in their own words." In knowledge-level learning, understanding is not necessarily required. In comprehension-level learning, however, students must understand concepts and principles and demonstrate this understanding by explaining the ideas in their own words.

Application.   Application-level learning is still more complex. Learning at and above this level typically is the goal of cognitively-oriented teachers. Application requires that a student use an abstraction in a concrete context (Bloom et al., 1956). A question such as "Given the following components of a chemical solution, determine its boiling point" requires application-level learning, as would the request "Given the proper equipment, take an accurate blood pressure reading from a patient." Students must be able to *use* concepts and principles (knowledge about solutions and boiling points or knowledge about taking blood pressures) in an applied problem.

Application is an important aim for instruction for most teachers. An example of an application-level objective is "In the lab period, the students will perform a titration and determine the acidity of their test solution within ± .04 pH." Other examples are "Given an array of circles, the students will correctly compute the area of five of them" and "Given specifications from a mechanic's manual and appropriate tools, students will set the correct gap for spark plugs on five different American engines within ± .001 inch."

Analysis.   Analysis-level learning also requires complex cognitive activity and is desired by most teachers. In analysis, students must be able to break down information into its component parts so that the relationship among all the components is clear (Bloom et al., 1956). A two-part question based on the novel *Watership Down* that would require analysis-level learning is "List and describe each of the forces acting on Hazel, the hero, which caused him to leave his original warren (a home for rabbits). What parts of Hazel's plans were based on Fiver's special skill?" (Fiver could see the future, especially to predict danger.) This question requires both comprehension (to answer the first part) and then analysis (to answer the second part). For students to analyze the situation they have to be able to comprehend it first. Thus, in Bloom's taxonomy learning is seen as *hierarchical*; higher levels of learning are built on lower levels.

Good analysis-level objectives are hard to write, and this is one reason they are sometimes neglected. Additionally, analysis sometimes can be confused with knowledge or comprehension. For example, if a teacher had discussed in class the parts of Hazel's plans that were based on Fiver's skill, the students could have memorized the information and given it back word for word in their answers. You must be sure that you avoid confusion and structure situations so that the analytic thinking required in an analysis-level objective is clear. Other examples of such analysis-level objectives are "In a five-page paper, the students will identify the limits placed on the executive and legislative branches by the judicial branch of the federal government" and "Given a sample of water from the Obion River, students in the chemistry laboratory will identify at least two major pollutants deriving from industrial sources."

Synthesis.   Synthesis-level learning requires that students put together old knowledge in new ways (Bloom et al., 1956). Synthesis involves high-level cognitive processes. It involves the analysis and recombination of bits of knowledge to develop a structure or pattern the students did not have prior to learning. A question that requires synthesis is "Using your knowledge about the geography and climate of Peru, write an essay describing the kinds of agricultural industries likely to exist there." Such a question demands more than simply describing or analyzing what the student knows about Peru. Facts about Peru must be recombined in a way that answers a question for which students previously had no answer. If the teacher has already given students some information about Peru's agricultural industries, such a question really would sample nothing more than knowledge- or comprehension-level learning. Synthesis requires original thinking—students must generate knowledge based on facts and principles they have learned.

Synthesis objectives often briefly describe the information available to students and then require the students to reorganize and extend this information. An example of a synthesis-level objective is "Given a description of the conditions on the planet Venus, the students will write a short story describing the ways in which explorers on the surface of Venus would live. Students must include descriptions of at least six problems and possible solutions." Again, you should carefully note that this objective would involve only comprehension if the students had previously learned how someone would live on Venus. Criteria are hard to set for synthesis objectives because subjective judgments often are required. If grades were to be assigned to the short stories about life on Venus, for example, the subjective judgment of the teacher would be needed to evaluate students' attainment of the objective.

Evaluation.   Evaluation-level learning requires the highest level of cognitive activity. Evaluation requires that students make judgments based on their knowledge about the *value* of methods and materials (Bloom et al., 1956). An evaluation-level question is "Ed must construct a model of an island and an ocean to demonstrate tides to his science class. Ed doesn't have much money, and he has only two days to build his model. Which of the following materials would be best suited for his model and why?" To answer such a question, students must be able to make judgments about each of the materials listed, determine which are the best for Ed's situation, and write a statement telling why.

Evaluation objectives ask students to make judgments based on their knowledge, and they frequently ask students to justify their decisions. Criteria tend to be qualitative and subjectively judged. An example of an evaluation-level objective is "Given the performance specifications for three new automobiles and information about a hypothetical family, the students will decide which automobile would be the most appropriate for that family's use.

Objectives at Different Levels.   The most important effect of Bloom's Taxonomy of Educational Objectives has been to draw attention to higher-level cognitive objectives in instruction. In spite of this, however, far too much emphasis still continues to be placed on the less complex forms of learning (Gagné & Driscoll, 1988; Pearson, 1985), such as remembering details from reading or discussions. Of course, teachers always will have some knowledge- and comprehension-level objectives for their students, but they also need to emphasize higher levels of learning. Most teachers feel that a balance of objectives across the six levels of learning enhances their instruction. As you will see in

Psychomotor objectives describe skilled physical movements. Many important objectives fall into the psychomotor domain.

Chapter Thirteen, a test blueprint can help you plan for the higher levels of learning you will want your students to attain.

Psychomotor Objectives   Psychomotor objectives are statements describing physical actions students are to perform. There is a cognitive component of most psychomotor objectives, but their basic purpose is to describe physical behavior. We tend to separate cognitive and psychomotor objectives because they usually require quite different practice conditions. The outcomes of cognitive learning ordinarily are inferred from verbal behavior, while in psychomotor learning changes in the speed, accuracy, integration, and coordination of body movements are directly observed.

Psychomotor objectives contain the same three components as other objectives—an action verb, criteria for performance, and conditions of assessment—as in the objective, "Given a hammer, a tenpenny nail, and a one-inch plank, students will drive the nail in five blows without bending it or marring the wood." Another psychomotor objective is "During the class period students will demonstrate the correct operation of a wood lathe." This example illustrates an important difference between many psychomotor objectives and cognitive objectives. Teachers tend to use terms like *correctly, appropriately,* or *efficiently* in writing psychomotor objectives because describing exactly what the "correct" procedure is would require so many words that the objective could end up being several paragraphs long. Imagine writing a detailed description of the "correct" way to hold a paper and pencil, place one's fingers on an oboe, or hit a baseball. "Correct" usually is specified by demonstration and description. In other words, the teacher shows students the "correct" way, describes the "correct" way, and helps students make at least one "correct" response by talking or guiding them through the movement, as we saw in the sections on modeling in Chapter Ten. "Correct," therefore, is the way the task is modeled for the students. Many teachers, in fact, write psychomotor objectives that specify "as demonstrated in class" or "as illustrated in the film" to guide students in seeing what is expected of them.

Affective Objectives

Affective objectives are statements of how we want our students to *feel* about things after a period of instruction. They have a high priority for most teachers (Prawat, 1985). What reading teacher would not want his students to "enjoy reading"? What science teacher would not want her students to be interested in "preserving the environment"? In fact, all teachers want their students to value, prefer, and be interested in the things they are taught.

Very often educational goals point directly to attitudes such as "appreciate" or "enjoy." There are some problems with this, as we saw when we tried to define such vague verbs earlier in the chapter. Another problem concerns the *use* of affective objectives. Suppose two high school students have identical averages on cognitive and psychomotor learning in one of their classes. Do teachers have the right to grade a student down because he or she "has a bad attitude" toward what was taught? It seems clear that teachers have the right and duty to evaluate cognitive and psychomotor learning for formal reports or grades. Do you have the same responsibilities for evaluating students' affective learning?

PRACTICE EXERCISE 12–2   IDENTIFYING LEVELS OF LEARNING

Below is a set of twelve statements taken from objectives. We have omitted conditions and criteria. Read each statement, and decide which level of learning it requires. Write your answer in the blank underneath each item.

1. Using a flame test, find the unknown in a chemical solution.

    _____

2. Name the fifty states of the Union.

    _____

3. Describe in your own words the three major causes of the War of 1812.

    _____

4. Given a news editorial about compulsory military service, students can detect those statements that reflect the writer's opinion regarding the rights of individuals versus the rights of the state.

    _____

5. Write an essay in which you judge which of the three methods of distillation would be safest and most efficient for the separation of benzene from carbon tetrachloride.

    _____

6. Given the characteristics of a species of antelope and the habits of wolves in an adjoining area, write an essay describing the possible effects of wolf predation on the antelope species after three seasons.

    _____

PRACTICE EXERCISE 12–2   *CONTINUED*

7. Given a description of salt marsh ecosystems, write a statement summarizing the probable effects of an oil spill on avian life.

   _____

8. Given a recording of an oboe quartet, students will identify and notate the melody line and the countermelody.

   _____

9. Define *perspective* in your own words.

   _____

10. Identify the places on the street that have been designated as the right places for crossing.

    _____

11. Using the criteria discussed in class for a news article, categorize each of the three following news articles, and write a statement telling which is the best, which is the worst, and why.

    _____

12. Employ the principles of nutrition and the following list of foods to plan three menus for well-balanced meals.

    _____

You may check your responses against the ones we present at the end of the chapter.

Teachers should be concerned with affective objectives.

We suggest that teachers use affective objectives but not to determine grades. When we teach educational psychology, we feel that we should teach it so that students enjoy it. We hope that students continue to study in the area and use the techniques they've learned. What value are teachers to their students if they do not believe that students should enjoy, appreciate, or like what is taught?

Writing Affective Objectives.   When writing affective objectives you should state one additional component—the affect (feelings, attitudes, and the like) that the teacher is trying to obtain. The other components—an action verb, the criteria, and the description of the conditions under which the behavior will be assessed—remain the same. Below are some examples of affective objectives that contain all four components.

> During the first semester, the students will voluntarily check out two or more books of their own choice from the school library as an indication of their enjoyment of reading

> During the semester, the students will make one or more unprompted comments per class period about pollution of the environment to indicate an appreciation of ecological concerns.

> In interactions with the teacher, the students will decrease the number of negative comments they make about themselves as an indication of a more positive self-concept.

These three objectives define affect as a set of behaviors. Each objective, however, is only one of many possible objectives for a particular affective state. The behaviors you select should be the ones you feel are most important. In other words, you want to choose behaviors such that a change in your students' behavior will indicate that your affective objective has been reached.

Cautions in Using Objectives

The truism that anytime you get something, you have to give something also holds for instructional objectives. We have stressed the very real advantages of using objectives, as any teacher who systematically uses them can attest. There are, however, certain costs associated with the use of objectives, and you should be familiar with them.

PRACTICE EXERCISE 12–3   WRITING INSTRUCTIONAL OBJECTIVES

Below is a list of three general educational goals. Choose one that strikes your interest and write one cognitive objective at each of Bloom's levels of learning, two psychomotor objectives, and two affective objectives relating to the goal. To check your responses, carefully examine the checklist we provide at the end of the chapter. If you have trouble, reread the chapter and try another of the three goals listed below.

Goal 1.   Develop an appreciation of and a respect for the role of the fine arts in our cultural heritage.

Goal 2.   Develop a positive attitude toward maintaining one's own physical, mental, and emotional health.

Goal 3.   Develop a concern for measures that conserve the world's energy reserves.

First, it is difficult to write good objectives. You will need to devote much time and thought to the development of objectives. Second, there is a tendency among some teachers to trivialize their courses by using too many objectives written at a knowledge or comprehension level. Third, our experience is that students who have been given objectives tend to control teachers so that they stay "on the subject." When you use objectives you run the risk of losing a part of your flexibility. Fourth, although student mastery of objectives will increase, many studies have indicated that the learning of information not directly mentioned in the objectives may actually decrease (see Hamilton, 1985, for a review). In other words, students *will* concentrate on the learning described by your objectives, but they will also pay less attention to learning material not covered by objectives.

Some investigators have argued that rigid adherence to objectives may cause the loss of one of the richest experiences for students—the unexpected happening. Also, cognitive goals involving problem solving and creativity cannot always be precisely specified in advance. For teachers interested in developing student cognition, *processes* are far more important than specific outcomes of learning. In general, however, we believe that the advantages of instructional objectives tend to

Make allowances for spontaneous exploration of topics. Planning and objectives are critical to good teaching, but sometimes the best learning is unplanned.

outweigh the disadvantages. Good evaluation *requires* specification of objectives (Gallini & Gredler, 1989). The effort you devote to developing objectives can reduce the work and uncertainty involved in deciding what and how to teach. Some reduction of incidental learning usually is more than made up for by greater mastery of those things you include as objectives because you judge them to be important. Teachers make decisions every day about what is important and what isn't. Your objectives communicate these decisions.

Trivialization can be avoided by having a distribution of objectives across the six levels of learning and across the different domains. Some knowledge- and comprehension-level objectives usually are necessary, but planning on your part should lead to the development of application, analysis, synthesis, and evaluation objectives linked to desired cognitive processes.

Having your students insist that you stick to the topic so they can master all the objectives also is not a bad idea. Remember, you always can add objectives. You also can make allowances in your instructional plan so that you and your students will be free to engage in spontaneous exploration of topics that weren't incorporated in the objectives.

Tips for Writing
Instructional Objectives

When you have a set of objectives such as those presented at the beginning of this chapter, you need not restate the conditions of assessment for each one.* Suppose you are teaching a one-week unit and you have developed twenty objectives for your students. If all the objectives are going to be assessed on an in-class examination, one statement prefacing your objectives should make very clear to your students the conditions under which assessment will occur. If you have one or two objectives that will be assessed under different conditions (on homework assignments or during an in-class laboratory period, for instance), you can specify the conditions for those objectives and note that all the rest will be assessed on an in-class examination. Our point is that you need not get bogged down in the petty details of writing objectives. The conditions for student performance are very important but you don't have to rewrite "on an in-class examination, without references" twenty times.

A second general point has to do with the criteria. Clearly, objectives with different criteria must have their criteria spelled out for the students. There will be occasions, however, on which several objectives have the same criteria (spelling errors and neatness, for example). If this is the case, one general statement telling students what criteria are in effect will suffice. Why write "with fewer than two misspelled words" twenty times when one general statement will do the job?

A final comment concerns the number of objectives that need to be written for any unit. Too many objectives may lead to a perception that the outcomes of learning will be trivial. On the other hand, too few objectives may result in vagueness and not direct the learner as well as more precise statements would. The "correct" number of objectives depends on many factors, of course, but perhaps most on the instructor's aims and the level of the learners (Ebel & Frisbie, 1986; Gallini & Gredler, 1989).

---

*Throughout our book we have opted to give you a shorthand form of objectives, omitting the criteria and conditions. This is because your professor will set the conditions and criteria to meet the needs of your class. Your professor is in the best position to make decisions about both conditions and criteria.

Use of Measurement in Educational Settings

Measurement is the process of assigning numbers to persons or objects based on the degree to which they possess a characteristic (Ebel & Frisbie, 1986). Some measurement is simple, such as determining the height of a chair. We simply stretch a tape measure or ruler from the ground to the top of the chair and read off the number of meters and centimeters indicated on the tape. Such measurement is easy, accurate, and repeatable. Unfortunately, most of the things educators must measure are far more complex and elusive than the height of a chair. We often are unsure about our ability to measure some things accurately, and sometimes don't even know quite what to measure. If you want to measure the attitudes of your students toward your last instructional unit, you must first decide what an attitude is and then how to measure it. You will be faced with similar definition problems in many of the units you teach that are concerned with hard-to-measure abilities like "inquiry skills." Other units may require the measurement of subtle aesthetic qualities like "expressiveness" or "visual literacy."

There are many forms of measurement teachers use to assess student progress. Tests, observations, work samples, self-reports, projects, and oral reports all are forms of educational measurement. When teachers seek to evaluate learning they must examine changes in

Teachers use many forms of measurement to assess student progress.

	1's	2's	3's	4's	5's	6's	7's	8's
Stacy H.	✶	★	★	★	★	✶		★
Maryann	✶	★	★	✶	★	★		★
Heidi	✶	★	★	★	★	✶		★
Scott V.	★	★	★	★	★	★		★
Barie	★	★	★	★	★	★		★
Jeremy	★	★	★	★	★	✶		★
Danielle	★	★	★	★	★	★		★

student behavior. But no matter how you choose to assess behavior, there is a set of principles that will help you select the best possible measures. One of our major goals in this chapter is to help you understand and apply these general principles so that your measurement practices as a teacher will be as useful and accurate as possible.

Measurement is a key to almost every aspect of the educational process. Formal education begins with measurement of children's abilities and aptitudes, and measurement continues to play an important role in elementary school, high school, and college. Even at the level of professional and graduate education, measurement is a critical tool. Measurement, of course, also is critically important to business and industry. The same principles we stress in education apply directly to other settings where human performance is evaluated. We need to determine which persons are qualified to be doctors, lawyers, and architects. These decisions, like the countless others that preceded them in the educational process, need to be based on the measurement of human qualities. We must know how skillful a person is, how comprehensive a person's knowledge is, how frequently an activity occurs, and how strong feelings are in order to make good decisions in education.

Measurement is useful for many purposes besides evaluation of student achievement. Students themselves benefit from the measurement of their skills and knowledge. Parents need to know about their children's progress. School administrators and the general public require information about education programs in order to make critical decisions on funding and program changes. Measurement can provide the necessary data on which to base these and many other decisions.

The Relationship of Measurement to Evaluation

We have mentioned some of the many educational uses of measurement, particularly those involving decision making. The process of using measurements in making decisions commonly is referred to as *evaluation*. Evaluation in education involves judging the quality of learning, teaching, and programs (see Keeves, 1988). There are four general categories of evaluation (DeLandsheere, 1988): formative, summative, placement, and diagnostic. In the following sections we examine how the uses of measurement can be related to each category.

Formative Evaluation

Formative evaluation takes place *during* instruction and is designed to help you adjust your instruction to help students meet their objectives. You may use homework as a source of formative evaluation. By scoring the homework you should be able to determine how well your students are progressing toward mastery of your objectives.

Because formative evaluation is designed to give teachers information about how student learning is progressing, it can and should take many forms, including quizzes, homework, oral responses to teacher questions, or observations. Many teachers have students solve math problems on the chalkboard and, by watching their performance, the teachers can determine how well the students are learning. Other teachers initiate class discussions and use their students' comments as a guide for their own actions.

Formative evaluation should occur frequently during instruction because it has several important functions: It provides feedback to students and to the instructor; it helps provide pacing and motivation for student learning; and, most important, it allows teachers to adjust their instructional activities to achieve meaningful learning (Gallini & Gredler, 1988).

The decision of whether to use the results of formative evaluation as a source of grades rests with each individual teacher. Many teachers believe that unless some sort of grade is attached to homework and quizzes (perhaps a check for completed homework or a number grade for quiz results), students will not be motivated to do their best. Other teachers, however, feel that the results of formative evaluation should not be used to determine grades. They reason that the students have not completed their learning and that the results of formative evaluation should be used primarily to help students correct errors (DeLandsheere, 1988). We are inclined to agree with this second line of thought. While some sort of acknowledgment may need to be made for completing assignments, formative evaluation, by its nature, is not suited for formal grading. (A thorough discussion of grading is presented in the next chapter.)

Formative evaluation is often neglected: Testing, homework, and other measurements are infrequently used. To neglect formative evaluation, however, is to squander a considerable resource for your teaching and for student learning.

Summative Evaluation

Summative evaluation typically occurs at the end of instruction and is designed to determine the extent to which the goals of instruction have been met. There are many ways in which summative evaluation can take place. Final examinations on a unit of instruction, term papers,

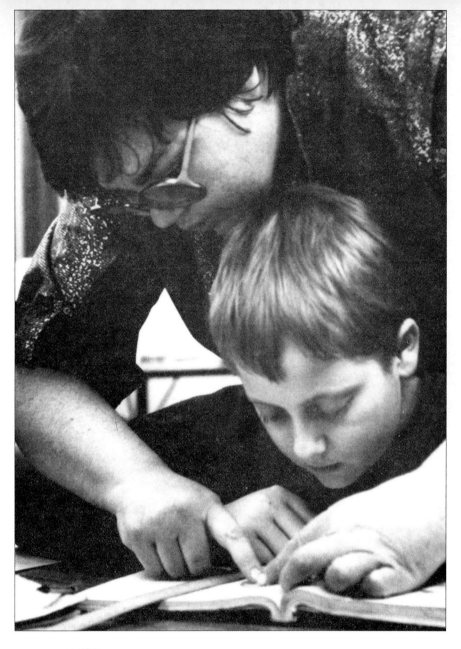

Formative evaluation can take many forms and should occur as often as possible. Here the teacher assesses how well the students understand the concept of "cube."

work samples (such as a painting, a sculpture, or a specific type of weld), performances, and ratings of attitudes all are possible forms of summative evaluation. Summative evaluation must be congruent with instructional objectives. It is administered not so much to direct learning as to determine if learning has taken place.

Placement Evaluation

Placement evaluation is done *before* the start of instruction. The goal of placement evaluation is to match students with beneficial instruction. Determining whether a child should enter kindergarten early is an example of a placement evaluation, as is deciding which instructional group a student should join.

Summative evaluations from prior learning can be used in making placement decisions. Grades, for example, can be used as a criterion for student participation in a program. Standardized tests also are frequently used for placement. Seldom, however, do standardized tests or other summative measures provide enough information for making decisions about instruction. The best placement decisions take both the learner and the setting into account. Instructional decisions require specific knowledge of how well the student's preparation and abilities are matched to what is to be learned. Such knowledge can best be gained by specific, teacher-designed measures that diagnose students' prior learning in relation to instructional objectives.

Diagnostic Evaluation   Diagnostic evaluation, which is used to determine why students are having problems in learning, usually is conducted *during* instruction. Teachers need to know if students' learning problems stem from their general background, perceptual abilities, motivational deficiencies, or the ineffectiveness of educational programs (Tittle, 1988). Ideally, diagnosis will lead to an effective remedial program. We know that this often does not happen, however. A behavioral disorder may be labeled and defined (as when a child is determined to be "emotionally disturbed"), but only a few diagnoses lead directly to a prescription of steps that will solve the problem. A diagnosis can be very useful when we try to experiment with ways of dealing with a child's problem. The more we know about the nature of a child's difficulty, the greater the likelihood of finding an effective program. A thorough diagnosis also may reveal that the problem is not within the child himself or herself but that the child's current program is ineffective. Proper motivational conditions may be lacking, for example, or the content may be poorly sequenced. When such factors are corrected, the child's "problem" may disappear.

Teacher-made tests can be effective diagnostic devices because of their close relationship to the curriculum, although traditionally most diagnostic tests have been standardized. Teacher-made tests may reveal specific areas of instruction in which a student needs remedial help. Standardized tests (discussed in detail in Chapter Fourteen) may be superior in a number of technical ways, but they may lack validity for the specific curriculum in which the student is involved (Berk, 1988).

Diagnostic evaluation sometimes resembles formative evaluation in that it is an ongoing process carried out during instruction. Formative assessment can identify failures in learning and imply alternative

PRACTICE EXERCISE 12–4   TYPES OF EVALUATION

For each of the following situations, classify the evaluation as (a) formative, (b) summative, (c) placement, or (d) diagnostic.

1. Each Friday, teachers in an experimental team-taught class collect "reaction cards" (on which students write whatever thoughts they have about the week's teaching), talk about the reaction cards as a team, and adjust their plans for the upcoming week.

2. The professor in Zoology 478 gives a comprehensive final examination of 100 multiple-choice questions and 6 short essay questions that cover the entire course.

3. An architect takes the examination of the state board of examiners in order to become fully certified as a practicing architect in the state of California.

4. For each forty units of instruction, the fourth-grade reading teachers devise their own brief skills test that is keyed to the objectives and that permits analysis of how well the objectives have been attained.

5. A second grader who has been referred to a school psychologist because of lack of success in the classroom is tested with a variety of measures, including the Wechsler Intelligence Scale for Children-Revised (WISC-R) and the McCarthy Scales of Children's Abilities.

6. Applicants for graduate study in a department of educational psychology (to which about 10 percent of applicants are admitted) are required to take the Graduate Record Examination as part of the admission process.

7. At a biweekly meeting, directors of a federal project intended to identify handicapped children who have been served by special education services evaluate their success and failure and set their goals for the next two weeks.

8. End-of-semester grades are used to "track" students into three levels of second-semester English.

9. Students in doctoral programs are required by the graduate college and their supervisory committees to take comprehensive written and oral examinations covering the general area of graduate training and their particular research specialty.

10. A university student who is troubled about who she is and and what she is going to be takes several personality and interest inventories as a part of her visits with a counselor at the university counseling center.

Properly used evaluation greatly aids student learning. The teacher's judgment of a student's negatives in a photography class helps the student see how well she has applied several new concepts.

approaches to instruction; but if failure continues, diagnostic evaluation may be necessary to more completely identify the causes of failure. Formative evaluation usually is more specific and keyed to particular units of instruction, while diagnostic evaluation is more general and organized around psychological characteristics of the student.

Summary of Formative, Summative, Placement, and Diagnostic Evaluation

Measurement is used in many different forms of evaluation. Formative evaluation usually is specific, frequent, and keyed to instructional units. It attempts to improve the learning processes as it occurs. Summative evaluation takes place at the culmination of learning for the purpose of grading or certifying student performance. It usually is more general than formative evaluation and occurs less frequently.

Placement evaluation occurs prior to instruction and is used to determine what kind of instruction students will benefit from. Diagnosis during instruction usually is problem oriented; that is, it is used to locate problems impeding learning. Failures in instruction and in subsequent attempts at remediation often lead to diagnostic evaluation.

Norm-Referenced and Criterion-Referenced Measures

An important distinction commonly is made between norm-referenced and criterion-referenced measures. **Norm-referenced** measures are constructed with the intent of ranking students on a numerical (0–100) or letter (A–F) scale. The major purpose of norm-referenced measures is to compare one person's performance *with the performance* *of others*. In standardized testing, an individual's score is compared with the performance of a carefully selected group of individuals (the "norm group"). In the classroom, other students make up the reference group to which an individual's score is compared.

Criterion-referenced measures compare an individual's score *to a standard of performance*, not to other students. A level of achievement ordinarily is set in advance; the learner then is judged as either having achieved or not having achieved the objectives satisfactorily. While criterion-referenced measures were developed at the turn of the century, they were not widely used until the past twenty-five years when they became an integral part of individualized instruction (Thomson & Sharp, 1988).

Determining the standard of performance often is the most difficult part of a criterion-referenced evaluation (Berk, 1988). If we are trying to set a standard for the quality of essays written by tenth-grade students, for example, we surely would have to spend a great deal of time thinking about such things as punctuation (How well do the students have to punctuate?), organization (What kinds of organization are acceptable? How many errors can students make in organization?), and many other important elements in producing an essay (spelling, grammar, style, consistency of tense, and so on). Finally, we would have to set a minimum standard for acceptable student performance in essay writing.

How does one decide whether to use a norm-referenced or a criterion-referenced form of measurement? It is not an either/or decision but rather a which/when decision (Berk, 1988). Because they provide a single score that summarizes a pupil's general level of achievement and not a list of objectives that have been attained, norm-referenced measures are most useful for summative, not formative, evaluation. They show how successful students' learning has been compared with others' learning and how successful teachers' efforts were in bringing about that learning.

Criterion-referenced measures seem to be especially valuable in judging the mastery of specific instructional objectives. They also provide information for decision making about instructional programs (have the instructional objectives been reached?). Similarly, criterion-referenced measures may be useful in diagnosing learning difficulties (on which objectives did a particular student do poorly?).

Generally speaking, criterion-referenced measurement is used when there is less concern about comparing students but more concern about ensuring competence. For an ambulance attendant, "fairly good" performance in applying an air splint to a fracture obviously is not good enough. A demonstration of full mastery of the skill is needed. Criterion-referenced measurement requires clear statements of objectives and a fixed level of judging satisfactory achievement (on each of five simulated victims, without leaving out any of the six steps in the procedure, the ambulance attendant can apply . . .). Typically, the form of evaluation best suited to individualized instruction and mastery-learning approaches is criterion-referenced (Berk, 1988).

Traditionally, however, the majority of educational measures have been of the norm-referenced type. Norm-referenced measures lend themselves well to grading (the person who earns 91 on a test can be compared with a person who scores 78 or 64). If norm-referenced tests are constructed carefully, they can provide the teacher and others with accurate and valid information on how students compare to one another. They also can provide invaluable feedback to learners on their achievement relative to others in the group (Vincent, 1988).

In sum, then, the major distinction in the designation of measurement as norm- or criterion-referenced is made on the basis of the form of the test or observation (for example, the choice between a rating scale and a checklist) and the use of the measure (comparing students versus assessing competence). If your purpose in measurement is to rank students and to be able to compare them to one another, your measurement should be of the norm-referenced type. If you want to determine whether your students meet a particular standard, then your choice should be criterion-referenced.

Reliability and Validity of Measures

We have seen that there are many uses for measurement in education and that the type of measurement chosen should relate closely to the purpose of that measurement. Regardless of the form of measurement chosen, however, the measurement must be consistent (it must be reliable), and it must measure what it claims to measure (it must be valid).

Reliability

A measure is reliable if it is consistent and accurate (Crocker & Algina, 1986). If a student took the same test twice in a row, scoring 91 on the first administration and only 64 on the second, we would say that the test was unreliable. Unreliable measures are of little, if any, value. What good is it to know that a student scored 91 on a test when this student scored quite differently on a retest? If we were to retest students using

In norm-referenced measures, our students' performances are compared with the performances of others.

the same test (assuming no learning or changes on their part) and find that their scores were almost identical, however, then we could have much greater confidence in our measurement. If our measurements are not reliable, we can never be sure whether the results mean anything. Our decisions concerning the future of students are far too important to trust to unreliable measurements. But how can we improve the reliability of our tests and observations? A good place to begin is with the cause of unreliability—measurement error.

Measurement error is the part of a person's score *unrelated* to the quality you are trying to measure. Suppose that you have constructed a test to measure your students' knowledge of American history in the period 1900–1910. If anything else besides their knowledge of American history affects their score, you are faced with a measurement error. A score on an essay examination may result from any of a variety of factors: how much the person knows about that period of history (which is what you are trying to measure), scoring mistakes, misreading of the questions by the student, a broken pencil at a crucial moment, critical lapses in memory at just the wrong times, or a poorly constructed test. All these factors, except knowledge of history, are sources of error and will make the test unreliable. Practically speaking, this means that we cannot completely trust such a score since retesting may result in a very different score, even if the student's knowledge remains relatively constant.

Applications for Teaching: Enhancing the Reliability of Your Measures

How can measurement error be reduced? Listed below are some general principles of measurement that can be incorporated into the design of any measurement device — quizzes, tests, observations, ratings, and checklists. Use of these principles will result in reliable measurement (see R. L. Thorndike, 1988).

1. Directions to the student should be clear and unambiguous. If students are faced with ambiguous directions and unclear descriptions of what you expect, error will be introduced into the measurement process. Unclear directions are likely to cause students to do things you don't want them to do. Wordy instructions can turn a mathematics quiz into a reading quiz, as students struggle to decipher the instructions. You don't want to have a measure of student learning ruined because your directions weren't clear.

Likewise, students need to understand the criteria for evaluation in performance areas such as music, speech, and athletics. If students know the factors on which their performance will be rated, they are more likely to give a performance representative of their capabilities. A student who performs poorly because he or she has not understood exactly what to do has not been rated on performance, but instead on ability to understand the directions.

2. Make your scoring or rating as objective as possible. One of the greatest sources of error in measurement is the changeability of graders and observers. Without clear guidelines, graders are likely to rate some answers or papers higher and some lower for the wrong reasons — their mood when grading, the neatness of the paper, their own misunderstanding of what criteria students are being evaluated on, or just plain fatigue. Graders of student work and raters of student performance need to have objective criteria to help them make their judgments. These criteria are statements or models that tell clearly what levels of student performances

are inadequate, adequate, or superior. Model answers, for example, provide a standard of comparison on which graders can base their judgments.

Sometimes different formats are called for. Compared to essay examinations, objective tests reduce the chances of error in scoring and increase reliability. Similarly, a checklist may serve to guide observers and reduce subjectivity in the observations they make. Any method that reduces subjectivity will help increase the reliability of measures.

3. Sample as much of the students' behavior as possible. You may not think of a test as a sample of behavior, but it most surely is: Each item or question requires students to make a response and samples some aspect of the students' abilities. In general, the longer tests are, the more likely they are to be reliable. Similarly, several samples of work (such as several short papers) are more likely to result in accurate measurement of the students' abilities than only one sample. In the performance areas, the more observations you make of students, the greater the likelihood that the composite of your observations will be a reliable assessment of the actual level of student performance. If you ask a student only one question about an entire chapter, for example, chances are that luck will play an important part in whether the student will answer that question correctly. The student may not know much about the chapter but just happen to know the one thing you asked. Conversely, it is possible for a student to know a great deal about the chapter but the single thing you asked turns out to be the one thing the student doesn't know.

If reliable measurement is your goal, it needs to be comprehensive enough to avoid errors in sampling. As the amount of student work you assess increases, so does the probable reliability. For reliability, the more the better! Of course, you need to balance the goal of reliability against what you can reasonably ask of your students (a four-hour test?) and of yourself.

Validity

Reliability is one essential characteristic of good measurement; **validity** is the other. A measurement is said to be valid if it measures what it is intended to measure. Validity requires reliability, but reliability does not assure validity. A test of aptitude for electronics is valid only if it truly measures this aptitude, that is, if it correlates closely with other known measures of this aptitude or it predicts future performance in the area of electronics.

There are several subcategories of validity (see Zeller, 1988). **Content validity** is the extent to which a measure samples and represents the content areas to be measured. A biology unit test, for example, would have content validity if and only if it accurately sampled the various areas covered in instruction. For a measure to be valid it must give the same emphasis to content and level of learning as given in instruction. On the other hand, almost everyone has had the depressing experience of a teacher presenting one set of materials and then testing something entirely different. This type of testing (besides being unfair) has very low content validity.

A second category of validity, **construct validity**, mostly is applied to psychological tests. A construct refers to an unobservable concept that is used by investigators to account for regularities in a person's behavior (Crocker & Algina, 1986). "Intelligence" and "motivation" are both constructs. Neither is directly observable. They are constructs used to explain why people behave in certain ways. A test is said to have construct validity if we can be reasonably confident that it measures the quality in question (that is, an "intelligence test" is a measure of the construct of intelligence and not some other quality such as motivation or creativity). Tests intended to measure a construct should correlate highly with other measures of the same construct. An example of construct validity would be taking scores from a test of sociability (which presumably measures the construct of sociability) and showing that students possessing more of this construct will have more friends than students possessing less of this construct.

If test performance differs from that predicted from the nature of the construct, the test has low construct validity. At that point, the test maker or user can doubt either the test *or* the theory, depending on which of the two he or she has the least confidence in. A test with construct validity will perform as expected if it is a measure of the trait in question and if the theory that is related to the trait is a sound one.

The degree to which a measure can accurately predict a future performance is called **predictive validity**. It is of great interest in the

PRACTICE EXERCISE 12–5   IMPROVING RELIABILITY AND VALIDITY

For each of the following measurement situations, a problem exists that will lead to lowered reliability and validity. Identify the primary problem as related to: (a) unclear directions given to the person being measured, (b) lack of objectivity in scoring, or (c) poor sampling of the person's behavior. Suggest a change in procedures to remedy the problem.

1. Professor Shaetz, in a class in music theory, gives a midterm essay examination that counts for 40 percent of the grade and a final examination (also an essay examination) that counts for 60 percent of the grade.

2. On a multiple-choice test, questions 6 through 10 all pertain to the situation described in question 5. Most students realize this and answer the questions correctly. Several students, however, didn't use the information from item 5. Most of those students miss three or four of the items.

3. The promotion and tenure committee is examining the file for Professor Bailey, who is being considered for promotion. Included in his file are student ratings of his teaching. For most classes he has taught, Professor Bailey has been able to get back ratings from about half of his students. Most are mildly positive.

4. As several professors look over the responses of Helen Dinsmore, a doctoral student, to her comprehensive examination, it is obvious that Helen has misread question 3 and given it an interpretation different from that intended by the writer of the question. Her response is excellent, but it doesn't answer the question. The professors are faced with a serious decision about what to do because her exam hangs in the balance.

5. Ms. Brenegan gives a single question on an examination that reads, "Discuss the theory of comprehensive musicianship."

6. Six members of the residence hall staff are interviewing a large number of applicants for several student-assistant positions. With some they talk about the weather, with others their studies, and with others their views of campus issues. They rate the applicants on a scale after spending about five

PRACTICE EXERCISE 12–5   CONTINUED

to ten minutes with each person. The five highest scorers are selected. Some people have a real doubt that the best people have been selected and that the process has been fair.

7. Halfway through a stack of term papers, Mr. Webb is interrupted by his two children, who are fighting. After separating them and sending both to their rooms, he resumes his reading of the papers and finishes them. As he is recording the grades the next morning, he discovers that the scores on the thirteen papers he graded after the interruption average nearly 5 points lower than those graded before.

8. Teachers at Belman Elementary School have been justifiably concerned about the noise level in the cafeteria, which ranges between a din and cacophony. Two psychologists monitor the noise level by means of a noise meter, preparing to set up a system in which the students are rewarded for lower noise levels. They find it interesting to note that teachers' judgments of the noise level bear little relation to the actual level. That is, the teachers often complain about the noise at times when it is actually lower than usual, and high-noise days are occasionally judged as "less noisy than usual."

9. The committee for the arts and crafts festival of Lakewood School must judge the entries in each of several categories, such as painting, woodworking, and lithography. Each person on the five-member committee is told to independently select a top-ranking entry in each of the categories. Four of the people are in general agreement on most of the categories but the judgments of the fifth person are "way out." His top choices in each category don't even appear on other people's lists.

10. In a group project in an adult education class, the groups turn in reports that vary widely in quality. Even though most groups appear to have worked hard, several projects are failed or are rated low. A talk with members of the groups reveal that many were unsure about what qualified as an acceptable project, how each member was to contribute, how long the report was to be, and how it was to be organized.

use of tests for selection and advisement purposes. If we used an interest inventory (a scale on which individuals indicate their likes and dislikes in interest, vocational, and scholastic areas) to guide students into vocational or career choices, we would need to feel confident that the inventory is meaningfully related to future job performance or satisfaction. What value would there be in giving students advice based on tests that have no predictive validity?

The most critical form of validity for the classroom teacher is content validity. Teachers need to know whether classroom tests accurately and fairly sample the content and the levels of learning they expect of students. The single best way to ensure that your tests and measures have content validity is to carefully match them to your instructional objectives by means of a blueprint (or, more formally, a table of specifications). The table of specifications ensures that any measure you construct fits the objectives and levels of learning that you require of your students. The process of constructing and using tables of specifications is described in detail in the next chapter, Chapter 13.

Summary of Reliability and Validity

The principles of reliability and validity enter into every measurement of human performance. They apply in any setting in which performance is judged: courtrooms, classrooms, homes, and the workplace. Questions of reliability will always be something like the following: "Can we be sure that we have made an accurate observation? Is our observation repeatable?"

Beyond accurate measurement is the question of *what* is being measured. Trivial outcomes can be measured accurately. In fact, many trivial outcomes are much easier to measure than more significant ones. Recall of facts is more readily measured than the ability to apply ideas, solve problems, or be creative, for instance. But is measurement of knowledge of facts valid for our instructional objectives? Usually not. Measures must measure what they are intended to measure. If the objectives of a course in Russian literature include knowledge of characters, recognition of recurring themes, and proper identification of metaphorical references, then a valid evaluation will assess all of these areas. In the same way, ratings of attitudes, interests, or psychomotor skills should measure what they are intended to measure, not attractiveness, personality, or some other dimension.

Choosing a Method of Measurement

A great many elements enter into the measurement decisions you make. The most basic judgment, of course, is determining whether measurement is needed and what the purpose of the measurement is. Is the measurement to be done in the cognitive, affective, or psychomotor domain? Is the measurement to be used for diagnostic, formative, summative, or placement purposes? Will norm-referenced or criterion-referenced measurement be best for your purposes? Also, does the measurement meet the necessary technical requirements for good measurement, that is, does it sample a representative part of what the student knows or can do, does it sample enough student behavior, and do the students understand clearly enough what is expected of them in order for you to obtain a reliable and valid measure?

The basic questions that arise in the measurement choices you make are summarized in Table 12–2. These will help you think about the choices you will constantly be making as an evaluator of student performance, of your own teaching, and of the worth of programs in which you are involved.

All the judgments you make relate to the central concern in measurement—is the method of measurement you use the best one for measuring the outcomes of learning and teaching? For affective outcomes, rating scales or behavioral observations may represent a

---

TABLE 12–2   KEY QUESTIONS IN DECISIONS ABOUT METHODS OF MEASUREMENT

1. Is there a purpose for the measurement?
2. Are the objectives being measured in the cognitive, affective, or psychomotor domain?
3. Is the measurement used for placement, diagnostic, formative, or summative evaluation?
4. Does the measure meet the requirements for reliability?
5. Does the measure meet the requirements for validity?
6. Is the measure feasible from the standpoint of administration, student time required, and scoring?

better choice than other methods, particularly testing. In psychomotor skill areas, checklists or rating scales are likely to match up most validly with the behaviors being measured. In the cognitive areas, a wide range of measurement methods is available. Your choice among types of tests, work samples, or other forms of assessment will be determined in large part by your instructional objectives (Berk, 1988; Zeller, 1988).

Summary

Teachers use broad educational goals as guides for their teaching. Because of the general nature of these goals, however, teachers must translate them into measurable, short-term statements of what students are to learn—instructional objectives. Instructional objectives ordinarily have three components: an action verb, the criteria for assessing students' performances, and a description of the conditions under which the evaluation is to take place. Objectives reflect three domains of learning: cognitive, psychomotor, and affective.

Cognitive objectives are focused on students' intellectual changes and have been organized by Bloom and his associates into a six-level taxonomy: knowledge, comprehension, application, analysis, synthesis, and evaluation. Different kinds of cognitive processes are required at each of these levels; higher-order cognitive goals are sought by many teachers. Psychomotor objectives describe physical actions students are to perform, while affective objectives indicate emotional states (attitudes, values, feelings, and so on) students should achieve as a result of instruction.

Determining whether or not instructional objectives have been met requires measurement. Measurement provides us with the data necessary for making educational decisions. The use of measurement in decision making is referred to as evaluation. Formative evaluation is designed to improve the learning process while it occurs. Summative evaluation occurs at the culmination of learning and is used to grade or certify students. Placement evaluation is designed to determine what kinds of instruction students will benefit from, and diagnostic evaluation is used to locate problems that may be impeding learning.

Criterion-referenced evaluation is based on the determination of whether learners have achieved a standard of performance. It is well suited for certifying competency and determining progress in individualized instruction. Norm-referenced evaluation, which compares a student's performance to that of others, is best suited for providing feedback on achievement relative to that of others in a group.

Since educational decisions only can be as good as the data on which they are based, measures must be chosen carefully so that they are reliable and valid. A reliable measure is consistent over multiple administrations, and a valid measure measures what it is intended to measure. As you continue through Chapters Thirteen and Fourteen, you will obtain the knowledge and skills necessary to make good measurement decisions. Chapter Thirteen presents a detailed discussion of the major forms of testing, observational methods, and product assessments available to classroom teachers. Chapter Fourteen presents the major categories of standardized testing.

Suggested Readings   Dick, W., & Carey, L. (1990). *The systematic design of instruction* (3rd ed.). Glenview, Illinois: Scott, Foresman.
> *This easy-to-read book provides a clear description of the process of developing instructional objectives and choosing instructional activities.*

Gagné, R. M., & Driscoll, M. P. (1988). *Essentials of learning for instruction* (2nd ed.). Englewood Cliffs, NJ: Prentice-Hall.
> *This incisive and easily followed volume clearly describes the relationship of goal setting to the choice of instructional activities and the assessment of learning.*

Gullicksen, H. (1987). *Theory of mental tests*. Hillsdale, NJ: Erlbaum.
> *Although highly theoretical, this volume is recommended because of its thorough coverage of test development.*

Keeves, J. P. (Ed.). (1988). *Educational research, methodology, & measurement: An international handbook*. New York: Pergamon Press.
> *This volume is one of the finest references available on educational measurement. Specific chapters detail an extraordinarily wide range of measurement topics. Highly recommended.*

Kubiszyn, T., & Borich, G. (1990). *Educational testing and measurement: Classroom application and practice* (3rd ed.). Glenview, Illinois: Scott, Foresman.
> *This text is representative of the many texts that provide a good introduction to the concepts and issues of educational measurement.*

Answers to Practice
Exercise 12-1

1. Number 1 is a poorly written objective. The verb form "develop an awareness" is vague and unclear. Students have no way of identifying the behavior they are supposed to perform. Conditions are specified and an attempt has been made to present a criterion, although the verb makes it hard to tell what the criterion means. A better form of this objective is "On an in-class examination the students will describe at least four of the seven major influences of Spanish culture on the American Southwest."

2. This is a well-written objective. It contains verbs that specify observable and measurable behaviors ("define" and "write") and it clearly states the criterion for acceptance and the conditions under which the behavior is expected to occur. No statements are made about spelling or neatness so we assume that such things are not important unless the teacher has specified them elsewhere.

3. This objective illustrates a common error. It contains an appropriate verb ("Identify") and it describes the conditions under which the behavior will occur ("while dissecting a frog"). Absolutely no mention is made of the criterion, however. A phrase describing the criterion, such as "at least five organs," could be inserted to improve this objective.

4. Number 4 is really in bad shape. The students won't know what they have to do—memorize, write, and so on. The conditions are explained, but no criteria for "really knowing" are provided. A better version is "Given the first part of each term in the multiplication tables, for example, $9 \times 9 = \underline{\hspace{1cm}}$, the students must be able to give the correct answer eight out of ten times on an oral quiz."

5. Objective 5 sounds very impressive, but it is also unclear. Just what is meant by "conceptualize"? What does "bring to bear" mean? Conditions are described but there is no mention of criteria. A clearer statement is "During a laboratory period students will demonstrate two methods of solving the problem, including at least five steps in the problem-solving process in each demonstration."

6. This objective definitely requires improvement. "Have a firm grasp" does not describe the students' behavior at all.

A statement is made about both conditions and criteria, but the criteria are unclear. A better way to write this objective is "On the final exam, the students will correctly solve 70 percent of the equations containing one unknown."

7. Objective 7 is well written. "Correctly pronounce" is an observable and measurable behavior. Both conditions of assessment and the criterion are clearly spelled out.

8. Number 8 is, frankly, terrible. It violates practically all the rules for writing objectives. What behavior does "remember" specify? What does "know for tomorrow's quiz" mean? Who "knows" (or better, who can say)? Rewriting this objective depends on what outcome the teacher actually wants. This objective could specify "list," "recognize," "define," or, in fact, any action verb that would describe the behavior the teacher wants from students. Conditions and criteria also need to be included in a rewritten objective.

9. This is a well-written statement. No mistake can be made about the behavior, the conditions, or the criteria.

10. Objective 10 is generally appropriate. The behavior, the conditions, and the criteria are clear.

Answers to Practice Exercise 12–2

1. Number 1 requires *application*-level learning. Students must be able to use an abstraction about solutions in a real situation.

2. The students are not required to be able to do anything more than name—no usage of the knowledge is required. Number 2 requires *knowledge*-level learning.

3. This requires *comprehension*-level learning. Students are asked to put knowledge into their own words, but no more is required.

4. *Analysis*-level learning is called for. Students must identify component parts of a complex idea and determine their relationship to the whole.

5. *Evaluation*-level learning is necessary for number 5. Students must make judgments about procedures based on their knowledge, and then they must support these judgments.

6. Number 6 requires *synthesis*-level learning. Students must break down knowledge they already have and recombine it in a new form.

7. This also calls for *synthesis*-level learning. Students may use knowledge about salt marshes, oil spills, and birds and break this knowledge down and recombine it into a new whole—a set of predictions.

8. *Analysis* is clearly called for in number 8. Students must break a musical presentation into its component parts and identify two of them.

9. *Comprehension*-level learning is the statement of knowledge in one's own words. This is required of students in number 9.

10. Number 10 asks for *knowledge*-level learning. Children are to identify, nothing more.

11. Number 11 cannot be resolved unless students engage in *evaluation*-level learning. Students are required to make judgments based on their knowledge and to support these judgments.

12. This requires *application*-level learning. An abstraction must be applied by students in a fairly concrete setting.

Checklist for Practice Exercise 12–3

Cognitive Objectives.   Check to see that each objective contains the three necessary components of a good instructional objective. Underline and label the components of each of your objectives. If you didn't use the three components, go back and start again. Remember, you must include (1) an action verb, (2) the conditions under which the students' behavior is expected to occur, and (3) the criterion for the students' behavior.

Check your knowledge-level objective to be sure that it calls for nothing more than the students' ability to recall or identify information.

Check your comprehension-level objective to be sure that it requires that students put some bit of information into their own words but nothing more.

Check your application-level objective to make sure that an abstraction is being applied to a concrete setting.

Check your analysis-level objective to be sure that it requires students to break information down into its component parts so that the relationships between the components are clear.

Check your synthesis-level objective to be sure that you are requiring the analysis and recombination of old bits of knowledge to develop something new.

Check your evaluation-level objective to be sure that you are requiring students to make judgments based on their knowledge about the *value* of methods and materials for some purposes.

Psychomotor Objectives. Your psychomotor objectives must also contain the same three components as the cognitive objectives. Carefully check to be sure that both of your psychomotor objectives contain all three components and that each actually calls for an observable physical activity.

Affective Objectives. You will remember that affective objectives must have four components: (1) the affect, (2) a behavioral specification of the affect, (3) conditions, and (4) criteria. Be sure both of your affective objectives contain all four of these components.

Answers to Practice Exercise 12–4

1. *Formative.* Information is collected during the educational experiences and is used to change or modify ongoing instruction.

2. *Summative.* The examination is at the conclusion of instruction and is intended as a general measure of achievement in the course.

3. *Placement.* In conjunction with other evidence, the examination results are used either to accept or reject the architect's application for full certification.

4. *Formative.* This example contains most of the characteristics of formative evaluation: It is keyed to specific objectives, occurs frequently during learning, and is used analytically.

5. *Diagnostic.* The purpose here is to identify more precisely the nature of the second grader's problems in terms of such variables as intelligence and developmental level.

6.   *Placement.* The examination is a part of the screening process by which applicants are selected for graduate study.

7.   *Formative.* This evaluation is used to guide the project. It takes place frequently within the project and is keyed to the project objectives.

8.   *Placement.* Summative evaluations from earlier experiences are sometimes used for subsequent placement. The particular use described in the example is not a good one, in the authors' opinion. A better approach would be to pretest students on the basis of their attainment of the objectives of the second course and modify instruction in light of the results.

9.   *Summative.* This is an end-of-learning evaluation intended to determine and certify the competence of the individual.

10. *Diagnostic.* The evaluations occur as a result of problems the student encountered. They are intended to further her and the counselor's understanding of why she is experiencing these difficulties and to help them work out solutions to the problem.

Answers to Practice Exercise 12–5

1.   *Poor sampling.* Only two examinations, particularly two essay examinations, do not constitute an adequate sample of what students may know and can do. More tests, shorter tests, shorter assignments, and other work samples would give the teacher a more reliable sample of student learning.

2.   *Unclear directions.* Confusion on an exam often results from lack of explanation of expected performance. Material relevant to answering questions should be clearly indicated and highlighted if necessary.

3.   *Poor sampling.* We don't know what the ratings would have been had all of them been received. Are the missing ratings positive or negative? We don't know, but might suspect that students who didn't like the course might not bother to turn in a student rating form. The best solution is to make sure ratings are obtained from all or nearly all of the students.

4. *Unclear directions.* Although misreading may be deliberate, the fault is usually in an unclear or poorly worded question. Essay questions on any exam should direct the learner to the type of response that will be acceptable. The solution, although it is too late for this situation, is to write unambiguous questions and to try them out on other people, such as another faculty member, in advance.

5. *Unclear directions.* This is only a little better than "Discuss the Civil War." Rewrite the question, focusing the student response on specific issues and areas.

6. *Poor sampling.* Each person is "tested" under different conditions and then only a brief sample of behavior is obtained. At the very least, interview conditions should be made standard. An even better approach would be to interview each person for a longer time (a larger sample) and to obtain other persons' judgments of their skills (more samples of behavior). Problems are also likely to exist in the areas of unclear directions (Does the applicant know what is expected of him or her?) and subjective scoring (What criteria form the basis for the rating?), but the sampling problem is especially severe.

7. *Lack of objectivity in scoring.* The lower scores seem to have resulted from a change in the scorer, rather than from any real differences in the papers. Having "model" answers, specifying criteria for scoring the questions, and scoring each question on all papers before scoring a second question are all ways to reduce this kind of error.

8. *Lack of objectivity in scoring.* Teachers' judgments form a kind of scale—terribly noisy, noisy, less noisy than usual. The point is that teacher judgments are highly subjective. Whereas the meter readings represent a more precise and objective measure, the teacher ratings obviously contain some sources of bias, such as whether the teacher feels good or bad, what the teacher is paying attention to, and to whom the teacher is talking. We need to confirm our judgments with others whenever possible. Better yet, we need to rely more on objective data—perhaps not noise meters, but information that is less subject to distortion.

9. *Lack of objectivity in scoring.* Here is an obvious example of different people having different ideas about excellence. To make this judgment fairer, criteria for making the judgment should be outlined. Each entry might be ranked by each judge for originality and technical execution, for example, with these characteristics defined as clearly as possible. In that case everyone would be rating approximately the same qualities.

10. *Unclear directions.* It is unlikely that people will reach a goal if they don't know what the goal is. What's more, the task of comparing one project to another becomes very difficult because there may be few criteria that cut across diverse projects. Most damaging, however, is that students are not judged on how well they can do the project but on how lucky they are in interpreting the assignment. The solution is simple. The professor should be clear in explaining what he or she expects the groups to do.

Teacher-Made Tests

TESTING
- ☐ Planning Tests
- ☐ Essay Questions
- ☐ Objective Questions

APPLICATIONS FOR TEACHING:
Item Analysis

OBSERVATIONAL METHODS
- ☐ Performance and Work Samples
- ☐ Rating Scales
- ☐ Checklists
- ☐ Behavioral Observation

OTHER EVALUATION METHODS
- ☐ Anecdotal Reports
- ☐ Sociometric Methods
- ☐ Self-Report Methods

GRADING
- ☐ Norm-Referenced Grading
- ☐ Criterion-Referenced Grading
- ☐ Grading on Improvement
- ☐ Grading on Expectations
- ☐ Grading by Contract

APPLICATIONS FOR TEACHING:
Mistakes to Avoid When Grading

SUMMARY

SUGGESTED READINGS

ANSWERS TO PRACTICE EXERCISES

OVERVIEW

An old saying in education is that the single best way to evaluate teachers is to look at the tests they give. Good tests and measures are the foundation of good teaching. The more adaptable and competent you are in measuring student knowledge and performance, the better your teaching will be.

For most people, the idea of measurement in education has always been synonymous with testing, that is, giving students a set of questions to which they must respond. Indeed, the title of this chapter recognizes their importance. Educational measurement, however, includes much more than testing.

In this chapter you will learn about a variety of methods for measuring the outcomes of learning. We hope that the acquaintance becomes more than a passing one. Skill in constructing and using a variety of measurement methods will greatly increase your overall effectiveness as a teacher.

OBJECTIVES

After reading this chapter, you should be able to meet the following objectives.

1. Develop tables of specifications for measures of student learning.

2. Construct appropriate essay questions and scoring guides.

3. Construct high-quality true-false, completion, matching, and multiple-choice items.

4. Perform an item analysis on a test.

5. Construct rating scales and checklists.

6. Use and interpret two forms of sociometric evaluations.

7. Make accurate decisions about the form of assessment to use in different educational settings.

Testing

Test is a common word that seldom is defined precisely. At the most general level of meaning, all of the measures we discuss in this chapter could be classified as tests; that is, they represent a systematic procedure for measuring a sample of behavior (Choppin, 1988). In this chapter, however, we will use a more specific and familiar definition. A

test is a sample of questions that requires students to select or supply written or oral responses. These responses then are judged and evaluated for accuracy and completeness. Testing defined in this way is the most frequently used and most important measure of achievement at every level of education (Ebel & Frisbie, 1986). By the time most people are adults, they have taken literally hundreds of tests ranging from classroom quizzes to standardized achievement tests. Testing is the cornerstone of measuring the cognitive goals of education: acquisition of knowledge, ability to analyze and synthesize, and capabilities for problem solving.

While the assessment of cognitive objectives is a major purpose of testing, tests also are frequently used to assist in the validation of complex psychomotor performances. Examinations for driver's licenses almost always include a test that assesses knowledge of driving laws and safe driving practices. The assumption, of course, is that this knowledge is related to the desired psychomotor performances, namely, safe driving habits. Coupled with appropriate psychomotor assessment, testing helps us make better judgments.

Testing also may be used as part of an overall assessment of students' attainment of affective objectives (Anderson, 1988). In many people's estimation, an affective objective such as "cultural appreciation" requires prior knowledge of historical information and current cultural practices (Tittle, 1988). Tests may be used to assess such basic knowledge. Of course, we need to realize that the testing of knowledge is not enough to assess whether affective goals have been attained, just as it is not enough to assure us that psychomotor objectives have been reached (Zeller, 1988). Other, additional measures are needed.

Planning Tests

High-quality testing begins with careful planning (Ebel & Frisbie, 1986). What is the purpose of the test? What should the test cover? What should the test be like—should it be essay, oral, or objective? Is a test really the best way of measuring the attainment of the objectives, or should observation or some other method be employed? These questions can best be answered if one begins at the right place—with your instructional objectives (Zeller, 1988). A test is developed from instructional objectives by means of a test blueprint or, as it is more formally called, a table of specifications.

A **table of specifications** contains a minimum of two parts: the areas (groupings of objectives) to be covered in the test and an indication of how much of the test will be assigned to each area (Herman, 1988). Many teachers also like to include some indication of

TABLE 13–1   INSTRUCTOR'S TABLE OF SPECIFICATIONS FOR A HYPOTHETICAL 50-ITEM TEST ON CHAPTER TWELVE, "AN INTRODUCTION TO MEASUREMENT"

Content Area	Time Spent Instructing (minutes)	Emphasis (% of total time)	Number of Test Items	Number of Test Items for Each Level of Learning	
				Knowledge/ Comprehension	Application/ Analysis/ Evaluation
Instructional objectives	40	13	6	3	3
Types of objectives	50	17	9	3	6
Cautions in using objectives	10	3	1	1	0
Uses of measurement	30	10	5	2	3
Measurement & evaluation	40	13	6	2	4
Norm- and criterion- referenced evaluation	50	17	9	3	6
Reliability	50	17	9	2	7
Validity	30	10	5	2	3
TOTAL	300	100	50	18	32

the level of learning being assessed. Table 13–1 shows a sample table of specifications for a test on Chapter Twelve, "An Introduction to Measurement." The general idea is that the test accurately represents the emphasis given in instruction and in the instructional objectives. Table 13–1 shows that the teacher has given most of the instructional emphasis to types of objectives (17%), norm- and criterion-referenced evaluation (17%) and to reliability (17%). The test reflects that emphasis by containing nine items from each of these three areas.

You can follow a similar plan for any test you construct. Place the content areas down the left-hand column. Then record how much time you spent on each content area (our example assumes six 50-minute periods, or 300 minutes). Calculate the percentage of emphasis placed on each instructional area and record this in the next column. Then derive directly from this percentage the number of test items for each area.

A second dimension of Table 13–1 is the use of Bloom's taxonomy to divide items into those measuring lower-level (knowledge and comprehension) and higher-level learning (application, analysis, synthesis, and evaluation). This division is particularly helpful as you make up the test. It ensures that higher levels of thinking are tested, not just rote recall. If your test items match well-written instructional objectives, you will avoid the cardinal sin of using trite, lower-order items to try to measure significant, higher-order learning.

The table of specifications helps ensure the content validity of the test, but it may have another use. Some test experts recommend sharing the table of specifications with students to help them prepare for the test, and in our experience, the table is quite useful to students and certainly is worth sharing with them.

The next part of planning any test is the choice of items. Classroom tests may by made up of two major categories of items: essay questions and objective questions. Types of essay questions include short-answer, discussion, and oral questions (Herman, 1988), and objective questions include completion, true-false, multiple-choice, and matching items. Each type of item has its strengths and weaknesses. Your approach should be to select those items that best measure the attainment of your instructional objectives. The following discussion should help you make that choice.

Essay Questions

Essay questions ask students to construct an answer in their own words and to respond either in writing or orally (Ebel & Frisbie, 1986). Essay questions can take many different forms and require a variety of mental processes including recall, organization of information, comparison, analysis, and evaluation. Essay questions may ask students to compare things, to make decisions for or against a controversial issue, to identify causes and effects, or to reorganize information (Kubiszyn & Borich, 1990).

Form of Essay Questions.   A common form of essay question is the *restricted-response* or *short-answer* form. In this type of question, the students are asked to respond briefly, usually in a half page or less, to a question that is fairly narrow in scope (Herman, 1988). An example of such a question is the following: "In three or four sentences, describe the general effect of shortening a test upon its reliability."

In an *extended-response* essay question, few restrictions are placed upon the person answering the question. The response may run from one to several pages, depending on the scope of question and the abilities and intent of the student (Herman, 1988). An example of such a question is "Take a position regarding your use of norm-referenced or criterion-referenced assessment in your first year of teaching. Defend your position by relating it to the nature of the subject matter you will teach, the level of the students you will have, and grading policies in your school district."

Both types of written essay questions require that students recall information, choose appropriate responses, and organize an answer in a logical and coherent fashion. Restricted-response questions permit a better sampling of content areas because more topics can be touched on in the same period of time (Kubiszyn & Borich, 1990). The extended-response essay suffers on the sampling dimension. No matter how well it is constructed, it will not be able to sample content as well as several short, carefully selected restricted-response questions can. The extended-response question is useful, however, in determining whether a student is able to organize large amounts of information into a coherent form and to construct logical arguments based on a wide range of information (Kubiszyn & Borich, 1990).

Oral essay questions differ from written essay questions in that the questions and responses are spoken. They require recall of information and construction of logical and organized answers. Oral questions allow for clarification of responses by the person answering the question and for detailed probing by the examiner. On the minus side, this method is extremely time-consuming since only one person can be examined at a time. There is a potential for unreliability in scoring because there usually is not a "product" to review after the interview has been completed. Also, reliability and validity may suffer if evaluation is made on factors unrelated to the objectives being assessed (social and expressive skills or appearance, for example). Further, as with all essay exams, sampling of content often is poor.

Oral questions usually are a part of the evaluation process for advanced degrees. Typically, however, the intent of such examinations is not to sample broadly across content areas, but rather to probe the depth of a student's knowledge in a restricted area of inquiry such as the topic addressed in a thesis or dissertation.

Scoring Essay Examinations. There are two general approaches for grading essay questions—the point method and the rating method. In the *point method* (sometimes called the *analytical method*) an "ideal" answer is envisioned by the teacher, and points are assigned to desired features of the ideal answer. The student's response then is compared to the ideal answer and scored on each of the desired dimensions. The student's score is the total number of points received.

Consider the 20-point question "Identify causes of low morale among the labor force at Consolidated Steel, Inc., and suggest steps for improving morale." The teacher might construct the following "ideal" answer and assign point values to parts of the answer.

1. Identifies three causes of low morale from the descriptions given (2 points for each cause, 6 points possible)

2. Suggests three or more workable steps to improve morale (2 points for each step, 6 points possible)

3. Places situation in general economic perspective (2 points possible)

4. Shows evidence of knowledge of prevailing working conditions in the industry (3 points possible)

5. Expresses self in an organized way (3 points possible)

A student may write an answer in which he or she identifies four causes (6 points) and suggests two steps to improve morale (4 points). Assuming the student shows some evidence of economic perspective (1 point), excellent knowledge of prevailing working conditions (3 points), and skill in organization and expression (3 points), he or she would receive a total of 17 points for this question.

In the *rating method* (sometimes called the *global* method), the ideal answer still serves as an overall standard for comparison, but it is not broken down into parts or features. There are several commonly used rating methods. One method involves establishing a series of categories (for example, a five-category scale ranging from "very poor quality" to "very superior quality"). The grader sorts the papers into the categories based upon how they compare to the "ideal" answer. A variation of this method is to select several papers at each rating level to serve as standards of comparison.

Generally the rating method is quicker than the point method and is appropriate if a large number of essay questions are to be read

(Kubiszyn & Borich, 1990). If you use the rating method you should read each essay a second time to be sure that it has been categorized properly. The point method focuses the grader's attention more closely on details of the answer and assists the grader in giving feedback to learners. The point method is used somewhat more frequently and is generally recommended for restricted-response essay questions where answers tend to be fairly specific.

A major problem of essay testing is that scoring, whether by the point or rating method, has been shown to be notoriously unreliable. Over the years, research has shown a low correspondence between scores given to the same answer by different graders, and even the same grader is likely to score an answer very differently on two different occasions (Myers, McConville, & Coffman, 1966; Starch & Elliott, 1912, 1913a, 1913b; Traxler & Anderson, 1935).

Teachers need to take special precautions to ensure fair grading. Generally the procedures outlined below will help you avoid the problems of unreliability associated with grading responses to essay questions.

Prepare a scoring key for each question. Nothing will reduce reliability more quickly than a changing standard. A scoring guide or ideal answer is essential.

Grade only one question at a time across all papers. This reduces the possibility that your judgment of one question may carry over to affect how you grade another question, a "halo" effect.

Shuffle the papers after each question. A random order helps reduce the possibility of systematic bias. Any bias that is present will be evened out over the grading of several questions.

If possible, grade the responses anonymously. While this is not always possible, it is desirable. The answers should speak for themselves, and your knowledge of other facts about students can unconsciously affect your grading.

Judge the mechanics of writing separately from the content. Often content and expression are not separated and students are graded on factors such as handwriting or grammar that are irrelevant to the objectives. If expression is one of your objectives for the exam, it should still be evaluated separately from content.

Avoid the use of optional questions. Optional questions remove the possibility of comparing everyone on the same standard, causing both reliability and validity to suffer.

In addition to the six guidelines for scoring essay questions, two other steps may be taken to improve reliability. First, better sampling of content can be accomplished by using more and shorter questions. Second, questions should direct the students to the nature of the response required. Ambiguous or completely open-ended questions ("Discuss the concept of validity") only cause students to become confused or to answer the "wrong" question. A good essay question should limit the area under consideration and should point to the expected nature and length of the answer. (See Table 13–2.)

TABLE 13–2   CONSTRUCTING GOOD ESSAY ITEMS

Advantages of the Essay Item

1. Measures higher-level abilities to organize, think logically, and express oneself effectively.

2. May stimulate desirable study habits, such as relating information, organizing, summarizing.

3. Usually relatively easy for the teacher to prepare.

Disadvantages of the Essay Item

1. Poorer sampling of content than that obtained by objective forms of testing.

2. Reliability is relatively low.

3. Difficult and subjective scoring.

4. Irrelevant factors such as spelling and handwriting may affect scoring of questions.

Suggestions for Constructing Essay Items

1. Make sure the question spells out the nature of the expected response to the student.

2. Use more restricted-response questions rather than fewer extended-response questions if better sampling is desired.

3. Use essay questions only where they are clearly the most suitable for measuring the learning outcomes.

4. Avoid giving optional questions.

Objective Questions

Objective questions require students to make very brief responses that are compared to predetermined answers (Choppin, 1988). Such items are called "objective" because they require little, if any, judgment for correct scoring. There are several formats that objective test items may take:

> *Completion:* The students must supply a word or phrase to complete an incomplete sentence or answer a question.

> *True-False:* The students must judge statements as either correct or incorrect.

> *Multiple-Choice:* The students must choose a correct answer from a set of alternative responses to a question.

> *Matching:* The students must match items from one list to corresponding items in another list.

A great deal of controversy surrounds the use of objective test items. Among the more frequently voiced criticisms are (1) that some teachers tend to use objective items to measure trivial outcomes, (2) that objective items do not assess students' abilities to organize and express themselves, and (3) that the possibility of guessing correct answers may lead to poor student preparation. Advocates of objective testing usually counter these arguments by stressing the potential for increased reliability and validity (Choppin, 1988; Ebel & Frisbie, 1986).

Advocates of multiple-item objective tests argue that they have a much better chance of adequately sampling course content than do essay tests limited to a few items. While the preparation of objective items usually is difficult, scoring is quick, accurate, and easy, thus facilitating rapid feedback. Additionally, objective items can be constructed that measure very complex abilities such as reasoning, problem solving, and data interpretation (Choppin, 1988; Ebel & Frisbie, 1986).

With proper care in the construction of objective items, very complex levels of learning can be assessed. Test authorities maintain that the testing of trivial outcomes by objective items is not an inherent problem of this form (see Ebel & Frisbie, 1986). Important gains in the reliability and content validity of a test often can be made through the use of objective items. A set of carefully constructed multiple-choice questions, for example, systematically can assess the comprehension, analysis, and evaluation capabilities of students while sampling a wide variety of content.

Objective testing certainly is not the answer to every assessment problem (there is a great deal you do *not* learn about a student if you use

objective testing alone). However, the potential of this method can be realized only if you acquire the skills necessary to construct excellent objective items.

Completion Items. **Completion questions** require a short answer—a word or a phrase—as the response. The item may be in the form of a question:

> In what form of item is either a word or phrase supplied as the correct answer? (completion)

or it may take a sentence-completion form:

> A word or phrase is supplied as the correct answer in (completion) items.

A similar format that can be used with proper instructions is the presentation of a list of items (for example, a set of dates) with blanks next to them. The students must give a response to each item on the list. For example:

> Below is a list of dates. Fill in the blank next to each date with the name of a major historical event that affected westward expansion.
>
> 1. 1845 (Texas admitted to Union)
>
> 2. 1848 (Gold discovered at Sutter's Mill)

3. 1853 (Gadsden Purchase)

4. 1865 (Civil War ends)

5. 1907 (Oklahoma admitted to Union)

Excessive use of completion items easily can encourage the learning of trivial information because of the nature of the required responses, but the ability to correctly label and recall is important in many subject areas, such as biology, foreign language, and medicine. Completion items permit a wide sampling of content with minimal response requirements, allowing students to answer a large number of questions in a relatively short period of time (see Table 13–3).

TABLE 13–3   CONSTRUCTING GOOD COMPLETION ITEMS

Advantages of the Completion Item

1. Ease of construction.
2. Can sample a wide range of subject matter.
3. Requires that a student supply the response from memory.

Disadvantages of the Completion Item

1. Not well suited to measuring complex learning outcomes.
2. Scoring can be quite subjective.

Suggestions for Constructing Completion Items

1. Write each item so that it has one and only one correct response.
2. Avoid verbatim quotations from the text.
3. Blanks should appear near the end of the sentence rather than toward the beginning.
4. Avoid excessive blanks in a single sentence.
5. All blanks for answers should be of the same length; avoid giving clues by the length of the line.

To write good completion items, avoid quoting directly from the text. Quotations often provide poor prompts for the correct answer and may lose much of their meaning by being lifted out of context. These verbatim items also tend to encourage rote recall. The items should be written as clearly as possible so that the sense of the item is understood prior to the point where the response is required. For this reason, blanks usually should appear later rather than earlier in the items.

True-False Items.   **True-false questions** are statements students must judge to be correct or incorrect (Ebel & Frisbie, 1986). Students may respond to them by marking true or false, yes or no, or correct or incorrect. Some examples are presented below.

   __(F)__   Completion items are statements students judge to be correct or incorrect.

   __(T)__   The highest level in Bloom's taxonomy is the evaluation level.

   __(F)__   Working memory has an unlimited capacity.

   __(F)__   Essay questions are usually more reliable than objective items.

True-false items are very widely used. They can be generated relatively quickly, scored rapidly and objectively, and *if constructed properly*, test higher levels of learning. A large number can be answered in a relatively short period of time—average secondary school students can complete about three to five true-false items per minute. True-false items generally are considered useful for younger students and for poorer readers, provided they are written in simple, direct language (see Table 13–4).

There are serious concerns about the true-false format, however. Good true-false items that are not completely obvious on the one hand or ambiguous on the other are sometimes difficult to construct. Other major criticisms include triviality, ambiguity, guessing, and encouragement of rote learning (Herman, 1988). The major defects of true-false questions may be removed by careful construction. However, most measurement specialists have strong reservations about the use of true-false items. Many items can be answered correctly regardless of the level of preparation of the student. Further, the diagnostic value of

TABLE 13–4   CONSTRUCTING GOOD TRUE-FALSE ITEMS

Advantages of the True-False Item

1. Provides a simple and direct means of assessing educational outcomes.
2. May be used to sample a wide range of subject matter.
3. Ease and objectivity of scoring.

Disadvantages of the True-False Item

1. Susceptibility to guessing is high.
2. Constructing statements that are neither obvious nor ambiguous is difficult.
3. May encourage poor preparation in students.

Suggestions for Constructing True-False Items

1. Absolute terms like *always* and *never* should be avoided since absolutely true or false statements are rare.
2. Avoid the use of negative statements and especially double negatives (such as "lengthening a test will *not* cause it to become *un*reliable").
3. Avoid complex statements containing two or more ideas.
4. True statements should not be longer than false statements.*
5. Avoid terms such as *usually* or *in general* that tend to indicate true items.

*A natural tendency is to insert extra qualifying words in true statements to ensure their correctness. Length of the statement then becomes a clue to the student.

any particular item is very low since chance plays such a strong part in the potential for getting a specific item correct. We recommend they be used very sparingly.

Multiple-Choice Items.   Like true-false items, **multiple-choice questions** present a limited number of possible responses to the student, who must choose the correct or best response. Typically, a multiple-choice item will consist of a *stem*, which may be either a question or an incomplete statement, and a set of *alternatives* (usually four or five) from which to choose the best or correct answer (Choppin, 1988; Herman, 1988). The multiple-choice item is adaptable to testing a variety of learning outcomes—from knowledge of specific facts to understanding and application of concepts and principles. The following item is an example:

> The average span of immediate memory is about how many units?
> a. 7
> b. 10
> c. 13
> d. 16

This item illustrates a common use for multiple-choice questions—testing for retention of specific facts (the correct answer is *a*, 7 units). Overuse of the multiple-choice item to measure knowledge of facts and terminology has led to a great deal of criticism of multiple-choice testing as unsuited for measuring many instructional outcomes. With careful construction, however, multiple-choice items can measure higher-order levels of learning quite effectively (see Choppin, 1988).

> You've all taken classes in which the teacher lectured profoundly and tested trivia. The testing concept that is lacking in this unfortunate state of affairs is
> a. item analysis of the test
> b. validity of the test
> c. reliability of the test
> d. norm-referenced testing

In order to answer the item correctly (unless you have studied this specific item or made a lucky guess), you need to understand certain concepts and make a decision about which best applies to the situation (alternative *b* is the correct choice). Simply memorizing the definition of validity isn't enough. If you want students to understand and apply information, tests should be aimed, at least in part, at this higher level of learning.

One excellent multiple-choice method for measuring higher levels of understanding is the interpretive exercise. An **interpretive exercise** consists of a descriptive statement or paragraph, pictorial materials, or both, followed by a series of multiple-choice questions that require the

PRACTICE EXERCISE 13–1   JUDGING AND WRITING MULTIPLE-CHOICE ITEMS

Correct each of the following objective items, using the suggestions in Table 13–5 as a guide. The first few items are keyed to particular suggestions. After that you're on your own. Our "better" versions are on page 443.

1. Reliability
    a. is that portion of any score caused by error
    b. refers to the consistency of measurement
    c. declines as the length of the test increases
    d. is the extent to which a measure represents the content it is supposed to measure
        (See suggestion number 2, Table 13–5.)

2. In norm-referenced testing, you are comparing an individual's performance to
    a. others
    b. the self
    c. "normal work"
    d. a preestablished standard of acceptable performance
        (See suggestion number 3, Table 13–5.)

3. A test that measures achievement against a standard (for example, many driver's license examinations) is called a
    a. norm-referenced test
    b. reliable test
    c. criterion-referenced test
    d. *a* and *c* above
    e. all of the above
        (See suggestion number 5, Table 13–5.)

4. The reliability of a test
    a. can best be improved by shortening the test
    b. will be strengthened by including a greater number of difficult items
    c. will increase upon the addition of additional items to the test
    d. will go down if the test is changed from criterion-referenced to norm-referenced
        (See suggestion number 2, Table 13–5.)

PRACTICE EXERCISE 13-1   *CONTINUED*

5. The most justifiable criticism of teacher-made objective tests is that they
   a. often emphasize rote learning
   b. discrimination against the poorer students
   c. broader sampling than is actually necessary
   d. less reliable than other forms of evaluation

6. If your goal was to sample students' recall of information from a wide variety of content areas, you would not be justified in using
   a. multiple-choice questions
   b. true-false questions
   c. short-answer questions
   d. all of the above
   e. none of the above

7. Grading essay items by counting number of lines would be
   a. somewhat reliable but not very valid
   b. somewhat valid but not very reliable
   c. neither somewhat valid nor partly reliable
   d. more often valid than somewhat reliable

8. Teacher-made tests typically are not
   a. checked for internal consistency
   b. standardized against norm groups
   c. highly reliable measures of learning
   d. not invalid measures of classroom learning

9. Rating scales
   a. are most commonly used for rote-level learning
   b. are occasionally used for knowledge-level learning
   c. can be used for application-level learning
   d. are very commonly used to assess psychomotor learning

10. Sociograms do not have which of the following uses:
   a. not establishing content validity nor internal consistency
   b. not identifying isolates nor group interactions
   c. assessing affective and psychomotor learning
   d. assessing cognitive and psychomotor learning

student to interpret the material (Kubiszyn & Borich, 1990). The following exercise is of this type:

A first-grade teacher, concerned about the inability of her students to follow directions, devises an instruction-following game to develop this skill. In a beginning phase, students are provided with boxes filled with a large variety of small objects. Working with small groups, the teacher gives instructions to do certain things with the objects and to interact with other group members. Each time an instruction is carried out, students are reinforced by means of approval and a check on a record form. Students can trade their checks for time in an area where they can play with toys from home, read, or engage in any activity they like. Following instructions on actual classroom tasks becomes the focus in later stages of training.

1. The category of learning that is the better explanatory model for the above is
    (a.) operant/instrumental conditioning
    b. respondent/classical conditioning

2. Within a reinforcement framework, the instructions given by the teacher are most appropriately conceptualized as
    a. reinforcers
    (b.) discriminative stimuli
    c. variable-ratio schedules
    d. respondent conditioning

3. Assume the teacher felt the children were having difficulty telling the difference between instructions and other kinds of things she said. She introduced a hand signal (such as an upraised hand) that meant, in effect, "Please pay attention. This is something to be acted on." She would have introduced an additional __?__ for the children's instruction—following.
    a. reinforcer
    b. extinction procedure
    c. reinforcement schedule
    (d.) discriminative stimulus

4. If the children learn that instruction following is rewarded when the hand signal is given, but that other verbalizations of the teacher don't require their attention they can be said to have acquired a
   a. shaping procedure
   b. behavioral chain
   (c.) discrimination
   d. generalization

Such exercises have been used extensively in standardized testing and are used by classroom teachers because of their ability to test higher levels of achievement (Choppin, 1988). While they are fairly difficult to prepare, interpretive exercises are well matched to objectives such as application of principles and evaluation of complex situations. The ability to make predictions about the effects of certain changes in a fragile environment or to make interpretations of poetry or prose passages might be tested by a series of interpretive questions.

A number of useful guides for constructing items to test higher levels of learning are available. The oldest and still the most complete guide is the *Taxonomy of Educational Objectives* (Bloom et al., 1956). Items are presented in the taxonomy that illustrate the assessment of learning outcomes at each level of learning. Another useful guide for the construction of higher-order test items is a chapter by DeLandsheere (1988) in which he gives excellent ideas for the development of sophisticated questions.

Multiple-choice items are one of the most versatile forms of testing. They can sample widely across content areas and, if well written, can measure the attainment of higher levels of learning. Moreover, the technique of item analysis (see page 421) can also be used on multiple-choice tests to detect and revise faulty items (see Table 13–5).

Matching Items. **Matching questions** consist of two parallel lists, one containing a series of words or phrases (stems) and the other made up of a series of responses. The student must match up the items in the response list with the items in the stimulus list.

Matching items have the advantage of being compact and easy to construct and there are a large number of relationships between two things that are important educational outcomes (Choppin, 1988). People and achievements, dates and historical events, symbols and con-

TABLE 13–5   CONSTRUCTING GOOD MULTIPLE-CHOICE ITEMS

Advantages of the Multiple-Choice Item

1. Better sampling of content than essay forms of testing.

2. Reliability can be relatively high.

3. Ease and objectivity of scoring.

4. Analysis of item performance and revision are possible.

Disadvantages of the Multiple-Choice Item

1. May encourage less than adequate preparation.

2. Sometimes misused to test only verbatim recall.

3. May encourage guessing.

4. Difficulty in preparation.

Suggestions for Constructing Multiple-Choice Items

1. Attempt to test for higher-order learning, not just verbatim recall of facts.

2. The stem of the item should present a meaningful problem.

3. Watch that the length of alternatives and the grammar don't give away the answers.

4. Make sure all alternatives are plausible, but that there is only one "best" or correct answer.

5. Where possible, eliminate negatively stated items (such as "which of the following is *not* . . .") and alternatives such as "none of the above," "all of the above," and "*a* and *b* above."

cepts, foreign words and English equivalents, plants and classifications, and authors and books are but a few of many important pairings.

Learning measured by matching items can be at a relatively low level—the association between two bits of factual information—but with some thought given to the construction of matching exercises, levels of learning well above rote recall can be measured. Consider the following example:

Directions: Write the letter of the concept in column B next to the situation in column A with which it best fits. Letters from Column B may be used once, more than once, or not at all.

		Column A		*Column B*
(E)	1.	High school grades are correlated with college grades.	A.	Internal consistency reliability
(D)	2.	For a new test of "locus of control," experts agree the test measures what it is intended to measure.	B.	Test-retest reliability
			C.	Content validity
(B)	3.	Students receive approximately the same score on an aptitude test the second time they take it.	D.	Construct validity
			E.	Predictive validity
(C)	4.	The teacher uses a table of specifications to match a test to instruction.	F.	Equivalent forms reliability
(A)	5.	In general, performance on individual items is correlated with performance on the total test.		
(E)	6.	Scholastic Aptitude Test scores correlate +.40 with grade-point average in freshman year of college.		
(C)	7.	The test over the geometry unit contains the same proportions of items per topic as did the geometry unit itself.		

Variations of matching items include having students match names with points on a map or parts of a diagram. Music teachers may require matching of keyboard locations to notes, while shop teachers may ask for correct labeling of tools used in projects. A football player may be asked to correctly associate blocking or tackling assignments with a given play. The variety of applications, plus the relative ease of preparation, makes matching items popular with many teachers. Like all item forms, however, they must actually measure the goals of learning for the classroom (see Table 13–6).

TABLE 13–6   CONSTRUCTING GOOD MATCHING ITEMS

Advantages of the Matching Item

1. Suited to measuring associations between concepts.

2. Requires little reading time.

3. Can be constructed with relative ease.

Disadvantages of the Matching Item

1. If used improperly, may encourage rote memorization of facts and figures.

2. Limited application to some higher levels of learning.

Suggestions for Constructing Matching Items

1. All parts of any one item should deal with a single topic.

2. Each list should contain no more than five to seven items.

3. The longer phrases should serve as stems and the shorter responses should be placed in the second column.

4. Unequal numbers of stems and responses should be used to diminish successful guessing.

5. Instruct learners that responses may be used once, more than once, or not at all in a given item.

Applications for Teaching: Item Analysis

One of the best arguments for using objective items, particularly multiple-choice items, is that they can be analyzed and improved. The techniques for doing this are called, collectively, *item analysis*. Item analysis provides two important kinds of information for each item on a norm-referenced test: how hard it is (item difficulty) and whether "good students" get the item right more often than "poor students" (item discrimination) (Ebel & Frisbie, 1986).

Items too difficult or too easy may make a test unreliable and so the test maker is usually looking for items of medium difficulty. If item analysis shows that almost everyone in the group got the item wrong, then perhaps some revision is in order.

An item also should distinguish between students who know more about the subject being tested and those who know less about it (Herman, 1988). For example, if most of the students in the lower half of the class got the item right and most of the students in the upper half of the class got it wrong, we would certainly question whether that item belonged on the test in its present form. That is exactly what happens in some cases, however. Poorly written items mislead the better students, while poorly prepared students answer correctly.

Professional test authors use computer programs to analyze the quality of their test items. Correlation techniques are used to determine if items are discriminating properly and to estimate the overall reliability of the test. If you're like many teachers, though, you may not have ready access to this kind of analysis. Nonetheless, some simple procedures are available that allow you to make substantial improvements in your items and greatly increase the overall quality of your tests. Many teachers develop pools of excellent items for their instructional objectives from which they can select

Many teachers develop pools of excellent items from which they can select items for their tests.

items for their tests. Each time an item appears on a test, student performance is used to analyze whether the item is of appropriate difficulty and whether it discriminates (distinguishes) between the better and the poorer students.*

---

*While many textbooks provide sets of objective items in their teachers' manuals, such items vary greatly in quality and many need substantial improvement. Item analysis will provide objective information to help you identify and improve defective items.

The following steps represent some agreed-upon procedures for item analysis. Although the example employs multiple-choice items, the procedures can easily be generalized to true-false items and to other item forms (Herman, 1988).

1. Type or write each item on a separate 5-by-7-inch card. Below is an item at the comprehension level for a cognitive development objective taken from an educational psychology course.

Course: 882   *Objective:* Cognitive Development   *Level:* Comprehension

Difficulty: _____   *Discrimination:* _____

Which of the following best distinguishes the period of formal operations from the period of concrete operations?

    a.   an increase in reflexive behavior
    b.   a tendency toward centrism
  (c.)   presence of propositional thinking
    d.   increasing belief in animistic concepts

Alternatives	*A*	*B*	*(C)*	*D*	*Omits*
Lower Group					
Upper Group					

By putting items on cards, you easily develop a file of items matched to your objectives. To construct a test, a sample of items matching your objectives can be pulled from the file and arranged in any order you desire.

2. After a test has been administered, rank the papers from top to bottom in terms of total score.

3. Divide the papers into two groups, upper and lower,* and count the number of stu-dents in each group who selected each alternative for each item. Enter these numbers on your card for the item. For the sample item, the result might be as follows for a 30-member class. "Omits" refer to people who did not answer the question at all.

Alternatives	A	B	(C)	D	Omits
Upper Group	1	1	12	1	0
Lower Group	2	6	5	2	0

4. Next, compute the *item difficulty* as follows:

$$\text{Difficulty} = \frac{\text{Number who got the item right}}{\text{Total number of students}} \times 100$$

For this item, $(12 + 5)$, or 17, out of 30 students chose *C*, the correct answer. Thus the difficulty is $(17 \div 30) \times 100$, or 57 percent, which indicates a relatively difficult item.*

5. The second computation is an estimate of item reliability or discriminating power. If the item is "working" properly, students who did well on the *total* test also should do well on *this item*, while those who scored less well on the test should do less well as a group on this item. This happened in our example—twelve out of fifteen people in the upper group got the item correct, compared to only five out of the fifteen in the lower group. The computation of *item discrimination* is as follows:

$$\text{Discrimination} = \frac{\begin{array}{c}\text{Number} \\ \text{correct} \\ \text{in upper} \\ \text{half}\end{array} - \begin{array}{c}\text{Number} \\ \text{correct} \\ \text{in lower} \\ \text{half}\end{array}}{\tfrac{1}{2}\,(\text{Total number of students})}$$

In this case we have $(12 - 5) \div [(\tfrac{1}{2})\,(30)]$, or $\tfrac{7}{15}$, or .47.

---

*Theoretically, the best result is obtained by selecting the upper 27 percent and the lower 27 percent as the upper and lower groups. For most classroom settings, however, groups may be too small to give reliable results, and simply dividing the class in half is a better procedure. The 27 percent figures are based on a normal curve model.

---

*The average score on the total test is related to the difficulty of the individual items. Thus, if items were to average around 50 percent difficulty, the average total test score would also be quite low.

The item discrimination index is a form of correlation coefficient. It either can be positive (up to +1.00) or negative (to −1.00). A clear problem exists with an item in which you get a very low positive (around zero) or negative discrimination index. A negative figure results when more students in the *lower* scoring group get an item right than do students in the *upper* group. Such items should be revised if possible or discarded if necessary. Something in the item—wording, ambiguity, or misinformation—usually is misleading the better students. Looking at the pattern of choices will help you determine what the problem is (Herman, 1988).

In general, *the higher the discrimination index,* the better your item. Certainly, low or negative discriminating items should be examined carefully. They either add little to or actually lower the reliability of your test.

For difficulty, a moderate range—neither too easy nor too hard—is recommended. In four-alternative multiple-choice tests, an average difficulty level of about 75 percent will result in the highest reliability (Wood, 1988). For motivational purposes, however, the test writer often will wish to include items easier than this, with difficulty levels of 85, 90, or even 100 percent. Although these items will not contribute to the reliability of your test, they will help students feel better about their overall performance.

Observational Methods

Teachers not only measure the achievement of cognitive goals, but they also are concerned with assessing skills and attitudes (Anderson, 1988). Physical education teachers, for example, need to determine student improvement in a variety of physical activities, such as tumbling, diving, and handball. In each performance area, teachers observe what students do, evaluate their performances, and provide feedback to encourage improvement. Music teachers evaluate their students on dimensions such as expression and accuracy. In home economics classes, teachers are likely to judge several different performances and products, such as diet selection, food preparation, and clothing construction. Vocational teachers must determine whether a drill press is operated properly or whether trainees can close a sale in a retail establishment. Is testing the best approach for assessing all these competencies? Probably not. A better way is a direct evaluation of actual task performance or an examination of a sample of completed work. Such methods of direct evaluation are known as *observational methods* (Kubiszyn & Borich, 1990).

Performances and Work Samples

The methods described in this section may be applied to activities in progress (performances) or to the products of those activities (work samples). Examples of performances are playing a song, drilling a hole, giving a speech, shooting a basket, administering cardiopulmonary resuscitation (CPR), and dismounting from parallel bars. Work samples may be as diverse as a plan for a solar heater, a papier-mâché model of a landscape, a birdhouse, a bookcase, a letter to the editor, or a report of activities. Most criteria applied in rating performances also can be applied in judging work samples. The job of the rater is much the same in both cases (Gullicksen, 1987).

There are times when observing performances is of greater benefit to the teacher than observing work samples. Naturally, the converse also is sometimes the case. Direct observation of tool handling, for instance, is much more valuable from a teaching standpoint than observing that a student's work sample is poorly constructed. On the other hand, direct observation sometimes isn't feasible or desirable. Students may complete projects in settings or at times when observation would be impossible, or the activity may be largely a mental one and there may not be anything to observe. Ideally, we want to provide as much relevant feedback to learners as possible and this includes feedback on both performance and product. In practice, teachers can observe only that which is possible within the limitations of class size, time, location, and the nature of the task.

Rating Scales

A rating scale typically indicates a trait or characteristic to be judged and a scale on which the rating can be made. Rating scales frequently are used to evaluate performance in the psychomotor and the affective domains (Anderson, 1988). Panels of judges, for example, give ratings to divers and gymnasts. Another common use of rating scales is in student evaluations of courses and instructors.

The simplest form of rating scale is the *numerical scale*, in which numbers indicate the degree to which a particular characteristic is present. The following is an example of a numerical scale:

Instructions: Please indicate your degree of confidence in using each of the following instructional methods. 1 = Little or no confidence; 2 = Some confidence; 3 = Great confidence.

1.	Inquiry teaching	1	2	3
2.	Classroom contracts	1	2	3
3.	Simulations	1	2	3

Another form of rating scale is the *graphic scale*, which requires that the rating be made by checking along a line. The purpose is identical to that of the numerical rating scale; only the method for indicating responses is different. The following sample of a graphic scale has been used to obtain the reaction of participants toward instructional sessions in adult education courses.

Instructions: Please indicate your reaction to the session by checking the point on the horizontal line that best represents your feelings.

1.   Topical importance to you

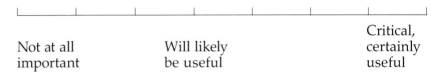

		Critical,
Not at all	Will likely	certainly
important	be useful	useful

2.   Would you recommend this session to future participants?

Strongly	Would	
suggest	generally	Would very highly
avoiding	recommend	recommend

A *comparative scale* provides samples of a product to be evaluated, usually at five to seven levels of quality. Examples of descriptive paragraphs, for instance, might be arranged into a scale of increasing quality for use by an elementary school language arts teacher. The teacher then can rate the paragraphs students write by matching them against samples representing the levels of quality. The following samples of children's writing define points of a comparative scale. As you can see, general writing skills (spelling, grammar, use of complex sentences, and so on) increase from level 1 to level 5.

Level 1. His a smartolk mean dumb and not ril nice.

Level 2. Scott is nice. I like him a lot. He's good in socker.

Level 3. Melissa is 10 years old and will be 11 in April. She's going to move at the end of the month.

Level 4. DeVone makes a good friend. She likes to have me come over and play and when we do, we have fun.

Level 5. Joette is a very pretty and intelligent girl. Sometimes she is very loud, but I really admire her. She is smart (I think) and very original.

Handwriting progress also can be measured by using a comparative scale to examine samples of students' writing on several occasions. Music teachers use taped performances of songs to rate how well current students are performing. Recordings of students' speeches of varying proficiency can help speech teachers judge how effective current student speeches are. Such standards greatly assist both teachers and students in attaining the highest possible level of performance.

For ratings to be most successful, the same principles of test construction that produce high reliability and validity must be followed. The behavior observed should be matched to instructional objectives and should be a representative sample of the students' actual performances. Only observable characteristics should be rated, and points on each scale should be defined clearly. Steps should be taken to reduce rater biases: Some raters are too lenient, others are too strict, and others rate everyone about average. Another possible bias to be avoided is the halo effect, in which the raters' knowledge of other traits of the persons being rated may affect their judgments. A popular teacher, for example, may be judged as more organized than he or she actually is, or the "class clown" may be rated as low in motivation by a teacher even though he or she generally turns in work as punctually as other members of the class.

Clear instructions to raters can help reduce rater biases. To counter the halo effect, raters should be told to rate each item independently and to judge the traits objectively. To cope with tendencies to be too strict, too lenient, or too cautious, raters should be instructed to use all points on the scale. Drawing attention to a comparison group ("compared to all instructors you have had, this instructor . . ."; "compared to other persons who have completed this minicourse, this student's performance . . .") can provide a more objective basis for making ratings and reducing biases (see Table 13–7).

Checklists

A **checklist** is a listing of steps, activities, or behaviors the observer records during an observation (Kubiszyn & Borich, 1990). Checklists are used to determine whether particular elements are present or absent in either a process or a product. They call for simple yes-no judgments. A chemistry instructor might use a checklist to see if students include all the necessary safety precautions in setting up an experiment. A vocational teacher can use a checklist to determine whether students can maintain a piece of machinery properly. In institutional settings, checklists often are used to assess the perfor-

---

TABLE 13–7   CONDUCTING GOOD RATING SCALES

Advantages of the Rating Scale

---

1. Useful for evaluating important learning objectives in the affective and psychomotor domain.

2. Can convey information on quality, frequency, and level of performance.

3. Useful for judging either performances or products.

Disadvantages of the Rating Scale

---

1. Subject to a variety of rater biases, including leniency, strictness, and the halo effect.

2. Subject to social expectations and, hence, susceptible to faking.

Suggestions for Constructing Rating Scales

---

1. Begin with a blueprint of the behaviors or traits in order to ensure valid sampling of the area.

2. Clearly define the traits to be rated in the most behavioral way possible.

3. Divide the rating continuum into as many points as are needed for clarity, usually from three to seven.

4. Clearly define the points on the continuum so there is no question as to what each rating means.

5. Train and motivate the raters to be as accurate and objective as possible.

---

mance of retarded individuals in self-care skills. Here is an example of a checklist used in determining whether students have acquired emergency cardiac care skills:

_____ Establishes unresponsiveness

_____ Calls out for help

_____ Properly tilts head with one hand on forehead, neck lift or chin lift with other

_____ Checks carotid pulse correctly on near side

_____ Stimulates activation of EMS system

_____ Produces proper body position for compression/ventilation cycles

_____ Does vertical compression

_____ Ventilates properly

_____ Checks pulse and breathing

Checklists are particularly helpful to teachers in diagnosing missing elements in performances, such as in the emergency cardiac care procedure above (see Table 13–8). By entering numbers rather than

---

TABLE 13–8   PREPARING GOOD CHECKLISTS

Advantages of the Checklist Format

---

1. Useful in analysis of learning of psychomotor performances and for determining growth in personal/social areas.
2. May be used for either processes or products.
3. May be used to analyze sequences and correct order of actions.
4. Simple and easy to use.

Disadvantages of the Checklist Format

---

1. Does not permit an estimate of the degree to which a behavior or trait is present.
2. Since only presence or absence of trait or behavior is noted, it is not useful in summarizing general impressions.

Suggestions for Constructing Checklists

---

1. Perform a task analysis on complex psychomotor performances to determine the component behaviors.
2. Clearly specify behaviors or traits to be observed, including any actions that represent common errors.
3. Arrange the behaviors or traits to be observed, including expected errors, in roughly the order they will occur.
4. Keep separate checklists for each person observed. For comparison, transfer information later to a master list.
5. Reduce invalid judgments by giving clear directions and training observers.

---

checks into the blanks (1 for the first action, 2 for the second, and so on) the sequence of actions can be analyzed, a factor that is very important in many performances.

Behavioral Observation   Behavioral observations are made of the occurrence or nonoccurrence of specified categories of behavior, such as talking, writing, reading, fighting, and the like. Typically, one or two categories of behavior are selected for observation and observations are repeated on several occasions to assess possible changes. The behaviors are defined carefully and specified (reading, for instance, may be defined by number of pages read), and then a count is made of the behavior over a period of days or weeks.

Informal behavioral observations can be very useful to you as a teacher. In monitoring group activity, for example, charting student participation can give some extremely useful information on the functioning of the group. By recording participation you can see how much interaction is taking place, who is doing most of the talking, and who is being left out.

Other Evaluation Methods

Anecdotal Records   **Anecdotal records** are written reports of specific incidents. They usually relate to areas of social adjustment, but they may pertain to any area of interest. Many supervisors of student teachers, for example, make extensive use of anecdotal records in which they write comments related to the students' teaching effectiveness.

Anecdotal records can provide information that more formal methods of observation often miss. They are most useful for noting unplanned but significant events that cannot be categorized easily. Although anecdotal records are not as systematic as many other recording methods, they can be rich sources of information to help make decisions concerning students (see Table 13–9).

Sociometric Methods   **Sociometric methods** are used to determine how well individual students are accepted by the class and the class's structure. (See Table 13–10.) One sociometric method is the *nominating technique*, in which students are asked to list a person or persons whom they would choose as companions for various work and play situations. Children are told that their responses will be held in confidence. They may be asked whom they would like to sit next to in the classroom or accompany on a trip. This device can help teachers identify isolated children (those no

---

TABLE 13–9   CONSTRUCTING GOOD ANECDOTAL RECORDS

Advantages of Anecdotal Records

---

1. Record spontaneous events that cannot be measured systematically.

2. Provide in-depth information about events.

3. Increase awareness of unique behaviors of students.

Disadvantages of Anecdotal Records

---

1. Time-consuming to write.

2. May become subjective and gossipy unless writer is well trained.

3. Tend to sample negative or problem behavior.

Suggestions for Constructing Anecdotal Records

---

1. The anecdotal records should be part of a general system for recording student behavior.

2. Each anecdote should be limited to a brief description of a single incident.

3. Record both positive and negative events.

4. Records should be as factual and objective as possible.

5. The record should reveal enough of the context of the behavior so that it is not subject to misinterpretation.

---

one chooses) and understand the general social structure of the classroom. Teachers then may use this information to incorporate isolated children into group activities or to structure groups in the classroom so that wider ranges of acquaintances are developed. Closely related to the nominating method is the *"Guess Who" technique.* Students are given a list of descriptions of persons (such as "this boy makes our class more fun") and are asked to name one or more persons who fit these descriptions.

The information from sociometric techniques can be reported in a variety of ways; for instance, the number of nominations simply can be tallied for each student. Often, however, we also are interested in who

Some children have few friends in their classes. Sociometric methods can help teachers identify such socially isolated students so that they can be helped to interact more with others.

made the nominations. For this purpose, a matrix constructed by listing group members along both the top and side of a grid can be used to tally who made the nominations *and* who received the nominations. Mutual choices can be circled. Students who are most popular (stars) and those who receive no choices at all (isolates) can be identified from this kind of graphical representation. A more complex method, the *sociogram* (Kubiszyn & Borich, 1990) can give us an even clearer picture of the social structure of a group. Isolates, stars, mutual choices, and rejections can be identified clearly by the use of a sociogram, such as the one pictured in Figure 13–1.

TABLE 13–10   USING SOCIOMETRIC METHODS

Advantages of Sociometric Methods

---

1.   Reveal judgments of peers about individuals in class or group.

2.   Relatively simple to design and employ.

Disadvantages of Sociometric Methods

---

1.   Relationships obtained may vary depending on the question asked.

2.   Relationships may be quite unstable, especially in younger children.

3.   Methods are susceptible to faking.

Suggestions for Using Sociometric Methods

---

1.   Write questions that fit the level of the students and that will elicit honest reactions.

2.   Match the number of choices students must make to the level of the students.

3.   Avoid asking negative questions (such as "Whom would you *not* like to go with on a field trip?").

Self-Report Methods   Knowledge of student activities and feelings is desired by many teachers. The more teachers know about students, the better they will be able to provide for their educational and social needs. In **self-reports** students furnish information by talking or writing about themselves; they provide a good way of obtaining in-depth information.

Personal interviews are an important form of self-report. Teachers with well-developed interviewing skills can learn a great deal about students, both cognitively and affectively. The key drawback to interviews, however, is the amount of time they require. With the number of students in most classrooms, an interview with each student is a luxury many teachers simply cannot afford. Other self-report methods are necessary. One such method is the activity checklist. A typical activity checklist asks students to check educational or cultural activities in which they participate outside of school. Activities students perform on their own are of interest to many teachers as they attempt to assess carry-over from classroom experiences.

FIGURE 13–1   A SIMPLE SOCIOGRAM

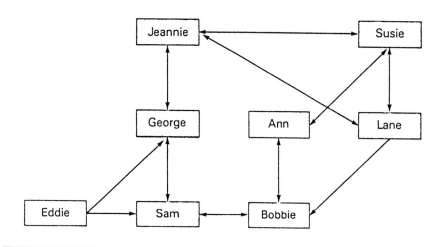

Note: This sociogram shows choices made by children in a fifth-grade class when they were asked, "Who would you like to work with on the project?" Each arrow indicates a positive choice. A two-way arrow indicates that the students chose each other.

Attitude scales are used frequently to allow students to report on feelings and opinions (Anderson, 1988). In an *attitude scale* a person can rate the extent of favorable or unfavorable feelings about a person, group, or topic. Although there are a number of highly sophisticated methods for formal construction of attitude scales, teachers can use attitude scales informally to help determine students' feelings about a variety of topics. The following items related to attitudes toward teaching handicapped students are intended for teacher trainees:

Instructions: Rate each of the following items in this set by circling your choice.
SD = strongly disagree, D = disagree, U = undecided, A = agree, and SA = strongly agree.

1. I'm not temperamentally suited to work with handicapped students.   SD D U A SA

2. I'm looking forward to the challenge of working with handicapped students.   SD D U A SA

This type of scale uses statements that are either positive or negative about the topic in question. Students then rate the degree of their agreement or disagreement with each statement. Of course, such scales are susceptible to "faking" and the possibility of a student's simply giving a socially desirable response should be recognized.

Simple attitude scales designed for children can be quite illuminating, however, since children are less likely to give socially desirable responses or to anticipate how the attitude data will be used. Even with adults, attitude scales can be useful and effective. Respondents must have trust in the person gathering the information, however, and be carefully instructed to respond openly and honestly (see Table 13–11). As you can see, attitude scales greatly resemble the rating scales discussed earlier. The major difference is that attitude scales are more likely to focus on the feelings of respondents than on the objective judgments of raters.

TABLE 13–11   CONSTRUCTING GOOD ATTITUDE SCALES

Advantages of Attitude Scales

---

1. Can be used to learn student feelings toward a variety of topics.

2. May be effectively used in self-appraisal.

Disadvantages of Attitude Scales

---

1. Highly susceptible to responses that are socially desirable and to faking.

2. Measures verbal behavior that may not relate to other forms of behavior.

Suggestions for Constructing Attitude Scales

---

1. Clearly identify the topic (focus) of the attitude measurement.

2. Write clear, direct, and simple statements about the topic.

3. Include both positive and negative statements on your scale.

4. Make sure each statement contains only a single idea.

5. Avoid factual statements.

6. Use the scale under conditions in which persons are likely to give honest and accurate responses.

Grading

Grading, or, as it is sometimes called, marking, is an evaluative activity involving some subjectivity and calling for comparisons. Your ability to use a grading method that actually reflects student achievement is a big step toward becoming an effective teacher. There are many ways of making comparisons but none is flawless—all have strong and weak points. We will examine five of the most common ways of grading and making comparisons.

Norm-Referenced Grading

Many teachers apply the concept of norm-referenced measurement (discussed in Chapter Twelve) to their grading. Norm-referenced grading (sometimes called "grading on the curve") involves evaluating students by comparing them to their classmates. Most teachers do not make arbitrary decisions about what percentage of students will obtain each grade, but this method can be tied to the normal curve by giving fixed percentages of each grade. An unfortunate result of this procedure is that some teachers become more concerned with the statistical distribution of grades than with what their students actually have learned (see Table 13–12).

The norm-referenced approach has some good features. It is based on the often correct assumption that ability and achievement are normally distributed.* When the norm-referenced approach is used,

TABLE 13–12	A GRADE DISTRIBUTION BASED ON THE NORMAL CURVE	
Letter Grade	*Percentage of Students to Receive Grade*
A	7
B	24
C	38
D	24
F	7

---

*At least this is so under ordinary instructional conditions. In criterion-referenced instruction that requires mastery learning (see Chapter Twelve) and in individual tutoring, the normal curve for achievement essentially disappears (Berk, 1988). The majority of students can successfully achieve most classroom goals under ideal instructional conditions.

PRACTICE EXERCISE 13–2   MAKING DECISIONS ABOUT METHODS OF
ASSESSMENT

For each setting use the list below to specify the assessment method
that would be your *first* (not necessarily your only) choice in
attempting to answer the question. Our responses are presented on
page 455.

Assessment Methods

a. Essay testing—restricted response, extended response, or
oral questioning

b. Objective testing—completion, true-false, multiple-choice, or
matching items

c. Ratings—process or product

d. Checklists—process or product

e. Self-report—activity, problem checklists, attitude scales

1. *Setting:* You ask, "I wonder if my students understand the
organization of Congress?"

Method: _____

2. *Setting:* You wonder if your biology students can properly
prepare a specimen for microscopic study.

Method: _____

---

teachers don't have to develop standards of performance—a savings in
time and effort. Additionally, no explanation of the norm-referenced
approach is needed for students, parents, or administrators—everybody has had experience with it. The method also has some severe
deficits. When only a limited number of A's are allowed, the difference
between the lowest A and the highest B often is trivial. The possibility
also exists than an entire class could work hard, learn a great deal, and

---

3.   *Setting:* "How successful has my unit in music appreciation been?"

     Method: _____

4.   *Setting:* Is little Al, who plays the tuba, ready to move into the senior band?

     Method: _____

5.   *Setting:* You wonder if your students read current events on their own.

     Method: _____

6.   *Setting:* You need to know if your students can relate the principles of civil liberties contained in the Constitution to today's news stories.

     Method: _____

7.   *Setting:* What knowledge do your students have of important accounting terminology?

     Method: _____

8.   *Setting:* Could your students tell the difference between a logical and an illogical argument?

     Method: _____

---

the majority still obtain only mediocre grades. There also is no way to differentiate between the "easy A" obtained in one class and the A in another class that required much more effort. Another shortcoming is the highly competitive atmosphere that can be generated in a classroom in which norm-referenced grading is used. In some classes students have actually sabotaged their classmates' work in order to win the competition for higher grades.

Criterion-Referenced
Grading

Criterion-referenced grading is based on the criterion-referenced measurement approach discussed in Chapter Twelve. In this method, teachers determine a standard of performance and grade students based on *how well they attain the standards* rather than comparing students to each other. A welding instructor, for example, may set a standard of five consecutive correct welds for students. For a class in chemistry, the teacher might require that students correctly identify the unknown element in two of three solutions.

One of the strongest points of the criterion-referenced approach is that students are not in competition with each other for a limited number of good grades. Instead, students compete with themselves to meet a well-defined standard of performance. A second advantage is that a student's relative standing in a class is not as important as the mastery of objectives. This eliminates the possibility of a student learning a great deal and still not obtaining a good grade. Criterion-referenced grading is especially well suited to all forms of individualized instruction.

The criterion-referenced approach also has disadvantages. The teacher, often without any firm guidelines from curricula or standardized measures, must set the standards of performance. If the standards are set too high it can result in an excessive number of failures. On the other hand, if the standards are set too low, students may obtain grades they really don't deserve (an A for little or no work, for instance). Criterion-referenced grading requires well-written objectives. While we certainly do not believe this is a major shortcoming, teachers who do not use objectives will have great difficulty in implementing a criterion-referenced approach. Well-written objectives that contain clearly specified criteria easily can be used, however, to set standards of performance.

A recurring problem with criterion-referenced grading is how to turn the results of comparisons with standards into number or letter grades. When students master objectives, their performance certainly deserves an A. But should students who just miss the standard of performance obtain F's? In a different vein, suppose you ask students to write a report about a field trip. One student turns in a report that meets all of your standards and, in fact, goes much further. Obviously, this paper deserves an A. But what about another student who turns in a report that just barely meets your standards with nothing extra at all? Does this student also obtain an A? Supporters of the criterion-referenced approach might say yes, but a lot of teachers might wish to give this second report a B or C.

"I'm afraid, Billy, there's no such thing as a no-fault math test."

One way to deal with these problems is to award grades on the basis of a percentage of objectives mastered. Students who master 90 percent or more of the objectives receive an A. Students who master between 80 and 89 percent obtain a B, and so on. This approach allows teachers to grade on the basis of standards of performance and further allows any number of students to make A's or B's and so on. Of course, some critics suggest that introducing percentages violates the criterion-referenced approach and is a form of norm-referenced evaluation.

Grading on Improvement

Some teachers feel that grades should be based on the amount of improvement or growth students demonstrate during a grading period. Those students who show the greatest improvement obtain A's; those with less improvement receive lower grades. This method actually is a norm-referenced approach using comparisons of improvement rather than absolute levels of achievement. With the addition of two disadvantages, the advantages and disadvantages of the norm-referenced approach apply here. First, the students who know the most about new material at the beginning of a unit are penalized, and, second, students might be encouraged to fake ignorance at the beginning of a unit so that their "growth" will seem greater than it is.

Grading on Expectations

There are teachers who believe they should assign grades to students on the basis of what the students are *capable* of doing, rather than by comparing their achievement to a standard of performance or norms. In this method, a student could achieve the highest score on a test and still be told, "Eddie, you're able to do a lot better than this. I'm not going to give you an A until you work up to your potential."

In contract grading, the teacher and student jointly determine objectives, how they will be used, and how each grade can be obtained.

We don't recommend this form of grading. The problems associated with it include the extreme difficulty of determining students' abilities, the difficulty of deciding if a student has actually worked up to his or her potential, and the punishment, on occasion, of high achievement. A teacher's grading decisions with this method largely are subjective and prone to errors.

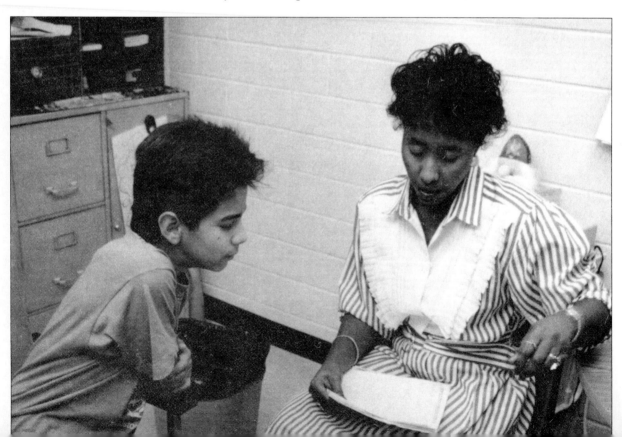

Grading by Contract   There are several different methods whereby the teacher and student can contract for grades in a course. In grading by contract the teacher and individual students jointly choose objectives to be met and the methods of demonstrating mastery of objectives. A student and teacher might agree that the student's completion of a book report meeting certain criteria, four summaries of short stories meeting specific standards, and one eight-stanza poem composed by the student will constitute a grade of A for a three-week grading period. In general, methods that involve grading by contract are best suited to programs where instruction is individualized. Contract grading allows the teacher to utilize standards of performance for the mastery of objectives while at the same time taking each student's entry level into account.

Applications for Teaching: Mistakes to Avoid When Grading

Several authors have provided excellent lists of commonly made mistakes in grading (see Hills, 1976; Palmer, 1962; Payne, 1974). We have prepared a composite list of seven errors in grading you should *avoid*.

1. Abdicating responsibility. Don't adjust your courses so that you can use tests developed by other teachers or textbook writers, regardless of how overworked you are.

2. Employing grades to alter attitudes. Don't give bonus points for good behavior or subtract points for misbehavior.

3. Becoming lazy. No matter how much you might dislike grading, don't base students' semester or course grades on a single test.

4. Going overboard. Don't make your courses an exercise in endurance in which students are assessed for everything short of the number of times they shift in their seat.

5. Using "special insight." Don't come to the conclusion that you have special insights allowing you to "see" how much students have learned without using any measurements.

6. Increasing difficulty levels. Don't change the difficulty level of your tests as the course progresses in an attempt to increase the standards of the course.

7. Demanding perfection. Students are human too.

Grading is a complex issue without clear-cut answers. Each grading method has strong and weak points. As you develop your own grading approach you may choose one of those we summarize or work out your own. No matter what the method, however, the most important factor is that grades should be a fair, objective reflection of student achievement.

Summary

This chapter was concerned with teacher-constructed forms of evaluation. The most widely used method of evaluating the mastery of cognitive objectives is testing, but testing also is used to evaluate components of psychomotor and affective learning. Teachers always should start the planning of a test from their objectives and the emphasis given to those objectives in their lessons. The best tests are constructed from tables of specifications, which help ensure that the levels of learning required in the objectives are reflected on the tests.

Test questions can be grouped into two major categories, essay and objective. Essay questions, whether open-ended, restricted-response, or oral, have the advantage of causing students to organize their thoughts and to present them in cogent oral or written form. Because of sampling and logistic problems, restricted response essay questions probably are best for most purposes.

Objective questions generally require far less subjectivity in scoring than do essay questions. Well-written objective items can sample higher levels of student learning and need not be restricted to assessing knowledge of facts. The most flexible form of objective question is the multiple-choice item, but true-false, matching, and completion items also are widely used.

Observational methods of evaluation typically are better suited to psychomotor and affective learning than are tests. Additionally, observational methods frequently can be used in conjunction with tests to evaluate the mastery of cognitive objectives.

Observations can be made of either process or products. Most observational evaluation methods are appropriate for either. Descriptions were provided for rating scales, checklists, behavioral observations, anecdotal records, sociometric methods, and self-report methods. Guides for the development and use of each form as well as the advantages and disadvantages of each were presented. Five methods of grading were discussed as well as several mistakes in grading that should be avoided.

Suggested Readings

Ebel, R. L., & Frisbie, D. A. (1986). *Essentials of educational measurement* (4th ed.). Englewood Cliffs, NJ: Prentice-Hall.

This book provides a good, intermediate-level discussion of teacher-made tests.

Herman, J. L. (1988). Item writing techniques. In J. P. Keeves (Ed.). *Educational research, methodology, and measurement: An international handbook.* New York: Pergamon Press.
  Although written at a high level, this chapter is an outstanding source for test development.

Kubiszyn, T., & Borich, G. (1990). *Educational testing and measurement: Classroom application and practice* (2nd ed.). Glenview, Illinois: Scott, Foresman.
  This book is an excellent source for teachers' test construction.

Wainer, H., & Braun, H. (1987). *Test validity.* Hillsdale, NJ: Erlbaum.
  Though advanced, this volume is an excellent exposition on the topic of test validity.

Answers to Practice Exercise 13-1

1. The flaw in the original item was the brevity of the stem. It did not communicate a meaningful problem to readers. A better version is:
    Reliability refers to the extent to which a test
    a.   measures the content it is supposed to measure
    (b.) consistently measures what it is supposed to measure
    c.   contains components of measurement error
    d.   loses value as its length decreases

2. The major flaw in the original item was the inordinate length of alternative *d*. The following item is much better:
    In norm-referenced testing you are comparing an individual's performance to
    (a.) the performance of   c.   a standard of "normal others   work"
    b.   a person's own   d.   a standard of excellence performance

3. Alternatives *d* ("*a* and *c* above") and *e* ("all of the above") in the original item were poor. They are likely to confuse students. Avoid such alternatives. Here is our improved item:
    A test that measures achievement against a standard of performance (for example, many driver's license examinations) is called a
    a.   norm-referenced test   (c.) criterion-referenced test
    b.   reliable test   d.   psychomotor test

4. The original item contained a stem too short to present a meaningful problem. The following is better:
The reliability of a test can best be improved by
    a.   shortening the test
    b.   including more difficult items
    (c.) lengthening the test
    d.   making it criterion-referenced

5. The correct answer was the only alternative (*a*) that agreed grammatically with the stem. An alternative could be:
The most justifiable criticism of teacher-made tests is that they
    (a.) often emphasize rote learning
    b.   discriminate against poorer students
    c.   sample more broadly than is actually necessary
    d.   are less reliable than other forms of evaluation

6. The original item was stated negatively ("not be justified in . . .") and alternatives *d* and *e* were inappropriate. Better phrasing would be:
If your goal were to sample students' recall of information from a wide variety of content areas, you would be justified in using
    (a.) multiple-choice questions
    b.   oral essay questions
    c.   restricted essay questions
    d.   open-ended essay questions

7. The original item contained alternatives that did not offer readers any clear distinctions. This version does:
Grading essay items by counting the number of lines would likely be
    a.   unreliable and invalid
    (b.) reliable and invalid
    c.   reliable and valid
    d.   valid and unreliable

8. The original item contained a negatively worded stem ("typically are not"). The new item avoids the problem:
Teacher-made tests usually have reasonably high
    (a.) content validity
    b.   internal consistency
    c.   test-retest reliability
    d.   construct validity

9. The original item had a stem so brief it could not communicate a meaningful problem to readers. The version below is better:
Rating scales are most commonly used for which forms of learning?
   a. rote and knowledge
   b. social and behavioral
   c. application and analysis
   (d.) psychomotor and affective

10. The original item was negatively worded, as were two of the alternatives. This item is much easier to understand:
Sociograms have two basic classroom uses. They are
   a. assessing cognitive and psychomotor learning
   b. assessing affective and psychomotor learning
   (c.) identifying isolates and group interactions
   d. establishing content validity and internal consistency

Answers to Practice Exercise 13–2

1. *(b) Objective testing.* Some form of objective testing probably is best for determining knowledge of a complex organization such as the Congress. In order to adequately sample all of these areas, multiple questions would be required.

2. *(d) Checklist.* A checklist would be our first choice. The steps involved in preparing a specimen could be outlined in detail and students could be assessed on their completion of these steps.

3. *(e) Self-report.* In order to assess the affective component, our choice would be self-report—either activity checklists (number of music pieces listened to, any records purchased, and so on) or simple attitude scales ("compared to six months ago, my enjoyment of music of the baroque period is (a) greater than it was then, (b) about the same, (c) less than it was then"). As mentioned in the chapter, basic knowledge in an area may be necessary in order for higher-level affective objectives to be reached. Some form of testing, either essay or objective, also may be appropriate. One caution, however, is that cognitive assessment should not be used in such a way that it generates negative attitudes toward the subject area.

4. *(c) Ratings.* A rating scale is probably most appropriate. A comparative scale, in which standard performances form the basis for judgment, may be useful.

5. *(e) Self-report.* The problem basically is one of determining motivation. Assessment of reading habits, however, can form an important basis for determining the appropriate levels of instruction for the students. An activity checklist would reveal a great deal to the teacher about students' reading habits.

6. *(a) Essay test.* This type of knowledge typically is assessed by essay examinations, often the extended-response type. In essay tests the student has the opportunity to organize his or her thoughts and to explain relationships between principles and events. An oral question also is well suited for this type of situation. The objective test, particularly multiple-choice questions, should not be eliminated from consideration, however. With proper construction, multiple choice items could measure students' abilities to apply principles.

7. *(b) Objective questions.* Knowledge of terminology is best assessed by means of objective questions. The multiple-choice format is quite versatile for most levels of learning.

8. *(a) Essay test.* The students could be instructed to judge each argument as logical or illogical in a restricted-response essay and to briefly outline the reasons for their judgment. If the argument is a complex one (for example, a court opinion), the extended-response essay would be required. Objective items such as multiple-choice questions should not be eliminated automatically. A series of well-constructed items in an interpretive exercise can effectively assess students' abilities to judge the logic in an argument.

CHAPTER

14

Standardized Tests

CHARACTERISTICS OF STANDARDIZED TESTS
- [ ] Achievement Tests
- [ ] Diagnostic Achievement Tests
- [ ] Single-Subject-Area Achievement Tests
- [ ] Survey Batteries
- [ ] Uses of Standardized Achievement Tests
- [ ] Summary of Achievement Tests

ABILITY TESTS
- [ ] Intelligence Tests and Scholastic Aptitude Tests
- [ ] Uses of Ability Test Results
- [ ] Summary of Ability Tests

MEASURES OF INTERESTS

INTERPRETING SCORES ON A STANDARDIZED TEST
- [ ] How Scores Are Described
- [ ] The Normal Curve
- [ ] Reporting Standardized Test Scores
- [ ] Imprecision of Scores: Standard Error of Measurement

PROFESSIONAL ETHICS AND STANDARDIZED TESTS

APPLICATIONS FOR TEACHING:
Ethical Test Use

SUMMARY

SUGGESTED READINGS

ANSWERS TO PRACTICE EXERCISE

OVERVIEW

Few educational issues have caused as much controversy as the use of standardized tests (Mehrens & Lehman, 1986). On the one hand, some persons have demanded that standardized tests not be used at all, declaring their use to be unethical, contrary to the aims of education, and against the best interests of children, especially minority group children (Cooper et al., 1988). On the other hand, proponents of standardized tests argue that they are excellent educational tools, among the most accurate and least biased measures of students' achievements, abilities, and interests (see Ebel & Frisbie, 1986; Gronlund, 1988).

Obviously, with such a marked divergence of opinion, they all can't be right: somebody has to be wrong—or everybody has to be at least partly wrong. In spite of this, it seems that standardized tests will be part of the educational scene for many years to come. No doubt their form will change from time to time, and the extent of their use will wax and wane, but they will continue to be used in education and it will be necessary for teachers to be knowledgeable about them.

As a teacher, you frequently will come into contact with standardized tests. You are likely to be asked to administer them and to interpret their results. The proper understanding and use of standardized tests can enhance your performance as a teacher. Their misuse can lead to poor decisions that may harm students' educational careers.

This chapter will provide you with basic information about standardized tests so that you will be able to weigh the issues with accuracy and to communicate with your future students and their parents about such tests. The chapter will survey the concepts and principles underlying all standardized tests and will deal specifically with the kinds of standardized tests used most often in education: achievement tests, ability tests, and interest inventories.

OBJECTIVES

After reading this chapter, you should be able to meet the following objectives.

1. Select the appropriate type(s) of standardized test(s) for given purposes.

2. Properly interpret test scores to students, parents, and others, correctly conveying meanings of such concepts as mean, median, mode, standard deviation, z-score, T score, percen-

tile rank, standard error of measurement, age and grade equivalents, and IQ scores.

3. Explain to students and parents their rights to privacy and the confidentiality of standardized test scores and other personal school records.

Characteristics of Standardized Tests

In Chapters Twelve and Thirteen we outlined the basic principles of measurement and discussed how you can create classroom tests based on sound measurement principles. This chapter shifts from teacher-made tests to commercially published standardized tests that schools purchase.

Standardized tests have three factors that set them apart from other forms of tests: (1) They have been carefully prepared, tried out, analyzed, and reviewed; (2) the instructions and conditions for administering and scoring them are uniform; and (3) the test results may be interpreted by comparison with tables of norms (Ebel & Frisbie, 1986).

Development of a typical standardized test begins with a table of specifications or plan that describes either curriculum content or specific mental abilities to be measured. Items then are carefully developed, reviewed, and revised. They are pretested, and the best items are chosen for the final form of the test.

Uniform directions make it possible to accurately interpret standardized test results over the wide range of users (Gronlund, 1988). If one test administrator were to allow thirty minutes for a part of a test and another only fifteen, the results of the two testing sessions would not be comparable. Uniform directions and administration are mandatory for valid standardized testing.

Tables of norms are developed by administration of the test to a standardized group. The **standardization sample** (norm group) is a carefully selected sample of persons representative of the individuals for whom the test is targeted. Their scores, called *norms*, serve as the frame of reference by which the scores of your students are evaluated. A 100-item test designed to measure reading comprehension among junior high school and high school students might first be given to several thousand representative junior high and high school students across the country. Care would be taken to represent all racial and

For today's students, veterans of a barrage of standardized tests, scenes like this one are familiar.

ethnic groups, socioeconomic levels, and areas of the country in the norm group. After the test is given, the test maker would have test scores that might show, for example, that beginning seventh graders in the norm group averaged 52 questions right, beginning eighth graders averaged 59 questions right, and so on. Future takers of the test then will have their performances compared to these scores.

How does one know whether a particular standardized test is valid for a given purpose? The starting point, of course, should be a specific definition of the kind of information sought through testing. To select the proper test, we first need to identify our reasons for testing. Are we interested in assessing attainment of instructional objectives, in grouping students, or in advising students about their vocational goals? Each different use, of course, implies a very different type of standardized test.

Although there are many ways in which standardized tests can be categorized, one of the most common is to group them according to their purposes into three broad classes: (1) achievement tests, (2) ability tests, and (3) interest inventories. Most schools have a standardized testing program that includes all three kinds of tests (Cooper et al., 1988).

Achievement Tests

Achievement tests are designed to measure the knowledge and abilities of students in subject matter areas (Gronlund, 1988). Table 14–1 contrasts standardized achievement tests to those constructed by classroom teachers. The amount of effort and expertise brought to bear on the development of a test and the goals of testing differ for these two types of tests. Commercial achievement tests usually are prepared by a team of measurement, research, and curriculum experts who work full-time on the development of a test, while a classroom teacher has to

---

TABLE 14–1   A COMPARISON OF TEACHER-MADE AND STANDARDIZED TESTS

Teacher-Made Achievement Tests	*Standardized Achievement Tests*
1. Directions sometimes are flexible, not uniform.	1. Directions for administering and scoring are uniform.
2. Test content is based on the teacher's own objectives. Content is specific to what has been taught.	2. Test content is determined by experts who survey texts and curricula to attempt to determine national trends.
3. Test construction is specific to the teacher's needs and time constraints. Less trying out or revision.	3. Test construction is meticulous. Tests are tried out and revised until they are at an excellent technical level.
4. Students' scores are compared only to the scores of students in the same classroom or to a criterion level established as a "passing" score.	4. Students' scores may be compared to national norms that usually include ages and grade equivalents.
5. Best suited for determining whether classroom objectives have been met. Useful as a basis for grading and marking.	5. Most appropriate for assessing broad curriculum goals, comparing students to national norms, and evaluating the performance of a teaching program.
6. Most useful for assessing specific weaknesses of individual students.	6. Most useful for identifying gaps in general ability or knowledge.
7. Prediction usually not advisable.	7. Prediction of future performance can often be made.

develop dozens of tests on top of all the other duties of teaching. Typically, standardized achievement tests are superior for estimation of overall student performance because of the care in their construction and the *availability of norms*. Teacher-made tests, in contrast, usually are superior for assessing the mastery of classroom objectives.

In general, there are three types of standardized achievement tests: (1) diagnostic tests, designed to identify patterns of students' strengths and weaknesses in specific areas; (2) single-subject-area tests, which assess students' general knowledge and abilities in a particular subject area; and (3) survey batteries (or, as they are sometimes called, multi-test batteries), which really are a set of single-subject-area tests standardized on the same norm group. All three forms of achievement tests are important to teachers. Because they have different purposes, cover different content, and are constructed differently (Sax, 1989) we shall examine each in more detail.

Diagnostic Achievement Tests

Diagnostic achievement tests are designed to identify weaknesses in students' knowledge or abilities in specific subject areas. They usually are employed when other information indicates the possibility of deficiencies in skills or knowledge. A diagnostic arithmetic test, for example, may help us determine if students have trouble with fractions, addition, or long division, while a diagnostic reading test may help us determine if students are poorly prepared in phonics, word-attack skills, vocabulary, or comprehension.

Diagnostic tests are very valuable for locating weaknesses, but they usually do not give us information about *why* weaknesses exist. Teachers must follow up diagnostic tests with direct observation of student performance to find out why difficulties exist.

Single-Subject-Area Achievement Tests

Single-subject-area achievement tests provide in-depth coverage of one subject area. In elementary school, the most common single-subject tests are those for reading and arithmetic. Reading-readiness tests, for example, often are administered near the end of the kindergarten year to identify students who are not yet ready for reading and to group students for instruction.

A wide range of single-subject-area tests also is available at the upper elementary and high school levels. Single-subject tests can be particularly appropriate in subjects, such as music and foreign languages, unlikely to be covered in a survey battery. Some schools rely on particular single-subject tests because their content coincides closely with the objectives of the schools' programs.

Survey Batteries

Wide-range achievement tests with several subtests that assess knowledge and abilities across many subject areas are referred to as *survey batteries*. Such broad-spectrum tests allow us to assess students' strengths and weaknesses in several subject areas. Survey batteries most commonly are used in the elementary grades, although there are several designed for use in secondary schools. The principle advantage of survey batteries is that each subtest has been standardized on the same norm group. This allows norm-based comparisons of students' relative performance across each of the subtests. The basic skills and subtests listed in Table 14–2 are typical of those appearing in such survey batteries as the California Achievement Tests, the Iowa Tests of Basic Skills, the Metropolitan Achievement Tests, and the Stanford Achievement Tests.

TABLE 14–2   BASIC SKILLS AND SUBTESTS IN A TYPICAL SURVEY BATTERY

Basic Skill	Subtest
Reading	Decoding (e.g., basic discrimination) Comprehension (i.e., constructing meaning) Vocabulary (giving meaning of words)
Writing, expression	Spelling Mechanics (e.g., punctuation, capitalization) Parts of speech (e.g., identifying verbs, nouns, adverbs)
Mathematics	Basic computation (addition, subtraction, multiplication, division) Definitions of mathematics concepts Solving story problems
Study Skills	Reading graphs, charts, and tables General library skills (e.g., using the card catalog)

Uses of Standardized Achievement Tests

Some schools purchase, administer, and score achievement tests and then simply file the scores. This practice is questionable both ethically and economically. Achievement tests have many potentially valuable uses for classroom teachers, counselors, administrators, and students themselves. Information that can be gleaned from achievement tests can be used in a variety of ways to help develop better educational programs.

Uses in Classroom Instruction.   Throughout this text we emphasize that instruction should begin at the point where students need it. Diagnostic tests and readiness tests help us determine where students are having difficulty and give us some basis for determining why the difficulties exist. Once teachers have identified the problem, they may begin to devise remedial instruction. This use alone makes standardized achievement tests potentially valuable. Single-subject tests and survey batteries also may be used to determine the strong and weak points of a class, allowing teachers to adjust their instructional techniques. Standardized test results can help identify objectives that have not been met and need to be reviewed.

Another classroom use of standardized achievement tests is to monitor grading procedures (Mehrens & Lehmann, 1986). We all have heard stories to the effect that Ms. Snell is a "hard grader" in math and Ms. Simms is an "easy grader." While standardized tests should not be used to assign grades (Gronlund, 1988), someone like Ms. Simms can compare the performance of her students to that of Ms. Snell's pupils on the same test. If Ms. Simms's students do not perform as well as Ms. Snell's on standardized measures of achievement, then perhaps Ms. Simms should consider adjusting her grading or teaching practices.

A more general use of standardized achievement test results is the overall determination of strengths and weaknesses of all students. As we noted in Chapter Thirteen, tests can be used to help place students in educational programs. Achievement test results allow us to make more accurate decisions in placing new or transfer students into appropriate educational experiences. The results of achievement tests also can be used to help determine who might benefit from enrichment activities and who needs remedial work. If it is instructionally sound to group students to provide more individualized instruction, standardized achievement test results can supply some of the information for that decision-making process.

It is important to remember that achievement tests should never be used as the sole source of information for instructional decisions (Mehrens & Lehmann, 1986). These tests can provide teachers with another perspective on the achievement of their classes that will complement their own observations and evaluations. They can add information about individuals and groups teachers should consider before making decisions.

Uses for Guidance.   Achievement test results can be used to help students make decisions about their educational and vocational goals. A student who professes a desire to become a research scientist, for example, might be asked some pointed questions by a counselor who notes that the student's achievement test scores in math and science are well below average. The counselor further may point out that the chances of success in the field, given such scores, have not been promising for similar students. The counselor would want the student to realize his or her strengths, weaknesses, and interests and to use these in making a decision. Given the information, the student may make a more realistic choice.

Uses for Evaluation of Instruction.   Standardized achievement tests may be used as a part of the process of evaluating instruction. The performance of students in one class may be compared to other local classes and to norm groups as a reference point in order to check progress. Caution must be urged, however, in the use of achievement tests for this purpose (see Porter, 1988). First, no two classes of students are identical. Second, like any test, achievement tests measure previous learning. A third-grade teacher may be very effective but not be able to make up everything that was badly taught in previous years. Third, no two teachers teach alike. Different skills are emphasized at different times by different teachers. Fourth, some teachers "teach for the test" when they know their teaching will be evaluated by a standardized test. Learning of test content occurs at the expense of concepts not specific to the test, and high scores on the test may not indicate a generally high level of knowledge.

Summary of Achievement Tests

Standardized achievement tests measure the knowledge and abilities of students in subject matter areas. Diagnostic and readiness achievement tests can help us identify student weaknesses and help provide the basis from which we develop remedial instruction. Single-subject achievement tests and survey batteries allow us to compare students' performances to one another and to national norms. Typically, the results of standardized achievement tests are used to help guide teaching practices, to provide guidance for students, and to help evaluate instruction.

Ability Tests

As we discussed in Chapter Four, intelligence tests are designed to measure students' general mental abilities. Like any other form of ability test, intelligence tests measure what the individual has learned. They provide a general estimate of how much people have profited from past experience and how well they will adapt to new situations.

The most prominent of the individual intelligence tests, the Stanford-Binet and the Wechsler Intelligence Scales, are discussed in Chapter Four. They are designed for administration to one person at a time. For most individual tests, a trained examiner is required to give directions, present problems, interpret answers, and score the overall test results.

While the term **intelligence test** is commonly used to refer to individual mental-ability tests such as the Stanford-Binet and the Wechsler Scales, its use is much less common in describing group tests of mental ability. Instead, these group tests often are referred to as **scholastic aptitude tests** (Cohen, 1988). There are several reasons for this difference in labeling: (1) many people wrongly associate the term *intelligence* with inherited ability, (2) there is a great deal of controversy over the concept of intelligence (what it means and what it includes), and (3) group tests usually are employed to predict later scholastic performance (Carey, 1988).

Unlike individual intelligence tests, scholastic aptitude tests are given in groups. They require the examinee to read questions and to mark responses on an answer sheet. There is little one-to-one contact with the examiner, whose role usually is restricted to reading test instructions, timing the test, and distributing and gathering up the answer sheets. Most scholastic aptitude tests consist of multiple-choice items presented in a booklet.

Compared to individual intelligence tests, these features might be considered disadvantages, but they are compensated for in part by the ease with which large numbers of people can be tested. Little time is spent in administering and scoring the tests. Additionally, if the test manual is followed carefully, the administrators need not have the level of skill required for administering individual measures of intelligence.

Scholastic aptitude tests sometimes yield a single score as a global measure of scholastic aptitude, but more often they provide a separate verbal (V) and quantitative (Q) score. The assumption behind separate verbal and quantitative scores is that the verbal scores best predict achievement in courses in which verbal concepts are emphasized (such as English, social studies) and quantitative scores best predict success in mathematics-based areas (algebra, chemistry, physics, and the like).

The separate scores generally provide a basis for differential prediction and may alert a teacher to areas in which students may encounter difficulties (Murphy & Davidshofer, 1988).

Many schools have testing programs in which scholastic aptitude tests are administered (Anastasia, 1988). Each year, for example, over two and a half million high school seniors take the Scholastic Aptitude Test (SAT), which has a major impact on admissions decisions in many colleges and universities. Similarly, a large number of students take the American College Testing (ACT) Program Test. Other examples of scholastic aptitude tests widely used at elementary and secondary levels are the Henmon-Nelson Tests of Mental Abilities, the California Tests of Mental Maturity, and the Otis-Lennon School Ability Test. An example of the types of items appearing on these tests is presented in Figure 14–1.

FIGURE 14–1   SAMPLE ITEMS FROM THE OTIS-LENNON SCHOOL ABILITY TEST

Practice Problems

V. △ is to ▲ as □ is to —   a. ▫   b. △   c. ■   d. ▴   e. ◼

W. The numbers in the box go together in a certain way. Find the number that goes where you see the question mark (?) in the box.

6	7	8
5	6	7
4	5	?

f. 9 g. 8 h. 7 j. 6 k. 5

X. What letter comes next in this series?
A   B   D   E   G   H   J   K   ?
a. N b. M c. L d. K e. I

Y. Hat is to head as shoe is to —
f. sock g. toe h. buckle j. leg k. foot

Z. The drawings in the first part of the row go together to form a series. In the next part of the row, find the drawing that goes where you see the question mark (?) in the series.

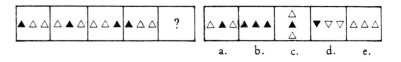

PRACTICE EXERCISE 14–1   REVIEWING STANDARDIZED TESTS

There is no better way to become acquainted with standardized tests than by reading them and their accompanying manuals. Utilizing your school's library, the counseling center, or a public school materials center, summarize on the following form an achievement test, a scholastic aptitude test, or an interest inventory. You may wish to consult with the Buros *Mental Measurement Yearbooks* for aid in reviewing the test you choose.

1. Test name _____

2. Publisher _____

3. Purpose of the test _____

    _____

    _____

    _____

4. Statements of validity and reliability (drawn from Buros or the test manuals)

    _____

    _____

    _____

5. Desirable features (if any) _____

    _____

Scholastic aptitude tests are generally considered somewhat less reliable and less valid than individual intelligence tests. An examiner giving an individual test can clear up misunderstandings and probe for more complete answers without damaging the standardized nature of the test, but this is not possible in a group test. Also, scholastic aptitude tests rely heavily on reading and reading speed so that poor or slow readers, regardless of their level of ability, may be penalized.

PRACTICE EXERCISE 14–1   CONTINUED

6. Undesirable features (if any) _____
    _____

7. Competitors (drawn from Buros) _____
    _____
    _____

8. General comments and recommendations on the use of the
    test _____
    _____
    _____

9. Personal, affective reactions to the test _____
    _____
    _____

A second activity that you may find helpful is to visit a counseling center and complete your own interest inventory. This is especially useful if you are still not quite sure what vocational and educational directions you wish to take.

---

*O. K. Buros's Mental Measurement Yearbooks (MMYs) contain expert critical reviews of all existing tests in print. The latest MMY is the tenth (Lincoln, NE: Buros Institute of Mental Measurements, 1989). Because of their objectivity, the MMYs are the most trustworthy source to consult in evaluating any standardized test.

Scholastic aptitude tests do *not* provide a good estimate of undeveloped learning potential for pupils from cultural minorities or disadvantaged homes or for students with poor reading skills. Neither scholastic aptitude tests nor intelligence tests measure native capacity or learning potential *directly*. Such tests are valid measures of learning potential only if all pupils have had an equal opportunity to learn the types of tasks presented on the test, are equally motivated, and have no hindrances (such as reading difficulties or emotional problems). Consequently, it is never proper to interpret scholastic aptitude scores as direct and unmodifiable measures of academic learning potential (see Anastasia, 1988; Cohen, 1988).

Uses of Ability Test
Results

Before discussing the uses of ability tests, we must point out that the results of any such test should be viewed very cautiously. An IQ or other mental-ability score is only one bit of evidence to be added to other information about a person. It is quite possible for a student to have a "bad day" when a test is given. Illness, hunger, fatigue, and just "feeling rotten" can lower a person's performance on standardized tests. Additionally, we should be alert to possible cultural biases in intelligence and scholastic aptitude tests. It is clear that environment (experience) directly influences the learned skills measured on ability tests. Obviously, for example, a student's vocabulary knowledge will be determined by the kind of vocabulary used in his or her immediate environment. The importance of one or two test scores should not be overemphasized in making decisions about students' futures.

Uses for Placement.   Intelligence and scholastic aptitude tests, along with other information about students, may help us identify those children who would benefit from special programs. The use of such tests in placement, particularly in the placement of mentally retarded students in special education, has been seriously challenged, however (see Chapter Fifteen).

Uses for Guidance.   A well-trained counselor's careful use of ability test results can be helpful in providing guidance for students and their parents who are making educational and vocational plans. Combined with achievement test results, grades, and indications of interests, a measure of general learning ability can help us give students a more complete picture of themselves.

Uses for Classroom Instruction.   There are few uses of ability tests in classroom instruction. It is possible to use ability test results to alter the form and pacing of your instruction to more closely meet your students' needs, but other information will likely be more valuable for instructional decisions than will knowledge of students' intelligence and aptitude test scores.

Summary of Ability Tests

Ability tests are designed to measure individuals' abilities to profit from experience and to adapt to new situations. They fall into two major categories. Individual intelligence tests have the advantage of the interaction of a trained examiner and a subject, a process usually resulting in a reliable and valid measure. Group tests, usually referred to as scholastic aptitude tests, are more efficient to administer to large numbers of people and do not require highly skilled testers. Intelligence and scholastic aptitude test results can be used in conjunction with other information in placement and guidance decisions, but they have limited application for classroom instruction. Teachers must recognize the role of cultural background and academic preparation in each student's score and should refrain from making any inferences about innate or native potential from a student's score.

Measures of Interests

The discussion so far has revolved around measures of achievement and ability, but we continually have emphasized that the results of achievement and ability measures must be used in conjunction with other information, particularly information about academic performance and interests. In this section, we shall briefly survey interest inventories.*

Interests usually are defined as feelings toward activities. **Interest inventories**, then, are designed to assess how people feel about various kinds of activities. The first interest inventory was developed by G. Stanley Hall in 1907 to assess children's interests in various types of recreation. It was not until 1919, however, during a summer institute at the Carnegie Institute of Technology, that an interest inventory was created based on formal scientific approaches. The Strong Vocational Interest Blank was developed from the work at that institute and

---

*There are other types of noncognitive measures besides interest inventories. You have probably heard of tests like the Rorschach "inkblot" test, the Minnesota Multiphasic Personality Inventory, and similar instruments. Such personality tests are not appropriate for general use in the schools and should not be administered as regular parts of school testing programs (see Mehrens & Lehman, 1986). They reveal little to the teacher that cannot be gained from a careful observation of a student's behavior.

remained the only standardized interest inventory available for twenty years. The Strong inventory since has been revised several times and now appears as the Strong-Campbell Interest Inventory (SCII).

Other measures of interest include the Kuder Preference Record, the Kuder Occupational Interest Survey, the Jackson Vocational Interest Survey, the Lee-Thorpe Occupational Interest Inventory, and Guilford's Interest Survey. In general, interest inventories are based on five assumptions:

1.   Interests are learned, not innate.

2.   Children's interests are unstable but become relatively permanent by early adulthood.

3.   People in specific occupations or educational programs have common likes and dislikes for activities.

4.   There are differences in how intensely people feel about participating in certain activities.

5.   Interests motivate people to select activities and to continue in them.

Typically, interest inventories contain several scales that have been standardized on specific vocational groups (artists, mechanics, photographers, psychologists) or specific educational groups (pre-med students, engineering students). People's responses on the inventory are compared to the norm group's responses. A counselor might say, "The results of your interest inventory indicate you have many interests in common with musicians and not so many in common with physicians or dentists. Perhaps it would clarify matters if we looked at what it is about medicine and dentistry that seemed to attract you at first."

One very important factor to keep in mind about interest inventories is that they are not really tests because no item has a "right" answer (Mehrens & Lehmann, 1986). There is nothing "right" or "wrong" about a young woman preferring the sciences to business, for example.

Faking is a problem with interest inventories. Suppose you were asked to respond to the following item:

Choose the one statement that you agree with the most.

a.   I very much enjoy gardening.

b.   I really enjoy playing cards.

c.   I like to contemplate my navel.

If for some reason you wanted to convey to the test administrator that you were industrious, you might mark *a*, even though you really didn't like gardening all that much.

Then, too, items such as this cannot possibly deal with people who like activities *a, b,* and *c* equally well. There is also no way for such items to reflect the intensity of a person's feelings. In general, the validity and reliability of interest inventories are lower than those of cognitive tests (Mehrens & Lehmann, 1986), and predictions based on interest inventories are much more general.

These problems, as well as sex biases that still crop up in some noncognitive tests, give us good reason to be cautious in the use of interest inventories. They may be helpful, however, in generating thoughtful discussions about vocational choices, especially in the hands of a well-trained counselor. Nonetheless, for the typical classroom teacher, we believe they probably provide less useful information than interviews and observational data for determining students' significant interests.

Interpreting Scores on a Standardized Test

In order to interpret standardized test results, you need to understand how norms are reported and how the scores of students taking the tests are compared to the norms. The following sections present important information for understanding and interpreting standardized test results.

How Scores Are Described

When a measurement is taken of any human characteristic—height, weight, reading test scores, or how far a ball is thrown—we do not expect each person to obtain the same score. If we examined the scores of twenty tenth-grade students on a reading comprehension test, the results might look like those pictured in Table 14–3. This tally of how many students obtained each score is called a **frequency distribution**. The scores being tallied are called **raw scores**—they are simply the number of items correct on the test.

Several concepts important to interpreting standardized test scores can be seen in a frequency distribution such as the one presented in Table 14–3. As you can see, the scores range widely, from a low of 53 to a high of 82, and they seem to bunch between 65 and 75.

The scores are spread out, but one score (70) was obtained more frequently than any other (three times). This most frequently occur-

TABLE 14–3	A FREQUENCY DISTRIBUTION FOR A CLASS OF TWENTY TENTH-GRADE STUDENTS ON A 100-ITEM READING COMPREHENSION TEST

Scores
82
80
78
77
75
74, 74
73
71, 71
70, 70, 70
69
67
66
65, 65
58
53

ring score is known as the **mode** (sometimes called the *modal score*).* The mode is one measure of **central tendency**, which refers to an average score or scores that best represent the performance of a group of students taking a test.

A second measure of central tendency is the **mean** (M). The mean is computed for a distribution by adding up all the scores (82 + 80 + 78 + 77. . .+ 53 = 1408) and dividing by the number of scores (20). The formula for mean (M) is as follows:

$$M = \frac{\Sigma X}{N}$$

where Σ = sum of; X = individual scores; N = number of scores.

In our example,

$$M = \frac{\Sigma X}{N} = \frac{1408}{20} = 70.4.$$

---

*Some distributions have more than one mode. In a different group, three students each might have scored at 71 and 73, with fewer students receiving other scores.

A third measure of central tendency is the median. The **median** is the midpoint of a set of scores—half the scores fall above it and half the scores fall below it. In our example, since there are 20 scores, we are looking for the point above which there are 10 scores and below which there are 10 scores.

If we count up from the bottom, we see that the tenth score from the bottom is 70 and the eleventh is 71. With an *even* number of scores, as in this example, the median is usually considered to be halfway between the two middle scores. Thus the median in this case is 70.5.

Things are even simpler if there is an *odd* number of scores in the distribution. In that case the middle score itself usually is considered to be the median since there are equal numbers of scores above and below it.*

You will find that measures of central tendency affect your interpretation of test results in two ways:

1.   The central tendency for a group is the best single indicator of that group's standing or performance. You can compare two sections of, say, freshman English by comparing their average scores on spelling or reading speed.

2.   Each individual in a group can be compared to others in the class. You can evaluate individuals by noting if they are higher or lower than the class average or if they achieve objectives more or less speedily than the class average.

It is a rather limited interpretation, however, to know only that one group is higher on the average than another or that an individual is above or below the class average. It often is necessary to know how

---

*There are more complex ways of determining the median. If we gave a 100-item test to 300 people, many would obtain the same scores. So by grouping scores into intervals (everyone who made between 51 and 55, and so on) and remembering some basic mathematical concepts (numbers and intervals have theoretical limits; the lower theoretical limit of 49 is 48.5), we would calculate the median with the following formula:

$$\text{Median} = L + \frac{(N/2) - F}{f_m}\text{(i)}$$

where L = the lower theoretical limit of the interval in which the median score is found; N = the number of scores; F = the total frequency below the interval in which the median score is found; f_m = the number of scores or the frequency within the median interval; and i = the size of the interval (the interval 51–55 spans five numbers and so its size is 5). For most classroom purposes, however, the simpler computation will suffice.

much the performances differ. To do this we must know how to measure the **variability** of test scores, that is, the way scores are spread around the measure of central tendency. Two sets of scores with identical means can be quite different in this respect.

Table 14–4 presents the results of the reading test we considered in Table 14–3 from a second class that has the same mean score as the first but with a quite different spread of scores. The second group clusters most closely around the mean. Its scores are much less *variable* than the scores in the first class.

The most common method for measuring the degree of variability of scores is the **standard deviation**, an index of how spread out scores are from the mean. It is an extremely important factor in interpreting test results. Tests in which scores are widely spread have large standard deviations, while tests with closely bunched distributions of

---

TABLE 14–4   FREQUENCY DISTRIBUTIONS FOR TWO CLASSES OF TWENTY TENTH-GRADERS ON A 100-ITEM READING COMPREHENSION TEST

Scores	
First Class	Second Class
82	
80	
78	
77	
	76
75	
74, 74	74, 74, 74
73	73, 73
71, 71	71, 71, 71
70, 70, 70	70, 70, 70, 70, 70
69	69, 69, 69
67	67
66	
65, 65	65
	62
58	
53	

IQ measures are sensitive to prior learning.

"You can't build a hut, you don't know how to find edible roots, and you know nothing about predicting the weather. In other words, you do *terribly* on our I.Q. test."

scores have smaller standard deviations. The standard deviation (SD) is found with the following formula.

$$SD = \sqrt{\frac{\Sigma(X-M)^2}{N}}$$

where Σ = the sum of; X = the individual scores; M = the mean of the distribution; and N = the number of scores.

Essentially, to find the standard deviation of a set of scores, (1) find each score's distance from the mean ($X - M$), (2) square the result (which will eliminate negative numbers), (3) total the squared numbers, and (4) divide the total by the number of scores (N). The result is called the *variance*. The square root of the variance is the standard deviation.

In both classes of 20 students, the mean was 70.4. Thus, for the first class, we would subtract 70.4 from 82, from 80, from 78, and so on, square each difference—$(11.8)^2$, $(9.6)^2$, and so on—and total the squared numbers. The total is then divided by the number of scores, in this case 20. The square root of this number is the standard deviation. Computation is as follows for the scores from the first class:

$$\text{SD} = \sqrt{\frac{\Sigma(X-M)^2}{N}} = \sqrt{\frac{930.8}{20}} = \sqrt{46.54} = 6.82.$$

For the second class:

$$\text{SD} = \sqrt{\frac{\Sigma(X-M)^2}{N}} = \sqrt{\frac{202.8}{20}} = \sqrt{10.14} = 3.18.$$

As you can see, the standard deviation for the second class is much smaller than for the first class. In a sense, the standard deviation is a kind of average—an average of how much the scores in a distribution deviate from the mean score. In standardized tests, the standard deviation is the measuring stick for describing how far above or below the mean a given student scores.

Test makers routinely compute the mean, median, mode, standard deviation, and other statistics for the norm group in order to develop norms for their tests. Norms might be available for each grade level of the norm group for the 100-item reading comprehension test mentioned earlier. Norms then become the point of comparison for your students' scores. Are your seventh graders above or below the mean as compared to the norm group? How far above or below the mean is a particular student? How do your students rank in reading achievement compared to other students? Standardized test results help provide teachers with answers to such questions.

The Normal Curve

As we noted earlier, tests are standardized on large groups rather than on the small classes of twenty we used to demonstrate the computation of the mode, mean, median, and standard deviation. When a test is given to a large group, there is the possibility of some students marking all items correctly and others marking none correctly. Most students would fall somewhere in between these extremes. Even in the two small classes we used as illustrations, scores tended to bunch toward the middle. Such a distribution is typical of most human characteristics. This phenomenon first was noted by the Belgian mathematician, Lambert Quetelet (1776–1874) when he was measuring soldiers' heights and weights. He graphed his results and determined they very nearly coincided with a mathematical distribution known as the Gaussian distribution, a bell-shaped curve.

PRACTICE EXERCISE 14–2   CALCULATING MODE, MEAN, MEDIAN, AND
STANDARD DEVIATION

Examine the data in the chart below:

94	86	75	68
93	86	73	67
90	86	72	66
88	86	71	65
87	80	70	64

These figures represent the scores on a 100-point math test. Using the information on the chart, answer the following questions:

1. What is the mode?

2. What is the mean?

3. What is the median?

4. What is the standard deviation?

Our answers appear on p. 481.

Quetelet's work came to the attention of many people (most notably Sir Francis Galton) and resulted in some misleading ideas. Since so many human (and animal) characteristics approximated the Gaussian distribution, with most measures falling close to the mean, deviations from the mean were thought of as "errors" because "nature's ideal" obviously was the mean (Kolstoe, 1973). Hence, this kind of distribution of scores came to be called the **normal curve**. The term normal curve has stayed in use although we no longer view deviations from the mean as errors.

Figure 14–2 presents a normal distribution of scores. Notice that the bottom line, the abscissa, represents scores, in this case the scores of several thousand randomly selected persons on the Wechsler Scales. It could be any human characteristic, of course—height, weight, or a measure of strength. The vertical line (ordinate) represents the number of times each score occurs (this vertical line usually is not present in most depictions of normal curves; we use it here to help you understand the meaning of the curve). The higher the point along the curve,

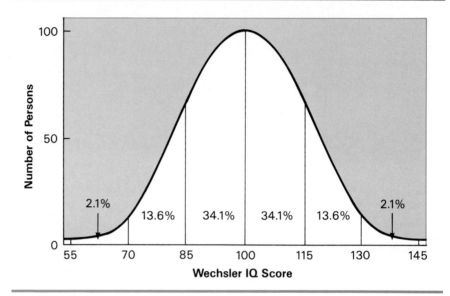

FIGURE 14–2   A NORMAL DISTRIBUTION OF INTELLIGENCE TEST
SCORES

the greater the number of scores at that point along the abscissa. In our example, 100 individuals have IQ scores of exactly 100.

In a **normal curve**, the mean, the median, and the mode will be identical; they all will fall at the same place on the curve, the center. The curve is symmetrical around this point, with the number of scores decreasing as we move in either direction from the midpoint. On the curve in Figure 14–2, we can see that 100 is the most common (modal) score, the mean score, and the midpoint (median) of IQ scores of the people in the sample. Fewer persons obtained scores of 85 or 115 and very few individuals scored either below 70 or above 130.

Reporting Standardized
Test Scores

In most standardized tests, the scores will approximate a normal distribution such as that in Figure 14–2. Test makers take advantage of this fact since predictable proportions of scores occur in each part of a normal distribution. The area between 100 and 115, for example, represents the range from the mean (100) to one standard deviation above the mean (in this case 115, since the standard deviation of the Wechsler Scales is 15). Approximately one-third of the scores (34.1%) fall in this area, the same number as fall between 100 and 85, that is, between the mean and one standard deviation *below* the mean. So approximately two-thirds (68.2%) of the population will score within one standard deviation of the mean on the Wechsler Scales and on most standardized tests.

Between +1 standard deviation and +2 standard deviations (between 115 and 130 in our IQ test example in Figure 14–2), we find another 13.6% of the scores. The same percentage falls between −1 and −2 standard deviations. Thus, a total of about 95% of the scores will fall between −2 standard deviations and +2 standard deviations. Almost all scores, 99.8%, fall between −3 standard deviations and +3 standard deviations. On the Wechsler Scale, this would mean that fewer than one out of a thousand persons would obtain IQ scores either below 55 or, alternatively, above 145. Extreme scores are very rare on standardized tests.

On standardized tests the raw scores (the actual scores received on the test, that is, the number of items correct) almost always are converted into standard scores. **Standard scores** are scores based on standard deviations and on the assumption that the distribution of scores is a normal one. By looking at a standard score, one can tell immediately how far above or below the mean a person's score is.

The simplest form of standard score is the z-score. The **z-score** simply gives a person's performance on a test in standard deviation units above or below the mean. For example, a z-score of +1.0 is equal to one standard deviation above the mean, a z-score of −2.0 is equal to two standard deviations below the mean, and so forth. Raw scores are turned into z-scores by the following formula:

$$z = \frac{X - M}{SD}$$

where X = the student's raw score; M = the mean of all scores; and SD = the standard deviation of the distribution.

As an example, suppose a student gets 79 items correct on our reading achievement test. Let's also say that the mean for her grade level in the norm group was 70 and the standard deviation was 5. The student's z-score would be:

$$z = \frac{X - M}{SD} = \frac{79 - 70}{5} = \frac{9}{5} = +1.8.$$

The student scored just less than two standard deviations *above* the mean, well above the average of the norm group.

Other kinds of standard scores include the T score (in which the mean is set at 50 with a standard deviation of 10), IQ scores (in which

PRACTICE EXERCISE 14–3   PLOTTING A NORMAL CURVE

One way to better understand how normal curves are constructed is to construct a graph yourself. Consider the frequency distribution below:

Score	Number of Persons Making the Score	Score	Number of Persons Making the Score
100	1	83	25
99	5	82	23
98	7	81	20
96	6	80	20
95	10	79	19
94	12	78	18
93	15	77	16
92	17	76	15
91	17	75	14
90	20	74	12
89	26	73	10
88	24	72	9
87	26	71	8
86	28	70	5
85	30	69	6
84	28	68	1

Using the graph framework we have constructed (below), plot the frequencies as dots and then connect the dots. We have plotted the first two points for you (i.e., one person scored 68, six scored 69).

the mean is 100 with a standard deviation of 15),* and scores used by the College Entrance Examination Board and many upper-level scholastic aptitude tests such as the Scholastic Aptitude Test (in which the mean is 500 and the standard deviation 100). Suppose you are looking over a high school senior's results on the Scholastic Aptitude Test. You notice that the student received a standard score of 600. This tells you immediately that the student scored one standard deviation above the mean on that test compared to the norm group.

---

*The Stanford-Binet has a standard deviation of 16.

PRACTICE EXERCISE 14–3   *CONTINUED*

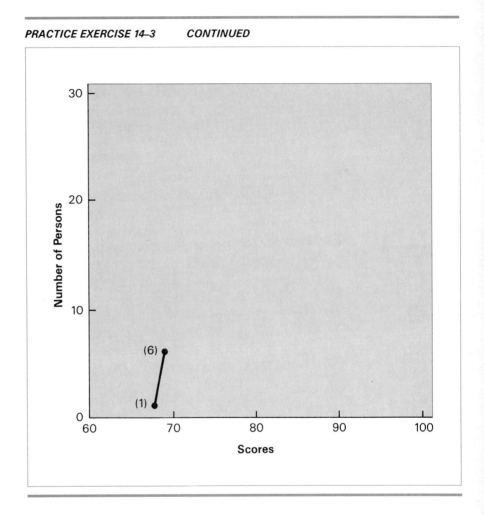

Other ways of comparing a student's performance to the norms are by grade-equivalent and age-equivalent scores. *Grade-equivalent scores* are best described with examples. If a child obtains a score on a test the same as the *median* score for all beginning fifth graders in the norm group (Grade 5.0), that child is given a grade-equivalent score of 5.0. Likewise, another child who makes a score identical to the median of beginning third graders is given a grade equivalent of 3.0. If the score were at the median of the end-of-year third graders (Grade 3.9), the grade equivalent would be 3.9. By examining the grade equivalents of students' test scores, we can compare them with the performance of norm-group students at various grade levels.

Age-equivalent scores are determined in the same way as grade equivalents except that chronological age rather than grade level is used (Ebel & Frisbie, 1986). An age-equivalent score of 10.0 means a particular student has scored at the median for individuals exactly ten years old. Age norms allow us to compare our students to the median performance of norm-group students at various ages. Like grade equivalents, they often are used to measure student growth over a period of time.

Another frequent way in which standardized test scores are reported is through **percentile rankings** or, simply, *percentiles*. A student's percentile on a standardized test tells us what proportion of students in the norm group obtained scores that were the same or lower than our target student. A student with a percentile of 89 did as well as or better than 89 percent of the norm group for that test. In contrast, a score at the 5th percentile is quite low, equaling or exceeding only five percent of the scores in the norm group. The relationship among the various kinds of standard scores is shown in Figure 14–3.

The information we obtain from tests with standardized scoring enables us to compare a student's performance with other students' performances across subtests and across tests. Standard scores are used to "make standard" the test scores by putting them on a common scale. Comparing the raw scores on thirty-item, forty-five-item, and twenty-four-item subtests would be nearly impossible, but in standardized tests the raw scores have been converted to standard scores with known means and standard deviations. Thus, rather than reporting a student received raw scores of, say, 24, 31, and 21 on the subtests, the subtest scores might be reported as *T* scores or as percentiles—for instance, the 80th percentile in spelling, 50th percentile in mathematics, and 98th percentile in language comprehension. From the standard score—the percentile—we can see immediately that the student scored above four-fifths of the students in spelling, was at the median in math, and was higher than all but 2 percent of the students in language comprehension. Standard scores make such comparisons possible.

Imprecision of Scores: Standard Error of Measurement

Imagine for a moment that, of all things, you're standing at the free-throw line of your local basketball court, basketball in hand. How many free throws can you make out of ten? "Well," you say, "I'll just shoot ten free throws and find out!" So you shoot ten and five go in. But is five what you will always score with ten tries? What if you were to be selected as a team member on the basis of this single score—would you

FIGURE 14–3   THE RELATIONSHIP OF STANDARD SCORES IN A NORMAL
                   DISTRIBUTION

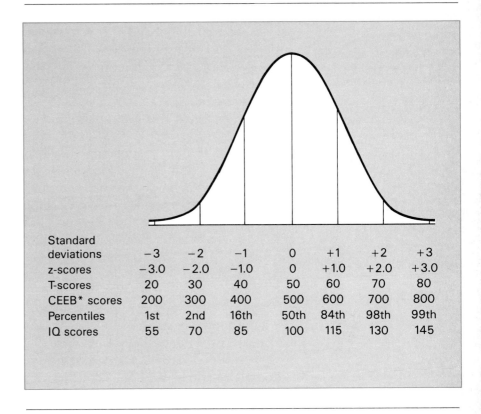

Standard deviations	−3	−2	−1	0	+1	+2	+3
z-scores	−3.0	−2.0	−1.0	0	+1.0	+2.0	+3.0
T-scores	20	30	40	50	60	70	80
CEEB* scores	200	300	400	500	600	700	800
Percentiles	1st	2nd	16th	50th	84th	98th	99th
IQ scores	55	70	85	100	115	130	145

*CEEB = College Entrance Examination Board

have confidence that this score represents your true ability? Probably not. So you shoot another ten and make six, another ten and you sink four, yet another ten and you make five. As you shoot more and more sets of ten, it becomes obvious that your scores are not always the same but vary around some average point. By shooting fifty sets of ten free throws, you may find that your average is 5.5, most of your scores are five or six, and that your best is eight and your worst is three.

To determine the typical spread of your scores in free-throw shooting, you could compute their standard deviation. The standard deviation of a set of an *individual's own scores* is referred to as the **standard error of measurement** (SEM). The standard error of measurement, then, can be thought of as the deviation of a person's observed scores around an average, "true" score.

The uses of the standard error of measurement are twofold. First, it conveys to us that any one score is imprecise. It is just one indicator of a person's actual ability and may be somewhat in error. Second, because of some statistical properties of the standard error of measurement, test users can estimate the probability that a person's "true" score lies within a certain interval. What are the chances, for example, that five of ten is a reasonable estimate of your free-throw shooting ability?

Let's see what this concept means for interpreting standardized tests. Because errors in measurement are assumed to be normally distributed, we can estimate that the chances are about two in three (68 percent), for instance, that a person's "true" score lies in an interval between one standard error below and one standard error above the actual score the person obtained on a test. Again, using what we know about the normal curve and the proportions in each part of it, we can guess the chances are about 95 percent that the person's true score is in an interval from two standard errors below to two standard errors above his or her observed score. The obtained score is the best estimate of what the person's true score would be if there were no measurement error.

Educational measurements, of course, seldom if ever are repeated as they were in our basketball example. A test taken over and over, for instance, soon is invalid. Even a second administration of a test often is impossible or at least impractical. How, then, is the standard error of measurement computed? Luckily, there is a simple method of estimating standard error based on (1) the overall reliability of the test (as described in Chapter Twelve) and (2) the standard deviation of the group taking the test. The formula for computing the standard error of measurement of a test is as follows:

$$\text{SEM} = \text{SD} \sqrt{1 - r}$$

where SEM = standard error of measurement; SD = standard deviation of the test; and r = the reliability coefficient of the test.

Suppose a test has a standard deviation of 8 and a reliability coefficient of .84. The standard error of measurement of this test would be $8\sqrt{1 - .84}$, or $8\sqrt{.16} = 8(.4) = 3.2$. You can see from the formula that as the reliability of the test decreases, the SEM increases. Also note that as the standard deviation of the test increases so does the SEM. You seldom will have to calculate the standard error of measurement of standardized tests, however. Test makers routinely report the standard error of measurement for tests and subtests. They do so to indicate that the score obtained is *only one estimate* of the person's true score. In other words, a person retaking the test is likely to receive a somewhat different score. As we have seen, the possibility of obtaining a different score depends to a great extent on the test's reliability and the standard deviation of the test.

Because there always is error in standardized test scores, percentile scores often are presented as *percentile bands*. This practice, used by such achievement tests as the California Achievement Tests, is based on the concept of standard error of measurement. Rather than report that a student scored at the 60th percentile, the test represents the student's score by a percentile band that ranges from, say the 52nd percentile to the 65th percentile. The best estimate of the student's true score is somewhere in this interval.

Percentile bands tell us there is a chance of error in the score obtained on any test. Shorter, less reliable tests, for example, will have wider percentile bands, while longer and more reliable tests will have narrower bands. The more reliable the test or subtest, the more confidence we have that the score a student obtains is reasonably accurate. Error never is completely removed, however, no matter how reliable a test may be. Teachers always should keep in mind that error is a part of any testing process, including standardized testing. A score is only an *estimate* of the trait or ability being measured.

Professional Ethics and Standardized Tests

The codes of ethics for the National Education Association and the American Psychological Association both assume test results are the property of the test taker (or his or her guardian). Therefore, teachers, psychologists, and schools are prohibited from releasing test results without the written consent of the test taker or his or her guardian.

This means that idle conversation about an individual's performance or any public release of test information gained by schools is unethical. There have been numerous cases in which individuals' rights to privacy have been violated by careless talk or improper dissemination of school records. To guard against unauthorized distribution of test results, most schools now have (or should have) forms on which students must specifically indicate they wish test scores to be released to potential employers or to other schools. In any event, the wise teacher will refrain from discussing performance on any standardized test.

Applications for Teaching: Ethical Test Use

The results of standardized tests can significantly aid a teacher's efforts if they are wisely employed. We have drawn the following set of guidelines for the use of standardized tests from the literature.

1. Be familiar with any test you use. Before using any standardized test, you should acquaint yourself thoroughly with the test itself and the manuals that accompany it. Specifically, you should know such information as the norm group used in the test, the means and standard deviations of the test and its subtests, the form of standard scores used, and the standard error of measurement for the test and its subtests. Such information will greatly affect your ability to administer the test competently and interpret the results accurately.

2. Follow all instructions for test administration exactly. Remember that any comparisons to the norm group are valid only if the test's instructions have been followed exactly. If you are involved in giving a standardized test, give it in a professional manner.

3. Treat all standardized test results as confidential. Do not discuss the results of standardized tests unless a student's parents or guardians have given you express permission to do so.

4. Keep test results in proper perspective. The results of a standardized test provide only one small sample of a student's abilities. While the score on a standardized test can help you make better educational decisions, it must be used in conjunction with other evidence, particularly your judgment of the student's in-class performance.

5. Interpret test results to parents and guardians accurately. Parents need to have valid feedback on their child's performance on measures of achievement, ability, and interest. Because they typically do not have the technical expertise to interpret test results, you must be prepared to explain the tests, what they measure, and what the results indicate. In particular, you need to stress the concept of measurement error — that the results of any one test represent a single measure subject to possible change. Often the best forum for sharing these results is a parent-teacher conference where you can answer parents' questions.

6. Prepare students for taking standardized tests. While "teaching to the test" is inappropriate, your students should be aware of the general purpose of tests and how they will be administered. For results to be valid, the students also need to be motivated to try to perform well on the tests. Try to reduce any anxiety but stress the fact that they are to work as hard as possible on the test.

7. Use tests for their intended purposes. Each standardized test has been developed for a specific purpose. Other uses of the test probably are unwise and may be unethical. Also, if a test requires a trained or licensed examiner and you do not have that credential, you have no business using that particular test.

8. Be aware of potential cultural biases in standardized test results. As we noted before, standardized tests provide only one bit of information about students. This information merely may reveal how discrepant a student's background is from the cultural framework represented by the test. Although test makers generally work hard at eliminating cultural biases, the possibility of biases still exists in most standardized measures.

Summary

Standardized tests have a carefully prepared set of test items, uniform procedures for administration and scoring, and norms based on a clearly defined norm group. Standardized achievement tests—diagnostic, single-subject-area, and survey achievement batteries—are designed to assess the knowledge and skills of students in specific subject areas. Diagnostic achievement tests are used when there is reason to believe a student has deficiencies in skills or knowledge. They are intended to furnish information that will help pinpoint the areas of deficiency. Single-subject-area tests survey the knowledge and skills of students in one content area. Survey batteries assess several content areas, allowing for comparisons of performance across areas. Intelligence tests are designed to measure the ability students have to profit from experience and to adapt to new situations. Individual intelligence tests are somewhat more reliable and valid, while group measures of scholastic aptitude are more convenient. Like any other test, intelligence tests and tests of scholastic aptitude are sensitive to prior learning. They should never be regarded as measures of innate ability or potential.

Interest inventories are designed to assess how students feel about certain activities. They are based on the assumptions that interests are learned, that interests are relatively stable by adulthood, that members of vocational groups share common interests, that there are differences in how intensely people feel about activities, and that interests are motivating factors in behavior. While there are problems with reliability and validity, interest inventories can help students develop an additional perspective on their own interests.

A number of statistical concepts underlie standardized testing—namely, the mean, median, mode, standard deviation, and the standard error of measurement. The concept of the normal distribution also is important to the reporting and interpretation of scores for most standardized tests. These concepts are used by test makers to convert raw scores—the actual number of items right—to standard scores. Standard scores then are used to report a student's scores across subtests and to compare students with the norms.

Measurement error always is a part of any test, and standardized tests are no exception. Standardized tests should never be used as the sole source of evidence for decision making, but they can help both teachers and students get a better picture of student achievement, ability, and interests. Standardized test scores always should be regarded with great caution and care. They are the property of the student and can be released only with consent.

Suggested Readings   Anastasia, A. (1988). *Psychological testing* (6th ed.). New York: Macmillan.

This well-regarded text provides detailed information on standardized tests, particularly those in the area of psychology.

Christiansen, H. D. (1988). *Casebook of test interpretation.* Tucson, AZ: Peter Juul Press.

Christiansen has produced an outstanding sourcebook for working through test interpretations.

Mehrens, W., & Lehman, I. J. (1986). *Using standardized tests in education* (4th ed.). New York: Longman.
> *This volume, now in its fourth edition, is a useful resource for professional educators.*

Murphy, K. R., & Davidshofer, C. O. (1988). *Psychological testing: Principles and applications.* Englewood Cliffs, NJ: Prentice-Hall.
> *With a title reminiscent of a fine educational psychology text, this volume offers solid coverage of basic educational measurement issues.*

Sax, G. (1989). *Principles of educational and psychological measurement and evaluation.* Belmont, CA: Wadsworth.
> *Sax's volume provides a firm foundation in educational measurement.*

Answers to Practice Exercise 14–2

1. Mode = 86
2. Mean = 78.35
3. Median = 77.5
4. Standard deviation = 9.94

PART FIVE

Thus far we have discussed how human beings learn and develop, how this knowledge may be applied in planning for instruction and in teaching, and how learning can be evaluated. In this final section of the text, we are primarily concerned with an issue that has become increasingly important in contemporary education—providing educational opportunities for students with special needs. Chapter Fifteen, *The Exceptional Student*, deals with the role of the regular classroom teacher in working with handicapped and gifted students. It describes how you can provide the most effective instruction to students with a wide range of academic ability.

The Special Needs Student

CHAPTER

15

The Exceptional Student

OVERVIEW

In any group of students you will see a wide range of individual differences. Physical differences are the most obvious—some students are tall, some are short, some are overweight, and others are thin. After only a short time, though, teachers note other kinds of differences—differences critical to instruction. Students vary greatly in their approaches to learning, in their abilities to remember, and in their abilities to think logically.

Students also approach challenges and problems in very different ways. Some plunge right into tasks, while others are cautious and hold back. Some students enjoy new activities, while others prefer the tried and true. Some are decisive, and others cannot make up their minds.

Individual differences such as these require teachers to adapt their teaching methods. Education should reach every individual. As we have stressed throughout this book, effective teachers always start with an analysis of the particular abilities of *each* student.

Students whose abilities and characteristics are furthest from the norm are the so-called exceptional students. Day and Borkowski (1988) suggest that exceptional students deviate from average children to an extent that they require a modification of school practices or special educational services in order to reach their potentials. These differences from average children may be in mental abilities, sensory abilities, physical characteristics, social behavior, or communication abilities. Exceptional students may differ in multiple ways.

As you can see, the term *exceptional student* includes both handicapped and academically talented students. It also emphasizes the need to modify education to fit individual differences. Academically talented students, for example, may become bored with unchallenging instruction, while mentally retarded children may find it difficult or impossible to learn when teaching methods designed for the average student are used.

Exceptional students—both handicapped and gifted—are now most often taught in the regular classroom. In order to maximize the learning of all of your students, you need to be aware of the special needs of exceptional learners. This awareness and the special techniques outlined in this chapter should help you teach all of your students more effectively.

| OBJECTIVES | After reading this chapter, you should be able to meet the following objectives. |

1. Recognize exceptional students' individual differences and the implications of individual differences for teaching.

2. Describe current practices in the education of handicapped students, based on an interview with a classroom teacher.

3. Assess your confidence in working with handicapped students and examine the basis for your assessment.

4. Make decisions about the best educational environment for several students, given brief descriptions of each student's capabilities and characteristics.

Individual Differences and Exceptionality

Modern psychology's beginnings can be traced back to the pioneering psychological laboratories devoted to the study of individual differences. Early researchers such as Wundt, Galton, and Cattell attempted to measure mental abilities by a variety of sensory and perceptual measures—by having people judge the passage of time, repeat letters, bisect a line, and discriminate colors, for example. While early investigators found that people vary greatly in their abilities to perform such tasks, none of these measures seemed related to anything important.

The first really significant step in the measurement of important individual differences in mental ability came with the work of Alfred Binet and Theodore Simon in France (see Chapter Four). They devised an "intelligence scale" that could distinguish normal children from mentally retarded children. This early scale led the way to the standardized testing of intelligence and other mental abilities.

Testing, as it was developed in the 1930s, 1940s, and 1950s, provided a reliable* method for assessing individual differences in cognitive ability. Because test scores are at least partly related to children's

---

*The concepts of reliability (measuring consistently) and validity (measuring what you say you are measuring) are both critical to mental-ability testing, particularly intelligence testing (see Chapters Twelve and Fourteen). There is little controversy about the reliability of most standardized mental-ability tests. Many persons, however, question the *validity* of what these tests measure, particularly across different cultural groups.

performance in school and other settings, the scores began to be used in educational decisions. On the basis of test scores, children were classified as "trainable," "educable," "borderline retarded," or "gifted," for example, and soon classes were formed for various categories of students.*

The practice of grouping exceptional students for instruction, however, was not limited to mentally retarded and academically talented students. Special classes and schools also were developed for other categories of exceptional students, such as orthopedically handicapped, visually impaired, deaf and hard-of-hearing, and learning-disabled students.

Categorization of Exceptional Students

By the 1960s, separate instruction for specifically categorized groups of exceptional students had become accepted practice. Such categories still are in use today, although they are somewhat less closely linked to separate instruction. Eligibility for accelerated programs, special education placement, and state and federal funding for the handicapped, however, all are still tied to categorization. Schools can be reimbursed by state governments for part of the expenses of educating a student if that student is classified as "mentally retarded," that is, if the student meets the state's criteria for mental retardation.

The practice of categorization has had both good and bad effects. On one hand, categorization has brought increased awareness that exceptional students have special needs. As a result, adapted materials, specially trained teachers, and structured classroom methods were developed to meet the problems of students with particular handicapping conditions.

On the other hand, categorization of handicapped students (and some say of gifted students) undeniably has led to negative stereotyped views and segregation (Smith, Price, & Marsh, 1986). Special schools, special classrooms, and labels based on categories ("emotionally disturbed" or "mentally retarded," for example) often unnecessarily separated children with special needs from their peers. Separate programs tend to magnify differences and reduce perceptions of similarity to other children.

---

*At one time, many decisions about students were based almost exclusively on intelligence test scores. One student whose IQ was 73 might be placed in a special education class, for example, while another with an IQ of 75 would not. Now intelligence tests usually are viewed as providing important information, but many other factors (such as social behavior, attention span) are taken into account in deciding what program is best for each student.

To call some students "normal" and others "retarded," for example, can reinforce the idea that all persons with a particular label are somehow alike and will act in the same way (Stephens, Blackhurst, & Magliocca, 1988). Categorization and labeling also can bring about a self-fulfilling prophecy in which handicapped children begin to view themselves as incapable of learning. Once they act on this view and reduce their efforts at learning, the prophecy is fulfilled—they do indeed fall further behind their peers (Stephens et al., 1988).

Categories of Exceptional Students

For good and bad, exceptional students continue to be grouped because of legislative requirements, tradition, or planning and administration. Federal legislation administered through the U.S. Office of Education, for instance, puts handicapped children into ten categories. In the following sections we will discuss several of these categories (see Table 15–1 for a summary of these categories). Our goal is to make you more aware of the special needs of each student. As you look at each category, remember every student is unique. There often are more differences among students within a category than there are differences between categories. Just because students fall in a given category does not mean grouping them for instruction is appropriate.

Handicapped Students   Overall, the number of children who have recognizable and significant handicaps—mental, emotional, and physical—is quite large. There is a strong likelihood you will teach handicapped students, and the need to be well prepared is obvious. Students who have one or more handicapping conditions make up more than a tenth of the school enrollment; nearly 4½ million children to age 21 are served by programs for the handicapped (United States Office of Education, 1988). Over two thirds of these handicapped children will spend part or all of their time in the regular classroom. At the elementary level, for instance, perhaps three or four students in a typical class will have a significant handicapping condition. At the secondary level, the numbers of handicapped students drop somewhat, reflecting maturation and the results of remedial teaching, but also the disproportionately high dropout rates of handicapped students.

Mentally Retarded Students.   All mental retardation involves below-average mental functioning. In IQ test performance, mental retardation is usually indicated by a score below 70 or 75, with the definition varying from state to state. As we saw in Chapter Fourteen, such

TABLE 15–1   CHARACTERISTICS OF SELECTED CATEGORIES OF
EXCEPTIONALITY

Category of Exceptionality	Characteristics	Critical Elements of Teaching
Mental retardation	Has difficulty remembering	Commence teaching at entry levels
	Lags significantly behind peers in academic achievement	Carefully sequence instruction
	Is behind in language development	Give reinforcement for small steps of achievement
	Has trouble making discriminations	Emphasize generalization of knowledge
	Has difficulty forming verbal and numerical concepts	Present only defining attributes of new concepts
Learning disability: general	Normal or above average intelligence	Pay careful attention to entry levels
	Uneven pattern of intellectual development	Adapt instruction to the student's abilities in different areas
	Typically does not progress well in reading or language-related skills	Carefully sequence instruction in difficult areas
		Reinforce language use and reading-related behaviors
		Attempt to develop intrinsic motivation
Learning disability: hyperactivity	Excessive activity, far beyond normal levels	Know about student's medical treatment and medications, if any
	Extremely short attention spans	Pay careful attention to classroom management techniques
	Frequent impulsive behavior	Arrange for school-home cooperation in behavior management programs
	High susceptibility to distraction	Assist other students in developing tolerance for the hyperactive student's behavior
	Disruptive behaviors	

Continued

TABLE 15–1   *CONTINUED*

Category of Exceptionality	Characteristics	Critical Elements of Teaching
Hearing impairment	Lack of attention	Speak clearly and face student when speaking
	Frequently needs oral directions repeated	Arrange preferential seating
	Turning or cocking of head	Employ written or mimed instructions
	Watches speakers' lips rather than making eye contact	Rephrase when repeating information
	Poor speech production	Use joint programming designed by resource teacher and parents
	Disruptive, stubborn, or shy	
	Difficulty in auditory tasks	Employ interpreter as needed
	Cannot locate direction of sounds	
Visual impairment	Rubs eyes frequently	Arrange preferential seating
	Complains of poor vision or of pains in eyes	Place emphasis on tactile and auditory learning
	Sensitivity to light	
	Holds books or other materials too close or far away	Obtain special materials (such as audiotapes of books) as needed from libraries for the visually impaired and blind
	Eyes water frequently	
	Holds head at odd angles when looking at things	For partially sighted, provide large-type materials
Speech and language disorders	Delayed language development	Model acceptable speech patterns
	Exhibits nasal or tremorous sound production	Give systematic reinforcement for language use in your class
	Lisps or stutters	Become aware of goals of speech therapy and reinforce achievement toward these goals
	Reverses sounds or words; "emeny" for "enemy" for example	
	Has vocabulary and speech of a much younger child	Do not show disapproval of student speech efforts

TABLE 15–1   *CONTINUED*

Category of Exceptionality	Characteristics	Critical Elements of Teaching
		Work toward developing the student's overall language development
Behavioral and emotional disturbances	Hostile aggressiveness	Use systematic behavioral management appraoches to provide a consistent environment
	Impulsive and disruptive	
	Withdrawn into a fantasy world	
	Socially isolated	Stay abreast of any psychological or medical treatment
	Depressed	
	Extremely self-deprecating	Identify target behaviors to reinforce
	Has unrealistic fears and phobias	
	Seeks attention despite negative consequences	Seek understanding of other class members both before and after problem behaviors occur
	Engages in self-injurious actions	
		Plan your actions before crises occur
		Work jointly on programs devised by you, the resource teacher, psychologists, and others
Orthopedic or other health impairment	Usually previously identified by medical personnel	Thoroughly familiarize yourself with the medical condition
		Attend to the comfort of the student
		Acquire appropriate skills for possible emergencies
		Provide or arrange for assistance in fulfilling basic needs (movement into inaccessible areas, and so on)
		Carefully nurture development of a positive self-concept

Continued

TABLE 15–1   CONTINUED

Category of Exceptionality	Characteristics	Critical Elements of Teaching
Gifted	Well above average in measured intelligence	Provide materials and activities that challenge the learner
	High levels of performance in academic tasks	Allow student to assume responsibility for structuring his or her own approaches to learning
	May be exceptional in one area but not in other areas	
	Generally reasonably healthy, active, and emotionally stable in relation to peers	Avoid unnecessary separation of the student from his or her peers

Note: Obviously we are suggesting all students receive meaningful instruction at their entry levels, and all students receive reinforcement for their achievements. In general, keep in mind that the most effective teaching procedures for exceptional students are adaptations of methods effective for all students. This table highlights the particular needs some exceptional students have for particular components of instruction.

scores would be in the lowest 2 to 5 percent of all IQ scores. A second criterion is that the mental retardation must have its onset sometime before late adolescence. Although some individuals who suffer brain damage from accidents or illness as adults have greatly reduced mental ability, they usually are not considered retarded. Third, there is an impairment in adaptive behavior in mental retardation. Adaptive behavior refers to sensorimotor development (walking, sitting up, talking) during the preschool years and, later, to a person's academic and social adjustment. Most mentally retarded students lag significantly behind their peers in reading, mathematics, and social development.

Retarded individuals sometimes have been divided into the following subgroups: (1) mildly or educably mentally retarded (approximate IQ range from 55 to 69), (2) moderately or trainably mentally retarded (approximate IQ range from 40 to 54), and (3) severely or profoundly retarded (IQs below 40).* By far the greatest number of mentally retarded children fall into the first category, mild retardation. Most mildly retarded individuals have significant difficulties with the challenges of the regular classroom if no special support is available. With appropriate planning and support, however, most mildly retarded children can benefit from instruction provided in the regular classroom. Certain special services, such as extra drill on particular skills, often are provided in part-time placement in special classes. Some mildly retarded students also may require assistance in social or economic adjustment, particularly under times of unusual stress. The majority of mildly retarded children can go on to become self-supporting and socially adjusted adults (Heward & Orlansky, 1988).

Special equipment, such as the computers available in this laboratory for handicapped students, can help handicapped students reach their fullest potential. The teacher, however, must remain alert to students' needs and, wherever necessary, tailor instruction to those needs.

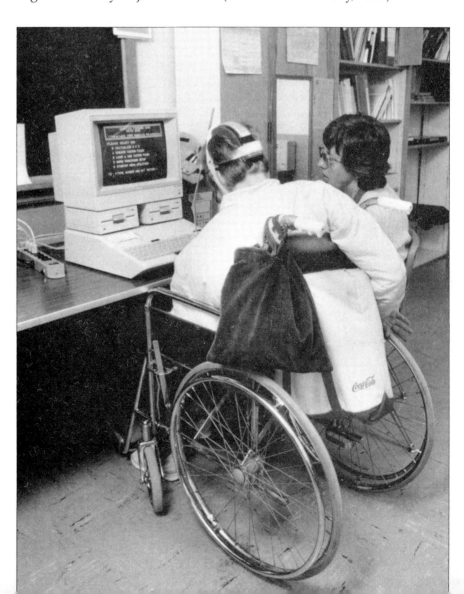

Kirk (1972) once estimated that, in an average community, about 2.5 percent of school-age children are mildly retarded, while perhaps five out of a thousand have more severe mental handicaps. The incidence of mental retardation, however, varies with the social and economic conditions of communities. Some areas have higher proportions of children with mental retardation, while other more advantaged areas have lower proportions. These differences across communities seem to relate to a number of factors—quality of prenatal care, nutrition, levels of stress, children's preschool experiences, language experience, social background, and parental education, to name only a few of many possible influencing effects (Stephens et al., 1988).

Learning-Disabled Students. Some students have very specific learning deficits, as opposed to the more general learning difficulties of mentally retarded students. The term *learning disabled* was suggested some time ago by Samuel Kirk (Kirk & Bateman, 1962) to describe this group of students. **Learning-disabled** students are a diverse group of children who have normal or near-normal intelligence levels but who have severe difficulties in understanding or using spoken or written language. About 44 percent of school-aged children receiving special programs have been classified as learning-disabled (United States Office of Education, 1988) (see Table 15–2). Typically, many more boys are identified as learning-disabled than girls, as much as six to ten times as many (see Stephens et al., 1988).

Some learning-disabled students have unusual problems in reading, writing, spelling, or arithmetic—unusual because adequate performance in these areas ordinarily is not difficult for children of near-normal or above-normal intelligence. Some learning-disabled students with normal mental ability may be able to read only at a third- or fourth-grade level upon entering high school, for example. Although the label *learning disabilities* has been greatly misused (for instance, calling every student who fails for unknown reasons "learning disabled"), there is a relatively small number of children for whom learning certain skills is extraordinarily difficult.

Some learning-disabled students also are hyperactive. Hyperactivity has been defined in a number of ways, but the typical hyperactive child engages in excessive activity, is inattentive, and behaves impulsively (Stephens et al., 1988). Hyperactive students are likely to talk, walk, fidget, and move about incessantly. They often have great difficulty in paying attention. They are disorganized, even chaotic, in their approaches to tasks. Hyperactive children are likely to follow instructions poorly and often do not complete their work. Further, they

TABLE 15–2   NUMBER OF STUDENTS AGED 0–21 BEING SERVED IN PROGRAMS FOR THE HANDICAPPED

Handicapping Conditions	Number	Percent of total
Learning disabled	1,926,097	43.60
Speech or language impaired	1,140,422	25.80
Mentally retarded	664,424	15.00
Emotionally disturbed	384,680	8.70
Hard of hearing and deaf	66,761	1.50
Orthopedically and other health impaired	110,986	2.50
Visually handicapped	27,049	0.61
Other	101,182	2.24
All conditions	4,421,601	100.00

Source: Statistics derived from The Tenth Annual Report to Congress on Implementation of the Education of the Handicapped Act Public Law 94-142, Washington, D. C.: Division of Innovation and Development, 1988.

tend to react quickly, resulting in sloppy work and low tolerance for frustration. It is not unusual for them to interrupt class or make strange sounds.

Hyperactivity may become apparent during toddlerhood—some babies literally wear out their cribs continually jumping, hopping, and climbing. The elementary school's demands for children to be reasonably attentive and restrained by the time they are five or six years old often clash with the characteristics of learning-disabled children, particularly those who are hyperactive. In addition, relationships with peers do not always go well. Impulsiveness and low frustration tolerance make it hard for peers to enjoy interacting with them. Problems also may arise during adolescence. Learning-disabled students show a higher-than-normal incidence of antisocial and destructive behavior and increased school failure and dropout rate. For hyperactive students, impulsiveness continues to be a severe problem in adolescence (Heward & Orlansky, 1988).

No one teaching method is likely to be effective for all learning-disabled students because their problems are so varied. Some authorities advocate using tactile and kinesthetic senses, for example, to assist the learning-disabled student who has problems in reading (see Hedley & Hicks, 1988). Many teachers have used behavioral programs for attempting to control hyperactivity. Often such behavioral programs are coupled with medical treatment, particularly with the use of stimulant drugs that, paradoxically, seem to improve attention span, reduce anxiety levels, and decrease impulsiveness in some hyperactive children.

A broad perspective needs to be maintained on the entire area of learning disabilities. The teacher must take many factors into account and no one approach—instructional, medical, or behavioral—is likely to be totally successful. Medications may be helpful for hyperactive children, but drugs alone are not enough to produce favorable outcomes (Heward & Orlansky, 1988). Teachers need to adapt instructional approaches to each student and use all the instructional techniques at their disposal.

Hard of Hearing and Deaf Students.   These two categories, although quite similar, usually are considered separately. **Hard of hearing** students have partial hearing while **deaf** students have no functional hearing at all. Hearing impairment may range from mild to severe. Mild hearing impairment may affect perception of only distant or faint sounds. Mildly impaired students may perceive nearby sounds or normal conversation, although they may need hearing aids. In severe hearing loss and deafness, even the loudest sounds are not heard.

About five children per thousand have hearing problems that require special attention in school, and of these a significant proportion may require special classes in speech reading (which involves deciphering the lip, face, and throat movements of speakers) or the use of sign language. The typical teacher might expect to have one or two hearing-impaired or deaf students over a three- or four-year span.

Teachers should be alert to identify hearing problems that may have slipped through health examinations or have developed recently. Signs of hearing impairment include instances in which students:

Are repeatedly inattentive

Mispronounce many words

Give "off-beat" answers to questions

Speak in a monotone or with inappropriately modulated words or sentences

Always turn one ear toward a speaker

Of course, some of these actions may be simple inattentiveness or incorrect learning. If the classroom management techniques described in Chapter Eleven are not effective, however, the possibility of hearing loss should be taken seriously and the child's hearing should be tested.

Teachers should expect to devote extra attention to the needs of hearing-impaired students. Children with impaired hearing often will miss information, explanations, descriptions, and directions. Always permit them to be seated where they can hear and see optimally. You will need to state instructions, directions, and important points slowly and clearly and to arrange for the students to signal when they have not understood.

Conceptual and language development will often be affected by more severe hearing loss. Deaf children, for instance, are often unable to develop verbal concepts and associated vocabulary. If hearing loss occurs early in life, deaf children may find some types of learning virtually impossible. Since their early experiences are largely visual and tactile, their first communication is usually through a gestural, or sign, language (Morariu & Bruning, 1984; Vaid, 1986). Learning to read and to use an auditory-based language such as English is difficult at best.

Children with severe hearing losses from birth will learn to speak only with the greatest difficulty. Correct speech and language use depend on hearing oneself and models speak. Without hearing, correct speech cannot be identified and mistakes cannot be corrected. Infants born deaf initially make the full range of sounds made by all children; however, vocalizations soon rapidly decrease, and they often cease well before the child is one year old. Without feedback, the making of sounds is extinguished (Rodda & Grove, 1987).

Most students with more than mild hearing impairment require significant amounts of time in special classrooms or schools in which skills in signing and speech reading are learned. In signing (signed communication), the language is gestural. American Sign Language, for example, is used by about a half-million deaf persons in the United States alone (Vaid, 1986), although many schools concentrate on signed English, a gestural language that relates signs to English-language equivalents. Speech reading is often useful if there is some functional hearing. To enable the more severely hearing-impaired students to take part in regular classroom activities, a teacher-interpreter fluent in signed communication usually is needed. Regular classroom teachers who have learned some sign language have found their ability to use signs has opened up a whole range of communication with hearing-impaired students in their classes. Additionally, many schools now teach some signing to their normal-hearing students to make possible more meaningful relationships with deaf and hard of hearing students.

Visually Handicapped Students.   Students are classified as **visually handicapped** if special adaptations of educational programs and materials are required because of their vision. Even after correction, visually impaired children have substantial impairment. While many children have imperfect vision, simply wearing glasses or contact lenses is not considered visual impairment.

Blindness usually is defined in terms of visual acuity (sharpness of vision), which often is measured by a wall chart containing letters or figures. On an eye chart the legally blind person (tested with corrective lenses on the person's better eye) can read letters from 20 feet away that a person with normal vision can read at 200 feet (20/200 vision). Other blind individuals, of course, have no vision at all. The degree of visual loss obviously dictates the types of adjustments that need to be made in instruction. Some visually impaired or legally blind students can read ordinary print with corrective devices, while others require Braille materials or audiotaped versions of reading materials and texts (Daneman, 1988).

Visually impaired and blind students constitute a relatively small but significant group of handicapped school-age children. Perhaps one in three thousand children is legally blind and about one in one thousand is visually handicapped (U.S. Office of Education, 1988). Despite the low incidence, visual impairment and blindness are severe problems. Daneman (1988) suggests that blindness prevents normal reading, limits the student's mobility in all but familiar surroundings, limits perception of the distant environment, and limits detection of social cues.

While some blind children attend special schools, most receive instruction in classrooms and schools in their own communities. Visually impaired and blind students were among the first handicapped students to be placed systematically in regular classrooms (Heward & Orlansky, 1988).

Although visually impaired and blind students are few in number, the nature of their handicap requires teachers to respond intelligently for meaningful learning to take place. Teachers should be aware that each state has one or more special libraries for the blind, with Braille, audiotape, and large-print materials available for instructional purposes. Instruction emphasizing kinesthetic and auditory learning will be of particular benefit to visually handicapped pupils. These students need to receive instruction in the perceptual modes from which they can gain the most.

Speech-Impaired Students.   Speech is a critical component of human communication. Language and conceptual development both are affected by the ability to pronounce words and sounds as meaningful units. Problems in the area of speech can cause several learning deficits. Speech handicaps generally involve (1) *articulation problems*, such as substituting or omitting sounds, (2) *voice problems*, in which the voice is pitched too high or there is poor-quality sound, and (3) *stuttering*, in which speech production is halting and erratic (see Heward & Orlansky, 1988). Additional speech problems include delayed speech, cleft palate, and speech difficulties associated with hearing impairment, cerebral palsy, or mental retardation. Speech disorders can occur alone or they may accompany other handicapping conditions. On the average, about one child in most classrooms may have a speech problem severe enough to warrant special attention.

Speech problems often result in other problems. Many students with speech impairments have difficulties with social adjustment. Special care must be taken to help them develop positive self-concepts and to help them meet their deficit needs to the greatest extent possible (see Chapter Eight). Future vocational limitations (there are professions in which speech impairments are a tremendous obstacle to success) largely can be avoided through programs jointly developed by speech therapists, parents, and teachers. Nonetheless, vocational guidance may be needed to help some speech-impaired students form realistic life goals.

Emotionally Disturbed Students.   A major factor in classifying children as emotionally disturbed is that the difficulty is severe and lasts over a long period of time. Behaviors such as impulsive, aggressive, and antisocial acts, as well as extreme withdrawal and depression, may lead to a student's classification as emotionally disturbed. Some emotionally disturbed children show extreme immaturity compared to their peers, others are involved in delinquent behavior, and still others are "troubled personalities" — chronically unhappy, anxious, fearful, or physically distressed.

Unfortunately, people often cannot agree about whether a behavior or behaviors should be called "disturbed." An action considered extremely serious by one person or group of people (hostility to authority figures, for instance) may be of little or no consequence to others. The severity of many problem behaviors at least partly is in the eyes of the beholder.

How many children have serious behavioral and emotional disorders? Because of the problems in definition, no one knows for certain, but a reasonable estimate is 2 to 3 percent (U.S. Office of Education, 1988). In some settings, however (such as in disadvantaged neighborhoods), there is a much higher proportion of emotional disorders. Less stressful settings produce significantly fewer problems.

Orthopedically or Other Health-Impaired Students.   Many children have medically related problems that interfere with their success in school. Not counting students with visual or auditory handicaps, about one in two hundred children has a significant orthopedic or health impairment. Some of these students have nervous system diseases such as cerebral palsy or epilepsy, while others may be crippled. Still other children have congenital heart problems, diabetes, severe asthma, or arthritis.

The instructional needs of students with such handicaps vary greatly depending on the nature of the handicap. Teachers first of all must know the appropriate responses to certain emergency conditions. If a teacher has a student with diabetes, he or she should be aware of the signs of an insulin reaction so that medically sound steps can be taken quickly if necessary. Teachers also should be thoroughly familiar with the workings and care of any prosthetic devices (such as wheelchairs or braces) used by their students. Because such devices often require periodic checking and adjustment, the teacher needs to monitor the posture and comfort of students using these aids. Other health-related handicaps require some teacher attention to activity levels or diet in accord with a physician's orders. Teachers may also need to provide assistance to physically handicapped students in toileting, dressing, or negotiating stairs.

Gifted Students

Definitions of the "gifted student" vary. Some definitions include only those students who have superior intellectual ability as measured by intelligence tests, while other definitions include students with superior talent in areas not strictly academic, such as art, writing, and music. Estimates of the number of **gifted students,** using intellectual ability as the definition, cluster around 3 percent (Borkowski & Day, 1988). In terms of measured intelligence, this figure would identify students with IQ scores above approximately 130. Some schools provide additional programs for "highly" gifted students, who are a much smaller group, with IQs of 145 or above.

Musical talent often appears early in young children. Several things must be present, however, to develop this talent to its fullest: excellent models, steady adult encouragement, time to practice, and feedback on performance.

Despite some negative stereotypes, gifted students actually tend to be larger, healthier, more active, more emotionally stable, and happier than the general school population (Cox, 1926; McLeod & Cropley, 1988; Terman et al., 1925). The image of scrawny, myopic bookworms without any social skills is simply not accurate in describing most gifted children. They seem to be favored in many aspects of their lives.

Differences between gifted and average students typically are described in terms of IQ or performance on achievement tests. Recently, however, psychologists have begun to address differences in the cognitive processes of gifted students and average students. Gifted students are able to manipulate information more rapidly in short-term memory, access long-term memory more quickly, and sequence unordered information more accurately. These differences in information-processing ability become greater as tasks become more difficult (Borkowski & Day, 1988).

For many handicapped students, adaptations in instruction must be made or learning will not occur at all. Changes in instruction for gifted students, however, are made to provide advanced programs and to increase flexibility beyond a basic program. Educators are sharply divided in their views of how education of the gifted should be conducted. Some (Stephens et al., 1988) argue that with proper organization and support, individualized programs for the gifted can and should be based in the regular classroom. These experts argue that gifted students should not be set apart from other students. Other educators, however, argue there should be special programs or even special schools for gifted students, particularly for the highly academically gifted and otherwise talented students. In a special setting, they say, the gifted can develop their abilities to the fullest by interacting with other gifted students and receiving special instruction (see Glenn, 1986).

The choice of educational programs for gifted students depends on people's values. While special programs may advance gifted students' abilities in one or more areas, those same programs may hinder their social development. Similarly, regular classroom-based programs may enhance social development but not maximize cognitive development. Some parents and teachers will choose to emphasize high intellectual or artistic achievement. Others set these goals as secondary to social adjustment goals they believe will be better for the students in the long run. Our view is that neither of these goals should take total precedence. Both society and gifted students are likely to be best served by programs that develop the special abilities of this group but that also do not neglect social development goals

Bilingual Students

Bilingualism, the speaking of two languages, has always been a part of our culture in the United States. One hundred years ago, many people in this country spoke Italian, German, Polish, or Russian as a first language and then became bilingual as they acquired English as a second language. In many areas of the United States today, there are large numbers of schoolchildren who speak Spanish, Vietnamese, or French as their first language. In some urban areas, schoolchildren may represent as many as twenty or more distinct language backgrounds. Many of these children know no English until they enter school.

Are bilingual students exceptional students? Strictly speaking, they are not. Language and cultural background cannot really be considered an exceptionality of any kind, at least not in the same way as giftedness or a learning disability is. Bilingualism, however, may have

PRACTICE EXERCISE 15–1   RATING YOUR CONFIDENCE IN TEACHING
SPECIAL NEEDS STUDENTS

1. On a five-point scale, rate your confidence in teaching students with the following special needs.

	No Confidence		*Some Confidence*		*Highly Confident*
a. Mentally retarded students	1	2	3	4	5
b. Learning-disabled students	1	2	3	4	5
c. Hard of hearing and deaf students	1	2	3	4	5
d. Visually handicapped students	1	2	3	4	5
e. Speech-impaired students	1	2	3	4	5
f. Emotionally disturbed students	1	2	3	4	5
g. Orthopedically and health-impaired students	1	2	3	4	5
h. Academically talented students	1	2	3	4	5

2. In which category were you *least* confident of your skills?
3. List one or more reasons for your lack of confidence below. For each reason, list a step you can take to help remove the reason.

Reasons for lack of confidence	*Action to eliminate this reason*
_____	_____
_____	_____
_____	_____
_____	_____

important implications for children's educational programs, and bilingual students form a distinct group.

Most favored are those children who have the language of the schools as their native tongue and who learn a second or even a third language. Many English-speaking students in the United States, for instance, study Spanish, French, or German and become bilingual. Similarly, children in Switzerland often study German, French, and Italian so that they are able to be effective citizens in their multilingual country. In these kinds of situations, bilingualism can be associated with real educational advantages.

A very different situation arises, however, when the child's first language is *not* the language of instruction. The problems most children face in learning and social adjustment are magnified greatly when classroom instruction, assignments, and reading materials are difficult or incomprehensible because of language differences (Vaid, 1986). Not only must these children learn to understand instruction and communicate with teachers and peers in an unfamiliar language, they also must cope with major differences in cultural habits, patterns, and values. Adequate self-expression can be nearly impossible.

Problems with comprehension can be solved to some extent by providing children with instruction in mathematics, science, history, health, or other subjects in their first language while they are at the same time learning the "mainstream" second language. Then, as the children progress in the second language, more and more of their instruction in other subjects can be shifted to it. Providing instruction in the first language for students who are not yet fully bilingual also should help reduce problems of separation. When children can question, talk, and react to the school experience in the framework of their own language and culture, adjustment is more likely. Resource persons with backgrounds in students' cultures are vital in aiding this transition.

Problems of cultural differences seem harder to resolve. Certainly teachers need to be knowledgeable about the cultures their students represent and sensitive to the cultural norms of their students. Teachers need to take great care not to devalue the language and culture of bilingual students. This plainly is undesirable and can take a severe toll on students' feelings of self-worth and pride.

A question raised in recent years is how far bilingual education should go. That is, should the emphasis in bilingual education be on readying children to interact primarily in the language of the majority

Children need a solid background in the language of instruction before they can function comfortably, both academically and socially, in the classroom.

or should basic competence in the second language be all that is required, with education in the first language continuing throughout the children's education? The issue has been hotly debated in recent years, and we suspect that arguments will continue in the United States until they are settled in the courts. At this point, however, we must reiterate what has been the major theme of our text: Learning is possible only when the information students are to learn is meaningful. Either instruction must be in the first language of the child or the child must be given all possible assistance to master the second language and become completely bilingual. Regardless of what the ultimate goal of bilingual education is determined to be, meaningful instruction, whether in English or another language, remains the primary purpose of education.

Programs for Handicapped Students

Public school programs for handicapped students are a relatively recent phenomenon. By the late nineteenth century, states had begun to accept responsibility for the care and better treatment of handicapped individuals. Indeed, the nineteenth century marked the real beginning of special education in facilities or institutions set aside for the care of the handicapped (Heward & Orlansky, 1988).

Residential Care

By the late nineteenth century, a number of private, city, or state-run institutions or "homes" had been established to provide residential care for handicapped individuals. In most instances, this care was more custodial than educational. Institutionalization often meant hope had been lost and custodial care was "all that could be done" for a handicapped person. A positive feature of this period, nonetheless, was a dawning recognition of the special needs of handicapped persons.

Residential care still is a major part of services to the handicapped, particularly those with severe disabilities. This care has been regulated more and more carefully, programs have been initiated to meet the individual needs of residents, and there now is the potential of leaving institutions for settings that integrate the handicapped into a community. Although there are some exceptions, residential facilities no longer are viewed as places where residents are permanently housed, but rather they are seen as places where people can develop skills that allow them to function outside the institutions.

Special Classes

At the turn of the twentieth century, public schools began to establish special classes for handicapped students, particularly mildly retarded and physically handicapped children. By the 1960s there were tens of thousands of special classes in the United States. Placement in these classes was based on the identification and labeling of children, with intelligence testing playing a key role in this process. Schools attempted to tailor classes to the needs of handicapped students by having separate classes for groups such as "trainable mentally retarded," "educable mentally retarded," and "learning-disabled" students.

As services to handicapped students increased, however, so did expectations for improvement. The solutions of the 1950s and 1960s, especially segregated classrooms, were increasingly questioned. In an influential article appearing in 1968, Lloyd Dunn argued that special

At its best, mainstreaming benefits both handicapped students, who are not isolated or stereotyped, and nonhandicapped students, who learn that diversity can be the source of many new and rewarding experiences.

class placement was a poor solution to the needs of mildly retarded students. He argued that special classes almost always included an overrepresentation of minority and lower-socioeconomic-status children, and he cited research results that demonstrated that mentally retarded students' academic achievement was no higher in special classes than it would have been in regular classrooms. Dunn also felt that improvements in regular education made it possible to provide better services to handicapped children than ever before. His most important point, however, was that labeling and stereotyping are an almost inevitable consequence of placement in special classes. As people considered these arguments, they soon began to search for new ways to educate handicapped students.

The Least Restrictive Environment and Mainstreaming

Rather than automatically teaching handicapped students in special classes, educators reasoned, why not try to find a **least restrictive environment** for each handicapped student?* The least restrictive environment is defined as the program or setting that provides the greatest opportunity for the individual development of a handicapped

---

*Some educators have found the term *least restrictive environment* to be more negative and legalistic than they would like. This term is a part of most legislation for the handicapped, however, and will likely remain in general use.

student—emotionally, socially, or intellectually. What is least restrictive for a particular student depends on the nature and severity of his or her handicap and on what is available in a school system.

The *regular classroom* currently is believed to be the least restrictive school environment for the majority of handicapped students. Most authorities now agree that most handicapped students will learn best, experience the greatest social benefits, and be labeled and segregated the least when most, if not all, of their school time is spent with their peers in regular classes. Special help almost always is needed, however, in providing handicapped students with meaningful instruction. A person with special-education expertise (a resource teacher) often will provide assistance to the regular classroom teacher in planning, evaluating, and, in some cases, delivering instruction to handicapped students.

Having handicapped students remain in the regular classroom is popularly referred to as **mainstreaming**. Mainstreamed handicapped children usually are those with mild to moderate handicaps. Many schools also have a resource room staffed by special-education teachers. Children with a handicap can spend varying amounts of time in the resource room depending on their need for specialized instruction. The major goal of the resource room, however, is to maximize the time students spend in the regular classroom. Typically, resource teachers help handicapped students develop the skills most likely to make their regular classroom experiences successful.

Children with severe handicaps are mainstreamed somewhat less often. Students who are deaf or blind or who have severe orthopedic handicaps often attend special classes or schools. More and more often the judgment is being made by many people that the regular classroom may be the best setting for learning, even for children with quite severe handicaps.

A Related Concept: Aptitude-Treatment Interaction.   You will recall that throughout this text we have stressed the need to assess each learner's capabilities and to modify instruction accordingly. An underlying assumption of this approach, and of the least restrictive environment concept, is that the teaching methods best for one learner are not necessarily best for another. Stated more technically, there is often an interaction of student capabilities (aptitudes) with the teaching method used (treatment). This interaction is called an *aptitude-treatment interaction* (Tobias, 1987). Figure 15–1 shows an aptitude-treatment interaction between (1) ability level of learners and (2) degree of structure of

FIGURE 15–1   SUCCESS IN LEARNING: AN INTERACTION OF ABILITY
LEVEL AND STRUCTURE OF TEACHING METHODS

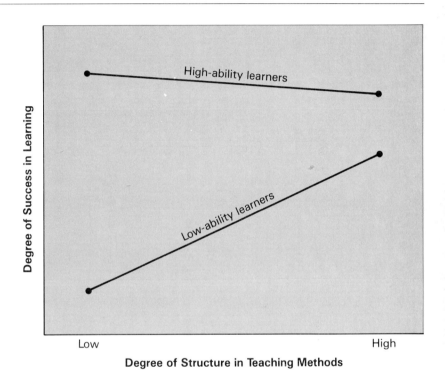

teaching methods. For students with low general ability, highly structured teaching activities work best. Examples of highly structured teaching include programmed instruction or instructional modules that very clearly specify objectives and activities. In contrast, less structured approaches, such as individual projects and discovery learning techniques, generally produce good results for higher-ability learners. For many students, standard conditions are not the best conditions for learning (Tobias, 1987). In other words, good instruction for some students may be poor instruction for others. A single approach to teaching is unlikely to be effective for all students.

Education for the Handicapped: Public Law 94-142.   The concepts of least restrictive environment and, by inference, mainstreaming also are key themes of a federal law, passed in 1975—Public Law 94-142, the

PRACTICE EXERCISE 15–2   CHOOSING A LEAST RESTRICTIVE
ENVIRONMENT

For each of the following, make a judgment about the type of services that would provide the *least restrictive environment* for the student. Which of the following settings are likely to be the best setting for the child to receive educational services the majority of the time? The choices are (a) regular (mainstreamed) classroom; (b) special classroom (resource room); (c) nonschool setting. Check your answers with ours at the end of the chapter.

1. Bill is a bright nine-year-old, but he is easily distracted and "hyper." He walks around the classroom frequently, constantly moves his hands or feet, and rocks in his chair. His classroom achievement is well below expected levels, and he does distract some other students, although most pay little attention to him.

2. Harriet has trouble keeping up. She is at or near the bottom of her sixth-grade class in most areas. She is very slow paced, mentally and physically. She is a large girl, "a little lazy," in her father's words, and not terribly well coordinated. Her measured intelligence (IQ) is around 80.

3. Natalie is thirteen years old. She has no verbal communication, bowel or bladder control, or self-care skills such as feeding or dressing. She does not sit up, crawl, or move about

Education for All Handicapped Children Act. This law brought together a large number of influences in education of the handicapped and gave them the force of law. In the past several years, the education of handicapped students has been strongly affected by the provisions of this law (U.S. Office of Education, 1988).

A free public education should be available to all handicapped children. Previously, many handicapped students were denied access to public schools if school personnel felt that they could not adjust to school requirements. Now the schools must provide education to all handicapped pupils or contract with someone else to provide it if no programs are available in the district.

PRACTICE EXERCISE 15–2   CONTINUED

> without someone's assistance. She has no measurable IQ level and has been classified as "profoundly retarded."
>
> 4. Kristen has a severe hearing impairment that has been related to her mother's contracting rubella (German measles) during pregnancy. She actually has no functional hearing. At age eight, Kristen does not have intelligible speech but does communicate some needs by short cries and vocalizations. She has a small vocabulary in American Sign Language. She cannot read speech (that is, she cannot lip-read) or print.
>
> 5. Jim, a fifth grader, has repeatedly attacked other students when he is angered, which occurs unpredictably and frequently. In the latest incident, another pupil required minor surgery after Jim bit his arm. Supervision is almost constant, but incidents have still occurred often, and other children and their parents are fearful for the children's safety.
>
> 6. Milton is a "slow learner." Classmates frequently ridicule him because he is uncoordinated and socially inept. He is below average in most school subjects but usually does not score the lowest in the class. Nonetheless, he is taunted with jeers of "Milton the Moron" by his classmates.

An individualized educational plan (IEP) must be written for each handicapped student. The IEP is a precisely written set of statements outlining the program of education for a handicapped student including its objectives, teaching methods, and measurement instruments. The time period to attain the objectives must also be indicated. Table 15–3 outlines the major components of an IEP.

Handicapped and nonhandicapped students should be educated together whenever possible. Special classes and schools for handicapped students are chosen only if there clearly is no alternative. The law doesn't require everyone receive the same instruction but that handicapped and nonhandicapped children be separated only when it is absolutely necessary.

TABLE 15–3	ELEMENTS OF A TYPICAL INDIVIDUALIZED EDUCATIONAL PLAN (IEP)	
1.	Personal data and general information	General descriptive data—name, address, age, grade, parents' names, and so on.
2.	Period of time covered by the IEP	IEPs are required by law to be prepared annually for handicapped students. Often an IEP will cover a shorter period of time, such as six months.
3.	Present performance levels in academic, social, self-help, language, vocational, and psychomotor areas	What can the student do now? Which performances are adequate and which need improvement? Performance levels usually are stated behaviorally.
4.	Program placement and justification	In what program/setting is the student now receiving education (regular classroom with resource teacher assistance, special classroom, part-time in resource room, homebound, and so on)? A statement is included justifying the placement.
5.	Annual or semiannual goals	What are the most important educational and social goals for this student in the time period covered by the IEP?
6.	Short-term, specific instructional objectives	Specific objectives with target dates for completion, locations of the experiences, times required per week, and responsible persons indicated for each objective.
7.	Methods for measuring attainment of the objectives (evaluation methods)	The methods of documenting progress are indicated for each objective. These may be in the form of behavior frequencies or rates, test scores, or ratings by observers.
8.	Signatures of the regular classroom teacher, the resource teachers, other school officials (as appropriate), and the parents	The signatures indicate that everyone, including the parents, agrees this is the best plan for this student at this time. Often, approval of this plan is obtained at a meeting in which all concerned persons are present.

Parental approval is required for special-education placement and programming. Previously, parents did not always have much influence on decisions made about their children. The law now specifies that parents must be consulted in placement decisions. Their permission or "informed consent" is required in all such decisions.

PRACTICE EXERCISE 15–3   TEACHERS' VIEWS OF EDUCATION OF THE HANDICAPPED

Interview an experienced teacher and ask how education of the handicapped has changed in the past five years. You will want to probe the following points:

1. How have school policies and procedures changed in the past five years, if at all?

2. Has the teacher's own role in the education of handicapped students changed in the past five years?

3. In the teacher's judgment, has education of the handicapped improved? If it has, what are some areas that need additional improvement? If it hasn't, what specifically needs to be accomplished?

Applications for Teaching: Working with Handicapped Students

Until relatively recently, many handicapped students were taught primarily by special-education teachers. Others received no special help at all. Because of mainstreaming, the regular classroom teacher now has a much greater role in the education of handicapped students. Teaching handicapped students requires a new and more adaptive set of instructional skills. The following are some guidelines for the regular classroom teacher who hopes to teach handicapped students effectively. The teacher should:

1. Expect to use resource personnel and services. The *resource teacher* is a trained special educator who has the role of helping regular classroom teachers work with handicapped students. He or she is trained not only in special education

skills but also as a consultant to other teachers. The IEP almost always is developed jointly by the resource teacher and the regular classroom teacher.

Other people in the school who provide assistance to classroom teachers are the school psychologist, the counselor, and the school nurse. Each has a role in planning education for handicapped students. Paid or volunteer aides often can be used effectively to help teachers individualize instruction for handicapped learners. Teachers also should be aware of the many services available for handicapped students in the community, state, and region. Local and state chapters of the Council for Exceptional Children, the Epilepsy Foundation, the Easter Seal Society, the United Cerebral Palsy Association, and other advocate groups can provide information about particular handicapping conditions. They also can help teachers locate needed instructional materials.

2. *Expect to adapt the goals, methods, and evaluation of your teaching.* Modifications often need to be made in the instructional materials used by handicapped students. Sometimes existing materials are unsuitable. The resource teacher usually can help in adapting materials or obtaining new materials. Goals also may need to be changed. It is rather silly to expect a student to learn American history by reading, for example, if that student's reading skills are extremely poor. The American history goals may need to be postponed or at least modified until the more basic goal of adequate reading is reached.

One controversial but often-needed modification is in the area of grading. Comparing mentally retarded students to other students on a norm-referenced grading system (see Chapter Thirteen) will be punishing to the retarded students, because even a high degree of accomplishment and effort will not result in a high grade when their performance is compared to that of their classmates. It is better to compare the retarded student's performance to objectives in a criterion-referenced system than to "reward" what may be exceptional effort with a D or F on a norm-referenced scale.

3. *Avoid labeling and categorization.* The problems with labeling are many. Labels often adversely affect teacher expectations. The use of labels also may produce isolation, stigmatization, and difficulty in gaining status (Glenn, 1986). Not only may handicapped students suffer from separation that stems from labeling, but the nonhandicapped students may develop erroneous concepts and stereotypes about what a handicap means.

4. *Work toward social as well as cognitive development.* Subject area knowledge is only one part of the educational picture. The school is a social setting in which students learn many things about themselves and others. If social learning is neglected, students may come to dislike and avoid people who are different. They may become prejudiced and belittle individuals with less ability. On the other hand, if social learning goals are fostered, students learn to interact as friends and companions and to treat their classmates with respect regardless of their abilities.

We now have more knowledge about how desired social interaction goals can be reached (see Graham, in press, for a review of research in this area). From the standpoint of developing positive social interactions and attitudes in both handicapped and nonhandicapped students, the following principles should be considered:

Verbal prompting and rehearsal. Preparation of both handicapped and nonhandicapped students can greatly improve the chances for good relationships. Often some discussion of the handicapping condition, the feelings of the students, and ways of interacting can be extremely useful.

Beyond this positive start, the teacher may want to describe situations likely to occur and perhaps rehearse some possible reactions. Rather than leaving reactions to chance, the teacher can make all the students much more at ease and eliminate potentially harmful situations.

Modeling desired interaction patterns. Teachers' actions will have a great effect on how their classes act. By drawing attention to some of their own behaviors, teachers can increase the chances that students will imitate them (for example, by making nonhandicapped students aware that working with a particular handicapped student is interesting and enjoyable). Teachers also can subtly draw attention to students who are interacting positively. Other students will observe this activity and be likely to imitate it.

Reinforcing appropriate social interactions. Teachers need to pay attention to exchanges between handicapped and nonhandicapped students and use their attention to strengthen positive interactions. When you see handicapped and nonhandicapped students together, for example, you can move toward them, visit with them, put your hand on their shoulders, smile, and so on, in confirmation of their exchange. Your attention will help increase the chances their interactions will continue.

Teachers also can reinforce nonhandicapped students for including handicapped students in social groups and making positive comments about them. In the same way, the positive social behaviors of handicapped students (initiating conversations, helping others) also can be prompted and reinforced.

Designing mutually rewarding situations. Many group activities are set up in such a way that the failure or slow work of one student leads to the failure of the entire group. If the group finishes last because of a handicapped student's performance, for example, other students may become angry and resentful. The fault, however, is with the person who designed the group activity, not the students. It is better to use only those group activities in which the roles of both handicapped and nonhandicapped students are linked to group success. It takes some thinking on the part of the teacher to do this, but by careful planning the teacher can find useful, productive roles for all children in group activities (Glenn, 1986). This may mean, however, that teachers must largely eliminate competitive group arrangements, particularly where one child's less than adequate performance can keep a group from being rewarded.

Developing independence and assertion in the handicapped student. Some handicapped stu-

dents, particularly those with physical and health-related handicaps, may develop a very passive approach to the world. For many reasons, some handicapped children may come to learn to depend on others to initiate activity, take care of their needs, and select their goals. Many of the methods of classroom management—selecting target activities that need to be increased, prompting assertive responses, and providing reinforcement for independence—can help such children work toward independence.

In some cases, a handicapped student (or any student) may not have the social skills that will encourage others to be friendly. Behaviors such as failure to listen, distractibility, clumsiness, loud yelling, bullying, or being withdrawn may make it very hard for the student to gain acceptance. If appropriate social skills are developed (see Chapter Ten) the way is opened for handicapped and nonhandicapped students to experience each other in the most positive way possible.

5. *Learn emergency procedures.* With some handicaps, emergencies may occur that require prompt, skilled actions to prevent mental or physical harm. Teachers should become familiar with the possible signs of emergencies in the handicapped students in their classrooms and should work out emergency procedures in advance. They should be alert for unusual signs in handicapped children, particularly those on medication or with chronic health problems.

Summary

Effective instruction must be based on the recognition of individual differences. Individual differences are most pronounced in exceptional students, who vary the most from the majority of students in one or more traits, abilities, or characteristics. Exceptional students include handicapped students, who may have a physical disability, a behavior disorder, or intellectual limitations. Exceptional students also include gifted students, who may have outstanding aptitude for academic work. Effective instruction for both handicapped and gifted students depends on matching instruction to the special needs of the learner.

Exceptional students traditionally have been categorized into groups, including the mentally retarded, learning disabled, hard of hearing or deaf, visually handicapped, speech impaired, emotionally disturbed, orthopedically or health impaired, and exceptionally academically talented. Many educators, however, have strong reservations about labeling and grouping exceptional students and believe it is harmful to base educational decisions on such categories.

An alternative approach grows out of the concepts of least restrictive environment, mainstreaming, and aptitude-treatment interaction. Least restrictive environment implies there is a "best" environment for each student, regardless of the category of handicap. *Mainstreaming* refers to teaching exceptional students together with their nonhandicapped peers in the regular classroom. The aptitude-treatment interaction concept implies that some methods of instruction are relatively more effective than others for students with different traits or levels of ability. The regular classroom, with appropriate resources, is the least restrictive environment for most handicapped students and provides the best opportunity for matching instruction to their needs.

Regular classroom teachers require a number of skills in order to make mainstreaming an effective approach. These skills include using resource personnel, adapting objectives, altering methods, employing alternative means of evaluation, and facilitating growth.

Suggested Readings

Borkowski, J. G., & Day, J. (1988). *Cognition in special children*. Norwood, NJ: Ablex.

> *Borkowski and Day have put together an outstanding volume. It is strongly recommended.*

Heward, W. L., & Orlansky, M. D. (1988). *Exceptional children: An introductory survey of special education*. Columbus, Ohio: Merrill.

> *A text for individuals who will work with handicapped students, this book provides basic descriptions of categories of handicaps.*

McLeod, J., & Cropley, A. (1988). *Fostering academic excellence*. New York: Pergamon.

> *The focus of this volume is on highly able students.*

Rodda, M., & Grove, C. (1987). *Language, cognition, and deafness.* Hillsdale, NJ: Erlbaum.
    This volume provides interesting information on language and cognition among the deaf.

Vaid, J. (1986). *Language processing in bilinguals.* Hillsdale, NJ: Erlbaum.
    This is a useful book devoted to understanding how bilingual individuals process information.

Answers to Practice Exercise 15–2

1. *Mainstreamed regular classroom.* Although Bill's behaviors are somewhat disruptive to others and often unproductive, he will do best in the regular classroom. A resource teacher or school psychologist may be of considerable assistance in helping the teacher devise a behavioral program for Bill.

2. *Mainstreamed regular classroom.* Formerly, many such children were placed in a special-education classroom. Most are now mainstreamed. The teacher will require special help from the school psychologist and resource teacher; with no help, the regular classroom would not be a good place for Harriet.

3. *Nonschool setting.* By careful programming, useful behaviors can be taught in many instances to profoundly retarded children such as Natalie. Because of the extensive nature of her disabilities, however, general care is required that ordinarily is now best provided in an institutional setting. This care includes programs to shape and teach basic skills whenever possible, nursing and other medical services, and round-the-clock supervision. A child like Natalie often will live in an institution for the mentally retarded. Individuals who have more skills than Natalie (such as mobility and self-care) may be placed in community-based programs, which often combine training with group-home living arrangements, and in some cases, the public schools.

4. *Nonschool setting.* Perhaps more than any other handicapped group, the deaf and hearing impaired have advocated a residential school approach. Many deaf and hard-of-hearing individuals strongly believe that the auditorily impaired student can be educated adequately *only* in a residential school. Specific skills such as signing and speech reading of-

ten are needed. The public schools often are not viewed as potential direct providers of much of this instruction. For those with less severe disabilities, however, mainstreaming has been attempted with many positive (but some negative) outcomes.

5. *Special classroom.* A temporary placement in a special class setting may be appropriate in this instance. Jim needs to learn self-control, which often is best taught by systematic programs in a *controlled* environment. The regular classroom might involve too many unpredictable factors and too large a student-teacher ratio to expect that self-control could be learned there. An effective program would be to establish self-control skills in the special class and then to gradually reintegrate Jim into the regular classroom.

6. *Mainstreamed regular classroom.* No other placement should even be considered, but conditions in the regular classroom certainly could use some improvement. The teacher needs to plan for individualized instruction, work with the class on social behavior, and improve Milton's interactive skills.

GLOSSARY

Accommodation: According to Piaget, accommodation is the process of modifying existing cognitive structures so that new information can be assimilated. (*See also* Assimilation.)

Achievement motivation: Acquired needs to perform successfully.

Achievement test: An achievement test is designed to measure the knowledge and abilities of students in subject matter areas.

Active response modes: Methods of enhancing reading comprehension that actively involve the reader.

Adjunct aids: Techniques designed to facilitate students' comprehension of reading materials.

Advance organizer: An overview of major ideas in reading materials designed to facilitate comprehension. Students read it prior to reading the materials.

Affective objective: An instructional objective that specifies learning outcomes related to students' values, preferences, and feelings.

Alphabetic writing: Alphabetic writing includes symbols for both consonant and vowel sounds. English and other Western languages use alphabetic writing.

Anecdotal record: A written report of specific incidents occurring in the classroom or elsewhere.

Applied research: Applied research in educational psychology is conducted to find solutions to actual educational problems.

Apply goal: The final goal to be reached in a means-end analysis of problem solving.

Aptitude test: Used to predict future cognitive or psychomotor performance.

Assimilation: In Piaget's theory, assimilation is the process of relating new information to already existing cognitive structures.

Attention: The focus of cognitive functions on particular aspects of tasks engaged in by an individual.

Attribute: *See* Concept attribute.

Attribution theory: Attribution theory seeks to explain behavior in terms of the kinds of interpretations people make about their experiences.

Basic research: Basic research in educational psychology is conducted to answer fundamental questions about the nature of learning or teaching without concern for any direct applications of the results.

Behavioral assessment: A method of judging educational processes and outcomes by systematically recording student behaviors.

Behavioral psychology: The study of the behavior of organisms. It focuses on observable events and has as its goal the prediction and control of behavior.

Being needs: In Maslow's hierarchy, being needs are based on the basic human desires for self-actualization, knowledge, and aesthetics.

Biculturalism: A situation in which individuals experience and assimilate the language and customs of two cultures. One possible goal of bilingual education is that students become bicultural.

Bilingualism: Strictly speaking, the ability to function fluently and interchangeably in two languages. Bilingualism may exist in degrees, however, ranging from complete competence in two languages to partial competence in either or both.

Causal attributions: The analyses we make of situations for which we seek "why" answers.

Causally-linked reactions: Reactions determined by people's analyses of *why* events occurred.

Central tendency: An average score or scores that best represent the performance of a group of students who have taken a test. The mean, median, and mode are measures of central tendency.

Checklist: A listing of steps, actions, or activities that an observer can mark as present or absent during an observation of student performance.

Classical conditioning: A form of learning in which a neutral stimulus, after being paired with an eliciting (unconditioned) stimulus, acquires the ability to bring forth the original reflex.

Cognitive objective: An instructional objective that specifies cognitive learning outcomes, such as concept learning or problem solving.

Cognitive processes: All the functions of the mind, including attention, memory, concept learning, problem solving, creative thinking.

Cognitive psychology: The systematic study of cognitive processes.

Cognitive style: Variations in how students typically approach, process, and remember information.

Completion question: A completion question, one type of objective test item, requires students to supply a word or phrase to complete an incomplete sentence or to answer a question.

Comprehension: The second stage of reading, in which the reader gains an overall understanding of the content.

Concept: A class of stimuli (information) that people group together on the basis of perceived commonalities.

Concept attribute: A similarity occurring across examples of a concept. Some attributes (defining attributes) are essential to defining the concept, while others (characteristic attributes) may pertain to only some examples.

Concrete operations: During the concrete operations stage (approximately seven to eleven years of age) of Piaget's stages of cognitive development, children develop the ability to apply logical thought to concrete problems.

Conditioned response: In classical conditioning, a response that is elicited by a formerly neutral stimulus (conditioned stimulus).

Conditioned stimulus: A formerly neutral stimulus that, through being paired with an eliciting (unconditioned) stimulus, comes to be able to elicit a conditioned response.

Conjunctive concept: A conjunctive concept is defined by common (shared) attributes. "Shoe" is a conjunctive concept because all shoes have in common the attributes of a sole and some means of being attached to a foot.

Conservation: In Piaget's theory, conservation means understanding that such features of objects as number, mass, and area are not changed by superficial transformations of the objects or set of objects.

Construct validity: How well a test or other instrument measures a psychological construct, which is an inferred state within a person such as creativity, intelligence, or personality that cannot be directly observed but must be inferred from visible evidence.

Content validity: The extent to which a test fairly samples and represents the content areas to be measured.

Contingency contract: *See* Individual contract.

Convergent thinking: The generation of ideas from given information with the emphasis on problem solutions that are conventionally acceptable.

Correlation coefficient: A numerical index of the degree of relationship between two sets of measures. The values of the correlation coefficient can range from $+1.00$ to -1.00.

Creative behavior: A behavior that is both novel and of value.

Criterion-referenced measure: A criterion-referenced measure (test) compares an individual's performance to a standard of performance, not to the performance of other persons.

Deafness: The absence of functional hearing.

Decay theory: Decay theory states that memories fade with the passage of time.

Decentration: In Piagetian theory, decentration occurs when children no longer focus on a single attribute of objects but begin to consider more than one feature at a time.

Declarative knowledge: The facts we possess and the beliefs we have about the world make up our declarative knowledge.

Decoding: Decoding is the initial stage of reading, in which the reader obtains the meaning of individual words.

Deficiency needs: In Maslow's hierarchy, deficiency needs are needs that humans are motivated to fulfill as a result of their lacking them.

Deictic tutoring: Deictic tutoring is a pattern of teaching young children in which objects are identified, looked at together, and named.

Diagnostic evaluation: Diagnostic evaluation is conducted to determine the reasons why a student is having problems in learning.

Discriminative stimulus: A cue for operant behavior.

Disjunctive concept: A concept defined by attributes of either one type or another type. An object is a member of a particular concept category if it possesses either one set of attributes *or* a second set of attributes.

Distinctiveness-of-encoding: In distinctiveness-of-encoding, based on the levels-of-processing perspective, the more distinctive events are, the more memorable they will be.

Divergent thinking: The generation of ideas from given information with the emphasis on variety and quantity of problem solutions.

Domain-specific knowledge: Knowledge about a specific area.

Educational psychology: The branch of psychology devoted to the study of how humans learn and how to help them learn.

Egocentrism: In Piaget's theory, egocentrism refers to the self-centered perspective of preoperational children, who cannot yet comprehend the viewpoints of others.

Elaboration-of-processing: In elaboration-of-processing, based on the levels-of-processing perspective, memory depends on how elaborately information is encoded.

Eliciting stimuli: Eliciting or unconditioned stimuli cause involuntary responses. A bright light shining in the eye is an eliciting stimulus for contraction of the pupil.

Encoding: The taking in of new information and the representation of it symbolically in thought.

Entity-oriented theory: A belief that personality characteristics are fixed and uncontrollable.

Episodic memory: A memory system that holds information about people's personal experiences.

Equilibration: Piaget referred to equilibration as the process that motivates humans to attempt to balance accommodation and assimilation.

Essay question: An essay question asks people to construct an answer in their own words in either written or oral form.

Evaluation: The process of using measurements to make a judgment of the value of something.

Extinction: In operant conditioning, extinction is a process in which a response occurs less and less frequently as a function of nonreinforcement. In classical conditioning, extinction of a conditioned response occurs when the conditioned stimulus is no longer paired with the eliciting (unconditioned) stimulus.

Fixation: In reading, fixation refers to the brief period of time in which the eyes come to rest on the text. (*See* Saccades.).

Flexibility: In measures of creativity, flexibility refers to the number of *different* kinds of ideas a person thinks of when faced with a problem.

Fluency: In measures of creativity, fluency refers to the number of ideas a person develops in response to a problem.

Formal operations: The last of the stages of cognitive development described by Piaget (eleven years through adulthood). During this stage many children are able to apply logic to a host of problems, both concrete and abstract. Some individuals apparently never attain formal operations.

Formative evaluation: Formative evaluation takes place during instruction and is designed to help teachers adjust their instruction to better help students meet their objectives.

Frequency distribution: A tally of how many students obtain each score on a test or other measure.

Functionalism: The first truly American school of thought in psychology. Its objectives were to determine how and why mental activity occurs.

Generalization: The making of the same response to two or more differing stimuli.

Gestalt psychology: A German school of thought, Gestalt psychology rejected atomism and reductionism and argued that humans perceive experiences as an organized field of events that interact and mutually affect one another. Gestalt psychology was the forerunner of much of contemporary cognitive psychology.

Gifted student: One who possesses superior intellectual or other abilities. The specific definitions vary from state to state but usually consist of criteria based on intelligence-test results, achievement test results, or creativity test results.

Goal state: In a problem representation, the goal state refers to the situation a person wants to be in when the problem is solved.

Good Behavior Game: A variant of the token economy in which group competition is coupled with token reinforcement procedures.

Group contract: An agreement negotiated between a teacher and a group of students that specifies both student and teacher behavior.

Hearing impaired: Hearing-impaired people have partial hearing. (*See* Deafness.)

Heuristic search: In problem solving, a heuristic search is one that is guided by some plan or body of knowledge.

Home-based contingencies: Behavior management programs in which the backup reinforcers are administered at home by the parents.

Hyperactivity: Hyperactivity (hyperkinesis) is a learning disorder characterized by excessive activity, inattentiveness, and impulsiveness.

Ill-defined problem: An ill-defined problem requires that the problem solver furnish the information necessary to solve the problem. Typically, there is not necessarily one right answer for ill-defined problems.

Imitation: The copying of the actions of one individual by another.

Individual contract: An agreement negotiated between one student and a teacher. The student generally agrees to change a behavior in return for reinforcement.

Information-processing model: A model of human cognition based on computers.

Initial state: In a problem representation, the initial state refers to conditions existing at the onset of a problem.

Instantiation: The process by which elements in the environment are correctly identified and matched to schemata.

Instructional objectives: An explicit statement of what students will be able to do as a result of instruction.

Intelligence quotient: The intelligence quotient (IQ) was originally defined as the ratio of mental age to chronological age, multiplied by 100. Newer tests of intelligence use an IQ measure derived from standard scores. (*See* Standard scores.)

Intelligence test: An intelligence test is designed to measure students' general mental abilities. It provides an estimate of how much a person has profited from past experience and how well he or she adapts to new situations.

Interest inventory: An interest inventory assesses how people feel about various kinds of activities and how closely their interests parallel those of individuals already holding jobs.

Interpretive exercise: An interpretive exercise consists of a descriptive statement or paragraph, pictorial materials, or both, followed by a series of multiple-choice questions that require the student to interpret the material.

Introspection: The major data-gathering method used by the structuralists. Introspection involves having experimental subjects report their mental events.

Item analysis: A set of techniques for judging the worth of questions. It provides two kinds of information: item difficulty and item discrimination (whether "good" students got the item right more often than "poor" students).

Item bias: The possibility that a text item may be biased toward or against certain individuals taking the test. For example, a standardized test item based on one American subculture may be inordinately difficult for members of another subculture.

Learning disability: Students with learning disabilities have normal or near-normal intelligence but have severe difficulties in understanding or using spoken or written language.

Least restrictive environment: An important part of the Education for All Handicapped Children Act (P.L. 94-142). The least restrictive environment for a special-needs student is the program or setting that provides the most normal but also the most effective environment for learning.

Levels-of-processing: A model for memory research developed by Fergus Craik and his associates that suggests that what a person remembers about an event is determined by the depth of the analysis of the material.

Locus of control: A term coined by Julian Rotter, refers to whether people feel the control of their successes and failures lies internally or externally to themselves.

Logography: A logography is a written language in which each word or concept is represented by a symbol for that word (a logogram).

Long-term memory: The permanent repository of information acquired from the world around us.

Mainstreaming: The education of handicapped students in the regular classroom for all or parts of the school day.

Matching questions: A form of objective question in which students match items from one list to corresponding items in another list.

Mean: The arithmetic average of a set of scores.

Meaningful learning: Learning is meaningful when it can be related to what is already known. Meaningful learning requires comprehension and understanding of the material to be learned.

Means-end analysis: A method of problem solving in which a problem is broken down into its component parts or subproblems and then solved using different means to resolve each subproblem.

Measurement error: The part of a person's score unrelated to the quality that was being measured. Measurement error is present in all test scores and ratings of performance.

Median: The median of a set of scores is that point above which half the scores fall and below which half the scores fall, that is, the midpoint of all scores.

Mediating responses: In Bandura's social learning theory, mediating responses are symbolic events (thoughts) that people envision when they encounter stimuli.

Mental age: The average raw score of children in the norm group of a specific age on measures of intelligence.

Mentally retarded students: Mentally retarded students have below-average mental functioning and ordinarily some delay in social or other areas of development.

Metacognition: In literal terms, metacognition means thinking about thinking. Metacognitive processes occur in working memory.

Metalinguistic awareness: The knowledge individuals acquire about language and their use of knowledge about language.

Metamemory: Knowledge people have about their own memory.

Mnemonic: A familiar word or image that is paired with new information to make the new information more meaningful.

Mode: The most frequently occurring score on a test.

Modeling: A demonstration of a behavior to be imitated by others.

Morphemes: The minimal units of meaning in spoken language.

Motherese: The special speech mothers and others direct to small children.

Multiple-choice question: A form of objective question that requires students to choose a correct answer from a set of alternative responses.

Nature-nurture question: The nature-nurture question concerns the relative influence of heredity (nature) and the environment (nurture) on individual abilities.

Negative reinforcer: A form of reinforcer that precedes the behaviors it strengthens. Negative reinforcers strengthen escape or avoidant behavior.

Network model: A model of semantic memory that pictures memories as hierarchical. Memories in such a hierarchy are thought to be connected to one another, with specific bits of knowledge placed at separate locations.

Neutral stimulus: A neutral stimulus is perceived by learners but has little or no effect on behavior.

Normal curve: In a normal curve (or normal distribution), the mean, the median, and the mode are identical, and they all fall at the same place on the curve, the center. The curve is symmetrical around this point with the number of scores decreasing away from the midpoint.

Norm-referenced measure: A norm-referenced measure is constructed to compare one person's performance with the performance of others.

Objective question: An objective question requires students to make very brief responses that are compared to predetermined answers.

Operant conditioning: Learning that is strengthened or modified by the consequences it produces.

Operating space: In Case's view, working memory has two aspects—operating space and short-term storage space. Operating space is used for actually processing information.

Operation: A scheme whose major characteristic is that it can be reversed.

Operator: In a problem representation, an operator is an action a person may take to reach the goal state.

Originality: In measures of creativity, originality refers to the development of rare or uncommon ideas.

Outcome-dependent reactions: Outcome-dependent reactions to events are reactions that are determined entirely by their results.

Parallel distributed processing: The theory of human memory that claims that humans are more flexible than computers because humans can consider pieces of information simultaneously.

Pattern matching: In problem solving, pattern matching is a form of heuristic search in which the problem solver attempts to recall previous actions that solved similar problems.

Percentile rank: A percentile rank (percentile) describes a particular student's test performance by giving the proportion of students in the norm group who obtained scores at or lower than the student's score.

Perception: In cognitive psychology, perception is the process of determining the meaning of what is sensed.

Phonemes: The smallest units of sound in which differences in sound result in differences in meaning.

Phones: Distinct, identifiable speech sounds are referred to as phones.

Phonetics: The study of human soundmaking.

Phonics: A common approach to the teaching of reading based on the decoding of sounds from letters and words.

Phonographic language: A form of written language in which the symbols represent the sounds of the spoken language.

Phonological recoding: When children can recode written symbols into sounds, they are engaged in phonological recoding.

Placement evaluation: Placement evaluation is made prior to the start of instruction to match students with instruction based on their entry characteristics.

Positive reinforcer: A reinforcing stimulus that occurs subsequent to behavior and strengthens the behavior that it follows. Positive reinforcers play a major role in operant conditioning.

Potency of reinforcement: The term *potency of reinforcement* refers to the ability of a stimulus to strengthen behaviors.

Pragmatics: The study of the effect of context on language.

Predictive validity: The degree to which a measure can accurately predict future performance.

Premack Principle: The Premack Principle states that for every pair of responses or activities in which an individual engages, the more probable one will reinforce the less probable one.

Preoperational stage: During the preoperational stage of cognitive development, as posited by Piaget, children rapidly develop language and conceptual thought. The stage is thought to begin at about age two and continue until approximately age seven.

Primary reinforcer: A stimulus that strengthens behaviors because of our biological nature.

Principle: A statement or rule that describes the relationship between two or more concepts.

Proactive interference: Proactive interference occurs when a learner is given a first set of information to learn followed by a second set of information to learn. Then, when the learner is tested on the second set of information, the first set inhibits the recall of the second set of information.

Problem: A problem exists when a person is in one situation, wants to be in another, but doesn't know how to get there.

Problem representation: Problem representation refers to how people understand problems. A complete problem representation involves understanding of the initial state, the goal state, the operators, and restrictions on the operators.

Problem space: The problem space is the total number of actions a problem solver considers possible in solving a problem.

Procedural knowledge: That knowledge we have that can be demonstrated through the performance of tasks.

Proposition: The smallest unit of information about which it makes sense to make a judgment of true or false.

Prototype: In human memory, a prototype is an identifiable case that is a good example of a concept.

Proximity search: In problem solving, proximity searches are heuristics that employ environmental feedback to determine whether the problem solver is moving closer to or further from the goal.

Psychometry: The measurement of psychological variables.

Psychomotor objectives: An instructional objective that specifies learning outcomes related primarily to skilled physical movements.

Punishing stimulus: A stimulus that occurs subsequent to behaviors and decreases the occurrence of the behaviors it follows.

Random search: In problem solving, a random search is one that is not guided by a plan or a body of knowledge.

Rating scale: A rating scale usually indicates a trait or characteristic to be judged and a scale on which the rating can be made.

Ratio IQ: An intelligence test score calculated by dividing an individual's mental age by his/her chronological age and multiplying by 100.

Raw score: A raw score is usually the number of items a student answers correctly on a test prior to any type of transformation of the score. (*See* Standard scores.)

Reciprocal determinism: Bandura's concept of reciprocal determinism holds that the social behavior of individuals occurs because of prior interactions with other people and with the immediate environment.

Reduction goal: In problem solving, reduction goals are subgoals met on the way to reaching the final goal.

Regression: A reader's eye movement back to an earlier segment of text; a "look-back."

Reinforcement potency: The effectiveness or potency of reinforcers is determined by their ability to strengthen behaviors. The greater the probability that a reinforcer will strengthen a behavior, the more potent it is said to be.

Reinforcing stimulus: A reinforcing stimulus (reinforcer) is a stimulus that, when applied to a behavior, strengthens it.

Relational concept: A relational concept is defined by a relationship between two or more of the concept's attributes (for example, north, above).

Reliability: A measure is reliable (has reliability) if it is a consistent and accurate measure.

Respondent conditioning: *See* Classical conditioning.

Response: A reaction by an organism to a stimulus.

Retrieval: The recall or recognition of information stored in memory.

Retroactive interference: Retroactive interference occurs when a person learns one set of information, followed by a second set of information, and the second set then inhibits recall of the first set of information.

Rote learning: Learning that has little or no meaning to the learner.

S^D: An S^D is a discriminative stimulus that signals that certain behaviors will be reinforced in its presence. For example, a green traffic light is an S^D for accelerating a car.

S$^\Delta$: An S$^\Delta$ (Ess-Delta) is a discriminative stimulus that signals that certain behaviors will not be reinforced in its presence. For instance, a red traffic light is an S$^\Delta$ for accelerating your car.

Saccade: The jump the eyes make from one fixation to the next during reading.

Satiation: Reinforcers often lose their potency as they are acquired in large amounts or in great numbers.

Schedule of reinforcement: The relationship of the number of reinforcers to the number of behaviors necessary to acquire the reinforcers. Common schedules include continuous, fixed-interval, variable-interval, fixed-ratio, and variable-ratio reinforcement.

Schema: A cognitive structure by which people organize events and objects on the basis of common characteristics.

Schema activation: Techniques designed to activate relevant schemata prior to a learning activity.

Schema theory: A modern view of human memory based, in part, on Piaget's ideas about schemata. In this perspective, schemata are knowledge structures of related information, and they provide frameworks for understanding new information and experiences.

Scheme: In Piaget's terms, a scheme is a cognitive structure by which people represent their operative knowledge.

Scholastic aptitude test: Scholastic aptitude test usually refers to group tests of general mental ability. They are used often to predict future academic performance.

Secondary reinforcer: A formerly neutral stimulus that has acquired some of the reinforcing value of primary reinforcers by being paired with them or other secondary reinforcers.

Self-concept: A person's view of himself or herself. People with a positive self-concept consider themselves worthwhile; people with a negative self-concept generally devalue their own worth.

Self-report: A record of information students have furnished by talking or writing about themselves.

Self-schema: The term *self-schema* is used by some cognitive theorists to describe the schema that people employ to make judgments about themselves.

Semantic memory: A memory system that stores memory for knowledge. The central feature of most models of semantic memory is the concept.

Semantics: The term used to refer to word meaning and the meaning of word combinations.

Sense receptors: The organs that allow us to contact the world and the information in it (eyes, ears, nose, mouth, and so on).

Sensing: In cognitive psychology, sensing refers to an awareness of an element of the environment prior to perception.

Sensorimotor stage: During the sensorimotor stage of cognitive development (birth to approximately two years of age), children's cognitive processes are closely linked to motor activity. Sensorimotor children do not yet think abstractly, although cognitive development can be observed as they display awareness of themselves and their surroundings.

Sensory registers: Holding systems that briefly maintain stimuli so they can be analyzed. It is thought that each of the senses has its own sensory register.

Set: A person's tendency to approach different problems in the same way.

Set-theoretic model: A set-theoretic model of semantic memory suggests that memory is stored as sets of elements such that each set includes all instances of that set as well as its attributes.

Shaping: A technique for modifying a response through reinforcement of successive approximations of that response.

Short-term memory: The part of the working memory in which incoming information is briefly stored.

Social behavior: Social behavior includes all the many kinds of interactions among people within a particular environment or geographic location.

Sociometric assessment: The evaluation of the level of social acceptance of students and the social structures of groups.

Solution path: In problem solving, a solution path refers to a way of employing operators that will take the problem solver from the initial state to the goal state.

Spontaneous recovery: The term used to denote the recurrence of an apparently extinguished response.

Standard deviation: An index of how spread out a set of test scores is from the mean of those scores.

Standard error of measurement: The standard deviation of a set of an individual's own scores. It is usually determined on the basis of a test's reliability and standard deviation and indicates the likelihood that an individual's obtained score is a good estimate of his or her true score.

Standard score: A test score based on standard deviations and the assumption that the distribution of scores is normal.

Standardized test: A standardized test is identified by three criteria: (1) it has been carefully prepared, tried out, analyzed, and reviewed; (2) the instructions and conditions for administering and scoring it are uniform; and (3) the results of the test may be interpreted by comparing them to tables of norms.

Standardization sample: The standardized sample (norm group) is a carefully selected sample of persons representative of the individuals for whom a standardized test is targeted. Their scores, called norms, serve as the frame of reference for evaluating the scores of future takers of the test.

Stimulus: A perceivable unit of the environment that may affect behavior.

Storage: In models of memory, storage refers to the holding of memories across time.

Storage space: In Case's view, working memory has two aspects—operating space and short-term storage space. Storage space is used for holding information in order to allow for processing.

Structuralism: The first school of thought in psychology. Founded by Wilhelm Wundt, it sought to identify basic cognitive processes, the ways in which the elements of thought combined, and the relationship of cognitive to physiological processes.

Summative evaluation: Summative evaluation occurs at the end of instruction and is designed to determine the extent to which the goals of instruction have been met.

Superstitious behavior: Superstitious behavior (superstition) is seen when reinforcement occurs on an accidental basis but a person nonetheless makes a connection between an action not associated with reinforcement and the occurrence of the reinforcement. Behavior is strengthened accidentally.

Syllabary: A syllabary is a form of written language in which there are written symbols for consonants and consonant-vowel combinations.

Syntax: The term used to refer to the ways that words are combined into larger meaningful units.

T score: A standard score with a mean of 50 and a standard deviation of 10.

Table of specifications: A blueprint for a test that relates the course objectives to the construction of the test.

Task analysis: The breaking down of an objective into a hierarchy of prerequisite knowledge and skills.

Task description: A step-by-step description of the sequence of things to be done in a task.

Test: A sample of questions that require students to select or supply written or oral responses.

Test-retest reliability: Test-retest reliability measures the stability of scores from one administration of a test to a second administration of the same test.

The "I": The part of the self that performs analyses—"I" does the thinking.

The "Me": The part of the self that is analyzed by the "I." The "Me" is that part of the self being thought about.

Time-out: The brief removal of a child from a reinforcing setting to one that is not reinforcing.

Token economy: A systematic method of providing students with immediate reinforcement for behavior using some form of tokens (checks, points, and the like).

True-false question: A form of objective question that requires students to judge statements as either correct or incorrect.

Unconditioned response: In classical conditioning, an unconditioned response is an unlearned, involuntary reaction to an eliciting (unconditioned) stimulus. The reflex linking the unconditioned stimulus and the unconditioned response is unlearned.

Unconditioned stimulus: An unconditioned or eliciting stimulus brings forth an unlearned, involuntary response. Unconditioned stimuli do not require learning to elicit a response (a puff of air on the eye brings forth a blink).

Validity: A measurement is said to possess validity (be valid) if it measures what it is supposed to measure.

Variability: The extent to which scores on a test are spread out around the measure of central tendency.

Vicarious reinforcement: The reinforcing effect of a person's observing models who receive reinforcement.

Visually impaired: Students are classified as visually impaired if special adaptations of educational programs and materials are required because of their vision. Blind people have no functional vision.

Well-defined problem: A well-defined problem presents a problem situation that contains all the necessary information for a solution. Usually there is only one (or a few) right answers to a well-defined problem.

Working memory: The component of cognitive models in which thinking occurs. It is the executive component of models of cognition.

Yodai mnemonics: Developed by Japanese researchers and used in the Suzuki method of teaching music, yodai mnemonics employ objects and events children know well as pegs on which they can hook to-be-remembered information.

z-score: A standard score that gives a person's performance on a test in standard deviation units above or below the mean. z-scores have a mean of 0 and a standard deviation of 1.

REFERENCES

Abravenel, E., & Gingold, H. (1985). Learning via observation during the second year of life. *Developmental Psychology 21*, 614–623.

Acredolo, L. P., Pick, H. L., & Olsen, M. G. (1975). Environmental differentiation and familiarity as determinants of children's memory for spatial location. *Developmental Psychology, 11*, 495–501.

Aiken, L. R. (1979). *Psychological testing and assessment* (3rd ed.). Boston: Allyn & Bacon.

Alexander, J. E. (1988). *Teaching reading* (3rd ed.). Glenview, IL: Scott, Foresman/Little, Brown.

Algozzine, B., & Korinek, L. (1985). Where is special education for students with high prevalence handicaps going? *Exceptional Children, 51*, 388–394.

Algozzine, B., Mercer, C. D., & Countermine, T. (1977). The effect of labels and behavior on teacher expectations. *Exceptional Children, 44*, 121–132.

Allen, D. I. (1970). Some effects of advance organizers and level of questions on the learning and retention of written social studies material. *Journal of Educational Psychology, 61*, 333–339.

Allport, F. H. (1924). *Social psychology.* Cambridge, MA: Riverside Press.

Allport, G. W. (1937). *Personality: A psychological interpretation.* New York: Holt, Rinehart & Winston.

Alpert, A. (1928). *The solving of problem situations by preschool children.* New York: Columbia University Press.

Alvord, M. K., & O'Leary, K. D. (1985). Teaching children to share through stories. *Psychology in the Schools, 22*, 323–330.

Ames, C., & Archer, J. (1988). Achievement goals in the classroom: Students' learning strategies and motivation processes. *Journal of Educational Psychology, 80*, 260–267.

Anastasia, A. (1988). *Psychological testing* (6th ed.). New York: Macmillan.

Anderson, J. R. (1983). A spreading activation theory of memory. *Journal of Verbal Learning and Verbal Behavior, 22*, 261–295.

Anderson, J. R., & Bower, G. H. (1973). *Human associative memory.* Washington, DC: Winston.

Anderson, J. R., Kline, P. J., & Lewis, C. H. (1977). A production system model of language processing. In M. A. Just & P. A. Carpenter (Eds.), *Cognitive process in comprehension* (pp. 192–207). Hillsdale, NJ: Erlbaum.

Anderson, L. W. (1988). Attitudes and their measurement. In J. P. Keeves (Ed.), *Educational research, methodology, & measurement: An international handbook.* New York: Pergamon Press.

Anderson, R. C. (1984). Role of the reader's schema in comprehension, learning, and memory. In R. C. Anderson, J. Osborn, & R. J. Tierney (Eds.) *Learning to read in American schools* (pp. 243–258). Hillsdale, NJ: Erlbaum.

Anderson, R. C., Reynolds, R. E., Schallert, D. L. & Goetz, E. T. (1977). Frameworks for comprehending discourse. *American Educational Research Journal, 14*, 367–381.

Anderson, R. C., Spiro, R. J., & Anderson, M. C. (1978). Schemata as scaffolding for the representation of information in connected discourse. *American Educational Research Journal, 15*, 433–439.

Anderson, R. C., Wilson, P. T., & Fielding, L. G. (1988). Growth in reading and how children spend their time outside school. *Reading Research Quarterly, 23*, 263–284.

Anderson, S., & Howess, C. M. (1987). *Getting ready for school: A calendar of practical activities.* Glenview, IL: Scott, Foresman.

Anderson, T., & Boyer, M. (1970). *Bilingual schooling in the United States* (Vols. 1 & 2). Washington, DC: U.S. Government Printing Office.

Anderson, T. N. (1981). Active response modes: Comprehension "aids" in need of a theory. *Journal of Reading Behavior, 21*, 221–229.

Andre, T. (1979). Does answering higher-level questions while reading facilitate productive learning? *Review of Educational Research, 49*, 280–318.

Andre, T. (1987). Processes in reading comprehension and the teaching of comprehension. In J. A. Glover & R. R. Ronning (Eds.), *Historical foundations of educational psychology.* New York: Plenum.

Anisfeld, M. (1984). *Language development from birth to three.* Hillsdale, NJ: Erlbaum.

Applebee, A. N. (1984). Writing and reasoning. *Review of Educational Research, 54,* 577–596.

Applebee, A. N. (1988). *The national assessment.* Paper presented to the annual meeting of the American Educational Research Association. New Orleans.

Armbruster, R. B., & Brown, A. L. (1984). Learning from reading: The role of metacognition. In R. C. Anderson, J. Osborn, & R. J. Tierney (Eds.), *Learning to read in American schools* (pp. 273–281). Hillsdale, NJ: Erlbaum.

Armstrong, S. L., Gleitman, L. R., & Gleitman, H. (1985). What some concepts might not be. In A. M. Aitkenhead & J. M. Slack (Eds.), *Issues in cognitive modeling* (pp. 121–179). Hillsdale, NJ: Erlbaum.

Aronson, E., Blaney, N., Sikes, J., & Snapp, M. (1978). *The jigsaw classroom.* Beverly Hills, CA: Sage Press.

Ashman, A. F., & Conway, R. N. (1988). *Cognitive interventions with intellectually disabled children.* New York: Routledge.

Atkinson, J. W. (1965). Some general implications of conceptual developments in the study of achievement-oriented behavior. In M. R. Jones (Ed.), *Human motivation: A symposium.* Lincoln: University of Nebraska Press.

Atkinson, J. W. (1966). Mainsprings of achievement oriented activity. In J. D. Krumboltz (Ed.), *Learning and the Educational Process.* Chicago: Rand McNally.

Atkinson, J. W. (1967, October). *Implications of curvilinearity in the relationship of efficiency of performance to strength of motivation for studies of individual differences in achievement-related motives.* Paper presented at the meeting of the National Academy of Sciences, University of Michigan, Ann Arbor, MI.

Atkinson, R. C., & Raugh, M. R. (1975). An application of the mnemonic keyword method to the acquisition of a Russian vocabulary. *Journal of Experimental Psychology: Human Learning and Memory, 104,* 126–133.

Atkinson, R. C., & Shiffrin, R. M. (1968). Human memory: A proposed system and its control processes. In K. W. Spence & J. T. Spence (Eds.), *The psychology of learning and motivation: Advances in research and theory* (Vol. 2) (pp. 96–143). New York: Academic Press.

Atwell, M. A. (1985). Predictable books for adolescent readers. *Journal of Reading, 29,* 18–22.

Ausubel, D. P. (1960). The use of advance organizers in the learning and retention of meaningful verbal material. *Journal of Educational Psychology, 51,* 267–272.

Ausubel, D. P. (1961). In defense of verbal learning. *Education Theory, 11,* 15–25.

Ausubel, D. P. (1962). A subsumption theory of meaningful verbal learning and retention. *Journal of General Psychology, 66,* 213–224.

Ausubel, D. P. (1963). *The psychology of meaningful verbal material.* New York: Grune & Stratton.

Ausubel, D. P. (1964). Some psychological aspects of the structure of knowledge. In S. Elam (Ed.), *Education and the structure of knowledge* (pp. 118–167). Skokie, IL: Rand McNally.

Ausubel, D. P. (1966). Early versus delayed review of meaningful learning. *Psychology in Schools, 3,* 195–198.

Ausubel, D. P. (1980). Schemata, cognitive structure, and advance organizers: A reply to Anderson, Spiro, and Anderson. *American Educational Research Journal, 17,* 400–404.

Ausubel, D. P., & Fitzgerald, D. (1961). The role of discriminability in meaningful verbal learning and retention. *Journal of Educational Psychology, 52,* 266–274.

Ausubel, D. P., & Fitzgerald. D. (1962). Organizer, general background, and antecedent learning variables in sequential verbal learning. *Journal of Educational Psychology, 53,* 243–249.

Ausubel, D. P., Novak, J. D., & Hanesian, H. (1978). *Educational psychology: A cognitive view.* New York: Holt, Rinehart & Winston.

Ausubel, D. P., & Youssef, M. (1963). Role of discriminability in meaningful parallel learning. *Journal of Educational Psychology, 54,* 331–336.

Ayers, L. P. (1918). History and present status of educational measurements. *Seventeenth Yearbook of the National Society for the Study of Education* (Part II). Bloomington, IL: Public School Publishing Company.

Ayllon, T., & Azrin, N. H. (1968). *The token economy: A motivation system for therapy and rehabilitation.* New York: Appleton-Century-Crofts.

Azrin, N. H., & Lindsley, O. R. (1956). The reinforcement of cooperation between children. *Journal of Abnormal Social Psychology, 52,* 100–102.

Baars, B. J. (1986). *The cognitive revolution in psychology.* New York: Guilford.

Baer, D., Peterson, R. F., & Sherman, J. A. (1967). The development of imitation by reinforcing behavioral similarity to a model. *Journal of Experimental Analysis of Behavior, 10,* 405–416.

Baer, D. M., & Sherman, J. A. (1964). Reinforcement control learning and retention of meaningful verbal material. *Journal of Educational Psychology, 51,* 267–272.

Bagley, W. C., Bell, J. C., Seashore, C. E., & Whipple, G. M. (1910). Editorial. *Journal of Educational Psychology, 1,* 1–3.

Bain, A. (1855). *The senses and the intellect.* London: Parker.

Baker, L., & Brown, A. (1985). Metacognitive skills of reading. In D. Pearson (Ed.), *Handbook of reading research* (pp. 231–272). New York: Longman.

Baldwin, J. (1913). *Social and ethical interpretation.* New York: Macmillan.

Ballou, F. W. (1915). *Scales for the measurement of English composition.* Cambridge: Harvard University Press.

Bandura, A. (1962). Social learning through imitation. In M. R. Jones (Ed.), *Nebraska Symposium on Motivation: 1962* (pp. 43–81). Lincoln: University of Nebraska Press.

Bandura, A. (1965). Influence of models' reinforcement contingencies on the acquisition of imitation responses. *Journal of Personality and Social Psychology, 1,* 589–595.

Bandura, A. (1969). *Principles of behavior modification.* New York: Holt, Rinehart & Winston.

Bandura, A. (1984). Representing personal determinants in causal structures. *Psychological Review, 91,* 508–511.

Bandura, A. (1985). Catecholamine secretion as a function of perceived coping self-efficacy. *Journal of Consulting and Clinical Psychology, 53,* 406–414.

Bandura, A. (1986). *Social foundations of thought and action: A social cognitive theory.* Englewood Cliffs, N.J.: Prentice-Hall.

Bardis, P. D. (1985). Jensen, Spearman's g and Ghazali's dates: A commentary on interracial peace. *The Behavioral and Brain Sciences, 8,* 219–220.

Barker, G. P., & Graham, S. (1987). Developmental study of praise and blame as attributional cues. *Journal of Educational Psychology, 79,* 62–66.

Barnes, B. R., & Clawson, E. V. (1975). Do advance organizers facilitate learning? Recommendations for further research based on an analysis of 32 studies. *Review of Educational Research, 45,* 637–660.

Barnes, E. J. (1974). Cultural retardation or shortcomings of assessment techniques? In R. J. Jones & D. L. MacMillan (Eds.), *Special education in transition* (pp. 121–162). Boston: Allyn & Bacon.

Barnes, J. M., & Underwood, B. J. (1959). "Fate" of first-list associations in transfer theory. *Journal of Experimental Psychology, 58,* 97–105.

Barrett, S. E., & Shepp, B. E. (1988). Developmental changes in attention skills: The effect of irrelevant variations on encoding and response selection. *Journal of Experimental Child Psychology, 45,* 382–399.

Barrish, H. H., Saunders, M., & Wolf, M. M. (1969). Good Behavior Game: Effects of individual contingencies for group consequences on disruptive behavior in a classroom. *Journal of Applied Behavior Analysis, 2,* 119–124.

Bartlett, F. C. (1932). *Remembering.* London: Cambridge University Press.

Barton, E. J., & Osborne, J. G. (1978a). The development of classroom sharing by a teacher using positive practice. *Behavior Modification, 2,* 231–250.

Barton, E. J., & Osborne, J. G. (1978b). *The development of physical sharing by a classroom teacher through the use of positive practice.* Paper presented at the Annual Convention of the Midwest Association of Behavior Analysis, Chicago.

Bates, E. (1976). *Language and context: The acquisition of pragmatics.* New York: Academic Press.

Bates, E., & MacWhinney, B. (1979). A functionalist approach to the acquisition of grammar. In E. Kennan (Ed.), *Developmental pragmatics* (pp. 221–236). New York: Academic Press.

Beach, R., & Bridwell, L. S. (1984). *New directions in composition research.* New York: Guilford.

Beardsley, L. V., & Marecek-Zeman, M. (1987). Making connections: Facilitating literacy in young children. *Childhood Education, 63,* 159–166.

Beck, A. T., Steer, R. A., Kovacs, M., & Garrison, B. (1985). Hopelessness and eventual suicide: A 10-year prospective study of patients hospitalized with suicidal ideation. *American Journal of Psychiatry, 142,* 555–563.

Beck, I. (1984). Development of comprehension: The impact of the directed reading lesson. In R. C. Anderson, J. Osborn, & R. J. Tierney (Eds.) *Learning to read in American schools* (pp. 3–20). Hillsdale, NJ: Erlbaum.

Beck, T. C. (1979). Cognitive therapy: Nature and relation to behavior therapy. *Behavior Therapy, 1,* 184–200.

Becker, W. C., Madsen, C. A., Arnold, C. R., & Thomas, D. R. (1967). The contingent use of teacher attention and praise in reducing classroom behavior problems. *Journal of Special Education, 1,* 287–307.

Begg, I., & Azzarello, M. (1988). Recognition and recall of invisible objects. *Memory & Cognition, 16,* 327–336.

Bellack, A. S., & Hersen, M. (1988). *Behavioral assessment* (3rd ed.). New York: Pergamon.

Belson, W. (1983). The effect of television violence on adolescent boys. *Revue Internationale de Criminologie et de Police Technique, 36,* 84–90.

Benton, S. L., & Blohm, P. J. (1985, March). *Effect of question type and position on measures of conceptual elaboration in writing.* Paper presented to the annual meeting of the American Educational Research Association, Chicago.

Benton, S. L., Glover, J. A., Monkowski, P. G., & Shaughnessy, M. (1983). Decision difficulty and recall of prose. *Journal of Educational Psychology, 75,* 727–742.

Bergeman, C. S., Plomin, R., DeFries, J. C., & Fulker, D.

W. (1988). Path analysis of general and specific cognitive abilities in the Colorado Adoption Project: Early childhood. *Personality and Individual Differences, 9,* 391–395.

Berk, R. A. (1988). Criterion-referenced tests. In J. P. Keeves (Ed.), *Educational research, methodology, & measurement: An international handbook.* New York: Pergamon Press.

Berliner, D. (1985, March). Discussant's comments. Given as part of a symposium on the history of educational psychology presented to the American Educational Research Association Convention, Chicago, Illinois.

Berlyne, D. E. (1960). *Conflict, arousal, and curiosity.* New York: McGraw-Hill.

Bernard, L. L. (1924). *Instinct.* New York: Holt, Rinehart & Winston.

Bernoulli, D. (1954). Exposition of a new theory on the measurement of risk (L. Sommer, Trans.). *Econometrica, 22,* 23–26.

Bialystok, E. (1988). Levels of bilingualism and levels of linguistic awareness. *Developmental Psychology, 24,* 560–568.

Bijou, S. W. (1955). A systematic approach to an experimental analysis of young children. *Child Development, 26,* 161–168.

Bijou, S. W., & Baer, D. M. (1963). Some methodological contributions from a functional analysis of child development. In L. P. Lipsitt & C. S. Spiker (Eds.), *Advances in child development and behavior* (pp. 165–192). New York: Academic Press.

Billings, D. C., & Wasik, B. H. (1985). Self-instructional training with preschoolers: An attempt to replicate. *Journal of Applied Behavior Analysis, 21,* 61–67.

Bilowit, D. W. (1979). Teaching children to "use" TV. *Television Quarterly, 15*(4), 27–29.

Bindra, A. (1969). *Motivation: A systematic reinterpretation.* New York: Ronald Press.

Binet, A., & Henri, V. (1896). La psychologie individuelle. *Année Psychologie, 2,* 411–465.

Binet, A., & Simon, T. (1905). Methodes nouvelles pour le diagnostic du niveau intellectuel des arnomaux. *Année Psychologie, 11,* 191–244.

Binet, A., & Simon, T. (1911). La mesure du développement de l'intelligence chex les jeunes enfants. *Bulletin de la Société Libra Pour L'étude Psychologique de l'Enfant, 12,* 187–248.

Binet, A., & Simon, T. (1979). The development of intelligence in children. In L. Willerman & R. G. Turner (Eds.), *Readings about individual and group differences* (pp. 32–51). San Francisco: Freeman.

Birnbaum, J. C. (1982). The reading and composing behaviors of selected fourth- and seventh-grade students. *Research in the Teaching of English, 16,* 241–260.

Bisanz, G. L., Vesonder, G. T., & Voss, J. F. (1978). Knowledge of one's own responding and the relation of such knowledge to learning. *Journal of Experimental Child Psychology, 25,* 116–128.

Blake, J., Austin, W., & Lowenstein, J. (1987). The effect of enactment upon sentence imitation in preschool children. *Journal of Psycholinguistic Research, 16,* 351–367.

Blanchard, E. G. (1970a). The generalization of vicarious extinction effects. *Behavior Research and Therapy, 8,* 323–330.

Blanchard, E. G. (1970b). The relative contributions of modeling, informational influences and physical contact in the extinction of phobic behavior. *Journal of Abnormal Psychology, 76,* 231–239.

Bloom, B. S. (1964). *Stability and change in human characteristics.* New York: Wiley.

Bloom, B. S. (1981). *The new direction in educational research and measurement: Alterable variables.* Address presented to the annual meeting of the American Educational Research Association, Los Angeles.

Bloom, B. S., Englehart, M. D., Furst, E. J., Hill, W. H., & Krathwohl, D. R. (1956). *Taxonomy of educational objectives. The classification of educational goals: Handbook I: Cognitive domain.* New York: McKay.

Bloom, L. (1970). *Language development: Form and function in emerging grammars.* Cambridge, MA: MIT Press.

Bloom, L. (1973). *One word at a time: The use of single word utterances before syntax.* New York: Humanities Press.

Bloomfield, L. (1933). *Language.* New York: Holt, Rinehart & Winston.

Bloomfield, L. (1942). Linguistics and reading. *Elementary English Review, 19,* 125–130, 183–186.

Bologna, N., & Brigham, T. (1978). *Analysis of procedures designed to increase the use of newly-acquired vocabulary words in essays.* Paper presented at the annual convention of the Midwest Association for Behavior Analysis, Chicago.

Boren, A. R., & Foree, S. B. (1977). Personalized instruction applied to food and nutrition in higher education. *Journal of Personalized Instruction, 2,* 39–42.

Boring, E. (1950). *A history of experimental psychology.* New York: Appleton-Century-Crofts.

Borkowski, J. G., & Day, J. (1988). *Cognition in special children.* Norwood, NJ: Ablex.

Borkowski, J. G., Milstead, M., & Hale, C. (1988). Components of children's metamemory: Implications for strategy generalization. In F. W. Weinert & M. Perlmutter

(Eds.), *Memory development: Universal changes and individual differences* (pp. 79–112). Hillsdale, NJ: Erlbaum.

Borkowski, J. G., Weyhing, R. S., & Carr, M. (1988). Effects of attributional retraining on strategy-based reading comprehension in learning-disabled students. *Journal of Educational Psychology, 80,* 46–53.

Bornstein, M. R., Bellack, A. S., & Hersen, M. (1977). Social-skills training for unassertive children: A multiple baseline analysis. *Journal of Applied Behavior Analysis, 10,* 183–185.

Bousfield, W. A. (1953). The occurrence of clustering and the recall of randomly arranged associates. *Journal of General Psychology, 49,* 229–240.

Bower, G. H. (1970). Analysis of a mnemonic device. *American Scientist, 58,* 496–510.

Bower, G. H., & Clark, M. C. (1969). Narrative stories as mediators for serial learning. *Psychonomic Science, 14,* 181–182.

Bowerman, M. (1978). Systematizing semantic knowledge: Changes over time in the child's organization of word meaning. *Child Development, 49,* 977–987.

Boyd, W. M. (1973). Repeating questions in prose learning. *Journal of Educational Psychology, 64,* 31–38.

Boyes, M. C., & Walker, L. J. (1988). Implications of cultural diversity for the universal claims of Kohlberg's theory of moral reasoning. *Human Development, 31,* 44–59.

Braine, M. D. S. (1987). What is learned in acquiring word classes—A step toward an acquisition theory. In B. MacWhinney (Ed.), *Mechanisms of language acquisition* (pp. 51–76). Hillsdale, NJ: Erlbaum.

Braine, M. D. S. (1988). *Categories and processes in language acquisition.* Hillsdale, New Jersey: Erlbaum.

Brainerd, C. J., & Pressley, M. (Eds.), (1985). *Basic processes in memory development.* New York: Springer-Verlag.

Bransford, J. D., & McCarrell, N. S. (1974). A sketch of a cognitive approach to comprehension. In W. B. Weimer and D. S. Palermo (Eds.), *Cognition and the symbolic processes* (pp. 103–123). Hillsdale, NJ: Erlbaum.

Bransford, J. D., & Stein, B. S. (1984). *The ideal problem solver.* San Francisco: Freeman.

Brennan, T., & Glover, J. A. (1980). A re-examination of the intrinsic-extrinsic reinforcement debate. *Social Behavior and Personality, 8,* 27–32.

Bridge, C. A. (1987). Strategies for promoting reader-text interactions. In R. J. Tierney, P. L. Anders, & J. N. Mitchell (Eds.), *Understanding Reader's Understanding* (pp. 283–305). Hillsdale, NJ: Erlbaum.

Bridges, K. R., Harnish, R. J., & Korber, K. (1987). The relationship of television viewing time to scores on the Fear Survey Schedules. *Personality & Individual Differences, 8,* 757–759.

Broadbent, D. E. (1958). *Perception and communication.* London: Pergamon.

Brocks, M., Armstrong, G. M., & Goldberg, M. E. (1988). Children's use of cognitive defenses against television advertising: A cognitive response approach. *Journal of Consumer Research, 14,* 471–482.

Brooks-Gunn, J., & Lewis, M. (1984). The development of early visual self-recognition. *Developmental Review, 4,* 215–239.

Brophy, J. (1981). Teacher praise: A functional analysis. *Review of Educational Research, 51,* 5–32.

Brophy, J. E., & Good, T. L. (1985). Teacher behavior and student learning. In M. Wittrock (Ed.), *Handbook of research on teaching* (3rd ed.) (236–271). New York: Macmillan.

Brown, A. (1987). Metacognition, Executive Control, Self-regulation, and other more mysterious mechanisms. In F. E. Weinert & R. N. Kluwe (Eds.), *Metacognition, motivation, and understanding* (pp. 41–54). Hillsdale, NJ: Erlbaum.

Brown, A. L., & Smiley, S. S. (1977). Rating the importance of structural units of prose passages: A problem of metacognitive development. *Child Development, 48,* 1–8.

Brown, F. G. (1976). *Principles of educational and psychological testing* (2nd ed.). New York: Holt, Rinehart & Winston.

Brown, J. F. (1936). *Psychology and the social order.* New York: McGraw-Hill.

Brown, J. S. (1961). *The motivation of behavior.* New York: McGraw-Hill.

Brown, R. (1973). *A first language: The early stages.* Cambridge, MA: Harvard University Press.

Brown, R. Cazden, C., & Bellugi, U. (1970). The child's grammar from I to III. In R. Brown (Ed.), *Psycholinguistics.* (pp. 213–234). New York: Free Press.

Brown, R. T. (in press). Creativity: What are we to measure? In J. A. Glover, R. R. Ronning, & C. R. Reynolds (Eds), *Handbook of creativity research.* New York: Plenum.

Bruner, J. (1966). *Toward a theory of instruction.* Cambridge, MA: Belknap Press.

Bruner, J. S. (1971). *The relevance of education.* New York: Norton.

Bruner, J. S. (1978). From communication to language: A psychological perspective. In I. Markova (Ed.), *The social context of language* (pp. 84–97). New York: Wiley.

Bruner, J. S. (1982). The organization of action and the nature of adult-infant transaction. In M. Cranach & R. Harre (Eds.), *The analysis of action* (pp. 93–110). New York: Cambridge University Press.

Bruner, J. S. (1983). *Child's talk.* New York: Norton.

Bruner, J. S., Goodnow, J. J., & Austin, G. A. (1956). *A study of thinking.* New York: Wiley.

Bruning, R. H. (1984). Key elements of effective teaching in the direct teaching model. In R. L. Egbert & M. M. Kluender (Eds.), *Using research to improve teacher education: The Nebraska Consortium* (Teacher Education Monograph No. 1) (pp. 146–165). Washington, DC: ERIC Clearinghouse on Teacher Education.

Bruning, R. H., Burton, J. K., & Ballering, M. (1978). Visual and auditory memory: Relationship to reading achievement. *Contemporary Educational Psychology, 3,* 340–351.

Bruning, R. H., Murphy, C. C., Bishop, J., & Wingrove, L. (1985). Learning word meanings from reading in the classroom under incidental and intentional conditions. Paper presented at the annual meeting of the National Reading Conference, San Diego, California.

Bryant, L. E., & Budd, K. S. (1984). Teaching behaviorally handicapped preschool children to share. *Journal of Applied Behavior Analysis, 17,* 45–56.

Buchwald, A. M. (1959). Experimental alterations in the effectiveness of verbal reinforcement combinations. *Journal of Experimental Psychology, 57,* 351–361.

Buchwald, A. M. (1960). Effects of "right" and "wrong" on subsequent behavior: A new interpretation. *Psychological Review, 76,* 132–145.

Bullock, M., & Lutkenhaus, P. (1988). The development of volitional behavior in the toddler years. *Child Development, 664*–674.

Buros, O. K. (1977). Fifty years in testing: Some reminiscences, criticisms, and suggestions. *Educational Research, 6,* 9–15.

Busemeyer, J. R., & Myung, I. J. (1988). A new method for investigating prototype learning. *Journal of Experimental Psychology: Learning, Memory, and Cognition, 14,* 3–11.

Bussey, K., & Bandura, A. (1984). Influence of gender constancy and social power on sex-linked modeling. *Journal of Personality and Social Psychology, 47,* 1292–1302.

Butler, S. R., March, H. W., Sheppard, M. J., & Sheppard, J. L. (1985). Seven-year longitudinal study of the early prediction of reading achievement. *Journal of Educational Psychology, 77,* 349–361.

Byrd, D. M., & Gholson, B. (1985). Reading, memory, and metacognition. *Journal of Educational Psychology, 77,* 428–436.

Cagel, M. (1985). A general abstract-concrete model of creative thinking. *Journal of Creative Behavior, 19,* 104–109.

Calfee, R. C. (1977). Assessment of independent reading skills: Basic research and practical applications. In A. S. Reber & D. L. Scarborough (Eds.), *Toward a psychology of reading* (pp. 237–268). Hillsdale, NJ: Erlbaum.

Canter, L. (1986). *Assertive discipline.* Santa Monica, CA: Canter & Associates.

Carden-Smith, L. K., & Fowler, S. A. (1984). Positive peer pressure: The effects of peer monitoring on children's disruptive behavior. *Journal of Applied Behavior Analysis, 17,* 213–227.

Carey, L. (1988). *Measuring and evaluating school learning.* Boston: Allyn & Bacon.

Carey, L. J., & Flower, L. (in press). Foundations for creativity in the writing process: Rhetorical representations of ill-defined problems. In J. A. Glover, R. R. Ronning, & C. R. Reynolds (Eds.), *Handbook of creativity research.* New York: Plenum.

Carlisle, K. E. (1985). Learning how to learn. *Teaching and Development Journal, 39,* 75–80.

Carney, R. N., Levin, J. R., & Morrison, C. R. (1988). Mnemonic learning of artists and their paintings. *American Educational Research Journal, 25,* 107–126.

Carpenter, P. A., & Just, M. A. (1982). What your eyes do while your mind is reading. In K. Rayner (Ed.), *Eye movements in reading: Perceptual and language processes* (pp. 47–91). New York: Academic Press.

Carpenter, P. A., & Just, M. A. (1985). Cognitive processes in reading. In J. Orasanu (Ed.), *Reading comprehension: From research to practice* (pp. 32–65). Hillsdale, NJ: Erlbaum.

Carr, E. G., & Durand, V. M. (1985). Reducing behavior problems through functional communication training. *Journal of Applied Behavior Analysis, 18,* 111–126.

Carr, H. A. (1925). *Psychology: A study of mental activity.* New York: Longmans, Green.

Carroll, J. B. (in press). New perspectives in the analysis of abilities. In R. R. Ronning, J. A. Glover, and J. C. Conoley (Eds.), *The impact of cognitive psychology on measurement.* Hillsdale, NJ: Erlbaum.

Carroll, J. B. (1988). Future developments in educational measurement. In J. P. Keeves (Ed.), *Educational research, methodology, & measurement: An international handbook.* New York: Pergamon Press.

Carver, R. P. (1972). Speed readers don't read; they skim. *Psychology Today, 6,* 22–30.

Case, R. (1978). A developmentally based theory and technology for instruction. *Review of Educational Research, 48,* 439–463.

Case, R. (1984a). The process of stage transition: A neo-Piagetian view. In R. J. Sternberg (Ed.), *Mechanisms of cognitive development* (pp. 19–44). New York: W. H. Freeman.

Case, R. (1984b). *Intellectual development: A systematic reinterpretation.* New York: Academic Press.

Case, R., Hayward, S., Lewis, M., & Hurst, P. (1988). Toward a neo-Piagetian theory of cognitive and emotional development. *Developmental Review, 8,* 1–51.

Cattell, J. McK. (1890). Mental tests and measurements. *Mind, 15,* 373–380.

Caudill, B. D., & Lipscomb, T. (1980). Modeling influences on alcoholics' rates of alcohol consumption. *Journal of Applied Behavior Analysis, 13,* 355–365.

Cautela, J. R. (1984). General level of reinforcement, *Journal of Behavior Therapy and Experimental Psychiatry, 15,* 109–114.

Ceci, S. J., & Liker, J. K. (1986). A day at the races: A study of IQ, expertise, and cognitive complexity. *Journal of Experimental Psychology: General, 115,* 255–266.

Ceci, S. J., & Liker, J. K. (1988). Stalking the IQ-expertise relation: When the critics go fishing. *Journal of Experimental Psychology: General, 117,* 96–100.

Chall, J. (1967). *Learning to read: The great debate.* New York: McGraw-Hill.

Charles, D. C. (1987). The early history of educational psychology. In J. A. Glover & R. R. Ronning (Eds.), *Historical foundations of educational psychology.* New York: Plenum.

Chase, C. I. (1968). The impact of some obvious variables on essay tests. *Journal of Educational Measurement, 5,* 315–318.

Chase, W. G., & Simon, H. A. (1973). The mind's eye in chess. In W. G. Chase (Ed.), *Visual information processing* (pp. 215–278). New York: Academic Press.

Chechile, R. A. (1987). Trace susceptibility theory. *Journal of Experimental Psychology: General, 116,* 203–222.

Chenfeld, M. B. (1985). *Creative activities for young children.* New York: Harcourt Brace Jovanovich.

Chenfeld, M. B. (1985). Words of praise. *Language Arts, 62,* 266–268.

Chomsky, N. (1957). *Syntactic structures.* The Hague: Mouton.

Chomsky, N. (1967). *Aspects of a theory of syntax.* Cambridge, MA: MIT Press.

Chomsky, N. (1980a). On cognitive structures and their development: A reply to Piaget. In M. Piattelli-Pal-marini (Ed.), *Language and learning: The debate between Jean Piaget and Noam Chomsky* (pp. 35–52). Cambridge, MA: Harvard University Press.

Chomsky, N. (1980b). The linguistic approach. In M. Piattelli-Palmarini (Ed.), *Language and learning: The debate between Jean Piaget and Noam Chomsky* (pp. 109–117). Cambridge, MA: Harvard University Press.

Choppin, B. H. (1988). Objective tests. Future developments in educational measurement. In J. P. Keeves (Ed.), *Educational research, methodology, and measurement: An international handbook.* New York: Pergamon Press.

Christiansen, H. D. (1988). *Casebook of test interpretation.* Tucson, AZ: Peter Juul Press.

Chukovsky, K. (1963). *From two to five.* Berkeley, CA: University of California Press.

Clark, E. (1987). The principle of contrast: A constraint on language acquisition. In B. MacWhinney (Ed.), *Mechanisms of language acquisition* (pp. 4–32). Hillsdale, NJ: Erlbaum.

Clark, E. V. (1983). Meanings and concepts. In P. H. Mussen (Ed.), *Handbook of child psychology* (Vol. 3) (pp. 361–382). New York: Wiley.

Clark, E. V. (1985, May). How children create new words. Presentation to the annual meeting of the University of Nebraska Reading Network, Lincoln, NE.

Clark, H. H., & Clark, E. V. (1971). *Psychology and language: An introduction to psycholinguistics.* New York: Harcourt Brace Jovanovich.

Clark, R., Gelatt, H. B., & Levine, L. (1965). A decision-making paradigm for local guidance research. *Personnel and Guidance Journal, 44,* 40–51.

Clawson, E. U., & Barnes, B. R. (1973). The effects of organizers on the learning of structured anthropology materials in the elementary grades. *Journal of Experimental Education, 42,* 11–15.

Cofer, C. N. (1957). Reason as an associative process. III: The role of verbal responses in problem solving. *Journal of General Psychology, 57,* 55–68.

Cohen, R. J. (1988). *Psychological Testing.* New York: Mayfield.

Cohn, S. J., Carlson, J. S., & Jensen, A. R. (in press). Speed of information processing in academically gifted youths. *Personality and Individual Differences.*

Coleman, L. M. (1988). Language and the evolution of identity and self-concept. In F. Kessel (Ed.), *The development of language and language researchers* (pp. 292–315). Hillsdale, NJ: Erlbaum.

Collins, A. M., & Loftus, E. F. (1975). A spreading activation theory of semantic processing. *Psychological Review, 82,* 407–428.

Collins, A. M., & Quillian, M. R. (1969). Retrieval time from semantic memory. *Journal of Verbal Learning and Verbal Behavior, 8,* 240–247.

Collins, H. F. *The influence of prosocial television programs emphasizing the positive value of differences on children's attitudes toward differences and children's behavior in choice situations.* Unpublished doctoral dissertation, Pennsylvania State University, 1974.

Coltheart, M. (1979). When can children learn to read—and when should they be taught? In T. G. Waller & G. E. MacKinnon (Eds.), *Reading research: Advances in theory and practice* (Vol. 1) (pp. 146–168). New York: Academic Press.

Coltheart, M. (1987). Functional architecture of the language-processing system. Published in M. Coltheart, R. Job, and G. Sartori (Editors), *The neuropsychology of language* (pages 3–26). Hillsdale, New Jersey: Lawrence Erlbaum.

Combs, M. (1987). Modeling the reading process with enlarged text. *The Reading Teacher, 40,* 422–426.

Commission on Reading (1985). *Becoming a nation of readers: The report of the Commission on Reading.* Washington, DC: Commission on Reading.

Conrad, C. (1972). Cognitive economy in semantic memory. *Journal of Experimental Psychology, 92,* 149–154.

Conrad, C. J., Spencer, R. E., & Semb, B. (1978). An analysis of student self-grading versus proctor grading in a personalized university course. *Journal of Personalized Instruction, 3* (1), 23–28.

Cook, T. P., & Apolloni, T. (1976). Developing positive social-emotional behaviors: A study of training and generalization effects. *Journal of Applied Behavior Analysis, 9,* 65–78.

Cooper, C. C., Benz, C. R., & Thompson, S. J. (1988). Design for excellence in teacher education: A developmental model for student assessment, selection, and retention. *Journal of Teacher Education, 39,* 15–20.

Cooper, H. M., & Burger, J. M. (1980). How teachers explain students' academic performance: A categorization of free response academic attributions. *American Educational Research Journal, 17,* 95–109.

Corey, G. (1977). *Theory and practice of counseling and psychotherapy.* Monterey, CA: Brooks/Cole Publishing Company.

Corkill, A. J. (1988). *Advance organizers: Consequences of encoding and retrieval manipulations on different types of textual recall.* Dissertation completed at the University of Nebraska, Lincoln, Nebraska.

Corkill, A. J., Glover, John A., Bruning, Roger H., and Krug, D. (1989). Advance organizers: Retrieval hypotheses. *Journal of Educational Psychology, 81,* pages 43–51.

Cormier, R., & Cormier, S. (1985). *Interviewing strategies for helpers.* San Francisco: Brooks/Cole.

Cosgrove, M., & McIntyre, C. W. (1974, March). *The influence of "Mister Rogers' Neighborhood" on nursery school children's prosocial behavior.* Paper presented at the meeting of the Southeastern Regional Society for Research in Child Development, Chapel Hill, NC.

Cote, J. E., & Levine, C. (1988). A critical examination of the ego identity status paradigm. *Developmental Review, 8,* 147–184.

Covington, M. V. (1985). Strategic thinking and fear of failure. In J. Segal, S. Chipman, & R. Glaser (Eds.), *Thinking and learning skills: Relating instruction to research* (pp. 389–416). Hillsdale, NJ: Erlbaum.

Covington, M. V., & Omelich, C. L. (1984). Task-oriented versus competitive learning structures: Motivational and performance consequences. *Journal of Educational Psychology, 76,* 1038–1050.

Covington, M. V., & Omelich, C. L. (1985). Ability and effort valuation among failure-avoiding and failure-accepting students. *Journal of Educational Psychology, 77,* 446–459.

Cox, D. (1926). *The early mental traits of three hundred geniuses: Genetic studies of genius* (Vol. 2). Stanford: Stanford University Press.

Craik, F. I. M., & Lockhart, R. S. (1972). Levels of processing: A framework for memory research. *Journal of Verbal Learning and Verbal Behavior, 11,* 671–684.

Craik, F. I. M., & Lockhart, R. S. (1978). Levels of processing: A reply to Eysenck. *British Journal of Psychology, 69,* 171–175.

Craik, F. I. M., & Tulving, E. (1975). Depth of processing and the retention of words in episodic memory. *Journal of Experimental Psychology: General, 104,* 268–294.

Crawley, S. J., & Mountain, L. H. (1988). *Strategies for giving content reading,* Boston: Allyn & Bacon.

Creer, T. L., & Miklich, D. R. (1979). The application of a self-modeling procedure to modify inappropriate behavior: A preliminary report. *Behavior, Research and Therapy, 8,* 91–92.

Crocker, L., & Algina, J. (1986). *Introduction to classical and modern test theory.* New York: Holt, Rinehart & Winston.

Cromer, R. F. (1988). The cognition hypothesis revisited. In F. Kessel (Ed.), *The development of language and language researchers* (pp. 230–246). Hillsdale, NJ: Erlbaum.

Cronbach, L. J. (1957). The two disciplines of scientific psychology. *American Psychologist, 12,* 671–684.

Cronbach, L. J. (1966). The role of the university in improving education. *Phi Delta Kappan, 47,* 539–545.

Cronbach, L. J. (1975). Course improvement through evaluation. In D. A. Payne & R. F. McMorris (Eds.), *Educational and psychological measurement* (pp. 241–260). Morristown, NJ: General Learning Press.

Cronbach, L. J., (1980). *Toward reform of program evaluation.* San Francisco: Jossey-Bass.

Cross, D. R., & Paris, S. G. (1988). Developmental and instructional analyses of children's metacognition and reading comprehension. *Journal of Educational Psychology, 80,* 131–142.

Crowell, C. R., Anderson, D. C., Abel, D. M., & Sergio, J. P. (1988). Task clarification, performance feedback, and social praise: Procedures for improving the customer service of bank tellers. *Journal of Applied Behavior Analysis, 21,* 65–71.

Crutchfield, R. W. (1969). Nurturing the cognitive skills of productive thinking. In *Life skills in school and society* (pp. 279–302). Washington, DC: Association for Supervision and Curriculum Development.

Damon, W., & Hart, D. (1982). The development of self-understanding from infancy through adolescence. *Child Development, 53,* 841–864.

Daneman, M. (1988). How reading braille is both like and unlike reading print. *Memory & Cognition, 16,* 497–504.

Dangel, R. F., & Hopkins, B. L. (1978). Be still, be quiet, be docile: What do the data say? *Journal of Applied Behavior Analysis, 10,* 127–133.

Dangel, R. F., & Polster, R. A. (1988). *Teaching child management skills.* New York: Pergamon.

Darwin, C. (1871). *The descent of man.* London: John Murray.

Davie, R., Butler, N., & Goldstein, L. (1972). *From birth to seven.* London, Longman.

Davis, G. A. (1966). Current status of research and theory in human problem solving. *Psychological Bulletin, 66,* 36–54.

Davis, G. A. (1973). *Psychology of problem solving: Theory and practice.* New York: Basic Books.

Day, J., & Borkowski, J. G. (1988). *Intelligence and exceptionality.* Norwood, NJ: Ablex.

deBono, E. (1985). The CoRT program. In J. W. Segal and S. F. Chipman (Eds.), *Thinking and learning skills* (Vol. 1) (pp. 171–184). Hillsdale, NJ: Erlbaum.

Dee-Lucas, D., & Larkin, J. H. (1988). Novice rules for assessing importance in scientific texts. *Journal of Memory and Language, 27,* 288–305.

DeGroot, A. D. (1965). *Thought and choice in chess.* The Hague: Mouton.

DeLandsheere, V. (1988). Taxonomies of educational objectives. In J. P. Keeves (Ed.), *Educational research, methodology, and measurement: An international handbook.* New York: Pergamon Press.

Dellarosa, D. (1988). A history of thinking. In R. J. Sternberg & E. E. Smith (Eds.), *The psychology of human thought* (pp. 1–18). New York: Cambridge University Press.

Dellarosa, D., & Bourne, L. E. (1985). Surface form and the spacing effect. *Memory & Cognition, 13,* 529–537.

Dempster, F. N. (1985). Proactive interference in sentence recall: Topic-similarity effects and individual differences. *Memory & Cognition, 13,* 81–89.

Derry, S. (1984). Effects of an organizer on memory for prose. *Journal of Educational Psychology, 76,* 98–107.

de Villiers, J. G., & de Villiers, P. A. (1978). *Language acquisition.* Cambridge, MA: Harvard University Press.

Detterman, D. K., & Spry, K. M. (1988). Is it smart to play the horses? Comment on "A day at the races: A study of IQ, expertise, and cognitive complexity." *Journal of Experimental Psychology: General, 117,* 91–95.

Dewey, J. (1886). *Psychology.* New York: Harper.

Dewey, J. (1898, November). *New York teachers' monographs.* New York: Teachers College Press.

Dewey, J. (1910). *How we think.* Boston: Heath.

Dewey, J. (1933). *How we think.* New York: Heath.

Diamond, B. J. (1985). The cognitive processes of competent third grade writers. A descriptive study. *Dissertation Abstracts International, 46,* 05A. (University Microfilms No. DA 8513892.)

Diamond, C. & Colletti, N. (1978). A training program in behavior modification. Paper presented to the annual meeting of the Midwestern Association for Applied Behavior Analysis, Chicago.

Dick, W. (1977). Summative evaluation. In L. J. Briggs (Ed.), *Instructional design* (pp. 68–79). Englewood Cliffs, NJ: Educational Technology Publications.

Dick, W., & Carey, L. (1978). *The systematic design of instruction.* Glenview, IL: Scott, Foresman.

Dinnel, D., & Glover, J. A. (1985). Advance organizers: Encoding manipulations. *Journal of Educational Psychology, 77,* 514–521.

Dinsmore, J. (1987). Mental spaces from a functional perspective. *Cognitive Science, 11,* 1–21.

Dixon, D. N. (1976, April). *A problem solving/relationship model for counseling.* Paper presented at the annual meeting of the American Educational Research Association, San Francisco.

Dixon, D. N. (1984). *Counseling: A problem solving approach.* New York: Wiley.

Dixon, D. N. (1987). A history of counseling psychology. In J. A. Glover & R. R. Ronning (Eds.), *Historical foundations of educational psychology.* New York: Plenum.

Dixon, D. N., Heppner, P. P., Petersen, C. H., & Ronning, R. R. (1979). Problem solving workshop training. *Journal of Counseling Psychology, 26*(2), 133–139.

Doll, E. A. (1962). A historical survey of research and management of mental retardation in the United States. In E. P. Trapp & P. Himmelstein (Eds.), *Readings on the exceptional child: Research and theory* (pp. 46–71). New York: Appleton-Century-Crofts.

Doll, E. A. (1965). *Vineland Social Maturity Scale.* Minneapolis, MN: American Guidance Service.

Dore, J. (1985). Children's conversations. In T. A. van Dijk (Ed.), *Handbook of discourse analysis: Vol. 3: Discourse and dialogue* (pp. 161–190). London: Academic Press.

Dornic, S. (1983). Proactive interference and language change: The effect of noise. *Reports from the Department of Psychology.* University of Stockholm, Stockholm, Sweden, No. 600, p. 7.

Dorval, B., & Eckerman, C. O. (1984). Developmental trends in the quality of conversation achieved by small groups of acquainted peers. *Monographs of the Society for Research in Child Development, 49*(2, Serial No. 206).

Downing, J. (1965). The initial teaching alphabet: Reading experiment. Glenview, IL: Scott, Foresman.

Downing, J. (1973). *Comparative reading.* New York: Macmillan.

Dowrick, P. W. (1978). Suggestions for the use of edited video replay in training behavioral skills. *Journal of Practical Approaches in Developmental Handicaps, 2,* 21–24.

Doyle, W. (1979). Making managerial decisions in classrooms. In D. Duke (Ed.), *Seventy-eighth Yearbook of the National Society for the Study of Education* (pp. 401–422). New York: National Society for the Study of Education.

Drumheller, S. J. (1971). *Handbook of curriculum design for individualized instruction: A systems approach.* Englewood Cliffs, NJ: Educational Technology Publications.

Dryden, W., & Golden, W. L., (1987). *Cognitive-behavioral approaches to psychotherapy.* New York: Hemisphere.

Duchastel, P. C., & Merrill, P. F. (1973). The effects of behavioral objectives on learning: A review of empirical studies. *Review of Educational Research, 43,* 53–69.

Duell, O. K. (1974). Effect and types of objectives, level of test questions, and judged importance of tested materials upon posttest performance. *Journal of Educational Psychology, 66,* 225–232.

Duffey, E. (1962). *Activation and behavior.* New York: Wiley.

Duncan, C. P. (1959). Recent research on human problem solving. *Psychological Bulletin, 56*(6), 397–429.

Dunker, K. (1945). On problem solving (L. S. Lees, Trans.). *Psychological Monographs, 58,* 407–416, 478.

Dunn, L. M. (1968). Special education for the mildly retarded: Is much of it justifiable? *Exceptional Children, 35,* 5–22.

Dunn, T. P., & Cardwell, J. D. (1984). Television and children: A symbolic interactionist perspective. *Psychology: A Quarterly Journal of Human Behavior, 21,* 30–35.

Durkin, D. (1974). A six year study of children who learned to read in school at the age of four. *Reading Research Quarterly, 10,* 9–16.

Durkin, D. (1978–1979). What classroom observations reveal about reading comprehension instruction in the first grade. *Reading Research Quarterly, 14,* 481–533.

Durkin, K. (1985). Sex roles and television roles: Can a woman be seen to tell the weather as well as a man? *International Review of Applied Psychology, 34,* 191–201.

Duryea, E. J., & Glover, J. A. (1982). A review of the research on reflection and impulsivity in children. *Genetic Psychology Monographs, 106,* 217–237.

Duyme, M. (1988). School success and social class: An adoption study. *Developmental Psychology, 24,* 203–209.

Dweck, C. S. (1988). Motivation. In R. Glaser & A. Lesgold (Eds.), *The handbook of psychology and education* (Vol. 1, pp. 187–239). Hillsdale, NJ: Erlbaum.

Dweck, C. S. & Leggett, E. L. (1988). A social-cognitive approach to motivation and personality. *Psychological Review, 95,* 256–273.

D'Zurilla, T. J., & Goldfried, M. R. (1971). Problem solving and behavior modification. *Journal of Abnormal Psychology, 78,* 107–126.

Ebbinghaus, H. (1913). Uber das gedachtnis. In H. A. Roger & C. Bossinger (Trans.), *On memory* (pp. 2–81). New York: Teachers College. (Original work published 1885.)

Ebel, R. L. (1978). The case for norm-referenced measurements. *Educational Researcher, 7,* 3–5.

Ebel, R. L., & Frisbie, D. A. (1986). *Essentials of educational measurement* (4th ed.). Englewood Cliffs, NJ: Prentice-Hall.

Education Development Center. (1975). *Comprehensive problem solving in secondary schools: A conference report.* Boston: Houghton Mifflin.

Ehri, L. C. (1978). Beginning reading from a psycholinguistic perspective: Amalgamation of word identities. In F. B. Murray (Ed.), *The recognition of words* (pp. 1–33). Washington, DC: IRA Series on the Development of the Reading Process, International Reading Association.

Eimas, P. D. (1985). The perception of speech in early infancy. *Scientific American, 252,* 46–52.

Eisner, E. W. (1967). Educational objectives, help or hindrance? *The School Review, 75,* 250–260.

Elardo, R. (1978). Behavior modification in an elementary school: Problems and issues. *Phi Delta Kappan, 59,* 334–338.

Elkind, D. (1973). Educational psychology. In P. Mussen & M. R. Rosenzweig (Eds.), *Psychology: An introduction* (pp. 41–50). Lexington, MA: Heath.

Elliot, A. J. (1981). *Child language.* London: Cambridge University Press.

Elliott, E. S., & Dweck, C. S. (1988). Goals: An approach to motivation and achievement. *Journal of Personality and Social Psychology, 54,* 5–12.

Ellis, A., & Beattie, G. (1986). *The psychology of language and communication.* New York: Guilford.

Ellis, N. R., Deacon, J. R., & Wooldridge, P. W. (1985). Structural memory deficits of mentally retarded persons. *American Journal of Mental Deficiency, 89,* 393–402.

Ellis, N. R., Palmer, R. L., & Reeves, C. L. (1988). Developmental and individual differences in frequency processing. *Developmental Psychology, 24,* 38–45.

Englehart, M. D., & Thomas, M. (1972). Rice as the inventor of the comparative test. In V. H. Noll, D. P. Scannell, & R. P. Noll (Eds.), *Introductory readings in educational measurements* (pp. 237–252). Boston: Houghton Mifflin.

Englert, C. S., Stewart, S. R., & Hiebert, E. H. (1988). Young writers' use of text structure in expository text generation. *Journal of Educational Psychology, 80,* 143–151.

Entwisle, D. R. (1977). A sociologist looks at reading. In W. Otto, C. W. Peters, & N. Peters (Eds.), *Reading problems, a multidisciplinary perspective.* Reading, MA: Addison-Wesley.

Ervin-Tripp, S. (1971). Wait for me, Roller Skate. In S. Ervin-Tripp & C. Mitchell-Kernan (Eds.), *Child discourse* (pp. 2–22). New York: Academic Press.

Estes, W. K. (1944). An experimental study of punishment. *Psychological Monographs, 57,* 1–40.

Estes, W. K. (1950). Toward a statistical theory of learning. *Psychological Review, 57,* 94–107.

Evertson, C. M., & Smylie, M. A. (1987). Research on classroom processes: Views from two perspectives. In J. A. Glover & R. R. Ronning (Eds.), *Historical foundations of educational psychology.* New York: Plenum.

Eysenck, H. J. (1971). *The I.Q. argument.* New York: Library Press.

Eysenck, H. J. (1987). Thomson's "bonds" or Spearman's "energy": Sixty years on. *Mankind Quarterly, 27,* 259–274.

Fabes, R. A., Eisenberg, N., McCormick, S. E., & Wilson, M. S. (1988). Preschoolers' attributions of the situational determinants of others' naturally occurring emotions. *Developmental Psychology, 24,* 376–385.

Fallen, N. H., & McGovern, J. E. (1978). *Young children with special needs.* Columbus, OH: Merrill.

Fancher, R. E. (1979). *Pioneers of psychology.* New York: Norton.

Farr, M. J. (1987). *The long-term retention of knowledge and skills.* New York: Springer-Verlag.

Faw, H., & Waller, T. G. (1976). Mathemagenic behaviors and efficiency in learning from prose. *Review of Educational Research, 46,* 691–720.

Feingold, B. F. (1974). *Why your child is hyperactive.* New York: Random House.

Feltovich, P. J. (1981). *Knowledge based components of expertise in medical diagnosis* (Technical Report Number PDS-2). Pittsburgh, Pennsylvania: University of Pittsburgh, Learning, Research, and Development Center.

Ferguson, C. A., & Slobin, D. I. (Eds.) (1973). *Studies of child language development.* New York: Holt, Rinehart & Winston.

Festinger, L. (1957). *A theory of cognitive dissonance.* Evanston, IL: Row, Petersen.

Festinger, L. (1959). *A theory of cognitive dissonance.* Stanford: Stanford University Press.

Fishman, D. B., Rotgers, F., & Franks, C. M. (1988). *Paradigms in behavior therapy.* New York: Springer.

Flavell, J. H. (1980). On Jean Piaget. *Newsletter, Society for Research in Child Development,* p. 1.

Flavell, J. H., Friedrichs, A. G., & Hoyt, J. D. (1970). Developmental changes in memorization processes. *Cognitive Psychology,* 324–340.

Flesch, R. (1955). *Why Johnny can't read and what you can do about it.* New York: Harper & Brothers.

Flower, L. S., & Hayes, J. R. (1983). Plans that guide the composing process. In C. H. Frederickson & J. F. Dominic (Eds.), *Writing: Process, development, and communication* (pp. 39–58). Hillsdale, NJ: Erlbaum.

Flowers, J. H., & Garbin, C. (in press). Perceptual processes in creativity. In J. A. Glover, R. R. Ronning, & C. R. Reynolds (Eds.), *Handbook of creativity research.* New York: Plenum.

Foch, T. T., DeFries, J. C., McClearn, G. E., & Singer, S. M. (1977). Familial patterns of impairment in reading disability. *Journal of Educational Psychology, 69,* 316–329.

Foorman, B. R., & Siegel, A. W. (1985). *Acquisition of reading skills.* Hillsdale, NJ: Erlbaum.

Foos, P. W., & Fisher, R. P. (1988). Using tests as learning opportunities. *Journal of Educational Psychology, 80,* 129–183.

Fox, R. A., & Roseen, D. L. (1977). A parent administered token program for dietary regulation of phenylketonuria. *Journal of Behavior Therapy and Experimental Psychiatry, 1977, 8,* 441–443.

Francis, R. (1983). BBC policy regarding the presentation of television violence. *Revue Internationale de Criminologie et de Police Technique, 36,* 91–99.

Franks, J. J., Plybon, C. J., & Auble, P. M. (1982). Units of episodic memory in perceptual recognition. *Memory & Cognition, 10,* 62–68.

Frase, L. T. (1967). Learning from prose material: Length of passage, knowledge of results and position of questions. *Journal of Educational Psychology, 58,* 266–272.

Frase, L. T. (1968). Effect of question location, pacing, and mode upon retention of prose material. *Journal of Educational Psychology, 59*(4), 244–249.

Frase, L. T., & Kreitzberg, V. S. (1975). Effects of topical and indirect learning directions on prose recall. *Journal of Educational Psychology, 67,* 320–324.

Frase, L. T., Patrick, E., & Schumer, H. (1970). Effect of question position and frequency upon learning from text under different levels of incentive. *Journal of Educational Psychology, 61,* 52–56.

Freeman, F. S. (1962). *Theory and practice of psychological testing* (3rd ed.). New York: Holt, Rinehart & Winston.

Freud, S. (1920). *A general introduction to psychoanalysis.* New York: Liveright.

Freud, S. (1922). *Beyond the pleasure principle.* London: International Psychoanalytic Press.

Freud, S. (1924). *Collected papers* (Vol. 1). London: Hogarth.

Friedman, F., & Rickards, J. P. (1981). Effect of level, review, and sequence of inserted questions on text processing. *Journal of Educational Psychology, 73,* 427–436.

Friedrich, L. K., & Stein, A. H. (1973). Aggression and prosocial television programs and the natural behavior of preschool children. *Monographs of the Society for Research in Child Development, 38*(51).

Friedrich, L. K., & Stein, A. H. (1975). Prosocial television and young children: The effects of verbal labeling and role playing on learning and behavior. *Child Development, 46,* 27–38.

Fries, C. C. (1952). *The structure of English: An introduction to construction of English sentences.* New York: Harcourt Brace & World.

Fries, C. C. (1962). *Linguistics and reading.* New York: Holt, Rinehart & Winston.

Froyen, L. (1988). *Classroom management.* Columbus, OH: Merrill.

Fuller, P. R. (1949). Operant conditioning of a vegetative human organism. *American Journal of Psychology, 62,* 587–590.

Funderbunk, F. R. (1976). Reinforcement control of classroom creativity. In T. Brigham, R. Hawkins, J. Scott, & T. F. McLaughlin (Eds.), *Behavior analysis in education: Self-control and reading.* Dubuque, IA: Kendall/Hunt.

Furth, H. G. (1989). Piaget's logic of assimilation and logic for the classroom. In G. Forman & P. B. Pufall (Eds.), *Construction in the computer age* (pp. 44–72). Hillsdale, NJ: Erlbaum.

Furth, H. G., & Wachs, H. (1975). *Thinking goes to school: Piaget's theory in practice.* New York: Oxford University Press.

Gagné, E. D., & Rothkopf, E. Z. (1975). Text organization and learning goals. *Journal of Educational Psychology, 67,* 445–450.

Gagné, R. M. (1964). Problem solving. In A. W. Melton (Ed.), *Categories of human learning* (pp. 41–59). New York: Academic Press.

Gagné, R. M. (1965). The analysis of instructional objectives for the design of instruction. In R. Glaser (Ed.), *Teaching machines and programmed learning, II: Data and direction* (pp. 32–41). Washington, DC: National Education Association.

Gagné, R. M. (1972). Domains of learning. *Interchange, 3,* 1–8.

Gagné, R. M. (1974a). *Essentials of learning for instruction.* New York: Holt, Rinehart & Winston.

Gagné, R. M. (1974b). Task-analysis—its relation to content analysis. *Educational Psychologist, 11,* 11–18.

Gagné, R. M. (1977). *The conditions of learning* (2nd ed.). New York: Holt, Rinehart & Winston.

Gagné, R. M. (1985). *The conditions of learning* (3rd ed.). New York: Holt, Rinehart & Winston.

Gagné, R. M. (1987). Peaks and valleys in educational psychology: A retrospective view. In J. A. Glover & R. R. Ronning (Eds.), *Historical foundations of educational psychology.* New York: Plenum.

Gagné, R. M., & Briggs, L. J. (1974). *Principles of instructional design.* New York: Holt, Rinehart & Winston.

Gagné, R. M., & Driscoll, M. P. (1988). *Essentials of learning for instruction* (2nd ed.). Englewood Cliffs, NJ: Prentice-Hall.

Galifret-Granjon, N. (1985). The emergence of symbols, cognition, and communication in infancy. *Psychologie Francaise, 30,* 88–94.

Gallini, J. K., & Gredler, M. E. (1989). *Instructional design for computers.* Glenview, IL: Scott, Foresman.

Gallup, G. H. (1980). The 12th annual Gallup poll of the public's attitudes toward the public schools. *Phi Delta Kappan, 61,* 34.

Galton, F. (1972). *Hereditary genius* (reprint). Gloucester, MA: Peter Smith.

Garber, H., & Heber, F. R. (1977). The Milwaukee Project: Indications of the effectiveness of early intervention in preventing mental retardation. In P. Mittler (Ed.), *Research to practice in mental retardation: Care and intervention* (Vol. 1) (pp. 212–231). Baltimore: University Park Press.

Garcia, J. (1972). I.Q. The conspiracy. *Psychology Today, 6*(4), 40–94.

Garner, R. (1987). Strategies for reading and studying expository text. *Educational Psychologist, 22,* 299–312.

Garvey, C. (1984). *Children's talk.* London: Fontana.

Gary, A. L., & Glover, J. A. (1974). *Modeling effects on creative responding.* Paper read at the Southeastern Psychological Association Convention, Hollywood, FL.

Gary, A. L., & Glover, J. A. (1975). Eye color and sex: Their relationship to modeled learning. *Psychotherapy: Theory, Research and Practice, 12*(4), 425–428.

Gates, A. I. (1922). *Psychology of reading and spelling with special reference to disability.* New York: Teachers College.

Gearheart, B. R., & Weishahn, M. W. (1976). *The handicapped child in the regular classroom.* St. Louis, MO: Mosby.

Gearheart, B. R., & Weishahn, M. W. (1980). *The handicapped student in the regular classroom* (2nd ed.). St. Louis, MO: Mosby.

Geisler, C., Kaufer, D., & Hayes, J. R. (1985, March). *Translating instruction into skill: Learning to write precisely.* Paper presented to the annual meeting of the American Educational Research Association, Chicago.

Gentner, D. (1982). Why nouns are learned before verbs: Linguistic relativity versus natural partitioning. In S. A. Kuczaj, II (Ed.), *Language development: Vol. 2: Language, thought, and culture* (pp. 168–181). Hillside, NJ: Erlbaum.

Gerrig, R. J. (1988). Text comprehension. In R. J. Sternberg & E. E. Smith (Eds.), *The psychology of human thought* (pp. 242–266). New York: Cambridge University Press.

Ghatala, E. S., Levin, J. R., Pressley, M., & Lodico, M. G. (1985). Training cognitive strategy monitoring in children. *American Educational Research Journal, 22,* 199–216.

Gibson, J. J. (1950). The implications of learning theory for

social psychology. In J. G. Miller (Ed.), *Experiments in social process* (pp. 189–201). New York: McGraw-Hill.

Gilley, M. C. (1988). Sex roles in advertising: A comparison of television advertisements in Australia, Mexico, and the United States. *Journal of Marketing, 52,* 75–85.

Gilligan, C. (1982). *In a different voice: Psychological theory and women's development.* Cambridge, MA: Harvard University Press.

Gilligan, C., & Attanucci, J. (1988). Two moral orientations: Gender differences and similarities. *Merrill-Palmer Quarterly, 34,* 223–238.

Ginsburg, H., & Opper, S. (1979). *Piaget's theory of intellectual development* (2nd ed.). Englewood Cliffs, NJ: Prentice-Hall.

Glaser, R. (1963). Instructional technology and the measurement of learning outcomes. *American Psychologist, 18,* 519–521.

Glaser, R. (1965). *Teaching machines and programmed learning, II: Data and directions.* Washington, DC: National Education Association.

Glaser, R. (1973). Educational psychology and education. *American Psychologist, 28,* 557–566.

Glass, A. L., & Holyoak, K. J. (1975). Alternative conceptions of semantic memory. *Cognition, 3*(4), 313–339.

Glasser, W. (1969). *Schools without failure.* New York: Harper & Row.

Glasser, W. (1977). 10 steps to good discipline. *Today's Schools, 66,* 61–63.

Glasser, W. (1981). *Stations of the mind: New directions for reality therapy.* New York: Harper & Row.

Glasser, W. (1986). *Control theory in the classroom.* New York: Harper & Row.

Glazer, S. M., & Searfoss, L. W. (1988). *Reading diagnosis and instruction.* Englewood Cliffs, NJ: Prentice Hall.

Gleitman, L. R., & Rozin, P. (1977). The structure and acquisition of reading, I: Relations between orthographies and the structure of language. In A. S. Reber & D. L. Scarborough (Eds.), *Toward a psychology of reading* (pp. 212–230). Hillsdale, NJ: Erlbaum.

Gleitman, L. R., & Wanner, E. (1984). Current issues in language learning. In M. H. Bornstein & M. E. Lamb (Eds.), *Developmental psychology: An advanced textbook* (pp. 55–89). Hillsdale, NJ: Erlbaum.

Glenn, C. G. (1986). New challenges: A civil rights agenda for the public schools. *Phi Delta Kappan, 67,* 653–656.

Glover, J. A. (1976a). Comparative levels of creative ability among elementary school children. *Journal of Genetic Psychology, 129,* 131–135.

Glover, J. A. (1976b). A comparison of the levels of creative ability between black and white college students. *Journal of Genetic Psychology, 128,* 95–99.

Glover, J. A. (1976c). *Predicting the unpredictable: Enhancing creative behavior.* Paper read at the Division 25 Symposium on Applied Behavior Analysis and Creativity at the American Psychological Association Convention, Washington, DC.

Glover, J. A. (1977). Risky shift and creativity. *Social Behavior and Personality, 5,* 317–320.

Glover, J. A. (1979a). Creative writing in elementary school students. *Journal of Applied Behavior Analysis, 12,* 483.

Glover, J. A. (1979b). *A parent's guide to intelligence testing.* Chicago: Nelson-Hall.

Glover, J. A. (1980). *Becoming a more creative person.* Englewood Cliffs, NJ: Prentice-Hall.

Glover, J. A. (1989). The testing effect: Not gone but nearly forgotten. *Journal of Educational Psychology.*

Glover, J. A., & Corkill, A. J. (1987). The "spacing" effect in memory for paragraphs and brief lectures. *Journal of Educational Psychology, 79,* 198–200.

Glover, J. A., & Dinnel, D. (1985, April). *Advance organizers and encoding procedures.* Paper presented to the annual meeting of the American Educational Research Association, Chicago.

Glover, J. A., & Gary, A. L. (1975). *Behavior modification: Enhancing creativity and other good behaviors.* Pacific Grove, CA: Boxwood.

Glover, J. A., & Gary, A. L. (1976). Procedures to increase some aspects of creativity. *Journal of Applied Behavior Analysis, 9,* 79–84.

Glover, J. A., & Gary, A. L. (1979). *Behavior modification: An empirical approach to self-control.* Chicago: Nelson-Hall.

Glover, J. A., Plake, B. S., Roberts, B., Zimmer, J. W., & Palmere, M. (1981). Distinctiveness of encoding: The effects of paraphrasing and drawing inferences on memory from prose. *Journal of Educational Psychology, 73,* 736–744.

Glover, J. A., & Ronning, R. R. (1987). About educational psychology. In J. A. Glover & R. R. Ronning (Eds.), *Historical foundations of educational psychology.* New York: Plenum.

Glover, J. A., Ronning, R. R., & Filbeck, R. W. (1977). *Teaching: Why not try psychology?* Des Moines, IA: Kendall/Hunt.

Glover, J. A., Ronning, R. R., & Reynolds, C. R. (Eds.). (in press). *A handbook of creativity.* New York: Plenum.

Glover, J. A., & Sautter, F. J. (1976). The effects of locus of control on four components of creative behavior. *Social Behavior and Personality, 4,* 257–260.

Glover, J. A., & Sautter, F. J. (1977a). Procedures for increasing four behaviorally defined components of creativity within formal written assignments among high school students. *School Applications of Learning Theory, 9*(4), 3–22.

Glover, J. A., & Sautter, F. J. (1977b). The relationship of risk taking to creative behavior. *Psychological Reports, 41,* 227–230.

Glover, J. A., & Trammel, S. (1976). Comparative levels of creative ability among behavioral problem and nonbehavioral problem students. *Psychological Reports, 38,* 1171–1174.

Glover, J. A., Ronning, R. R., & Bruning, R. H. (1990). *Cognitive psychology for teachers.* New York: Macmillan.

Glover, J. A., Timme, V., Deyloff, D., & Rogers, M. (1987). Memory for student-performed tasks. *Journal of Educational Psychology, 79,* 445–452.

Gnagey, W. J. (1981). *Motivating classroom discipline.* New York: Macmillan.

Goelman, H., Oberg, A., & Smith, F. (1984). *Awakening to literacy,* Exeter, NH: Heinemann.

Goetz, E. M., & Baer, D. M. (1971). Descriptive social reinforcement of "creative" blockbuilding by young childen. In E. Ramp & B. L. Hopkins (Eds.), *A new direction for education: Behavior analysis* (pp. 63–81). Lawrence, KS: Support and Development Center for Follow-Through.

Goetz, E. M., & Baer, D. M. (1973). Social control of form diversity and the emergence of new forms in children's blockbuilding. *Journal of Applied Behavior Analysis, 6,* 209–218.

Goetz, E. M., & Salmonson, M. (1972). The effects of general and descriptive reinforcement on "creativity" in easel painting. In G. Semb (Ed.), *Behavior analyses and education* (pp. 82–93). Lawrence, KS: Support and Development Center for Follow-Through.

Gold, S. (1987). Predicting reading achievement using an individual reading readiness inventory. *Child Study Journal, 17,* 97–103.

Goldin-Meadow, S., & Feldman, H. (1977). The development of language-like communication without a language model. *Science, 197,* 401–403.

Goldsmith, R. E. (1984). Personality characteristics associated with adaption-innovation. *Journal of Psychology, 117,* 159–165.

Good, T., Biddle, B. J., & Brophy, J. E. (1975). *Teachers make a difference.* New York: Holt, Rinehart & Winston.

Good, T., & Grouws, D. (1977). Teaching effects: A process-product study in fourth grade mathematics classes. *Journal of Teacher Education, 28,* 49–54.

Goodman, C., & Gardiner, J. M. (1981). How well do children remember what they have recalled? *British Journal of Educational Psychology, 51,* 97–101.

Goodman, K. S. (1970). Reading: A psycholinguistic guessing game. In H. Singer & R. B. Ruddell (Eds.), *Theoretical models and processes of reading* (pp. 46–81). Newark, DE: International Reading Association.

Gordon, T. (1974). *Teacher effectiveness training.* New York: McKay.

Gordon, T. (1977). *Teacher effectiveness training.* New York: Random House.

Gordon, W. J. J. (1961). *Synetics: The development of creative capacity.* New York: Harper & Row.

Gormezano, I., Prokasy, W. F., & Thompson, R. F. (1986). *Classical conditioning.* Hillsdale, NJ: Erlbaum.

Gottlieb, J. (1980). Improving attitudes toward retarded children by using group discussion. *Exceptional Children, 47,* 106–111.

Gottlieb, M. I., & Williams, J. E. (1987). *Textbook of developmental pediatrics.* New York: Plenum.

Graham, S. (in press). Review of attribution research. *Educational Psychology Review.*

Gray, W. S. (1922). Remedial cases in reading: Their diagnosis and treatment. *Supplementary Educational Monographs* (No. 22). Chicago: University of Chicago Press.

Greene, R. L. (1988). Generation effects in frequency judgment. *Journal of Experimental Psychology: Learning, Memory, & Cognition, 14,* 298–304.

Greenfield, P. M., & Smith, J. H. (1976). *The structure of communication in early language development.* New York: Academic Press.

Greeno, J. (1974). Hobbits and orcs: Acquisition of a sequential concept. *Cognitive Psychology, 6,* 270–292.

Greenwood, C. R., Carta, J. J., & Hall, R. V. (1988). The use of peer tutoring strategies in classroom management and educational instruction. *School Psychology Review, 17,* 258–275.

Gronlund, N. E. (1976). *Measurement and evaluation in teaching* (3rd ed.). New York: Macmillan.

Gronlund, N. E. (1978). *Stating objectives for classroom instruction.* New York: Macmillan.

Gronlund, N. E. (1985). *Measurement and evaluation in teaching* (5th ed.). New York: Macmillan.

Gronlund, N. E. (1988). *How to construct achievement tests.* Englewood Cliffs, NJ: Prentice-Hall.

Grueneberg, M. (1973). The role of memorization techniques in final examination preparation. *Educational Research, 15,* 134–139.

Guilford, J. P. (1936). *Psychometric methods.* New York: McGraw-Hill.

Guilford, J. P. (1959). Three faces of intellect. *American Psychologist, 14,* 469–479.

Gullicksen, H. (1987). *Theory of mental tests.* Hillsdale, NJ: Erlbaum.

Gunter, B., & Furnham, A. F. (1985). Androgyny and the perception of television violence as perpetrated by males and females. *Human Relations, 38,* 535–549.

Guthrie, E. R. (1935). *The psychology of learning.* New York: Harper & Row.

Gutkin, T. B. (1978). Modification of elementary students' locus of control: An operant approach. *Journal of Psychology, 100,* 107–115.

Haefele, J. W. (1962). *Creativity and innovation.* New York: Reinhold.

Hakes, D. T. (1982). The development of metalinguistic abilities: What develops? In S. Kuczaj, II (Ed.), *Language development* (Vol. 2), (pp. 216–232). Hillsdale, NJ: Erlbaum.

Haley, J. (1987). *Problem-solving therapy* (2nd ed.). San Francisco: Jossey-Bass.

Hall, G. S. (1887). Editorial. *American Journal of Psychology, 1,* iii–vi.

Hall, G. S. (1891). Children's lies. *Pedagogical Seminary, 1,* 211–218.

Hall, G. S. (1891). Editorial. *Pedagogical Seminary, 1,* iii–viii.

Hall, R. H., Rocklin, T. R., Dansereau, D. F., Skaggs, L. P., O'Donnell, A. M., Lambiotte, J. G., & Yount, M. D. (1988). The role of individual differences in the cooperative learning of technical material. *Journal of Educational Psychology, 80,* 172–178.

Hall, R. V., & Hall, M. C. (1980). *How to use time-out.* Washington, DC: Professional Education.

Hall, V. C., & Kaye, D. B. (1980). Early patterns of cognitive development. *Monographs of the Society for Research in Child Development, 45* (Whole No. 184).

Halliday, M. A. K. (1975). *Learning how to mean: Explorations in the development of language.* New York: Elsevier.

Halliday, M. A. K., & Hasan, R. (1976). *Cohesion in English.* London: Longman.

Halpain, D., Glover, J. A., & Harvey, A. L. (1985). Differential effects of higher- and lower-order questions: Attention hypotheses. *Journal of Educational Psychology, 77,* 703–715.

Halpern, A. S. (1979). Adolescents and young adults. *Exceptional Children, 45,* 518–523.

Hamachek, D. (1987). A history of humanistic psychology. In J. A. Glover & R. R. Ronning (Eds.), *Historical foundations of educational psychology.* New York: Plenum.

Hamilton, R. J. (1985). Adjunct questions and objectives. *Review of Educational Research, 55,* 47–86.

Hampton, J. A. (1988). Overextension of conjunctive concepts: Evidence for a unitary model of concept typicality and class inclusion. *Journal of Experimental Psychology: Learning, Memory, and Cognition, 14,* 12–32.

Hampton, J. A., & Taylor, P. J. (1985). Effects of semantic elaborations on same-different decisions in a good-bad categorization task. *Journal of Experimental Psychology: Learning, Memory and Cognition, 11,* 85–93.

Harburton, E. C. (1981). *Study skills for college.* Cambridge MA: Winthrop.

Harris, A. J. (1970). *How to increase reading ability* (5th ed.). New York: McKay.

Harris, A. J., & Sipey, E. R. (1979). *How to teach reading.* New York: Longman.

Harris, A. J., & Sipey, E. R. (1980). *How to increase reading ability.* (7th ed.). New York: Longman.

Harris, A. J., & Sipey, E. R. (1983). *Readings on reading instruction.* (2nd ed.). New York: Longman.

Harris, F. R., Wolf, M. M., & Baer, D. M. (1969). Effects of adult social reinforcement on child behavior. *Young Children, 20,* 8–17.

Harris, M. B. (1970). Reciprocity and generosity: Some determinants of sharing in children. *Child Development, 41,* 222–245.

Hart, D. (1988a). A longitudinal study of adolescents' socialization and identification as predictors of adult moral judgment development. *Merrill-Palmer Quarterly, 34,* 245–260.

Hart, D. (1988b). The development of personal identity in adolescence: A philosophical dilemma approach. *Merrill-Palmer Quarterly, 34,* 105–114.

Harvard College. (1895). *Reports on composition and rhetoric.* Cambridge, MA: Harvard University Press.

Hawkins, R. P., Pingree, S., & Adler, I. (1987). Searching for cognitive processes in the cultivation effect: Adult and adolescent samples in the United States and Australia. *Human Communication Research, 13,* 553–577.

Hayden, A. H. (1979). Handicapped children, birth to age three. *Exceptional Children, 45,* 510–516.

Hayes, C. (1951). *The ape in our house.* New York: Harper.

Hayes, J. R. (1978). *Cognitive psychology: Thinking and creating.* Homewood, IL: Dorsey.

Hayes, J. R. (1986). *The complete problem solver.* Homewood, IL: Dorsey.

Hayes, J. R. (1988a). Characteristics of notable composers and painters. Unpublished manuscript. Carnegie-Mellon University, Pittsburgh, Pennsylvania.

Hayes, J. R. (1988b). *The complete problem solver* (2nd ed.). Hillsdale, NJ: Erlbaum.

Hayes, J. R. (in press, a). *Cognitive psychology: Thinking and creating* (2nd ed.). Homewood, IL: Dorsey.

Hayes, J. R. (in press, b). A cognitive model of creative thought. In J. A. Glover, R. R. Ronning, & C. R. Reynolds (Eds.), *Handbook of creativity research.* New York: Plenum.

Hayes, J. R., & Flower, L. S. (1980) Identifying the organization of writing processes. In L. W. Gregg & E. R. Steinberg (Eds.), *Cognitive processes in writing* (pp. 3–30). Hillsdale, NJ: Erlbaum.

Hayes, J. R., & Flower, L. (1986). Writing research and the writer. *American Psychologist, 41,* 1106–1113.

Hayes, J. R., & Simon, H. A. (1974). Understanding written problem instructions. In L. W. Gregg (Ed.), *Knowledge and cognition* (pp. 202–220). Potomac, MD: Erlbaum.

Hayes, J. R., & Simon, H. A. (1976). Psychological differences among problem isomorphs. In N. Castellon, Jr., D. Pisoni, & G. Potts (Eds.), *Cognitive theory* (Vol. II) (pp. 81–96). Potomac, MD: Erlbaum.

Hayes, J. R., Waterman, D. A., & Robinson, C. S. (1977). Identifying relevant aspects of a problem text. *Cognitive Science, 5,* 297–313.

Hayes, S. C., Rosenfarb, I., Wulfert, E., Munt, E. D., Korn, Z., & Zettle, R. D. (1985). Self-reinforcement effects: An artifact of social standard setting. *Journal of Applied Behavior Analysis, 21,* 201–214.

Hearnshaw, L. S. (1979). *Cyril Burt, psychologist.* Ithaca, NY: Cornell University Press.

Hebb, D. O. (1949). *The organization of behavior.* New York: Wiley.

Heber, R., Garber, H., Harrington, S., Hoffman, C., & Falender, C. (1972, February). *Rehabilitation of families at risk for mental retardation.* Progress report of the Rehabilitation Research and Training Center in Mental Retardation, University of Wisconsin, Madison.

Hebert, E. F., Winograd, P. N., & Danner, F. W. (1984). Children's attributions for failure and success in different aspects of reading. *Journal of Educational Psychology, 76,* 1139–1148.

Hedegaard, M. (1984). Non-instructional concept learning. *Psykologisk Skriftserie Aarhus, 9,* 27–37.

Hedley, C. N., & Hicks, J. S. (1988). *Reading and the special learner.* Norwood, NJ: Albex.

Heider, F. (1944). Social perception and phenomenal causality. *Psychological Review, 51*, 358–374.

Heider, F. (1958). Social perception and phenomenal causality. *Psychological Issues, 1*, 35–52.

Henry, G. K. (1987). Symbolic modeling and parent behavioral training: Effects on noncompliance of hyperactive children. *Journal of Behavioral Therapy and Experimental Psychiatry, 18*, 105–113.

Hergenhahn, B. R. (1976). *An introduction to theories of learning.* Englewood Cliffs, NJ: Prentice-Hall.

Herman, J. L. (1988). Item writing techniques. In J. P. Keeves (Ed.), *Educational research, methodology, and measurement: An international handbook.* New York: Pergamon Press.

Herriman, M. L., & Myhill, M. E. (1984). Metalinguistic awareness and education. In W. E. Tunmer, C. Pratt, & M. L. Herriman (Eds.), *Metalinguistic awareness in children* (pp. 221–236). Berlin: Springer-Verlag.

Herrnstein, R. (1973). IQ. *The Atlantic, 28*, 43–64.

Hersen, M., & Barlow, D. H. (1976). *Single case experimental designs.* New York: Pergamon.

Hersen, M., & Last, C. G. (1988). *Child behavior therapy casebook.* New York: Plenum.

Hershberger, W. (1974). Self-evaluational responding and typographical cueing: Techniques for programming self-instructional reading materials. *Journal of Educational Psychology, 66*, 288–296.

Herzberg, O. E. (1926). *A comparative study of different methods used in teaching beginners to write.* New York: Teachers College, Columbia University Press.

Heward, W. L., & Orlansky, M. D. (1988). *Exceptional children: An introductory survey of special education.* Columbus, OH: Merrill.

Higbee, K. L., & Kunihara, S. (1985). Cross-cultural applications of Yodai mnemonics in education. *Educational Psychologist, 20*, 57–64.

Higgins, S. T., & Morris, E. K. (1985). A comment on contemporary definitions of reinforcement as a behavioral process. *Psychological Record, 35*, 81–88.

Hilgard, E. R. (1987). Perspectives on educational psychology. In J. A. Glover & R. R. Ronning (Eds.), *Historical foundations of educational psychology.* New York: Plenum.

Hilgard, E. R., & Bower, G. H. (1975). *Theories of learning* (4th ed.). Englewood Cliffs, NJ: Prentice-Hall.

Hilgard, E. R. (1987). *Psychology in America: A historical survey.* New York: Harcourt Brace Jovanovich.

Hiller, J. H. (1974). Learning from prose text: Effects of readability level, inserted question difficulty, and individual differences. *Journal of Educational Psychology, 66*, 202–211.

Hillinger, M. L. (1980). Priming effects with phonetically similar words: The encoding-bias hypothesis reconsidered. *Memory and Cognition, 8*, 115–123.

Hills, J. R. (1976). *Measurement and evaluation in the classroom.* Columbus, OH: Merrill.

Hinsely, D., Hayes, J. R., & Simon, H. A. (1977). From words to equations. In P. Carpenter & M. Just (Eds.), *Cognitive processes in comprehension* (pp. 54–68). Hillsdale, NJ: Erlbaum.

Hitch, G. J., Halliday, S., Schaafstal, A. M., & Schraagen, J. M. C. (1988). Visual working memory in young children. *Memory and Cognition, 16*, 120–132.

Holt, E. B. (1931). *Animal drive and the learning process.* New York: Holt, Rinehart & Winston.

Holt, J. (1964). *How children fail.* New York: Pitman.

Holt, J. (1970). *What do I do Monday?* New York: Dutton.

Holtzman, J. M., & Akiyama, H. (1985). What children see: The aged on television in Japan and the United States. *Gerontologist, 25*, 62–68.

Homme, L., Csanyi, A. P., Gonzales, M. A., & Rechs, J. R. (1969). *How to use contingency contracting in the classroom.* Champaign, IL: Research Press.

Homme, L. E., DeBaca, P. C., Devine, J., Steinhorst, R., & Rickert, E. J. (1963). Use of the Premack Principle in controlling the behavior of nursery school children. *Journal of Experimental Analysis of Behavior, 6*, 43–54.

Hoppe, F. (1930). Erfolg und misserfolg. *Psychologische Forschung, 14*, 1–62.

Horn, J. M. (1983). The Texas adoption project: Adopted children and their intellectual resemblance to biological and adoptive parents. *Child Development, 54*, 268–275.

Horn, J. M. (1985). Bias? Indeed! *Child Development, 56*, 779–780.

Houston, J. P. (1966). Stimulus recall and experimental paradigm. *Journal of Experimental Psychology, 72*, 619–621.

Hoyt, F. S. (1906). The place of grammar in the elementary curriculum. *Teachers College Record, 7*, 467–500.

Huey, E. B. (1908). *The psychology and pedagogy of reading.* New York: Macmillan.

Huey, E. B. (1968). *The psychology and pedagogy of reading.* Cambridge, MA: MIT Press. (Original work published 1908.)

Hoyer, W. J., & Familant, M. E. (1987). Adult age differences in the rate of processing expectancy information. *Cognitive Development, 2*, 59–70.

Hughes, J. N. (1988). *Cognitive behavior therapy with children in schools.* New York: Pergamon.

Hull, C. L. (1943). *Principles of behavior.* Englewood Cliffs, NJ: Prentice-Hall.

Hull, G. (1987). The editing process in writing: A performance study of more skilled and less skilled college writers. *Research in the Teaching of English, 21,* 8–29.

Humphrey, G. (1921). Imitation and the conditioned reflex. *Pedagogical Seminary, 28,* 1–21.

Humphrey, J. E. (1978). Increasing school attendance with the aid of peer helpers and rewards: A case study. Paper presented at the annual meeting of the Midwestern Association of Behavior Analysis, Chicago.

Hunkins, F. P. (1969). Effects of analysis and evaluation questions on various levels of achievement. *Journal of Experimental Education, 38,* 45–58.

Hunt, E. (1978). Mechanics of verbal ability. *Psychological Review, 85,* 109–130.

Hunt, E. (in press). Science, technology and intelligence. In R. R. Ronning, , J. A. Glover, & J. Conoley (Eds.), *The impact of cognitive psychology on measurement.* Hillsdale, NJ: Erlbaum.

Hunt, E., Frost, N., & Lunneborg, C. (1973). Individual differences in cognition: A new approach to intelligence. In G. Bower (Ed.), *The psychology of learning and motivation* (Vol. 7) (pp. 86–112). New York: Academic Press.

Hunt, E., Lunneborg, C., & Lewis, J. (1975). What does it mean to be high verbal? *Cognitive Psychology, 7,* 194–227.

Hunt, E., Lunneborg, C., & Lewis, J. (1979). What does it mean to be high verbal? In L. Willerman & R. G. Turner (Eds.), *Readings about individual and group differences* (pp. 121–146). San Francisco: Freeman.

Hunt, E., & Pellegrino, J. (1985). Using interactive computing to expand intelligence testing. *Intelligence, 9,* 167–176.

Hunt, J. McV. (1961). *Intelligence and experience.* New York: Ronald Press.

Hursh, D. E. (1976). Personalized systems of instruction: What do the data indicate? *Journal of Personalized Instruction, 1,* 91–105.

Inhelder, B., de Caprona, B., & Cornu-Wells, A. (Eds.), (1988). *Piaget today.* Hillsdale, NJ: Erlbaum.

Isaksen, S. G., & Parnes, S. J. (1985). Curriculum planning for creative thinking and problem solving. *Journal of Creative Behavior, 19,* 1–29.

Itard, J. (1817). Memoire sur le begaiement [A memoir on stuttering]. *Universel des Sciences Medicales, 7,* 129–144.

Itard, J. M. G. (1962). *The wild boy of Aveyron.* New York: Appleton-Century-Crofts.

Jackson, C. D. (1970). On the report of the Ad Hoc Committee on Educational Uses of Tests with Disadvantaged Students: Another psychological view from the Association of Black Psychologists. *American Psychologist, 30,* 86–90.

Jacobs, J. E., & Paris, S. G. (1987). Children's metacognition about reading: Issues in definition, measurement, and instruction. *Educational Psychologist, 22,* 255–278.

Jacobs, J. F., & Degraaf, C. A. (1973). *Expectancy and race: The influences upon the scoring of individual intelligence tests.* Paper presented at the annual meeting of the American Educational Research Association, New Orleans.

Jacoby, L. L. & Craik, F. I. M. (1979). Effects of elaboration of processing at encoding and retrieval. Trace distinctiveness and recovery of initial content. In L. S. Cermak & F. I. M. Craik (Eds.), *Levels of processing and human memory* (pp. 1–22). Hillsdale, NJ: Erlbaum.

Jacoby, L. L., Craik., F. I. M., & Begg, I. (1979). Effects of decision difficulty on recognition and recall. *Journal of Verbal Learning and Verbal Behavior, 18,* 585–600.

James, W. (1890). *The principles of psychology* (Vols. 1 & 2). New York: Holt.

James, W. (1899). *Talks to teachers on psychology and to students on some of life's ideals.* New York: Holt.

James, W. (1909). *Pragmatism: A new name for old ways of thinking.* New York: Longmans, Green.

Jarvik, L. F., & Erlenmeyer-Kimling, L. (1967). Survey of familial correlations in measured intellectual functions. In J. Zubin & G. A. Jervis (Eds.), *Psychopathology of mental development* (pp. 323–360). New York: Grune & Stratton.

Jenkins, J. G., & Dallenbach, K. M. Oblivescence during sleep and waking. (1924). *American Journal of Psychology, 35,* 605–612.

Jenkins, J. J. (1974). Remember that old theory of memory? Well, forget it! *American Psychologist, 29,* 785–795.

Jenkins, J. R., & Deno, S. L. (1971). Influence of knowledge and type of objectives on subject-matter learning. *Journal of Educational Psychology, 62,* 67–70.

Jenkins, J. R., & Neisworth, J. T. (1973). The facilitative influence of instructional objectives. *Journal of Educational Research, 66,* 254–256.

Jennings, J., Geis, F. L., & Brown, V. (1980). Influence of television commercials on women's self-confidence and independent judgment. *Journal of Personality and Social Psychology, 38*(2), 203–210.

Jensen, A. R. (1969). How much can we boost I.Q. and scholastic achievement? *Harvard Educational Review, 39,* 32–112.

Jensen, A. R. (1980) *Bias in mental testing.* New York: Free Press.

Jensen, A. R. (1985). The nature of the black-white difference on various psychometric tests: Spearman's hypothesis. *The Behavioral and Brain Sciences, 8*, 193–219. (commentary from 220–263).

Jensen, A. R. (1987). A history of the study of individual differences. In J. A. Glover & R. R. Ronning (Eds.), *Historical foundations of educational psychology*. New York: Plenum.

Jensen, A. R. (in press). The *g* beyond factor analysis. In R. R. Ronning, J. A. Glover & J. C. Conoley (Eds), *The impact of cognitive psychology on measurement*. Hillsdale, NJ: Erlbaum.

Jensen, A. R., Larson, G. E., & Paul, S. M. (1988). Psychometric *g* and mental processing speed on a semantic verification task. *Personality and Individual Differences, 9*, 243–256.

Johnson, D. W., & Johnson, R. (1981). Effects of cooperative and individualistic learning experiences on interethnic interaction. *Journal of Educational Psychology, 73*, 444–449.

Johnson, D. W., Johnson, R. T., Nelson, D., & Read, S. (1978). *Mainstreaming: Development of positive interdependence between handicapped and nonhandicapped students*. Minneapolis, MN: National Support Systems Project.

Johnson, R. T. (1988). Cooperative learning. Paper given to Ball State University's annual learning colloquium. Muncie, IN.

Johnson, R. T., & Johnson, D. W. (1981). Building friendships between handicapped and nonhandicapped students: Effects of cooperative and individualistic instruction. *American Educational Research Journal, 18*, 415–423.

Jones, F. H. (1988). *Positive classroom discipline*. New York: McGraw-Hill.

Jones, W. P., & Anderson, J. R. (1987). Short- and long-term memory retrieval: A comparison of the effects of information load and relatedness. *Journal of Experimental Psychology: General, 116*, 137–153.

Judd, C. H. (1903). *Genetic psychology*. New York: Doran.

Jung, C. (1912). *The psychology of the unconscious*. Leipzig: Franz Deuticke.

Jung, C. (1923). *Psychological types or the psychology of individuation*. New York: Harcourt, Brace.

Just, M., & Carpenter, P. (1987). *The psychology of reading and language comprehension*, Boston: Allyn and Bacon.

Just, M. A., & Carpenter, P. A. (1980). A theory of reading: From eye fixations to comprehension. *Psychological Review, 87*, 329–354.

Kail, R. (1984). *The development of memory in children (2nd ed.)*. San Francisco: Freeman.

Kail, R. (1988). Developmental functions for speeds of cognitive processes. *Journal of Experimental Child Psychology, 45*, 339–365.

Kamfer, F. H., & Schefft, B. K. (1988). *Guiding the process of therapeutic change*. Champaign, IL: Research Press.

Kann, R. (1984). Increasing motivation and reading comprehension of exceptional learners: Three modeling techniques. *Pointer, 29*, 20–22.

Kanner, L. (1943). Autistic disturbances of affective contact. *Nervous Child, 2*, 217–250.

Kapfer, P. G., & Ovard, G. F. (1971). *Preparing and using individualized learning packages*. Englewood Cliffs, NJ: Educational Technology Publications.

Kaplan, M. (1966). *The essential works of Pavlov*. New York: Bantam.

Kaplan, R. (1974). Effects of learning with part vs. whole presentations of instructional objectives. *Journal of Educational Psychology, 66*, 787–792.

Kaplan, R., & Rothkopf, E. Z. (1974). Instructional objectives as directions to learners: Effect of passage length and amount of objective-relevant content. *Journal of Educational Psychology, 66*, 449–456.

Kaplan, R., & Simmons, F. G. (1974). Effects of instructional objectives used as orienting stimuli or as summary/review upon prose learning. *Journal of Educational Psychology, 66*, 614–622.

Karlin, R., & Karlin, A. R. (1987). *Teaching elementary reading*. New York: Harcourt Brace Jovanovich.

Katona, G. (1940). *Organizing and memorizing*. New York: Columbia University Press.

Kaufman, R. A. (1976). *Identifying and solving problems: A systems approach*. LaJolla, CA: University Associates.

Kazdin, A. E. (1981). Applied behavioral principles in the schools. In C. R. Reynolds & T. E. Gutkin (Eds.), *A handbook for school psychology* (pp. 761–795) New York: Wiley.

Kazdin, A. E. (1984). *Behavior modification in applied settings*, (3rd ed.). Homewood, IL: Dorsey.

Kazdin, A. E. (1988). *Child psychotherapy*. New York: Pergamon.

Kazdin, A. E. (1988). Childhood depression. In J. C. Witt, S. N. Elliott, & F. M. Gresham (Eds.), *Handbook of behavior therapy in education* (pp. 526–561). New York: Plenum.

Keane, K. J., & Kretschmer, R. E. (1987). Effect of mediated learning intervention on a cognitive task performance with a deaf population. *Journal of Experimental Psychology: Learning, Memory and Cognition, 79*, 49–53.

Kegan, R. (1982). *The evolving self: Problem and process in human development*. Cambridge, MA: Harvard University Press.

Keller, F. S. (1937). *The definition of psychology.* New York: Appleton-Century-Crofts.

Keller, F. S. (1965). *The definition of psychology* (2nd ed.). New York: Appleton-Century-Crofts.

Keller, M. F., & Carlson, P. M. (1974). The use of symbolic modeling to promote social skills in pre-school children with low levels of social responsiveness. *Child Development, 45,* 912–919.

Kennedy, M. M. (1978). Findings from the Follow Through planned variation study. *Educational Researcher, 7*(6), 3–11.

Keough, D. A., Faw, G. D., Whitman, T. L., & Reid, D. H. (1984). Enhancing leisure skills in severely retarded adolescents through a self-instructional treatment package. *Analysis and Intervention in Developmental Disabilities, 4,* 333–351.

Kershner, J. R., & Ledger, G. (1985). Effect of sex, intelligence, and style of thinking on creativity: A comparison of gifted and average IQ children. *Journal of Personality and Social Psychology. 48,* 1033–1040.

Khan, M., & Paivio, A. (1988). Memory for schematic and categorical information. *Journal of Experimental Psychology: Learning, Memory, and Cognition, 141,* 558–561.

Kiewra, K. A. (1985). Investigating notetaking and review: A depth of processing alternative. *Educational Psychologist, 20,* 23–32.

Kilpatrick, J. (1985). Doing mathematics without understanding it: A commentary on Higbee and Kunihara. *Educational Psychologist, 20,* 65–68.

Kintsch, W. (1972). Notes on the structure of semantic memory. In E. Tulving & W. Donaldson (Eds.), *Organization of memory.* New York: Academic Press.

Kintsch, W. (1974). *The representation of meaning in memory* (pp. 68–79). Hillsdale, NJ: Erlbaum.

Kintsch, W., Miller, J. R., & Polson, P. G. (1984). *Methods and tactics in cognitive science.* Hillsdale, NJ: Erlbaum.

Kintsch, W. (1988). The role of knowledge in discourse comprehension: A construction-integration model. *Psychological Review, 95,* 163–182.

Kirk, S. A. (1972). *Educating exceptional children* (2nd ed.). Boston: Houghton Mifflin.

Kirk, S. A., & Bateman, B. (1962). Diagnosis and remediation of learning disabilities. *Exceptional Children, 29,* 72.

Klatzky, R. L. (1980). *Human memory: Structures and processes* (2nd ed.). San Francisco: Freeman.

Klazky, R. L. (1984). *Memory and awareness.* San Francisco: Freeman.

Klausmeier, H. J. (1988). The future of educational psychology and the content of the graduate program in educational psychology. *Educational Psychologist, 23,* 203–220.

Klesges, R. C. Malott, J. M., & Ugland, M. (1984). The effects of gradual exposure and parental modeling on the dental phobias of a four-year old girl and her mother. *Journal of Behavior Therapy and Experimental Psychiatry, 15,* 161–164.

Kliegl, R., Smith, J., Heckhausen, J., & Baltes, P. B. (1987). Mnemonic training for the acquisition of skilled digit memory. *Cognition and Instruction, 4,* 203–223.

Kline, C. L. (1972). The adolescents with learning problems: How long must they wait? *Journal of Learning Disabilities, 5,* 262–271.

Kniveton, B. (1987). Misbehaving peer models in the classroom: An investigation of the effects of social class and intelligence. *Educational Studies, 13,* 161–168.

Knott, G. P. (1980). Communicative competence and secondary learning disabled students. *Directive Teacher, 2,* 22–24.

Knox, B. J., & Glover, J. A. (1978). The effects of pre-school experience on I.Q., creativity and readiness to learn among black and white first graders. *Journal of Genetic Psychology, 132*(1), 151.

Kohlberg, L. (1958). The development of models of moral thinking and choice in the years 10 to 16. Unpublished doctoral dissertation, the University of Chicago, Chicago, IL.

Kohlberg, L. (1984). *Essays on moral development: Vol. II. The psychology of moral development.* New York: Harper & Row.

Kohlberg, L. (1987). *Childhood psychology and childhood education: A cognitive developmental view.* New York: Longman.

Kohlberg, L. (in press). *Essays on moral development: Vol. III. Moral education.* New York: Harper & Row.

Köhler, A. (1925). *The mentality of apes.* New York: Harcourt, Brace.

Kohler, F. W., & Fowler, S. A. (1985). Training prosocial behaviors to young children: An analysis of reciprocity with untrained peers. *Journal of Applied Behavior Analysis, 18,* 187–200.

Kolers, P. A., & Roediger, H. (1984). Procedures of mind. *Journal of Verbal Learning and Verbal Behavior, 23,* 425–449.

Kolodner, J. L. (1984). *Retrieval and organizational strategies in conceptual memory: A computer model.* Hillsdale, NJ: Erlbaum.

Kolstoe, R. H. (1973). *Introduction to statistics for the behavioral sciences.* Homewood, IL: Dorsey.

Kontos, S. (1988). Development and interrelationships of reading knowledge and skills during kindergarten and first grade. *Reading Research and Instruction, 27,* 13–28.

Koppenall, R. J. (1963). Time changes in the strength of A-B, A-C lists: spontaneous recovery? *Journal of Verbal Learning and Verbal Behavior, 2,* 310–319.

Krathwohl, D. R., Bloom, B. S., & Masia, B. B. (1964). *Taxonomy of educational objectives. The classification of educational goals. Handbook II: Affective domain.* New York: McKay.

Kratochwill, T. R., & Bijou, S. W. (1987). The impact of behaviorism on educational psychology. In J. A. Glover & R. R. Ronning (Eds.), *Historical foundations of educational psychology.* New York: Plenum.

Kreutzer, M. A., Leonard, S. C., & Flavell, J. H. (1975). An interview study of children's knowledge about memory. *Monographs of the Society for Research in Child Development, 40*(1, Serial No. 159).

Krumboltz, J. D., & Thoresen, C. E. (Eds.). (1976). *Counseling methods.* New York: Holt, Rinehart & Winston.

Kubiszyn, T., & Borich, G. (1990). *Educational testing and measurement: Classroom application and practice* (3rd ed.). Glenview, IL: Scott, Foresman.

Kulhavy, R. (in press). Another look at feedback. *Educational Psychology Review.*

Külpe, O. (1893). *Outline of psychology.* Leipzig: Engleman.

Kuo, L. Z. (1921). Giving up instincts in psychology. *Journal of Philosophy, 17,* 645–664.

Lakoff, G. (1972). *Hedges: A study in meaning criteria and the logic of funny concepts.* Paper presented at the Eighth Regional Meeting, Chicago Linguistic Society, University of Chicago Linguistics Department, Chicago.

Lambert, W. E., & Tucker, G. R. (1972). *Bilingual education of children.* Rowley, MA: Newbury House.

Landers, S. (1988). Pulling the punches from children's TV. *Monitor, 19,* 22–23.

Lansman, M., & Hunt, E. (1982). Individual differences in secondary task performance. *Memory & Cognition, 10,* 10–24.

Lapsley, D. K., & Power, F. C. (1988). *Self, ego, and identity.* New York: Springer-Verlag.

Larkin, J. H. (1985). Understanding, problem representation, and skills in physics. In S. F. Chipman, J. W. Segal, & R. Glaser (Eds.), *Thinking and learning skills* (Volume 2) (pp. 160–183). Hillsdale, NJ: Erlbaum.

Lawson, T. E. (1974). Effects of instruction objectives on learning and retention. *Instructional Science, 3,* 1–21.

Lawton, J. T., & Wanska, S. K. (1977). Advance organizers as a teaching strategy: A reply to Clawson and Barnes. *Review of Educational Research, 47,* 233–244.

Lefcourt, H. M. (1976). *Locus of control: Current trends in theory and research.* Hillsdale, NJ: Erlbaum.

Leinhardt, G. (1987). Development of an expert explanation: An analysis of a sequence of subtraction lessons. *Cognition and Instruction, 4,* 225–282.

Lenneberg, E. H. (1967). *Biological foundations of language.* New York: Wiley.

Leonard, J. P. (1931). English language. *Review of Educational Research, 1,* 345–353.

Lesgold, A. (1988). Problem solving. In R. J. Sternberg & E. E. Smith (Eds.), *The psychology of human thought* (pp. 188–213). New York: Cambridge University Press.

Levin, J. R. (1981). The mnemonic '80s: Keywords in the classroom. *Educational Psychologist, 16,* 65–82.

Levin, J. R. (1985). Yodai features = mnemonic procedures: A commentary on Higbee and Kunihara. *Educational Psychologist, 20,* 73–76.

Levy, Y. (1988). The nature of early language: Evidence from the development of Hebrew morphology. In Y. Levy, I. M. Schlesinger, & M. D. S. Braine (Eds.), *Categories and processes in language* (pp. 72–91). Hillsdale, NJ: Erlbaum.

Lewin, K. (1936). *Principles of topological psychology.* New York: McGraw-Hill.

Li, Y., & Reames, F. M. (1977). Physics education needs PSE: A report on its use at Tuskegee Institute. *American Journal of Physics, 45,* 208–209.

Liebert, R. M., Neale, J. M., & Davidson, T. (1973). *The early window: Effects of television on children and youth.* New York: Pergamon.

Liebert, R. M., & Sprafkin, J. (1988). *The early window: Effects of television on children and youth* (3rd ed.). New York: Pergamon.

Lindsley, O. R. (1971). Precision teaching in perspective: An interview with Ogden R. Lindsley. *Teaching Exceptional Children, 3*(3), 114–119.

Lindquist, E. F. (Ed.). (1951). *Educational measurement.* Menasha, WI: Banta.

Loftus, G. R., & Loftus, E. F. (1977). *Human memory: The processing of information.* New York: Wiley.

Loney, J. (1980). Hyperkinesis comes of age: What do we know and where should we go? *American Journal of Orthopsychiatry, 50,* 28–42.

Lowth, R. (1762). *A short introduction to grammar.* London: John Murray.

Luchins, A. S. (1942). Mechanization in problem solving: The effect of Einstellung. *Psychological Monographs, 54* (Whole No. 6).

Lukens, J. (1988). Comparison of the fourth edition and the L–M edition of the Stanford-Binet used with mentally retarded persons. *Journal of School Psychology, 26,* 87–89.

Lund, N. J., & Duchan, J. F. (1983). *Assessing children's language in naturalistic contexts.* Englewood Cliffs, NJ: Prentice-Hall.

Lundberg, I., Frost, J. & Peterson, O. (1988). Effects of an extensive program for stimulating phonological awareness in preschool children. *Reading Research Quarterly, 23,* 263–284.

Lundin, R. W. (1972). *Theories and systems of psychology.* Lexington, MA: Heath.

Lundin, R. W. (1985). *Theories and systems of psychology* (3rd ed.). Lexington, MA: Heath.

Lunzer, E. A. (1976). Jean Piaget: A biographical sketch. In N. P. Varma & P. Williams (Eds.), *Piaget, psychology and education* (pp. i–vii). Itasca, IL: Peacock.

Luria, A. R. (1982). *Language and cognition.* New York: Wiley.

Lyman, R. L. (1929). Summary of investigations relating to grammar, language, and composition. *Supplementary Education Monographs,* No. 36. Chicago: University of Chicago Press.

Lyon, D. O. (1914). The relation of length of material to time taken for learning and the optimum distribution of time. *Journal of Educational Psychology, 5,* 1–9, 85–91, 155–163.

MacKinnon, D. W. (1968). Selecting students with creative potential. In P. Heist (Ed.), *The creative college student: An unmet challenge* (pp. 57–91). San Francisco: Jossey-Bass.

MacLeod, C. M. (1988). Forgotten but not gone: Savings for pictures and words in long-term memory. *Journal of Experimental Psychology: Learning, Memory and Cognition, 14,* 19s–21c.

MacLeod, C. M., Hunt, E. B., & Mathews, N. N. (1978). Individual differences in the verification of sentence-picture relationships. *Journal of Verbal Learning and Verbal Behavior, 17,* 335–357.

MacNamara, J. (1972). Cognitive basis of language learning in infants. *Psychological Review, 79,* 1–13.

MacWhinney, B. (1982). Basic syntactic processes. In S. Kuczaj (Ed.). *Language development* (Vol. 1) (pp. 22–59). Hillsdale, NJ: Erlbaum.

MacWhinney, B. (1987) (Ed.), *Mechanisms of language acquisition.* Hillsdale, NJ: Erlbaum.

Mace, F. C., & Kratochwill, T. R. (1988). Self-monitoring. In J. C. Witt, S. N. Elliott, & F. M. Gresham (Eds.), *Handbook of behavior therapy in education.* (pp. 325–361). New York: Plenum.

Madsen, C. H., Becker, W. C., & Thomas, D. R. (1968). Rules, praise and ignoring: Elements of elementary classroom control. *Journal of Applied Behavior Analysis, 1,* 139–151.

Madsen, C. H., Madsen, C. K., Sandargas, R. A., Hammon, W. R., & Edgar, D. E. (1970). Classroom RAID (rules, approval, ignore, disapproval): A cooperative approach for professionals and volunteers. Unpublished manuscript. University of Florida.

Madsen, K. B. (1973). Theories of motivation. In B. Wolman (Ed.). *Handbook of general psychology* (pp. 121–150). Englewood Cliffs, NJ: Prentice-Hall.

Madsen, K. B. (1974). *Modern theories of motivation.* New York: Wiley.

Maehr, M. L. (1984). Meaning and motivation: Toward a theory of personal investment. In R. Ames & C. Ames (Eds.), *Research on motivation in education: Student motivation* (Vol. 1, pp. 115–144). New York: Academic Press.

Maehr, M. L., & Sjogren, D. D. (1971). Atkinson's theory of achievement motivation: First step toward a theory of academic motivation? *Review of Educational Research, 41,* 143–159.

Mager, R. (1962). *Preparing instructional objectives.* Palo Alto, CA: Fearon.

Mager, R. (1976). *Preparing instructional objectives* (2nd ed.). Palo Alto, CA: Fearon.

Mahoney, M. J. (1974). *Cognition and behavior modification.* Cambridge, MA: Ballinger.

Mahoney, M. J., & Thoresen, C. E. (1974). *Behavioral self-control.* New York: Holt, Rinehart & Winston.

Maier, H. W. (1969). *Three theories of child redevelopment* (rev. ed.). New York: Harper & Row.

Maier, N. R. F. (1933). An aspect of human reasoning. *British Journal of Psychology, 24,* 144–155.

Maltzman, I. (1955). Thinking from a behavioristic point of view. *Psychological Review, 62,* 275–286.

Maltzman, I., Bogartz, W., & Bregar, L. (1958). A procedure for increasing word association originality and its transfer effects. *Journal of Experimental Psychology, 56,* 392–398.

Maltzman, I., Simon, S., Raskin, D., & Licht, L. (1960). Experimental studies in the training of originality. *Psychological Monographs: General and Applied, 74*(6), 1–17.

Mandler, G. (1975). *Mind and emotion.* New York: Wiley.

Mandler, G. (1985). *Cognitive psychology: An essay in cognitive science.* Hillsdale, NJ: Erlbaum.

Mandler, J. M. (1984). *Stories, scripts, and scenes: Aspects of schema theory.* Hillsdale, NJ: Erlbaum.

Mandler, J. M., & Johnson, N. S. (1977). Remembrance of things parsed: Story structure and recall. *Cognitive Psychology, 9,* 111–151.

Manis, F. R. (1985). Acquisition of word identification skills in normal and disabled readers. *Journal of Educational Psychology, 77,* 78–90.

Mann, H. (1845). Boston grammar and writing schools. *Common School Journal, 7,* 289–368.

Maratsos, M. (1988). Cross-linguistic analysis, universals, and language acquisition. In F. Kessel (Ed.), *The development of language and language researchers,* (pp. 192–207). Hillsdale, NJ: Erlbaum.

Marsh, H. W., Byrne, B. M., & Shavelson, R. J. (1988). A multi-faceted academic self-concept: Its hierarchical structure and its relation to academic achievement. *Journal of Educational Psychology, 80,* 366–380.

Marshall, A. M., & Sherman, J. A. (1978). *Token economies: An incomplete technology?* Paper presented at the annual convention of the Midwest Association for Behavior Analysis, Chicago.

Marshall, K. (1977). You can turn around the failing student. *Learning, 6,* 50.

Martin, J. A. (1971). The control of imitative and non-imitative behavior in severely retarded children through "generalized instruction following." *Journal of Experimental Child Psychology, 11,* 390–400.

Maslow, A. H. (1987). *Motivation and personality* (3rd ed.). New York: Harper & Row. Revised by Robert Frager, James Fadiman, Cynthia McReynolds, and Ruth Cox.

Maslow, A. H. (1968). *Toward a psychology of being* (2nd ed.). Princeton: Van Nostrand.

Maslow, A. H. (1970). *Motivation and personality* (2nd ed.). New York: Harper & Row.

Maslow, A. H. (1971). *The further reaches of human nature.* New York: Viking.

Masur, E. F., McIntyre, C. W., & Flavell, J. H. (1973). Developmental changes in apportionment of study time among items in a multitrial free recall task. *Journal of Experimental Child Psychology, 15,* 237–246.

Matson, J. L., & Ollendick, T. N. (1988). *Enhancing children's social skills.* New York: Pergamon.

May, Y. (1977). Personalized self-instruction at the Cambridge School. *The Science Teacher, 44,* 22–23.

Mayer, R. E. (1984). Aids to text comprehension. *Educational Psychologist, 19,* 30–42.

McAllister, L. W., Stachowiak, J. G., Baer, D. M., & Conderman, L. (1969). The application of operant conditioning techniques in a secondary school. *Journal of Applied Behavior Analysis, 2,* 277–285.

McCall, R. B. (1977). Childhood IQ's as predictors of adult educational and occupational status. *Science, 197,* 482–483.

McCall, W. A. (1920). A new kind of school examination. *Journal of Educational Research, 1,* 33–46.

McCall, W. A. (1922). *How to measure in education.* New York: Macmillan.

McClelland, D. C. (1961). *The achieving society.* Princeton: Van Nostrand.

McClelland, J. L. (1988). Connectionist models and psychological evidence. *Journal of Memory and Language, 27,* 107–123.

McCormick, C. B., & Levin, J. R. (1984). A comparison of different prose-learning variations of the mnemonic keyword method. *American Educational Research Journal, 21,* 379–398.

McCrudden, T. (1979). *A contextualist analysis of adjunct aids in prose processing.* Unpublished doctoral dissertation, University of Nebraska, Lincoln.

McDaniel, M. A., Einstein, G. O., & Lollis, T. (1988). Qualitative and quantitative considerations in encoding difficulty effects. *Memory and Cognition, 16,* 8–14.

McDaniel, T. R. (1980). Exploring alternatives to punishment: The keys to effective discipline. *Phi Delta Kappan, 61*(7), 455–458.

McDougall, W. (1908). *Introduction to social psychology.* London: Methuen.

McGeoch, J. A. (1932). Forgetting and the law of disuse. *Psychological Review, 39,* 352–370.

McGeoch, J. A., & McDonald, W. T. (1931). Meaningful relation and retroactive inhibition. *American Journal of Psychology, 43,* 579–588.

McGraw, B., & Grotelueschen, A. (1972). Direction of the effect of questions in prose material. *Journal of Educational Psychology, 63,* 580–588.

McKeown, M. G. (1985). The acquisition of word meaning from context by children of high and low ability. *Reading Research Quarterly, 20,* 482–496.

KcKeown, M. G., & Curtis, M. E. (1987) (Eds.), *The nature of vocabulary acquisition.* Hillsdale, NJ: Erlbaum.

McKinney, C. W., Larkins, A. G., & Burts, D. C. (1984). Effects of overt teacher enthusiasm on first-grade students' acquisition of three concepts. *Theory and Research in Social Education, 11,* 15–24.

McKinnon, D. W. (1962). The nature and nurture of creative talent. *American Psychologist, 16,* 484–495.

McKoon, G., & Ratcliff, R. (1988). Contextually relevant aspects of meaning. *Journal of Experimental Psychology: Learning, Memory, and Cognition, 14,* 331–343.

McLeod, J. & Cropley, A. (1988). *Fostering academic excellence.* New York: Pergamon.

McNamara, T. P., & Healy, A. F. (1988). Semantic, phonological, and mediated priming in reading and lexical decisions. *Journal of Experimental Psychology: Learning, Memory, and Cognition, 14,* 398–409.

McNeill, D. (1970). *The acquisition of language: The study of developmental psycho-linguistics.* New York: Harper & Row.

Meador, B. D., & Rogers, C. R. (1974). Client-centered therapy. In R. Corsini (Ed.), *Current psychotherapies* (pp. 236–274). Itasca, IL: Peacock.

Mednick, S. A. (1962). The associative basis of the creative process. *Psychological Review, 69,* 220–232.

Mehan, H. (1985). The structure of classroom discourse. In T. A. van Dijk (Ed.). *Handbook of discourse analysis: Vol. 3: Discourse and dialogue.* London: Academic Press.

Mehrens, W. A., & Lehmann, I. J. (1975). *Measurement and evaluation in education and psychology* (2nd ed.). New York: Holt, Rinehart & Winston.

Mehrens, W. A., & Lehmann, I. J. (1978). *Measurement and evaluation in education and psychology* (3rd ed.). New York: Holt, Rinehart & Winston.

Mehrens, W., & Lehman, I. J. (1986). *Using standardized tests in education* (4th ed.). New York: Longman.

Meichenbaum, D., & Turk, D. C. (1987). *Facilitating treatment adherence.* New York: Plenum.

Meichenbaum, D. H. (1977). *Cognitive behavior modification.* New York: Plenum.

Meichenbaum, D. H., & Goodman, K. S. (1971). Training impulsive children to talk about themselves: A means of developing self-control. *Journal of Abnormal Psychology, 77,* 115–126.

Melton, J. W. (1959). The science of learning and the technology of educational methods. *Harvard Educational Review, 29,* 96–106.

Melton, J. W. (1963). Implications of short-term memory for a general theory of memory. *Journal of Verbal Learning and Verbal Behavior, 2,* 1–21.

Melton, J. W., & Irwin, J. M. (1940). The influence of degree of interpolated learning on retroactive inhibition and the overt transfer of specific responses. *American Journal of Psychology, 53,* 173–203.

Melton, J. W., & Martin, E. (Eds.). (1972). *Coding processes in human memory.* Washington, DC: Winston.

Meltzoff, A. N. (1988). Infant imitation after a 1-week delay: Long-term memory for novel acts and multiple stimuli. *Developmental Psychology, 24,* 470–476.

Mendonca, J. D., & Seiss, T. F. (1976). Counseling for indecisiveness: Problem solving and anxiety management training. *Journal of Counseling Psychology, 23*(4), 339–347.

Mercer, J. F. (1972). I.Q.: The lethal label. *Psychology Today, 6*(4), 44–97.

Mervis, C. B., & Rosch, E. (1981). Categorization of natural objects. *Annual Review of Psychology, 32,* 89–115.

Messick, S. (Ed.) (1976). *Individuality in learning. Implica-*

tions of cognitive styles and creativity for human development. San Francisco: Jossey-Bass.

Messick, S. (1984). The nature of cognitive styles: Problems and promise in educational practice. *Educational Psychologist, 19,* 59–74.

Metcalf, J., & Wiebe, D. (1987). Intuition in insight and noninsight problem solving. *Memory and Cognition, 15,* 238–246.

Metfessel, N., Michael, W. B., & Kirsner, P. A. (1969). Instrumentation of Bloom's and Krathwohl's taxonomies for the writing of behavioral objectives. *Psychology in the Schools, 6,* 227–231.

Meyer, B. J. F. (1975). *The organization of prose and its effects on recall.* Amsterdam: North-Holland.

Meyer, B. J. F., Young, C. J., & Barlett B. S. (1988). *Memory improved: Reading and memory enhancement across the lifespan through strategic text structure.* Hillsdale, NJ: Erlbaum.

Meyer, D. E. (1970). On the representation and retrieval of stored semantic information. *Cognitive Psychology, 21,* 242–300.

Meyer, M. (1908) The grading of students. *Science, 28,* 243–250.

Mezynski, K. (1983). Issues concerning the acquisition of knowledge: Effects of vocabulary training on reading comprehension. *Educational Research, 53,* 253–279.

Michael, W. (1988). Issues in the measurement of creativity. Paper presented as part of an invited symposium to the annual meeting of the American Psychological Association, Atlanta.

Michael, W. (in press). Psychometric issues in the study of creativity. In J. A. Glover, R. R. Ronning, & C. R. Reynolds (Eds.), *Handbook of Creativity Research.* New York: Plenum.

Miller, G. A. (1956). The magical number seven, plus or minus two: Some limits on our capacity to process information. *Psychological Review, 63,* 81–97.

Miller, G. A. (1962). Some psychological studies of grammar. *American Psychologist, 17,* 748–762.

Miller, G. A. (1964). *Mathematics and psychology.* New York: Wiley.

Miller, G. A. (1969). Psychology as a means of promoting human welfare. *American Psychologist, 24,* 1026–1075.

Miller, G. A. (1981). *Language and speech.* San Francisco: Freeman.

Miller, H. G., Williams, R. G., & Haladyna, R. M. (1978). *Beyond facts: Objective ways to measure thinking.* Englewood Cliffs, NJ: Educational Technology Publications.

Miller, J. G., & Bersoff, D. M. (1988). When do American

children and adults reason in social conventional terms? *Developmental Psychology, 24,* 366–375.

Miller, J. R., & Kintsch, W. (1980). Readability and recall of short prose passages: A theoretical analysis. *Journal of Experimental Psychology: Human Learning and Memory, 6,* 335–353.

Miller, N. E., & Dollard, M. J. (1941). *Social learning and imitation,* New Haven: Yale University Press.

Miller, R. B. (1953a). *Handbook in training and training equipment design.* Technical Report. 53–137. Wright-Patterson AFB, OH: Wright Air Development Center.

Miller, R. B. (1953b). *A method for man-machine test analysis.* Technical Report 53–136.. Wright-Patterson AFB, OH: Wright Air Development Center.

Miller, R. B. (1956). *A suggested guide to position-task description.* Technical Memorandum ASPRL-TM-56-6. Lackland AFB, TX: Air Force Personnel and Training Research Center.

Mischel, W. (1968). *Personality and assessment.* New York: Wiley.

Mitchell, J. V. (Ed.). (1985). *The ninth mental measurements yearbook.* Lincoln: University of Nebraska Press.

Moates, D. R., & Schumacher, G. M. (1980). *An introduction to cognitive psychology.* Belmont, CA: Wadsworth.

Monroe, W. S. (1935). Hazards in the measurement of achievement. *School and Society, 41,* 38–49.

Monroe, W. S. (1945). Educational measurement in 1920 and 1945. *Journal of Educational Research, 38,* 334–340.

Morariu, J., & Bruning, R. H. (1982, March). *Differential cognitive processing by deaf and hearing high school students using printed English and American Sign Language passages.* Paper presented to the annual convention of the American Educational Research Association, New York City.

Morariu, J. A., & Bruning, R. H. (1984). Cognitive processing by prelingual deaf students as a function of language context. *Journal of Educational Psychology, 76,* 844–856.

Morgan, C. L. (1931). *Habit and instinct.* London: Arnold. (Original work published 1896.)

Morphett, M., & Washburne, C. (1931). When should children begin to read? *Elementary School Journal, 31,* 496–503.

Morris, C. J., & Kimbrell, G. (1972). Performance and attitudinal effects of the Keller method in an introductory psychology course. *Psychological Record, 22,* 523–530.

Morris, C. J., & Kimbrell, G. Individual differences and PSI: A reanalysis. *Journal of Personalized Instruction, 2,* 47–49.

Morrow, L. M. (1988). Young children's responses to one-to-one story readings in school settings. *Reading Research Quarterly, 23,* 89–107.

Moses, M. (1985). Thinking and excellence in education: Pieces of the same puzzle? *Journal of Creative Behavior, 19,* 13–119.

Murphy, G. (1947). *Personality.* New York: Harper.

Murphy, K. R., & Davidshofer, C. O. (1988). *Psychological testing: Principles and applications.* Englewood Cliffs, NJ: Prentice-Hall.

Murray, F. S., & Rowe, F. B. (1979). Psychological laboratories in the United States prior to 1900. *Teaching of Psychology, 6,* 19–21.

Murray, H. A. (1938). *Explorations in personality.* New York: Oxford University Press.

Myers, A. E., McConville, C., & Coffman, W. E. (1966). Simplex structure in the grading of essay tests. *Educational and Psychological Measurement, 26,* 41–54.

Myles-Worsley, M., Johnston, W. A., & Simons, M. A. (1988). The influence of expertise on x-ray image processing. *Journal of Experimental Psychology: Learning, Memory, and Cognition, 14,* 553–557.

Naglieri, J. (1988). Interpreting the subtest profile on the fourth edition of the Stanford-Binet scale of intelligence. *Journal of Clinical Child Psychology, 17,* 62–65.

Nagy, W. E., & Herman, P. A. (1984). Grade and reading ability effects on learning words from context. Paper presented at the annual meeting of the National Reading Conference, St. Petersburg Beach, FL.

Nagy, W. E., & Herman, P. A. (1985). The influence of word and text properties on learning words from context. Paper presented at the annual meeting of the American Educational Research Association, Chicago.

Nagy, W. E., & Herman, P. A., (1987). Breadth and depth of vocabulary knowledge. In M. G. McKeown & M. E. Curtis (Eds.), *The nature of vocabulary acquisition* (pp. 23–41). Hillsdale, NJ: Erlbaum.

National Society for the Study of Education. (1945). *Forty-fifth yearbook. Part I: Measurement of understanding.* Bloomington, IL: Public School Publishing Company.

Neisser, U. (1967). *Cognitive psychology.* New York: Appleton-Century-Crofts.

Nelson, D. L., & Archer, C. S. (1972). The first letter mnemonic. *Journal of Educational Psychology, 63,* 482–486.

Nelson, K. (1973). Structure and strategy in learning to talk. *Monographs of the Society for Research in Child Development, 38*(1–2, Serial No. 149).

Newell, A., Shaw, J. C., & Simon, H. A. (1960). Report on a general problem-solving program for a computer. *Information processing: Proceedings of the International Conference on Information Processing.* Paris: UNESCO.

Newell, A., & Simon, H. A. (1956). The logic machine: A complex information processing system. *IRE Transactions on Information Theory, 2,* 61–79.

Newell, A., & Simon, H. A. (1972). *Human problem solving.* Englewood Cliffs, NJ: Prentice-Hall.

Newman, H. H., Freeman, F. N., & Holzinger, K. J. (1937). *Twins: A study of heredity and environment.* Chicago: University of Chicago Press.

Newport, E. L., Gleitman, H., & Gleitman, L. R. (1977). Mother, I'd rather do it myself: Some effects and non-effects of maternal speech style. In C. E. Snow & C. A. Ferguson (Eds.), *Talking to children: Language input and acquisition* (pp. 73–88). New York: Cambridge University Press.

Ninio, A., & Bruner, J. S. (1978). The achievement and antecedents of labelling. *Journal of Child Language, 5,* 1–15.

Ninio, A., & Snow, C. (1988). Language acquisition. In Y. Levy, I. M. Schlesinger, & M. D. S. Braine (Eds.), *Categories and processes in language acquisition* (pp. 9–29). Hillsdale, NJ: Erlbaum.

Nisan, M., & Kohlberg, L. (1982). Universality and variation in moral judgment: A longitudinal and cross-sectional study in Turkey. *Child Development, 53,* 865–876.

Noble, C. E. (1952). An analysis of learning. *Psychological Review, 59,* 421–430.

Noble, C. E. (1963). Meaningfulness and familiarity. In C. N. Cofer & B. S. Musgrave (Eds.), *Verbal behavior and learning: Problems and processes* (pp. 168–185). New York: McGraw-Hill.

Noppe, L. D. (1985). The relationship of formal thought and cognitive styles to creativity. *Journal of Creative Behavior, 19,* 88–96.

Norman, D. A., & Bobrow, D. G. (1975). On data-limited and resource-limited processes. *Cognitive Psychology, 7,* 44–64.

Norman, D. A., & Bobrow, D. G. (1979). Descriptions: An intermediate stage in memory retrieval. *Cognitive Psychology, 11,* 107–123.

Nosofsky, R. M. (1988). Similarity, frequency, and category representations. *Journal of Experimental Psychology: Learning, Memory, and Cognition, 14,* 54–65.

Novick, L. R. (1988). Analogical transfer, problem similarity, and expertise. *Journal of Experimental Psychology: Learning, Memory, and Cognition, 14,* 510–520.

O'Brien, E. J., Shank, D. M., Myers, J. L., & Rayner, K. (1988). Elaborative inferences during reading. *Journal of Experimental Psychology: Learning, Memory, and Cognition, 14,* 410–420.

Ochs, E., & Schieffelin, B. (Eds.) (1979). *Developmental pragmatics.* New York: Academic Press.

O'Connor, R. D. (1973). Relative efficacy of modeling, shaping and the combined procedures for modification of social withdrawal. In C. M. Franks & G. T. Wilson (Eds.), *Behavior therapy and practice* (pp. 131–160). New York: Brunner/Mazel.

Odom, S. L., Hoyson, M., Jamieson, B., & Strain, P. S. (1985). Increasing handicapped preschoolers' peer social interactions: Cross-setting and component analysis. *Journal of Applied Behavior Analysis, 18,* 3–16.

Odoroff, E. (1985, March). *Learning from revisions.* Paper presented to the annual meeting of the American Educational Research Association, Chicago.

O'Leary, K. D. (1972). Behavior modifications in the classroom: A rejoinder to Winnet and Winkler. *Journal of Applied Behavior Analysis, 5,* 505–511.

O'Leary, K. D., & Becker, W. C. (1967). Behavioral modification of an adjustment class: A token reinforcement program. *Exceptional Children, 3,* 637–642.

O'Leary, S. G., & Dubey, D. R. (1979). Applications of self-control procedures by children: A review. *Journal of Applied Behavior Analysis, 12,* 449–466.

O'Leary, K. D., Kaufman, K. F., Kass, R. C., & Drabman, R. S. (1970). The effects of loud and soft reprimands on the behavior of disruptive students. *Exceptional Children, 57,* 145–155.

O'Leary, K. D., & O'Leary, S. G. (1972). *Classroom management: The successful use of behavior modification.* New York: Pergamon.

O'Leary, K. D., & Wilson, G. T. (1975). *Behavior therapy: Application and outcome.* Englewood Cliffs, NJ: Prentice-Hall.

Ollendick, T. H., & Francis, G. (1988). Behavioral assessment and treatment of childhood phobias. *Behavior Modification, 12,* 165–205.

Oney, B., & Goldman, S. R. (1984). Decoding and comprehension skills in Turkish and English: Effects of the regularity of grapheme-phoneme correspondences. *Journal of Educational Psychology, 76,* 557–568.

Orton, S. T. (1937). *Reading, writing and speech problems in children.* New York: Norton.

Ortony, A. (1979). Beyond literal similarity. *Psychological Review, 86,* 161–180.

Osherson, D., & Markman, E. (1975). Language and the ability to evaluate contradictions and tautologies. *Cognition,* 213–226.

Outhwaite, W. (1983). *Concept formation in social science.* Boston: Routledge & Kegan Paul.

Owen, F. (1974, June). *Familial studies of learning disabled children.* Paper presented to the Interdisciplinary Institute on Reading and Child Development, Newark, DE.

Owen, F. W. (1968). Learning disability—a familial study. *Bulletin of the Orton Society, 18,* 33–39.

Packard, R. G. (1970). The control of "classroom attention": A group contingency for complex behavior. *Journal of Applied Behavior Analysis, 3,* 13–28.

Page, E. B. (1958). Teacher comments and student performance: A seventy-four classroom experiment in school motivation. *Journal of Educational Psychology, 49,* 173–181.

Paige, J. M., & Simon, H. A. (1966). Cognitive processes in solving algebra word problems. In B. Kleinmuntz (Ed.), *Problem solving: Research, method, and theory* (pp. 177–201) New York: Wiley.

Paivio, A., & Desrochers, A. (1981). Mnemonic techniques in second-language learning. *Journal of Educational Psychology, 73,* 780–795.

Palincsar, A. S., Brown, A. L., & Martin, S. M. (1987). Peer interaction in reading comprehension instruction. *Educational Psychologist, 22,* 231–254.

Palmer, J. & Jonides, S. (1988). Automatic memory search and the effects of information load and irrelevant information. *Journal of Experimental Psychology, Learning, Memory and Cognition, 14,* 136–144.

Palmer, J., MacLeod, C., Hunt, E., & Davidson, J. (1985). Information processing correlates of reading. *Journal of Memory and Language, 24,* 59–88.

Palmer, O. (1962). Some classic ways of grading dishonestly. *The English Journal, 52,* 464–467.

Paris, S. G. (1987). Introduction to current issues in reading comprehension. *Educational Psychologist, 22,* 209–212.

Parish, T. S. (1977). The enhancement of altruistic behavior in children through the implementation of language conditioning procedures. *Behavior Modification, 1,* 283–306.

Pavlov, I. P. (1928). *Lectures on conditioned reflexes* (W. H. Gantt, Trans.). New York: International Press.

Payne, D. A. (1974). *The assessment of learning: Cognitive and affective.* Lexington, MA: Heath.

Pearson, D. P. (1985). The comprehension revolution: A twenty-year history of process and praise related to reading comprehension. Reading Education Report No. 57, Center for the Study of Reading, University of Illinois at Urbana-Champaign.

Perkins, D. N. (1988). Creativity and the quest for mechanism. In R. J. Sternberg & E. E. Smith (Eds.), *The Nature of Creativity* (pp. 305–336). New York: Cambridge.

Perl, E., & Lambert, W. E. (1962). The relation of bilingualism to intelligence. *Psychological Monographs, 76,* 1–23.

Peters, R. D., & McMahon, R. J. (1987). *Social learning and systems approach to marriage and family.* New York: Brunner-Mazel.

Petersen, C. P. (1979). *Problem solving among the aged.* Unpublished doctoral dissertation, University of Nebraska.

Petitto, L. (1988). "Language" in the pre-linguistic child. In F. Kessel (Ed.), *The development of language and language researchers* (pp. 217–229). Hillsdale, NJ: Erlbaum.

Petry, S., & Meyer, G. E. (1987). *The perception of illusory contours.* New York: Springer-Verlag.

Pfiffner, L. J., & O'Leary, S. G. (1987). The efficacy of all positive management as a function of the prior use of negative consequences. *Journal of Applied Behavior Analysis, 20,* 315–321.

Pfiffner, L. J., Rosen, L. A., and O'Leary, S. G. (1988). The efficacy of an all positive approach to classroom management. *Journal of Applied Behavior Analysis, 18,* 257–261.

Pflaum, S. W., Walberg, H. J., Karegianes, M. L., & Rasher, S. P. (1980). Reading instruction: A quantitative analysis. *Educational Research, 9,* 12–18.

Phillips, R. H. (1984). Increasing positive self-reinforcement statements to improve self-esteem in low-income elementary school children. *Journal of School Psychology, 22,* 155–163.

Piaget, J. (1926). *The language and thought of the child.* London: Routledge & Kegan Paul.

Piaget, J. (1932). *The moral judgement of the child.* London: Routledge & Kegan Paul.

Piaget, J. (1952). *The origins of intelligence in children* (M. Cook, Trans.). New York: International Universities Press.

Piaget, J. (1969). *The mechanisms of perception* (G. N. Seagrim, Trans.). London: Routledge & Kegan Paul.

Piaget, J. (1970a). *The child's conception of movement and speed* (M. J. MacKensie, Trans.). London: Routledge & Kegan Paul.

Piaget, J. (1970b). Piaget's theory in P. Mussen (Ed.), *Carmichael's manual of child psychology* (3rd ed.) (pp. 236–288). New York: Wiley.

Piaget, J. (1973). *To understand is to invent: The future of education* (G. Robers & A. Robers, Trans.). New York: Grossman.

Piaget, J. (1976). *Le comportement moteur de l'évolution.* Paris: Gallimand.

Piaget, J. (1977). Problems of equilibration. In M. H. Appel & L. S. Goldberg (Eds.), *Topics in cognitive development* (Vol. 1) (pp. 2–41). New York: Plenum.

Piaget, J. (1978). A summary of the theory of Jean Piaget. In D. K. Gardiner (Ed.), *Readings in developmental psychology* (pp. 3–23). New York: Holt.

Piaget, J. (1980). Schemes of action and language learning. In M. Piatelli-Palmarini (Ed.), *Language and learning: The debate between Jean Piaget and Noam Chomsky* (pp. 22–31). Cambridge, MA: Harvard University Press.

Piaget, J., & Inhelder, B. (1969). *The psychology of the child* (H. Weaver, Trans.). London: Routledge & Kegan Paul.

Piaget, J., & Inhelder, B. (1973). *Memory and intelligence* (A. J. Pomerans, Trans.). London: Routledge & Kegan Paul.

Pichert, J. W., & Anderson, R. C. (1977). Taking different perspectives on a story. *Journal of Educational Psychology, 69,* 309–315.

Pillow, B. (1988). The development of children's beliefs about the mental world. *Merrill-Palmer Quarterly, 34,* 1–32.

Plake, B. S. (1980). A comparison of a statistical and subjective procedure to ascertain item validity: One step in the test validation process. *Educational and Psychological Measurement, 40,* 397–404.

Plomin, R. (1987). The nature and nurture of cognitive abilities. In R. Sternberg (Ed.), *Advances in the psychology of human intelligence* (pp. 11–36). Hillsdale, NJ: Erlbaum.

Plomin, R., & DeFries, J. C. (1983). The Colorado adoption project. *Child Development, 54,* 276–289.

Plomin, R., Loehlin, J. C., & DeFries, J. C. (1985). Genetic and environmental components of "environmental" influences. *Developmental Psychology, 21,* 391–402.

Pluck, M., Ghafari, E., Glynn, T., & McNaughton, S. (1984). Teacher and parent modeling of recreational reading. *New Zealand Journal of Educational Studies, 19,* 114–123.

Polya, G. (1946). *How to solve it.* Princeton: Princeton University Press.

Popham, W. J. (1978). The case of criterion-referenced measurements. *Educational Researcher, 7,* 6–10.

Popham, W. J. & Husek, T. F. (1969). Implications of criterion-referenced measurement. *Journal of Educational Measurement, 6,* 1–9.

Porter, A. C. (1988). Understanding teaching: A model for assessment. *Journal of Teacher Education, 39,* 2–7.

Postman, L. Stark, K., & Henschel, D. (1969). Conditions of recovery after unlearning. *Journal of Experimental Psychology Monograph, 81*(1, Pt. 2).

Postman, L., & Underwood, B. J. (1973). Critical issues in interference theory. *Memory and Cognition, 1,* 19–40.

Powers, F. F. (1929). Psychology of language learning. *Psychological Bulletin, 26,* 261–274.

Prakesh, A. O. (1973). *Effects of modeling and social reinforcement on the racial preferences of children.* ERIC Document Reproduction Service, ED 086 357. Washington, DC: U.S. Government Printing Service.

Prawat, R. S. (1985). Affective versus cognitive goal orientations in elementary teachers. *American Educational Research Journal, 22,* 587–604.

Premack, D. (1959). Toward empirical behavioral laws: I. Positive reinforcement. *Psychological Review, 66,* 219–233.

Premack, D. (1965). Reinforcement theory. In D. Levine (Ed.), *Nebraska Symposium on Motivation* (pp. 3–41). Lincoln: University of Nebraska Press.

Pressey, S. L. (1955). Concerning the nature and nurture of genius. *Scientific Monthly, 81,* 123–129.

Pressey, S. L. (1979). An interview with S. L. Pressey. *Directive Teacher, 2,* 1, 23–24.

Pressley, M. (1977). Children's use of the keyword method to learn simple Spanish vocabulary words. *Journal of Educational Psychology, 69,* 465–472.

Pressley, M. (1985). More about Yodai mnemonics: A commentary on Higbee and Kunihara. *Educational Psychologist, 20,* 69–72.

Pressley, M., Borkowski, J. G., & O'Sullivan, J. T. (1984). Memory strategy instruction is made of this: Metamemory and durable strategy use. *Educational Psychologist, 19,* 94–107.

Pressley, M., Levin, J. R., & Delaney, H. D. (1981). *The mnemonic keyword method.* Theoretical Paper No. 92. Madison, WI: Wisconsin Research and Development Center for Individualized Schooling.

Pressley, M., Levin, J. R., & Delaney, H. D. (1982). The mnemonic keyword method. *Review of Educational Research, 52,* 61–92.

Pribram, R. H. (1971). *The language of the brain.* Englewood Cliffs, NJ: Prentice-Hall.

Proger, B. B., Carter, C. E., Mann, L., Taylor, R. G., Jr., Bayuk, R. J., Jr., Morris, V. R., & Reckless, D. E. (1973). Advance and concurrent organizers for detailed verbal passages used with elementary school pupils. *Journal of Educational Research, 66,* 451–456.

Pryor, R. W., Haig, R., & O'Reilley, J. (1969). The creative porpoise: Training for novel behavior. *Journal of the Experimental Analysis of Behavior, 12,* 653–661.

Quinn, K. B., & Matsuhashi, A. (1985, March). Stalking ideas: The generation and elaboration of ideas in writing based on reading. Paper presented to the annual meeting of the American Educational Research Association, Chicago.

Rachlin, H. (1976). *Introduction to modern behaviorism* (2nd ed.). San Francisco: Freeman.

Radgowski, T. A., Allen, K. E., Ruggles, T. R., Schilmoeller, G., & LeBlanc, J. M. (1978). *Training of a foresight language in preschool children using a delayed pre-*

sentation of feedback. Paper presented at the annual convention of the Midwest Association for Behavior Analysis, Chicago.

Rank, O. (1932). *Art and the artist: Creative urge and personality development.* New York: Tudor.

Raphael, T. E., & Kirschner, B. (1985, March). Improving expository writing ability: Integrating knowledge of information sources and text structures. Paper read to the annual meeting of the American Educational Research Association, Chicago.

Rayner, K., & Bertera, J. H. (1979). Reading without a fovea. *Science, 206,* 468–469.

Rayner, K., & McConkie, G. W. (1977). Perceptual processes in reading: The perceptual spans. In A. S. Rebert & D. L. Scarborough (Eds.), *Toward a psychology of reading* (pp. 31–50). Hillsdale, NJ: Erlbaum.

Rayner, K. & Pollatsek, A. (1989). *The psychology of reading.* Englewood Cliffs, New Jersey: Prentice-Hall.

Raz, N., Willerman, L., & Yama, M. (1988). One sense and senses: Intelligence and auditory information processing. *Personality and Individual Differences, 8,* 201–210.

Recht, D. R., & Leslie, L. (1988). Effect of prior knowledge on good and poor readers' memory of text. *Journal of Educational Psychology, 80,* 16–20.

Reese, H. W., & Parnes, S. J. (1972). Programming creative behavior. *Child Development, 41,* 83–89.

Reese, S. L. & Smith, J. J. (1977). Behavior modification approaches. Paper presented to the annual meeting of the Midwestern Association for Applied Behavior Analysis, Chicago.

Reichle, J., Siegel, G., & Rettie, M. (1985). Matching prosodic and social features: Performance of Down's syndrome preschoolers. *Journal of Communication Disorders, 18,* 149–159.

Reid, H. P., Archer, M. B., & Friedman, R. M. (1977). Using the personalized system of instruction with low-reading-ability middle school students: Problems and results. *Journal of Personalized Instruction, 2,* 199–203.

Reimer, J., Paolitto, D. P., & Hersh, R. H. (1983). *Promoting moral growth: From Piaget to Kohlberg.* New York: Longman.

Reiser, R. A., Tessmer, M. A., & Phelps, D. C. (1984). Adult-child interaction in children's learning from "Sesame Street." *Educational Communication and Technology Journal, 32,* 217–223.

Reissland, N. (1988). Neonatal imitation in the first hour of life: Observations in rural Nepal. *Developmental Psychology, 24,* 464–469.

Reitman, W. R. (1964). Heuristic decision procedures, open constraints, and the structure of ill-defined problems. In M. W. Shelly & G. L. Bryan (Eds.), *Human judgments and optimality* (pp. 176–197). New York: Wiley.

Reitsma, P. (1988). Reading practice for beginners: Effects of guided reading, reading-while-listening, and independent reading with computer-based speech feedback, *Reading Research Quarterly, 23,* 219–235.

Remmers, H. H., Bloom, B. S., Krathwohl, D. R., Burros, O. K., Mowrer, O. H., & Stalnaker, J. M. (1951, August 31–September 5). *Symposium: The development of a taxonomy of educational objectives.* Fifty-ninth annual meeting of the American Psychological Association, Chicago.

Rescorla, L. A. (1980). Overextension in early language development. *Journal of Child Language, 7,* 321–335.

Resnick, D. P. (1981). Testing in America: A supportive environment. *Phi Delta Kappan, 62,* 625–628.

Resnick, L. B. (1976). Task analysis in instructional design: Some cases from mathematics. In D. Klahr (Ed.), *Cognition and instruction.* Hillsdale, NJ: Erlbaum.

Resnick, L. B., & Wang, M. C. (1969). Approaches to the validation of learning hierarchies. *Proceedings of the Eighteenth Annual Regional Conference on Testing Problems.* Princeton: Educational Testing Service.

Rest, J. R. (1983). Morality. In P. H. Mussen (Ed.), *Handbook of child psychology, Vol. 3. Cognitive development* (pp. 556–629). New York: Wiley.

Reynolds, G. S. (1975). *A primer of operant conditioning* (2nd ed.). Glenview, IL: Scott, Foresman.

Reynolds, M. C., & Balow, B. (1972). Categories and variables in special education. *Exceptional Children, 38,* 357–366.

Reynolds, M. C., & Birch, J. W. (1977). *Teaching exceptional children in all America's schools.* Reston, VA: Council for Exceptional Children.

Reynolds, R. E., Standiford, S. M., & Anderson, R. C. (1979). Distribution of reading time when questions are asked about a restricted category of text information. *Journal of Educational Psychology, 71,* 183–190.

Rice, J. M. (1897). The futility of the spelling grind. *Forum, 23,* 163–172, 409–419.

Rickards, J. P., & DiVesta, F. S. (1974). Type and frequency of questions in processing textual material. *Journal of Educational Psychology, 66,* 354–362.

Riley, M. S., & Greeno, J. G. (1988). Developmental analysis of understanding about quantities and of solving problems. *Cognition and Instruction, 5,* 49–101.

Rincover, A., Cook, R., Peoples, A., & Packard, D. (1979). Sensory extinction and sensory reinforcement principles for programming multiple adaptive behavior change. *Journal of Applied Behavior Analysis, 12,* 221–234.

Rips, L. J., Shoben, E. J., & Smith, E. E. (1973). Semantic distance and the verification of semantic relations. *Journal of Verbal Learning and Verbal Behavior, 12,* 1–20.

Ritchie, D., Price, V., & Roberts, D. F. (1987). Television, reading, and reading achievement: A reappraisal. *Communication Research, 14,* 292–315.

Rivlin, R., & Gravelle, K. (1985). *Deciphering the senses: The expanding world of human perception.* New York: Simon & Schuster.

Roberts, R. N., Nelson, R. O., & Olson, T. W. (1987). Self-instruction: An analysis of the differential effects of instruction and reinforcement. *Journal of Applied Behavior Analysis, 20,* 235–242.

Robinson, F. (1972). *Effective study.* New York: Macmillan.

Rock, I. (1984). *Perception* (2nd ed.). San Francisco: Freeman.

Rodda, M., & Grove, C. (1987). *Language, Cognition, and Deafness.* Hillsdale, NJ: Erlbaum.

Roe, A. (1953). *The making of a scientist.* New York: Dodd, Mead.

Roediger, H. L. (1980). Output interference in the recall of categorized and paired-associate lists. *Journal of Experimental Psychology: Human Learning and Memory, 6,* 91–105.

Rogers, C. R. (1942). *Counseling and psychotherapy: Newer concepts in practice.* Boston: Houghton Mifflin.

Rogers, C. R. (1951). *Client centered therapy.* Boston: Houghton Mifflin.

Rogers, C. R. (1965). Client-centered therapy. In E. Shostrom (Ed.), *Three approaches to psychotherapy* (pp. 101–178). Santa Ana, CA: Psychological Films.

Rogers, C. R. (1983). *Freedom to learn for the 80s.* Columbus, OH: Merrill.

Rogers-Warren, A., & Baer, D. M. (1976). The role of offer rates in controlling sharing by young children. *Journal of Applied Behavior Analysis, 9,* 491–497.

Rohwer, W. D. (1984). an invitation to an educational psychology of studying. *Educational Psychologist, 19,* 1–14.

Rosch, E. (1973). On the internal structure of perceptual and semantic categories. In T. E. Moore (Ed.), *Cognitive development and the acquisition of language* (pp. 81–126). New York: Academic Press.

Rosch, E. (1975). Cognitive representations of semantic categories. *Journal of Experimental Psychology: General, 104,* 192–223.

Rosch, E. (1977). Human categorization. In N. Warren (Ed.), *Advances in crosscultural psychology,* Vol. 1 (pp. 261–273). London: Academic Press.

Rosch, E., & Lloyd, B. B. (1978). *Cognition and categorization.* Hillsdale, NJ: Erlbaum.

Rosenbaum, M. S., & Drabman, R. S. (1979). Self-control training in the classroom: A review and critique. *Journal of Applied Behavior Analysis, 12,* 467–486.

Rosenshine, B. (1971). *Teaching behaviors and student achievement.* London: National Foundation for Educational Research.

Ross, C. C. (1947). *Measurement in today's schools.* New York: Prentice-Hall.

Ross, E. A. (1901). *Social control.* New York: Macmillan.

Ross, E. A. (1908). *Social psychology.* New York: Macmillan.

Rothkopf, E. Z. (1965). Some theoretical experimental approaches to problems in written instruction. In J. D. Krumboltz (Ed.), *Learning and the educational process* (pp. 191–213). Chicago: Rand McNally.

Rothkopf, E. Z. (1966). Learning from written instructive materials: An exploration of the control of inspection behavior by test-like events. *American Educational Research Journal, 3,* 241–249.

Rothkopf, E. Z. (1970). The concept of mathemagenic activities. *Review of Educational Research, 40,* 325–336.

Rothkopf, E. Z. (1972). Variable adjunct question schedules, interpersonal interaction, and incidental learning from written material. *Journal of Educational Psychology, 63,* 87–92.

Rothkopf, E. Z., & Bisbicos, E. E. (1967). Selective facilitation effects of interspersed questions on learning from written materials. *Journal of Educational Psychology, 58,* 56–81.

Rothkopf, E. Z., & Bloom, R. D. (1970). Effects of interpersonal interaction on the instructional value of adjunct questions in learning from written material. *Journal of Educational Psychology, 61,* 417–422.

Rothkopf, E. Z., & Kaplan, R. (1972). Exploration of the effect of density and specificity of instructional objectives on learning from text. *Journal of Educational Psychology, 63,* 295–302.

Rotter, J. B. (1954). *Social learning and clinical psychology.* Englewood Cliffs, NJ: Prentice-Hall.

Rotter, J. B. (1966). Generalized expectancies for internal versus external control of reinforcement. *Psychological Monographs, 80*(1), Whole No. 609.

Rowe, D. W., & Rayford, L. (1987). Activating background knowledge in reading comprehension assessment. *Reading Research Quarterly, 22,* 160–176.

Royce, J. (1898). The psychology of invention. *Psychological Review, 5,* 123–144.

Rozin, P., & Gleitman, L. R. (1977). The structure and acquisition of reading. II: The reading process and the acquisition of the alphabetic principle. In A. S. Reber &

D. L. Scarborough (Eds.), *Toward a psychology of reading* (pp. 222–246). Hillsdale, NJ: Erlbaum.

Rubin, A. M. (1979). Television use by children and adolescents. *Human Communication Research, 5*(2), 109–120.

Ruch, G. M. (1924). *The improvement of the written examination.* Chicago: Scott, Foresman.

Ruch, G. M., & Stoddard, G. D. (1927). *Tests and measurements in high school instruction.* Yonkers, NY: World Book.

Rudd, J. R. & Geller, E. S. (1985). A university-based incentive program to increase safety belt use: Toward cost-effective institutionalization. *Journal of Applied Behavior Analysis, 18,* 215–226.

Rumelhart, D. E. (1980). *An introduction to human information processing.* New York: Wiley.

Rumelhart, D. E., Lindsay, P. H., & Norman, D. A. (1972). A process for long-term memory. In E. Tulving & W. Donaldson (Eds.). *Handbook of Memory* (pp. 206–232). Hillsdale, NJ: Erlbaum.

Rush, J. (1893). *The philosophy of the human voice* (7th ed.). Philadelphia: The Library Company.

Russell, B. (1921). *The analysis of mind.* London: George Allen & Unwin.

Russell, W. A. (1970). *Milestones in motivation: Contributions to the psychology of drive and purpose.* New York: Appleton-Century-Crofts.

Salmon-Cox, L. (1981). Teachers and standardized achievement tests: What's really happening? *Phi Delta Kappan, 62,* 631–634.

Sang, R. C. (1987). A study of the relationship between instrumental music teachers' modeling skills and pupil performance behaviors. *Bulletin of the Council for Research in Music Education, 91,* 155–159.

Sapir, E. (1949). The status of linguistics as a science. In D. G. Mandelbaum (Ed.), *Selected writings of Edward Sapir in language, culture, and personality* (pp. 2–34). Berkeley: University of California Press. (Article originally published, 1929.)

Sattler, J. M. (1974). *Assessment of children's intelligence.* Philadelphia: Saunders.

Satz, P. (1977). Reading problems in perspective. In W. Otto, C. W. Peters, & N. Peters (Eds.), *Reading problems: A multidisciplinary perspective.* Reading, MA: Addison-Wesley.

Sautter, F. J., & Glover, J. A. (1978a). *Behavior, development and training of the dog.* New York: Arco.

Sautter, F. J., & Glover, J. A. (1978b). The relationship of perceived reinforcement potential on the production of creative behaviors. *The Journal of Genetic Psychology, 131,* 129–136.

Sax, G. (1989). *Principles of educational and psychological measurement and evaluation.* Belmont, CA: Wadsworth.

Saywitz, K., & Wilkinson, L. C. (1982). Age-related differences in metalinguistic awareness. In S. Kuczaj, II (Ed.), *Language development* (Vol 2) (pp. 259–283). Hillsdale, NJ: Erlbaum.

Schlaefli, A., Rest, J. R., & Thomas, S. J. (1985). Does moral education improve moral judgment? A meta-analysis of intervention studies using the defining issues test. *Review of Educational Research, 55,* 319–352.

Schneider, W., & Pressley, M. (1988). *Memory development between 2 and 20.* New York: Springer-Verlag.

Schnell, T. R. (1973). The effect of organizers on reading comprehension of community college freshmen. *Journal of Reading Behavior, 5,* 169–176.

Schofield, N. J., & Ashman, A. F. (1987). The cognitive processing of gifted, high average, and low average ability students. *British Journal of Educational Psychology, 57,* 9–20.

Scholnick, E. K., & Wing, C. S. (1988). Knowing when you don't know: Developmental and situational considerations. *Developmental Psychology, 24,* 190–196.

Schroth, M. L. (1984). Memory for intratrial events in concept formation. *Perceptual and Motor Skills, 59,* 23–29.

Schulman, C. S. (1982). Educational psychology returns to the school. In A. G. Kraut (Ed.). *The G. Stanley Hall Lecture Series* (Vol. II), (pp. 73–118). Washington, DC: American Psychological Association.

Schunk, D. (1987). Peer models and children's behavioral change. *Review of Educational Research, 57,* 149–174.

Schwartz, R. G., & Leonard, L. B. (1985). Lexical imitation and acquisition in language-impaired children. *Journal of Hearing and Speech Disorders, 50,* 141–149.

Scott, J., Williams, J. M. G., & Beck, A. T. (1988). *Cognitive therapy in clinical practice.* New York: Routledge.

Scripture, E. W. (1902). *Elements of experimental phonics.* New York: Charles Scribner's Sons.

Searle, J. (1969). *Speech acts: An essay in the philosophy of language.* London: Cambridge University Press.

Sears, P. S. (1940). Levels of aspiration in academically successful and unsuccessful children. *Journal of Abnormal Social Psychology, 35,* 498–536.

Sechenov, I. M. (1863). *Reflexes of the brain.* Moscow: Russian Academy of Sciences.

Seiler, T. B., & Wannemacher, W. (1983). *Concept development and the development of word meaning.* New York: Springer-Verlag.

Seligman, M. E. P. (1966). Chronic fear produced by unpredictable shock. *Journal of Comparative and Physiological Psychology, 66,* 402–411.

Semb, G. (1974). The effects of mastery criteria and assignment length on college student test performance. *Journal of Applied Behavior Analysis, 7,* pages 61–69.

Semb, G. (1976). Building an empirical base for instruction. *Journal of Personalized Instruction, 1,* 11–12.

Shallerick, M. E., & Barnes, W. (1936). *The situation as regards English.* Ninth Yearbook, National Education Association, Washington, DC: National Education Association.

Shannon, C. E., & Weaver, W. (1949). *The mathematical theory of communication.* Urbana: University of Illinois Press.

Shell, D. F., Murphy, C. C., & Bruning, R. H. (1989). Self-efficacy and outcome expectancy mechanisms in reading and writing achievement. *Journal of Educational Psychology, 81,* 91–100.

Sherman, J. A., & Bushell, D. (1974). Behavior modification as an educational technique. In F. D. Horowitz (Editor), *Review of child development research* (Volume 4) (pages 170–198). Chicago: University of Chicago Press.

Sherman, J. L., & Kulhavy, R. W. (1980). Processing flexibility in connected discourse. *Contemporary Educational Psychology, 5,* 41–64.

Sherrington, C. S. (1906). *The integrative action of the nervous system.* New Haven, Connecticut: Yale University Press.

Shields, J. (1962). Monozygotic twins: Brought up apart and brought up together. London: Oxford University Press.

Shiffrin, R. M., Pisoni, D. B., & Casteneda-Mendez, R. (1974). Is attention shared between the ears? *Cognitive Psychology, 6,* 190–215.

Shirey, L. L., & Reynolds, R. E. (1988). Effects of interest on attention and learning. *Journal of Educational Psychology, 80,* 159–166.

Shirley, K. W. (1974). *The prosocial effects of publicly broadcast children's television.* Unpublished doctoral dissertation, University of Kansas, Lawrence.

Shoben, E. J., & Ross, B. H. (in press). Structure and process in cognitive psychology using multidimensional scaling and related techniques. In R. R. Ronning, J. A. Glover, & J. C. Conoley (Eds.), *The relationship of cognitive psychology to measurement.* Hillsdale, NJ: Erlbaum.

Shockley, W. (1971). Negro I.Q. deficit: Failure of a "malicious coincidence" model warrants new research proposals. *Review of Educational Research, 41*(3), pages 227–248.

Siegler, R. S. (1980). When do children learn? The relationship between existing knowledge and learning. *Educational Psychologist, 15,* 135–150.

Siegler, R. S. (1980). Recent trends in the study of cognitive development: Variations on a task-analytic theme. *Human Development 23,* 278–285.

Siegler, R. S. (1984). Mechanisms of cognitive growth: Variation and selection. In R. J. Sternberg (Ed.), *Mechanisms of cognitive development* (pp. 141–162). New York: Freeman.

Siegler, R. S. (1987). The role of learning in children's strategy choices. In L. S. Liben (Ed.), *Development and learning conflict or congruence?* (pp. 61–79). Hillsdale, NJ: Erlbaum.

Simon, H. A. (1973). The structure of ill-structured problems. *Artificial Intelligence, 4,* 181–201.

Simon, H. A., & Chase, W. G. (1973). Skill in chess. *American Scientist, 61,* 394–403.

Simon, H. A., & Gilmartin, K. (1973). A simulation of memory for chess positions. *Cognitive Psychology, 5,* 29–46.

Simon, H. A., & Hayes, J. R. (1976). The understanding of process: Problem isomorphs. *Cognitive Psychology, 8,* 165–190.

Simon, H. A., & Newell, A. (1971). Human problem solving: The state of the theory in 1970. *American Psychologist, 26*(2), 154–159.

Singer, H., & Donlan, D. (1988). *Reading and learning from text* (2nd ed.). Hillsdale, NJ: Erlbaum.

Singer, J. L., & Singer, D. G. (1984). Psychologists look at television: Cognitive, developmental, personality, and social policy implications. *Annual Progress in Child Psychiatry and Child Development, 11,* 488–506.

Skager, R. W. (1978). *The great criterion-referenced test myth.* Los Angeles: Center for the Study of Evaluation, UCLA Graduate School of Education.

Skeels, H. M., & Dye, H. B. (1939). A study of the effects of differential stimulation on mentally retarded children. *American Association of Mental Deficiency Proceedings, 44,* 114–136.

Skinner, B. F. (1938). *The behavior of organisms.* New York: Appleton-Century.

Skinner, B. F. (1953). *Science and human behavior.* New York: Macmillan.

Skinner, B. F. (1957). *Verbal behavior.* New York: Appleton-Century-Crofts.

Skinner, B. F. (1961). The science of learning and the art of teaching. In B. F. Skinner (Ed.), *Cumulative record* (pp. 143–182). New York: Appleton-Century-Crofts.

Skinner, B. F. (1968). *The technology of teaching.* New York: Appleton-Century-Crofts.

Skinner, B. F. (1983). *A matter of consequences: Part three of an autobiography.* New York: Knopf.

Skinner, B. F. (1984). The shame of American education. *American Psychologist, 39,* 947–954.

Slamecka, N. J., & Katsaiti, L. T. (1987). The generation effect as an artifact of selective displaced rehearsal. *Journal of Memory and Language, 26,* 589–607.

Slavin, R. (1978). Student teams and comparisons among equals: Effects on academic performance and student attitudes. *Journal of Educational Psychology, 10,* 532–533.

Slavin, R. E. (1980a). Cooperative learning. *Review of Educational Research, 50,* 314–342.

Slavin, R. E. (1980b). Cooperative learning in teams: State of the art. *Educational Psychologist, 15,* 93–111.

Slavin, R. E. (1981). A policy choice: Cooperative or competitive learning. *Character, 2,* 1–6.

Slavin, R. E. (1984). Students motivating students to excel: Cooperative incentives, cooperative tasks, and student achievement. *Elementary School Journal, 85,* 53–63.

Sledd, J. (1959). *A short introduction to English grammar.* Chicago: Scott, Foresman.

Slobin, D. I. (1971). Developmental psycholinguistics. In W. O. Dingwall (Ed.), *A survey of linguistic science* (pp. 229–256). College Park: University of Maryland.

Slobin, D. I. (1973). Cognitive prerequisites for the development of grammar. In C. A. Ferguson & D. I. Slobin (Eds.), *Studies of child language development* (pp. 113–132). New York: Holt, Rinehart & Winston.

Slobin, D. I. (1988). From the Garden of Eden to the Tower of Babel. In F. Kessel (Ed.), *The development of language and language researchers* (pp. 8–26). Hillsdale, NJ: Erlbaum.

Small, M. A., Raney, J. F., & Knapp, T. J. (1987). Complex reaction time and general intelligence. *Journal of Genetic Psychology, 148,* 405–414.

Small, M. A., Raney, J. F., & Knapp, T. (1988). Complex reaction time and general intelligence: A refinement. *Journal of Genetic Psychology, 148,* 405–414.

Smith, E. E., Shoben, E. J., & Rips, L. J. (1974). Structure and process in semantic memory: A featural model for semantic decisions. *Psychological Review, 81,* 214–241.

Smith, F. (1978). *Reading.* Cambridge: Cambridge University Press.

Smith, T. E. C., Price, B. J., & Marsh, G. E. (1986). *Mildly handicapped children and adults.* St. Paul, MN: West.

Snarey, J. R., Reimer, J., & Kohlberg, L. (1985). Development of social-moral reasoning among kibbutz adolescents: A longitudinal study. *Developmental Psychology, 21,* 3–17.

Snow, C. E. (1977). Mothers' speech research: From input to interaction. In C. E. Snow & C. A. Ferguson (Eds.), *Talking to children: Language input and acquisition* (pp. 302–320). New York: Cambridge University Press.

Snow, C. E., & Ferguson, C. A. (Eds.) (1977). *Talking to children: Language input and acquisition.* New York: Cambridge University Press.

Snow, R. E. (1980). Aptitude, learner control, and adaptive instruction. *Educational Psychologist, 15,* 151–158.

Snowman, J., & Cunningham, D. J. (1975). A comparison of pictorial and written adjunct aids in learning from text. *Journal of Educational Psychology, 67,* 307–311.

Sodian, B., & Wimmer, H. (1987). Children's understanding of inference as a source of knowledge. *Child Development, 58,* 424–433.

Solomon, R. L. (1964). Punishment. *American Psychologist, 19,* 239–253.

Solso, R. L. (1988). *Cognitive Psychology* (2nd ed.). Boston: Allyn & Bacon.

Spache, G. D. (1976). *Diagnosing and correcting reading disabilities.* Boston: Allyn & Bacon.

Spearman, C. (1904). "General intelligence," objectively determined and measured. *American Journal of Psychology, 15,* 201–293.

Spearman, C. (1927). *The abilities of man.* London: Macmillan.

Sprafkin, J., Gadow, K. D., & Kant, G. (1988). Teaching emotionally disturbed children to discriminate reality from fantasy on television. *Journal of Special Education, 21,* 99–107.

Spring, C. (1978). Automaticity of word recognition under phonics and whole-word instruction. *Journal of Educational Psychology, 70,* 445–450.

Stallings, J. (1975). Implementation and child effects of teaching practices in Follow Through classrooms. *Monographs of the Society for Research in Child Development, 40*(7), 1–133.

Stam, J. H. (1980). An historical perspective on "linguistic relativity." In R. W. Rieber (Ed.). *Psychology of language and thought* (pp. 134–167). New York: Plenum.

Starch, D. (1916). *Educational measurement.* New York: Croft.

Starch, D., & Elliott, E. C. (1912). Reliability of grading work in high school English. *School Review, 20,* 442–457.

Starch, D., & Elliott, E. C. (1913). Reliability of grading work in mathematics. *School Review, 21,* 254–257.

Starch, D., & Elliott, E. C. (1913). Reliability of grading work in history. *School Review, 21,* 676–681.

Stein, B. (in press). Memory systems in creativity. In J. A. Glover, R. R. Ronning, & C. R. Reynolds (Eds.). *Handbook of creativity research.* New York: Plenum.

Stephens, T. M. (1981). Teaching social behavior—the schools' challenge in the 1980's. *Directive Teacher, 3,* 4–10.

Stephens, T. M., Blackhurst, A. E., & Magliocca, L. A. (1988). *Teaching mainstreamed students* (2nd ed.). New York: Pergamon.

Stern, W. (1924). *On the psychology of individual differences* (A. Barwell, Trans.). New York: Holt.

Sternberg, R. J. (1981). Testing and cognitive psychology. *American Psychologist, 36,* 1181–1189.

Sternberg, R. J. (1982). *What cognitive psychology can (and cannot) do for test development.* Paper presented to First Annual Buros-Nebraska Symposium on Measurement and Testing, Lincoln, NE.

Sternberg, R. J. (1982). *Handbook of human intelligence.* New York: Cambridge University Press.

Sternberg, R. J. (1985). *Beyond IQ: A triarchic theory of intelligence.* New York: Cambridge University Press.

Sternberg, R. J. (Ed.), (1987). *Advances in the psychology of human intelligence.* Hillsdale, NJ: Erlbaum.

Sternberg, R. J. (1988). *The triarchic mind: A new theory of human intelligence.* New York: Viking.

Sternberg, R. J. (Ed.), (1988). *The nature of creativity.* New York: Cambridge.

Sternberg, R. J. (1988). Intelligence. In R. J. Sternberg & E. E. Smith (Eds.), *The psychology of human thought* (pp. 267–308). New York: Cambridge.

Stevens, R. J. (1988). Effects of strategy training on the identification of the main idea of expository passages. *Journal of Educational Psychology, 80,* 21–26.

Stipek, D. J., & Daniels, D. H. (1988). Declining perceptions of competence: A consequence of changes in the child or in the educational environment? *Journal of Educational Psychology, 80,* 352–356.

Stone, C. W. (1908). *Stone arithmetic test.* New York: Teachers College.

Stone, J. (1983). *Parallel processing in the human information processing system.* New York: Plenum.

Sullivan, H. S. (1931). The modified treatment of schizophrenia. *American Journal of Psychiatry, 11,* 519–540.

Sully, J. (1884). *Outlines of psychology with special reference to the theory of education.* New York: D. Appleton & Company.

Sulzer-Azaroff, B., & Mayer, G. R. (1977). *Applying behavior analysis procedures with children and youth.* New York: Holt, Rinehart & Winston.

Surbeck, E., & Endsley, R. C. (1979). Children's emotional reactions to television violence: Effects of film, charac-

ter, reassurance, and sex. *Journal of Social Psychology, 109,* 269–282.

Swanson, D. H., & Denton, J. J. (1977). Learning for mastery versus personalized systems of instruction: A comparison of remediation strategies with secondary school chemistry students. *Journal of Research in Science Teaching, 14,* 515–524.

Taft, M. L., & Leslie, L. (1985). The effects of prior knowledge and oral reading accuracy on miscues and comprehension. *Journal of Reading Behavior, 17,* 163–179.

Talmage, H., Pascarella, E. T., & Ford, S. (1984). The influence of cooperative learning strategies on teacher practices, student perceptions of the learning environment, and academic achievement. *American Educational Research Journal, 21,* 163–179.

Tambs, K., Sundet, J. M., & Magnus, P. (1988). Genetic and environmental effects on the covariance structure of the Norwegian Army ability tests. A study of twins. *Personality and Individual Differences, 9,* 791–800.

Tarde, G. (1903). *The laws of imitation.* New York: Holt.

Taylor, C. W. (1961). A tentative description of the creative individual. In W. B. Waetjen (Ed.), *Human variability and learning* (pp. 202–240). Washington, DC: American Society for Child Development.

Taylor, C. W. (1984). Developing creative excellence in students. *Gifted Child Quarterly, 28,* 106–109.

Taylor, M., & Kratochwill, T. R. (1978). Modification of preschool children's bathroom behaviors by contingent teacher attention. *Journal of School Psychology, 16,* 64–71.

Telford, C. W., & Sawrey, J. M. (1977). *The exceptional individual.* Englewood Cliffs, NJ: Prentice-Hall.

Terman, L. M. (1916). *The measurement of intelligence.* Boston: Houghton Mifflin.

Terman, L. M. (Ed.). (1925). *Genetic studies of genius. Vol. I. Mental and physical traits of a thousand gifted children.* Stanford: Stanford University Press.

Terman, L. M., & Merrill, M. A. (1937). *Measuring intelligence.* Boston: Houghton Mifflin.

Terman, L. M., & Merrill, M. A. (1973). *Stanford-Binet intelligence scale: Manual for third revision.* Boston: Houghton Mifflin.

Thompson, M., Brassell, W. R., Persons, S., Tucker, R., & Rollins, H. (1974). Contingency management in the schools: How often and how well does it work? *American Educational Research Journal, 1,* 19–28.

Thompson, M. E. (1911). *Psychology and pedagogy of writing.* Baltimore: Warwick & York.

Thorndike, E. L. (1898). Animal intelligence: An experimental study of the associative processes in animals.

Psychological Review, Monograph Supplement (Whole No. 8).

Thorndike, E. L. (1903). *Educational psychology.* New York: Teachers College.

Thorndike, E. L. (1904). *An introduction to the theory of mental and social measurements.* New York: Teachers College.

Thorndike, E. L. (1906). *Principles of teaching: Based on psychology.* New York: Seiler.

Thorndike, E. L. (1910a). The contribution of psychology to education. *Journal of Educational Psychology, 1,* 5–12.

Thorndike, E. L. (1910b). *Thorndike handwriting scale.* New York: Teachers College.

Thorndike, E. L. (1911a). *Animal intelligence.* New York: Macmillan.

Thorndike, E. L. (1911b). A scale for merit in English writing by young people. *Journal of Educational Psychology, 2,* 361–368.

Thorndike, E. L. (1913). *Educational psychology* (Vols. 1–3). New York: Teachers College.

Thorndike, E. L. (1917). Reading as reasoning: A study of mistakes in paragraph reading. *Journal of Educational Psychology, 8,* 325–332.

Thorndike, E. L. (1918). The nature, purposes, and general methods of measurements of educational products. *Seventeenth yearbook of the National Society for the Study of Education. Part II.* Bloomington, IL: Public School Publishing Company.

Thorndike, R. L. (1963). The measurement of creativity. *Teacher's College Record, 54,* 422–424.

Thorndike, R. L., & Hagen, E. P. (1977). *Measurement and evaluation in psychology and education* (4th ed.). New York: Wiley.

Thorndike, R. L. (1988). Reliability. In J. P. Keeves (Ed.), *Educational research, methodology, and measurement: An international handbook.* New York: Pergamon Press.

Thurstone, L. L. (1938). Primary mental abilities. *Psychometric Monographs* (No. 1). Chicago: University of Chicago Press.

Thurstone, L. L. (1952). Creative talent. In L. L. Thurstone (Ed.). *Applications of psychology.* New York: Harper.

Tinbergen, N. (1951). *The study of instinct.* New York: Oxford University Press.

Tinker, M. A. (1965). *Basis for effective reading.* Minneapolis: University of Minnesota Press.

Tisak, M. S., & Turiel, E. (1988). Variation in seriousness of transgressions and children's moral and conventional concepts. *Developmental Psychology, 24,* 352–357.

Titchener, E. B. (1898). The postulates of a structural psychology. *Psychological Review, 7,* 449–465.

Titchener, E. B. (1909). *Lectures on the experimental psychology of thought processes.* New York: Macmillan.

Tittle, C. K. (1988). Test bias. In J. P. Keeves (Ed.), *Educational research, methodology, and measurement: An international handbook.* New York: Pergamon Press.

Tobias, S. (1987). Mandatory text review and interaction with student characteristics. *Journal of Educational Psychology, 79,* 154–161.

Tolman, E. C. (1932). *Purposive behavior in animals and man.* New York: Naiburg.

Tolman, E. C. (1938). The determiners of behavior at a choice point. *Psychological Review, 45,* 1–41.

Torrance, E. P. (1965). *Creativity in the classroom.* Englewood Cliffs, NJ: Prentice-Hall.

Torrance, E. P. (1980, June). *The state of the art of education for the gifted and talented.* Presented to the first annual Nebraska Symposium on the Education of Gifted Children, Lincoln, NE.

Torrance, E. P. (1988). The nature of creativity as manifest in its testing. In R. J. Sternberg (Ed.), *The nature of creativity* (pp. 43–75). New York: Cambridge.

Touhey, J. C., & Villamez, W. J. (1980). Ability attribution as a result of variable effort and achievement motivation. *Journal of Personality and Social Psychology, 38,* 211–216.

Traxler, A. E., & Anderson, H. A. (1935). The reliability of an essay examination in English. *School Review, 43,* 534–539.

Trevarthen, C. (1979). Communication and cooperation in early infancy: A description of primary intersubjectivity. In M. Bullowa (Ed.), *Before speech: The beginning of interpersonal communication.* New York: Cambridge University Press.

Trotter, R. J. (1972). This is going to hurt you more than it hurts me. *Science News, 18,* 332.

Tuckman, B. (1988). *Testing for Teachers.* New York: Harcourt Brace Jovanovich.

Tuckman, B. W. (1975). *Measuring educational outcomes: Fundamentals of testing.* New York: Harcourt Brace Jovanovich.

Tulving, E. (1985). On the classification problem in learning and memory. In Nilsson, L., & Archer, T. (Eds.), *Perspectives on learning and memory* (pp. 73–101). Hillsdale, NJ: Erlbaum.

Tunmer, W. E., Pratt, C., & Herriman, M. E. (Eds.). (1984). *Metalinguistic awareness in children.* Berlin: Springer-Verlag.

Tyler, R. W. (1942). General statement on evaluation. *Journal of Educational Research, 35,* 492–501.

Underwood, B. J. (1957). Interference and forgetting. *Psychological Review, 64,* 49–60.

United States Commission on Civil Rights. (1967). *Report on the effectiveness of compensatory educational programs.*

United States Department of Education. (1988). *Tenth annual report to Congress on the implementation of the Education of the Handicapped Act.* Washington, DC: U.S. Department of Education.

United States Office of Education (1988). *Implementation of the Education of the Handicapped Act Public Law 94–141.* Tenth Annual Report to Congress, Washington, DC: Division of Innovation and Development.

Urban, H. B., & Ford, D. H. (1971). Some historical and conceptual perspectives on psychotherapy and behavior change. In A. E. Bergin & S. L. Garfield (Eds.), *Handbook of psychotherapy and behavior change: An empirical analysis* (pp. 216–233). New York: Wiley.

Vaid, J. (1986). *Language processing in bilinguals.* Hillsdale, NJ: Erlbaum.

Vandierendonk, A. (1984). Concept learning, memory, and transfer of dot pattern categories. *Acta Psychologica, 55,* 71–88.

Van Hoaten, R. V., Morrison, E., Jarvis, R., & McDonald, M. (1974). The effects of explicit timing and feedback on compositional response rate in elementary school children. *Journal of Applied Behavior Analysis, 7,* 547–555.

Vargas, J. S. (1977). *Behavioral psychology for teachers.* New York: Harper & Row.

Vasudev, J. (1988). Sex differences in morality and moral orientation: A discussion of the Gilligan and Attanucci study. *Merrill-Palmer Quarterly, 34,* 239–244.

Vellutino, F. R. (1977). Alternative conceptualizations of dyslexia: Evidence in support of a verbal deficit hypothesis. *Harvard Educational Review, 47,* 112–221.

Venezky, R. L. (1975). Prereading skills: Theoretical foundations and practical applications. In T. A. Brigham, R. Hawkins, J. W. Scott, & T. F. McLaughlin (Eds.), *Behavior analysis in education: Self-control and reading* (pp. 216–242). Dubuque, IA: Kendall/Hunt.

Venezky, R. L. (1980). *Orthography, reading, and dyslexia.* Baltimore: University Park Press.

Vernon, P. E. (in press). The nature-nurture problem. In J. A. Glover, R. R. Ronning, & C. R. Reynolds (Eds.), *Handbook of creativity research.* New York: Plenum.

Vincent, D. (1988). Norm-referenced assessment. In J. P. Keeves (Ed.), *Educational research, methodology, and measurement: An international handbook.* New York: Pergamon Press.

Vosniadou, S., Pearson, P. D., & Rogers, T. (1988). What causes children's failures to detect inconsistencies in text? Representation versus comparison difficulties. *Journal of Educational Psychology, 80,* 27–39.

Vygotsky, L. S. (1962). *Thought and language.* Cambridge, MA: MIT Press. (Originally published in Russian, 1934.)

Vygotsky, L. S. (1978). *Mind in society.* Cambridge, MA: Harvard University Press.

Wade, S. E. (1983). A synthesis of the research for improving reading in the social studies. *Review of Educational Research, 53,* 461–498.

Wagner, R. R., & Sternberg, R. J. (1984). Alternative conceptions of intelligence and their implications for education. *Review of Educational Research, 54,* 179–223.

Wahler, R. G. (1969). Setting generality: Some specific and general effects of child behavior therapy. *Journal of Applied Behavior Analysis, 2,* 239–246.

Wainer, H., & Braun, H. (1987). *Test validity.* Hillsdale, NJ: Erlbaum.

Waite, C. J., Blick, K. A., & Boltwood, C. E. (1971). Prior use of the first letter technique. *Psychological Reports, 29,* 630.

Walker, E., & Emory, E. (1985). Commentary: Interpretive bias and behavioral genetic research. *Child Development, 56,* 775–778.

Walker, N. (1986). Direct retrieval from elaborated memory. *Memory and Cognition, 14,* 321–328.

Walker, W. H., & Kintsch, W. (1985). Automatic and strategic aspects of knowledge retrieval. *Cognitive Science, 9,* 261–283.

Wallach, M. A., & Kogan, N. (1965). *Modes of thinking in young children: A study of the creativity-intelligence distinction.* New York: Holt, Rinehart & Winston.

Waller, T. G. (1976). Children's recognition memory for written sentences: A comparison of good and poor readers. *Child Development, 47,* 90–95.

Waltz, D. L., & Pollack, J. B. (1985). Massively parallel parsing: A strongly interactive model of natural language interpretation. *Cognitive Science, 9,* 51–74.

Ward, H. M., & Baker, B. L. (1968). Reinforcement therapy in the classroom. *Journal of Applied Behavior Analysis, 1,* 323–328.

Ware, H. W. (1985). Thinking skills: The effort of one public school system. In J. W. Segal & S. F. Chipman (Eds.), *Thinking and reasoning skills* (Vol. 1) (pp. 207–229). Hillsdale, NJ: Erlbaum.

Waring, D., Johnson, D. W., Maruyama, G., & Johnson, R. (1985). Impact of different types of cooperative learning on cross-ethnic and cross-sex relationships. *Journal of Educational Psychology, 77,* 53–59.

Waters, H. S., & Tinsley, V. S. (1982). The development of verbal self-regulation: Relationships between language, cognition, and behavior. In S. Kuzcaj, II (Ed.), *Language Development* (Vol. 2), Hillsdale, NJ: Erlbaum.

Waters, G. S., Bruck, M., & Malus-Abramowitz, M. (1988). The role of linguistic and visual information in spelling: A developmental study. *Journal of Experimental Child Psychology, 45,* 400–421.

Watkins, C. E., McKay, B. L., Parra, R., & Polk, N. E. (1988). Using WAIS-R short forms with clinical outpatients: A cautionary note. *Professional Psychology: Research and Practice, 19,* 397–398.

Watson, D. L., & Tharp, R. G. (1985). *Self-directed behavior* (4th ed.). Monterey, CA: Brooks/Cole.

Watson, J. B. (1913). Psychology as the behaviorist views it. *Psychological Review, 20,* 158–177.

Watson, J. B. (1928). *Psychological care of infant and child.* New York: Norton.

Watson, P. (1972). I.Q.: The racial gap. *Psychology Today, 6*(4), 48–99.

Waugh, N. C., & Norman, D. A. (1965). Primary memory. *Psychological Review, 72,* 89–104.

Wechsler, D. (1949). *Manual for the Wechsler Intelligence Scale for Children.* New York: Psychological Corporation.

Wechsler, D. (1955). *Manual for the Wechsler Adult Intelligence Scale.* New York: Psychological Corporation.

Wechsler, D. (1967). *Manual for the Wechsler Preschool and Primary Scale of Intelligence.* New York: Psychological Corporation.

Wechsler, D. (1974). *Manual for the Wechsler Intelligence Scale for Children—Revised.* New York: Psychological Corporation.

Wechsler, D. (1981). *Manual for the Wechsler Adult Intelligence Scale—Revised.* New York: Psychological Corporation.

Weiner, B. (1980). May I borrow your class notes? An attributional analysis of judgments of help giving in an achievement-related context. *Journal of Educational Psychology, 72,* 676–681.

Weiner, B. (1985). An attributional theory of achievement motivation and emotion. *Psychological Review, 92,* 548–573.

Weiner, B., & Kukla, A. (1970). An attributional analysis of achievement motivation. *Journal of Personality and Social Psychology, 15,* 1–20.

Weinert, F. E., & Kluwe, R. H. (Eds.). (1987). *Metacognition, motivation, and understanding.* Hillsdale, NJ: Erlbaum.

Weinstein, M. (1988). Preparation of children for psycho-therapy through videotaped modeling. *Journal of Clinical Child Psychology, 17,* 131–136.

Wertheimer, M. (1978). *A brief history of psychology.* New York: Holt, Rinehart & Winston.

Wesman, A. G. (1970). Intelligent testing, In B. L. Kintz & J. L. Bruning (Eds.), *Research in psychology* (pp. 207–231). Glenview, IL: Scott, Foresman.

Whipple, G. M. (1910). *Manual of mental and physical tests.* Baltimore: Warwick & York.

Whipple, G. M. (1925). *The twenty-fourth yearbook of the National Society for the Study of Education. Part I. Report of the National Committee on Reading.* Bloomington, IL: Public School Publishing Company.

White, E. E. (1886). *The elements of pedagogy.* New York: American Book.

White, R. T., & Gagné, R. M. (1974). Past and future research on learning hierarchies. *Educational Psychologist, 11,* 19–28.

Whiteman, M. F. (1983). *Variation in writing.* Hillsdale, NJ: Erlbaum.

Whorf, B. L. (1952a). *Collected papers on metalinguistics.* Washington, DC: Department of State, Foreign Service Institute.

Whorf, B. L. (1952b). Language, mind, and reality. *Etc.: A Review of General Semantics, 9,* 167–188.

Whorf, B. L. (1956). Languages and logic. In J. B. Carroll (Ed.), *Language, thought, and reality: Selected writings of Benjamin Lee Whorf.* Cambridge, MA: MIT Press. (Article originally published, 1941.)

Whorf, B. L. (1956). Science and linguistics. In J. B. Carroll (Ed.), *Language, thought, and reality: Selected writings of Benjamin Lee Whorf* (pp. 212–256). Cambridge MA: MIT Press.

Wickelgren, W. A. (1974). *How to solve problems.* San Francisco: Freeman.

Wickens, D. D., Moody, M. J., & Vidulid, M. (1985). Retrieval time as a function of memory set size, type of probes, and interference in recognition memory. *Journal of Experimental Psychology: Learning, Memory, and Cognition, 11,* 154–164.

Wigfield, A. (1988). Children's attributions for success and failure: Effects of age and attentional focus. *Journal of Educational Psychology, 80,* 76–81.

Wilde, O. (1904). *Intentions: The decay of lying and other essays.* Portland, ME: Mosher.

Wilkinson, L. C., & Rembold, K. (1982). The communicative context of early language development. In S. Kuczaj (Ed.), *Language development* (Vol. 2) (pp. 43–61). Hillsdale, NJ: Erlbaum.

Willerman, L. (1979). *The psychology of individual and group differences.* San Francisco: Freeman.

Willerman, L., & Turner, R. G. (1979). *Readings about individual and group differences.* San Francisco: Freeman.

Williams, J. (1977). Building perceptual and cognitive strategies into a reading curriculum. In A. S. Reber & D. L. Scarborough (Eds.), *Toward a psychology of reading* (pp. 303–320). Hillsdale, NJ: Erlbaum.

Williams, R. L. (1987). Classroom management. In J. A. Glover & R. R. Ronning (Eds.), *Historical foundations of educational psychology.* New York: Plenum.

Williams, R. L. (in press). The current status of locus of control research. *Educational Psychology Review.*

Wilson, P. T. (1985). Amount of reading, reading instruction, and reading achievement. Paper presented at the National Reading Conference, San Diego, CA.

Winett, R. A., & Winkler, R. C. (1972). Current behavior modification in the classroom: Be still, be quiet, be docile. *Journal of Applied Behavior Analysis, 5,* 499–504.

Wishbow, N. (1988). *Creativity in poets.* Unpublished doctoral dissertation, Carnegie-Mellon University, Pittsburgh, PA.

Witt, J. C., Elliott, S. N., & Gresham, F. M. (1988). *Handbook of behavior therapy in education.* New York: Plenum.

Wittrock, M. C. (1979). The cognitive movement in instruction. *Educational Researcher, 8,* 5–11.

Wittrock, M. C. (1985). *Handbook of research on teaching* (3rd ed.) New York: Macmillan.

Wolf, R. L., & Simon, R. J. (1975). Does busing improve the racial interactions of children? *Educational Researcher, 4,* 5–10.

Wong, B. Y. L. (1985). Self-questioning instructional research: A review. *Review of Educational Research, 55,* 227–268.

Wood, R. (1988). Item analysis. In J. P. Keeves (Ed.), *Educational research, methodology, and measurement: An international handbook.* New York: Pergamon Press.

Woodworth, R. S. (1918). *Dynamic psychology.* New York: Columbia University Press.

Worthen, B., & Sanders, J. R. (1973). *Educational evaluation: Theory and practice.* Worthington, OH: Jones.

Worthen, B., & Sanders, J. R. (1987). *Educational evaluation: Alternative approaches and practical guidelines.* New York: Longman.

Wright, B. J., & Bell, S. R. (1984). Item banks: What, why, how. *Journal of Educational Measurement, 21,* 331–345.

Yantis, S., & Meyer, D. E. (1988). Dynamics of activation in semantic and episodic memory. *Journal of Experimental Psychology: General, 117,* 130–147.

Yoakam, G. A. (1955). *Basal reading instruction.* New York: McGraw-Hill.

Young, P. T. (1936). *Motivation of behavior.* New York: Wiley.

Yuill, N., & Perner, J. (1988). Intentionality and knowledge in children's judgments of actor's responsibility and recipient's emotional reaction. *Developmental Psychology, 24,* 358–365.

Yule, W., & Carr, J. (1988). *Behavior modification for people with mental handicaps.* New York: Routledge.

Zeller, R. A. (1988). Validity. In J. P. Keeves (Ed.), *Educational research, methodology, and measurement: An international handbook.* New York: Pergamon Press.

Zentall, T., & Galef, B. G. (1988). *Social learning: A comparative approach.* Hillsdale, NJ: Erlbaum.

Zimmer, J. W. (1978a). *A level of processing analysis of memory for prose.* Paper presented at the annual meeting of the American Educational Research Association, Toronto.

Zimmer, J. W. (1978b). *A processing activities approach to memory for prose.* Paper presented at the annual meeting of the American Psychological Association, Toronto.

Zimmer, J. W., & Glover, J. A. (1979). *Logical inferences and prose processing.* Paper presented at the annual meeting of the Western Psychological Association, San Diego.

Zimmer, J. W., Petersen, C. H., Ronning, R. R., & Glover, J. A. (1978). The effects of adjunct aids in prose processing: A re-examination. *Journal of Instructional Psychology, 5,* 27–34.

NAME INDEX

SUBJECT INDEX